Multicultural Writers *since* 1945

An A-to-Z Guide

*Edited by Alba Amoia
and
Bettina L. Knapp*

GREENWOOD PRESS
Westport, Connecticut • London

Library of Congress Cataloging-in-Publication Data

Multicultural writers since 1945 : an A-to-Z guide / edited by Alba Amoia and Bettina L. Knapp.
    p. cm.
  Includes bibliographical references and index.
  ISBN 0–313–30688–5 (alk. paper)
  1. Authors—20th century—Biography. 2. Literature, Modern—20th century—Bio-bibliography. 3. Multiculturalism in literature. I. Amoia, Alba della Fazia. II. Knapp, Bettina Liebowitz, 1926–
PN452.M88   2004
809′.045—dc21
[B]   2003048541

British Library Cataloguing in Publication Data is available.

Library of Congress Catalog Card Number: 2003048541
ISBN: 0–313–30688–5

First published in 2004

Greenwood Press, 88 Post Road West, Westport, CT 06881
An imprint of Greenwood Publishing Group, Inc.
www.greenwood.com

Printed in the United States of America

The paper used in this book complies with the Permanent Paper Standard issued by the National Information Standards Organization (Z39.48–1984).

10 9 8 7 6 5 4 3 2 1

Writers are citizens of many countries: the finite and frontiered country of observable reality and everyday life, the boundless kingdom of imagination, the half-lost land of memory.

—*Salman Rushdie, Text delivered to the International Parliament of Writers (Strasbourg, November 1993)*

CONTENTS

CONTENTS

Contents

CONTENTS

Contents

CONTENTS

PREFACE AND ACKNOWLEDGMENTS

World War II (1939–45) marked a turning point no less portentous than any of the earlier major transformations in world history. New departures in human affairs became more sharply defined both chronologically and geographically. Communication among nations made giant strides; inhabitants of the planet were no longer isolated; and the attributes and problems of one region affected every other. Emigration and immigration increased, provoking clashes as well as convergences among ethnicities. Scientific experiments and discoveries long dreamed about went forward, from the outermost reaches of space to the innermost recesses of the human mind.

National identities and cultural allegiances became increasingly intertwined in an ongoing human symposium and in its opposite—vicious bouts of hatred and mass exterminations. Intellectual and cultural concerns broadened, in part through decolonization and the emergence of new nations, to include formerly unnoticed cultures that now clamored for recognition. East and West drew closer, writing took on an international flavor, and a new literary geography was molded.

The whole idea of multiculturalism, hitherto confined to some dozen major linguistic groups or ideologies—or both—expanded as new literary voices were translated and disseminated internationally. Some of the world's finest minds consciously or unconsciously combatted the nationalisms of the twentieth century. Authors who crossed borders and changed their perceptions of other cultures became valuable witnesses to the broader changes in society.

The notion of multiculturalism, which has come to serve as a kind of common denominator for a group as diverse as it is numerous, admittedly has powerful enemies. Should people reject their inherited culture and attempt to assimilate and build on the values of another? What are the merits or demerits of multiculturalism as a way of life and of literature?

The editors of this volume believe that such epochal multicultural events as the diaspora of writers and artists during the Nazi-Fascist and Communist eras and the displacement of colonized peoples will promote greater understanding among ethnic, racial, religious, and linguistic groups.

Conceived under the sign of pluralism and dialogue among diverse civilizations, the newly constructed (2002) Alexandrian Library in Egypt aims at becoming the cultural center of the Eastern and Western worlds. Like the ancient Mouseion, where Alexandria's multicultural coterie gathered, the new nonsectarian institution will house a massive collection of writings from every corner of the world—the almost surrealistic literary dream of Jorge Luis Borges's *Biblioteca de Babel* come true. Such cosmopolitanism harbors diversified creeds, traditions, and cultures. The cosmopolite, in extreme opposition to the fanatic who believes there is but a single truth that must prevail, upholds pluralism and the relativity of truth.

For the purposes of this volume, *multicultural authors* are those who voluntarily have lived in a culture other than their own or were wrenched from one culture into another and who have written about their experiences. In a few rare cases, they are authors who may never have left their homelands, but who so strongly underwent the influence of foreign cultures that their writings bear transnational imprints.

The volume comprises more than one hundred entries on authors from various countries and cultures, many of whom have been enriched by contact with a new language. "Notitia linguarum est prima porta sapientiae" (knowledge of languages is the doorway to wisdom), wrote Roger Bacon (1214–94), the thirteenth-century English Franciscan known as "Doctor Mirabilis" in his *Opus tertium* (quoted in Edwards, *Multilingualism*, 4), and nearly a century ago Ludwig Wittgenstein acknowledged that the limits of his language signified the limits of his world. Elias Canetti (Nobel Prize for Literature, 1981), the Bulgarian-born German writer who lived in England for almost 50 years, according to his autobiography, *Die gerettete Zunge: Geschichte einer Jugend* (1977), ascribes his ability to grasp the multiplicity of existence to his ability to speak five languages.

Nonetheless, the majority view among transplanted intellectuals is that one's first language constitutes one's person. Three Americans who have won the Nobel Prize for Literature—Czesław Miłosz, Isaac Bashevis Singer, and Joseph Brodsky—were immigrants still writing in their native, non-English tongues. But some multicultural writers abandoned their original language, as did the Hungarian author Arthur Koestler, and some still use both languages as a homage to their indigenous literature. Joseph Brodsky (Nobel Prize for Literature, 1987) was so inspired by John Donne, T. S. Eliot, and W. H. Auden that he tried writing verse in English. The South African Breyten Breytenbach, despite living in Paris for three decades, has produced no creative work in French, writing most of his prose in English and his poetry in his mother tongue, Afrikaans. Milan Kundera's recent novels were written in French rather than in his native Czech. Vladimir Nabokov, Samuel Beckett, and others adopted the language of their host country, whereas Marguerite Yourcenar and Ingeborg Bachmann, for example, resided in foreign countries but continued to write in their native tongue. Likewise, the Chinese author Gao Xingjian (Nobel Prize for Literature, 2000) and Albanian novelist Ismail Kadare live abroad but write in their own languages. Witold Gombrowicz and Joseph Brodsky lived between two worlds and two languages, as do Andrei Makine and others today.

The entries in this volume offer a sampling of diverse linguistic, ethnic, and cultural writings and focus specifically on the effects of multiculturalism or lack of acculturation on selected authors. Mention is made throughout the preface and introduction of many bilingual and multicultural authors for whom entries regrettably were excluded for lack of space. Their names and the titles of some of their works appear in the bibliography and index at the end of the book.

For easier reference, the entries are presented in alphabetical rather than chronological or geographical order. Each entry generally includes: (1) an outline of the author's particular intercultural career and its repercussions on his or her works; (2) a discussion of multicultural themes; (3) critical material on his or her life and work; and (4) a bibliography stressing the author's works that reflect a multicultural perspective and offering pertinent critical material. The volume also contains a general bibliography that includes a wide range of works directly or indirectly related to the subject of multiculturalism. The index highlights the writers' multicultural contacts, influences, and themes.

The preparation of this reference volume was made possible by the scholarship and generosity of our contributors, who have adroitly shed light on the meaning of multiculturalism in literature. We are especially indebted to Professor Giorgio Amitrano for his general guidance through the field of Oriental literatures and for his specialized knowledge of Japanese literature. We thank Professor Maria Antonietta Saracino of the University of Rome for sharing with us her expertise in postcolonial literatures in English. The collaboration of Professor Maria Cristina Pisciotta in the area of Chinese literature and Professor Maurizio Riotto in Korean literature were indispensable to us. We thank also Professor James O. Pellicer for guidance in the field of Hispanic American literature; Professor Ingeborg Baumgartner for German literature; Professor Susan Brantly for Scandinavian literature; and Professor Bruce Merry for Greek literature.

A word of special appreciation for his valuable comments and suggestions must go to Dr. Richard Poate Stebbins, scholar, humanist, and linguist of Boston, Massachusetts. Professor Paul Archambault, Professor Marlène Barsoum, Professor Stuart Knee, Professor Arianna Maiorani, and Professor Beatrice Stiglitz are to be thanked in particular for their cooperation and support.

INTRODUCTION
Alba Amoia and Bettina L. Knapp

The Epicurean philosopher Philodemus of Gadara (first century B.C.E.) exhorts us to "save one another," thus providing an aphorism for a multicultural approach to literature and culture. Broadening our understanding of and compassion for foreigners and their mores may enhance our understanding of ourselves with respect to others (Gnisci and Sinopoli, eds., *Letteratura comparata*, 213–14).

THE WATERSHED YEAR OF 1945 AND BEYOND, ORIENT AND OCCIDENT

Africa

Contemporary African literature, straddling diverse social, cultural, religious, and political convictions, in the end crystallizes as a literary search for the African author's own identity. Some African writers (Sembene Ousmane, b. 1923; Ngūgī wa Thiong'o, b. 1938) relate the rise of national consciousness in Africa to World War II, when Africans fought side by side with whites against fascism, xenophobia, and racism, and realized that blacks and whites had similar qualities and defects (Jameson and Miyoshi, eds., *The Cultures of Globalization*, 114).

The "New African literature" emerged around 1960 concomitantly with the acquisition of independence by many African states. African writers, shifting from oral to written texts, used the former colonizers' linguae francae to replace their own spoken tribal languages. The Nigerian author Chinua Achebe (b. 1930) focuses on the importance of the linking language that permitted separate linguistic communities to communicate. The Somali novelist Nuruddin Farah (b. 1945), who went into exile to flee persecution by the Siyad Barre regime in 1974, declared in 1986: "I write in English and continue to be heard. . . . [O]therwise I would be easily silenced" (quoted in Sturrock, ed., *The Oxford Guide to Contemporary Literature* [hereafter abbreviated as *Oxford*], 14).

The exiled Mazisi Kunene (b. 1930, South Africa, an active member of the banned African National Congress) worked on an epic poem in praise of the early-nineteenth-century Zulu emperor Shaka that evokes the prowess of precolonial Africa. The English version of *Emperor Shaka the Great: A Zulu Epic* (1979) is his translation from his own Zulu original (*Oxford*, 6, 8).

South Africa's Nadine Gordimer (b. 1923; Nobel Prize for Literature, 1991), whose earlier bleak novels on life under apartheid helped to project a bridge to the outside world, tackles the theme of South Africa's new racism against clandestine immigrants in *The Pickup* (2001), about the love of a young Arab in Johannesburg for a white woman.

In North Africa, *pied-noir* literature was one of a migratory elite, written by men and women who were often of mixed European background, who wrote in French, and who lived in Algeria. Some authors, such as Albert Camus (1913–60; Nobel Prize for Literature, 1957) and Emmanuel Roblès (1914–95), did not limit their settings to Algeria. Camus described the Netherlands (in *La chute*, 1956) and Paris and Brazil (in two short stories in *L'exil et le royaume*, 1957); Roblès portrayed Mexico (in *Les couteaux*, 1956), Japan (in *L'homme d'avril*, 1959), and Italy (in *Le Vésuve*, 1961) (King, Connell, and White, eds., *Writing Across Worlds*, 134, 138).

With the coming of independence in 1962, most *pied-noir* writers left Algeria. Algerian-born Assia Djebar, following in Camus's footsteps, narrates the confining condition of double belonging (to Algeria and to France) in *Vaste est la prison* (1995), among other highly acclaimed works, and in *Ces voix qui m'assiègent . . . en marge de ma francophonie* (1999) she explores the question of identity and writing.

Second-generation Algerian migrants who live in France, such as the novelist and filmmaker Mehdi Cheref (b. 1952), declare that they feel "neither French nor Algerian" (quoted in Mahjoub, "An Interview with Mehdi Charef," 37).

Lusophone Africa boasts such internationally known writers as José Craveirinha (b. 1922) and Bernardo Mia Couto (b. 1955) from Mozambique, and Luandino Vieira (b. 1935) and Carlos Pepetela (b. 1941) from Angola. Also from Angola is the mestizo writer Mário António Fernandes de Oliveira (b. 1934), who, even while remaining deeply conscious of his African heritage, extended his vision to Europe, where he spent most of his life (Moser, "Neglected or Forgotten Authors of Lusophone Africa," 19).

Israel

The year 1948 marked the founding of the State of Israel, with an influx of refugees and a new literary scene. Older writers such as S. Yizhar

(b. 1916), Yehuda Amichai (1924–2000), and Aharon Appelfeld (b. 1932) concerned themselves mainly with the general history of the Jews. The younger generation of writers (born between 1949 and 1972), however, turned to personal analyses of individual experiences and the psychological effects of the Holocaust (Riggan, "Hebrew Literature in the 1990s," 477).

After a long silence in Israel on the subject of the Arabs' loss of their land, A. B. Yehoshua in 1968 published a volume of stories, *Mul haye'arot; sipurîm* (1968, English trans. *Facing the Forests*), a radical critique of the founding generation who repressed the Arabs in their midst and a plea that the unhealthy silence at the heart of Israeli society be addressed (*Oxford*, 241). Yehoshua's *Masa' el Tom ha-elef: Roman bi-sheloshah halakim* (1997, English trans. *Voyage to the End of the Millennium*) examines the very nature of Jewry in all its cultural, philosophic, religious, and ethnic aspects, and his collection of literary essays *Kohah ha-nora shel ashmah ketanah: Ha-heksher ha-musari shel ha-tekst ha-sifruti* (1998, English trans. *The Terrible Power of a Minor Guilt: Literary Essays*) explores the relationship between literature and morality through new interpretations of Euripides, Fedor Dostoevsky, William Faulkner, Albert Camus, Raymond Carver, and S(hmuel) Y(osef) Agnon.

India

Ever since India gained independence in 1947, there has been a huge Indian migration to Western English-speaking countries, particularly to Great Britain. Literary talent abounded in the post-1947 Indian government: President Radhakrishnan, Prime Minister Jawaharlal Nehru, Krishna Menon, and C. J. Rajagopalachari. The future of Indian literature lay, ironically, in English rather than in the Hindi language spoken by the majority of Indians or in any of the country's twelve other major tongues.

Conflict between Hindi and Urdu, the cultivated language of literary tradition spoken prevalently by Muslims, is flagrant, as illustrated in Anita Desai's (b. 1932) *In Custody* (1984). In *Baumgartner's Bombay* (2000), narrating India as seen through the eyes of a German Jew fleeing from Nazi persecution, Desai writes: "India was two worlds, or ten" (quoted in Saracino, *Altri lati del mondo*, 145).

With exceptions such as Mulkraj Anand (b. 1905), R. K. Narayan (b. 1907), and Raja Rao (b. 1909), few Indian writers before the 1930s had attempted prose fiction in English. Two major writers in the Indian languages were Rabindranath Tagore (b. 1861), who wrote in Bengali, and Premchand (b. 1880), who wrote in both Hindi and Urdu. Modern Indian writers suffer what Anand referred to as "the double burden on my shoulders, the Alps of the European tradition and the Himalaya of my Indian past" (quoted in Mishra, "A Spirit of Their Own," 47).

The Malayalam language has a form of literature that combines Sanskrit and Malayalam and is best represented by Kavalam Madhava Panikkar (1895–1963), playwright and novelist who wrote books on history and politics (e.g., *Asia and Western Dominance: A Survey of the Vasco da Gama Epoch of Asian History, 1498–1945*, 1953; and *The Afro-Asian States and Their Problems*, 1959). Panikkar wrote partly in English and partly in Malayalam.

Rajagopal Parthasarathy (b. 1934) announced in his essay "Whoring after English Gods" (1976) that his "prolonged and tempestuous affair with the English language" was over and that henceforth he would write in Tamil (quoted in *Oxford*, 208).

Vikram Seth (b. 1952)—author of the "great California novel" *The Golden Gate: A Novel in Verse* (1986) and of books with local characters set in the United States, India, and China, as well as an admirable translator of Chinese poems—is a new kind of international writer. It is as though Indian, Chinese, and American cultures were all available to him (*Oxford*, 219), a proof that national boundaries are falling.

Nor can one compartmentalize a Salman Rushdie (b. 1947; living in England and the United States, but born in Bombay of Muslim parents now in Pakistan); a V. S. Naipaul (who was born [1932] in Trinidad, of Indian descent, but left his distressed family to live in London and turn himself into a writer); a Hanif Kureishi (born [1954] and raised in England by a Pakistani father and an English mother), whose *The Buddha of Suburbia* (1990) explores so well the experience of living within an Asian community in a foreign land. The multicultural Indian novelist Amit Chaudhuri (b. 1962) sprinkles his works with a "drizzle of nostalgia-tinted impressions of Oxford and India" (Mishra, "A Spirit of Their Own," 52).

Sinhalese literature owes much to Michael Ondaatje (b. 1943) and to the Sri Lankan poet Romesh Gunesekera (b. 1954). Ondaatje, originally of Sri Lanka, moved to England in 1954 and emigrated to Canada in 1962. Winner of the 1992 Booker Prize, he produced the multiform, multivocal book *Running in the Family* (1982), which retraces the roots and the story of his European Ceylonese family and re-creates the multicultural reality of his country's colonial society before World War II. *The English Patient* (1992), set in Africa and in Italy, is based on four main characters, each a foreigner in an exotic country and in a situation of historical crisis where East and West meet. Gunesekera weaves themes of memory and exile, of history and postcolonial upheaval, and, rooting his narrations in both Asian and European culture, he sets some of his short stories (those of *Monkfish Moon*, 1992, for example) in Sri Lanka and England.

Ediriwira R. Sarachchandra (b. 1914) served in Paris as ambassador of Sri Lanka (1974–77), a sojourn that inspired the novel *With the Begging Bowl* (1986). In addition to his theatrical adaptations of various European and Japanese classics, he also translated into English his novel *Malagiya atto* (1959) and its sequel *Malavunge avurudu* (1965) under the title *Foam upon the Stream: A Japanese Elegy* (1987), set in Japan (Didier, *Dictionnaire universel des littératures*, 3: 3547–48).

China

Politics dictated literary practice in twentieth-century China. In the name of the Communist Revolution and of Mao Tse-tung's disastrous Cultural Revolution (1966–76), attacks on traditional culture practically smothered all literature. Most Western books were prohibited from the early 1960s to the mid-1980s—restrictions that only aroused hunger for non-Communist writings. The crackdown on intellectuals has often been referred to in China as its own Holocaust. The mainlanders who fled to Taiwan wrote stories centering on the homesickness felt by the exiles. Similarly, after the Tiananmen massacre of 1989, a large number of Chinese intellectuals went into exile. The diasporic existence of Taiwanese poet Dominic Cheung (Chang Ts'o) (b. 1943) resonates in his *Drifting* (2000), poems imbued with a longing for anchor and mooring. Ba Jin (b. 1904) of Chengdu was discovered in France, and French culture became an essential point of reference in his bilingual literary production; Ha Jin (pen name of Jin Xuefei), born in 1956 in Liaoning Province (southern Manchuria), moved from China to the United States in 1985 and now writes in English.

Gao Xingjian (b. 1940; Nobel Prize for Literature, 2000), having vowed never to return to China until the totalitarian system has been overthrown, is now a naturalized French citizen. His writings address fundamental issues of human existence. In his long novel *Lingshan* (1989, English trans. *Soul Mountain*), for example, he relates his five-month, 15,000-kilometer journey from central China to the east coast—a record of a lonely individual's quest for his soul, at the end of which he declares, "I comprehend nothing, I understand nothing" (cited in Wu, "Gao Xingjian: *Soul Mountain*," 101).

Japan

After Nagai Kafū (b. 1879) had prowled the Yoshiwara brothel district of Tokyo searching for material for his novels until his death in 1959, Suga Atsuko (b. 1929) learned in France and Italy to look at Japanese life with different eyes, and thus she crossed all barriers of time and culture. The early novels and short stories of Murakami Haruki (b. 1949) in the 1980s abound in references to Western culture; but his four years spent in the United States filled him with feelings of being a foreigner in his own homeland.

Vietnam

Vietnamese author Nhât Linh emigrated to China in 1945 (Didier, *Dictionnaire universel des littératures*, 3: 4035), while the years 1954–75 saw massive emigrations of North Vietnamese to the South. After the Vietnam War ended in 1975 with a Communist victory, almost 2 million Vietnamese emigrated to the West, among them the writers Nguyên Văn Sâm, who fled to the United States in 1979. In one short story of his collection *Khói sóng trên sông* (2000), an "overseas Vietnamese-American" yearns to return to his old way of life.

Despite the haven that France offers writers, exiled Linda Lê declares in *Fuir* (1988) that "the man who leaves his country is condemned to carry a goblin on his back to remind him of his betrayal" (quoted in Mai Mouniama's entry on Lê).

Korea

After regaining national sovereignty at the end of Japanese colonial rule (1910–45), Korea was then divided into North and South, even as writers strove to create a modernized Korean national literature. Up to the mid-1980s, Korean writers who remained in their homeland were subjected to strict censorship and a highly limited freedom of movement. Today the country's best-known author is Yi Munyŏl (b. 1948), whose concept of freedom is evocative of that of the French existentialist Jean-Paul Sartre. Other Korean writers living outside of their native land and adopting the language of the host country include Yu Miri in Japan and Yi Ch'angnae in the United States.

Australia and New Zealand

Out of an Australian cultural history already isolated by distance has sprung a vital and creative multicultural society bubbling with fresh immigrant blood from southern Europe, the Middle East, and Asia. Australians, as illustrated by the prolific David Malouf (b. 1934 in Brisbane of Lebanese and English parents), are the children of two worlds. Author of novels, short stories, poetry, and several opera libretti, Malouf features in *An Imaginary Life* (1978) the poet Ovid, banished from Rome, and creates a marriage of I and the not-I in a borderless, seamless universe.

Charles Brasch, the editor of *Landfall*, the dominant postwar literary magazine, wrote that New Zealand was indeed a long way from Europe, but that Europe could take root and flower there. C. K. Stead (b. 1932) identifies himself as a New Zealander, but he insists on the importance of European tradition. His *The New Poetic* (1964, rev. ed. 1987) is a study of Yeats, Eliot, and Pound (*Oxford*, 290–91), and the repertoire of his recent work *The Right Thing* (2000) ranges from variations on ancient classical poets (Horace, Catullus, etc.) to explorations of the Bible.

Although Brasch's Eurocentric generation felt their isolation, by the 1980s New Zealand came more into line with the rest of the world, thanks to some young writers who had begun to experiment with a new style of fiction à la Jorge Luis Borges, Samuel Beckett, Alain Robbe-Grillet, Italo Calvino, and other foreign writers. Additional inspirational French texts were those of Roland Barthes, Jacques Lacan, Jacques Derrida, and so forth. New Zealand writers born right after World War II were saturated with American culture, and in due course an American poetry class was established at Auckland University (*Oxford*, 284, 288, 292, 294).

Europe

Post-1950 **English literature** became invigorated with writers from North America, Australia, the Caribbean, South Asia, and Africa. British novelist Doris Lessing, born in Iran in 1919, dedicated to Southern Rhodesia (today's Zimbabwe) her unforgettable novel *The Grass Is Singing* (1950). Later expelled from that country, she has written several successful works, the latest of which is *Mara and Dann* (1999), in which she imagines life in the next ice age, when western Europe will have disappeared, the Mediterranean will have dried up, and human life on the continent now known as Ifrik (Africa) will have been reduced to a few warring tribes struggling to obtain food and water.

Talented young writer Justin Hill (b. 1971) portrays a young Englishman abroad, staggered by the cultural differences between China and the West, in *A Bend in the Yellow River* (1997), and in *The Drink and Dream Teahouse* (2001) he succeeds in letting his Chinese characters speak with their own voices in the absence of a Western narrator.

In **France,** Marguerite Duras (1914–96) narrated her own childhood in French Indochina in *Barrage contre le Pacifique* (1950), and journalist Claude Ollier (b. 1922) focused on landscapes and lifestyles in sundry foreign lands (in the fictional cycle *Le jeu d'enfant*, 1958–75; *Marrakch medine*, 1979; and *Mon double à Malacca*, 1982).

Jean-Marie Gustave Le Clézio's (b. 1940) mixed origins and international travel have inspired him to write works reflecting the combined influences of the South Seas, Central and North America, France, and Africa. A plethora of motley types, races, and religions simmer and steam in his poetic prose, transforming the act of writing into a cosmic experience.

Postwar **Italy** erupted into modernity with its rapid industrialization. The writer-filmmaker Pier Paolo Pasolini (1922–75) foresaw that Italy inevitably would become the future promised land for Indian, Arab, and African immigrants (Saracino, *Altri lati del mondo*, 23). Many writers drew their material from prewar experiences, as did Carlo Levi in *Cristo si è fermato a Eboli* (1945, English trans. *Christ Stopped at Eboli*), but Primo Levi focused on the twentieth-century Jewish experience in *Se questo è un uomo* (1947, English trans. *Survival in Auschwitz: The Nazi Assault on Humanity*).

The writings of both Elsa Morante (1912–85) and Alberto Moravia (1907–90), although not strictly multicultural, crossed the boundaries of insular Italy and are known worldwide. The contemporary Italian writers best known internationally are Umberto Eco (b. 1932), whose Italian Academy Lectures *Serendipities: Language and Lunacy* (1998, trans. William Weaver) delve into the mystery of the origin of languages and communication in general; and the journalist and novelist Oriana Fallaci (b. 1929), whose on-the-spot observances of the Vietnam War (*Niente e così sia*, 1969), of the Lebanese war (*Insciallah*, 1990), and of post–September 11 New York City (*La rabbia e l'orgoglio*, 2001), have made her into a quarrelsome cult figure.

Greek literature, for the first 15 years after World War II, concerned itself with the war against Italy (1940–41), the Axis occupation (1941–44), and the Resistance. The traumatic civil war and the defeat of the Communist left led to imprisonment or exile of thousands of Greeks, but from around 1960 to the establishment of the military dictatorship (1967), literature enjoyed a remarkable flowering with three dominant poets of the "Generation of 1930": Odysseas Elytis (b. 1911, Nobel Prize for Literature, 1979); Yannis Ritsos (1909–90), whose verse reflects opposition to the Greek junta that resulted in his exile; and George Seferis (1900–71, Nobel Prize for Literature, 1963), who also wrote poems on the theme of exile.

Nikos Kazantzakis, best known for his *Bíos kaì politeía toû Aléxi Zórmpa* (1946, later translated as *Zorba the Greek*), lived in France "in a kind of temperamental exile from Greece" (quoted from Bruce Merry's entry on Kazantzakis). Under the military dictatorship of the Greek colonels (1967–74), serious writers refused to publish their work, but a large group of young nonconformist poets known as "the poets of *amfisvitisi*" (challenge to accepted values) and later as the "Generation of 1970" emerged to give voice to new international influences and the impact of American culture (*Oxford*, 188, 189).

In 1960, **Spain** began to emerge from the isolated, oppressive years of Francisco Franco's dictatorship. In *Tiempo de silencio* (1962, English trans. *Time of Silence*), Luis Martin-Santos (1924–64) introduced new literary devices in the Spanish novel. The underground playwright Fernando Arrabal (b. 1932) fled to Paris, where he founded the "panic theater"— his brand of theater of the absurd. Only after Franco's death could his plays be performed in Spain.

Juan Goytisolo (b. 1931 in Barcelona), cofounder of the "Turia" literary group, also fled Spain for France. *Señas de identidad* (1966, English trans. *Marks of Identity*) is the first novel in a trilogy that also includes *Reivindicación del Conde don Julián* (1970, English trans. *Count Julian*) and *Juan sin tierra* (1975, English translation, *Juan the Landless*). The trilogy is about a Barcelonan's increasing alienation, while in Paris, from his identity as a member of a Spaniard family with a slave-owning colonial past. The novel *Las virtudes del pájaro solitario* (1988, English trans. *The Virtues of the Solitary Bird*) juxtaposes medieval Spain's Christian and Sufi mysticism, its Catholicism and Islamism, even while demystifying homo-sexuals and AIDS victims (*Oxford*, 379–80).

In **Spanish America,** Pablo Neruda (1904–73; Nobel Prize for Litera-ture, 1971) had completed most of his important poetic work before 1960 (especially his celebrated *Veinte poemas de amor y una canción deses-perada*, 1924). In the 1960s, as though in response to Fidel Castro's 1959 revolution, the need for a Spanish American cultural voice became overt and manifested itself in a veritable literary boom. A generation of writers came of age at much the same time: Argentinian Julio Cortázar, Cuban Guillermo Cabrera Infante, Peruvian Mario Vargas Llosa, Mexican Car-los Fuentes, Colombian Gabriel García Márquez (Nobel Prize for Liter-ature, 1982), and Chilean José Donoso. With them, Spanish American fiction found new confidence and a sense of its place in the world (*Oxford*, 393). The Mexican poet and critic Octavio Paz (1914–98; Nobel Prize for Literature, 1990) underscored the coexistence of a variety of civilizations and historical pasts in Spanish Americans.

With the departure of the Fascist dictatorship of António de Oliveira Salazar and Marcello Caetano (1925–74), the progress of the proletariat became the subject of **Portugal**'s neorealist literature; subsequently the concern was with the middle class and their problems (*Oxford*, 311–12). The Nobel Prize for Literature was bestowed in 1998 on José Saramago (b. 1922), but his subject matter is mainly Portuguese Iberian or allegor-ical rather than multicultural.

In the **Netherlands,** Cees Nooteboom (b. 1933) developed the travel narrative in the direction of the personal essay. His *De Zucht naar het Westen* (The longing for the West, 1985) grew out of a series of visits to the United States during the 1970s and the 1980s. But his love of Spain dominates, as reflected in *Omweg naar Santiago* (1992, English trans. *Roads to Santiago: Detours and Riddles in the Lands and History of Spain*).

For many years after 1945, **Scandinavian** writers focused on the after-effects of World War II, Finland's war against Russia, Germany's occupa-tion of Norway and Denmark, and Sweden's compromised neutrality. But Swedish literature extended its horizons more than that of Norway and Denmark. The Swedish author Jan Myrdal (b. 1927), originally a novelist, turned away from fiction, considering it a form of lying that drove readers away from purposeful action to change the world. His *Rap-port från kinesisk by* (1963, English trans. *Report from a Chinese Village*) is an unbiased account of a trip to China and Mao's new society, and *Samtida bekännelser av an Europeisk intellektuell* (1964, English trans. *Con-fessions of a Disloyal European*) critically assesses Western society and Myrdal's own role as an intellectual (*Oxford*, 341).

Another Swedish writer to abandon fiction—in this case for reportage—is Sara Lidman (b. 1923), who eventually left Sweden for South Africa. There she produced two novels in English about apartheid, was arrested, and then expelled. During the Vietnam War, she visited

Hanoi, recording in *Samtal i Hanoi* (1966) her observations of events and her support of the Vietnamese harrowed by U.S. bombings.

The Danish poet Henrik Nordbrandt (b. 1945), having lived in Greece and Turkey, romantically rejects what he considers the North's cold rationality in order to embrace southern experiences of sensuousness and mysticality (*Oxford*, 351).

In **Germany,** writers of the generation of Hans Werner Richter (1908–93) and Alfred Andersch (1914–80), originators of the Gruppe '47, found themselves looking to the United States (Ernest Hemingway and William Faulkner), France (Albert Camus and Jean-Paul Sartre), and Italy (Elio Vittorini, Cesare Pavese, Alberto Moravia) for literary models. The antiwar novel *Blechtrommel* (1959, English trans. *The Tin Drum*) by Günter Grass (b. 1927; Nobel Prize for Literature, 1999), informed by a sense of the fragility of the concept of "enemy," became an international best-seller. It inaugurated the West German literature of the 1960s, contributing to a new sense of East German–West German identity (*Oxford*, 166). Although a recurrent theme in Grass's writings is that of refugees and flight, in his most recent works he has manifested a universal interest in embracing life and history as a whole.

Ingeborg Bachmann's (1926–73) poems include many inspired by her life in Italy and several that originated on a trip to Prague ("Wenzelsplatz," "Jüdischer Friedhof," and "Poliklinik Prag," 1963–65). She had much in common, poetically and politically, with the Romanian German-language poet Paul Celan.

After World War II and the Communist takeover in **Poland,** the cultural clock stopped. Czesław Miłosz (b. 1911; Nobel Prize for Literature, 1980) emigrated to France, then in 1960 went to Berkeley, California, which permitted him to publicize the suffocation of literary and other freedoms in Poland. His *Widzenia nad Zatoką San Francisco* (1969, English trans. *Visions from San Francisco Bay*) places an American location within a larger historical context, even while helping to alter visions of the New World in the European mind. The American poet laureate Robert Pinsky has referred to Miłosz as "an essential American poet—perhaps even the most important living American poet" (quoted in Carpenter, "The Gift Returned," 631).

Soviet leader Josef Stalin's death freed theater directors to produce their new brand of absurdist plays such as those by Stanislaw Ignacy Witkiewicz (1885–1939). And the eclectic fusion of Eastern and Western theatrical styles in the work of Jerzy Grotowski (b. 1933) demonstrated that, ironically, the agony of Communist rule stimulated rather than annihilated theater.

Life under Communist rule was the subject matter for **Czechoslovakian** novelists in exile (Josef Škvorecký, Milan Kundera) and for those in the homeland writing as dissidents (Ivan Klíma, Ludvík Vaculík, Pavel Kohout). In his memoir, translated as *Headed for the Blues* (1996, 1997), the émigré Škvorecký (b. 1924), now living in Canada, continues to inveigh against the regime's thwarting of his own and others' literary talents. Kundera (b. 1929), whose first novel, *Žert* (1967), brought official disfavor and loss of citizenship, moved to France and became a French citizen in 1980. He has turned to more general themes in his four most recent books, originally written in French: *L'art du roman* (1986), *Les testaments trahis* (1993), *La lenteur* (1995), and *L'identité* (1997).

The displacement process that took place during World War II and immediately afterward in Europe is described by **Slovenian** authors whose autobiographical or purely fictional narratives treat the myth of the New World as one of their main themes. The protagonist in *He, the Father* (1950), by Slovene American Australian author Frank Mlakar (1913–61), sees America as a land of opportunity, but only for the diligent, the brave, and the daring. On returning to his homeland, he finds it as impoverished and corrupt as ever (King, Connell, and White, eds., *Writing Across Worlds*, 168).

Similarly, in *Men Who Built the Snowy* (1984), Australian Slovene Ivan Kobal (b. 1928) reiterates Mlakar's observation that the fairytale aspect of the New World gives way to brutal reality. Other Slovene Australian and Slovene Canadian authors continue to cherish their dreams in the New World until they feel the lack of their old-fashioned ways and find nothing to replace them. Others return to their homeland, but ironically fare no better.

Albania's writers and intellectuals underwent a purge in 1973 that represented a serious setback for the development of literature and culture. The geopolitically isolated country was edging in the 1970s toward the nadir of the era of Enver Hoxha, Albania's Communist leader and general. Ties with the Soviet Union had been severed in 1961 and with China in 1976–77. During this period, Ismail Kadare (b. 1936), the leading exponent of literary creativity, wrote a succession of historical novels. *Nepunesi i pallatit te ëndrrave* (1981, English trans. *The Palace of Dreams*) is set in a fantastic nineteenth-century Istanbul, and *Pluhuri mbreteror* (1995, English trans. *The Pyramid*), unfolds in ancient Egypt. He has "his own complex loyalties to an inner, mythic world, while never ceasing to be an employee of the Palace of Nightmares that was Enver Hoxha's Albania" (Malcolm, "In the Palace of Nightmares," 24). Kadare fled to Paris in 1990 and has become an established figure on the French and European scene. He revised his novel *Nëntori i një kryeqyteti* (1975), deleting much of the period propaganda from a plot that was politically conformist. It appeared in French translation in 1998 (*Novembre d'une capitale)*.

The Soviet Union and Russia

Writers who remained in the Soviet Union could not but recognize the superior quality of works written by Russians abroad. Vladimir Nabokov

(1899–1977) in the United States had made his mark as one of the most original masters of twentieth-century fiction.

From Paris came the brilliant comedy *Zhizn' i neobychainye prikliucheniia soldata Ivana Chonkina* (1975, English trans. *The Life and Extraordinary Adventures of Private Ivan Chonkin*), and its sequel, *Pretendent na prestol: Novye prikliuchenie soldata Ivana Chonkin* (1979, English trans. *Pretender to the Throne*) by the banned writer Vladimir Voinovich (b. 1932). Also in Paris the political refugee Andrei Makine (b. 1957?) wrote several novels in French, especially *Le testament français* (1995, Prix Goncourt and Prix Medicis *ex aequo*, English trans. *Dreams of My Russian Summers*, 1997), in which he questions the nature of cultural belonging, and *Au temps du fleuve Amour* (1994, English trans. *Once upon the River Love*, 1998), which examines the divide between East and West and in what ways they meet. Makine has been compared to Vladimir Nabokov in that they both return to the memory of speaking in a foreign language.

United States, Canada, and the Caribbean

For post–World War II **American literature,** mention must be made again of Nabokov, who wrote so intriguingly in his native Russian while he was in England and Germany and so brilliantly in English about the myths of post–World War II America in *Lolita* (1953). His cross-cultural ties can be recognized easily in his writings completed during his "American" years.

Writing in the American idiom, poet William Carlos Williams (1883–1963) was seen by some as a multiculturalist who counterposed his Spanish Caribbean heritage and a Eurocentric world.

The explosive growth of **Asian American literature** in the United States reflects the unique place held by Asian Americans in their new culture. Korean America is represented in *East to America: Korean American Life Stories* (1996) by Elaine H. Kim and Eui-Young Yu, spirited stories that present a complex web of historical and cultural forces that shape and are shaped by the protagonists.

The Chinese American experience is reflected in the works of Ha Jin. Having studied American literature at Shandong University, he chooses to write in English, but his linguistic dissections of Chinese society retain a definite Chinese flavor (*Ocean of Words*, 1996; *Under the Red Flag*, 1997; *In the Pond*, 1998; *Waiting*, 1999).

Protagonists are poised between Chinese and American identities in the work of Maxine Hong Kingston (b. 1940), in particular *The Woman Warrior* (1976), which describes a Chinese childhood in California, and *China Men* (1980), which goes back in time to her father's and grandfather's generations, when the tide of Chinese immigrants shaped so many of New York's laundry shops and restaurants (*Oxford*, 415).

Asian American culture is characterized by class, gender, and intergenerational conflict, and Asian Americans remain anachronistic. Lisa Lowe's critical writings of the 1990s show the complications of class differences in the heterogeneous Asian American culture group and contextualize the dominated-dominator relationship between East and West. The fiction of Chitra Banerjee Divakaruni (b. 1957) of India, who now lives in California, is based on biculturalism. In her novel *The Mistress of Spices* (1997), she narrates the Indian experience of isolation in the immigrant world of California, where Indians try to carve out an identity for themselves. *Sister of My Heart* (1999) links two women who fit into each other's lives—one in India, one in California.

Bharati Mukherjee (b. 1940), whose childhood was multilingual and multiethnic, went from Bengal to the United States and is claimed as both an Indian and an American writer. In *Darkness* (1985) and *The Middleman and Other Stories* (1988), she offers her readers insights into the positive and negative force of tradition and inherited traits (*Oxford*, 419). Declaring her literary preference for Asian immigration stories, Mukherjee urges Asian-born writers in North America to reject tales set in India in favor of narrated experiences of immigrants.

Pakistani writer Bapsi Sidhwa (b. 1938), now a citizen of the United States, focuses in *An American Brat* (1993) on both her contemporary Parsi life in Pakistan and her immigrant experience in the United States.

Jewish American writing made a breakthrough on the American scene in the 1950s and 1960s with the Polish-born Isaac Bashevis Singer (1904–91), winner of the Nobel Prize for Literature in 1978. He wrote in New York, in Yiddish, about the degeneration of a Jewish family in Warsaw from 1900 to World War II; about the destinies of Holocaust survivors searching for answers to life's questions; and about the problems of a Polish Holocaust survivor living in Brooklyn. Kurt Vonnegut Jr. (b. 1922) protested the horrors of the twentieth century in *Player Piano* (1951), *Slaughterhouse Five* (1969), *Deadeye Dick* (1982), and *Hocus Pocus* (1990).

By the 1990s, a few Jewish writers sought the panacea of cultural syncretism. The Buddhist Jewish encounter is illustrated in *High Holiday Sutra* (1997) by Allan Appel (b. 1945) and in *The Jew in the Lotus: A Poet's Rediscovery of Jewish Identity in Buddhist India* (1994) by Rodger Kamenetz (b. 1950).

Although the 1960s saw many **Canadians** expatriating themselves to Great Britain, most had returned to their roots by 1975, when the multiculturalist era in Canada was already under way. After the 1970s, the palette of early and traditional Anglophone and Francophone literatures of Canada became more complex, as immigrant authors exploring their cultural roots emerged on the Canadian literary scene: Michael Ondaatje of Sri Lanka, Rohinton Mistry (b. 1952) of India, Cyril Dabydeen (b. 1945) of Guyana, M. G. Vassanji (b. 1950) of Tanzania, Joy Kogawa (b. 1935) of Japan, and Sergio Kokis (b. 1944) of Brazil. Kokis's *Le pavillon* *des miroirs* (1999), for example, focuses on the narrator's experiences of the antipodal cultures of Brazil and Canada, between which he oscillates to discover who he is.

A London-based Canadian expatriate, Michal Ignatieff (b. 1944), became director of the Carr Centre of Human Rights Policy. He searches for his family's Russian past and reflects on self and identity in the novels *The Russian Album* (1987) and *Isya* (1991).

In the **Caribbean,** the Atlantic slave trade serves as the impetus for a complex exploration of what constitutes home (see the later discussion of Derek Walcott). The strong nationalist movements that accelerated in the 1940s and eventually led to self-government did not radically change the basic social and linguistic structure of the Caribbean. The Africans imported as slaves, unable to use their own native languages, had to learn the Creole languages that were also adopted by indentured East Indians. The twentieth-century Anglophone Caribbean thus inherited a structure in which standard English was the language of officialdom and education, of the expatriate plantocracy and the middle class, white and mulatto, whereas the first language of the workers and peasants (Indian or black) was Creole (*Oxford*, 449–50).

Patrick Chamoiseau's *Solibo Magnifique* (1988, English trans. *Solibo Magnificent*) was a translation challenge with its three linguistic modes— French, Creole, and the idiom of the current Creolist group. Raphaël Confiant, writing in his customary blend of standard French and Creole, stresses in *Eloge de la créolité* (1989, coauthored with Jean Bernabé and Patrick Chamoiseau), *Commandeur du sucre* (1994), and *Régisseur du rhum* (1999) the heterogeneity and hybridity of Martinique's people and an economy that rests on racial inequality.

POSTCOLONIAL MULTICULTURALISM

Imperialist nations assumed that colonial conquest "civilized," that colonized peoples needed to be guided and vivified by ever-renewed European intelligence. (A recent thesis, however, argues that the British Empire rested not on postulations of inferiority and subordination but rather on the construction of a comfortingly analogous Other [David Cannadine in *Ornamentalism: How the British Saw Their Empire* (2001) reviewed by Smith, "Refuge for the Aristocracy," 30].)

Before the appearance of the new African, Caribbean, and Indian literatures, Western writers had ventriloquized the voices of colonized people. In the postcolonial period, however, the new writers spoke for themselves. Some attached cultural prestige to the use of English and French, but in the main they continued to use both native and adopted languages. Léopold Sédar Senghor of Senegal (1906–2001), embodying both an African cultural, psychological, and spiritual identity and an undeniable "Frenchity," used to say that he thought in African but wrote in French. The Moroccan author Tahar Ben Jelloun (b. 1944; Prix Goncourt, 1987) paved the way for Maghrebian writers who, owing to their heavy colonial heritage, still today express themselves in French. The Egyptian Nagib Mahfouz (b. 1911; Nobel Prize for Literature, 1988) opened the doors for authors who wrote in their native Arabic.

Many African and Maghrebian intellectuals, ironically forced to emigrate to the very countries that had colonized their own lands, wrote of the conflict between their traditional cultures and those of contemporary western Europe. They moved between two worlds and two identities, either separating or linking the two cultures—or both. The Sudanese novelist al-Tayyib Salih (b. 1929), writing in Arabic, confronts his own society with that of London of the 1950s and underscores the plight of the African intellectual in Europe in *Mawsim al-Hijrah ila᾽ al-Shamal* (1966, English trans. *A Season of Migration to the North*) (Saracino, *Altri lati del mondo*, 121).

African writers focus on the dichotomies of tradition and modernity. The two long poems *Song of Lawino: A Lament* and *Song of Ocol*, by Okot p'Bitek (1931–82), capture town and village, the European and the African: an Acoli (native African) wife derides her husband for his affair with a totally Westernized woman *(Song of Lawino)*. Her husband's reply *(Song of Ocol)* recalls the past nostalgically but laments bitterly that the postcolonial ideal has not been realized *(Oxford*, 9).

The "new" literature is profiting from the postcolonial wisdom of its authors. Chinua Achebe (b. 1930), a pioneer among Africans actually writing in English, tells the story of a Nigerian village at the time of the whites' arrival *(Things Fall Apart*, 1958). He does not try to convince his readers that, prior to the whites' arrival, Nigeria lived in a sort of Golden Age. Nonetheless, he believes that the English did not have the right to destroy the villages' ancient mores. Under the dictates and the violence of the English, everything "fell apart."

The Francophone *négritude* movement that rejected the French policy of assimilation and affirmed the African heritage, was pioneered in the 1930s by Senghor and Aimé Césaire and was nurtured in Paris after World War II. Writers abandoned their *Francité* (Frenchity) to embrace *négritude*, looked to Africa for inspiration, and experimented with their own genres (for example, Senghor's seminal 1948 anthology of black poetry, *Anthologie de la nouvelle poésie nègre et malgache de langue française*). Martinican Frantz Fanon (1925–61), in *Peau noire, masques blancs* (1952, English trans. *Black Skin, White Masks*), describes the blacks' feelings of inferiority and how Antillean blacks lost their identity both at home and abroad. Fanon rejected assimilation and *négritude*: he was for worldwide struggles for independence (King, Connell, and White, eds. *Writing Across Worlds*, 111–12). Fanon's compatriot Édouard Glissant (b. 1928) also insisted on the value of cultural specificity. His experiences of exile in Paris led to the formulation of his theory of an Antillean identity,

"Antillanité" (cf. his novel *Tout-monde*, 1993). From the 1970s, Glissant had called for West Indian culture to repatriate itself to the Caribbean—not to France, not to mythical Africa, not to utopian revolution. He concocted a melange of European, African, and other Antillean traditions, anchored firmly in the Creole islands—*Créolité*—that crystallized in the 1980s. For Glissant, the West Indies should have its own cultural and linguistic syncretism. The West Indian identity should be represented by contact between and intermixture of cultural systems as an alternative to racism, differential attitudes, and religious fundamentalism (King, Connell, and White, eds., *Writing Across Worlds*, 105, 120).

Guadeloupean Maryse Condé (b. 1937) chronicles the black diaspora to the Caribbean. *Hérémakhonon* (1976) tells of a black West Indian who, in search of her identity, goes to Africa to find her roots, is disabused, and goes to the United States, where she realizes the relative unimportance of having a country, a language, or even a particular place of origin. Condé likes to explore the evolution of Creole culture in multigenerational novels, to show how culture can cause human beings and their personalities either to blossom or to wither.

Gisèle Pineau (b. 1956), the author of *L'exil selon Julia* (1996), belongs to both Guadeloupe and France, whose linguistic, spatial, and cultural differences she explores in her works based on personal experience.

David Dabydeen (b. 1955 in Guyana), author of *A Harlot's Progress* (1999), about the terrible voyages of African slaves and indentured Indian servants to the Caribbean, focuses in other novels on the personal and historical complexities of migration to England. Caryl Phillips (b. 1958 on St. Kitts) is a Briton, but he also belongs to the African diaspora. He makes the parallel between the sufferings of the Jews of Europe and those of Africans (*The Nature of Blood*, 1997). His recent work, *The Atlantic Sound* (2000), retraces the routes of slave ships from Europe to Africa and then to the New World. Where must the African diaspora see its future?

The West Indian Derek Walcott (b. 1930; Nobel Prize for Literature, 1992) explores the pros and cons of the West Indian mixed society (*In a Green Night*, 1962, and the autobiographical *Another Life*, 1973). *Omeros* (1990) echoes the travels in Homer's *Iliad* and *Odyssey*, as Walcott examines the Caribbean tapestry of Europeans, Africans, and Indians. His "black Homer" says: "A drifter is the hero of my book" (quoted in King, Connell, and White, eds., *Writing Across Worlds*, 103). In *What the Twilight Says* (1998), Walcott's Caribbean man cannot go back to Africa, and he cannot be white, so he must create a new literature.

Indian literature mixes adopted European values and unrepudiated Indian claims and assumptions, with the result that Indian characters in immigrant milieus live out the most that an exile can expect: only "half a life," the title of V. S. Naipaul's recent novel (2001). Many important Indian and Pakistani writers, expatriates from the subcontinent for economic or academic reasons, or the offspring of emigrated families abroad, have become citizens of the country that has received them—for example, Salman Rushdie, Hanif Kureishi, and Naipaul. Naipaul (Nobel Prize for Literature, 2001), a confirmed expatriate formed by three cultures (Hindu, Trinidadian, and English), explores the condition of the colonial or marginal individual. He continues to search for himself in his labyrinthine and ever more difficult wanderings between Orient and Occident, suspended as he is between England and India. In later autobiographical works, he makes the story of his own "an archetype of colonial experience" (*Oxford*, 133).

EXILE, EXPATRIATION, AND ESCAPE: LEITMOTIFS OF POSTWAR LITERATURE

War deracinated many modern authors, and generations of refugee and emigrant writers were uprooted by twentieth-century restlessness. The exile experience was marked by an uneasy clinging to old habits and tenacious remembrance of what could not be reconstructed. Exiled writers usually started publishing works about the political events in the country they fled, and later, when they sought a homeland abroad, their themes were of alienation, of being a stranger in a strange land. The Somalian Nuruddin Farah (b. 1945), escaping on four continents from the ruthless dictator Siyad Barre, "in many respects emblemizes the archetypal twentieth-century condition of exile" (Riggan, "Nuruddin Farah's Indelible Country of the Imagination: The 1998 Neustadt International Prize for Literature," 701). André Aciman (b. 1951), the author of *Out of Egypt: A Memoir* (1996), as an exile in New York from Alexandria writes: "[A]n exile is not just someone who has lost his home; it is someone who can't find [or think of] another" ("Shadow Cities," 35).

Young authors who were bred in Algeria but live in France and then "return" to Algeria depict this land in the blackest of colors as a place to flee forever (King, Connell, and White, eds., *Writing Across Worlds*, 89, 136). Malika Mokeddem (b. 1956), in *L'interdite* (1993), tells of an Algerian woman doctor who, after experiencing political violence, flees to France, where she is made to feel a marginalized foreigner. Subsequently she returns to her primitive native village, where she tries to integrate two different cultures in her life.

Exile or study overseas have helped South African writers to address apartheid. After a long detention in South Africa, Breyten Breytenbach (b. 1939) moved to Paris, took a Vietnamese wife, and became a citizen of France. He renounced his Afrikaner birthright in *The True Confessions of an Albino Terrorist* (1982) (*Oxford*, 18). Bessie Head (1937–86), when her native South Africa closed its doors to her, gathered and transcribed oral testimony from villagers in Botswana (*Serowe: Village of the Rain Wind*, 1981), thereby saving Serowe's history from oblivion.

East European exiles who influenced world poetry—Joseph Brodsky, Czesław Miłosz, and the Lithuanian poet Tomas Venclova (b. 1937)—all in some way evoke the estrangement, bitterness, and disorientation of their lives in absence from their countries.

Exile is often juxtaposed with escape—the yearning to redefine one's identity or to live out an imagined life elsewhere. The Albanian writer Fatos Kongoli (b. 1944), author of *Dragoi i fildishtë* (1999, French trans. *Le dragon d'ivoire*), relates (probably autobiographically) the decisive years of an Albanian student in China in the 1960s as he comes into contact with students from other parts of the world. Thirty years later, back in stifling postcommunist Albania, he is an isolated and despairing alcoholic.

Writers who chose exile or escaped to produce their work include Samuel Beckett (1906–89; Nobel Prize for Literature, 1969), who fled Ireland, Gabriel García Márquez (b. 1928; Nobel Prize for Literature, 1982), and Günter Grass (b. 1927), the latter two writing their "national" novels in Paris: *Cien años de soledad* (1967, English trans. *One Hundred Years of Solitude*), and *Blechtrommel* (1959, English trans. *The Tin Drum*), respectively. Some emigrant Irish authors recognized the ignorance and bigotry of their own country while they were in exile. Some, such as Beckett, merged into their host society to embrace its literary, philosophical, and cultural preoccupations; others, such as Edna O'Brien (b. 1930), denounced the society from which she came (King, Connell, and White, eds., *Writing Across Worlds*, 20). The New York–based Irish author Frank McCourt (b. 1932) depicts the poverty and desolation of his miserable Irish Catholic childhood in his memoir *Angela's Ashes* (1996), and in *'Tis: A Memoir*, its sequel (1999), he tells the story of his American journey from impoverished immigrant to brilliant teacher and raconteur.

African, Middle Eastern, Caribbean, and West Indian writers realized that they could better launch their works through self-exile to the world's great metropolitan centers. Paris and London, for example, have become leading centers of Arabic intellectual life and publishing. The Moroccan Tahar Ben Jelloun, the Lebanese Adonis (b. 1930, pseudonym of Ali Aḥmad Saiʾīd Esber), and the Syrian Mahmoud Darwish (b. 1941) live and write in Paris, as does the Lebanese-born Egyptian Andrée Chedid (b. 1920), who publishes her novels in French, having made Paris her home since 1946 (*Oxford*, 37).

Lebanon's cultural life had been enriched by an inflow of exiled Palestinian writers, but after the Lebanese civil war (1975–91) there was a noticeable outflow of writers and intellectuals to Paris, London, and the United States (*Oxford*, 26). Three contemporary Lebanese authors—all concerned with the complexities of survival during the war, self-identification, and life in exile—are Rabih Alameddine (in his forties, now residing in San Francisco, author of *Homesick*, 1997), Tony Hanania (b. 1964, now living in London, author of *Unreal City*, 1999), and Hani Hammoud (b. 1963, now the director of Radio Orient in Paris and author of *L'Occidentaliste*, 1997).

George Lamming (b. 1927 in Barbados) has written novels about postwar migration to England, the first of which, *In the Castle of My Skin* (1953), addresses the destructive aspects of the education he received under colonialism and the pressures that forced him into exile. Themes of exile also characterize his works *The Emigrants* (1954) and *Water with Berries* (1971) (*Oxford*, 454). In *The Pleasures of Exile* (1960), Lamming writes: "To be colonial is to be in a state of exile" (quoted in King, Connell, and White, eds., *Writing Across Worlds*, 59).

In *The Lonely Londoners* (1956), Samuel Selvon (1923–94) of Trinidad gives tragic undertones to the plight of unemployed West Indian exiles in London, but he also brings out the comic side of their natures. The protagonist of his *Moses Ascending* (1975) and *Moses Migrating* (1983) eventually returns to the Caribbean but, with a premonition of making a mistake, purposely does not sell his house in London (*Oxford*, 455–56).

In Jamaica Kincaid's autobiographical *At the Bottom of the River* (1983) and *Annie John* (1985), the heroine, Annie, wonderfully content in her Antiguan "paradise," goes to live in the United States, where slowly it becomes clear to her how tradition bound are her mother and her island society.

And Tamai Kobayashi sets her short stories (*Exile and the Heart*, 1998) in moving, recollected landscapes of North America and Japan.

Holocaust Literature

Patrick Modiano (b. 1945), author of *Voyage de noce* (1990, English trans. *Honeymoon*), explains contemporary feelings of uprootedness, estrangement, and existential anguish as deriving from the unassimilated horrors of the Holocaust (*Oxford*, 147).

The Holocaust has produced a mass of literature (by writers such as Paul Celan, Primo Levi, and others). In particular, the powerful writings of Elie Wiesel (Nobel Peace Prize, 1986) have established him as the bard of Jewish suffering. The literature of the Shoah, combining testimony, document, and fiction, desperately attempts to "give verbal expression to an experience that challenges and defies the boundaries of language yet emerges through it" (Ramras-Rauch, "Aharon Appelfeld: A Hundred Years of Jewish Solitude," 493).

The Hebrew writer who has painted Jewish suffering most movingly is Israel's Aharon Appelfeld (b. 1932 in Romania). He does not merely narrate his pain and distress. He tries to explain the reasons for the Holocaust. His masterpiece, *Tor ha-pela'ot* (1978, English trans. *The Age of Wonders*), a novel about the frustration among Jewish intellectuals in central Europe in the 1930s, telescopes time and crystallizes the horrors of

Appelfeld's past (*Oxford*, 243). The author expands the broad historical scope of his earlier works to concentrate on the inner world of Shoah victims in *Kutonet Veha-passim* (1983, English trans. *Tzili: The Story of a Life*), *Mikreh Ha-Kerah* (1997, English trans. *The ice mine*), and *Mesilat barzel* (1991, English trans. *The Iron Tracks*).

David Grossman (b. 1954), who knows both Hebrew and Arabic, is "an unflinching commentator on Jewish-Palestinian relations." His novel *ᶜAyen ᶜerekh—ahavah* (1986, English trans. *See Under—Love*) is about Israeli society's silence on the subject of its damaged national psyche because of the Holocaust (*Oxford*, 247–48).

TRAVEL AND EXOTIC LITERATURE AND THE EFFECTS OF DISTANCE

Fictional visions of new worlds materialized in the works of travel writers who labored under the illusion that life elsewhere must be different, that extreme climates and bizarre landscapes must breed human beings quite unlike us. This universal delusion is fast disappearing.

In the past, the point of travel was chiefly commercial, exploratory, and scientific. Subsequently it became more personally oriented—a self-evaluation through "getting to know" the other. It served also to construct one's identity through encounter with the exotic "elsewhere." About 20 years ago, the English review *Granta* relaunched "travel writing" in a form similar to the classical travel narrative. *Granta* gathered into its ranks journalists and writers of talent (Jonathan Raban, Bruce Chatwin, Salman Rushdie, Neal Ascherson, James Fenton, Ryszard Kapuściński). Today, imitators of the restless Bruce Chatwin (1940–89) abound. He traveled to the Sudan, where he lived with nomads, and wrote about Dahomey. Many of his works focus not on countries but on places between and beyond nations: *In Patagonia* (1977), the semiarid, windswept plateau of southern Argentina; *The Viceroy of Ouidah* (1980), the old kingdom of Dahomey; *On the Black Hill* (1982), the Welsh Marches; and *The Songlines* (1987), the Australian Outback. His urge to travel he explained by the nomadic imperative—that humans are fitted for wandering and not for a sedentary life and that nomadism is the true condition of humans, for, in his phrase, "possessions exhaust us" (quoted in Ryle, "Nomad," 7).

The poetics of travel has gained ground (Didier, *Dictionnaire universel des littératures*, 3: 4071); today's travel writers blend history, myth, technology, and poetic imagination. Jean-Marie Gustave Le Clézio (b. 1940) portrays humans as errant, obsessed with death and dissatisfaction, in a search to quench their spiritual thirst. The French poetic prose writer Julien Gracq (b. 1910) glorifies Venice and creates a mythical landscape for his novel *Le rivage des Syrtes* (1951); but he denigrates Rome, describing his own disappointed reactions rather than reality in his peremptory *Autour des sept collines* (1988).

The Austrian writer Peter Handke (b. 1942) wrote 17 colorful journals on trips around the world (for example, *Noch einmal für Thukydides*, 1990, English trans. *Once Again for Thucydides*). The Italian novelist and short story writer Alberto Moravia (1907–90) was also a travel writer of ilk, whose probing accounts of visits to China, India, and Africa are still read today.

The Polish writer and journalist Ryszard Kapuściński (b. 1932) offers major reportages on the Soviet Union and Africa that break new ground in their treatment of history, in particular his volumes *Imperator* (1992, English trans. *Imperium*), on the fall of the Soviet Union, and *Heban* (1998, English trans. *The Shadow of the Sun*), on the life he shared with ordinary people across the African continent.

Ingo Schulze (b. 1963 in Dresden, East Germany) gained profound insights into the life and thinking of the Russian people after six months in St. Petersburg. The result was *Augenblicke des Glücks* (1995, English trans. *33 Moments of Happiness: St. Petersburg Stories*)—"a fusion of travel writing and fiction, some of it surrealist, some Chekovian" (Annan, "Nesting Dolls," 35). In Schulze's 1998 heroless novel *Simple Storys: Ein Roman aus der ostdeutschen Provinz*, a trip to Assisi helps to define the unfortunate condition of living in East Germany.

The much-traveled New Yorker Paul Bowles (1910–99), who lived for 50 years in Morocco, produced a travel book from his own particular point of view: disgust with Western civilization. Its significant title is *Their Heads Are Green and Their Hands Are Blue* (1963).

Mexican Octavio Paz, attracted by the mystery of the Orient, traveled to India and Japan—a journey that had an enormous influence in his life (see his *Ladera este*, 1969). The adventures of the hero of *The Circle of Reason* (1986), the first novel by Amitav Ghosh (b. 1956), take him from his home in an Indian village through the slums of Calcutta, to Goa, to Africa. Ghosh's *In An Antique Land* (1992) emphasizes the historical relationship between Egypt and India. Ontario-based Steven Heighton (b. 1961) explores Japan and the differences between East and West as witnessed by a young traveler in some of the stories contained in *Flight Paths of the Emperor* (1992).

Freya Stark (1893–1993), the doyenne of travelers, wrote that writers, like painters, need to stand back from what they want to see in order to acquire the right perspective. She called it "the eye of distance" (quoted in Mondesir, "Far from the Madding Crowd," 52). The Indian-born English author Lawrence Durrell writes at the beginning of *Justine* (1957), the first novel in *The Alexandria Quartet*, his great work about expatriate life: "I have had to come so far away from it in order to understand it all!" (17). Exiled Nuruddin Farah, writing about his native Somalia, says: "For me, distance distills. . . . To write a 'truly inspired work of fiction' about Somalia, I had to leave it" (quoted in Riggan, "Nuruddin Farah's Indelible Country of the Imagination," 701).

INTRODUCTION

There are various reasons why writers distance themselves from their homelands. Sometimes they seek to escape boredom and the static routine of home life; sometimes they are political escapees from tyranny; sometimes they are refugees from war-torn lands. Distance has brought to many of them an increased clarity of vision that has crystallized in some memorable literary creations.

Multicultural and multilingual writers through the ages set out on their various earthly peregrinations to search for freedom and well-being or for fresh images and new challenges. The liberating effects of voluntary emigration seem to be undeniable. Not a few authors have yearned for interplanetary discovery and have filled interstellar space in their own literary way: Cicero's dream voyage to the moon and beyond in *Somnium Scipionis* (52 B.C.E); Savinien Cyrano de Bergerac's two novels of imaginary travel, *Etats et empires de la lune* (1657) and *Histoire comique des états du soleil* (1662); Carlo Goldoni's text for Franz Josef Haydn's *Il mondo della luna* (1777); Edgar Allan Poe's cosmic fantasy *Eureka* (1848); Jules Verne's *De la terre à la lune* (1865); Louis Auguste Blanqui's *L'éternité par les astres* (1872); Karl Kraus's *Die Letzten Tage der Menscheit* (1918), planned out in his mind for a theater on Mars; Claude Ollier's *La vie sur Epsilon* (1972); and, today, Fred Hoyle's science fiction and the writings of Stephen Hawkings and Carl Sagan.

Carl Sagan (1934–96), whose foreknowledge never ceases to impress us, addressed "two parallel but related multicultural themes, the terrestrial and the extraterrestrial, . . . [seeking in both] to bring in the outsider, the disenfranchised Other" (quoted from Richard Sussman's entry on Sagan). With him, we wander among survivals of a world that, to an extent, can still be read and understood, even while we simultaneously project our imaginations into a multigalaxial universe.

CHINUA ACHEBE
(1930–)

Joseph Nnadi

BIOGRAPHY

In his partial autobiography "Named for Victoria, Queen of England," Chinua Achebe wrote with his characteristic humor: "So if anyone asks you what Her Britannic Majesty Queen Victoria had in common with Chinua Achebe, the answer is: They both lost their Albert!" (*Hopes and Impediments: Selected Essays*, 33). Baptized Albert Chinualumogu (Achebe), he, as a young university student, "dropped the tribute to Victorian England" (*Hopes and Impediments*, 33) and cut the twelve-letter middle name in two, "making it more businesslike without . . . losing the general drift of its meaning" (*Hopes and Impediments*, 34). If his two given names are symbolic of the two cultures he inherited, his choice to drop one and shorten the other is equally symbolic of his rejection of any form of cultural imposition, be it Western or African. When necessary, Achebe distanced himself even from his own culture, a gesture he compares to "a backward step which a judicious viewer may take in order to see a canvas steadily and fully" (*Hopes and Impediments*, 35). By so doing, he emerged as a cultural mulatto.

Achebe's cultural crossbreeding was a consequence of colonial history. He was born in Ogidi (Eastern Nigeria) into an extended family that had just been culturally torn apart by the advent of Christianity in the land of the Igbo (Ibo). His austere father, then a catechist in the service of the Church Missionary Society, became the instrument of Achebe's Westernization, which came to a head at the London University College in Ibadan (Western Nigeria). There Achebe graduated with an honors degree in English.

By contrast, his informal education was under the tutelage of his father's maternal uncle, Chief Osinyi, the epitome of traditional Igbo culture and worldview, who offered young Achebe a solid foundation in African culture. Achebe paradoxically was both the angelic choirboy at Sunday services and the zealous frequenter of Osinyi's compound, to which he was irresistibly drawn by the aroma of well-cooked "rice and stew" (*Hopes and Impediments*, 35). For the child Achebe, "heathen" food was no less tasty than that of the "people of the Church" (*Hopes and Impediments*, 30), just as traditional Igbo culture would be no less valid and nourishing for the adult than the Western one.

Although Igbo society and worldview were literally shattered in the aftermath of colonization and imported religions, as suggested by the title of Achebe's first novel, *Things Fall Apart* (1958), his personal world did not fall apart despite his adventures into the two conflicting cultures: "We lived at the crossroads of cultures. . . . We still do. . . . But . . . the crossroads does have a certain dangerous potency; dangerous because a man might perish there wrestling with multiple-headed spirits, but he might be lucky and return to his people with the boon of prophetic vision. . . . What I do remember is a fascination for the ritual and the life on the other arm of the crossroads" (*Hopes and Impediments*, 34–35). Achebe achieved a near magic harmony between all the arms of his cultural crossroads and "returned to his people" (*Hopes and Impediments*, 35) armed with a vision that would illuminate his professional and literary careers.

Achebe's worldwide experience is extensive: "he studied at the B.B.C. in London in 1956 and was appointed the first Director of External Broadcasting in Nigeria in 1961. In 1960–61 he traveled in East Africa on a Rockefeller Fellowship, and in the USA, Brazil and Britain in 1963 on a UNESCO Fellowship" (Carroll, *Chinua Achebe*, 25). Later on, having lectured at universities in Nigeria, Massachusetts, and Connecticut, Achebe attained international repute and won numerous prestigious awards, including a fellowship of the Modern Languages Association of America, eleven honorary doctorates from universities in Great Britain, the United States, Canada, and Nigeria, as well as the Scottish Arts Council Neil Gunn Fellowship and the Nigerian National Merit Award—the country's highest recognition for intellectual achievement.

Since 1988, Achebe has lived in the United States, continuing to give lectures, grant interviews, and write.

MAJOR MULTICULTURAL THEMES

A major theme of Achebe's writings is the futility of a North-South dialogue. He recalls a negative comment on his *Arrow of God* (1969) by "an American reviewer with the amazing name of Christ" (*Hopes and Impediments*, 26). " 'Perhaps no Nigerian at the present state of his culture and ours can tell us what we need to know about that country, in a way that is available to our understanding . . . in a way W. H. Hudson made South America real to us, or T. E. Lawrence brought Arabia to life' " (*Hopes and Impediments*, 26). For Achebe, this Christ has a problem: the belief that "only his brothers can explain the world, even the alien world of strangers, to him!" (*Hopes and Impediments*, 26); hence his disbelief in a Nigerian's account of Nigeria. Achebe deplores the racist stance of those Westerners who, arrogating to themselves the monopoly of knowledge, refuse to see the black man as a potential contributor to world dialogue. Achebe's writing is primarily a crusade for the dignity of the black man, for the respect of all races and cultures.

This view explains his criticism of Joseph Conrad's well-known novel: "*Heart of Darkness* projects the image of Africa as 'the other world,' the antithesis of Europe and therefore of civilization, a place where man's vaunted intelligence and refinement are finally mocked by triumphant bestiality" (*Hopes and Impediments*, 2). Achebe's self-appointed mission was to produce an antidote to the racist poison discharged by Conrad's pen. The first dose of this antipoison was *Things Fall Apart*.

This novel narrates the fate of Okonkwo, an Igboman whose stubborn resistance to colonial cultural imperialism earned him an untimely suicide. In many respects, the novel is a compendium of Igbo cosmology, but it is also the story of a conversion. Toward the end of the novel, the district commissioner, a white man, is deeply touched by the words of Obierika, the deceased man's best friend, who stands under the tree where Okonkwo committed suicide: "That man was one of the greatest men in Umuofia. You drove him to kill himself; and now he will be buried like a dog" (*Things Fall Apart*, 187). Obierika continues: "In the many years in which he had toiled to bring civilization to different parts of Africa, he had learnt a number of things" (187). The all-knowing white man's admission to learning something, anything, from contact with Africa is a novelty. In his impending retirement, he will write a book whose title, *The Pacification of the Primitive Tribes of the Lower Niger*, descends on him, like a revelation, under the tree of Okonkwo's suicide. Although he still conceives of the natives as "primitive tribes," the word *pacification* must sound like a neologism in the context of the colonial rhetoric of conquest, civilization, and Christianization.

To be able to write this novel, Achebe had to purge himself of the dose of poison he had unwittingly imbibed from Conrad and his kind: "At the university I read some appalling novels about Africa (including Joyce Cary's much praised *Mister Johnson*) and decided that the story we had to tell could not be told for us by anyone else no matter how gifted or how well intentioned. Although I did not set about it consciously in that solemn way, I now know that my first book, *Things Fall Apart*, was an act of atonement with my past, the ritual return and homage of a prodigal son" (*Hopes and Impediments*, 38). Achebe shares the *négritude* philosophy that for the black man a return to his past is the antidote to his cultural alienation.

Arrow of God, the second novel of a proposed Okonkwo trilogy that Achebe admits was never completed, won the first New Statesman Jock Campbell Prize.

Nearly 30 years after *Things Fall Apart*, Achebe produced his most accomplished novel, *Anthills of the Savannah* (1987), essentially a sad reflection on the political life of an independent African country. Government officials and the local populace are juxtaposed with expatriate characters to simulate North-South encounters. These encounters reveal that the old prejudices and obstacles of the pre-independence era still persist. But, more important, in this novel Achebe raises his artistic gaze to a universal plane, as he identifies with and embraces all humanity. Underscoring the close relationship, in his worldview, between feminism, *négritude*, and humanism, he writes: "The women are, of course, the biggest single group of oppressed people in the world and, if we are to believe the Book of Genesis, the very oldest. But they are not the only ones. There are others—rural peasants in every land, the urban poor in industrialized countries, Black people everywhere including their own continent, ethnic and religious minorities and castes in all countries" (*Anthills of the Savannah*, 98). In a sense, all of Achebe's works convey the same messages, but *Anthills of the Savannah* proves that the pointedly antiracist stance of his first novels was only the first phase of a universal humanism.

SURVEY OF CRITICISM

David Carroll's volume (1970) is one of the early groundbreaking critical works on Achebe. In addition to biography, it provides an overview of the social and cultural background of Igbo society and a chapter on each of Achebe's earliest novels. Nadine Gordimer's 1975 article reviews the cultural dilemmas and difficult choices of African writers who, like Achebe, had to write in foreign languages. Diana-Akers Rhoads's 1993 study is an in-depth analysis of the promotion of African culture and the subversion of Western cultures in Achebe's work. She argues that Achebe saw it as a duty to show his people the dignity they lost during the colonial period. As she explains it, he set himself two concrete objectives: to present the peculiarities of Igbo culture and to reveal "a common humanity which transcends the European and the African, which belongs to both but is peculiar to neither" (61–62). She also touches on the unique role assigned to women in Igbo society and in Achebe's novels, underscoring the theme of the supremacy of motherhood common to both *Things Fall Apart* and *Arrow of God*.

In her 1993 article, Chelva Kanaganayakam emphasizes the social, political, and cultural realism of *Anthills*. The first full biography of Achebe is by Ezenwa-Ohaeto (1997).

SELECTED BIBLIOGRAPHY

Works by Achebe

Things Fall Apart. London: Heinemann Educational Books, 1958.
Arrow of God. New York: Doubleday, 1969.
Anthills of the Savannah. London: Heinemann, 1987.
Hopes and Impediments: Selected Essays. New York: Doubleday, 1989.

Selected Studies of Achebe

Adeeko, Adeleke. "Contests of Text and Context in Chinua Achebe's *Arrow of God.*" *Ariel: A Review of International English Literature* (Calgary) 23, no. 2 (April 1992): 7–22.

Carroll, David. *Chinua Achebe.* New York: Twayne, 1970.

Ezenwa-Ohaeto. *Chinua Achebe: A Biography.* Bloomington: Indiana University Press; London: James Currey, 1997.

Gordimer, Nadine. "At the Crossroads of Cultures." *Times Literary Supplement* (London) (October 17, 1975): 1227.

Kanaganayakam, Chelva. "Art and Orthodoxy in Chinua Achebe's *Anthills of the Savannah.*" *Ariel: A Review of International English Literature* (Calgary) 24, no. 4 (October 1993): 35–51.

Rhoads, Diana-Akers. "Culture in Chinua Achebe's *Things Fall Apart.*" *African Studies Review* 36, no. 2 (1993): 61–72.

Sengova, Joko. "Native Identity and Alienation in Richard Wright's *Native Son* and Chinua Achebe's *Things Fall Apart:* A Cross-Cultural Analysis." *Mississippi Quarterly: The Journal of Southern Culture* 50, no. 2 (spring 1997): 327–51.

Sharma, Govind-Narain. "The Christian Dynamic in the Fictional World of Chinua Achebe." *Ariel: A Review of International English Literature* (Calgary) 24, no. 2 (October 1993): 85–99.

ANDRÉ ACIMAN
(1951–)

Susan D. Cohen

BIOGRAPHY

In 1951, André Aciman was the first on his father's side of his Jewish Sephardic family to be born in Egypt, as was his mother in the maternal line. His paternal relatives came from Turkey, which, beginning in 1905, they had left for Alexandria in search of a better life. Aciman never became an Egyptian citizen, for, as Egypt gained statehood, it refused citizenship to the Jews in its population, regardless of how long they and their ancestors had lived there. After Gamal Nasser seized power in 1952, Alexandria's Jews were expelled in the wake of Islamification: the Islamic fundamentalism that fused with and was confused with a brand of Egyptian nationalism, and that fostered anti-Semitism and excluded native Jews, no matter how the latter identified and defined themselves. After the confiscation of their cloth factory, the freezing of their assets, and the daily and nightly harassment, the Acimans left Alexandria in 1965.

Departure meant dispersal—a familial diaspora. Aciman and his nuclear family, except for his father, went to Italy, where they lived in straitened circumstances for three years. His paternal grandmother went to France and then to Brazil. A great-uncle settled in England. His father went to France, where Aciman himself spent long vacation months each year. After Aciman completed secondary school in Rome, he and both parents emigrated to New York, where he pursued his higher education at Lehman College and then earned his master's and doctoral degrees in comparative literature at Harvard University. As professor of comparative literature, he has taught at Princeton University (1990–97), Bard College (1997–2001), and the Graduate Center of the City University of

New York (2001). Author of numerous scholarly essays and articles, Aciman was made famous by his work *Out of Egypt: A Memoir* (1994), which won the Whiting Writers Award that year. This memoir was followed in 2000 by *False Papers*, on the theme of exile and memory. He is currently completing a novel, *Over the Footbridge* (forthcoming, Farrar, Straus and Giroux), a book on Marranism in the seventeenth century, and one on Marcel Proust.

From 1996 to 2000, Aciman was a member and judge of the PEN Club and in 2001 was a judge for the National Book Award. He was president of the Italo Svevo International Association, a board member of the New York Council for the Humanities, and the recipient of several prizes for essays on comparative literature. Three of these essays were selected for *Best American Essays* collections. He contributes to *The New Yorker*, the *New York Review of Books*, the *New York Times*, *The New Republic*, and *Commentary*.

MAJOR MULTICULTURAL THEMES

As Aciman remarks, "You realize you're multicultural only when you go to a society that is monocultural" (interview with Susan D. Cohen, December 14, 2001). He lived in a city, Alexandria, in which so many nationalities and languages coexisted that multiplicity constituted the very nature of its culture. Between themselves and with older relatives, his parents often spoke Ladino, the "native" language of Sephardic Jews separated from their native land and dispersed throughout Europe and the Ottoman Empire after expulsion from Spain in the fifteenth century. With their son, however, they spoke only French. Aciman was sent to an English school where the teachers, mostly Arab after 1952, frequently broke into Arabic. Various members of the family spoke Italian, Greek, English, or German. Ignorant of formal spoken Arabic, they communicated with poorer Arabs in a mélange that everybody understood. Like them, middle-class and wealthy Arabs largely chose English or French.

The notion of a native tongue further divides along oral and written lines. Aciman learned to write in English but spoke French at home with his deaf mother, who oddly spoke this "maternal" language in a strange voice. "This was part of my problem all around," writes Aciman; "I spoke several languages with a French accent, except French" (*False Papers*, 51). Unremarkable in Alexandria, this polyglotism became anomalous in monocultural countries where identity, nationality, and language operate in the singular. As the syntax of Aciman's sentence proves, an "otherness" of other languages marks his English. Traces of the linguistic severalness of his native tongues color his word order and word choice. In addition to the thematic content of his work, the very matter of his writing conveys some of the multiplicity of the culture producing it. His original cultural plurality nourishes both of his careers, that of author and that of professor of comparative literature, the latter presupposing the very multiplicity that made him.

What lies at the heart of Aciman's writing is Alexandria, the city he had lost even before leaving it. Many of his relatives having already been exiled, his childhood ended before the expulsion of 1965. The combination of catastrophic political forces and affectionate portraits of generations of family members in Alexandria enlarges *Out of Egypt*, expanding it from the personal to the historical, and becoming the theme and subject of the essays he wrote as well.

Aciman's texts revolve around return. *Out of Egypt* thematizes a process of reconstruction. The narrator physically returns to Europe, which elicits the return of memories through association, conversation, and imagination during visits to his great-uncle Vili in England, to his aunt Flora in Venice, and to his great-aunt and grandmother, who live together in Paris. The visits convey the loss of togetherness in diasporic exile and set the stage for evocations of their earlier life in Alexandria and its painful demise. Aciman uses a vocabulary of archaeology, in which memory is also a retrieval of various "ruins" covered by accretions of time after the destruction by an historical cataclysm. In Paris with his wife 20 years after his first return, when his great-aunt and grandmother are dead, Aciman notes the "too late[ness]" (214) of revisiting their apartment, site of one of his mnemonic digs into the first lost site. Assuming that artifacts "dusted off from an ancient find" (214) would have appeared quaint to his wife, he leaves them buried for her, yet he excavates them for himself and for the reader in the very act of imagining and recording their would-have-been words. Elsewhere he reconstitutes conversations in Alexandria that occurred before his birth as well as those he actually heard.

In *Letters of Transit: Reflections on Exile, Identity, Language, and Loss* (1999), the narrator does go back to Alexandria. Aciman's theme of return, analyzed in the essays in its reciprocal relationship to memory, predicates a gaze rarely turned toward the place in which the narrator finds himself. Return consists of shuttling back and forth in space and time, of projection into the past and into a future envisaged as memory of the present but from another site. It entails permanent lodgings only in a domicile "not fully here," of an exile whose home, the multiple culture of Alexandria, has been destroyed. Multiplicity is rendered, but only with time and space lags. Throughout the essays, Aciman calls this "travel" a back-and-forth "traffic," "arbitrage" (a literary and mnemonic speculation based on absence), or "palintrope" (a returning from and to).

Themes of snobbery, contempt, insecurity, language, and identity intertwine in Aciman's work to form one indivisible whole. If he acknowledges and mocks his paternal grandmother's snobbery toward the "Arab Jews" on the maternal side (something characteristic of upper-class Sephardim) and the family's contempt for Arabs generally, he also contextualizes these attitudes as primarily a class prejudice, shared in the latter case by upper-class Arabs. He shows how his family's contempt is a function of deep, historically motivated insecurity, repeatedly experienced. During the family's ironic last seder in Egypt before their expulsion, dispossession, and destitution, the crushed grandmother laments that "this was the ninth time she had seen the men in her life lose everything; first her grandfather, then her father, her husband, five brothers, and now her son" (*Out of Egypt: A Memoir*, 304). Who one is connects to where one belongs, and past persecutions of the Jews explain Uncle Vili's bragging about his chameleon-like prowess in switching nationalities, languages, and allegiances among various countries in Europe. If at first this bravado produces amusement or annoyance, we understand and admire it on a more profound level when we recognize it as a survival tactic requiring extraordinary pluck, intelligence, and skill. Even the pleasurable mastery of many languages is based on continual uprooting. The text poignantly indicates its connection to a nonbelonging that will assail the family once they scatter. In the anti-Jewish atmosphere of the Suez crisis, the family huddles together, listening to a French-language radio station during a blackout: "Everyone . . . sensed something solemn in the sonorous voice that suddenly spoke from the old Philco in a stately French accent so different from ours. Radio Monte Carlo! It was the French of movie stars, the French my uncles mimicked but never mastered, the French one made fun of but secretly envied, the French one claimed one didn't care to speak. . . . It was a French that made us feel remote, dated, inferior" (*Out of Egypt: A Memoir*, 169).

Intertextuality marks Aciman's memoir and essays, and it joins the basic trope of plural in-betweenness. The major intertexts concern wandering (Homer), exile (Dante), memory (Marcel Proust), and reimagination of all of these things (like Konstantinos Cavafy's rereading of *The Odyssey*, in which the wanderer chooses to remain away from home, accepting Calypso's offer of immortality). They deploy the languages Aciman has learned in his life: Greek, Italian, French, and the English of his own text. Writing constitutes his permanent lodgings, perhaps this wanderer's own stab at immortality, englobing that of his remembered Ithaca. Through the continuous use of the first person, writing also allows him to recover, albeit with postexpulsion temporal and spatial lags, a bit of his initial beloved centrality in a plurality that displacement, diaspora, and adulthood dissipated.

Aciman defines love as longing hinging on loss, but also as multiplicity in time. The back-and-forth traffic entails love of all the places involved. With places as with people, you "never really unlove anyone" (*False Papers*, 175); you love new people, more people. Aciman writes in tones of nostalgia and elegy, but the key is love, and the results are revival and that most Jewish of acts, bearing written witness.

SURVEY OF CRITICISM

Roger J. Porter (2001) notes that in writing postexilic autobiography Aciman forges a complex identity, a component of which is the discovery of the increased resonance that the multicultural aspect of his childhood milieu began to acquire once he lost it. Departure heightens his consciousness of how this identity constitutes him, as he negotiates between nostalgia and freedom. He makes literary capital out of a loss that makes him a writer, which enables him to surmount despair as he writes himself into a new person, enriched by memory, by the plural nature of his native culture, and by the multiplicity of cultures he has inhabited since he was exiled. No one replaces the other. They become acquisitions despite constituting repeated losses. Memory affords retrieval as compensation, a renewed self-knowledge, even a substitution of the present, remembering self, for the disappearance of the remembered one.

Michael André Bernstein (1996) distinguishes between expatriation, which is a voluntary undertaking, and exile, which is an often brutally imposed condition. He records the enduring fascination that exile as a literary topos exercises on readers, whether used, as in European texts from the Renaissance (Dante) through the nineteenth century, to critique Europe's social and political order or, as more recently, to describe the final moments of a culture, especially one whose existence was abruptly and unexpectedly terminated (as in literature of the Shoah). Noting the penury in English of stories about the once thriving Jewish cultures of Alexandria, Cairo, Baghdad, and Constantinople that were also, if less murderously, liquidated, Bernstein heralds Aciman's memoir as a text that begins to fill this gap.

Exile literature succeeds, writes Bernstein, when it treats the wider history in terms of individual experience, which Aciman does. For Aciman, identity is the central question of the text, exemplified in the signature challenge proffered constantly by Uncle Vili: "Siamo o non siamo?" (Are we or aren't we?). The tension between identity, for this Jewish family from Turkey, and identifying, or the fabrication of a mostly imaginary descent from well-born Spanish Jewish refugees, extended to language. They spoke French, Italian, and imperfect Arabic, and they sent their son to an English school. Bernstein perceives the uneasiness underlying their dogged identification with the West and consequent rejection of whatever Europeans deemed repellent. No one in the family can answer the question "Are we or aren't we?" simply or straightforwardly without revealing networks of poses and fictions that partake of a necessary strategy of survival.

SELECTED BIBLIOGRAPHY

Works by Aciman

Out of Egypt: A Memoir. New York: Riverhead, 1994.
Letters of Transit: Reflections on Exile, Identity, Language, and Loss. Ed. André Aciman. New York: New Press, 1999.
False Papers. New York: Farrar, Straus and Giroux, 2000.

Selected Studies of Aciman

Bernstein, Michael André. "Exile, Cunning, and Loquaciousness." *Salmagundi* 111 (Summer 1996): 182–94.

Cohen, Susan D. Unpublished interview with André Aciman in New York City, December 14, 2001.

Porter, Roger J. "Autobiography, Exile, Home: The Egyptian Memoirs of Gini Alhadeff, André Aciman, and Edward Said." *Biography* 24 (Winter 2001): 302–13.

VASSILIS ALEXAKIS
(1943–)

Bruce Merry

BIOGRAPHY

This contemporary bilingual French novelist was born a Greek. His family lost their property on the Aegean island of Santorini in the earthquake of 1956 and moved to Athens. In his childhood, Vassilis wrote his name, a title, three pages of text, and one of illustration in exercise books stitched together by his mother. In the mid-1960s, he obtained a scholarship to study journalism at Lille (France). Having finished these studies, he returned to Greece to do military service and left again at the onset of the Colonels' regime in 1967, living in Paris from that date. He has contributed to the newspaper *Le Monde* and to other French papers and has held exhibitions of his humorous drawings in Paris (1976, 1981). Although he directed the film *Milo-Milo* in 1979, his first full-length feature film was *Oi Athinaioi* (1990), which juxtaposes a classical drama below the Acropolis with a soccer match, a watermelon rolling across Athens, and the profit-spinning invention of a coffin for two. Ironically, in this urban antifilm, Alexakis plots a supposed state of ethnic weariness, with a tired thief, an exhausted electrician, and a worn-out actress.

For a series called "Guide to Present-Day Travel," Alexakis published the essay *Les Grecs d'aujourd'hui* in 1979. He published three novels in French in the 1970s: *Le sandwich* (1974); *Les girls du City-Boum-Boum* (1975), a charmingly silly book about a journalist who wants the best for himself while spraying obscenity or innuendo at chic society; and *La tête du chat* (1978); the last two were also published in Greek (1985 and 1979, respectively). He is the author of irreverent, cosmopolitan collections of sketches and aphorisms as well: *Gdusou* (*Déshabille-toi, dessins humoris-*

tiques, 1982) contains his own humorous drawings, some with captions. (One man asks another if *communism* is written with one *m* or two; his friend answers "one doesn't write it"; this cartoon first came out in the Athenian newspaper *To Vima* of October 27, 1973.) More of his drawings can be found in *I skia tou Leonida* (*L'ombre de Léonidas, histoires dessinées*, 1984), a series of six illustrated stories, and in *Le fils de King Kong, aphorismes* (1987).

MAJOR MULTICULTURAL THEMES

Talgko (1980) was the first of Alexakis's novels written directly in Greek. Its exotic title is a Spanish acronym for "light train of linked carriages invented by Guoikotsea and financed by Oriol" (88). It is the name of the express train that takes the narrator-heroine Eleni from Paris to Barcelona and back. The book purports to be a heartfelt reflection by a Greek married woman on her affair with a married Greek intellectual living in Paris. They spend a week together in Barcelona, but shortly after the holiday is concluded, he suggests ending the affair. Eleni notes that he looks at every woman who passes by; he comments that he must devour the appearance of each one because he is devoted to them all. Intermittently the book succeeds in flouting most feminist standards on love and commitment. *Talgko* was filmed by Giorgos Tseberopoulos as *Xafnikos erotas*.

The sociological thriller *La tête du chat*, was made by Dimitris Stavrakas into a television serial under the same name. A French romantic author with servants, dictation typists, and an aristocratic wife is pitted against a disaffected clerk in a medical firm who leaves dead animals in the author's house and car and announces that he will kill the author. The clerk outwits the member of the establishment by crouching in the back of his car as he leaves a nightclub (a familiar Hollywood motif). After the showdown on a freeway near Saint-Cloud on the Seine, the clerk dumps the author's body in the forest. Alexakis makes use here of the modern theme of urban stalking, combining it with the staple beliefs of Cold War leftist activists that it should be illicit for the rich to enjoy their wealth and that large incomes should be outlawed.

La langue maternelle: Roman (1995, winner *ex aequo* of the Prix Médicis for that year) pursues an obsession with the Greek letter epsilon (short *e*), and the narrator's curiosity at its unexpanded, unexplained appearance over the oracle at the temple of Delphi, which was held to be the center of the civilized world. He wonders whether this *e* is a misprint for *ai* (as in *ainigma*) and therefore a historical spelling error. He consults the Bostanzoglous antilexicon and learns an alternative word for *prophylactic*. He analyzes the euphemistic numeral terms that his mother used to replace Greek Demotic words for the body's waste matter. He learns that at Delphi, during the German occupation, when radios were prohibited, the news was broadcast from a hilltop by a megaphone (280). The spoken or written Greek word, with its historical primacy, is the unstated hero of this Mediterranean pilgrimage, where fiction strays into the subgenre of archaeological survey.

Le coeur de Marguerite (1999) roams over the Greek islands and France. A German contemporary novelist, who is an imaginary ideal of the narrator's self, is a man with a foot in two countries (France and Greece). He also puts a hand on the females who come into his reach, while his father gets rid of a mistress and prepares to act in *Faust*. Alexakis plays up the adulterous affair, but the reader is more interested in *where* Marguerite and the narrator are parted or reconciled, rather than how. As in many such metanarrative documents with an experimental thrust, the novelist-within-the-novel is not sure how to begin or end his text, so his German double, Eckermann (alluding to the writer associated with Goethe), instructs him as an initiate. The narrator goes to Australia to film the Greek community there (and to visit a brothel for $120), and he learns the Aborigines' phrase *"Wada ningango jambiri"* (110), which means "I love you" and with which he ends the book (427). The text is replete with reflections on language—for example, that the interrogative semicolon in Greek is less "seductive" than the French question mark (363)—and with word puzzles that lovers invent for each other. A chauvinist Hellenist says that when the Greeks were writing *Electra* and building the Parthenon, the Bulgarians were living in trees and talking in onomatopoeia (322).

In *Avant* (1992), the few inhabitants of a small Parisian cemetery, basking in their Woody Allen–type humor, meet in their underground chambers to plan their escape from the world of silence and death. The book treats en passant some of the major social problems of the day: unemployment, racism, and homelessness.

SURVEY OF CRITICISM

Alexakis is known as a debunking intellectual who executes several genres at once (art, cartoon, film, and fiction). Paul Côté (1996) sees the sought object of travel in *La langue maternelle* as less important than the "wisdom which the process of exploration can procure" (138). Dimitri Mitropoulos (1997) compares Alexakis's expatriate status with that of Margarita Karapanou, Vassilis Vassilikos, and Aris Fakinou, who made careers as Greek writers in Paris. Alexakis's case may show that contemporary Greek writing is "better off in other language environments" (188). Artemis Leontis (1997) considers that Alexakis's novel *Paris-Athènes* (1997) reflects the recent ambition of Greek intellectuals to define a new, decentralized locus for the old-fashioned trope of Hellenism. Alexakis's book sets the tone of intellectual displacement and ease of movement across a frontierless, liberated Europe by shifting its characters between two different capitals. It also invites the reader to visit different centers of Greek immigration (e.g., Montreal and New York). It gives rise to the oldest trope of all—namely *xenitiá*, the sojourn of Greeks across the world. Some of Alexakis's characters start to weep as soon as they leave Greece, and they go on weeping for the entire time they live abroad. Thus, Leontis can refer to the Hellenism of Alexakis as "suspended between worlds," able to move beyond its container and "foreground other histories in the scattered communities of the Greek diaspora" (227).

SELECTED BIBLIOGRAPHY

Works by Alexakis

Le sandwich: Roman. Paris: Julliard, 1974.

Les girls du City-Boum-Boum: Roman. Paris: Julliard, 1975. [*Ta koritsia tou Situ Boum-Boum.* Trans. Vassilis Alexakis. Athens: Exantas, 1985.]

La tête du chat. Paris: Seuil, 1978. [*To kefali tis gatas.* Trans. Marika Kilitsoglou. Athens: Exantas, 1979.]

Les Grecs d'aujourd'hui. Paris: A. Balland, 1979.

Talgko. Athens: Exantas, 1980. [*Talgo: Roman.* Trans. Vassilis Alexakis. Paris: Seuil, 1983.]

Déshabille-toi, dessins humoristiques. Athens: Exantas, 1982. [*Gdusou.* Trans. Vassilis Alexakis. Athens: Exantas, 1982.]

L'ombre de Léonidas, histoires dessinées. Athens: Exantas, 1984. [*I skia tou Leonida.* Trans. Vassilis Alexakis. Athens: Exantas, 1984.]

Contrôle d'identité: Roman. Paris: Seuil, 1985.

Le fils de King Kong, aphorismes. Geneva: Les Yeux Ouverts, 1987.

Paris-Athènes. Paris: Seuil, 1989.

Pourquoi tu pleures? Nouvelles. Cologne: Romiosini-Schwarze Kunst, 1991. [*Warum weinst du denn?* Trans. Niki Eidener. Cologne: Romiosini-Schwarze Kunst, 1991.]

Avant: Roman. Paris: Seuil, 1992. [*Prin.* Trans. Karina Lampsa. Athens: Exantas, 1994.]

I mitriki glosa: Mythistorima. Athens: Exantas, 1995. [*La langue maternelle: Roman.* Trans. Vassilis Alexakis. Paris: Fayard, 1995.]

Le coeur de Marguerite: Roman. Paris: Stock, 1999.

Selected Studies of Alexakis

Côté, Paul. "*La langue maternelle.*" *French Review* 70, no. 1 (October 1996): 137–38.

Leontis, Artemis. "Beyond Hellenicity: Can We Find Another Topos?" *Journal of Modern Greek Studies* 15, no. 2 (1997): 217–31.

Mitropoulos, Dimitri. "On the Outside Looking In: Greek Literature in the English-Speaking World." *Journal of Modern Greek Studies* 15, no. 2 (1997): 187–96.

Oktapoda-Lu, Efstratia. "Vassilis Alexakis ou la quête de l'identité." *Littérature et Nation* 24 (2001): 281–96.

ISABEL ALLENDE
(1942–)

Martha L. Rubí

BIOGRAPHY

Isabel Allende was born in Lima, Peru, where her early years were marked by constant cultural uprooting. At the time of her birth, her father, Tomás Allende Pesce de Bilbaire, cousin of the future socialist president of Chile, Salvador Allende, was serving as diplomatic attaché in Chile. Her mother, Francisca Llona-Barros, endearingly called "doña Panchita," against parental wishes had wed the debonair Allende, a refined social dandy 15 years her senior. From the outset, the marriage was plagued by Tomás's constant absence from home, his mysterious trips, and strong devotion to his own circle of friends. His highly publicized comportment finally caused doña Panchita to leave him, taking the 3-year-old Isabel to Santiago, Chile, where she found refuge in her father's home. Doña Panchita's marital problems were not solved by the subsequent birth of two other children, Juan and Francisco, which only strengthened her decision to divorce her husband—an action very much frowned upon in traditional Chilean society.

Isabel's widowed grandfather, Augustín Llona Cuevas, provided shelter for his own daughter and for his three young grandchildren. In later years, the writer remembered him lovingly as austere and proud, and, above all, she forever immortalized the big ancestral house of her childhood in her best-selling novel *La casa de los espíritus* (1982).

After the permanent disappearance of her husband from her life, doña Panchita saw to the educational needs of her children and nurtured Isabel's admiration for independent and willful women characters. The tight bond between mother and daughter persists to this day.

Isabel's mother formed a union in 1953 with Ramón Huidobro, "Uncle Ramón," a diplomat by career, sent on missions to Bolivia and Beirut. Once more the mother defied traditional social norms by falling in love with a married man separated from his wife, who refused him a divorce.

Isabel attended a private American school in Bolivia (1953–58), where she became conscious of class differences between the Indian populace and others of Chilean or European roots. Keeping very much to herself, she became an avid reader of fiction, an activity that saved her from boredom and loneliness. At the American school, she learned to speak and write English, which prepared her for attendance at an English school in Beirut. Here the confusion of four languages and cultures—Spanish spoken at home, English in the private British school, and Arabic and French in public—manifested itself in her extreme shyness. She preferred being left alone with her books to conversing at social gatherings. During this period, the sensuous world of the tales of the *Arabian Nights*—the forbidden book Ramón painstakingly locked in a glass cabinet, unaware that the children cleverly unlocked it at night—whetted her appetite for exotic adventure. The exemplary of Sheherazade provided the future writer with a rich tapestry of detailed stories woven by a woman narrator as a means of survival. This early contact with Arabic culture offered Allende much literary material for her novels: *Eva Luna* (1987), *Cuentos de Eva Luna* (1989), and *Afrodita* (1997).

Allende returned to Chile in 1958 to complete her education as the Suez Canal crisis deepened in the Middle East and then worked for the United Nations Food and Agricultural Organization in Santiago (1959–65). Duties in the Department of Information included journalism and the production of a television program. In 1962, at the age of twenty, she married a Chilean engineer, Miguel Frías, and a year later gave birth to a daughter, Paula. She traveled throughout Europe and lived in Brussels and in Sweden with her husband and child. Back in Chile in 1966, she gave birth to a son, Nicolás, and in 1967 was called upon to collaborate on a magazine, *Paula*, where she directed a humorous feminist column, "Los impertinentes" ("Impertinent Men"), and contributed a series of articles entitled "Civilizing Your Troglodyte." Her multiple talents led her to write theatrical works, among them *El embajador* (1971), *La balada del medio pelo* (1973), and *Los siete espejos* (1974).

During General Augusto Pinochet's coup d'état on September 11, 1973, her uncle, Salvador Allende, met his death. It is suspected that he was assassinated by the military regime. Fearing for her family's safety, Allende procured safe haven for herself, her husband, and her children in Venezuela, where they remained for 13 years during the dictatorship in Chile. In Venezuela, she worked as an administrative assistant in a high school and as a writer for the newspaper *El Nacional* of Caracas.

Upon receiving news in 1981 that her 99-year-old grandfather was dying, Allende began to write a letter that later became the manuscript of

La casa de los espíritus. The following year marked the beginning of her international recognition when the Spanish publisher, Plaza y Janés, took the risk of distributing the unknown Chilean woman writer's novel, a risk that paid off with such overwhelming success that the novel was then translated into English and other languages and made into a highly publicized film in 1993. Subsequent works displayed Allende's talents and met with popular demand. Immediately following her best-seller, she published *La gorda de porcelana* (1984), a short humorous novel she had written in 1974, and a second novel, *De amor y de sombra* (1984, film adaptation 1994). Her third novel, *Eva Luna*, was published in 1987, the year she divorced her husband. In 1988, at the age of 45, she met and married her second husband, an American, and left Venezuela to reside in San Rafael, California.

After the publication in Spain of *Cuentos de Eva Luna* (1989), Allende returned to Chile, where President-elect Patricio Aylwin presented her with the prestigious Gabriela Mistral literary award (1990).

Her daughter's untimely death in 1992 was a devastating blow, but Allende learned to use her narrative talents in a therapeutic attempt to come to grips with the tragedy. Her memoirs, *Paula* (1994), although written in Spanish, also appeared in German, Dutch, and English with the subtitle *Novel*. The next book reinstated Allende's fine humor and an unforeseen zest for life in her delightfully erotic, recipe-related narrative *Afrodita* (1997), translated into Italian and English in 1998 and published in certain pirated editions as well. The long list of international prizes Isabel Allende has won during her lifetime includes the Dorothy and Lillian Gish Prize awarded to those who "contribute beauty to the world."

Another novel, *Hija de la fortuna*, followed in 1999, and translations of her most recent novel, *Retrato en sepia* (2000), are in progress.

MAJOR MULTICULTURAL THEMES

Isabel Allende's multicultural experiences provide a myriad of sources and literary material for her works. *La casa de los espíritus* draws motifs from her childhood and the big old house in Chile, filled with family history and secrets. The events of the story are seen through the magical eyes of a little girl who identifies with strong women characters. Allende captures the refined social standing that "white linen" evokes in a traditional upper-class South American family. The sense of magic and nostalgia quickly turns to shattering confrontation with the cruelty and stark realism of a military regime (Pinochet's). This work reveals Allende's Hispanic roots and her familiarity both with tragic reality and with the literary use of magic realism as a Latin American trademark. Writers such as Gabriel García Márquez (Colombia), Alejo Carpentier (Cuba), Julio Cortázar (Argentina), and Carlos Fuentes (Mexico), among others, have used magic realism to criticize unjust political systems by combining reality with mythic elements.

In *Eva Luna* and *Cuentos de Eva Luna*, multicultural characters coexist in a sensuous tropical surrounding extracted from Allende's years in Venezuela. The character Eva Luna is both narrator and main protagonist of the stories. Modeled after Sheherazade of the *Thousand and One Nights*, Eva Luna weaves her tales for the sake of survival, in exchange for food and shelter. The name Eva Luna is a composite. *Eva* symbolizes the birth of the new woman, a new kind of mestiza (of European and Indian blood) who is independent and in control of her life. Eva, like the biblical Eve, is first in the line of a new breed. *Luna* (moon) symbolizes the passion for life and instinct for survival that she inherits from her nomadic Indian father. Other characters of Arabic and European background derive from Allende's many travels and from the ethnic characteristics of cultures that she experienced firsthand. Memorable are the erotic, sensuous Zulema; the good friend and protector Ryad Halabí, of Arabic origin; and Rolf and his cherublike cousins, of Belgian stock. All these characters are made to exist and blend in a tropical culture where guerrilla warfare, romance, and Eva Luna's adventures are a modern retelling of the Sheherazade saga.

In later works (*Hija del la fortuna* and *Retrato en sepia*), Allende was highly influenced by American culture and history. Her residence and American lifestyle in California provide a historical backdrop for new characters in her novels, and her American husband, Willie Gordon, was her inspiration for *El plan infinito* (1991). The California Gold Rush serves as the stage for a Chilean family epic centered on a strong-willed and independent great-grandmother who makes the family fortune in the New World.

SURVEY OF CRITICISM

Celia Correas-Zapata's biography (1998) re-creates Isabel Allende's life and works in a unique way: in the format of an interview. Correas-Zapata juxtaposes questions and answers to construct Allende's multidimensional life chronologically: her personal history and her professional contributions—novels, short stories, theatrical works, children's books, memoirs, television programs, and movie adaptations. Correas-Zapata approaches the novels in particular from the point of view of multicultural influences, making this biography rich in cultural sources. She considers all the countries that have left an indelible mark on Allende's personal vision of the world.

In a critical analysis of Allende's works, Susan Frank (1996) traces the origins of and the influences on the author's writing. Equally revealing is John Rodden's (1999) edited volume of biographical interviews.

SELECTED BIBLIOGRAPHY

Works by Allende

La casa de los espíritus (1982). [*The House of the Spirits.* Trans. Magda Bogin. New York: Knopf, 1985.]

La gorda de porcelana. Madrid: Alfaguara, 1984.

De amor y de sombra (1984). [*Of Love and Shadows.* Trans. Margaret Sayers Peden. New York: Knopf, 1987.]

Eva Luna (1987). [*Eva Luna.* Trans. Margaret Sayers Peden. New York: Knopf, 1988.]

Cuentos de Eva Luna (1989). [*The Stories of Eva Luna.* Trans. Margaret Sayers Peden. New York: Bantam Books, 1992.]

El plan infinito (1991). [*The Infinite Plan: A Novel.* Trans. Margaret Sayers Peden. New York: HarperCollins, 1993.]

Paula (1994). [*Paula.* Trans. Margaret Sayers Peden. New York: HarperCollins, 1995.]

Afrodita (1997). [*Aphrodite: A Memoir of the Senses.* Trans. Margaret Sayers Peden. New York: HarperCollins, 1998.]

Hija de la fortuna (1999). [*Daughter of Fortune: A Novel.* Trans. Margaret Sayers Peden. New York: HarperCollins, 1999.]

Conversations with Isabel Allende. Ed. John Rodden. Foreword Isabel Allende. Trans. from Spanish Virginia Invernizzi. Trans. from German and Dutch John Rodden. Austin: University of Texas Press, 1999.

Retrato en sepia. Barcelona: Plaza y Janés, 2000.

Selected Studies of Allende

Correas-Zapata, Celia. *Isabel Allende: Vida y espíritu.* Barcelona: Plaza y Janés, 1998.

Frank, Susan. "The Wandering Text: Situating the Narratives of Isabel Allende." In *Latin American Women's Writing*, ed. Anny Brooksbank Jones and Catherine Davies, 66–84. Oxford: Clarendon Press, 1996.

Rojas, Sonia R., and Edna A. Rehbein. *Critical Approaches to Isabel Allende's Novels.* New York: Peter Lang, 1991.

KATERINA ANGHELAKI-ROOKE
(1939–)

Bruce Merry

BIOGRAPHY

Born in Athens into a family of intellectuals, Katerina Anghelaki-Rooke published her first verses in 1956, studied English literature for a year at Athens University, and then went to southern France for further courses. She earned her degree from Geneva University and in 1962 won the City of Geneva's first prize for poetry. Later she traveled extensively, giving poetry readings and lecturing at Canadian or U.S. universities, among them Cornell, Harvard, the State University of New York, Princeton, Dartmouth, and Columbia. In the United States, she has conducted seminars on the twentieth century's best-known Greek writer, Nikos Kazantzakis, a family friend whom she had known since childhood.

Her early verse came out in a clutch of small and now forgotten journals such as *Parallax, Vapori, Sima, Epopteia,* and *I Nea Poiisi.* With the advent of the Colonels' dictatorship (1967–74), her voice was silenced, but her poems and essays then made their way into 10 other languages, and she has won several international prizes and grants. For her, history became a more basic consideration than politics.

She has published in Athens her translations into Greek of an eclectic range of modern classics including Dylan Thomas's *Under Milk Wood* (Ermias, 1973), Andrey Voznesensky's poems (Boukoumanis, 1974), Shakespeare's *The Taming of the Shrew* (Evangelatos, 1988), Vladimir Mayakovsky's *Kak delat' stikhi?* (Hypsilon, 1988), Seamus Heaney's *Bog Poems* (Kastaniotis, 1996), Sylvia Plath's *Poems* (Patakis, 1996), Aleksandr Pushkin's *Evgeni Onegin* (Kastaniotis, 1999), Mikhail Lermontov's *Geroi nashego vremini* (Kastaniotis, 1998), and a selection of 20 contemporary American poets (Hypsilon, 1983).

Eleni Fourtouni has described Anghelaki-Rooke as living in Athens half the time and dedicating the other half to her home on the isle of Aegina, "writing poetry, cultivating her pistachio orchard, and healing her friends' wounds with her laughter and love" (*Contemporary Greek Women Poets*, 35).

MAJOR MULTICULTURAL THEMES

Anghelaki-Rooke's allusive, anti-elegiac, nonrhyming verse, in asymmetrical bundles of loosely connected, unpunctuated strophes, moves from grand historical symbols back to the individual, futile body. Alexander the Great, the Sphinx, Christ, Satan, the belly, and the navel (a favorite word in her poems) taper down to the "museless worm / Tightly folded in the leaf of the myrtle" (*Piimata '63–'69*, 54). Womanhood may be glorious, but the international lesson of feminism is never far from sight in Anghelaki-Rooke's tumbling homily. She records that mothers before World War II led lives at complete variance from those of women who lived in the postwar society, where choices began to exist. Perhaps for her mother and grandmother's generation, love was "actually a large bag, / Tied tight / With animals inside that kick, / And bad dreams" (*Magdalini, to megalo thilastikó*, 23). She asks, "Did my mother actually want something, / Or did she just sigh in silence, / With all the 'I want' phrases / Coiled round her voice box?" The individual who writes this verse can know as little as the next person, but at least she can establish "what I am in life / And what defeats me in love" (*Magdalini, to megalo thilastikó*, 22). Often Anghelaki-Rooke talks of getting down to the "pith" *(koukoutsi)* and using words on the page to tease out the essence of things. Her imagery draws on the exotic panoply of her experience and reading: so the ground splits "like a watermelon," or the names "Catherine! Heathcliff" (*Magdalini, to megalo thilastikó*, 41) are heard in a dark, north wind, or she takes us on tour in Amherst, Massachusetts, past a taciturn "Emilu" (i.e., Emily Dickinson), who "paints magic / On the vapors of the twilight" (*O thriambos tis statherís apoleias*, 31). She reinterprets the cloistered American writer, placing Dickinson among brocades and painted tableware as a pursuer of angels (a common image in the work of Anghelaki-Rooke, whose own surname literally means "little angel"). At times, the whiff of sacrilege that earned anathema for her godfather, Nikos Kazantzakis, tempts her own iconoclastic tendencies: thus, the Virgin Mary becomes the "belle of the ball" on Good Friday, and angels are the whores of heaven, "but their wings caress the oddest / Psychologies" (*O thriambos tis statherís apoleias*, 62). She alludes nonchalantly in her verse to icons of multicultural awareness such as Beethoven's *Ode to Joy* or Picasso's *Guernica*. But she also makes room for the fauna and flora of her international itinerary. Squirrel, heron, snake, pine-marten, black-bird, hedgehog, hibiscus, hyacinth, lilac, grapevine arbor, nettle, eucalyptus, scarab, spider, locust, and ant lurk in her lines. She understands the role in history of the minor figure beside the Titan. She poses Alexander's soldiers before Babylon and observes his "troubadour" in a recital on fame, standing in the shadow of his "tropical" commander, a general blind with springtime, guided by rivers, destined for cities, and "drawing the bow of the sea" (*Piimata '63–'69*, 27, 29, 31).

Anghelaki-Rooke's assessment of poetry from other cultures is full of contrasts. She defines the seen-unseen in Marianne Moore, stresses William Carlos Williams's insistence on the primacy of object over ideas, and examines Hart Crane's notion that a hierarchy of beliefs can emerge in America more readily than elsewhere. In the poetic act, the person counts more than the personal. The *ego* counts more than the *he*. Hidden elements are made public by poetry, such as Anne Sexton's suicide attempts, Sylvia Plath's insanity, Robert Lowell's drinking, and Allen Ginsberg's and Robert Duncan's homosexuality. John Ashbery and Robert Creely are poets who also succeeded in deforming the reality of the personal. She approves Lawrence Ferlinghetti's dictum that modern poetry should avoid making poetry its own theme. American verse historically has had two poles: Puritanism and Walt Whitmanism. Chinese ideograms and Sanskrit phrases creep into Ezra Pound's verse and move the U.S. tradition beyond Europe toward the Middle East and Asia. Robert Bly and W. S. Merwin translated Swedish or Arabic writers, and Philip Lamantia was the only authentic surrealist poet in the United States. Pound and Eliot's influence was too strong to allow the European subconscious (surrealism) to cross the Atlantic or the English Channel. The "Red Indians'" poetry, in dance and song, had already reached Greek epic levels before the white invaders finished them off. They had personal songs that nobody was authorized to sing without the consent of those who "owned" them. In fact, the poem would affect only the single American Indian who owned it, rather than his hearers. Many of Anghelaki-Rooke's own poems seem to display a private ownership similar to that of the North American indigenous singer, with titles such as "My Head," "Stories of Eyes," "My Feet," "My Heart at Night," and "Poetry Is the Torment of Material." They include warnings to herself, such as "Most humans / Are bad lovers / Of the particular, / Let us ponder this well / Before / We again fall in love with the stars" (*O thriambos tis statherís apoleias*, 52), or the highly self-deprecating "I inflate my body each morning / And the balloon-vendor / Then goes away, / Bearing the pump" (*Magdalini, to megalo thilastikó*, 9). Here, in sum, Anghelaki-Rooke defers to the primacy of a plebeian, folk tradition, while maintaining the abstract intellectualism of her own modest place in history: "I hear my head / And its beat is the tune of a musician in love, / Who once loved chaos" (*O thriambos tis statherís apoleias*, 11).

SURVEY OF CRITICISM

Most critics refer to the eroticism of Anghelaki-Rooke's poetry, and they accept her deployment of the idea that a poet's governing theme is her own living body. Minas Savvas (1998) notes the omnipresent "heartrending allusions with a buoyant resonance" in her writing (429). John E. Rexine (1987) observes that "love seems to be at the center of being" (328), and Thomas Stravelis (1985) draws attention to her presentation of "love and death and the lucid suffering between them" (637). Thanasis T. Niarchos, in his interview with Anghelaki-Rooke in *Kibotos* (1980), questions what drew her to Penelope betrayed, to Alexander the Great as cultural time traveler, and to Magdalene the mammal; she replies that poems are biographies, and she felt she was marked physically by fate to write them. She continues by saying that many contemporary Greek poets have to compose in a language that is known to only 8 or 9 million people in the world, so they were influenced by the Beat poets. For many Greeks, writers such as T. S. Eliot are fatally mediated by being read in translation, and in much Greek verse it is difficult to distinguish the message or content. She has learned from the American poet Robert Bly that a poem is an extension of a person's being, entirely different from the skin and hands of its actual writer. Her own place in contemporary literature is balanced between different generations, either that of the 1950s–1960s or that of the 1970s, but she belongs to neither. Her favorite poets were Aleksandr Pushkin, Friedrich Hölderlin, Rainer Maria Rilke, and Dionysios Solomos, but the multicultural transfer of words in and out of competing languages fascinated her. Nikos Karouzos put the words *"cinturato Pirelli"* (Pirelli reinforced rubber) into one of his Greek poems, so she spent ages wondering whether she could get the word *ascenseur* into one of her own.

SELECTED BIBLIOGRAPHY

Works by Anghelaki-Rooke

Piimata '63–'69. Athens: Ermeias, 1971.

Magdalini, to megalo thilastikó. Athens: Ermis, 1974.

O thriambos tis statherís apoleias. Athens: Kedros, 1978.

Synghroni amerikani piités. Ed. and trans. Katerina Anghelaki-Rooke. Athens: Hypsilon, 1983.

I mnistires. Athens: Kedros, 1984.

Beings and Things on Their Own. Trans. Katerina Anghelaki-Rooke and Jackie Willcox. Brockport, N.Y.: Boa Editions, 1986.

Oraia erimos i sarka: Piimata. Athens: Kastaniotis, 1995.

From Purple into Night. Trans. Katerina Anghelaki-Rooke and Jackie Willcox. Introduction by David Constantine. Nottingham, England: Shoestring, 1997.

Selected Studies of Anghelaki-Rooke

Fourtouni, Eleni, ed. and trans. *Contemporary Greek Women Poets*, 35–45. New Haven, Conn.: Thelphini Press, 1978.

Niarchos, Thanasis Th., ed. *Kibotos: Synomolies me tous Katerina Angelake-Rouk.* Athens: Egnatia, 1980.

Rexine, John E. "Translations." *World Literature Today* 61, no. 2 (Spring 1987): 328.

Savvas, Minas. "Katerína Anghelaki-Rooke. *From Purple into Night.*" *World Literature Today* 72, no. 2 (Spring 1998): 429.

Stravelis, Thomas. "Katerína Angheláki-Roúk: *I mnistíres.*" *World Literature Today* 59, no. 4 (Autumn 1985): 636–37.

W. H. AUDEN
(1907–1973)

Jane Benardete

BIOGRAPHY

Born in York, England, Wystan Hugh Auden grew up in what he called "a middle-class professional family": "My father was a doctor, my mother had a university degree. The study was full of books on medicine, archaeology, the classics. . . . In one way we were eccentric: we were Anglo-Catholics." In this home, he said, he learned "certain attitudes": "that knowledge is something to seek for its own sake; an interest in medicine and disease, and theology; . . . a dislike of strangers and cheery gangs; and a contempt for businessmen and all who work for profits" (*The English Auden: Poems, Essays, and Dramatic Writings, 1927–1929*, 397). After attending St. Edmund's school in Surrey (where he met the English author Christopher Isherwood) and Gresham's in Holt, he entered Christ Church College, Oxford, in 1925. His first ambition was to be a mining engineer, but after studying with Nevill Coghill—Oxford don and tutor, known as a medievalist—he chose to concentrate in English. He was also influenced by the critic I. A. Richards (Davenport-Hines, *Auden*, 78).

His adult life was peripatetic. He spent a year, 1928–29, in Berlin, and from 1930 to 1935 he was a master at the Downs school in Cornwall. In May 1935, he married Erika Mann, daughter of Thomas Mann, solely to give her British citizenship and safety from Nazism. In 1936, he went with the Irish poet and classicist Louis MacNeice to Iceland (see their *Letters from Iceland*, 1937), and in 1937 he traveled to Spain, where he briefly wrote propaganda for the Loyalists. In 1938, with Christopher Isherwood, he went to China (see their *Journey to a War*, 1939) and for the first time visited the United States. He returned to the United States in January 1939 and in April that year met Chester Kallman, with whom he celebrated a "honeymoon" tour across the country the following summer. They remained together for the rest of Auden's life, coauthoring articles and libretti (e.g., "Translating Opera Libretti," in *The Dyer's Hand*, 483–99).

From his college years, Auden was outstanding among his contemporaries, who included such writers as Christopher Isherwood, Stephen Spender, and Cecil Day-Lewis. Auden's enthusiasm for the United States and his residence there was criticized in England, especially during the emotional war years. His revisions of his work (which coincided with his residence in the United States and his return to practicing Anglo-Catholicism) also stirred disapproval. In an edition of his poems published in 1945, *The Collected Poetry of W. H. Auden*, he made "alterations, excisions, and additions" that led some critics to an "equivocal" view of the poetry written after 1939 (Bahlke, ed., *Critical Essays on W. H. Auden*, 2). He became a U.S. citizen in 1946 and until 1972 lived in his adopted country for at least part of every year. During this time, he taught or lectured at various U.S. colleges, among them Bennington, Swarthmore, Barnard, Mount Holyoke, and Smith. He received many prizes and awards, including in 1948 a Pulitzer Prize for *The Age of Anxiety* and in 1957 the Feltrinelli Prize for Literature. From 1951 to 1959, he edited the Yale Series of Younger Poets, selecting for publication one book a year by such then-unknowns as Adrienne Rich, John Ashbery, James Wright, and W. S. Merwin. From 1948 to 1958, he spent his summers in Italy and from 1958 until his death in Kirchstetten, Austria. In 1956, he was elected to a five-year term as professor of poetry at Oxford. In 1972, he returned to Oxford, planning to live thereafter at Christ Church. He died in Vienna in September 1973 and was buried at Kirchstetten.

MAJOR MULTICULTURAL THEMES

Living through two world wars, as well as the Spanish civil war and the Cold War, Auden experienced and recorded radical cultural changes, first as an Englishman, then as a world traveler, and finally as a citizen of the United States. The "provincial England of 1907" into which he was born, was, he said, "Tennysonian in outlook," whereas "the England of 1925 when [he] went up to Oxford was *The Waste Land* in character" (quoted in Carpenter, *W. H. Auden: A Biography*, 12). Auden was, at that time in Oxford, a self-styled "anarchist individualist," often a social critic and spokesman for the left. Although he felt that "in a critical period . . . the poet must have direct knowledge of major political events," he disowned the notion that "poetry need or even should be directly political" (*The English Auden*, xviii). His insistence on the apolitical nature of poetry persisted through the Cold War era. In 1972, he told an interviewer that he had "come to realize that, in cases of social or political injustice . . . [t]he arts can do nothing" (*Writers at Work: The "Paris Review" Interviews*, 251).

For many years, Auden enthusiastically embraced the United States and distanced himself from England. His decision to remain in the United States through World War II may have been strengthened by his relationship with Chester Kallman, but he often expressed the importance of the United States to him as a writer. Living there was, he said in 1939, "[t]he most decisive experience of my life so far. It has taught me the kind of writer I am, i.e. an introvert. . . . All Americans are introverts"; in the same year, he wrote a friend that he "never wish[ed] to see England again" (quoted in *The English Auden*, xx). Auden's subject matter and poetic manner soon changed: one reason he left England, he wrote in later years, "was precisely to stop me writing poems like 'September 1, 1939' " (quoted in *The English Auden*, xx). He studied American writers and at times adopted an American voice, for example in "A Walk after Dark" in the laconic "down East" manner of Robert Frost (*W. H. Auden: Collected Poems*, 267–68). In his introduction (1946) to an edition of Henry James's *The American Scene*, Auden identifies himself with James's fictitious "recent immigrant," noting details such as the Americans' "magnificent boots and teeth," and he praises America as a country "where liberty is prior to virtue . . . for freedom of choice [is] . . . the human prerequisite without which virtue and vice have no meaning" (*The Dyer's Hand*, 318).

SURVEY OF CRITICISM

Though many of the critics who disapproved of Auden's revisions of his work were English (see John Haffenden [1983]), not all were. An American, Joseph Warren Beach (1957), concluded that "we are most satisfied when there is a consistent thread running through the whole . . . body of an artist's work. . . . With Auden we are not sure of this. We know that he is a very gifted actor and mimic. . . . But we cannot give ourselves up to him without certain reservations" (253). In a 1960 review entitled "What's Become of Wystan?" the English poet Philip Larkin asserted that after 1940 Auden betrayed his admirers by remaking "his entire poetic equipment" and becoming "too verbose to be memorable and too intellectual to be moving" (cited in Jacobs, *What Became of Wystan*, xiii).

Auden's literary executor, Edward Mendelson, notes that "the history of Auden's reputation has consistently followed a pattern in which initial outrage at new developments in manner and subject is supplanted by gradual acceptance and understanding of the merits of Auden's changes" (*W. H. Auden: Collected Poems*, 11). Mendelson's two volumes of history, criticism, and interpretation are *Early Auden* (1981) and *Later Auden*

(1999). Biographies include those by Humphrey Carpenter (1981) and Richard Davenport-Hines (1995). Auden also figures in Christopher Isherwood's account of his Berlin years, *Christopher and His Kind: 1929–1939* (1976). The "Berlin years" are also the subject of Norman Page's *Auden and Isherwood: The Berlin Years* (1998).

SELECTED BIBLIOGRAPHY

Works by Auden

Auden, W. H., and Louis MacNeice. *Letters from Iceland*. Faber and Faber, 1937.

Auden, W. H., and Christopher Isherwood. *Journey to a War*. London: Faber and Faber, 1939.

The Collected Poetry of W. H. Auden. New York: Random House, 1945.

The Age of Anxiety. New York: Random House, 1947; London: Faber and Faber, 1948.

The Dyer's Hand. New York: Random House, 1948. [Includes a reprint of Auden's 1946 introduction to Henry James's *The American Scene*, as well as other "Americana."]

W. H. Auden: Collected Poems. Ed. Edward Mendelson. New York: Random House, 1976.

The English Auden: Poems, Essays, and Dramatic Writings, 1927–1929. Ed. Edward Mendelson. London: Faber and Faber, 1977.

Auden, W. H., and Christopher Isherwood. *Plays and Other Dramatic Writings by W. H. Auden, 1928–1938*. Ed. Edward Mendelson. Princeton, N.J.: Princeton University Press, 1988.

Selected Studies of Auden

Bahlke, George W., ed. *Critical Essays on W. H. Auden*. New York: G. K. Hall, 1991.

Beach, Joseph Warren. *The Making of the Auden Canon*. Minneapolis.: University of Minnesota Press, 1957.

Carpenter, Humphrey. *W. H. Auden: A Biography*. Boston: Houghton Mifflin, 1981.

Davenport-Hines, Richard. *Auden*. London: Heinemann, 1995.

Haffenden, John, ed. *W. H. Auden: The Critical Heritage*. London: Routledge and Kegan Paul, 1983.

Isherwood, Christopher. *Christopher and His Kind: 1929–1939*. New York: Farrar, Straus and Giroux, 1976.

Jacobs, Alan. *What Became of Wystan*. Fayetteville: University of Arkansas Press, 1998.

Mendelson, Edward. *Early Auden*. New York: Viking, 1981.

———. *Later Auden*. New York: Farrar, Straus and Giroux, 1999.

Page, Norman. *Auden and Isherwood: The Berlin Years*. New York: St. Martin's Press, 1998.

Plimpton, George, ed. *Writers at Work: The "Paris Review" Interviews*. New York: Viking Press, 1958.

PAUL AUSTER
(1947–)

Robert E. Clark

BIOGRAPHY

Paul Auster was born in Newark, New Jersey, and grew up in South Orange and Maplewood, bland and prosperous Jersey suburbs. His father was a landlord, his mother a homemaker. Neither had strong literary interests. The professor and translator Allen Mandelbaum, however, was Auster's uncle. Part of Mandelbaum's library (left with his family while Mandelbaum was in Europe) spurred Auster's interest in canonical European literature and incidentally suggested the eclectic learning of a prominent scholar. After high school, Auster toured Spain, Italy, France, and Ireland (in particular Dublin as the setting for *Ulysses*). As in American romantic fiction before Henry James, Europe promised greater cultural variety and an artistic apprentice ground.

Auster wrote about books and film for student publications at Columbia University, where he earned the bachelor of arts degree in 1969. He had lingered in Paris beyond the administrative limits of a junior year abroad, but a generous dean saved him from the Vietnam draft by reinstating him. He earned Columbia's master of arts degree with concentration in Renaissance literature in 1970.

The jobs he held were possibly more odd and possibly more international than those of other young writers: helping to translate the Vietnamese Constitution in Paris; following an enigmatic international crew to Mexico for a project about Quetzalcoatl; working briefly on an oil tanker traveling down the U.S. eastern seaboard; writing catalog copy for Ars Libris, a Manhattan book and print firm specializing in the twentieth-century European avant-garde. Auster describes those times in *Hand to Mouth: A Memoir of Early Failures* (1997), in which he focuses on the low wages of translating and writing, the lure of travel, and friendships with an assortment of eccentrics from various social classes and cultures. Some of the same material had taken more engaging form in an earlier novel with a Columbia student-protagonist, *Moon Palace* (1989), in which bildungsroman fuses with road trip.

Indeed, autobiography is in constant interplay with Auster's fiction: he is insistent on the complex relationship between life and art and forthcoming about close parallels, often noted by interviewers. His fiction and autobiography share many motifs: dramatic chance events, synchronicity and magical-seeming coincidence, love of baseball, inspiration from wide reading in European literatures, and appreciation for humble genres (detective fiction, science fiction, and travel tales).

Auster devoted the 1970s to translating from the French (business documents as well as literature) and to writing poetry and literary journalism in English. He began the decade living in France (1971–74), often in company with the writer and translator Lydia Davis. They married in 1974. On their return to the United States, he became a figure in the downtown and Brooklyn literary, fine arts, and performance scenes. Although solitary in writing habits, he is a charming and gracious presence; interviews mention friendships with poets, painters, performance artists, and film directors across the international arts world.

Financial difficulties contributed to the gradual end of Auster and Davis's marriage. After a period of separation and solitude, he met another writer and translator, Siri Hustvedt, whom he married in 1981. Like Davis's father, Hustvedt's father was a prominent professor (of Norwegian literature). Auster had a strong interest in the Norwegian writer Knut Hamsun long before his second marriage, and his fiction has affinities with the feminism and concern about poverty in modern Scandinavian literature. Both topics are important in his earlier fiction, in particular *In the Country of Last Things* (1987).

Auster's breakthrough as a novelist came in the 1980s with *The New York Trilogy* (*City of Glass*, 1985; *Ghosts*, 1986; *The Locked Room*, 1986). The trilogy is a brilliant and incisive exploration of American culture and detective fiction; and in the two later volumes, language play and experimental techniques make evident the author's command of contemporary European, especially French, fiction.

Among Auster's later fiction, *Timbuktu* (1999) is a moving tale accessible to younger readers, narrated by a dog cared for by an unpublished homeless writer. As well as appealing to younger readers, Auster seems to have broadened his approach to a general audience in other ways, encouraging them to share his excitement about literature that embraces several cultures and respects social outcasts. (Early in his career, he had translated the challenging work of living French poets for American readers and had edited *The Random House Book of Twentieth-Century*

French Poetry [1982], translating many poems himself.) By hosting a public radio program, Auster recently collected tales from nonprofessional writers of a wide variety of cultures and classes for his edition of *I Thought My Father Was God* (2001).

Critical insight into Auster's place in a specifically American avant-garde (on Manhattan's Upper West Side; in 1970s and 1980s Soho; in the galleries and neighborhood hangouts of Soho, New York, and Park Slope, Brooklyn) may also offer historical perspective on the reciprocal exchange between Europe and the United States in the literary and film world over the past three decades.

In the 1990s, Auster reached a world audience by writing and assisting in directing the very successful independent film *Smoke* (1995). (The first critically successful film based on his fiction was *The Music of Chance* [1990]). He next directed *Lulu on the Bridge* (1998), a fusion of Louise Brooks's life, G. W. Pabst's silent classic *Pandora's Box*, and a modern romance with a supernatural element. With Hustvedt, Auster more recently helped write the film *The Center of the World* (2001).

MAJOR MULTICULTURAL THEMES

Auster weds commercial genres to serious investigation of identity, freewill and fate, spirituality, and, lately, love. His writing has always shown tenderness for people at the margins of cultures or torn between two cultures—from the poor in a consumption-mad United States to Americans who have metaphysical affinities with the Asian cultures (*Moon Palace* and *Lulu on the Bridge*). His prototypically American resilience, generosity, and wry humor may account for some of his popularity in Europe, especially because his work also pokes fun at the excesses of America and its popular culture. (He also burnishes legends about the great immigrant and tourism cities of Manhattan and Brooklyn.) Perhaps those qualities also make his work intriguing—if not exotic—to the relatively homogenous societies of Japan and Scandinavia.

Throughout his career, Auster has borrowed from the world's most culturally diverse literary corpus, including medieval and Renaissance quest, quest-romance, and quest-epic forms that by the early modern period had absorbed tales from Christian, Arabic, and Mediterranean sources for many centuries. (He also admires parody forms such as *Don Quixote* and *Orlando Furioso*.) From such quest literature, he takes the peripatetic plot, the road story, for *The Music of Chance, Moon Palace, In the Country of Last Things* (1987), *Leviathan* (1992), and *Timbuktu: A Novel*, in parables and fables of moral complexity.

Quest literature is also a precedent for the search for identity, purpose, and (although rare in his early work) redemption that characterizes his fiction. The unsentimental attitude toward sex in his early work also accords with ancient epic-quests. In later works, however—*In The Country of Last Things, Smoke, Lulu on the Bridge*, and *Timbuktu*—love becomes a suitable aim for a quest, even if unrealized or disastrous.

The panorama of social class among Auster's characters—observed by rogue-wanderer narrators—derives in part from the Spanish picaresque novel (*Lazarillo de Tormes* and *Don Quixote*), as do passages that underline the torments of bureaucracy and misery of family life, with a nod to Kafka.

Much critical attention has gone to the centrality of randomness and accident in Auster's work. Although the limited metaphysical realm of French existentialism is relevant, early modern British fiction and theater also contribute to this motif, not just in *Tristram Shandy*–like comic accident, but in larger narrative structures, including Shakespearean reversals of fortune, revealed hidden identities, and whimsical providential grace or retribution.

SURVEY OF CRITICISM

Reviews and journalism make up the bulk of Auster criticism, much of it currently accessible on Web pages devoted to him and often superior to academic studies that tend toward jargon and unimaginative response. Auster has also reprinted his own revealing early literary essays and many interviews he has given about his work.

Source studies linking Auster to Samuel Beckett, Knut Hamsun, Franz Kafka, and others have been popular in Europe and America—as have thematic studies of his interest in the limits of language, the process of self-creation, and the puzzles of shifting identity. Some critics have grouped him with contemporary postmodern writers such as Don Delillo and have deployed the predictable Continental literary theory of the 1970s and 1980s to explicate his work.

SELECTED BIBLIOGRAPHY

Works by Auster

The New York Trilogy. London: Faber and Faber, 1987. [Includes *City of Glass*, 1985; *Ghosts*, 1986; *The Locked Room*, 1986.]

In the Country of Last Things. New York: Viking, 1987.

Moon Palace. New York: Viking, 1989.

The Music of Chance. New York: Viking, 1990.

Leviathan. New York: Viking, 1992.

Smoke and Blue in the Face: Two Films. Preface by Wayne Wang. New York: Hyperion, 1995.

Hand to Mouth: A Memoir of Early Failures. New York: Henry Holt, 1997.

Lulu on the Bridge: A Film. New York: Henry Holt, 1998.

Timbuktu: A Novel. New York: Henry Holt, 1999.

Translations and Anthologies

A Little Anthology of Surrealist Poems. Trans. Paul Auster. New York: Siamese Banana Press, 1972.

The Random House Book of Twentieth-Century French Poetry. Ed. Paul Auster. New York: Random House, 1982.

The Notebooks of Joseph Joubert: A Selection. Ed., trans., and preface by Paul Auster. Afterword by Maurice Blanchot. San Francisco: North Point Press, 1983.

A Tomb for Anatole, by Stéphane Mallarmé. Bilingual edition. Trans. and introduction by Paul Auster. San Francisco: North Point Press, 1983.

On the High Wire, by Philippe Petit. Trans. Paul Auster. Preface by Marcel Marceau. New York: Random House, 1985.

Vicious Circles and After the Fact, by Maurice Blanchot. Trans. Paul Auster. Barrytown, N.Y.: Station Hill Press, 1985.

Poems, by Jacques Dupin. Ed. Paul Auster. Trans. Paul Auster, Stephen Romer, and David Shapiro. Preface by Mary Ann Caws. Winston-Salem, N.C.: Wake Forest University Press, 1992.

Chronicles of the Guayaki Indians, by Pierre Clastres. Trans. and foreword by Paul Auster. London: Faber and Faber, 1998.

I Thought My Father Was God. Ed. Paul Auster. New York: Henry Holt, 2001.

Selected Studies of Auster

Barone, Dennis. *Beyond the Red Notebook: Essays on Paul Auster.* Philadelphia: University of Pennsylvania Press, 1995.

Clark, Robert. "Paul Auster" (essay and interview). *Columbia Magazine* (Fall 1999): 50–51.

Duperray, Annick. *Colloque Paul Auster.* Arles: Actes Sud; Marseille: Université de Provence-IRMA (Grena), 1995.

Herzogenrath, Bernd. *An Art of Desire: Reading Paul Auster.* Amsterdam and Atlanta, Ga.: Rodopi, 1999.

BA JIN
(1904–)

M. Cristina Pisciotta

BIOGRAPHY

Known as the leading exponent of anarchist literature in China, as one of
the most popular and well-loved Chinese novelists, and as a 1975 candidate for the Nobel Prize for Literature, Ba Jin has had an extraordinarily
long and fruitful life and career. Born in Chengdu of a rich mandarin
family, Li Feigan (his real name) lost both his parents at a very early age.
A number of traumatic childhood experiences marked him for life and
made him particularly sensitive to human pain and suffering.

After studying French and English in a Western-oriented language
school, he became impatient with traditional education and morals.
Receptive to the new anarchist ideas, he left Chengdu to study at Nanjing and later at Shanghai, thereafter embarking for France in 1927.
The occupant of a garret in an antiquated pension in the Latin Quarter
of Paris, he lived a solitary and studious life "in that foreign country
where I knew no one, had neither relatives nor friends, and the fate of
my country tormented me. . . . But over the past fifty years, I have often
thought that those days spent on the banks of the Seine or the Marne
were the most important of my life" (preface to *Famille: Roman* [Chi-
nese: *Jia*], 22–23).

This was in fact the most formative period of his life, the time that saw
the development of those ideas and passions that led him to literature; for
it was precisely in those years 1927–28 that French culture was becoming
an essential point of reference in his artistic production, one that would
always serve as a kind of counterweight to the civilization of his own land.

In France, he deepened his knowledge of anarchist theories, associating with the Chinese anarchist groups in Paris and adopting a pseudonym, Ba Jin (the first syllable is borrowed from the last name of the celebrated anarchist Mikhail Aleksandrovich Bakunin, and the second comes from the last syllable of the name Pyotr Alekseyevich Kropotkin, another leading anarchist). He studied the French Revolution but was interested above all in literature, particularly in the works of the French realists and naturalists, who became his masters. The defeat of the revolutionary forces in his own homeland brought him to the verge of nihilism. His first novel, *Miewang* (1929), published in the narrative monthly *Xiaoshuo yuebao*, brought him immediate popularity.

Returning to Shanghai, Ba Jin continued to concern himself with the libertarian movement but dedicated the bulk of his time to literary writing, which attained considerable proportions. The two most important works, in terms of scale and quality, are the two trilogies *Aiqingde sanbuqu* (1931–34) and *Jiliude sanbuqu* (1931–40). The first depicts the hesitations and doubts of a youth poised between sentimental life and revolution. The second is composed of three largely independent parts, *Jia* (1931), *Chun* (1938), and *Qiu* (1940). *Jia*, considered Ba Jin's masterpiece, seems to have been inspired by personal experience: the plot unfolds at Chengdu and reveals the progressive disintegration of a clan whose different generations are no longer able to live together and in which the characters of the three brothers clash, to the great distress of their loved ones.

During the Second Sino-Japanese War (1937–45), Ba Jin, escaping to Guilin and later to Chongqing, wrote the small masterpiece entitled *Qiyuan* (1944), in which we again encounter French and Chinese culture, antique splendor and decadence, and China's past and present as revealed in the history of a great Chengdu family. He also wrote *Hanye* (1946), one of his most touching novels, about a young woman who is obliged to leave her husband when he, weak and gravely ill, is unable to free himself from his cruel mother.

Ba Jin wrote nothing further after the Chinese Communist victory in 1949, but his popularity continued to increase. Editor in chief of two important reviews, *Shouhuo* and *Shanghai Wenxue*, he continued to exercise great influence over Chinese public opinion. Though separated from the literary world during the Cultural Revolution and severely criticized for his youthful anarchistic beliefs, Ba Jin was rehabilitated after the fall of the Gang of Four and laboriously resumed writing, greeting the end of the "dark years" as "a second liberation" (quoted in Levy, ed., *Dictionnaire de littérature chinoise*, 6).

The unequaled popularity and profound liking for Ba Jin in China and abroad are certainly owing not only to the quality and special humanity of his literary works, but also to ideas that have always remained distinct from Marxist orthodoxy and to a lifetime of terrible trials.

Ba Jin

MAJOR MULTICULTURAL THEMES

Returning to Paris with a delegation of Chinese writers in 1979, Ba Jin recalled the importance of his first sojourn in France in a series of essays ("Nice," "Return to Marseilles," "Lyons," "Château-Thierry," "A Sea of Friendship") that collectively illustrate the depth of his affinity with French history and literature (*Suixiang lu*, 1980, translated as *Random Thoughts*, 1984). "It was in France that I began my career as a writer. I began writing my first novel in Paris in 1927 and finished it at Château Thierry in 1928. . . . My sojourn at that time amounted to only two years, but French culture, which appealed to me greatly, began from that time onward to be coupled with my own" (preface to *Famille: Roman*, 22).

The Chinese anarchist movement developed primarily among Chinese students in France in the first two decades of the twentieth century and was at one and the same time "the antithesis and the predecessor of Marxism-Leninism in China" (Guillermaz, *Storia del Partito Comunista Cinese—1921–1949*, 36). Chinese intellectuals seem to have been attracted by revolutionary anarchism much more than by socialism. The rejection of society and the exaltation of individual liberty possessed a certain affinity with ancient Taoist currents and were perhaps more comprehensible in China for that reason.

For Ba Jin, involvement in Parisian anarchist groups was decisive in determining ideological choices that are very evident in all his writings. France, for him, however, was above all the country of the Great Revolution of 1789: he began to study that upheaval while in Paris and later continued his studies in China, where he wrote a long and detailed essay on the history of the French Revolution based on the idea that its true hero "was not Mirabeau, nor Danton, nor Robespierre, but the French people" ("Faguo Gemingde lishi," 261).

Yet many of the prominent personalities of the French Revolution became protagonists of Ba Jin's narratives. "Luobosibierde mimi" (1934) presents to us a heroic figure (Maximilien Robespierre) who is always ready to affirm the republican ideal to the very depths, but who is lacerated by the hallucinations and torments of his conscience; and "Malade si" (1934) is imbued with Ba Jin's affectionate admiration for a man (Jean-Paul Marat) who loves the people more than himself. "I have read all the books there are about Marat," Ba Jin writes. "I know him as a friend knows a good friend" ("Mala Gedai he Yatang Lukesi," 122).

Others who figure in his stories are Charlotte Corday ("Mala Gedai he Yatang Lukesi," 1955) and Georges-Jacques Danton ("Dandongde bei ai," 1936). "I too have often been inspired by [Danton's] words: Courage, courage, and still more courage," Ba Jin writes (quoted in Lang, *Pa Chin and His Writings*, 247); and Jean-Jacques Rousseau will always remain for him the "great inspirer" and the "conscience of the eighteenth century." "One evening I approached the statue of Rousseau on foot," Ba Jin

59

recounts, "and automatically began to caress the cold stone base as if I were caressing a beloved person. Then, raising my head, I remained standing for a little while and gazing at this great hero, forgetting my grief" ("Xiezuo shenghuode huigu," 1936, 3). Rousseau, too, becomes a character in a story, "Lusao yu Luobosibier" (1933): here the author imagines an encounter and a dialogue between Robespierre and Rousseau, in which the philosopher Rousseau reproves the revolutionary Robespierre for having wanted to realize his ideals with the help of the guillotine.

Although the political experience in Paris and the study of French history were clearly decisive in the formation of Ba Jin's revolutionary and social ideals, his immersion in French literature was no less important for the maturing of his literary output. He chose his basic readings from among the representatives of *la littérature engagée* and the realist school: Victor Hugo, Guy de Maupassant, André Gide, Romain Rolland. The young revolutionaries who people Ba Jin's novels have a particular affinity with Jean Christophe, the German musician who is the passionate hero of Rolland's eponymous novel.

But the French author whom Ba Jin considers most congenial, the one whom he constantly quotes and whose works he takes as the model for some of his novels, is Émile Zola. Many are the stories in which Ba Jin's characters quote sentences from Zola in the course of conversation. In "Masaide ye" (1932, included in vol. 7 of *Ba Jin xuanji shijuanben*, 1982), Ba Jin tells of his first moving encounter with the French writer: "in my room I did nothing but read the novels of Zola, at any hour of the day or night" (150).

The cyclical structure of Ba Jin's novels shows clearly his derivation from the French literary tradition and, more directly, from Zola. Moreover, when Ba Jin attacks the familiar Chinese patriarchal family system that he considers one of the greatest social evils in contemporary China, he actually uses Zola's famous phrase, *J'accuse*, as a title (1941).

The novel *Xue* (1933, originally entitled *Mengya*, meaning "seeds") is one of the clearest examples of Zola's influence, in a narrative all too plainly modeled on Zola's *Germinal*. Like Zola before him, Ba Jin also spent a week at a coal mine in order to achieve a thorough understanding of the life and problems of the miners; and both books, traveling as it were on parallel tracks, explore the birth (or "seeds") of a new workers' force and denounce the injustices done to it. Another famous novel by Ba Jin, *Hanye* (1947) closely follows, though in a less spectacular fashion, the techniques and themes of Zola's *Thérèse Raquin*.

But to retrieve Ba Jin's French life and Parisian panoramas with the "dolorous carillon of Notre Dame" (*L'automne dans le printemps* [*Chuntian li de qiutian*], 225); to learn about the French friends he saw in his numerous trips to their country; to enter into his feelings as an exile in a foreign land and his passionate participation in Parisian political affairs;

or, finally, to be present at his French language lessons at the lycée of Château-Thierry, we must read his early stories (collected in *Ba Jin xuanji shijuanben*, 1982), especially "Fangdong taitai" (1929), "Aide cuican" (1930), "Yalianna," "Yi feng yin" and "Hao ren" of 1931, and "Masaide ye" (1932).

SURVEY OF CRITICISM

The work of Olga Lang (1976) is fundamental for anyone wishing to approach Ba Jin's writings. She analyzes his entire narrative work and provides a detailed and exhaustive overview of his life, his cultural formation, and the successive stages of his literary output.

In a different way, Jean Monsterleet (1952, 1954), a personal friend of the Chinese writer, studies Ba Jin's relations with French culture and the varied aspects of his multiculturalism, dwelling in particular on French authors and intellectuals who played a fundamental role in his artistic formation: Victor Hugo, Guy de Maupassant, André Gide, Romain Rolland, Émile Zola. In the case of Rolland, for example, toward whom Ba Jin felt a profound affinity based on humanitarianism, moral integrity, and courage, Monsterleet establishes precise relationships between the characters of Rolland's novels (especially *Jean-Christophe*) and those of Ba Jin's novels, who see in art a fundamental instrument of struggle against injustice and who are imbued with a strong anarchistic sentiment. Monsterleet makes an especially careful comparative analysis of Zola's *Germinal* and *Xue*. Although Zola and Ba Jin represent two geographically and chronologically different realities (a mining town of northern France in 1860 and a coal mine in northern China around 1930), the aspects of the first phases of industrialization are similar, as are the miners' working conditions, their lifestyles, and the taverns where they meet to discuss the sociopolitical problems that concern them. Both novelists cry out against social injustices, emphasizing the contrast between the comfortable and corrupt world of the managers and the poor, painful one of the workers; both use an outsider, a newcomer, to describe life in the mines with an unprejudiced eye; both liken this reality to a volcano on the point of erupting.

Li Zhichang (1930) confronts the wider problem of the influence of French naturalism, especially of Zola, in Ba Jin's works, pointing out that Ba Jin did not particularly absorb the theoretical articles collected above all in *Le roman expérimental* and made little use of the expression *experimental novel*. The Chinese writer seems less interested in scientific-physiological discussion than in the representation of a violent milieu that destroys individual freedom—the novel of denunciation—but that never manages to develop, as in Zola, into an objective and journalistic description concealing rage and bitterness.

The work of Marián Gálik (1986) is itself a milestone in the study of the relations between modern Western and Chinese culture; she gives us a general view of Ba Jin's Western readings, showing what the great writer makes his own and how he transforms and assimilates it.

Ng Yok-Soon (1987) is chiefly concerned with Ba Jin's life and travels in France and with his relationships with French intellectuals. A detailed list of the translations of Ba Jin's works in France and of Ba Jin's own Chinese translations of French works reflects the enormous good fortune and popularity the author has enjoyed and still enjoys in that country, to the point where François Mitterand conferred on him in 1983 the ribbon of commander of the Legion of Honor for his "contribution to world civilization" (200).

A further contribution to the understanding of Ba Jin's multiculturalism is Robert A. Scalapino and George T. Yu's study of the Chinese anarchist movement (1961), which examines the birth of his anarchistic ideas, his relations with French groups (including his articles published in *Le Libertaire*, the weekly organ of the Anarchist-Communist Union of Paris), and his connections to the great names of world anarchist literature.

SELECTED BIBLIOGRAPHY

Works of Ba Jin

Miewang (1929). Beijing: Kaiming, 1950.

Jia. Beijing: Renmin wenxue chubanshe, 1931. [*Famille: Roman*. Preface by Ba Jin. Trans. Li Tche-houa and Jacqueline Alézaïs. Paris: Flammarion, 1979.]

Aiqingde sanbuqu (1931–34). In *Ba Jin wenji*, vol. 3. Beijing: Renmin wenxue chubanshe, 1958.

Chuntian li de qiutian (1932). In *Ba Jin xuanji shijuanben*, 5: 90–186. Chengdu: Sichuan renmin chubanshe, 1982. [*L'automne dans le printemps*. Trans. Li Meiying and Hansheng. Beijing: Littérature Chinoise, 1982.]

Xue (1933). Shanghai: Wenhua shenghuo, 1946.

"Lusao yu Luobosibier" (1933). In *Ba Jin sanwen xuan*, 118–19. Beijing: Xinhua, 1955.

"Luobosibierde mimi" (1934). In *Ba Jin xuanji shijuanben*, 7: 238–50. Chengdu: Sichuan renmin chubanshe, 1982. [*Secret de Robespierre et autres nouvelles*. Paris: Mazarine, 1980.]

Ba Jin xuanji. Shanghai: Zhongyang shudian, 1936.

"Xiezuo shenghuode huigu." In *Ba Jin xuanji*, 1–15. Shanghai: Zhongyang shudian, 1936.

Lishi xiao pinji. Shanghai: Chenzhong, 1936.

"Faguo Gemingde lishi." In *Lishi xiao pinji*, 260–64. Shanghai: Chenzhong, 1936.

"Dandongde bei ai." In *Lishi xiao pinji*, 237–60. Shanghai: Chenzhong, 1936.

Jiliude sanbuqu (1931–40). [Trilogy: *Jia*. Beijing: Renmin wenxue chubanshe, 1931. *Chun*. Shanghai: Kaiming, 1938. *Qiu*. Beijing: Renmin wenxue chubanshe, 1940.]

Kongsu (J'accuse). Shanghai: Wenhua shenghuo, 1941.

Qiyuan (1944). In *Ba Jin xuanji shijuanben*, 5: 187–370. Chengdu: Sichuan renmin chubanshe, 1982. [*Le jardin du repos: Roman*. Trans. Nicolas Chapuis and Roger Darrobers. Paris: Robert Laffont, 1979.]

Aiqingde sanbuqu (1940–45). In *Ba Jin wenji*, vol. 3. Beijing: Renmin wenxue chubanshe, 1958.

Hanye (1946). In *Ba Jin xuanji shijuanben*, 6: 209–482. Chengdu: Sichuan renmin chubanshe, 1982. [*Nuit glacée*. Trans. M.-J. Lalitte. Paris: Gallimard, 1978.]

Ba Jin sanwen xuan. Beijing: Xinhua chubanshe, 1955.

"Mala Gedai he Yatang Lukesi." In *Ba Jin sanwen xuan*, 120–30. Beijing: Xinhua chubanshe, 1955.

Ba Jin wenji. 14 vols. Beijing: Renmin wenxue chubanshe, 1958–62.

Suixiang lu. Beijing: Renmin wenxue chubanshe, 1980. [*Random Thoughts*. Trans. Geremie Barmé. Hong Kong: Joint, 1984.]

Ba Jin xuanji shijuanben. 10 vols. Chengdu: Sichuan renmin chubanshe, 1982. [Includes "Fangdong taitai" (1929, 6: 172–93); "Aide cuican" (1930, 7: 11–26); "Yalianna" (1931, 7: 79–82); "Hao ren" (1931, 8: 60–79); "Yi feng xin" (1931, 9: 330–37); and "Masaide ye" (1932, 7: 146–59).]

"Malade si" (1934). In *Ba Jin xuanji shijuanben*, 7: 251–72. Chengdu: Sichuan renmin chubanshe, 1982.

Selected Studies of Ba Jin

Galik, Marian. *Milestones in Sino-Western Literary Confrontation (1898–1979)*, 203–24. Wiesbaden, Germany: Otto Harrassowitz, 1986.

Lang, Olga. *Pa Chin and His Writings: Chinese Youth between the Two Revolutions*. Cambridge, Mass.: Harvard University Press, 1967.

Levy, André, ed. *Dictionnaire de littérature chinoise*. Paris: Quadrige-PUF, 2000.

Li Zhichang. "Ziranzhuyide Zhongguo wenxue lun." In *Xin wenyi pinglun*, ed. Zhang Ruoying, 27–38. Shanghai: Wenyi chubanshe, 1950.

Monsterleet, Jean. "Pa Kin." *France-Asie* (Saigon) 1 (January 1952): 732–45.

———. "Note sur Pa Chin et les maîtres qui l'ont formé." *Revue de Littérature Comparée* 28, no. 1 (January–March 1954): 89–94.

Ng Yok-Soon. "Ba Jin et la France." In *Ba Jin: Le brouillard*, 197–208. Paris: Cent Fleurs, 1987.

Scalapino, Robert A., and George T. Yu, *The Chinese Anarchist Movement*. Berkeley: Center for Chinese Studies, Institute of International Studies, University of California, 1961.

Related Work:

Guillermaz, Jacques. *Storia del Partito Comunista Cinese—1921–1949*. Milan: Feltrinelli, 1970.

INGEBORG BACHMANN
(1926–1973)
Ingeborg Baumgartner

BIOGRAPHY

Ingeborg Bachmann, twentieth-century Austria's foremost lyric poet and prose fiction writer, absorbed multiculturalism with the very air she breathed. Born on June 25, 1926, as the first child of the schoolteacher Mathias Bachmann and his wife, Olga, Bachmann grew up during the war years in Klagenfurt, Austria, located near the border of former Yugoslavia and Italy. Early on she displayed exceptional gifts as a writer of dense prose and mellifluous lyrics, demonstrating keen awareness of political conflict and a sensitivity to cultural differences. Indeed, her first prose work, *Das Honditschkreuz*, written probably in 1944 (published posthumously in 1978 in *Werke*, vol. 2), takes its theme from Napoleonic history and juxtaposes protagonists from Austria and France—an apposition Bachmann expands on in later works (Hapkemeyer, *Ingeborg Bachmanns früheste Prosa*, 24).

After completing secondary school in Klagenfurt, she enrolled briefly at the universities in Innsbruck (1945) and Graz (1946) before moving to Vienna (fall 1947). In her words, this was "the longest road" she ever traveled (*Werke*, 4: 301). Studying German literature, psychology, and philosophy, she completed her dissertation on Martin Heidegger in 1950. After graduation, she traveled first to Paris, visiting Paul Celan (himself an Austrian from the Bukowina), then to London, where she gave her first reading of her work at the Anglo-Austrian Society. Returning to Vienna, she worked first for the American Occupation Forces Network, then for the Austrian Radio Rot-Weiss-Rot, writing scripts and both translating and adapting plays by Thomas Wolfe and Louis MacNeice.

Although she had made her debut as the author of a short story ("Die Fähre," 1946) and a radio play ("Ein Geschäft mit Träumen," first broadcast in 1952), she came to be known primarily as a lyricist. In 1952, an invitation to a reading before Gruppe '47, the organization of German writers founded by Hans Werner Richter in 1947, opened up opportunities for broader exposure, especially to German writers and publishers. It also occasioned her friendship with composer Hans Werner Henze, with whom she maintained a long-lasting relationship. The following year brought Bachmann not only honors but also major changes in her personal life: Gruppe '47 awarded her its prize, providing a modicum of financial security, and she saw the publication of her first volume of poetry, *Die gestundete Zeit, Gedichte*, which includes poems inspired by her travels abroad. Two years later, her text *Der Idiot: Ballett-Pantomime nach F. M. Dostojewski von Tatjana Gsovski*, for Henze's ballet pantomime (1955), followed. Most important for Bachmann, she moved to Italy, the country that had such a profound and permanent impact on her. First residing in Ischia and later in Naples, by 1954 she established residence in Rome, a city she would come to call home. In addition to working as a freelance writer and even as a newspaper correspondent, she composed most of the poems later published in her second volume, *Anrufung des Großen Bären* (1956), which includes her explicit homage to Italy. Her brief visit to the United States at this time as participant in the International Seminar at Harvard University yielded not only the poems "Harlem" and "Reklame," but also the radio play *Der gute Gott von Manhattan* (1958).

After a year-long stint in Munich serving as dramaturge for Bavarian Television, Bachmann lived alternately in Rome and Zürich between 1958 and 1963. As guest professor (1959–60) at the University of Frankfurt am Main, she delivered five lectures on contemporary literature. She furnished texts for Hans Werner Henze's opera *Der Prinz von Homburg* (1960), prepared her first volume of prose narratives, *Das dreißigste Jahr* (1961), and an edition of poems by Giuseppe Ungaretti with her own German translations. These diverse literary contributions earned her prestigious prizes, such as the Berliner Kritikerpreis (1961) and the Georg-Büchner Preis (1964), and membership in the literature section of the Academy of Arts in Berlin (1961) and in the Comunità Europea degli Scrittori (COMES) in 1965. A Ford Foundation stipend enabled her in 1963 and 1964 to live and work in Berlin. Here she completed another libretto for Hans Werner Henze, began work on a novel tentatively titled "Todesarten," and undertook more travels. Her visit to Prague is reflected in poems such as "Prag Jänner 64" and "Böhmen liegt am Meer." Her stay in Egypt and the Sudan finds its way into narratives such as *Der Fall Franza: Requiem für Fanny Goldmann* (1979).

Bachmann's return to Rome at the end of 1965 signaled a less peripatetic existence, interrupted briefly by sojourns to Germany to give readings and to Austria to visit her family. She continued work on her projected cycle of novels "Todesarten," coming out in 1971 first with *Malina*, whose hard-to-define genre met with puzzling critical response, but whose undisputed originality was affirmed after feminists embraced it. The last published work during her lifetime, *Simultan* (1972), a volume of prose narratives, unites in its title story Bachmann's major cultural interests: Slavic and Italian themes expressed by unnamed protagonists who traverse countries, communicate in different languages, and work as translators. Bachmann's last and perhaps most significant journey was made in the spring of 1973, when an invitation by the Austrian Cultural Institute provided the opportunity to give readings in several Polish cities and to visit Auschwitz. In the fall of that year, in her Rome apartment, an accidental fire inflicted severe burns on her, ultimately causing her death on October 17, 1973. She was 47 years old.

MAJOR MULTICULTURAL THEMES

An obsessive reader and compulsive writer, fluent in four languages, intimately familiar with most countries of western Europe, Ingeborg Bachmann encompasses and transforms these experiences in her works. The quest for foreign lands, escape from the ordinary, and flight into utopia characterize her early poems in *Die gestundete Zeit, Gedichte*—for example, "Abschied von England" and "Paris"; her longing for exotic landscapes is manifest in "Herbstmanöver." The theme of escape reappears in her three radio plays: in *Ein Geschäft mit Träumen* (written 1952, published posthumously in 1976), an office worker fleeing from ordinary life finds solace in dreams; in *Zikaden* (1955), an entourage of international cohorts, one aptly named Robinson, seeks refuge on a Mediterranean island; and in *Der gute Gott von Manhattan* (1958), set in "the city of cities" (*Werke* 1: 288), the demands of a capitalistic society and personal fulfillment clash, and escape now becomes an escape into a hotel room (Achberger, *Understanding Ingeborg Bachmann*, 43). These works reveal Bachmann to be a keen observer of landscape, cityscape, and social order, masterfully sublimating these elements into imaginary topography (Weigel, *Ingeborg Bachmann: Hinterlassenschaften unter Wahrung des Briefgeheimnisses*, 221). The title story of her last publication, *Simultan*, representative of Bachmann's sovereign command of languages, is imbued with non-German phrases; mastering simultaneous translation, the characters easily move from language to language, from country to country, and, like Bachmann, are at home in all cultures (Meise, "Topographien," 94).

Though feeling at ease in the Slavic world, Bachmann, like many German writers of the eighteenth and nineteenth centuries, is drawn to Italy, specifically to Rome. Unlike these German writers, however, Bachmann regards Rome not as a place of pilgrimage but as "eine selbstverständliche Stadt" (a matter-of-fact city) (Hapkemeyer, *Ingeborg Bachmanns früheste Prosa*, 126), where she liked to live and felt at home—something that her essay "Was ich in Rom sah und hörte" (first published in 1973) underscores. Indeed, throughout her work Bachmann professes the deepest affection for Italy, a land where her creative imagination soared: "war ich zum Schauen erwacht. / Da fiel mir Leben zu" (I was awakened to see. / Then my life began) (*Anrufung des Großen Bären*, 53). In many poems—for example, "Brief in zwei Fassungen" and "Römisches Nachtbild"—she focuses "on the mythological and metaphysical in the context of the largely Mediterranean landscape" (Achberger, *Understanding Ingeborg Bachmann*, 16). So pervasive is Bachmann's bond with Italy that editors saw fit to collect pertinent lyrics and prose narratives in a volume entitled *Mein erstgeborenes Land: Gedichte und Prosa aus Italien* (1978, 2d ed. 1992).

SURVEY OF CRITICISM

Although multicultural themes in Bachmann's work are woven like fine threads into a colorful, dense tapestry, their presence has attracted only sporadic attention. One reason may be that Bachmann's familiarity with diverse cultures is taken for granted and deemed less deserving of special attention than themes of gender relations, escapism, or language crisis; see, for example, the work by Ulrich Thiem (1972), Manfred Jurgensen (1981), and Andreas Hapkemeyer (1982). Furthermore, critics mourn the fact that no definitive biography of Bachmann has heretofore been published. Nevertheless, accessible, sound interpretations of Bachmann's work abound. The finest book happens to be the most recent one: Sigrid Weigel (1999) has accomplished the prodigious task of assembling and organizing the convolutes of archival material, secondary sources, and interviews to produce a comprehensive picture of the poet that punctures persistent legends. Equally thorough and persuasively argued is the work by Kurt Bartsch (1988), which, along with Karen Achberger's fine study (1995), focuses on the philosophical and poetic language and the feminist themes, even while making ample references to multicultural topics. A number of anthologies include discussion of the impulses Bachmann received from journeys and poets: Heinz Arnold's edited volume (1984), for example, contains Helga Meise's essay on topographies; the more recent volume edited by Dirk Göttsche and Herbert Ohl (1993) offers articles on Bachmann and modern French lyrics, Elsa Morante, and Marcel Proust.

SELECTED BIBLIOGRAPHY

Works by Bachmann

Die gestundete Zeit, Gedichte. Frankfurt am Main: Frankfurter, 1953.

Der Idiot: Ballett-Pantomime nach F. M. Dostojewski von Tatjana Gsovski. Mainz: Schott, 1955.

Anrufung des Großen Bären. Munich: R. Piper, 1956.

Der gute Gott von Manhattan. Munich: R. Piper, 1958.

Das dreißigste Jahr; Erzahlungen. Munich: R. Piper, 1961.

Malina: Roman. Frankfurt am Main: Suhrkamp, 1971.

Simultan; neue Erzahlungen. Munich: R. Piper, 1972.

Werke. 4 vols. Munich: R. Piper, 1978.

Mein erstgeborenes Land: Gedichte und Prosa aus Italien (1978). Ed. Gloria Keetman-Maier. Munich: R. Piper, 1992.

Der Fall Franza: Requiem für Fanny Goldmann. Munich: R. Piper, 1979.

Letzte, unveröffentlichte Gedichte, Entwürfe und Fassungen. Ed. Hans Höller. Frankfurt am Main: Suhrkamp, 1998.

Selected Studies of Bachmann

Achberger, Karen R. *Understanding Ingeborg Bachmann.* Columbia: University of South Carolina Press, 1995.

Arnold, Heinz Ludwig, ed. *Ingeborg Bachmann.* Munich: Text und Kritik, 1984.

Bartsch, Kurt. *Ingeborg Bachmann.* Stuttgart: J. B. Metzlersche, 1988.

Böschenstein, Bernhard. "Ingeborg Bachmann und die moderne französische Lyrik." In *Ingeborg Bachmann: Neue Beiträge zu ihrem Werk*, ed. Dirk Göttsche and Hubert Ohl, 353–63. Würzburg: Königshausen und Neumann, 1993.

Göttsche, Dirk, and Hubert Ohl, eds. *Ingeborg Bachmann: Neue Beiträge zu ihrem Werk.* Würzburg: Königshausen und Neumann, 1993.

Hapkemeyer, Andreas, ed. *Ingeborg Bachmanns früheste Prosa: Struktur und Thematik.* Bonn: Herbert Grundmann, 1982.

Höller, Hans. *Ingeborg Bachmann: Das Werk von den frühesten Gedichten bis zum "Todesarten" Zyklus.* Frankfurt am Main: Athenäum, 1987.

———. "Ingeborg Bachmanns Rom-Poetik." In *Il viaggio a Roma: Da Freud a Pina Bausch*, ed. Flavia Arzeni, 83–91. Rome: Edizioni di Storia e Letteratura, 2001.

———, ed. *Der Dunkle Schatten, dem ich schon seit Anfang folge: Ingeborg Bachmann, Vorschläge zu einer neuen Lektüre des Werks.* Vienna: Löcker, 1982.

———, ed. *Ingeborg Bachmann, Bilder aus ihrem Leben: Mit Texten aus ihrem Werk.* Munich: R. Piper, 1983.

Johnson, Uwe. *Eine Reise nach Klagenfurt.* Frankfurt am Main: Suhrkamp, 1974.

Jurgensen, Manfred. *Ingeborg Bachmann: Die neue Sprache.* Bern: Peter Lang, 1981.

Kaiser, Gerhard R. "Kunst nach Auschwitz oder: 'Positivist und Mystiker.' Ingeborg Bachmann als Leserin Prousts." In *Ingeborg Bachmann: Neue Beiträge zu ihrem Werk*, ed. Dirk Göttsche and Herbert Ohl, 329–52. Würzburg: Königshausen und Neumann, 1993.

Meise, Helga. "Topographien." In *Ingeborg Bachmann*, ed. Heinz Ludwig Arnold, 93–108. Munich: Text und Kritik, 1984.

Svandrlik, Rita. " 'Die Fremde als Bestimmung': Ingeborg Bachmann und Elsa Morante." In *Ingeborg Bachmann: Neue Beiträge zu ihrem Werk*, ed. Dirk

Göttsche and Herbert Ohl, 365–79. Würzburg: Königshausen und Neumann, 1993.

Swiderska, Malgorzata. *Die Vereinbarkeit des Unvereinbaren: Ingeborg Bachmann als Essayistin.* Tübingen: Max Niemeyer, 1989.

Thiem, Ulrich. "Die Bildsprache der Lyrik Ingeborg Bachmanns." Inaugural diss., University of Cologne, 1972.

Weigel, Sigrid. *Ingeborg Bachmann: Hinterlassenschaften unter Wahrung des Briefgeheimnisses.* Vienna: Paul Zsolnay, 1999.

SAMUEL BECKETT
(1906–1989)

Robert E. Clark

BIOGRAPHY

A central figure in modern English, French, and Irish literature—who drew inspiration from the Italian and French canon throughout his life—Samuel Beckett enjoys international acclaim as the author of *En attendant Godot* (1952) and *Fin de partie* (1957), two of the world's most frequently staged modern plays. The potential influence of a scholarly literature on him that rivals the critical work on his friend James Joyce (the most studied modern writer in English) did not undermine his ability to reach a world audience. Admiration from critics, a Nobel Prize (1969), and 50 years of international scrutiny of his work and private life have only increased Beckett's eminence.

He was born at Foxrock, outside Dublin, on April 13, 1906, to prosperous Protestant merchants and builders established among Ireland's elite. His father, Frank, was a quantity surveyor, a type of architectural and engineering consultant for construction projects. May, Beckett's beloved and difficult mother, had been Frank's nurse while he recovered from an illness and a failed love affair (Beckett found a mate in somewhat similar circumstances). Beckett's first culture was thereby that of an Irish gentry passionate about country pleasures, drinking, and sport. His mother was skilled at acerbic verbal sparring, and his father was a hearty raconteur—stereotypical Irish styles of wit reflected in Beckett's work (Cronin, *Samuel Beckett: The Last Modernist*, 13–56).

Although from childhood he was happiest when alone, Beckett excelled at cricket, tennis, and boxing. His athleticism matched a love of the physical comedy of Charlie Chaplin and Buster Keaton, a fondness carried over into the acrobatic tramps and downtrodden but resilient characters of his texts. He was also a gifted student of languages, in particular French and Italian, at Earlesfort House, Dublin, then at Portora Royal School (where Oscar Wilde had studied), where he earned a bachelor's degree; later he earned a master's degree from Trinity College, Dublin. His second culture stretched from canonical world literature to American popular film (Knowlson, *Damned to Fame: The Life of Samuel Beckett*, 23–63; Cronin, *Samuel Beckett*, 1–50).

Beckett completed his only academic publication, a compact and brilliant master's thesis about the recently deceased Marcel Proust, in 1930. Withdrawing gradually from sporadic teaching and academia, he assisted James Joyce in writing *Finnegan's Wake* (in a collection by Joyce's disciples, Beckett thumbed his nose at readers lacking the humor, adventurousness, or erudition to appreciate *Wake's* modernism [*I can't go on, I'll go on: A Selection from Samuel Beckett's Work*, 105]). He also wrote a collection of short stories, *More Pricks Than Kicks* (1933), and a novel, *Murphy* (1938). Now Beckett's culture was the international yet insular bohemia of writers, painters, and performers in expatriate Paris of the 1930s—a culture famous also for drinking bouts, marathon talk, and hostility to (other) outsiders (Knowlson, *Damned to Fame*, 243; Cronin, *Samuel Beckett*, 67–102). When he was stabbed and nearly killed in a street episode in 1937 (Cronin, *Samuel Beckett*, 284–91), a French friend, Suzanne Deschevaux-Dusmesnil, helped nurse him back to health, becoming his lover and lifelong companion. Thus, his third culture involved a deep intellectual and personal immersion in the literary, philosophical, and cultural preoccupations of Paris (Knowlson, *Damned to Fame*, 243–73).

After Germany's rout of France during World War II, Beckett and his wife joined the Resistance, narrowly escaping Gestapo arrest. They fled Paris for Roussillon in the south, where Beckett enjoyed a prolific golden period, producing what became the masterpieces of the 1950s. His first novel written in French, *Mercier et Camier*, contained the seeds for *En attendant Godot*, which in Roger Blin's Paris postwar production (1953) kicked off Beckett's ascent to international fame (early productions at San Quentin Prison and Miami Beach suggest *Godot's* astonishing breadth of appeal). Beckett also composed a tour de force fiction trilogy in French (*Molloy, Malone meurt*, and *L'innommable*), which he himself translated into English as *Molloy, Malone Dies*, and *The Unnamable* (1950–52), as well as a dark comic novel, *Watt* (1953) (Knowlson, *Damned to Fame*, 273–309).

These works were followed by triumphs in the theater from the 1960s onward: *Fin de partie, La dernière bande* (1959), and *Happy Days* (1961). As had French intellectual discourse, Beckett turned increasingly toward preoccupation with communication, language, identity, and mind, consonant with broader currents in postwar Continental thought. Yet theater audiences still heard resonances of Dante, the music hall, silent film, and Irish blarney holding off despair. Beckett's masterworks created their own culture and world—stirring responses at a pace and volume in paradoxical relation to a slim, tightly focused, and repetitive oeuvre (Knowlson, *Damned to Fame*, 351–77; Cronin, *Samuel Beckett*, 421–46).

During the 1970s, Beckett, almost always his own translator in French and English, spent a great deal of time translating and directing his own plays. He was particularly fond of working in Germany and with director Alan Schneider in the United States. In both cases, his exacting technical and linguistic standards were met. Beckett continued to write major prose works up until *Stirrings Still* (1988); even during his final illness he worked on a poem, "What is the Word," writing in bed. He died on December 22, 1989, a few months after the death of his wife (Knowlson, *Damned to Fame*, 509–601; Cronin, *Samuel Beckett*, 559–93).

MAJOR MULTICULTURAL THEMES

Although the Irish-born Beckett, like Joyce, had an encyclopedic knowledge of English, French, and Italian literature, his mature work is not primarily multicultural.

Yet his huge appeal across time and cultures suggests an uncanny ability to write at a depth that resounds in all cultures without relying on the particulars of a given culture. He confronts culture by posing questions of isolation, communication, survival, resistance, self-destruction, and endurance. His social concerns are similarly primal: life outside society, poverty, fierce conflict between friends and family, resistance to institutions, faint hopes for freedom, the evanescence of pleasure.

From *More Pricks Than Kicks* to the play *Compagnie* (1980), isolation, not culture, is the chosen state of Beckett's characters. Human cruelty, vacuity, and inability to love make contact painful. In his great trilogy of novels that describes the struggles of a storyteller—or of anyone possessed of memory—uncertain identity, imaginary company, and isolation are necessary for creativity. If one type of hell is other people, Beckett's infernal vision is of solitude, in which reverie, dream, and the struggle to invent are concentrated. His multicultural significance is to ask whether culture is possible or inevitably something to flee.

Nonetheless, Beckett's work is not finally misanthropic. His protagonists are heroes of patience and invention. Didi and Gogo are too poor to own much more than a rope to hang themselves, but witty enough to entertain one another, us, and possibly Godot. Krapp has little but his tapes, yet they encapsulate a prototypical life. *Oh les beaux jours* vanquishes the body, not the spirit. Beckett's universe has a perverse plenitude, hinted at by irrational numbers, signaled by people who make much from nothing and by other intersections of the void and infinite. The cosmos is malevolent, yet wildcards of diminution and renewal are miraculous, if faint, rewards for tenacity.

SURVEY OF CRITICISM

An immense critical corpus in all major European research languages has abundantly completed source and contextual studies of Beckett—from Dublin to Berlin. David Pattie's guide (2000) cleverly divides Beckett criticism into successive periods—"Cartesian" (1959–69), "the Beckett Industry" (1970–80), and so forth. Hugh Kenner's classic *A Reader's Guide to Samuel Beckett* (1973) is still helpful, particularly if teamed with P. J. Murphy and colleagues' (1994) overview of criticism in major European research languages, usefully categorized by nation and genre.

Among edited collections of essays, Cathleen Culotta Andonian's volume (1998) complements John Pilling's (1994), which includes an important essay by Ann Beers on Beckett's bilingualism, and Harold Bloom's (1985), which reprints essays by Wolfgang Iser, Theodor W. Adorno, and Northrop Frye. Lance St. John Butler collects no fewer than 83 influential essays in his 1994 work.

Beckett's habits of privacy and solitude are reflected in the main title of his authorized biography, *Damned to Fame*, by James Knowlson (1996). This work, the useful biography by Anthony Cronin (1996), and articles in the *Journal of Beckett Studies* (published by Florida State University) have corrected and amended the work of Deirdre Bair (1978).

SELECTED BIBLIOGRAPHY

Works by Beckett

Molloy; Malone Dies; and, The Unnamable: Three Novels (1950–52). New York: Grove, 1959.
I can't go on, I'll go on: A Selection from Samuel Beckett's Work. Ed. Richard W. Seaver. New York: Grove, 1976.
The Complete Dramatic Works. London and Boston: Faber and Faber, 1986.
Stirrings Still. London: John Calder, 1988.
The Theatrical Notebooks of Samuel Beckett. Ed. James Knowlson. London: Faber and Faber, 1992.
Samuel Beckett: The Complete Short Prose, 1929–1989. Ed. S. E. Gontarski. New York: Grove Press, 1995.

Selected Studies of Beckett

Armstrong, Gordon. *Samuel Beckett, W. B. Yeats, and Jack Yeats: Images and Words*. Lewisburg, Pa.: Bucknell University Press; London and Toronto: Associated University Presses, 1990.
Bair, Deirdre. *Samuel Beckett: A Biography*. New York: Harcourt Brace Jovanovich, 1978.
Birkett, Jennifer, and Kate Ince, eds. *Samuel Beckett*. New York: Longman, 2000.
Blau, Herbert. *Sails of the Herring Fleet: Essays on Beckett*. Ann Arbor: University of Michigan Press. 2000.
Bloom, Harold, ed. *Samuel Beckett*. New York: Chelsea House, 1985.

Breuer, Rolf, Harald Gundel, and Werner Huber. *Beckett Criticism in German: A Bibliography.* Munich: W. Fink, 1986; Paderborn, Germany: Schoning, 1996.

Buning, Marius, Matthijs Engleberts, Sjef Houppermans, and Emmanuel Jacquart, eds. *Samuel Beckett: Crossroads and Borderlines.* Amsterdam and Atlanta, Ga.: Rodopi, 1997.

Cohn, Ruby. *A Beckett Canon.* Ann Arbor. University of Michigan Press, 2001.

Cronin, Anthony. *Samuel Beckett: The Last Modernist.* London: HarperCollins, 1996.

Culotta Andonian, Cathleen, ed. *The Critical Response to Samuel Beckett.* Westport, Conn.: Greenwood Press, 1998.

Davies, Paul. *Beckett and Eros: the Death of Humanism.* New York: St. Martin's Press, 2000.

Friedman, Alan Warren, ed. *Beckett in Black and Red: The Translations for Nancy Cunard's "Negro."* Lexington: University Press of Kentucky, 1999.

Juliet, Charles. *Conversations with Samuel Beckett and Bram van Velde.* Trans. Janey Tucker. Leiden: Academic Press, 1995.

Junker, Mary. *Beckett: The Irish Dimension* (1995). Niwot, Ireland: Irish American Book Company, 1997.

Kennedy, Sighle. *Murphy's Bed: A Study of Real Sources and Surreal Associations in Samuel Beckett's First Novel.* Lewisburg, Pa.: Bucknell University Press, 1971.

Kenner, Hugh. *A Reader's Guide to Samuel Beckett.* New York: Farrar, Straus and Giroux, 1973.

———. *Samuel Beckett: A Critical Study* (1961). New ed. Berkeley: University of California Press, 1968.

Knapp, Bettina. *Off-stage Voices: Interviews with Modern French Dramatists.* Ed. Alba Amoia, 31–36. Troy, N.Y.: Whitston, 1975.

Knowlson, James. *Damned to Fame: The Life of Samuel Beckett.* New York: Simon and Schuster, 1996.

Murphy, P. J., Werner Huber, Rolf Breuer, and Konrad Schoell, eds. *Critique of Beckett Criticism: A Guide to Research in English, French, and German.* Columbia, S.C.: Camden House, 1994.

Pattie, David. *The Complete Critical Guide to Samuel Beckett.* London and New York: Routledge, 2000.

Pilling, John. *The Cambridge Companion to Beckett.* Cambridge, England, and New York: Cambridge University Press, 1994.

St. John Butler, Lance, ed. *Critical Essays on Samuel Beckett.* Aldershot, England: Scholar Press; Brookfield, Vt.: Ashgate, 1994.

TAHAR BEN JELLOUN
(1944–)

Abdellatif Attafi

BIOGRAPHY

Writer Tahar Ben Jelloun was born in Fez, Morocco, at a time when the country was a protectorate of both France and Spain. The modest family home had no running water, and its large interior courtyard was open to the sky. Winters were freezing, and summers were hot. Ben Jelloun attended a Koranic school where he learned verses of the Koran and was taught the difference between good and evil, love of God, respect for all his prophets, and equality of humankind. He learned as well that the differences in people lie in the quality of their souls and their beliefs.

His family moved to Tangier in 1955. The city was prosperous and, under its international statute, was a haven for many different communities. Ben Jelloun quickly adopted Tangier, a crossroad between the Atlantic Ocean and the Mediterranean Sea. Naturally projected toward Europe, yet deeply rooted in Africa, the city was populated by Arabs, Africans, and Europeans. After his philosophical studies and poetic contributions to the review *Souffle* under the direction of the Moroccan poet Abdellatif Laabi, Ben Jelloun went to France to pursue a doctorate in social psychiatry.

Upon his arrival in Paris in 1971, he started to write for the national French newspaper *Le Monde*. At the time of his first essay, "La plus haute des solitudes"(1977), derived from his doctoral research related to the Moroccan immigrant community in France—his primary source of inspiration—he was already well known to the French public.

His journey to France and his decision to settle in Paris as a writer allowed him to look closely and differently at the dilemma of being a

Moroccan writer who writes in French rather than in Arabic. From his first poems, in which the frustrated poet asks his illiterate readers to set fire to his work, to his later novels, accepted and respected by a large audience all over the world today, Ben Jelloun is at ease with French, a language that he considers liberating.

In a multicultural Europe, the majority, no longer silent, supports a multicultural France. Ben Jelloun's literary work is still in progress. There are as many Ben Jellouns as novels he has written. Although his work is sometimes not well understood by his own countrymen, he is without a doubt the best-known Moroccan writer both within and outside of Morocco.

MAJOR MULTICULTURAL THEMES

Ben Jelloun's first literary works, "L'aube des dalles" and "Homme sous linceul de silence" (1971), were poetry, a medium he considers the most urgent means of expression. But he is mostly known for his abundant fiction, in which sociology mixed with free imagination and poetic rhythm create a pell-mell narration of real and ferric structure. Conformist readers find his writing difficult to grasp because it transgresses the traditional references they use to decode text.

The fiction of Ben Jelloun, set in multicultural situations, is the product of a writer with a large base of inspiration and creativity, including themes such as Islam, Africa, Arab heritage, Berber heritage, colonialism, immigration, oppression, and racism. In his first novels, *Harrouda* (1973) and especially *Moha le fou, Moha le sage* (1978), the narration is discontinued, delirious, and violent, containing references directly related to the writer's educational background and his travels. A harsh, critical look at the position of the North African woman is the basis of the first novel, dedicated to his mother. The fact that she could not read French served as a liberating factor and inspiration for Ben Jelloun, who feels confined writing in Arabic, the language of the Koran.

The resolution of his own cultural conflict seems to inspire him in *Les yeux baissés* (1991) and in *Les raisins de la galère* (1996). The two novels are indeed entirely centered on the deconstruction and reconstruction of cultural identity in a multicultural situation. In the beginning of the first story, the reader discovers the hard conditions of living in small Moroccan villages, which push people to emigrate. The heroine, a shepherd in her village, leaves with her family to go to France, where she experiences culture shock. First, she is completely disoriented in time as well as in space. She does not understand why the Parisians are not speaking Berber (her native tongue). Then, as she adapts to her host society, she finds herself in conflict with her parents, especially with her father. With the crumbling of the myth and the beginning of disillusionment, the main character begins to have ambivalent feelings, such as love for a country in which she can never be entirely accepted as Berber French.

Away from her native society and not yet totally integrated in France, she feels caught in between yet cut off from both cultures.

The girl goes back to her native village only to be told from those who stayed behind that she is perverted and has forgotten everything. At the end of the story, she realizes she has a double personality: one is more inclined to accept the norms of her native land, whereas the other is attracted by the norms of French society. She takes her bags and leaves the village again, saying good-bye to the first aspect of her double personality, as though she has accepted letting go of some part of who she is in order to live fully her new life in France. The heroine avoids enculturation as well as acculturation by engaging herself in a process of biculturation. By interiorizing what is good in the two cultures through education and experience, she manages to create her own space where she can finally breathe. A correlation may be established here between the heroine's tale and the author's own trajectory.

The title of Ben Jelloun's novel *Les raisins de la galère* evokes the sweet fragility and the exclusion of a lost generation—those born in France of North African immigrant parents. The characters are torn between the absence of a parental model and the racist rejection they experience daily at different levels of French society. Despite the narrow margin for maneuvering, the heroine, in a very difficult environment, manages to educate herself at the university level and even tries to pursue a political career. But around her, the future of the other characters is potentially disastrous.

As a new literary space, Italy appears in *Les raisins de la galère*. Ben Jelloun expanded the journey connecting North Africa to France, often emphasized in his work, to include Italy for the first time. As a logical next step, he then set entire novels in Italy: *Labyrinthe des sentiments* (1999) and *L'auberge des pauvres* (1999), which perfectly characterize the African quarter of Naples.

The seriousness of the racial situation inspired Ben Jelloun to write *Le racisme expliqué à ma fille* (1998), a short book for children about racism. He obviously believes that work in building social consciousness aimed at tolerance and respect of others' differences should start at an early age. Europe has been very receptive to the book, which has reignited animated discussions and debates in schools, in homes, on radio, on television, and in the newspapers, as the collective consciousness is again forced to face the reality of racism and its consequences.

Ben Jelloun's valuable contribution to the understanding of the complexity of immigration and of the identity crises that follow such journeys provides a stimulating space for more dialogues, exchanges, and rapprochement between peoples on both sides of the Mediterranean Sea.

SURVEY OF CRITICISM

Rachida Saigh Bousta (1999) offers an extensive analysis of Ben Jelloun's writings as well as insightful cultural information on topics such as

North Africa, Morocco, Islam, women in Islam, the Koranic school, and so forth, which are important in gaining a better understanding of the author's background and writings. Included in Bousta's book is an exhaustive list of additional bibliographical references to Ben Jelloun.

SELECTED BIBLIOGRAPHY

Works by Ben Jelloun

Harrouda (1973). Paris: Denoel, 1982.
La réclusion solitaire. Paris: Seuil, 1976.
Moha le fou, Moha le sage. Paris: Seuil, 1978.
Les amandiers sont morts de leurs blessures. Paris: Maspéro, 1983.
L'enfant de sable. Paris: Seuil, 1985.
Hospitalité française. Paris: Seuil, 1985.
La nuit sacrée. Paris: Seuil, 1987.
Les yeux baissés. Paris: Seuil, 1991.
Les raisins de la galère. Paris: Fayard, 1996.
Le racisme expliqué à ma fille. Paris: Seuil, 1998.
Labyrinthe des sentiments. Paris: Stock, 1999.
L'auberge des pauvres. Paris: Seuil, 1999.

Selected Studies of Ben Jelloun

Bousta, Rachida Saigh. *Lecture des récits de Tahar Ben Jelloun: Ecriture, mémoire et imaginaire*. Casablanca: Afrique Orient, 1999.
Kaye, Jacqueline, and Abdelhamped Zoubir. *Language, Literature, and National Identity in Algeria and Morocco*. London and New York: Routledge, 1990.
Madelain, Jacqueline. *L'errance et l'itinéraire*. Paris: Sindbad, 1983.
Mousouni, Lahcen. *Le roman marocain de langue française*. Paris: Publisud, 1987.
Tenkoul, Abderrahman. *Littérature marocaine d'expression française: Essais d'analyse sémiotique*. Casablanca: Afrique Orient, 1985.

ISAIAH BERLIN
(1909–1997)

Stuart Knee

BIOGRAPHY

Isaiah Berlin was a fortunate pilgrim. Despite upheaval in the world in general and in Jewish society in particular during the first half of the twentieth century, he led a privileged and surprisingly cloistered existence. As an exile, a minority group member, and a public intellectual, he sought to fuse the three primary cultures of his being into a single philosophy of freedom. In so doing, he challenged powerful authoritarian beliefs and, by the end of his life, achieved a personal sense of belonging.

Berlin's expressive qualities of voice and intellect were Russian, Jewish, and English. The first two matured over the course of four score years but were products of his ethnicity and youthful environment; the last was cultivated in a western European milieu of tolerance and liberty. It seemed that one mode of expression enhanced the others, ceaselessly mixing and mingling from the hour of his 1909 birth in Riga, Latvia, to doting, financially secure parents whose relatives were both secular and Hassidic. He was an only child, introspective, watchful, and self-absorbed. A withered arm limited his active participation in sports, and he did not attend school, so his formal introduction to secular education and the company of peer groups was delayed until he was nearly a teenager. Instead, he sought and received the counsel and affection of his mother, a revered figure from whom he absorbed Jewish culture, a love for Zionism, and some regard for ritual. Also, he was no stranger to the library or the riches therein. While the czarist regime crumbled around him, between 1916 and 1919 he imbibed the *Jewish Encyclopaedia* and the works of Lev Tolstoy, Ivan Turgenev, Aleksandr Pushkin, Heinrich

Heine, Johann Wolfgang von Goethe, Jules Verne, Alexandre Dumas, and Mayne Reid, a popular author of cowboy tales.

As refugees of war and revolution, the Berlin family escaped unharmed from Russia in 1921 to find permanent asylum in England. There Berlin developed a layered personality that employed the English language as a conduit for expressing prerevolutionary Russian, Hebraic, and British values. First at Corpus Christi College and then at All Souls College, both of Oxford, he explored his own personality. It unfolded in its preoccupation with concepts of liberty and freedom and with the philosophy of history. None of these topics really moved his peers and colleagues in the radical 1930s, except perhaps when they wished to take issue with Berlin's apparent lack of enthusiasm for scientific determinism and dogma-driven ideological systems. Although Berlin was always at ease with this sort of skepticism, detractors always thought of him as an equivocator. He occasionally thought of himself in a similar way but was never troubled by any lasting guilt pangs. Before Berlin departed All Souls for a more engaging world, he completed and published his only monograph, an original and highly critical study of Karl Marx (1939).

World War II offered Isaiah Berlin an opportunity to redirect his scholarly commitments. No longer was he insular: he grew as an individual, utilizing his past but never really returning to it. His vision, both academic and personal, was involving, dynamic, and forward looking; it remained so until his retirement.

Performing on the "real" stage of global conflict and diplomacy as a propagandist for the British Foreign Office working out of the British embassy in Washington, D.C., he interested prominent American Jews and Jewish organizations in the British war effort while interpreting the British Empire's Palestine stance in a less anti-Zionist fashion. He learned of but never wrote about the Holocaust; however, he did utilize two 1945 encounters with suppressed literary lights Boris Pasternak and Anna Akhmatova in the shaping of his postwar, anti-Stalinist worldview.

For the final quarter century of his creative life, Berlin became an anti-Soviet sage, a world-renowned essayist on the subjects of personal choice and historical relativism, guiding spirit, fund-raiser for and president of Oxford University's Wolfson College, and husband to Aline, an aristocratic French woman with prerevolutionary Russian Jewish lineage. Of all these achievements, the most significant for him, perhaps, was the last because it provided him with a sense of physical and emotional completion.

MAJOR MULTICULTURAL THEMES

In works such as *Russian Thinkers* (1978) and *The Roots of Romanticism* (1999), Isaiah Berlin became a preeminent political philosopher and historian of ideas during the Cold War because the questions he posed and attempted to answer related significantly to that era. Drawing on a skep-

ticism derived at least in part from his Jewish ethnicity and on an admiration for indigenous critics of nineteenth-century Russian culture
(notably Ivan Turgenev and Alexander Herzen), Enlightenment philosophers such as Voltaire, the Neapolitan thinker Giambattista Vico, the
German romantic Johann Gottfried Herder, and the best of Britain's tradition of humane scholarship as advanced by John Stuart Mill, Berlin
sought the ultimate meaning of freedom, not so much as a political
choice, but as a moral choice. A convivial and social person by inclination
and not much given to systematic writing and archival research, his
proper mediums were the public address, the public forum, and the essay,
where his extraordinary talents as synthesizer and conversationalist were
most compelling.

In 1949, Berlin was teaching Russian thought to undergraduates at
Harvard while working on several projects at the university's Russian
Research Center. He was in between careers, and an article he published
in *Foreign Affairs* (1950) was, at once, a farewell to his role as Soviet analyst and his inaugural as seminal thinker. Although he demonstrated his
predictable opposition to Stalinist monism, he broke new ground by calling for choice and individual freedom as realizations of "human good"
(Ignatieff, *Isaiah Berlin: A Life*, 198). Shortly thereafter, he composed a
pioneering essay on Lev Tolstoy's philosophic underpinnings. He concluded that the great Russian author appeared to be a seeker of multiple
truths but was, in fact, a tragic idealist who hoped to realize the unity of
humankind through some mathematically precise, immutable natural
law. This piece appeared in 1951 with a nondescript title but reappeared
two years later renamed *The Hedgehog and the Fox: An Essay on Tolstoy's
View of History*; it enhanced Berlin's reputation as a man who understood
passions, identity crises, and anguish.

Drawing on his distaste for absolutes in an age whose insecurities were
driven by them, Berlin discovered their provenance in the Enlightenment, a problematic period whose failure, he felt, was inscribed on the
present. Assuredly, Jean-Jacques Rousseau and Maximilien Robespierre
were no Marxists, but they were nonetheless ideologues and dogmatists:
in their haste to liberate France from despotism, they would "force men
to be free" (quoted in Rogers, ed., *Aspects of Western Civilization* 2: 110).
Stunned by the oxymoronic simplicity of this belief system, Berlin studied
it relative to the belief system of the romantics, among them the Germans
Friedrich von Schiller, Johann Gottfried Herder, and Johann Gottlieb
Fichte. He concluded that the Enlightenment was deeply flawed because
the values of natural law to which it subscribed in no way correlated to the
exercise of either free choice or free will. Berlin named his synthetic construct, which implied moral choice and individual accountability as defin-
ers of civilization, *historical inevitability*, or *pluralism* (Ignatieff, *Isaiah
Berlin: A Life*, 205–6, 286). He broadcasted and lectured on the topic of
each individual's obligation to choose a path rather than obey a system,

liberal or otherwise. As such, each man, each woman, bore the responsibility, the consequence, even the pain, of that choice. If they chose poorly, they could not escape history's judgment. Berlin's encounter with truth would resonate in Jerusalem, where SS officer Adolf Eichmann was held responsible for his collusion in genocidal acts, and in ensuing years its echo would resound in Cambodia, Bosnia, and Rwanda.

After completing an article comparing the identity quests of Benjamin Disraeli and Karl Marx, Berlin defined "two concepts of liberty," one positive, one negative, in his inaugural lectures as Oxford University's Chichele Professor of Social and Political Theory. According to him, "positive" liberty was coercive and from it emerged forms of totalitarianism, which were nothing more than misunderstood or misapplied Enlightenment and romantic doctrines. By contrast, "negative" liberty, "the core of a properly liberal political creed" (Ignatieff, *Isaiah Berlin: A Life*, 226), was authentic in its emphasis on social justice, its burden of moral choice, its commitment to freedom, and its possibility for tragic failure. He offered no solution for ongoing crises of national liberation and national revival in the 1960s in Hungary, Cuba, Israel, and Algeria and therefore incurred the displeasure of leftists and cold warriors alike. Consequently, his legacy is not an answer, but rather a continuing debate.

SURVEY OF CRITICISM

Henry Hardy, once a postgraduate student in philosophy at Wolfson College and, after that, an editor at Oxford University Press, is responsible for gathering the disparate essays of Isaiah Berlin and placing them before scholarly and lay audiences in a systematic fashion. The bulk of Hardy's work on Berlin's published materials was completed in the 1970s, and a significant body of collections have appeared since 1978. Hardy also established a Berlin archive for unpublished or incomplete manuscripts, lectures, correspondence, personal letters, and family memorabilia. Without a doubt, the most important, even indispensable, book published on Berlin is Michael Ignatieff's 1998 biography. It is an honest, unsentimental, and vivid portrait. Only in one area do I feel that he did not "find" the man. Why did Berlin, until he was past 40, settle on the role of platonic confidante and father confessor to a succession of attractive women? Was it his fear of involvement, his accommodating, chameleon-like personality, or something else? With regard to his professional achievements, some intellectuals do not find him above reproach either. In a recent very long, complex article, Roger Sandall (2000) sees Berlin's romanticized view of Herder as addleheaded and implies that the ostensibly great scholar Berlin was an overindulged underachiever. Marxist historians take Berlin to task also. One of the most persistent is Edward Hallett Carr, whose reply to Berlin's "historical inevitability" appears in his classic 1961 study *What Is History?*

SELECTED BIBLIOGRAPHY

Works by Berlin

Karl Marx: His Life and Environment (1939). 4th ed. New York: Oxford University Press, 1978.

The Hedgehog and the Fox: An Essay on Tolstoy's View of History. New York: Simon and Schuster, 1953.

Russian Thinkers (1978). Ed. Henry Hardy and Aileen Kelly. New York: Penguin, 1984.

Personal Impressions. Ed. Henry Hardy. Introduction by Noel Annan. New York: Viking Press, 1981.

The Crooked Timber of Humanity: Chapters in the History of Ideas. Ed. Henry Hardy. 1st American ed. New York: Knopf, distributed by Random House, 1990.

The Sense of Reality: Studies in Ideas and Their History (1997). Ed. Henry Hardy. Introduction by Patrick Gardiner. New York: Farrar, Straus and Giroux, 1998.

The Roots of Romanticism. Ed. Henry Hardy. Princeton, N.J.: Princeton University Press, 1999.

Selected Studies of Berlin

Bullock, Alan. "A Hedgehog or a Fox?" *Time International* (November 23, 1998): 88.

Carr, Edward Hallett. *What Is History?*, 169–72. New York: Vintage, 1961.

Clausen, Christopher. "Ich Bin ein Berliner." *The New Leader* 81 (December 14, 1998): 9–10.

Gray, John. "Isaiah Berlin: A Life." *New Statesman* 127 (November 20, 1998): 48.

Grayling, A. C. "Meditations on a Thinker." *Financial Times*, November 21, 1998, 5.

Hoffman, Stanley. "Isaiah Berlin: A Life." *Foreign Affairs* 78 (May 1999): 140.

Ignatieff, Michael. *Isaiah Berlin: A Life.* New York: Metropolitan, 1998.

Meyerhoff, Hans, ed. *The Philosophy of History in Our Time*, 225–28, 249–71. Garden City, N.Y.: Doubleday Anchor, 1959.

Roazen, Paul. "Isaiah Berlin: A Life." *American Scholar* 68 (Spring 1999): 152–54.

Rogers, Perry M., ed. *Aspects of Western Civilization.* Vol. 2. Englewood Cliffs, N.J.: Prentice Hall, 1988.

Sandall, Roger. "The Book of Isaiah." *Quadrant* 44 (June 2000): 10–22.

Sieff, Martin. "Saving Isaiah." *National Review* 51 (February 8, 1999): 55–56.

YVES BONNEFOY
(1923–)

Lorena Zaccagnino

BIOGRAPHY

Two places from Bonnefoy's childhood have left their mark: Tours, the town where he was born into a family of peasant origin in 1923, in a poor neighborhood whose deserted streets remain in his memory; and Toirac, where he went every year with his family until 1936, the year of his father's death, to spend the summer holidays at his maternal grandfather's home. For him, this village in the Lot Valley was a timeless place; its fruits went on ripening from one summer to the next, and summer seemed endless. But, of course, come September, he had to leave this special place—his "there"—and return to the ordinary, everyday life of Tours. This image of fullness has seduced him throughout his life, allowing him to believe in the possibility of escaping the finite nature of being and withdrawing into an ideal space. Since that time, he has succumbed to the fascination of images whose power lies in creating worlds that are released from the sufferings reality brings, in separating him from the imperfect transitoriness of existence. The means he was to use for his *retour au sol* (return to the soil), to paraphrase his beloved Arthur Rimbaud, was poetry.

In the early 1940s, Bonnefoy studied mathematics, formal logic, and history of sciences at the University of Poitiers. In 1943, he left for Paris, where he attended Gaston Bachelard's courses at the Institut d'histoire des sciences. During this period, he was fascinated by abstract thought and found deep contentment in constructing concepts and pure relationships. In addition to mathematics, he studied philosophy, attending Jean Wahl's and Jean Hyppolite's courses at the Sorbonne. His *licence* in philosophy was followed by a diploma for which he studied the work of Charles Baudelaire and Søren Kierkegaard. He had been interested in philosophical thought even before studying at the Sorbonne, and it was his lycée philosophy master in Tours who had introduced him to Georges Hugnet's *Petite anthologie du surréalisme*, in which he discovered the poetry of André Breton, Benjamin Péret, and Paul Eluard and admired Giorgio De Chirico, Alberto Giacometti, and the early Joan Miró.

Bonnefoy's debut as a poet with "L'Anti-Platon," published in 1947 in a magazine he founded *(La Révolution la Nuit)*, in effect reflects the play of hallucination as explored by the surrealists. However, that same year he refused to sign the surrealist manifesto *Rupture inaugurale*, thus irretrievably distancing himself from the Breton whose passion for enigma and whose superior intellect and lucid political agenda he had so admired. It seemed to Bonnefoy that the surrealists limited themselves to playing games with existence, whereas he himself felt the full burden and complexity of it.

From 1949 to 1953, he traveled in Europe and especially in Italy, whose artistic output from Roman art to Piero della Francesca, Andrea Palladio, Michelangelo Buonarroti, the baroque and Caravaggio, and Nicolas Poussin and Giacometti, was to be central to his studies in the history of art. In this period, he also worked on his first poetry collection, *Du mouvement et de l'immobilité de Douve*, published in 1953 to extraordinary critical and public acclaim. After *Hier régnant désert* (1958), in which the poetry—still brimming with anger and the surrealists' need to desecrate—searches for the *vrai lieu* (true place) *(L'Arrière-pays*, 16) in the space of becoming, *L'improbable* appeared in 1959. This collection of essays is a dense and evocative reflection on poetry and art—in particular painting, which represents a fundamental part of Bonnefoy's creative inspiration. In 1968, he married Lucy Vines, and in 1972 their daughter Mathilde was born. In the years that followed, he traveled to the United States, India, Japan, Cambodia, and Iran.

From 1960 onward, Bonnefoy was appointed to teaching posts in a number of universities, including those of Geneva, Vincennes, and Nice; then from 1981 to 1993 he was a professor of comparative studies in poetic function at the Collège de France.

His poetry output was continually interrupted by his writings in art and literary criticism: *Pierre écrite* (1965), a collection of poems in which the solitary search for the self becomes a sharing and discovers in the space of obviousness a connection with the Other; *Rome, 1630; l'horizon du premier baroque* (1970), an admirable essay on the Roman baroque in which we see again the poet's interest in Italian art and culture; *L'Arrière-pays* (1972), a major prose work in which poetry is omnipresent; and *Dans le leurre du seuil* (1975). The latter are Bonnefoy's mature verses, in which he seeks to regain a lost unity, having escaped the deception that the objects of everyday life can be accommodated elsewhere, outside of poetry.

The 1980s and 1990s saw the publication of poetry collections such as *Ce qui fut sans lumière* (1987), *Récits en rêve* (1987), *Début et fin de la neige* (1991), *La vie errante* (1993), as well as essays and translations. In 1981, the *Dictionnaire des mythologies et des religions des sociétés traditionnelles et du monde antique* was published under Bonnefoy's editorship.

Today, in addition to his poetical works, Bonnefoy still devotes himself to reflections on literature and on the figurative arts and their relationship to poetry, as well as to translation of works by Shakespeare, William Butler Yeats, and Giacomo Leopardi, which constitutes a large part of his work. In 1999, he published *Lieux et destins de l'image, cours de poétique au Collège de France*, about the conflict between image and presence, and in 2000 *La communauté des traducteurs*, in which he poses the theoretical problem of translation, beginning with the question of whether it is possible to translate poetry. He has received honorary degrees from the University of Chicago and Trinity College, Dublin, and was honored again in January 2001 by the Third University of Rome.

MAJOR MULTICULTURAL THEMES

Poetry and travel share the same bloodline, Bonnefoy wrote in an essay titled "Les tombeaux de Ravenne" (in *L'improbable*), and of all the actions humans can perform they are perhaps the most useful and the only ones with a purpose. Here he is not just alluding to the many countries whose culture, language, or landscape he has loved. Travel, whether real or in dreams, is the experience of the "elsewhere." The great works we admire in a foreign land leave open the possibility that the language of their creators might produce unimagined categories of thought. So the traveler rebels against his own language with impatience and dreams of what it cannot give him. This jolt is already poetry, says Bonnefoy. The traveler who goes in search of unknown places is really looking for the starting point of a journey that is spiritual. He sets off only after he has found the long-awaited land. This interior exploration leaves the discoverer at the entrance to an *"arrière-pays,"* a mysterious hinterland made up of emotions, memories, and aspirations. Travel, love, and architecture for Bonnefoy are merely human rituals to welcome presence—in other words, the instant of absolute absorption in the real, when the ideal world meets the material one, setting free the poet's longed-for unity.

Bonnefoy's first trip to Italy in the early 1950s was a revelation to him. Italy, the chosen land that he would later call the "Méditerranée de l'esprit" (Mediterranean of the spirit) (quoted in Jackson, *Yves Bonnefoy*, 10), became his model of the art of living and creating. In an unforgettable moment, he discovered that the world painted by De Chirico, which he had believed to be imaginary, does exist on this earth. Italy is the *vrai lieu* that embodies the wonders of the elsewhere and contains the infinity of presence within the finiteness of a real entity. Stone, trees, the sea, the warmth of Tuscany, and all perceptible species that until then had moved under his gaze now came back to him as though desiccated. In *L'Arrière-pays*, whose prose is a melting pot of distant or vanished civilizations—from Greece to Egypt, from Iran to Cambodia—that for Bonnefoy have the "qualité de distance, d'inconnu" (quality of distance, of the unknown) (*L'Arrière-pays*, 34), he describes his encounter with Italy as a rebirth into the world because it allows him to return to the place of those *"années profondes"* (deep years) in Toirac (quoted in Jackson, *Yves Bonnefoy*, 12).

A few countries in central Asia—the mountains of Armenia, the Caucasus—actually represent for Bonnefoy societies that are "aware" of presence; in these places he senses the mythical importance of presence released from a land mass that is not precisely locatable on the map. In *L'Arrière-pays*, he wonders about the place of Tibet or the Gobi desert in his theology of the Earth, tracing a map of the "hinterland" stretching from Ireland to Alexander's distant empire and taking in Asia's Islamic cities and the countries of the Mediterranean (one of the stories that left an impression in his childhood imagination, *Dans les sables rouges*, is set in the Gobi desert). These civilizations, he explains, are born of a desire to lay foundations, and their image of themselves is the circle, the floor plan, and the dome, figures that he imbues with existential time, far removed from the atemporal perfection of the rectangle of Greek temples, so that they have the possibility of lighting upon presence.

Bonnefoy's work as a translator of Shakespeare, Yeats, and Leopardi has also guided him in experiencing otherness and in comparing different ways of being in the world. The English and Italian poems he has "renewed" allow him to slip into the language produced by other cultures, by unknown rhythms and musicalities. Translation for him is making poetry anew, following an autonomous path separate from the original author's path. But it is undoubtedly also a meeting with the voice coming from other places; it is the desire and the curiosity for an encounter with that which is different.

The course of his transition from the temptation to escape into alternative worlds that are produced by the imagination to the acceptance of the transitoriness of the real involves of necessity a changed approach to subjectivity. It is only in dreams and in places imagined by the ideal that subjectivity is rampant and lacking the boundary that allows it to be identified. The act of limiting subjectivity and recognizing its limits makes it possible for humans to acknowledge the presence of the other and to engage in a relationship with it. In a 1979 essay titled "Yves Bonnefoy, la poésie entre deux mondes," Jean Starobinski maintains that although Bonnefoy's poetry is dominated by the first person, it is not at all a narcissistic creation. He justifies this assertion by emphasizing the otherness present in Bonnefoy's poems, where the subjective statement is only the first element in a relationship that needs difference for comparison. Bonnefoy's writings are thus directed outward and have as their object the relationship with the world—they are not an internal reflection of the I. The attention to the other, to difference, allows for a return to simple reality and to the demystification of the omnipotent I. The themes of death, multiplicity, and diversity are thus synonyms for a rediscovery of the real.

The space in which Bonnefoy finds a relationship with the other is obviousness. What he desires is for the image—the ideal world that seduces him—to be integrated with reality and for each person to be part of the existence of others and in this way share the same world. He sees it as the special task of poetry to prepare the ground for this union, this encounter with presence. Even the nobility and beauty of the poems must defer to the deeper aim of their existence, which is exchange, the communication between people. Thus, even the simplest dialogue between two individuals can create presence if there is an eagerness for reciprocal understanding, which is the only possible cure for the world's solitude.

SURVEY OF CRITICISM

John E. Jackson's admirable study (1976) assigns a fundamental role to Bonnefoy's discovery of Italy, a country that came to symbolize the elsewhere and the real for the poet. Jean Starobinski (1976) distinguishes the narcissistic *me* from the *I* with which Bonnefoy vindicates his ethical choice of responsibility. In an article published a few years later, Starobinski (1979) emphasizes the openness of the poet's writings to the external world as they seek a relationship with otherness and diversity. Georges Poulet (1976) illustrates the distance between the idea and the authentic presence of being. In another essay (1985), Poulet shows that in going in search of a place, the traveler is doing nothing more than seeking after the starting point of a journey that is spiritual.

SELECTED BIBLIOGRAPHY

Works by Bonnefoy

L'improbable (1959); *suivi de Un rêve fait à Mantoue.* Paris: Mercure de France, 1980.
Rome, 1630; l'horizon du premier baroque. Paris: Flammarion, 1970.
L'Arrière-pays (1972). Geneva: A. Skira, 1992.
Poèmes: L'Anti-Platon, Du mouvement et de l'immobilité de Douve, Hier régnant désert, Dévotion, Pierre écrite, Dans le leurre du seuil. Paris: Mercure de France, 1978.
Dictionnaire des mythologies et des religions des sociétés traditionnelles et du monde antique. Ed. Yves Bonnefoy. Paris: Flammarion, 1981.

Roméo et Juliette, Macbeth, précédé de L'inquiétude de Shakespeare. Paris: Gallimard, Folio, 1985.

Récits en rêve. Paris: Mercure de France, 1987.

Ce qui fut sans lumière. Paris: Mercure de France, 1987.

Début et fin de la neige; suivi de Là où retombe la flèche. Paris: Mercure de France, 1991.

La vie errante (1993); *suivi de Une autre époque de l'écriture et de Remarques sur le dessein* (1993). Paris: Mercure de France, 1997.

Lieux et destins de l'image, cours de poétique au Collège de France. Paris: Seuil, 1999.

La communauté des traducteurs. Strasbourg: Presses Universitaires de Strasbourg, 2000.

Selected Studies of Bonnefoy

Blanchot, Maurice. "Comment découvrir l'obscur?" *Nouvelle Revue Française* 83 (1959): 867–79.

Finck, Michèle. *Yves Bonnefoy: Le simple et le sens.* Paris: J. Corti, 1989.

Jackson, John E. *Yves Bonnefoy.* Paris: Seghers, 1976.

Poulet, Georges. "Un idéalisme renversé." *L'Arc* 66 (1976): 58–66.

———. "Yves Bonnefoy". In *La pensée indéterminée*, 261–79. Paris: Presses Universitaires de France, 1985.

Richard, Jean-Pierre. "Yves Bonnefoy, entre le nombre et la nuit." *Critique* 168 (1961): 387–411.

Starobinski, Jean. "La prose du voyage." *L'Arc* 66 (1976): 3–8.

———. "Yves Bonnefoy, la poésie entre deux mondes." *Critique* 385–86 (1979): 505–22.

PIERRE BOULLE
(1912–1994)
Lucille Frackman Becker

BIOGRAPHY

The French novelist and short story writer Pierre (François Marie-Louis) Boulle was born in Avignon on February 20, 1912, to Eugène and Thérèse (Seguin) Boulle. In an autobiographical work titled *L'îlon: Souvenirs*, published when he was 78 years old, Boulle evoked images of his early years in Provence, eschewing strict chronology to follow the order of memory. These images, he wrote, "with their mixture of joy, of anguish, of hope, and of disappointment, constitute a store of riches which I never tire of counting, as an old miser counts his coins" (7). His native Provence would provide the background for *Le bon Léviathan* (1978), *Miroitements* (1982), and *À nous deux, Satan!* (1992).

The most important person during his formative years was his father, a brilliant lawyer whose legal world of Avignon is portrayed by Boulle in the novel *La face* (1953). Despite his great love and respect for his father, he did not feel that he himself was suited for the law, and, after completing his secondary studies at the lycée, he went to Paris to study science and engineering at the Sorbonne. The style and content of his fiction bear the mark of his scientific education; he attributes to it his "somewhat cruel taste for the bizarre together with great formal simplicity and rigorous logic" (*My Own River Kwai*, 26). It is also apparent in his essay on cosmology, *L'univers ondoyant* (1987), and in his works of science fiction, most notably *La planète des singes* (1963).

Boulle received his *licence ès sciences* in 1931 and an engineering diploma from the École supérieure d'electricité in 1933. He then worked as an engineer for two years in Clermont-Ferrand. Boredom, restlessness, and a desire to travel led him to accept a position abroad as an electrical engineer. So, at the age of 24, he left France for a rubber plantation in British Malaya. A fictionalized account of his years in Southeast Asia until the outbreak of World War II can be found in *Le sacrilège malais* (1951), Boulle's only novel of an autobiographical nature. In the pages of this work, we find atmosphere, local color, characters, and incidents that reappear in the novels and short stories set in Asia: *Le pont de la rivière Kwaï* (1952), *Le bourreau* (1954), *L'épreuve des hommes blancs* (1955), *Les voies de salut* (1958), *Les oreilles de jungle* (1972), *Les vertus de l'enfer* (1974), *Histoires perfides* (1977), and *Le malheur des uns . . .* (1990).

The account of Boulle's war years in Southeast Asia as a Resistance fighter and as a secret agent in Indochina can be found in *Aux sources de la rivière Kwaï*, published much later in 1966. At the outbreak of World War II in 1939, he enlisted in the French army in Indochina. After the collapse of France, he went to Singapore and joined the Free French, who trained him as an intelligence agent and saboteur. On December 7, 1941, when Japan attacked Pearl Harbor, the Pacific Islands, Malaya, and the British possessions in China, the Free French decided to transfer their mission to Kunming, China. From Kunming, Boulle departed by mule train for a desolate Chinese mountain post en route to Moung-La, a Thai village on the banks of the Nam-Na River, six miles from the Indochinese border. After several months of fruitless efforts to infiltrate Indochina, then held by Vichy forces, he entered the French colony in 1942 after a hair-raising descent of the Nam-Na River on a raft he had constructed of bamboo held together by rushes. He was promptly arrested by the French authorities, and in October 1942 he was court-martialed, found guilty of treason, reduced to the ranks, deprived of French nationality, and sentenced to hard labor for life. During his time in prison, having nothing to do—for, ironically, no job was assigned to this man sentenced to forced labor for life—Boulle began to write to pass the time. On little bits of paper filched here and there, he scribbled some recollections of his adventures during the raft trip on the Nam-Na. In September 1944, when Allied victory appeared certain, the prison authorities decided to organize Boulle's "escape," and he spent the rest of the war with the Free French in Calcutta.

Sick with malaria and dysentery, Boulle returned to Paris on January 3, 1945, where he was awarded the French Légion d'Honneur, the Croix de Guerre, and the Médaille de la Résistance. He returned to the rubber plantation in Malaya in 1945 in an attempt to resume his life where the war had interrupted it, but he was unable to follow this sensible course, for the war had made him incapable of doing an ordinary job. In 1948, he decided abruptly that writing was to be his life; he left his job, went back to Paris, sold all his possessions, moved into a little hotel on the Left Bank, and started writing a novel, taking a vow to undertake nothing else ever again. "I have kept my word," Boulle wrote at the end of *Aux sources de la rivière Kwaï*. "I have done practically nothing else ever since, and this foolhardy decision, taken some twenty years ago among the fireflies piercing the equatorial darkness of a Malayan plantation, still strikes me today as the worthy conclusion to a series of incongruous adventures" (*My Own River Kwai*, 214).

MAJOR MULTICULTURAL THEMES

Five of Boulle's novels provide a guide to colonial mentality within the framework of a broad historical overview of Southeast Asia during the first three-quarters of the twentieth century: from the re-creation in *Le sacrilège malais* of the early years of colonialism inherited from the nineteenth century, through World War II, which was to undermine that colonialism (in *Le pont de la rivière Kwaï* and *L'épreuve des hommes blancs*), to the nationalistic liberation movements unleashed by the war that would put an end to colonialism (*L'épreuve des hommes blancs* and *Les voies de salut*), and, finally, to the casting off of what Kipling called the "White Man's burden" (in *Les oreilles de jungle*). Dr. Moivre, a character in *L'épreuve des hommes blancs* who serves as Boulle's alter ego, expresses the author's ideas on colonialism: "From a strictly moral point of view, the expropriation of one nation by another could not be justified by any means or by any argument which had even the remotest claim to rationalism" (*The Test*, 83). In the same novel, Boulle refutes another colonialist misconception that maintains that the ordinary people of Southeast Asia immediately loved the white strangers who came to their lands and would willingly sacrifice themselves on their behalf. On the contrary, the Malay fishermen in the novel refuse to help the white men in their desperate flight from the Japanese. Their only concern is for survival, and they are indifferent to the outcome of the war being waged around them. The new Japanese order is as alien to the Malays as the European organization had been.

SURVEY OF CRITICISM

Louis Allen, in his 1986 article, finds Boulle's novel *Le pont de la rivière Kwaï* successful in depicting the courage of resistance but a failure in its account of the nature of the Japanese enemy. Lucille Frackman Becker, in her literary biography of Pierre Boulle (1996), details the author's experiences in Southeast Asia and devotes a chapter to an in-depth analysis of the novels situated there. Edgar C. Knowlton (1982) observes that the use Boulle makes of his firsthand experience in Southeast Asia is persuasive in its sympathy for the cultures, languages, and peoples of the area. Judith D. Suther (1983) discusses several French novels on U.S. involvement in Vietnam, including Boulle's *Les oreilles de jungle*, which she characterizes as arch satire on the continued U.S. saturation bombing of Vietnam following the Tet Offensive of 1968. Ian Watt (1959) analyzes *Le pont de la rivière Kwaï* in the light of his own experiences as a Japanese prisoner of war who was forced to work on the Burma-Siam railway. Although Boulle's picture bears little direct resemblance to what Watt saw on the Kwai, Watt feels that the author's ultimate purpose was to dramatize the ridiculous disparity between the West's rational technology and its self-destroying applications. The translation of the novel into film is the object of studies by Michael Anderegg (1984), Ian Watt (1968), and most critics of Boulle's oeuvre.

SELECTED BIBLIOGRAPHY

Works by Boulle

Le sacrilège malais. Paris: Julliard, 1951.

Le pont de la rivière Kwaï. Paris: Julliard, 1952.

L'épreuve des hommes blancs. Paris: Julliard, 1955. [*The Test.* Trans. Xan Fielding. New York: Vanguard Press, 1957.]

Les voies de salut. Paris: Julliard, 1958.

Aux sources de la rivière Kwaï. Paris: Julliard, 1966. [*My Own River Kwai.* Trans. Xan Fielding. New York: Vanguard Press, 1967.]

Les oreilles de jungle. Paris: Flammarion, 1972.

L'îlon: Souvenirs. Paris: Editions de Fallois, 1991.

Selected Studies of Boulle

Allen, Louis. "To Be a Prisoner." *Journal of European Studies* 16, no. 64 (December 1986): 233–38.

Anderegg, Michael A. "*The Bridge on the River Kwaï* (1957)." In *David Lean*, 91–102. Boston: Twayne, 1984.

Becker, Lucille Frackman. *Pierre Boulle.* New York: Twayne, 1996.

Ganne, Gilbert. "L'obsédé de la rivière Kwaï." *Nouvelles Littéraires* 2018 (May 5, 1966): 1, 11.

Knowlton, Edgar C. "Southeast Asia in the Works of Francis de Croisset and Pierre Boulle." *Proceedings of the 43rd Annual Symposium on Asian Studies* 3 (1982): 451–61.

Suther, Judith D. "French Novelists and the American Phase of the War in Indochina." *Selecta: Journal of the Pacific Northwest Council on Foreign Languages* 4 (1983): 1–9.

Watt, Ian. "Bridges over the Kwai." *Partisan Review* (Winter 1959): 83–94.

———. "The Myth of the River Kwai." *Observer* (September 1968): 18–21, 23–26.

PAUL BOWLES
(1910–1999)

Patricia Perkins

BIOGRAPHY

At the age of 19 and as a student at the University of Virginia, Paul Bowles flipped a coin to decide whether he should commit suicide or leave immediately for Europe, a sudden compulsion. Heads, Europe won. Without telling his parents or the college, he sold all his furniture and booked passage on an ocean liner and arrived at his destination with $24 in his pocket. He stayed six months, working, mooching off friends, and hiking in the Black Forest and the French Alps. Every night he washed out his one shirt and tacked it to the hotel room door. A year later, after another semester at college dictated by his parents, he decided to leave home forever.

He traveled continuously to Europe, North Africa, Cuba, Mexico, Central America, India, Thailand, and Sri Lanka through the 1930s, 1940s, and 1950s, never staying anywhere more than a few months. He was acquainted with important figures in music and literature: Gertrude Stein, Aaron Copland, Virgil Thompson, Jean Cocteau, Truman Capote, Tennessee Williams, and William Burroughs, to name a few.

Before 1950, he devoted himself to music, becoming such a successful composer that he supported himself through the depression. He had already published surrealist poems in the prestigious Parisian magazine *transitions*. But when Gertrude Stein told him he was not a poet, he quit writing and concentrated on music for the next 15 years. Stein also told him that the weather of Tangier would suit him. When he saw the North African coast for the first time in 1931, he wrote: "It was as if some interior mechanism had been set in motion by the sight of the approaching land. I based my sense of being in the world on an unreasoned conviction that certain areas of the earth's surface contained more magic than others, a secret connection between the world of nature and the consciousness of man, a hidden but direct passage which bypassed the mind. Like any Romantic, I had always been vaguely certain that during my life I should come to a magic place, which in disclosing its secrets, would give me wisdom and ecstasy—perhaps even death" (*Without Stopping*, 125). He waited until 1947 to heed that "interior mechanism." Going to Tangier, he lived in a succession of hotel rooms and apartments. "If I am here now," he wrote, "it is only because I was still here when I realized to what an extent the world had worsened, and that I no longer wanted to travel" (*Without Stopping*, 369).

Inspired by his wife's literary efforts, Bowles began writing short stories. When Doubleday publishers told him they would rather have a novel, he wrote *The Sheltering Sky*, which, though Doubleday rejected it, ended up on the *New York Times* best-seller list for 11 weeks in 1950. In all, he produced four novels—*The Sheltering Sky* (1949), *Let It Come Down* (1952), *The Spider's House* (1955), and *Up above the World* (1966)—as well as numerous short stories; travel essays and one travel book, *Their Heads Are Green and Their Hands Are Blue* (1963); poetry, *Points in Time* (1982); a lyrical history of Morocco; and translations of Moroccan stories.

Composer in the 1930s and 1940s, existential novelist and darling of the Beats in the 1950s, pothead guru of the 1970s with an interview in *Rolling Stone Magazine*—Bowles was reinvented by each succeeding generation in its own image. At a concert series and symposium at New York's Lincoln Center and the New School for Social Research in 1955, he was rediscovered as a composer. The 1980s and 1990s have seen a heightening of critical interest in Bowles, especially from a multicultural standpoint.

He died of a heart attack in Tangier in 1999 at the age of 88.

MULTICULTURAL THEMES

As a writer, Bowles is a kind of tabula rasa—because both love and religion were considered unmentionable and obscene in his family, because he was isolated and never at ease in his own culture, because of his existentialism—a clean slate on which is written both the "alien" cultures and the reactions of Westerners to encounters with them. Bowles is Observer. On one level, he simply presents the stories, the logic, the untranslated reasoning of the Other. He neither mediates nor explains. Nobody can explain, finally, so he gives us the bizarre, the cruel, the absurd as unvarnished construct, matter-of-factly. He does not pretend to understand the logic—though as a long-term resident in Morocco and a veteran traveler, he understands more than most—he just puts it on the reader's plate. He quotes without comment a Moroccan saying, "You tell me you are going to Fez. Now, if you say you are going to Fez, that means you are not going. But I happen to know that you are going to Fez. Why have you lied to me, you who are my friend?" (quoted in Caponi, *Paul Bowles*, 51).

On another level, Bowles gives us the Western point of view: dissociation of meaning from context, time distortion, questions about the nature of perception, head-on collision. His Western characters are never strong enough. They let the menace of the landscape and its people, the ones who *belong* to a place, overpower them. His characters die horrible deaths—all described in crystal precision prose, one tinkling syllable after another, one clean, clear sentence following the next.

Like the sound of one hand clapping, the encounter between one mindset and another is a koan, a Zen puzzle that defies rational analysis. Bowles gives us the koan in a hundred different ways, in a hundred different stories, in stories within stories. His particular point of view, stemming from his disgust with Western civilization, is obvious. His goal, he proclaimed in one interview, was to "help society go to pieces, make it easy. . . . Who doesn't want to [destroy it]?" he asked. "I mean, look at it!" (Caponi, *Conversations*, 94–95). It was this disgust—a sure conviction that Westerners are doomed, rudderless, decadent, commercialized, and blind—that allowed him to turn toward the field of encounter, to collide with the Other, and to record the fallout.

His early stories are about the indifference of the Other to our civilized ideas about civilized behavior, our rules of fair play, what we would call human decency. The desert does not care. The sheltering sky does not care. The tribesmen do not care. We are foolhardy to venture out into their world. Scratch the veneer of our touted civilization, and we bleed, great copious clots that Bowles gathers in a big bowl and offers up to the ceremony of beating drums and stamping feet.

In his later work, Bowles was less bitter and had less need to show us how weak and stupid we are. *Points in Time* (1982), his lyrical history of Morocco, includes history, popular songs, legends, and stories in what amounts to a literary collage. His later work has been called "cool" and "remarkable." He simply stated the koan, stories about encounter, about misunderstanding, about miscues and missed signals. He translated stories that his illiterate Moroccan friends told to his tape recorder, acknowledging even then that they told of "violence and bloodshed and hatred" because they knew he liked that kind of story (Elghandor, "Atavism and Civilization: An Interview with Paul Bowles," 28).

SURVEY OF CRITICISM

The critic, attempting to confront Paul Bowles on multicultural territory, is presented with a unique problem. Bowles himself never believed he understood the Moroccan mind. What, then, the critics have asked, does he come up with in his encounter with Morocco, where he lived for 50 years? John Maier (1996) believes that Bowles's early work demonstrates the belief that one can never really know the Other, that the gulf is too great (29). He insists that in Bowles's later work "his serious preoccupation with Moroccan thinking in his fiction has been sustained for over five decades, and goes far beyond the Orientalist fascination with the exotic East" (144). He likens Bowles's quest to that of Paul Ricoeur: "the comprehension of the self by the detour of the comprehension of the other" (22).

Paul Keegan (1988), reviewing *Call at Corazon and Other Stories*, says he finds "insistence on a single theme: the irreducibility of cultural difference" (526). Geoffrey O'Brien (1986) adds: "The self, which senses its fundamental emptiness, gawks in amazement at shrubs and sidewalks and pebbles. It wants to make contact: but between the I and the Other a wedge has been driven. That jagged fissure is the world" (13).

There are those—notably the Moroccan intelligentsia as represented by Abdelhak Elghandor—who feel Bowles has completely misrepresented North Africa and the Arabo-Islamic culture. Although Bowles demurred that he was only writing narrative, not trying to explain or show anything at all about Moroccan culture, Elghandor, in his 1994 interview with the author, accused Bowles of "ignoring of Arabo-Islamic institutional, written culture—its poetry, its prose, its philosophy, and its scripturalist theology." He continued: "your exclusive concentration on the oral, the folkloric, the visual, the mystic, the intuitive and cult orders have created in your writing a biased, incomplete, sometimes even a lopsided and erroneous view of Arabo-Islamic culture" (12). "I don't see that it's desirable that there should be a homogeneous mass," responded Mr. Bowles at a later point in the interview (29).

SELECTED BIBLIOGRAPHY

Works by Bowles

The Sheltering Sky. New York: New Directions, 1949.
Let It Come Down. New York: Random House, 1952.
The Spider's House. New York: Random House, 1955.
Their Heads Are Green and Their Hands Are Blue. New York: Random House, 1963.
Up above the World. New York: Simon and Schuster, 1966.
Without Stopping. New York: G. P. Putnam's Sons, 1972.
Points in Time. London: Peter Owen, 1982; New York: Ecco Press, 1984.
Call at Corazon and Other Stories. London: Peter Owen, 1988.

Selected Studies of Bowles

Caponi, Gena. *Paul Bowles*. New York: Twayne, 1998.
———, ed. *Conversations with Paul Bowles*. Jackson: University of Mississippi Press, 1993.

Elghandor, Abdelhak. "Atavism and Civilization: An Interview with Paul Bowles." *ARIEL: A Review of International English Literature* 25, no. 2 (April 1994): 7–30.

Keegan, Paul. "Americans in Foreign Parts." *Times Literary Supplement* 4441 (May 13–19, 1988): 526.

Maier, John. *Desert Songs: Western Images of Morocco and Moroccan Images of the West.* Albany: State University of New York Press, 1996.

O'Brien, Geoffrey. "White Light White Heat." *Voice Literary Supplement* 44 (April 1986): 10–13.

Weiss, Timothy. "Oriental Terrains in Paul Bowles' *Their Heads Are Green and Their Hands Are Blue.*" *Journal of African Travel Writing* 6 (1999): 40–51.

JOSEPH BRODSKY
(1940–1996)

Henry Urbanski

BIOGRAPHY

Joseph Brodsky, Russian poet and writer, was born on May 24, 1940, in the former Soviet Union, in the city of Leningrad (originally and now again named Saint Petersburg). Even as a child, he realized that he did not fit into the fabric of accepted Communist Russian society. Because he was Jewish, Brodsky was persecuted by his teachers and at the age of 15 dropped out of school. In order to help support his family, he took a job in a factory. In his spare time, to escape the bleakness of his life and the world around him, he began writing poems that expressed his pain, disenfranchisement, and loss of spirit. His poetry was printed in the underground literary papers—*samizdat* (literally, "self-published" works circulated, recopied, and passed on by readers). He was soon subjected to government-sponsored terror for his nonconformity.

In 1963, Brodsky was denounced by a Leningrad newspaper that referred to his poetry as "pornographic and anti-Soviet." He was placed in a mental institution and in 1964 was arrested and brought to trial as a "literary parasite." He was asked by the judge: "Who has recognized you as a poet? Who has enrolled you in the ranks of poets?" His response was: "No one. Who enrolled me in the ranks of the human race?" (quoted in McFadden, "Joseph Brodsky, Exiled Poet Who Won Nobel, Dies at 55," B5).

Brodsky was sentenced to five years hard labor in the Arctic Circle for failing to do his "constitutional duty to work honestly for the good of the motherland" (McFadden, "Joseph Brodsky, Exiled Poet," B5). By this time, however, he had a following both at home and abroad, so, owing to international protest, he was released after serving only 18 months. In 1971, he declined two invitations to immigrate to Israel. In spite of enduring persecution as both a Jew and a poet, he did not want to leave his homeland. He wrote, "For everything I have in my soul, I am obliged to Russia and its people" (quoted in Bethea, *Joseph Brodsky and the Creation of Exile*, 42). The Soviet government, however, considering Brodsky's poetry dangerous and anti-Soviet, believed that exile would result in the poet's loss of touch with the Russian language and culture and therefore in the loss of his influence. Brodsky's poetry was confiscated, and he was placed on a plane to Vienna.

In 1972, with the help of the poet W. H. Auden, Brodsky immigrated to the United States, where he became poet in residence at the University of Michigan. This was a critical period in his life as a writer. While still in Russia, he had taught himself English and Polish in order to read in the original and translate the poems of his favorite authors, such as John Donne and Czesław Miłosz. After arriving in the United States, he began to translate his own poetry into English. Through the new language, he was coming to terms with his separation from his country, adjusting to his new life in the United States, and, at the same time, retaining his Russian heritage.

Brodsky enjoyed great professional success and eventually became a professor at Mount Holyoke College. He continued to write verse in Russian and then translate it into English. He wrote prose, mostly essays, in English. He referred to himself as a Russian poet and an American prose writer. His prose writing exhibits the same feeling for language as does his poetry. It is rich in metaphors, with layers of images and creative use of vocabulary.

In addition to his positions at the University of Michigan and Mount Holyoke College, he was a professor at Queens College of the City University of New York. His writings appeared in *The New Yorker* and the *New York Review of Books*. He published several volumes of poetry and prose, and his work was included in anthologies. He was the recipient of an honorary doctorate in literature from Oxford University, the 1981 MacArthur Award, the 1986 National Book Critics Circle Award, and the Nobel Prize in Literature in 1987 for his lifetime of achievements. In 1991, Brodsky was named Poet Laureate of the United States, the first time this honor was bestowed on an émigré who was not a native speaker of English. In spite of three heart attacks, he continued to smoke and drink heavily, which eventually led to his untimely death in 1996.

MAJOR MULTICULTURAL THEMES

In the United States, Brodsky immersed himself in the literature and culture of his adopted country. Yet exile was difficult for him. In one poem, he describes an exiled writer as one "who survives like a fish in the sand" (*A Part of Speech*, 114). At the same time, however, he believed that exile is, in a sense, the poet's "natural condition" (quoted in Kline, "Variations on the Theme of Exile," 56). George Kline, a Brodsky critic and translator, observed a sharp difference between the poems Brodsky wrote during his temporary Arctic exile, those he wrote just before his 1972 permanent exile, and those he wrote after he found himself in the West. The poems of the first group convey a sense of shock and loss, a sense of "being overboard" and in "no-man's land" (Kline, "Variations on the Theme of Exile," 56), of going deaf, blind, and mad, of losing his memory. The second group of poems, Kline asserts, express Brodsky's anticipation and fear of impending personal loss—that of his wife and son. The latter poems in this group juxtapose the empire—a huge, amoral, fear-inspiring force—against the freedom-seeking individual. These poems express a sense of the poet who, only 32 years old, feared growing old and decrepit, of lapsing into "non-speaking," of losing his "verbs and endings" (Kline, "Variations on the Theme of Exile," 56–57). Losing touch with one's native tongue is a frightening prospect for anyone, especially a poet. For Brodsky, this fear was understandable because he believed that exile and language are intertwined:

> For one in our profession, the condition we call exile is, first of all, a linguistic event: an exiled writer is thrust, or retreats, into his mother tongue. From being his, so to speak, sword, it turns into his shield, into his capsule. What started as a private intimate affair with the language, in exile becomes fate—even before it becomes an obsession. (*On Grief and Reason: Essays*, 32)

To Brodsky, a poet in exile must retain absolute control of his native tongue. He also felt that he needed to write in the language of his adoptive country and to continue as a poet and a writer. He was keenly aware of the importance of language, literature, and poetry in forming and shaping the culture of a nation. He stated in his Nobel lecture that "[i]f what distinguishes us from other members of the animal kingdom is speech, then literature—and poetry in particular, being the highest form of locution—is, to put it bluntly, the goal of our species" (*On Grief and Reason*, 50). In the same Nobel lecture, he draws on his own experience of being persecuted by the Soviet state and observes:

> Language and presumably, literature, are things that are more ancient and inevitable, more durable than any form of social organization. The revulsion, irony, or indifference often expressed by literature toward the state is essentially the reaction of the permanent—better yet, the infinite—against the temporary, against the finite. (*On Grief and Reason*, 47)

Because Russian writers and poets have always been very important to the Russian people, Brodsky was keenly aware of the power and impact language and the process of writing had on the reader and subsequently on the poet himself or herself. "A poet," he says, "is someone intoxicated by language's capability to extend man's consciousness" (*On Grief and Reason*, 58).

Brodsky could not understand why poetry did not have the kind of powerful influence in the United States that it did in Russia. He thought that inexpensive anthologies of the best American poets should be made available in hotels, airports, hospitals, and supermarkets: "By failing to read or listen to poets, society dooms itself to inferior modes of articulation, those of the politician, the salesman or the charlatan. . . . In other words, it forfeits its own evolutionary potential" (*On Grief and Reason*, 205).

SURVEY OF CRITICISM

According to James H. Billington (1996), "Joseph Brodsky sustained and exemplified the mysterious power of poetry both in the repressive Soviet culture from which he was exiled and in the permissive American culture to which he came." Billington goes on to point out that Brodsky popularized poetry in the United States, whereas in his former country, Russia, poetry "had to follow a much straighter and narrower path" (D1). He suggests that the key to Brodsky's poetry, both in his native and adopted languages, is the sonority of languages for which Brodsky had one of the most sensitive ears.

Writing in the *New York Review of Books*, Czesław Miłosz (1980) states: "Behind Brodsky's poetry is the experience of political terror, the experience of debasement of man and the growth of the totalitarian empire. . . . I find it fascinating to read his poems as part of his larger enterprise, which is no less than an attempt to fortify the place of man in a threatening world" (23).

Victor Erlich (1974), another critic, agrees. He refers to "the richness and versatility of Brodsky's talent, the liveliness and vigor of his intelligence, and his intimate bond with the Anglo-American literary tradition" (621). There is no doubt that Brodsky was well on his way to bridge the gap between his Russian heritage and the culture of his adopted country.

SELECTED BIBLIOGRAPHY

Works by Brodsky

Chast' rechi: Stikhotvoreniia, 1972–1976. Ann Arbor: Ardis, 1977. [*A Part of Speech*. New York: Farrar, Straus and Giroux, 1980.]
Mramor. Ann Arbor: Ardis, 1984. [*Marbles: A Play in Three Acts*. New York: Farrar, Straus and Giroux, 1989.]
Less Than One: Selected Essays. New York: Farrar, Straus and Giroux, 1986.
Uraniia: Novaia kniga stikhov. Ann Arbor: Ardis, 1987. [*To Urania: Selected Poems, 1965–1985*. New York: Farrar, Straus and Giroux, 1988.]
Watermark. New York: Farrar, Straus and Giroux, 1992.

On Grief and Reason: Essays. New York: Farrar, Straus and Giroux, 1995.

So Forth: Poems. New York: Farrar, Straus and Giroux, 1996.

Collected Poems in English. Ed. Ann Kjellberg. New York: Farrar, Straus and Giroux, 2000.

Selected Studies of Brodsky

Bethea, David M. *Joseph Brodsky and the Creation of Exile.* Princeton, N.J.: Princeton University Press, 1994.

Billington, James H. "The Poet Who Proved the Power of Words." *Washington Post,* January 30, 1996, D1.

De Witt, Karen. "Poet Laureate on Mission to Supermarket's Masses." *New York Times,* December 10, 1991, B15.

Erlich, Victor. "A Letter in a Bottle." *Partisan Review* 41, no. 4 (Fall 1974): 617–21.

Kline, George L. "Variations on the Theme of Exile." In *Brodsky's Poetics and Aesthetics,* ed. Lev Loseff and Valentina Polukhina, 56–88. London: Macmillan, 1990.

McFadden, Robert D. "Joseph Brodsky, Exiled Poet Who Won Nobel, Dies at 55." *New York Times,* January 29, 1996, A1, B5.

Miłosz, Czesław. "A Struggle against Suffocation." *New York Review of Books* (August 14, 1980): 23–25.

PEARL S. BUCK
(1892–1973)

Arianna Maiorani

BIOGRAPHY

Pearl Comfort Sydenstricker was born in Hillsboro, West Virginia, but her parents, southern Presbyterian missionaries, took her with them to China when she was only three months old. She grew up in Chen-chiang (Zhenjiang), a small town in Kiangsu (Jiangsu) Province, learning both English and Chinese. Her teachers were her mother and a Chinese tutor, a certain Mr. Kung; her father spent months away from home in search of new converts. During the Boxer Uprising in 1900, Mrs. Sydenstricker and her children were evacuated to Shanghai, where Pearl attended a boarding school (1907–9) and began working for the Door of Hope, a shelter for Chinese slave girls and prostitutes. She was then sent back to the United States to continue her education, remaining in Virginia until 1914, when she graduated from Randolph-Macon Woman's College. She returned to China to care for her mother and to work as a teacher for the Presbyterian Board of Missions. In 1915, she met John Lossing Buck, an agricultural economist who became her first husband in 1917 and from whom she was divorced in 1934.

After their marriage, they moved to Nanhsuchou (Nanxuzhou) in Anhwei (Anhui) Province, where the couple traveled extensively throughout the countryside. Through her experiences among the people of the rural community, she gathered an abundance of material that she would use in her Chinese stories. She worked as a teacher and interpreter with her husband and gave birth in 1921 to a mentally disabled daughter; in 1925, the couple adopted a baby girl. Now settled in Nanking (Nanjing) (1920–33), they both taught at Nanking University until the terrible battle of 1927 in that city between Chiang Kai-shek's Nationalist troops, the Communists, and warlords, in which several Westerners were killed. The Bucks remained in hiding for a day until rescued by U.S. gunboats. After this incident, they moved to Unzen, in Japan, where they spent a year before returning to Nanking.

Buck had begun publishing her stories and essays in the 1920s in the magazines *Asia*, *The Nation*, and the *Atlantic Monthly*. After her return to the United States, she published her first novel, *East Wind, West Wind* (1930). Her second and most famous novel, *The Good Earth*, published in 1931 and adapted as a film by Metro-Goldwyn-Mayer in 1937, was a best-seller in both 1931 and 1932, earning her the Pulitzer Prize and the Howells Medal in 1935, the year of her marriage to the New York publisher Richard Walsh.

An old farmhouse, Green Hills Farm, in Bucks County, Pennsylvania, that Buck purchased in 1934, is now included in the Registry of Historic Buildings. In 1936, she was named member of the National Institute of Arts and Letters; and she was the first American woman to receive the Nobel Prize for Literature (1938).

During World War II, she and her second husband actively defended civil and women's rights as well as antiracist and humanitarian causes; in 1941, they founded the East and West Association for educational exchange, which became a target of McCarthyism: an FBI file on Pearl Buck had already been initiated in 1937 and reached nearly 300 pages. For more than a decade, she and Richard Walsh were also editors of the magazine *Asia*, and they led a campaign against the national Chinese exclusion laws and the U.S. government's internment of Japanese Americans. From 1934, Buck was also a regular contributor to *Crisis*, the magazine of the National Association for the Advancement of Colored People, and to *Opportunity*, published by the National Urban League. She served on the board of the Urban League and was a trustee of Howard University. Throughout her life, she devoted much of her time and money to mentally or physically disabled children, founding in 1949 a Welcome House for Asian and Amerasian children considered unadoptable by adoption agencies (she and Walsh adopted six of them). She was elected to the American Academy of Arts and Letters (1951) and in 1964 created the Pearl Buck Foundation, which provides medical care and education for thousands of Amerasian children in many Asian countries. She died in Danby, Vermont, and is buried at Green Hills Farm.

MAJOR MULTICULTURAL THEMES

During her lifetime, Buck published more than 70 books, including novels, collections of poems and stories, children's books, translations, essays, biographies, and an autobiography. A great part of her literary production focuses on multicultural themes that underscore her deep interest not only in Chinese culture, but also in racial equality and in the relationship between East and West. The title of her autobiography, *My Several Worlds, A Personal Record* (1954), is revealing in this respect. She always affirmed that the ancient indigenous Chinese novel was her first inspirational model—a tradition that taught her flexibility and independence of style and enabled her to identify with her characters but to tell their stories without revealing her role as narrator. Her first novel, *East Wind, West Wind*, is based on her experience of life in China and focuses on the world of Chinese women. In her best-known novel, *The Good Earth*, she uses both the classic Western novel style and the Chinese saga narrative rhythm to tell the story of a Chinese peasant family who, through hard work and sacrifice, become rich and highly respected; it is a story of struggle for life and wealth, of human attachment to the earth, of famine and rebellion, of marriage and parenthood—a novel that also reveals very crude aspects of the world of Chinese women. Buck does not write from the external point of view of a Westerner: she tells the whole story from within, almost as though she were a member of the family, using the extensive material she had gathered during her years in China. *Dragon Seed* (1942) is also a story about a family of Chinese peasants who are deeply attached to the earth and to traditions and who try to resist the Japanese invasion, and *The Mother* (1934) is a novel about a peasant woman forced to struggle against poverty, brutality, and violence during the Japanese invasion of northern China.

The Exile (1936) and *Fighting Angel; Portrait of a Soul* (1936) are biographies of Buck's parents: the first is the story of a missionary's wife who leaves her own healthy family to follow her husband to China, where she fights against conditions of disease, poverty, and ignorance; the second is the story of a very brave and stubborn missionary who, during the Boxer Uprising and the Japanese occupation of China, persists in preaching his creed.

Each of Buck's novels is a study of an aspect of Eastern life that implies an implicit confrontation with the Western world. Simply by depicting the culture and history of the East through her characters' stories, she describes a world still unknown to the majority of her readers and at the same time gives them the opportunity of meeting and comparing two cultures. Thus, she has often been considered a cultural bridge between East and West, describing to the Western world the true China, the East she had lived in and known since her childhood, not the mythical country of fairytales and ancient travel books. She further develops multicultural themes revolving around the meeting of East and West in later novels and stories that reveal differences and prejudices on both sides and deal with the many cultural and social issues raised by the encounter—for example, *Peony* (1948), a depiction of the life of Jews in China; *The Hidden Flower* (1952), the story of a Japanese girl who upsets her family by falling in love with an American soldier; *The New Year; A Novel* (1968); *The Three Daugh-*

ters of Madame Liang; A Novel (1969); *All Under Heaven; A Novel* (1973); and *East and West: Stories* (1975). Her nonfiction works focusing on the culture and history of the East and its relationship with the West, such as *American Unity and Asia* (1942), *The People of Japan* (1966), and *China Past and Present* (1972), are also significant contributions to a multicultural oeuvre that has only recently become appreciated.

SURVEY OF CRITICISM

Pearl Buck's works, despite their great public success and the many awards they earned for their author, were almost disregarded by literary critics, especially immediately after World War II. Critics have focused more on her eventful life, praising her as a social activist, and less on her artistic achievements. The most recent books about Buck's life and work, however, reveal an increasing interest in her as a historical and cultural figure between East and West and a desire to rediscover this long-forgotten writer. Kang Liao (1997) discusses Buck's works from the Chinese perspective, studying contents and characters from a multicultural point of view and considering Buck's novels as a means through which Americans may better understand China past and present. Peter Conn (1996) has written a comprehensive cultural biography of Buck in which he examines the reasons for her fall into oblivion and focuses on those books he considers of prime importance in the contemporary American discussion of gender and of social and civil rights. Nora Stirling (1983) is the author of another biography based on interviews with people who knew Buck. The important collection of essays emanating from the Pearl S. Buck Centennial Symposium, edited by Elizabeth Lipscomb, Frances Webb, and Peter Conn (1994), covers a wide range of aspects of Buck's work and life. Yü (1981) offers an interesting perspective of Buck as a writer between two worlds and Irvin Block (1973) deals with multiculturalism in the author's life and works.

SELECTED BIBLIOGRAPHY

Works by Buck

East Wind, West Wind. New York: John Day, 1930.
The Good Earth. New York: John Day, 1931.
The Mother. New York: John Day, 1934.
The Exile. New York: Reynal and Hitchcock, 1936.
Fighting Angel; Portrait of a Soul. New York: Reynal and Hitchcock, 1936.
The Chinese Novel (Nobel Prize lecture). New York: John Day, 1939.
Dragon Seed. New York: John Day, 1942.
American Unity and Asia. New York: John Day, 1942.
Peony. New York: John Day, 1948.
The Hidden Flower. New York: John Day, 1952.
My Several Worlds, A Personal Record. New York: John Day, 1954.

The People of Japan. New York: Simon and Schuster, 1966.
The New Year; A Novel. New York: John Day, 1968.
The Three Daughters of Madame Liang; A Novel. New York: John Day, 1969.
Mandala. New York: John Day, 1970.
China Past and Present. New York: John Day, 1972.
All under Heaven; A Novel. New York: John Day, 1973.
East and West: Stories. New York: John Day, 1975.

Selected Studies of Buck

Block, Irvin. *The Lives of Pearl Buck: A Tale of China and America.* New York: Thomas Y. Crowell, 1973.

Conn, Peter. *Pearl S. Buck: A Cultural Biography.* Cambridge, England, and New York: Cambridge University Press, 1996.

Liao, Kang. *Pearl S. Buck: A Cultural Bridge across the Pacific.* Westport, Conn.: Greenwood Press, 1997.

Lipscomb, Elizabeth J., Frances E. Webb, and Peter Conn, eds.: *The Several Worlds of Pearl S. Buck: Essays Presented at a Centennial Symposium, Randolph-Macon Woman's College, March 26–28, 1992.* Westport, Conn.: Greenwood Press, 1994.

Rizzon, Beverly. *Pearl S. Buck: Good Earth Mother.* Philomath, Ore.: Drift Creek Press, 1992.

Sherk, Warren. *Pearl Buck: A Woman in Conflict.* Piscataway, N.J.: New Century, 1983.

Stirling, Nora. *Pearl Buck: A Woman in Conflict.* Piscataway, N.J.: New Century, 1983.

Waldron, Ann. *Pearl S. Buck: Compassion for Two Worlds.* Las Cruces, N.M.: Softwest Press, 1998.

Yü, Yüh-chao. *Pearl S. Buck's Fiction: A Cross-Cultural Interpretation.* Nanking and Taipei: Academia Sinica, Institute of American Culture, Republic of China, 1981.

IVAN BUNIN
(1870–1953)
B. Amarilis Lugo de Fabritz

BIOGRAPHY

Ivan Alekseevich Bunin was born in Voronezh, Russia, to an impover-ished noble family. He completed four years in the gymnasium in the town of Elets, after which his brother Iulii tutored him privately. Author of both poetry and prose, he became better known as a poet during the first half of his life; he also was a talented translator—of works by Alfred Tennyson, Alfred de Musset, Lord Byron, Charles-Marie Leconte de Lisle, and Adam Mickiewicz, among others. One of his best-known translations is that of *The Song of Hiawatha* by Henry Wadsworth Longfellow, based on native North American lore and structured metri-cally on a Finnish epic. Bunin received the Pushkin Prize in 1903 for his own verse and for his translations of Byron and Longfellow, as well as another Pushkin Prize in 1909. By then, he had published collections of original verse and more than 20 short prose works. That year the Acad-emy of Sciences recognized his contribution to Russian literature by electing him a member. His best-known works of prose appeared after 1909: *Derevnia* (1910), *Sukhodol: Povesti i rasskazy 1911–1912 g.* (1912), and the short story "Gospodin iz San-Frantsisko" along with the six-volume *Polnoe sobranie sochinenii* (complete collected works) in 1915.

Bunin's interest in foreign aesthetics derived not only from reading, but also from the extensive travels he undertook prior to the Russian Revolution of 1917. His travels included visits to Switzerland and Ger-many in late 1900 and to Constantinople in 1903, which led to a fascina-tion with the Middle East that he did not shake for the rest of his life. He also traveled to Egypt, Syria, Palestine, and Ceylon (Sri Lanka). Following the start of the Bolshevik Revolution in 1917, Bunin and his second wife, Vera Nikolaevna Muromtseva, took refuge in Odessa, Ukraine, and on February 9, 1920, they left Russia forever to settle finally in Grasse in the south of France, where Bunin enjoyed an active social life within the émigré community. During his first four years in exile, he published no fewer than 11 anthologies of prose, poetry, and translations with Russian-language houses in Paris, Prague, and Berlin, and as a member of the Russian émigré community in France he became a visible vocal opponent of the Soviet regime. On November 9, 1933, he won the Nobel Prize for Literature.

After 1945, poor health and poverty limited Bunin's activities. He became dependent on contributions from friends and admirers to pay for his living expenses and medical bills. In spite of these difficulties, he still remained active within the Russian community in Paris. The speech he presented to an audience at the Soviet embassy in Paris during the autumn of 1945 led to a number of rumors that appeared in print in émigré journals, accusing him of supporting the Soviet regime. He refuted these accusations in person and through letters to the editors of the leading Russian émigré publications of the time. This was the last major political debate to engage him. The few stories he wrote after 1945 appeared in the last collection of his of his work to be published during his lifetime: *Vesnoi, v Iudee: Roza Ierikhona* (1953). He died on November 8, 1953. His book on Chekhov, *O Chekhove: Nezakonchennaia rukopis*, was published posthumously in 1955.

MAJOR MULTICULTURAL THEMES

Bunin's first encounter with multicultural themes through translations of European and American works expanded into serious literary exploration of Eastern philosophical concepts following the outbreak of World War I. Prior to this period, he had been interested in the central questions of being, and he had sought illumination from a number of sources, including the religious literature of the Middle East. Following his trip to Ceylon, however, he found himself struck in particular by Buddhism. His best-known work dealing with the issue of the vanity of self-assertion is the short story "Gospodin iz San Frantsisko," in which, through a combination of skillful description and representation of points of view, he provides insight into the gentleman's psyche and reveals a society dominated by egocentricity, hypocrisy, and self-indulgence. It is a skillful Buddhist reflection on the moral decay of early-twentieth-century western Europe.

Bunin also tried in his later prose to integrate his impressions of some of the exotic locales he had visited. The story collection *Vesnoi, v Iudee: Roza Ierikhona* includes a number of short stories and poems that almost resemble a travelogue of his later life. "Vesnoi, v Iudee" features a male character who visits the East for the first time. "I saw a completely new world in front of me" (14), he says as he records his impressions of bazaars and deserts. The poem "Nel Mezzo del Camin di Nostra Vita" presents an impressionistic picture of Naples in April as the gardens start coming alive in days that are "perpetually memorable to me" (89). Thus, Bunin's work in emigration demonstrates two distinct emotional registers: in one, there is a somber awareness of the passage of time and how it undermines all human endeavors; in the other, the author in exile shows a desire to enjoy the full range of life's experiences.

SURVEY OF CRITICISM

Scholarship on Bunin can be divided into Soviet and non-Soviet scholarship prior to and following the fall of the Soviet Union. Soviet scholarship disregarded the foreign influences that affected Bunin's works, focusing instead on his contribution to early-twentieth-century Russian literature. Soviet scholars had difficulty gaining access to Bunin's works, in particular those works from his time in exile, which were banned from publication and distribution in the Soviet Union. Scholarship outside of the Soviet Union acknowledged these works to a certain extent but emphasized Bunin's anti-Bolshevik stance rather than analyzing critically his overall aesthetic systems.

Analysis of Bunin's oeuvre has benefited from the reduction of political tension in the post-Soviet era. For a comprehensive overall view of Bunin's career, Julian W. Connolly's 1982 biography is still the essential text. A number of scholars both in Russia and outside of Russia have undertaken studies of the different facets of Bunin's plurinational interests. Scholarship in the United States has focused primarily on the Buddhist elements in Bunin. Thomas Gaiton Marullo (1998) offers probably the most complete treatment of this influence. Marullo traces how key concepts of self, craving, enlightenment, regression, and rebirth are seminal motifs in the author's works.

Among Russian scholars, E. M. Volkov has undertaken research on Bunin's contribution as a translator. In an essay published in 2000, he speaks about the broad range of translations undertaken by Bunin and how they influenced Russian literary development throughout the twentieth century.

Bunin also left his impressions of his time abroad in a number of diaries, letters, and articles. Thomas Gaiton Marullo has collected and translated the majority of the documents from Bunin's first decade in exile in *Ivan Bunin: From the Other Shore, 1920–1933*, published in 1995. O. N. Mikhailov has gathered an even greater number of these documents in *I. A. Bunin: Publitsistika 1918–1953 godov* (1998). These texts serve to show the wide range of contacts and interests Bunin maintained while he was still in exile.

SELECTED BIBLIOGRAPHY

Works by Bunin

Derevnia. Moscow: Moskovskoe knigoizdatel'stvo, 1910. [*The Village.* Trans. Isabel F. Hapgood. New York: A. A. Knopf, 1923.]

Sukhodol: Povesti i rasskazy 1911–1912 g. Moscow: "Knigoizdatel'stvo pisatelei," 1912.

Polnoe sobranie sochinenii. 6 vols. Saint Petersburg: A. F. Marks, 1915.

Gospodin iz San-Frantsisko: Proizvedeniia 1915–1916 g. Moscow: Kn-vo pisatelei, 1916. [*The Gentleman from San Francisco, and Other Stories.* Trans. S. S. Koteliansky and Leonard Woolf. Richmond, England: Hogarth Press, 1922.]

Zhizn' Arsen'eva: Istoki dnei. Paris: Izd-vo "Sovremennyia zapiski," 1930. [*The Life of Arseniev: Youth.* Books 1–4 trans. Gleb Struve and Hamish Miles; book 5 trans. Heidi Hillis, Susan McKean, and Sven A. Wolf. Ed. and introduction by Andrew Baruch Wachtel. Evanston, Ill.: Northwestern University Press, 1994.]

Okaiannye dni. Berlin: Petropolis, 1935. [*Cursed Days: A Diary of Revolution.* Trans. and introduction by Thomas Gaiton Marullo. Chicago: Ivan R. Dee, 1998.]

Osvobozhdenie Tolstogo. Paris: YMCA Press, 1937. [*The Liberation of Tolstoy: A Tale of Two Writers.* Trans. and introduction by Thomas Gaiton Marullo and Vladimir T. Khmelkov. Evanston, Ill.: Northwestern University Press, 2001.]

Temnye allei. Paris: La Presse Française et Etrangère, 1946. [*Dark Avenues, and Other Stories* (1949). Trans. Richard Hare. Westport, Conn.: Hyperion Press, 1977.]

Vesnoi, v Iudee: Roza Ierikhona. New York: Izdatel'stvo imeni Chekhova, 1953.

O Chekhove: Nezakonchennaia rukopis. New York: Izdatel'stvo imeni Chekhova, 1955.

Ustami Buninykh: Dnevniki Ivana Alekseevicha i Very Nikolaevny I drugie arkhivnye materialy (Diaries of Ivan Alekseevich and Vera Nikolaevna). Frankfurt am Main: Posev, 1977.

Ivan Bunin: Russian Requiem, 1885–1920: A Portrait from Letters, Diaries, and Fiction. Ed. with an introduction and notes by Thomas Gaiton Marullo. Chicago: Ivan R. Dee, 1993.

Ivan Bunin: From the Other Shore, 1920–1933: A Portrait from Letters, Diaries, and Fiction. Ed. and trans. Thomas Gaiton Marullo. Chicago: Ivan R. Dee, 1995.

I. A. Bunin. Publitsistika 1918–1953 godov. Ed. O. N. Mikhailov. Moscow: Nasledie, 1998.

Selected Studies of Bunin

Bakhrakh, Aleksandr. *Bunin v khalate: Po pamiati, po zapisiam.* Bayville, N.J.: T-vo zarubezhnykh pisatelei, 1979.

Connolly, Julian W. *Ivan Bunin.* Boston: Twayne, 1982.

Ivan Bunin

I. A. Bunin i mirovoi literaturnyi protsess: Materialy mezhdunarodnoi nauchnoi konferentsii posviashchennoi 130- letiiu so dnia rozhdeniia pisatelia: 20–22 sentiabria 2000 g (Proceedings of literary conference held September 20–22, 2000, on the 130th anniversary of Ivan Bunin's birth). 2 vols. Orel, Russia: Orlovskii gosudarstvennyi universitet, 2000.

Marullo, Thomas Gaiton. *If You See the Buddha: Studies in the Fiction of Ivan Bunin*. Evanston, Ill.: Northwestern University Press, 1998.

Roshchin, Mikhail. *Ivan Bunin*. Moscow: Molodaia gvardiia, 2000.

Volkov, E. M. "I. A. Bunin—perevodchik 'Pesni o Gaiavate'" In *I. A. Bunin i mirovoi literaturnyi protsess: Materialy mezhdunarodnoi nauchnoi konferentsii posviashchennoi 130-letiiu so dnia rozhdeniia pisatelia: 20–22 sentiabria 2000 g*, 2: 17–23. Orel, Russia: Orlovskii gosudarstvennyi universitet, 2000.

GUILLERMO CABRERA INFANTE

(1929–)

James O. Pellicer

BIOGRAPHY

Guillermo Cabrera Infante was born in 1929 in Gibara, in the province of Oriente on the northeastern Atlantic coast of Cuba, to Zoila Infante Castro and Guillermo Cabrera López. Both parents were active in the foundation of the Communist Party in their local town, a highly risky activity in those days. As a matter of fact, when Guillermo was seven years old and his brother, Sabá, only three, the police invaded their home with weapons and aimed at their mother, who tried to hide compromising political literature and to flee. Both parents were taken to Santiago and thrown into jail, while the boys looked for refuge at their neighbors' homes.

His parents' financial problems from several months of incarceration caused the family to seek better chances in the big city. By 1941, the family was installed with relatives in a poor and crammed tenement in Havana, where his father found a job with the Communist newspaper *Hoy.* Despite his firm political beliefs, Cabrera López sent his son to a local English school because of his conviction that English would open the boy's future. By 1946, at age 17, the young Cabrera Infante obtained a certificate of completion and started to look for a job in that direction even while translating articles from the American socialist press for his father's employer.

After finishing high school, Cabrera Infante began his career as a journalist. In this new environment, he met people and made important friends. One of them was a young Communist named Carlos Franqui, who combined his political ideology with a deep love for the arts. Thanks to his friend's influence, Cabrera Infante started to read the works of two important Nobel Prize authors, the Guatemalan Miguel Angel Asturias and the American William Faulkner. According to his biographer Raymond D. Souza, Franqui gave him a copy of Faulkner's *The Wild Palms* translated into Spanish by Jorge Luis Borges, "a rendering that now Cabrera Infante considers superior to the original" (*Guillermo Cabrera Infante: Two Islands, Many Worlds*, 21). From Faulkner, he moved to John Steinbeck, Ernest Hemingway, and especially James Joyce. Souza affirms that Joyce's "works have been one of the most enduring influences on [Cabrera Infante's] writings" (*Guillermo Cabrera Infante*, 22).

Under the influence of Asturias, Cabrera Infante launched his literary career with a short story, "Aguas de recuerdo," which Franqui found worth publishing, encouraging the author to take it to *Bohemia*, the most popular magazine in Cuba. Cabrera Infante himself commented: "To my regret (and that of others as well) and to my surprise, the story was accepted" (quoted in Torres Fierro, "Entrevista con Danubio Torres Fierro," 1078). It was his entrée into the world of writing; the owner of *Bohemia*, the Spaniard Antonio Ortega, employed him and later named him secretary to the editorial staff of the magazine *Carteles*. By his twenty-third birthday, Cabrera Infante was recognized as a young man of letters working for several publications in Havana—*Hoy, Bohemia, Carteles*—and then creating one of his own, the literary magazine *Nueva Generación*. In addition, he hosted in his humble apartment a cultural gathering that became the basis for the foundation of the organization Cinemateca de Cuba, dedicated to the development of cinematography in the country.

Two hobbies, going to the movies and reading comics, marked not only the future course of his life but also his peculiar style as a writer and his multicultural personality. Every Hollywood actress, actor, and novel converted into a movie influenced his formative years, and comic strips acquainted him with action seen in successive detailed frames that give a total picture. Both techniques characterize his very peculiar writing style, essentially cinematic and culturally enriched.

Meanwhile, in 1952, army sergeant Fulgencio Batista took over the flimsy Cuban government left after the ousting of the dictator Gerardo Machado Morales. Batista sought to rule the country as his private household and suddenly found the second story published by Cabrera Infante in *Bohemia*, "Balada de plomo y yerro," to be disagreeable. The writer landed in jail, was condemned to pay a fine, and was forbidden to sign anything with his name. As a result, in 1953 "G. Caín" was born ("Ca" for Cabrera and "in" for Infante). With this pseudonym, he signed his first cinematic chronicle and started a series of movie critiques, a task that entirely suited the real love of his life—the cinema.

Thanks to publisher Antonio Ortega's protection, Cabrera Infante contributed film reviews and critiques, now in his own section of the weekly magazine *Carteles*, of which he later became managing editor. He went to New York, among other reasons, to establish a loan agreement between the Film Library of the Museum of Modern Art and the Cinemateca. He took advantage of this trip to see as many movies as he could and even interviewed American and foreign movie stars passing through New York, where he seriously pursued another hobby of his younger days—theater and musical comedy.

As opposition to the Batista dictatorship grew, Cabrera Infante participated with his friend Carlos Franqui in subversive movements that culminated in the revolutionary action started by Fidel Castro, who, in 1959, appointed Cabrera Infante editor of the cultural journal *Lunes de Revolución*. This appointment, in addition to his previous cinematic enterprises, truly made Cabrera Infante the leader of Cuba's official culture. He published his first volume of short stories, *Así en la paz como en la guerra; cuentos* (1960) and married the actress Miriam Gómez in 1961.

Under his direction, *Lunes de Revolución* called for an open approach to culture that would include black and Cuban folklore and a totally eclectic orientation. Cabrera Infante was a true believer in José Martí's motto: "Culture brings freedom" (quoted in Souza, *Guillermo Cabrera Infante*, 37). Everything pointed to a happy future, but soon reality distorted the picture: the Castro government, adamant in its intention to dictate the role of the intellectual in the revolution, censured the movie *P.M.*, made by Cabrera Infante's brother, Sabá. When Cabrera Infante attempted to show it, the Official Commission seized it. Cabrera Infante's insistence on free artistic expression for *Lunes de Revolución* only led to the government's intervention and the final closing of the journal. No longer welcomed in Cuba's cultural life, he received in 1961 an urgent appointment as cultural attaché to the Cuban embassy in Belgium. During this time abroad, he published *Un oficio del siglo veinte, por G. Caín* (1963), a collection of his film reviews.

His mother's mortal illness call him back to Cuba in 1965, only to find her dead. Even worse, his beloved Cuba was also dead. He decided to return to Europe; with great difficulty, he obtained visas for himself, his wife, and two daughters and established the family in Spain, where he published his first novel, *Tres tristes tigres* (1965). Franco's regime unfortunately decided that Cabrera Infante's presence in Spain was not welcome. Encouraged by the first royalties obtained from a film script of an English movie, he put to work his certificate of English proficiency and moved to England with his family. After a difficult start, the family finally established itself in South Kensington, on Gloucester Road.

In England, Cabrera Infante continued writing both literature and film reviews and scripts. Contrary to Castro's explicit command, he contributed his first political manifesto against the dictator in 1968 to *Mundo Nuevo*, a prestigious popular South American magazine. In 1969, he became a British citizen; in 1970, he went to Hollywood to arrange for the financing of a film script and then to New York. In the United States, he received a Guggenheim fellowship. In 1976, he published in Spain his favorite work, *Exorcismos de esti(l)o*, an ingenious exercise on the relation of the parts to the whole; and in 1979 *La Habana para un Infante difunto*, "the first serious erotic novel ever written in Spanish since 1515 when Francisco Delicado published *La lozana andaluza*" (Montenegro and Santi, eds., *Infantería*, 44).

Since 1978, Cabrera Infante has lectured and taught courses at Yale, West Virginia, Virginia, Wellesley College, and the University of California in Los Angeles. He has traveled extensively and received distinctions such as *doctor honoris causa* from the Universidad Internacional de la Florida, the Medal of Sancho IV from the Universidad Complutense in Spain, and especially the Premio Cervantes (1997), a prize equivalent in the Spanish world to the Nobel Prize.

MAJOR MULTICULTURAL THEMES

As previously stated, Cabrera Infante's major multicultural achievement is his association between literature, cinema, and comic strips as a means of expression. This multimedia liaison is quite original and permeates all his work. It characterizes his way of writing as well. Passing from one frame of action to another without an apparent connection and superimposing action, he forces his reader to make correlations. For instance, his first major work, *Tres tristes tigres*, suddenly and unexpectedly begins with a superimposition of languages in a nightclub's opening show. The medley continues by combining a quotation from Lewis Carroll with Afro-Cuban mythology. The narrative style mixes Spanish with Cuban jargon and an epistolary approach with description in the first and third persons.

In his stories, the characters go to the movies and remember or comment on films. Thus, the action narrated in the foreground is reflected at subordinated levels. In *Ella cantaba boleros*, the main character, who is always a narrative "I," quickly passes from an Argentine movie star, Hugo del Carril, to a Mexican star, Cantinflas. From this vantage point, he remembers the film *Abismos de pasión* based on *Cumbres borrascosas (Wuthering Heights)*, which causes him to remember both Luis Buñuel and Emily Brontë. Moments later, when the main character is making love, something interrupts him, and he thinks: "Impudent Proustians, Huxleys in Havana, it is necessary to recover lost time" ("le temps perdu") (150).

This technique of mixing literature and cinema from different cultures is extremely common in Cabrera Infante's narrative and is efficacious in enriching one text by means of another. The use of puns in surrealistic fashion is reminiscent of the Spaniard Ramón Gómez de la Serna. In an interview published by the magazine *Contacto*, Jesús Hernández Cuellar asked Cabrera Infante which was his favorite work and why. The writer answered: "Probably *Exorcismos de esti(l)o* because in that book I brought the Cuban language to a kind of wordplay that no one has ever achieved in Spanish before, with the exception of Gómez de la Serna, although there were antecedents in French like Jarry, Satie, and Queneau, as well as in English like Lewis Carroll and Joyce."

The reader has to be on the alert when reading Cabrera Infante's works because the context continuously opens up to wider multicultural connotations. When the writer indicates that his character is serious, he does not say so simply, but rather uses the more complex "Charles Voyeur's seriousness." When the main character touches his mistress, the narrator states: "in the darkness, he touched the *Braille* of her skin." In the enormous and demanding work at the printing press, he is "the galleys' Ben-Hur." When he is tempted to suicide because of his girlfriend's rejection, he thinks of "opening his veins in a warm bath—Petronius servant of my Caesar," and returning from his own house to hers becomes "Upon returning from Rome" (*Ella cantaba boleros*, 89, 90, 91). Cabrera Infante's production is incessantly opened to massive multicultural references not only within the Spanish or Hispanic American cultures, but within a universal context that encompasses the arts and history. Notwithstanding, the common reference is to his beloved Havana; all his literature is imbued with feelings of both nostalgia and wrath owing to the conflict between the various Cuban regimes and his own convictions.

SURVEY OF CRITICISM

The best biography of Guillermo Cabrera Infante is the one by Raymond D. Souza (1996), who in 12 substantial chapters comprehensively studies Cabrera Infante's life and oeuvre and presents a flawless portrait of the Cuban writer as well as a wide-ranging exploration of his published and unpublished works. The author's environment and his relationships appear in a vivid presentation that gives depth to the biographical inquiry. One of the greatest values of this book is its comprehensive bibliography, which includes English translations of his works, unpublished film scripts, interviews, criticism, and history.

Reynaldo L. Jiménez (1977), in addition to a general study of the Cuban narrative of the revolution, presents an in-depth exploration of Cabrera Infante's life and evolution. He also offers a very appealing analysis of humor in Cabrera Infante's work, humor as an attitude toward life and humor as a deconstructive tool in facing reality. This work includes a very helpful bibliography.

Rosemary Geisdorfer Feal's (1986) study is of paramount interest in the analysis of contemporary Hispanic American narrative. The work begins by a theoretical exploration of the very nature of autobiography. Then it presents a structural analysis of autobiography based on *Infante's*

Inferno and concludes with a study of Vargas Llosa's *La tía Julia y el escribidor.*

A voluminous work of more than 1,000 pages, entitled *Infantería* (1999), starts with an introduction by editor Nivia Montenegro and a preliminary analysis of Cabrera Infante's literature by coeditor Enrico Mario Santi, followed by a very helpful chronology of the writer's life and works. The main corpus is a well-selected anthology of every work by Cabrera Infante. A 1986 interview with Danubio Torres Fierro closes the book; it focuses on Cabrera Infante's early work, or as Torres Fierro says, his "prehistoric" moments, better to appreciate the "awakening of a Latin American conscience" ("Entrevista con Danubio Torres Fierro," 1094).

SELECTED BIBLIOGRAPHY

Works by Cabrera Infante

Así en la paz como en la guerra; cuentos. Montevideo: Ediciones R., 1960. [*Rites of Passage.* Trans. John Brookesmith, Peggy Boyars, and Guillermo Cabrera Infante. London: Faber and Faber, 1993.]
Un oficio del siglo veinte, por G. Caín. Havana: Ediciones R., 1963. [*A Twentieth-Century Job.* Trans. Kenneth Hall and Guillermo Cabrera Infante. London: Faber and Faber, 1991.]
Tres tristes tigres. Barcelona: Editorial Seix Barral, 1965. [*Three Trapped Tigers.* Trans. Donald Gardner and Suzanne Jill Levine, with Guillermo Cabrera Infante. New York: Harper and Row, 1971.]
Exorcismos de esti(l)o. Barcelona: Editorial Seix Barral, 1976.
La Habana para un Infante difunto. Barcelona: Editorial Seix Barral, 1979. [*Infante's Inferno.* Trans. Suzanne Jill Levine with Guillermo Cabrera Infante. New York: Harper and Row, 1984.]
Holy Smoke. London: Faber and Faber, 1985 [original in English].
Ella cantaba boleros. Madrid: Santillana, 1996.
Infantería. Ed. Nivia Montenegro and Enrico Mario Santi. Mexico City: Fondo de Cultura Económica, 1999.
Hernández Cuellar, Jesús. Interview with Guillermo Cabrera Infante. *Contacto* magazine. Available at: http://www.contactomagazine.com/infante.htm.

Selected Studies of Cabrera Infante

Feal, Rosemary Geisdorfer. *Novel Lives: The Fictional Autobiographies of Guillermo Cabrera Infante and Mario Vargas Llosa.* Chapel Hill: University of North Carolina Press, 1986.
Hall, Kenneth E. *Guillermo Cabrera Infante and the Cinema.* Newark, Del.: Juan de la Cuesta, 1989.
Jiménez, Reynaldo L. *Guillermo Cabrera Infante y "Tres tristes tigres"* (1976). Miami: Ediciones Universal, 1977.
Machover, Jacobo. *El heraldo de las malas noticias: Guillermo Cabrera Infante (Ensayo a dos voces).* Miami: Ediciones Universal, 1996.

Nelson, Ardis L. *Cabrera Infante in the Menippean Tradition*. Newark, Del.: Juan de la Cuesta, 1983.

Pereda, Rosa María. *Guillermo Cabrera Infante*. Madrid: Edaf, D.L., 1979.

Sánchez-Boudy, José. *La nueva novela hispanoamericana y "Tres tristes tigres."* Miami: Ediciones Universal, 1971.

Souza, Raymond D. *Guillermo Cabrera Infante: Two Islands, Many Worlds*. Austin: University of Texas Press, 1996.

Torres Fierro, Danubio. "Entrevista con Danubio Torres Fierro." In *Infantería*, ed. Nivia Montenegro and Enrico Mario Santi, 1066–97. Mexico City: Fondo de Cultura Económica, 1999.

———. *Memoria Plural: Entrevistas a escritores latinoamericanos*. Buenos Aires: Editorial Sudamericana, 1986.

ALBERT CAMUS
(1913–1960)
Paul J. Archambault

BIOGRAPHY

Albert Camus was born in Mondovi, Algeria. His mother, Catherine Sintès, was of Majorcan origin; his father, Lucien, came from an Alsatian family that had settled in Algeria after 1871. Mobilized as an infantryman when World War I broke out, Lucien was killed at the Battle of the Marne. His wife then moved from Mondovi with their two sons to the working-class neighborhood of Belcourt, in Algiers, of which Camus later drew unforgettable pictures of merchants, street vendors, carpenters, coopers (like his uncle, Etienne Sintès), and storekeepers. She earned a living by working in a munitions factory and cleaning homes. An unschooled woman afflicted by deafness, she rarely spoke, and in Camus's literary work she is often portrayed as a modest, unspeaking, working-class woman who is the picture of Stoic endurance (as in "Les Muets," one of the stories in *L'exil et le royaume*). She died in September 1960 in Belcourt, outliving Albert by nine months.

Camus attended the *école communale* of Belcourt (1918–23), where one of his teachers, Louis Germain, took notice of this gifted boy and arranged for him to obtain a scholarship to attend the lycée in Algiers. (Camus dedicated his 1957 Nobel Prize speech to Louis Germain.) In his lycée years (1923–30), Camus studied traditional humanistic disciplines, especially French and Latin, preparing to become a schoolteacher, as any young *bachelier* of his class might. He also developed a passion for soccer and was goalie on the junior team of the Racing universitaire algérois (RUA). "What I know most surely about morality and the duty of man," he observed later, "I owe to sport, and learned it in the RUA" (quoted in Lottmann, *Albert Camus: A Biography*, 40).

Camus passed his baccalaureate examinations in June 1930 and during his subsequent preparation for the *licence ès lettres* discovered his taste for writing, an inclination that was much encouraged by his philosophy professor, Jean Grenier, one of the most profound influences in Camus's life, himself a writer and thinker of some note. It was also around the time of his baccalaureate that Camus discovered that he was stricken with tuberculosis, an illness with which he was to struggle during his entire life.

While at the University of Algiers, Camus joined the Algerian Communist Party, of which he was a member from autumn 1935 to November 1937, and from which he was expelled for his dissident ideas. He also was married briefly to Simone Hié, an attractive and flirtatious young woman he met at the university, but that marriage ended in divorce a year later. Camus later married Francine Faure, an Algerian French woman from a respectable *pied-noir* family, a lasting marriage (although Albert was never a faithful husband and Francine was afflicted with depression for many years) that produced two children, Jan and Catherine.

In 1936, Camus wrote a thesis on the relationship of Hellenism and Christianity in the works of Plotinus and Saint Augustine. After a month of travel in central Europe and Italy, he created at the Maison de la culture of Algiers a theater troupe, the Théâtre du travail, which produced plays such as Fernando de Rojas's *La Celestina* and adaptations of Fedor Dostoevsky's *The Brothers Karamazov*, in which Camus himself performed as an able actor and director. He worked concomitantly as a journalist for *L'Alger Républicain*, directed by Pascal Pia, writing a great variety of articles, including a celebrated series on the economic miseries of the region of Kabylia, published as "Misère de Kabylie" (1939).

When war broke out in Europe in September 1939, Camus had been planning his first trip to Greece. He had spent most of his life in Algeria, as he had little money for extensive traveling. The trip did not materialize; instead he continued to work for the *Alger Républicain* and was offered a job by its director to work in Paris for *Paris-Soir* from March until June 1940. He then left Paris for Clermont-Ferrand with the *Paris-Soir* group on June 9 as the Germans advanced on the capital. From Clermont-Ferrand, he returned to Oran, where he spent the years 1941 and 1942, returning then to the continent, to Lyons, where he wrote for the underground newspaper *Combat*.

At war's end in May 1945, Camus settled in Paris with Francine and their two children. Having gained sufficient celebrity to be in demand as a lecturer, he traveled to North America in 1946 and to South America in 1949, recording his impressions in his *Carnets* (1964), but remaining generally unenthusiastic about the New World. (Extracted jottings from the *Carnets* were published separately as *Journaux de voyage* [1978] in France and as *American Journals* [1987] in the United States.)

Paris was to be Camus's intellectual home until his death in 1960, although he ever longed for the sun, the mountains, and the beaches of his native Algeria, to which he returned whenever he could. He had become an increasingly famous light in the Parisian literary establishment, largely because of his publication of *L'étranger* and *Le mythe de Sisyphe* in 1942, and *La peste* in 1947, the latter book providing one of the greatest best-sellers in the history of French publication. The inherent pessimism and the terse, minimalistic writing *("écriture blanche")* of the first two works attracted the attention and the favorable criticism of Jean-Paul Sartre, and Camus's name became increasingly associated with Sartre and existentialism during the years 1945–52.

In point of fact, Camus never considered himself an existentialist and pointedly answered in the negative whenever he was questioned on that matter. His mentor in philosophy, Jean Grenier, wrote of Camus that he represented quite the opposite of existentialism. His rigor and his confidence in reason, Grenier wrote, "placed him in opposition to existentialist philosophies" (*Théâtre, récits, nouvelles*, xx). As for Camus's personal relationship with Sartre, it was always a distant one. He was never a member of the editorial staff of *Les Temps Modernes*, created by Sartre and Simone de Beauvoir in 1946, where Marxist figures such as Sartre, Beauvoir, and Francis Jeanson dominated the ideological scene. Camus's politics was never as radically to the left as that of the *Temps Modernes* group. He shared neither Sartre's Marxist vision of history nor his attraction to Soviet-style communism nor his visceral anti-Americanism.

The Sartre-Camus relationship came to an abrupt end after the publication of Camus's *L'homme révolté* in 1951. Jeanson gave the book a scathing review in *Les Temps Modernes*, even to the point of suggesting that the book had been financed by the U.S. Central Intelligence Agency (CIA), given its staunch pro-Western, antitotalitarian stance. Camus wrote a stiff, cold letter of protest to the director of *Les Temps Modernes*, Sartre, who responded with a savage personal attack on Camus himself. The two never saw each other again. Sartre did write a moving, almost affectionate obituary on Camus in *Les Temps Modernes* after Camus's tragic death in a car accident on January 4, 1960, wherein he deplored the premature loss of a former friend who had always remained (Sartre said, somewhat condescendingly) "Ce petit voyou d'Alger" (That little ruffian from Algiers).

The break with Sartre in 1952 very probably propelled, rather than hindered, Camus's projection to international fame, culminating with his receiving the Nobel Prize for Literature in the fall of 1957. During the Cold War period of the 1950s, he was progressively considered a liberal, humanistic alternative to the revolutionary, anti-imperialist, anticapitalistic posturing of the Sartre-Beauvoir tandem and of the extreme Parisian left in general. Camus's writing reached its highest point of sophistication with the publication of a series of short stories entitled *L'exil et le royaume* and *La chute* (1956), with the staging of plays such as *Caligula* (1944) and *Le malentendu* (1944), and with brilliant adaptations of Pedro Calderón de la Barca's *La dévotion à la croix*, William Faulkner's *Requiem pour une nonne*, and Fedor Dostoyevsky's *Les possédés*, among others.

Several posthumous works have appeared since Camus's death: among them are *La mort heureuse* (1971), the sketch of what was to become *L'étranger;* early essays in a collection entitled *Le premier Camus* (1973); and *Le premier homme* (1994), a largely autobiographical novel he was writing about his family history at the time of his car accident.

MAJOR MULTICULTURAL THEMES

The multiculturalism in Camus's writing is based on a series of oppositions that recur frequently and at times too easily—explainable, however, when one remembers that Camus was an Algerian Frenchman, a Mediterranean born in poverty, who saw himself, somewhat defensively, in opposition to the French intellectual and bourgeois establishment of the left that based its very raison d'être on symbols such as continental European culture, Paris, knowledge of German philosophy (especially Hegel and Marx), and prestigious university diplomas and pedigrees.

He considered himself a Mediterranean, not a continental or Parisian intellectual; he was a pagan born in Christian and post-Christian times, a lover of nature caught up in the vagaries of history. The Mediterranean, the Greeks in particular, had introduced into Western thought the idea of nature, with its sense of boundaries and limitations both aesthetic and moral. Christianity, largely through the thinking of Saint Augustine (whom Camus had read and admired as a student) had introduced into Western thought the idea of history as process, as linear advancement toward a final end. With the secularization of Christianity, there had entered into Western thought, largely though the Germanic North, a sinister historicism, entirely immanentistic and creator of its own laws, best represented by Hegel and Marx. Camus saw in German historicism the roots of twentieth-century totalitarianism with the disastrous effects wreaked upon humanity by communism and Nazism in particular. The Greeks might have killed and did kill one another in many an internecine war, Camus reasoned; but Greek thought at its worst could never have invented the death camps of World War II.

One of the first ideologies Camus seems to have taken seriously might be called the "Mediterranean ideology." During the years following his baccalaureate, he was being "pumped full" of "the conceit of [the] Mediterranean man . . . that these sun-blessed shores breed men who know their limits and the just measure of things"—an ideology not to be construed as being in any way fascist or even nationalistic, seemingly having been bred more by Camus's reading of favorite French writers such as André Gide, Henry de Montherlant, Pierre Louÿs, and his philosophy professor Jean Grenier, transplanted intellectuals who had invented a North Africa of their own (Lottmann, *Albert Camus*, 69). The best symbol of the Mediterranean in Camus's mind was the romantic excavation site of Tipasa (a seaside village some 45 miles east of Algiers), with its Roman ruins and its adjacent sea. Well before he was 20, he had written an enthusiastic if somewhat untalented poem containing verses such as "Mediterranean! Your world is on our scale" ("Mediterranean," translated by and quoted in Lottmann, *Albert Camus*, 69).

In a lecture given at the Maison de la culture of Algiers on February 8, 1937 (later published in the monthly bulletin of that institution, called *Jeune Méditerranée*), Camus, although making it clear that the Mediterraneanism he subscribed to was not to be confused with Mussolini-style fascism, maintained that it was nevertheless a recognizable feeling. There is such a thing, he said, as a Mediterranean *"patrie."* Having recently spent two months traveling through Austria and Germany, he wondered why he felt so awkward in the presence of these people who are always "buttoned up to the neck" and who may know how to laugh, but do not know what joy is. What a relief it was to reach Provence and Italy and to find that "vie forte et colorée" (strong, colorful life) that tells a Mediterranean that he is back in his *patrie!* Christianity, Camus continued, became a world religion only after its encounter with the Mediterranean, being at its inception a "moving but closed doctrine, Judaic above all, ignorant of concessions, harsh, exclusive and admirable." It was a Mediterranean, Francis of Assisi, who made of Christianity an interior and tormented religion, "a hymn to nature and to naïve joy." Once again Camus could not refrain from opposing this type of Mediterranean, Franciscan Christianity against its Nordic counterpart: "The only attempt ever made to separate Christianity from the world we owe to a Nordic, Luther. Protestantism is literally a Catholicism that has been wrenched from the Mediterranean and to its influence, which is at the same time dangerous and exciting." Fascism, he adds, has a far more human, less militaristic face in Italy than in Germany: "the Mediterranean miracle is to allow men who live humanely in a country [Italy] with inhuman laws" (*Essais*, 1322–23).

Whether one agrees with such touching and romantic formulations or not, one thing is clear: Camus never rid himself of this naive Mediterraneanism that was based on a bogus conception of cultural unity derived from the unity of the Romance languages and from the root contributions of Graeco-Roman culture, and that took no account of the fact that, already in 1937, a majority of the inhabitants of the Mediterranean, at least on its southern shores, spoke Arabic. In the resounding conclusion to *L'homme révolté*, (1952), Camus sounded very much like the young man of 1937, propounding Mediterraneanism as the one reply to the unbridled absolutism of German philosophy: "The deep conflict of this century is perhaps not between the German philosophies of history and

Christian politics, which to a certain extent are in complicity, but between German dreams and the Mediterranean tradition, between the violences of eternal adolescence and virile strength, between nostalgia, made more acute by knowledge and books, and courage, hardened and enlightened in the course of life; between history, in short, and nature. . . . But historical absolutism, in spite of its triumphs, has never ceased running up against an invincible exigency of human nature, of which the Mediterranean, where intelligence is the sister to harsh light, keeps the secret. . . . We Mediterraneans always live from the same light" (*Essais*, 703).

SURVEY OF CRITICISM

At the time of Camus's death in 1960, the Camus bibliography already numbered in the thousands of items. To summarize the "new" Camus scholarship that has appeared since that date, we may mention among the significant works of criticism Conor Cruise O'Brien's highly readable *Albert Camus of Europe and Africa* (1970). O'Brien was one of the critics to raise the question of the "silent Arab" in Camus's works—that is, of Camus's consideration of Algerian Arabs as secondary figures in terms of both their literary presence and their political importance. Camus was very sensitive on this question and was quick to respond that he never considered Arabs as second-rank literary figures or second-rate citizens of Algeria, although the political solution he did favor for Algeria would at best have made it a part of a larger Franco-Arab federation. Camus never favored total independence for Algeria.

English Showalter (1984) provides a deep and sensitive reading of Camus's *L'exil et le royaume*; his work is worth pointing out among the fine, quiet works of criticism on Camus written in the past two decades. Perhaps the most brilliant work of collective criticism is that edited with an introduction by Harold Bloom, Sterling Professor of the Humanities at Yale University. In the Modern Critical Views Series, Bloom's 1985 volume contains signal essays by Victor Brombert, Roger Shattuck, Paul de Man, Jacques Guicharnaud, and René Girard, among other Camus scholars. We should note, finally, two exhaustive biographies of Camus written in the past 25 years: Herbert R. Lottmann's *Albert Camus: A Biography* (1979), an excessively thorough and perhaps too detailed study of every particular of Camus's life; and the masterful biography by Olivier Todd, *Albert Camus: Une vie* (1996, English translation 1998), a sympathetic, beautifully written work that probes the mind as well as the heart of Albert Camus.

SELECTED BIBLIOGRAPHY

Works by Camus

L'étranger. Paris: Gallimard, 1942.

Le mythe de Sisyphe. Paris: Gallimard, 1942.

Caligula. Paris: Gallimard, 1944.

Le malentendu: Paris: Gallimard, 1944.

La peste. Paris: Gallimard, 1947.

L'homme révolté. Paris: Gallimard, 1951.

La chute. Paris: Gallimard, 1956.

L'exil et le royaume. Paris: Gallimard, 1957.

Théâtre, récits, nouvelles. Ed. Jean Grenier and Roger Quilliot. Paris: Gallimard, 1962.

Carnets, mai 1935–février 1942. Paris: Gallimard, 1962.

Carnets, janvier 1942–mars 1951. Paris: Gallimard, 1964.

Essais. Ed. R. Quilliot and L. Faucon. Paris: Gallimard, 1965.

La mort heureuse. Ed. Jean Sarocchi. Paris: Gallimard, 1971.

Le premier Camus: Suivi de Écrits de jeunesse d'Albert Camus. Ed. Paul Viallaneix. Paris: Gallimard, 1973.

Journaux de voyages. Ed. Roger Quilliot. Paris: Gallimard, 1978.

Le premier homme. Paris: Gallimard, 1994.

Selected Studies of Camus

Bloom, Harold, ed. *Albert Camus.* Modern Critical Views Series. New York: Chelsea House, 1985.

Knapp, Bettina L., ed. *Critical Essays on Albert Camus.* Boston: G. K. Hall, 1988.

Lottmann, Herbert R. *Albert Camus: A Biography.* Garden City, N.Y.: Doubleday, 1979.

O'Brien, Conor Cruise. *Albert Camus of Europe and Africa.* New York: Viking Press, 1970.

Showalter, English. *Exiles and Strangers: A Reading of Camus's "Exile and the Kingdom."* Columbus: Ohio State University Press, 1984.

Todd, Oliver. *Albert Camus: Une vie.* Paris: Gallimard, 1996. [*Albert Camus: A Life.* Trans. Benjamin Ivry. London: Vintage, 1998.]

ELIAS CANETTI
(1905–1994)

Elizabeth Powers

BIOGRAPHY

From the evidence of his autobiography, Elias Canetti came into the world in an exemplary multicultural setting. He was born in Ruse, a town on the Danube River in northern Bulgaria, a region that only 30 years earlier had been part of the Ottoman Empire. His family on both sides was a large one of merchants and tradesmen of Sephardic Jewish origin, but the culture in which Canetti spent the first six years of his life was not the narrow one of East European Jewish peasantry; it was rather Oriental-worldly and cosmopolitan. When he writes in his autobiography that everything he went on to experience in life was already foreshadowed by events in Ruse (*Die gerettete Zunge: Geschichte einer Jugend*, 11), he is referring both to the tyranny of power in the patriarchal setting presided over by his father's father and to his mother's chauvinism concerning her illustrious Spanish ancestors. Canetti's life journey, literally and figuratively, was away from the confines of such power relations and local clan pride to a setting of universalist, liberal values, to the source of the Enlightenment, to western Europe.

His first languages were Ladino, the language of Jews from the Iberian peninsula, and Bulgarian, but seven or eight languages were commonly spoken in Ruse, especially by tradesmen like his ancestors. Unlike other Jewish writers of eastern European background (e.g., Franz Kafka or Paul Celan), he came to his German literary inheritance in a roundabout way. His parents, who had met in Vienna as students, spoke German with one another, a memento of their common love for theater, but Elias the child was excluded from this intimate linguistic sphere. In 1911, when he was about to enter school, his parents moved to Manchester, England, where his father, besides extolling English institutions, encouraged his son's rapid progress in learning the English language. Yet, at his father's sudden death, his mother returned to the continent with her three sons, to Vienna, and she forced Elias to learn German within a matter of months. By the time he entered school in Vienna in 1913, he had become his mother's literary intimate, and the autobiography portrays the school years in Vienna (1913–16) and later in Zürich (1916–21) as ones of growing literary precocity. It was because of his mother's enthusiasm for the languages that to her represented high culture that his own tongue was set free, so to speak: "under my mother's influence I was born again, to the German language, and from the pain of this birth arose the passion that united me to both, to the language and to my mother" (*Die gerettete Zunge: Geschichte einer Jugend*, 94).

The idyllic years of early literary formation were interrupted in 1921, when his mother insisted that he learn about "the real world." The family spent the next three years (1921–24), a time of raging inflation, in Frankfurt, where Canetti saw spontaneous protest demonstrations of *die Masse*—the crowd, the mob—at the murder of Walter Rathenau, the German statesman, industrialist, and philosophical writer. The crowd's "complete change of consciousness" (*Die Fackel im Ohr: Lebensgeschichte 1921–1931*, 80) contributed to Canetti's early interest in the psychology of the crowd, which bore fruit in his later study *Masse und Macht* (1960).

He began the "practical" study of chemistry at the University of Vienna in 1924. While he was pursuing his Ph.D., his friendships and activities centered on the cultural life of Vienna, including attendance at the celebrated lectures of the cultural critic Karl Kraus. At one of these lectures, Canetti met Veza Taubner-Calderon, likewise a Sephardic Jew, whom the eight years younger Canetti married in 1934. Ideas for a mammoth literary undertaking of eight novels began to take shape (1926–28)—a "Comédie Humaine of the Insane" (*Die Fackel im Ohr: Lebensgeschichte 1921–1931*, 200). In the tradition of totalizing accounts of modernity by Viennese intellectuals—Robert Musil, Herman Broch, Karl Kraus, Ludwig Wittgenstein, Sigmund Freud—Canetti intended to concern himself with the gathering political disorder in Europe at that time. He completed only one of the novels, however: *Die Blendung* (literally "the blinding" or "the dazzlement"), which has provoked "a wide range of interpretations . . . from a misogynist account of the battle of the sexes to a narrative about the embattled and ultimately disintegrating position of the individual in modern society" (Eigler, "Elias Canetti," 169). Its reception was fatally undermined by political currents at its appearance in 1935.

In January 1939, Canetti and his wife arrived in England, where he returned to his meditations on the nature of the crowd, meditations that were extended, in the wake of Adolf Hitler, to a consideration of the phenomenon of power. When *Masse und Macht* was published in 1960, it went relatively unnoticed. Canetti was isolated from intellectual currents in Germany, and he was somewhat of an outsider in England, despite powerful friendships, including with the writer Iris Murdoch. Nevertheless, the friendly reception of the English translation of this work (see Murdoch's review) and of *Die Blendung* traveled back to the continent, and in the following years Canetti began to garner literary recognition in Germany and Austria. The appearance of the first volume of his autobiography, *Die gerettete Zunge: Geschichte einer Jugend* (1977), also increased interest in this major, if neglected, European writer, and in 1981 he was awarded the Nobel Prize for Literature. He completed two additional autobiographical volumes, *Die Fackel im Ohr: Lebensgeschichte 1921–1931* in 1980 and *Das Augenspiel: Lebensgeschichte 1931–1937* in 1985. His oeuvre also includes numerous essays, some plays, and a book of travel impressions (*Die Stimmen von Marrakesch: Aufzeichnungen nach einer Reise*, 1967). In the late 1980s, Canetti returned to Zürich, where he died in 1994.

MAJOR MULTICULTURAL THEMES

Like many twentieth-century intellectuals, Canetti was appalled by the condition of the modern world, but unusual for a European writer is the vast range of non-European sources on which he drew to illuminate this condition. Stripped of its outward forms, the modern condition is a human one, shared by all peoples of the earth, past and present: it is a condition in which the powerful dominate the weak and in which individual freedom and individuality are continuously compromised.

Canetti's immersion in non-European cultures is exemplified, in exaggerated aspect, by the central character of *Die Blendung*, who in his earliest conception was called the *Büchermensch*, or bookman. He appears in the novel as Peter Kien, a world-famous, if unworldly, Sinologist who possesses a library of 25,000 volumes, one that contains everything "the world considered important, books concerning all religions, all thinkers, those of all Eastern literatures, of Western ones" (*Das Augenspiel: Lebensgeschichte 1931–1937*, 9).

Canetti's interests extended back to the earliest human textual records. He claims that "literally no work of literature" had a greater influence on him than the ancient Mesopotamian epic *Gilgamesh* (*Das Gewissen der Worte: Essays*, 277). Gilgamesh, in his failed attempt to find the secret of eternal life, nevertheless serves as an example of what should be the goal for humans: rejection of our preoccupation with the afterlife in favor of embracing and perfecting the human situation in the present one.

An essay on Confucius speaks of the aspects of the Chinese sage's influence on Canetti as a young man: lifelong interest in learning and veneration for the past, again for the purpose of offering models for the present order of human things (*Das Gewissen der Worte: Essays*, 200–206). Canetti's research on crowds in the 1920s led him anew to Asian thinkers ("Chinese and soon Japanese names were familiar to me" [*Die Fackel im Ohr: Lebensgeschichte 1921–1931*, 238]), but when *Masse und Macht* appeared in 1960, much of its material also derived from anthropological and ethnographic accounts (e.g., of Kalahari Bushmen and native Australians) for the evidence they gave of humankind in its most unadulterated form.

For Canetti—and for his early mentor Karl Kraus—the integrity of words was an ethical issue. Canetti's term *acoustical masks* refers to "the linguistic shape of a human being" (Durzak, "The Acoustic Mask: Toward a Theory of Drama," 94), the idiosyncratic ways in which people express themselves. In attending to these sounds, in listening to the words of another person, one grants that person moral status (*Die Fackel im Ohr: Lebensgeschichte 1921–1931*, 207). The conviction that sounds can express "everything that goes on inside a human being" (Durzak, "The Acoustic Mask," 94) is one of the subjects of Canetti's account of his only non-European journey, a 1954 trip to Morocco, where he understood not a word of the spoken language. The book ends with a moving account of a beggar who has taken up residence in the middle of the marketplace in Marrakech. Canetti ponders the possibilities of the being that is concealed under a pathetic bundle of rags (perhaps it has no arms, perhaps it has no tongue), but that nevertheless alerts us to its human status and makes its insistent claim on us with a single repeated sound: "ä-ä-ä-ä-ä-ä-ä." "Ich war," writes Canetti, "stolz auf das Bündel, weil es lebte" (I was proud of that bundle, because it lived) (*Die Stimmen von Marrakesch: Aufzeichnungen nach einer Reise*, 87).

SURVEY OF CRITICISM

The multitude of non-European sources on which Canetti drew has elicited two schools of critical reaction. Susan Sontag (1980), speaking of a childhood "rich in displacements," has referred to Canetti as a "writer in exile" (47), one who is not "Eurocentric" and who, because he is "[c]onversant with Chinese as well as with European thought, with Buddhism and Islam as with Christianity," is indeed free "from reductive habits of thinking" (50). Although Dagmar Barnouw (2000) disagrees with the description of Canetti as an exile (because Canetti has always written in German, he "has not been subjected to the profound disruption of language and culture that exile has meant for so many writers" [15]), she too finds that Canetti's "abstinence from ideology of any shade or substance seems to be related to his early exposure to many different languages, cultures, and temperaments" (18).

A divergent but representative view, that of Hansjakob Werlen (2000), asserts that Canetti is ideological, that his descriptions of non-Western cultures, particularly in *Masse und Macht*, constitute "white writing": that is, they are written according to the anthropological conventions of Europeans and to the unquestioning use of the writer's privileged position to create meaning out of distant events and cultures. Canetti is thus guilty of Orientalism: "While centuries of European civilization have softened ritualistic expressions of power, the true face of power still appears unmasked in the customs of the Oriental rulers" (183). Ergo, Hitler as a despotic and barbarian Mongolian prince.

These contrasting points are grounded in Canetti's biography. Though it has not yet been mentioned in the critical literature, his work has much in common spiritually with that of the great sages of the European Enlightenment—Voltaire, Montesquieu, Goethe—who brought the intellectual riches of the non-European world to our attention as evidence of their own universalist ideals.

SELECTED BIBLIOGRAPHY

Works by Canetti

Die Blendung. Vienna: Herbert Reichner, 1935; Frankfurt am Main: Fischer, 1965. [*Auto-da-Fé.* Trans. C. V. Wedgwood. London: Cape, 1946; *Tower of Babel.* Trans. C. V. Wedgewood. New York: A. A. Knopf, 1947.]

Masse und Macht. Hamburg: Claassen, 1960. [*Crowds and Power.* Trans. Carol Stewart. New York: Viking Press, 1962.]

Die Stimmen von Marrakesch: Aufzeichnungen nach einer Reise. Munich: C. Hanser, 1967. [*The Voices of Marrakesh: A Record of a Visit.* Trans. J. A. Underwood. London: M. Boyars, 1978.]

Das Gewissen der Worte: Essays. Munich: C. Hanser, 1975; 10th ed., 1998. [*The Conscience of Words.* Trans. Joachim Neugroschel. New York: Seabury Press, 1979.]

Die gerettete Zunge: Geschichte einer Jugend. Munich: C. Hanser, 1977.

Die Fackel im Ohr: Lebensgeschichte 1921–1931. Munich: C. Hanser, 1980.

Das Augenspiel: Lebensgeschichte 1931–1937. Munich: C. Hanser, 1985.

Selected Studies of Canetti

Barnouw, Dagmar. "Elias Canetti—Poet and Intellectual." In *Critical Essays on Elias Canetti*, ed. David Darby, 15–34. New York: G. K. Hall, 2000.

Bayley, John. "Canetti and Power." *London Review of Books* (December 17, 1981–January 20, 1982): 5–7.

Durzak, Manfred, in conversation with Elias Canetti. "The Acoustic Mask: Toward a Theory of Drama." In *Critical Essays on Elias Canetti*, ed. David Darby, 93–108. New York: G. K. Hall, 2000.

Eigler, Friederike. "Elias Canetti." In *Encyclopedia of German Literature*, ed. Matthias Konzett, 1: 168–70. New York: Fitzroy Dearborn, 2000.

Murdoch, Iris. "Mass, Might, and Myth." In *Critical Essays on Elias Canetti*, ed. David Darby, 154–57. New York: G. K. Hall, 2000. [Reprinted from *The Spectator* (London) (September 6, 1962): 337–38.]

Sontag, Susan. "Mind as Passion." *New York Review of Books* (September 25, 1980): 47–52.

Werlen, Hansjakob. "Destiny's Herald: Elias Canetti's *Crowds and Power* and Its Continuing Influence." In *Critical Essays on Elias Canetti*, ed. David Darby, 171–85. New York: G. K. Hall, 2000.

Witte, Bernd. "Elias Canetti." In *Kritisches Lexikon zur deutschsprachigen Gegenwartsliteratur*, ed. Heinz Ludwig Arnold, n.p. Munich: Edition Text und Kritik, 1999.

TRUMAN CAPOTE
(1924–1984)

John Dolis

BIOGRAPHY

Christened Truman Streckfus Persons, Truman Capote was born in New Orleans, the son of Archulus Persons and Lillie Mae Faulk. The marriage was insecure from the outset, setting the tenor of Truman's formative years, shuttled among various relatives in Louisiana, Mississippi, and Alabama. Precocious, gifted, and uncommonly bright, he had acquired by the age of nine an appreciation for the works of Gustave Flaubert and Marcel Proust and had already written his first (never published) book. Throughout his grade school years, he wrote essays, fiction, and poems, publishing several short stories. His mother remarried in 1932, and Truman's surname was changed in 1935 to that of his legally adoptive father, Joseph Garcia Capote. Taken to live with his mother and stepfather in New York, he attended schools in the East before enrolling at Greenwich High School in Connecticut (1939), where he wrote for the school paper and published both fiction and poetry in its literary journal. He later graduated from the Franklin School in New York, where, after a short-lived job as copyboy with *The New Yorker,* he began his full-time career as a writer.

His earliest publications in *Harper's Bazaar* and *Mademoiselle* won him immediate fame. Following the publication of his first novel, *Other Voices, Other Rooms* (1948), Capote left the United States for his first trip overseas—a three-month stint in Europe, including London, Paris, and Venice. He revisited Europe the following year (1949), living and writing on the island of Ischia off the coast of Naples, then traveling to Tangier and finally Paris before returning to New York in December. He collected and prepared for publication nine travel articles under the title

Local Color (1950) before boarding a Norwegian freighter bound for Italy in April 1950. Arriving at Taormina, a hill town in Sicily, he rented the top two floors of a villa, the Fontana Vecchia, in which D. H. Lawrence had lived for two years in the 1920s. After finishing *The Grass Harp* (1951), Capote went to Venice and then returned to the United States. The following spring (1952) saw him in Taormina again, and that autumn he moved to Rome. In early 1953, he went to Ravello, where he was commissioned to write the screenplay for *Beat the Devil* (released in 1954), starring Humphrey Bogart. He then settled in Portofino to work on the play version of his short story "House of Flowers" (1951), returning to New York in 1954 to attend his mother's funeral. He flew to London in June 1954 to collaborate with Harold Arlen on the musical version of "House of Flowers" (produced in 1954; new production, 1968).

As a reporter for *The New Yorker*, he journeyed to Russia in December 1955 with the American cast of *Porgy and Bess*, detailing its production in *The Muses Are Heard: An Account* (1956), and to Japan the following year—also spending two weeks in Hong Kong, Thailand, and Cambodia—to write a biographical piece about Marlon Brando during the filming of *Sayonara* in Kyoto. Funded once again by *The New Yorker*, Capote was back in Moscow in 1958, commissioned to write a piece about its unofficial "other" side; thence to Denmark, where he visited Isak Dinesen, whose writing he greatly admired. His sketch of Dinesen appeared in *Observations* (1959), a book of photographic portraits by Richard Avedon accompanied by Capote's own prose portraits. After summering in Greece, he sailed back to the United States in October 1958, returning one final time to Moscow in early spring 1959 to research a piece he never completed. He spent the summer of 1960 in Palamós, Spain, and autumn in Verbier, Switzerland, then moved on to London, where, in roughly eight weeks, he wrote the screen adaptation of Henry James's *The Turn of the Screw*, titled *The Innocents* (1961). During the next two years, he spent the spring and summer in Palamós and the autumn and winter in Verbier. He returned to the United States in March 1963, where, except for winters in Verbier, frequent vacations, and business trips, he lived the remainder of his life.

Following the publication of *In Cold Blood: A True Account of a Multiple Murder and Its Consequences* (1965), Capote's writing took a back seat to basking in his fame and fortune, traveling, and socializing with the rich and famous, while becoming more and more dependent on drugs and alcohol. He published little else until 1979, when he produced several new pieces that, together with previous publications, were collected in *Music for Chameleons* (1980). For the final two decades of his life, he claimed to be working on his "Proustian" masterpiece, *Answered Prayers*, of which three sections were posthumously published (1987). During his final years, Capote succumbed to what he called his "demons," buttressed by drugs, alcohol, convulsive seizures, and hallucinations. He died on August 25, 1984.

MAJOR MULTICULTURAL THEMES

Capote lists among the authors who influenced him most Gustave Flaubert, Jane Austen, Charles Dickens, Marcel Proust, Anton Chekhov, Katherine Mansfield, E. M. Forster, Ivan Turgenev, and Guy de Maupassant. He especially admired Flaubert's sense of control and his perfectionism, values that manifest themselves in the precision of Capote's own prose style. The spectrum of Capote's broad aesthetic taste is echoed in the multicultural dimensions of his oeuvre, much of which thematically revolves around people, places, and the subject of travel itself. In *The Dogs Bark: Public People and Private Places* (1973), he observed of his first trip to Europe that it enabled him to look at things once again with wonder. He comments on this sense of wonderment in essays that attempt to capture the sense and spirit of "place," pieces devoted to local color and its effects, ranging from locations in the American South to New York and far beyond—Europe, Asia, and Africa. The nine vignettes collected in *Local Color*, for instance, constitute a representative cross-section of places to which he traveled and in which he lived: "New Orleans," "New York," "Brooklyn," "Hollywood," "Haiti," "To Europe," "Ischia," "Tangier," and "A Ride through Spain." Elsewhere he deals with other cultures and other places: a study of Sicily against the backdrop of his rented villa in Taormina, sketches of various islands in the Adriatic along the Yugoslavian coast, and vignettes of cruises to various Greek islands.

Place, however, does not occupy a privileged position as such. Capote often deploys place in the service of configuring a personality defined and demarcated by his or her cultural space. In "House of Flowers," for example, Haiti provides the background for Ottilie, a prostitute in Port-au-Prince, who marries Royal Bonaparte and lives in his "house of flowers," where she suffers torments doled out by her mother-in-law, Old Bonaparte. Similarly, *Music for Chameleons* (written in 1979) portrays a Fort-de-France aristocrat against the backdrop of Martinique.

Capote considered one of his earliest aesthetic influences to be Frederik Mariko, a Japanese florist in New Orleans who made toys as well as flower arrangements that exemplified Japanese culture, perfectly pitched in shape and color. Japanese culture served as the sometimes divergent, sometimes complementary cultural background against which Marlon Brando's portrait emerges in Kyoto. Diverse cultural spaces similarly background the biographical vignettes Capote designed to accompany Richard Avedon's photos in *Observations*, sketches, for example, of Pablo Picasso, Marcel Duchamp, and André Gide.

In *The Muses Are Heard* as well, Capote, exploring political and cultural differences, is less concerned with place as such and more occupied with personalities and situations. Whereas he seems genuinely captivated by and sympathetic to Japanese tradition, his chiefly negative judgments of the Russian people, their politics and culture, are more consonant with the climate of opinion during the early Iron Curtain years.

Beyond the sense of place and personality, Capote's oeuvre frequently engages the subject of travel itself, often in the figure of the traveling subject. His most legendary fictional heroine, Holly Golightly, in *Breakfast at Tiffany's* (1958), does just as the name on her calling card suggests: "Miss Holiday Golightly . . . Traveling.". In her desire to escape to anywhere, she flees the clutches of Sally Tomato's drug syndicate—with operations in Mexico, Cuba, Sicily, Tangier, Tehran, and Dakar—by going to Rio, then to Buenos Aires, thence on to Africa (perhaps), traveling lightly, indeed, and leaving but the barest trace of her final whereabouts, a photograph of an African wood carving that bears a striking resemblance to Holly herself. In his preface to *The Dogs Bark: Public People and Private Places*, Capote considers himself a "Holly," a vagrant, "a planet wanderer." His fiction is populated by many such vagabonds— exotic, unconventional, bizarre—who, in their search for self-knowledge and identity, seek a place in the world. They exceed, necessarily, all sense of boundaries precisely because they are extraordinary and extravagant, and they refuse to be defined. Such tension, structured in the vagabond who seeks to place his or her self, yet cannot be confined to one particular province or region, configures much of the machinery that drives the oeuvre. In the end, the vagabond—whether in the guise of Ottilie in "House of Flowers" or Holly in *Breakfast*—reflects a single, cosmopolitan persona, a multiple personality at odds with himself or herself, crosspurposes deflected in the multicultural currents of an oeuvre signed "Truman Capote." "I move in all worlds," he once remarked (quoted in Long, "In Cold Comfort," 181). In short, Capote, like "Father" Knapp in *A House on the Heights* (1959), is both world traveler and collector of odds and ends. Capote's own passion to collect was provoked, he declared, by the French writer Sidonie-Gabrielle Colette. His travel, too, amassed essays that fashion a cultural collage—one that bears an uncanny resemblance to George Knapp's store: a collection of English brass, Barcelona lamps, French paperweights, Greek icons, Korean cabinets—a jumble, a bricolage of foreign parts.

SURVEY OF CRITICISM

Not surprisingly, perhaps, most Capote criticism addresses his domestic oeuvre, primarily the early fiction (*Other Voices, Other Rooms, The Grass Harp*, etc.) and his "nonfiction novel" *In Cold Blood: A True Account of a Multiple Murder and Its Consequences*. For the most part, critics have remained eerily silent regarding his foreign oeuvre—that is, the travel writing and journalism devoted to other places, people, and cultures. In his definitive biography, Gerald Clarke (1988) examines this latter facet of Capote's oeuvre in passing but is concerned more with the life than with the writing as such. William L. Nance, in *The Worlds of Truman Capote* (1970), likewise seems content to focus on domestic worlds, yielding only several pages to *Local Color*, several to *The Muses Are Heard*, an occasional page to Capote's travel and life abroad—but entirely glossing over the promise that the title of his work holds forth. Jean Mouton (1967) reads *In Cold Blood* in light of André Gide, Paul Claudel, and Albert Camus. The volume edited by Joseph J. Waldmeir and John C. Waldmeir (1999) includes several essays that touch tangentially on multicultural concerns, most notably the chapters by Cecil Brown and John C. Waldmeir, but once again it generally ignores Capote's multicultural concerns.

SELECTED BIBLIOGRAPHY

Works by Capote

Other Voices, Other Rooms. New York: Random House, 1948.
Local Color. New York: Random House, 1950.
The Grass Harp. New York: Random House, 1951.
Capote, Truman, and Harold Arlen. *House of Flowers* (1954). New York: Random House, 1968. [Libretto of short story "House of Flowers" (1951)].
The Muses Are Heard: An Account. New York: Random House, 1956.
Breakfast at Tiffany's. New York: Random House, 1958.
A House on the Heights (1959). New introduction by George Plimpton. New York: Little Bookroom, 2002.
Observations (with Richard Avedon). New York: Simon and Schuster, 1959.
The Innocents (1961). Twentieth Century Fox videocassette. Beverly Hills, Calif.: Fox Video, 1996.
In Cold Blood: A True Account of a Multiple Murder and Its Consequences. New York: New American Library, 1965.
The Dogs Bark: Public People and Private Places. New York: Random House, 1973.
Music for Chameleons. New York: Random House, 1980.
Answered Prayers: The Unfinished Novel. New York: Random House, 1987.

Selected Studies of Capote

Brown, Cecil. "Plat du jour: Soul Food. Truman Capote on Black Culture." In *The Critical Response to Truman Capote*, ed. Joseph J. Waldmeir and John C. Waldmeir, 31–36. Westport, Conn.: Greenwood Press, 1999.
Clarke, Gerald. *Capote: A Biography*. New York: Simon and Schuster, 1988.
Cowley, Malcolm, ed. *Writers at Work: The "Paris Review" Interviews*. New York: Viking, 1958.
Fowles, John. "Capote as Maupassant." *Saturday Review* 7 (July 1980): 52–53.
Garson, Helen S. *Truman Capote*. New York: Frederick Ungar, 1980.
Grobel, Lawrence. *Conversations with Capote*. Foreword by James A. Michener. New York: New American Library, 1985.

Long, Barbara. "In Cold Comfort." *Esquire* 25 (June 1966): 124, 126, 128, 171–3, 175–6, 178–81.

Mouton, Jean. *Littérateur et sang-froid: Un récit véridique de Truman Capote pose des questions au roman.* Paris: Desclee De Brouwer, 1967.

Nance, William L. *The Worlds of Truman Capote.* New York: Stein and Day, 1970.

Reed, Kenneth T. *Truman Capote.* Boston: Twayne, 1981.

Waldmeir, John C. "Religion and Style in *The Dogs Bark* and *Music for Chameleons.*" In *The Critical Response to Truman Capote,* ed. Joseph J. Waldmeir and John C. Waldmeir, 155–66. Westport, Conn.: Greenwood Press, 1999.

Waldmeir, Joseph J., and John C. Waldmeir, ed. *The Critical Response to Truman Capote.* Westport, Conn.: Greenwood Press, 1999.

PAUL CELAN
(1920–1970)
Arta Lucescu Boutcher

BIOGRAPHY

Paul Celan was born Paul Antschel in the town of Czernowitz, which was then considered the capital of Bukovina—a region of Romania. Yet, culturally speaking, his upbringing was Austro-German and Jewish. This combination was not unusual in a city with a population of 100,000 Jews, a city that was then called "Little Vienna" because it had been for many years a province of the Hapsburg monarchy. Celan was brought up speaking High German; he always remembered his mother, Fritzi Antschel, as the person closest to his heart—it was she who introduced her son to the German classics (Friedrich von Schiller, Johann Wolfgang von Goethe, Rainer Maria Rilke, Heinrich Heine) and encouraged his intellectual development. His first poems were written in keeping with the German romantic tradition. His father, Leo Antschel, aimed for a more Orthodox upbringing, an education that Celan continuously resisted. Nevertheless, he was fluent in Hebrew before he spoke Romanian at the state school he attended in 1930.

He was sent to Paris in 1938 to pursue a medical career because Romanian schools were anti-Semitic and imposed quotas for Jews. Once in Paris, Celan became interested in the avant-garde surrealists. He returned to Czernowitz in 1939, where he began to study romance philology. After an overnight visit with friends in June 1942, he returned home only to find both of his parents gone: they had been deported to a concentration camp in Transnistria, Russia, where both died. Scarred for life, Celan forever mourned the death of his parents; nor would he ever forget the years (July 1942 to February 1944) he spent at hard labor in

Romanian camps: in Tăbăreşti (Wallachia), then, closer to Czernowitz, in Piatra-Neamţ and Paşcani, and in Pleşeşti in the western mountains. He once wrote to his best friend, the German Jewish poet Nelly Sachs, that "all things are unforgotten," referring to his experience as a Jew during the Holocaust era and to the loss of his family and his native Czernowitz (Felstiner, *Paul Celan: Poet, Survivor, Jew*, 197). The atrocities that he, his family, and his friends suffered eventually brought on several nervous breakdowns.

Celan left Czernowitz and moved to Bucharest in 1945, where he lived for two years working as a translator and writing poetry (mostly in German and some in Romanian). His friend Petre Solomon, the writer, described this period as a happy one. Because he saw no future in the contemporary era of socialist realism, Celan crossed the Romanian border on foot and managed to escape to Austria in 1947. In Vienna, although his work gained recognition, he sometimes felt misunderstood by his fellow writers; nor was he able to find permanent employment. Therefore, in 1948, just before the publication of his early poems, *Der Sand aus den Urnen*, he moved to Paris, where a period of silence followed (1948–52) during which he wrote very few poems. He married Gisèle de Lestrange in 1952 and a year later their first child, François, was born but survived for only a few days.

After the publication in Stuttgart of his first major collection of poems, *Mohn und Gedächtnis* (1952), written abroad between 1944 and 1952, he continued to write poetry in German, receiving recognition from the Germans who were at the time supporting the effort of young postwar writers. *Von Schwelle zu Schwelle* was published in Paris in 1955 and was dedicated to his wife. Just as for Kafka's character in "Before the Law" (in *Parables and Paradoxes*), the poet's anguish centers around the impossibility of reaching beyond the thresholds of his life in the West. This was the point in his life at which Celan felt that his poetry was misunderstood, and he doubted that he could succeed as a writer in exile.

He received the Literature Prize of the Free Hanseatic City of Bremen in 1958 and was awarded the Georg Büchner Prize, Germany's premier literary award, in 1960. His success as a writer was acknowledged everywhere, to a great extent thanks to the poem "Todesfuge" (in *Mohn und Gedächtnis*), which has been named the *Guernica* of postwar European literature. Depicting Jews forced to play music while their fellow prisoners were digging graves, it presents striking surrealist metaphors associated with death camps, each image reinforced by rhythm and repetition. Indeed, the poem became required reading for young Germans. Many other publications were very well received everywhere in Europe, even though Celan felt that his work had been forgotten and his private life was not faring well. Although a second child was born to the couple and his wife gave Celan her continued support, their marriage fell apart in 1967, contributing to his worsening state of mind.

The first cycle of poems in the collection *Fadensonnen* (1968) had been written in collaboration with his wife, Gisèle, who illustrated them with her own engravings. Created during moments of extreme depression, however, these poems reveal a sense of excoriating loneliness and despair—his writing having crystallized without being able to heal his wounds. Following a visit to Israel in October 1969, where he was warmly welcomed by many Jewish scholars, he returned to Paris and suffered one last mental breakdown: he committed suicide in March 1970.

MAJOR MULTICULTURAL THEMES

Having been raised in a multicultural environment, Celan was a polyglot fluent in German, Hebrew, and Romanian, and later on in Russian and French. After World War II, in 1947, Paul Antschel changed his name to Paul Celan (reversing the second and the first syllables), marking a new beginning in his life as a writer. His real home was to become *the word itself*, and German the language that was to keep him connected to his life in Czernowitz and to his family.

Being a polyglot and a migrant was both a blessing and a misfortune that caused Celan to feel lost and to question his identity; he wished he could return to his native Czernowitz and to the family he had lost forever. However, he never felt disconnected from his Jewishness, and although he claimed his poetry was nonreligious, his verse was often spiritual. The collection of poems entitled *Atemwende* (1967) marks the beginning of his spiritual search and mystical statement in which his breath will turn inward in order to claim that "there are still songs to sing beyond humankind" (*Selected Poems and Prose of Paul Celan*, trans. John Felstiner, 241).

His poetics revolve around many of the newly invented words he created, words as messages that he would send to his readers. He declared that the "poem, being an instance of language, hence essentially dialogue, may be a letter in a bottle thrown out to sea with the—surely not always strong—hope that it may somehow wash up somewhere, perhaps on a shoreline of the heart" ("Speech on the Occasion of Receiving the Literature Prize of the Free Hanseatic City of Bremen," in *Collected Prose*, trans. Rosmarie Waldrop, 34).

The poet's intention in formulating his poetics was to depict reality, and he found a unique way of bringing the truth of the Holocaust years into a present reality; his description "a word—you know a corpse" is revealing in that by calling the word a corpse he transforms verse into a message capable of disclosing all truths about its past (Felstiner, *Paul Celan: Poet, Survivor, Jew*, 149). He could not escape the suffering that marked his youth, and consequently poetry for him became the receiver of this past, a way of life, and his only true home.

In many ways, Celan was a citizen of the twenty-first century: he lived his life in the East, the West, and the South of Europe in a multicultural environment of many languages and people. He also bridged the gap between postwar Germany and the rest of Europe during a period when writing in German, especially by a Jew, was very unpopular. Theodor Adorno criticized Celan for writing beautiful poetry with the Holocaust as a theme—a "barbaric" act for a Jew after Auschwitz. Yet his beautiful poems were, above all, truth embodied in verse, truth about his own past: "something standing in question," as Celan stated while preparing his Bremen acceptance speech (quoted in Felstiner, *Paul Celan: Poet, Survivor, Jew*, 118).

Celan's mentor, Alfred Margul-Sperber, thought that his poetry was comparable to Kafka's writings, and he praised Celan in a letter of introduction as being "the poet of our west-easterly landscape . . . the most original and unmistakable of the recent German generation" (quoted in Felstiner, *Paul Celan: Poet, Survivor, Jew*, 51).

SURVEY OF CRITICISM

John Felstiner's book *Paul Celan: Poet, Survivor, Jew* (1995) is an indispensable work of reference encompassing both Celan's life and his works and demonstrating how they relate to each other. His chronological presentation touches on all the profound issues that make up the alchemy of Celan's poetics: his youth and closeness to his mother, his labor camp experience, his life as a multicultural European citizen, his Jewishness, his married life, his psychological traumas, and, most of all, the sense of loss he felt as a Jew writing in German in a foreign land. The reader also gains a thorough understanding of Celan's poetry, which is analyzed in all of its complexity by connecting it to Celan's real life in a most sensitive way. Felstiner also wrote the introduction to the translations (1955, by Christopher Clark) of Paul Celan's correspondence with Nelly Sachs, illuminating this important relationship. Israel Chalfen (1991) presents Celan's life in Czernowitz and his early years of study in Paris; this work recaptures Celan's youth and how it was changed by the war and the loss of his parents and concludes with Czernowitz and Romania transformed into Celan's alien homeland. Clarise Samuels's *Holocaust Visions: Surrealism and Existentialism in the Poetry of Paul Celan* (1993), a study based on her doctoral dissertation, is a helpful analysis of Celan's work.

Anne Carson's work (1999) is a comparative study of Celan and the ancient Greek lyric poet, Simonides of Keos. Both poets understand that brevity is essential to clarity, and Carson presents them as crafting each word to reproduce the quintessence of their philosophy.

SELECTED BIBLIOGRAPHY

Works by Celan

Der Sand aus den Urnen. Vienna: Sexl, 1948.
Mohn und Gedächtnis. Stuttgart: Deutsche Verlags-Anstalt, 1952.

Von Schwelle zu Schwelle; Gedichte. Stuttgart: Deutsche Verlags-Anstalt, 1955.

Atemwende. Frankfurt am Main: Suhrkamp, 1967. [*Breathturn.* Trans. Pierre Joris. Los Angeles: Sun and Moon Press, 1995.]

Fadensonnen. Frankfurt am Main: Suhrkamp, 1968. [*Threadsuns.* Trans. Pierre Joris. Los Angeles: Sun and Moon Press, 2000.]

Gesammelte Werke in Fünf Bänden. Ed. Beda Alleman and Stefan Reichert. Frankfurt am Main: Suhrkamp, 1983.

Collected Prose. Trans. Rosmarie Waldrop. Manchester, England: Carcanet Press, 1986.

Paul Celan, Nelly Sachs Correspondence. Ed. Barbara Wiedmann. Trans. Christopher Clark. Introduction by John Felstiner. Riverdale-on-Hudson, N.Y.: Sheep Meadow Press, 1995.

101 Poems. Trans. Nikolai Popov and Heather McHugh. Hanover, N.H.: University Press of New England, 2000.

Selected Poems and Prose of Paul Celan. Trans. John Felstiner. New York: W. W. Norton, 2001.

Selected Studies of Celan

Carson, Anne. *Economy of the Unlost: Reading Simonides of Keos with Paul Celan.* Princeton, N.J.: Princeton University Press, 1999.

Chalfen, Israel. *Paul Celan: A Biography of His Youth* (1979). Trans. Maximilian Bleyleben. Introduction by John Felstiner. New York: Persea Books, 1991.

Felstiner, John. *Paul Celan: Poet, Survivor, Jew.* New Haven, Conn.: Yale University Press, 1995.

Samuels, Clarise. *Holocaust Visions: Surrealism and Existentialism in the Poetry of Paul Celan.* Columbia, S.C.: Camden House, 1993.

PATRICK CHAMOISEAU
(1953–)

Kaiama L. Glover

BIOGRAPHY

Patrick Chamoiseau was born in Fort-de-France, Martinique, and continues to live and write there to this day. Aside from a relatively brief stay in Paris, where he studied law, and travels to various other parts of the world, he has essentially remained rooted to his native island. Despite his ostensible insularity, however, this Martinican writer-theorist represents one of the principal promulgators of a multicultural aesthetic to emerge in the Francophone Caribbean during the latter half of the twentieth century.

There does not yet exist any source of extensive biographical information on Patrick Chamoiseau. One must look to the author himself for details of his childhood and young adulthood. More specifically, Chamoiseau's two autobiographical accounts of his early days in Martinique, *Antan d'enfance* (1993) and *Chemin d'école* (1994), reveal much about the period of his life from his very first thoughts on the world around him to his experiences as a young student in the classroom. Writing about himself in the third person, he recounts the most minute recollected details of his early days in Martinique, providing countless anecdotes that emphasize the island's rich Creole culture. These stories, written in a French infused with a distinct vernacular flavor, capture the author's first impressions of the splendor, vibrancy, and mystery of Martinique—its landscape, its culture, and its people. Indeed, Chamoiseau has long been preoccupied by Creole culture and its value with respect to the creation of a Martinican identity. An avid reader of world literatures from a very young age, he constantly found himself frustrated by the fact that none of the authors he admired actually came from Martinique. He quickly became resentful of the cultural lack he perceived in the Caribbean. Where, he wonders in his autobiographical-theoretical work *Écrire en pays dominé* (1997), was he to find a voice that resembled his own—that understood and expressed his vision of the world? Where was he to find a voice that told histories (as opposed to a History), that appreciated the nonlinear temporality of the islands, that recognized identity as fundamentally amalgamated and multicultural?

Chamoiseau first heard this voice in the fictional works of Martinican writer Édouard Glissant. More specifically, Glissant's 1975 novel *Malemort* deeply impressed Chamoiseau and seemed to him the first truly authentic representation of a distinctly Caribbean cosmos. Pursuing the continued expression of this reality has since served as Chamoiseau's primary aesthetic motivation and has become the foundation of his philosophy not only as an artist but also as a citizen of the Francophone Caribbean. As part of this pursuit, Chamoiseau is currently employed as a full-time probation officer in Fort-de-France, working most often with young offenders. The execution of a tangible social role in Martinique has enabled him to maintain a direct connection with the Creole community and has provided him directly and indirectly with the people, places, and situations that appear in his fiction.

MAJOR MULTICULTURAL THEMES

A close look at the fictional and theoretical works of Patrick Chamoiseau indicates clearly that his perspective on both literature and society is fundamentally dedicated to and entirely founded on the expression of a multicultural ideal. In effect, the basic premise of Chamoiseau's socioaesthetic philosophy, the *Créolité* movement, necessarily implies the juxtaposition of and exchange between culturally different populations in the physically restricted island space. According to Chamoiseau, who developed the notion of *Créolité* along with author-theorist Raphaël Confiant and grammarian Jean Bernabé, the brutal confrontation between diverse peoples with distinct and, at times, conflicting beliefs and practices led to the growth of a profoundly syncretic New World culture both in Martinique and throughout the Caribbean.

Convinced that the evolution of the Antillean collective depends primarily on establishing and embracing an authentic Creole identity, Chamoiseau and his collaborators published *Éloge de la créolité* in 1989. This text essentially announces its authors' refusal of exteriority, their rejection of the assumption that Martinican culture is somehow inferior to either European or African culture, the island's principal cultural influences. Chamoiseau and his associates are convinced that Martinicans' unquestioning acceptance of all things European and, more specifically, of all things French, prevents them from discovering their true selves. They contend that the pervasive presence of a "filter of Occidental values" (Bernabé, Chamoiseau, and Confiant, *Éloge de la créolité*, 14) creates an atmosphere of cultural dependence in the Francophone Caribbean and therefore cultivates a sense of collective self-loathing. By the same token, the *négritude*-inspired idealization of the African continent represents an equally counterproductive approach to identity construction. The Creolists maintain that the near-exclusive reliance on an African past for the construction of a present identity is as harmful an illusion as the desire for assimilation to a Franco-European sociopolitical, intellectual, and aesthetic value system.

The Creolist response to such a priori exteriorizing tendencies is simply to acknowledge and embrace a multicultural identity; to promote the "annihilation of false universality, monolingualism and purity" (Bernabé, Chamoiseau, and Confiant, *Éloge de la créolité*, 28). Borrowing heavily from Glissant's philosophy of "relation," Chamoiseau proposes a celebration of Martinique's unique cultural makeup and an exploration of the multiple influences (African, Indian, European, etc.) that define Martinicans on both a collective and an individual level. In effect, he views his island and the Caribbean in general as a veritable melting pot out of which something entirely unique has been created: an intrinsically multicultural—Creole—identity. And, of course, this identity is by no means static. Rather, it must be accepted as pluralized, inclusive, and open-ended. The Creole individual should therefore be understood as a being engaged in a constant struggle toward a more harmonious identity. Chamoiseau's perspective on identity and culture is based, therefore, on a dialogic and at times paradoxical understanding of the world—an understanding that actually finds value in the destabilization, conflict, and even chaos that are inherent to a multicultural environment. He therefore views Martinique and the Caribbean neither as a tragic postcolonial dead end nor as a passive satellite of France. Instead, he perceives his homeland as a rich source of social, aesthetic, and linguistic exchange—an example for the entire world to follow.

Solibo Magnifique (1988) tells the tale of a Creole storyteller and his audience, presenting the at once comic and tragic realities of life in a heteroglossic society. This novel in particular reveals Chamoiseau's approach to the text as a veritable linguistic playground as well as an inherent means of resisting the dominating presence of the French language, imposed on France's former colonies from without.

As the authors of *Éloge de la créolité* so eloquently put it, inhabitants of the Caribbean islands must recognize their culture as "the anticipation of the contact between cultures, already the heralds of the future world . . . a maelstrom of signifieds in one signifier: a Totality" (27). Indeed, for Chamoiseau, this "product and consequence of colonialism" (Burton, "Debrouya pas peche, or il y a toujours moyen de moyenner: Patterns of Opposition in the Fiction of Patrick Chamoiseau," 469) that is the Antilles can and should set the example for an increasingly multi-cultural world.

No other of Chamoiseau's works of fiction provides a better example of the quotidian manifestations of Creole reality in Martinique than his award-winning epic novel *Texaco* (1992). Entirely faithful to the theoretical construction of *Créolité* presented in *Éloge de la créolité*, this novel offers an exhaustive portrait of a profoundly multicultural community. With its polyvocal narrative style and vague temporal structure, it is a veritable mosaic of the Creole universe. The text traces the physical development of the Texaco neighborhood and simultaneously recounts the multiple overlapping (hi)stories that make up this community's History. In describing the origins and evolution of a seemingly banal Martinican shantytown, Chamoiseau succeeds in producing what is at once a richly documented anthropological study and a delicately crafted fiction. The result is a decided tension between the author's preservation of the mystery and magic in this multicultural community and his apparent desire to penetrate and explain as much as possible. Peppered with characters from various social, racial, and ethnic backgrounds, the novel challenges traditionally Occidental notions of individual identity, time, space, and language. Chamoiseau approaches these concepts from a distinctly insular and multicultural perspective, painting an exceptionally detailed picture of an authentic Creole community.

SURVEY OF CRITICISM

Critical work on Patrick Chamoiseau's multiculturalism tends to focus primarily on the author's use of language, arguably one of the most original aspects of his aesthetic strategy. Although a great many of his fictional works are written in French, he is celebrated by numerous theorists for his consistent exploration of the "heteroglossic potential" (Burton, "Debrouya pas peche," 467) of Francophone Caribbean communities. Marie-Agnès Sourieau, in her article "Patrick Chamoiseau, *Solibo Magnifique:* From the Escheat of Speech to the Emergence of Language" (1992), maintains that the composite language employed by Chamoiseau perfectly reflects the composite nature of the Caribbean.

Richard Burton, in his article "Debrouya pas peche, or il y a toujours moyen de moyenner: Patterns of Opposition in the Fiction of Patrick Chamoiseau" (1993), writes extensively on Chamoiseau's fluid movement between "standard" European French, basilectal Creole, and a creolized French or frenchified Creole called the interlect. Burton views this constant switching among linguistic codes as emblematic of the cultural mix Chamoiseau celebrates in his work. Critic Delphine Perret's essays "La parole du conteur créole: *Solibo Magnifique* de Patrick Chamoiseau" (1994) and "Lire Chamoiseau" (1995) focus on the potentially problematic aspects of multilingualism in Chamoiseau's fiction. She poses the question of whether or not a non-Creolophone reader might ever truly access the polysemic vertigo that often results from Chamoiseau's particular brand of multiculturalism. Finally, in *Rayonnants écrivains de la Caraïbe* (1998), Régis Antoine celebrates Chamoiseau's writing style as an effective means of challenging Eurocentric notions of language and culture in the Caribbean.

SELECTED BIBLIOGRAPHY

Works by Chamoiseau

Solibo Magnifique. Paris: Gallimard, 1988. [*Solibo Magnificent.* Trans. Rose-Myriam Réjouis and Val Vinokurov. New York: Pantheon, 1998.]

Bernabé, Jean, Patrick Chamoiseau, and Raphaël Confiant. *Éloge de la créolité.* Paris: Gallimard, 1989.

Texaco. Paris: Gallimard, 1992.

Antan d'enfance. Paris: Gallimard, 1993.

Chemin d'école. Paris: Gallimard, 1994.

Écrire en pays dominé. Paris: Gallimard, 1997.

Selected Studies of Chamoiseau

Antoine, Régis. *Rayonnants écrivains de la Caraïbe: Haiti, Guadeloupe, Martinique, Guyane: Anthologie et analyses.* Paris: Maisonneuve and Larose, 1998.

Burton, Richard D. E. "Debrouya pas peche, or il y a toujours moyen de moyenner: Patterns of Opposition in the Fiction of Patrick Chamoiseau." *Callaloo* 16, no. 2 (1993): 466–81.

Perret, Delphine. "Lire Chamoiseau." In *Penser la créolité*, ed. Maryse Condé et Marie Cottenet-Hage, 153–72. Paris: Karthala, 1995.

———. "La parole du conteur créole: *Solibo Magnifique* de Patrick Chamoiseau." *French Review* 67, no. 5 (April 1994): 824–39.

Sourieau, Marie-Agnès. "Patrick Chamoiseau, *Solibo Magnifique*: From the Escheat of Speech to the Emergence of Language." *Callaloo* 15, no. 1 (1992): 131–37.

Additional Work

Glissant, Édouard. *Malemort: Roman.* Paris: Seuil, 1975.

ANDRÉE CHEDID
(1920–)
Judy Cochran and Anne D. Craver

BIOGRAPHY

Of Lebanese and Syrian descent, Andrée Chedid (née Saab) was born on the banks of the Nile in Cairo, Egypt, where she spent her childhood years, visiting Paris frequently. She became a naturalized citizen of France and has made Paris her home since 1946. She completed her secondary education in Paris, returned to Cairo to study journalism at the American University, and received her undergraduate degree in journalism. After she married Louis Chedid, the couple lived in Beirut for three years before establishing themselves permanently in Paris.

Chedid's distinguished career has bridged French and Middle Eastern cultures for more than half a century. One of the most highly acclaimed authors in the French language today, she is first and foremost a poet, insisting that poetry has always been the wellspring of all her writing. Her poetic works, dating from the 1940s to the present, have been reedited in anthology form. She is also the author of three volumes of short stories, two collections of plays, three short prose works or *récits*, and 11 novels, all of which resonate with her multicultural heritage. Her works have been translated into 15 languages. She is the recipient of numerous prestigious literary awards for both poetry and prose in Europe and the Mediterranean, including the highest award of the Académie Mallarmé for poetry (1976), the Prix Goncourt for the short story (1979), and the Prix Albert Camus for the novel (1996). She received the French Légion d'Honneur title of *commandeur* (2000), and the Académie française bestowed on her the Grand Prix Paul Morand (2001) in recognition of the magnitude and universality of her contribution to French letters.

MAJOR MULTICULTURAL THEMES

Universality is the true hallmark of Andrée Chedid's writing. Whether her poetry and prose reflect landscapes specific to Europe and the Middle East is of less importance than the vision of human solidarity and responsibility the author strives to communicate. Scholar and critic Richard Stamelman suggests that Chedid's poetic reality is not found so much in landscape, but in "le visage," the face of the other ("Le visage triomphant: The Poetry of Andrée Chedid," 32). The repeated image of the primordial or naked face in her poetry is an allusion to our common ancestry as members of the human race. In the verse anthology *Territoires du souffle: Poèmes* (1999), the Face acquires the archetypal force of religious icons: "Le Visage / Régna / Sur toute la creation" (The Face / Reigned / Over all creation) (96). Indeterminable yet incarnate, this image projects the possibility of human perfectibility within the realm of duality, for mortality is one of the fundamental questions to which Chedid continually returns.

War is a constant thread in her work. The collection *Cérémonial de la violence* (1976) may be read as the author's anguished protest against the incessant conflict and destruction in Lebanon at that time. Nicole Trèves suggests a link between the uncharacteristically abrupt and fragmented style of these poems and the dismemberment suffered by the country and its inhabitants ("Andrée Chedid et le geste exemplaire," 86). Novels such as *La maison sans racines* (1985), set in Beirut, and *Le message* (2000), which might take place in Sarajevo or in any city torn by warring factions, illustrate the devastation that results from the desire for dominance in a deadly game where all are victims. In Chedid's work, a poem or short story may contain the seed of a novel, as was the case for *La maison sans racines*, in which the friendship between two young women—Miriam, a Christian, and Ammal, a Muslim, prefigured in the short story "Un jour l'ennemie" (in *Les corps et le temps suivi de L'étroite peau*, 1978)—provides a model of the everyday kinship and understanding that might lead to peace. Thus, Évelyne Accad explains the symbolic death of Sybil, a young girl killed by a sniper's bullet at the end of the novel, as an image of Lebanon, the metaphoric child victimized by war ("Andrée Chedid: Amour et vision," 101).

In Chedid's works, it is characteristically women who, as a result of the suffering and loss they experience during war, join together and exhibit the generosity, initiative, and vision necessary to achieve peace. The play *Les nombres* (1981), based on the Old Testament story of Deborah, illustrates the ideal of the strong yet compassionate woman divided between her sense of obligation to her people along with the attendant necessity to incite them to war and her intrinsic love for humanity, *les nombres*. Bettina Knapp describes Chedid's Deborah as a woman who must assume male responsibilities in a patriarchal society (*Andrée Chedid*, 67). Renée Linkhorn employs the term *feminitude* to denote Chedid's sense of woman's true role as a person who fully assumes her womanhood yet does not make gender a political issue (*The Prose and Poetry of Andrée Chedid: Selected Poems, Short Stories, and Essays*, 6).

Chedid's writing is rooted in the universality of collective memory rather than in the personal and anecdotal. In a 1991 interview with Lebanese critic Alīs Sallūm, she speaks of the genesis of her first novel, an account of the subjugation of Samya, a young Egyptian woman in an arranged marriage: "*Le sommeil délivré* is the actualization of a human cry that lives within me, and perhaps this cry is there to represent the Arab woman's voice. . . . I lived my childhood in Egypt, and I saw examples of this oppressed woman" ("Andrīyah Shadīd: Ṣarkhah fī Wajh Jidār," 30–31). At the source of Andrée Chedid's writing is the concern not for one race or gender over another, but for the spiritual liberation and self-realization of all human beings. Her vision of universality is encapsulated in the title of the collection of poems *Fraternité de la parole* (1976), in which she defines a poetics of fraternity through words that express the commonality of human destiny. Bernard Mazo attributes the universality Chedid voices to her roots in the Near East, a land the author herself describes as a land of earth and poetry ("Andrée Chedid ou l'appétit d'être au monde," 85). Indeed, as the critic Jérôme Garcin declares, Andrée Chedid has chosen the single yet multiple nationality of poetry: "l'écriture de cette femme, qui entre Egypte, Liban et France a choisi la nationalité 'poésie,'—on y entre sans passeport, et on demeure en liberté" (the writing of this woman who, between Egypt, Lebanon, and France, chose the nationality "poetry"—one enters there without a passport and one moves about freely; "Epreuves du vivant," 143).

Universally proclaimed a major voice of our times, Andrée Chedid defies any attempt to confine or contain her. In her world of fraternal words, the *I* of poetry belongs to all.

SURVEY OF CRITICISM

Andrée Chedid's works have been analyzed in the East and the West, in French, Arabic, and English. Both Egypt and Lebanon claim her as their own (see the unsigned articles "Adībah wa-Shaʾirah min Lubnān Taʾīsh fī Bārīs" [1963] and "Andrīyah Shadīd: Min Aʾmāq Adībah Faransīyah Miṣrīyah" [1982]; see also Muḥammad Yūsuf al-Quʾayd, [1988]). Alīs Sallūm (n.d.) remarks that Chedid is "one of the most famous Arab writers who does not write in her native tongue" (44). Egyptian critic Isá Makhlūf (1986) also places Chedid's work within the canon of Arabic literature, and Lebanese journalist Sharbal Dāghir (1995) uses Chedid's own words in summarizing her multiculturalism and insistence on a global identity—one with humanity: "I don't find it necessary to say that my identity is this and nothing else but this—whether it is Lebanese, Egyptian, French, or anything else. I wrote several books, especially novels and short stories, whose main events come from Egyptian or Lebanese history—but I've always strived to look for the universal and humanity in its totality" (16).

Translator and critic Michael Bishop (1995) describes Chedid as "France's most vigorous, accessible and widely read woman poet of the past forty years" (17) and notes that both French and American critics refer to her as "d'origine libanaise, écrivain d'expression française" (109). Whereas in Francophone anthologies she is frequently listed as a Lebanese or Egyptian writer, in anthologies of French literature she is found among other French women writers or contemporary French poets. Scholars such as Jacques Izoard (1977), Bettina Knapp (1984), Renée Linkhorn (1990), and Sergio Villani (1996) reject any classification of her work.

SELECTED BIBLIOGRAPHY

Works by Chedid

Le sommeil délivré. Paris: Stock, 1952. Reprint, Paris: Flammarion, 1976.
Jonathan: Roman. Paris: Seuil, 1955. [Second version entitled *Mon ennemi, mon frère.* Tournai: Casterman, 1982.]
Cérémonial de la violence. Paris: Flammarion, 1976.
Fraternité de la parole. Paris: Flammarion, 1976. Reprinted in *Poèmes pour un texte.* Paris: Flammarion, 1991.
Les corps et le temps suivi de L'étroite peau. Paris: Flammarion, 1978.
Théâtre. Paris: Flammarion, 1981. [Includes *Bérénice d'Egypte, Les nombres, Le montreur.*]
La maison sans racines: Roman. Paris: Flammarion, 1985.
The Prose and Poetry of Andrée Chedid: Selected Poems, Short Stories, and Essays. Trans. and introduction by Renée Linkhorn. Birmingham, Ala.: Summa, 1990.
Selected Poems of Andrée Chedid. Trans. and ed. Judy Cochran. Lewiston, N.Y.: Edwin Mellen Press, 1995.
Lucy: La femme verticale. Paris: Flammarion, 1998.
Territoires du souffle: Poèmes. Flammarion, 1999.
Le message: Roman. Paris: Flammarion, 2000.

Selected Studies of Chedid

Accad, Évelyne. "Andrée Chedid: Amour et vision." In *Des femmes, des hommes et la guerre: Fiction et réalité au proche Orient,* 95–115. Paris: Côté-femmes, 1993.
"Adībah wa-Shāʾirah min Lubnān Taʿīsh fī Bārīs." *al-Anwār* (January 28, 1963): n.p.
"Andrīyah Shadīd: Min Aʿmāq Adībah Faransīyah Miṣrīyah." *Uktūbir* (May 2, 1982): 34–35.
Bishop, Michael. "Andrée Chedid." In *Contemporary French Women Poets: From Chedid and Dohollau to Tellermann and Bancouart,* 1: 17–35. Amsterdam: Rodopi, 1995.
Dāghir, Sharbal. "Shāʾirah wa-Ruwāʾīyah Lubnānīyah wa-Miṣrīyah . . . wa-Bārīsīyat al-Hawá." *al-Ḥayāh* (April 19, 1995): 16.

Garcin, Jérôme. "Epreuves du vivant." *Sud* 94–95 (1991): 143–45.

Izoard, Jacques. *Andrée Chedid.* Paris: Seghers, 1977.

Knapp, Bettina. *Andrée Chedid.* Amsterdam: Rodopi, 1984.

Makhlūf, Isá. "7 Textes pour un chant." *al-Yawm al-sābiʾ* (June 9, 1986): 40.

Mazo, Bernard. "Andrée Chedid ou l'appétit d'être au monde." *Poésie I* 21 (March 2000): 85–92.

al-Qaʾayd, Muḥammad Yūsuf. "Andrīyah Shadīd: Qalamuhā fī Bārīs wa-Qalbuhā fī al-Qāhirah." *al-Muṣawwar* (June 24, 1988): 46–47.

Sallūm, Alīs. "Andrīyah Shadīd: Ṣarkhah fī Wajh Jidār." *al-Dawlīyah* 47 (1991): 30–31.

———. "Andrīyah Shadīd Tataḥaddath ilá 'Kull al-ʿArab': Adabī Yakhfiq bil-Raghbah fī al-Ḥurrīyah." *Kull al-ʿArab* (n.d.): 44–46.

Stamelman, Richard. "Le visage triomphant: The Poetry of Andrée Chedid." *L'Esprit Créateur* 32, no. 2 (Summer 1992): 31–42.

Trèves, Nicole. "Andrée Chedid et le geste exemplaire." *Dalhousie French Studies* 13 (Fall/Winter 1987): 80–88.

Villani, Sergio, ed. *Andrée Chedid: Chantiers de l'écrit.* Woodbridge, Ontario: Albion Press, 1996.

J. M. COETZEE
(1940–)

Diego Saglia

BIOGRAPHY

Born in Cape Town on February 9, 1940, J. M. Coetzee was educated at the University of Cape Town, where he received his first degree in 1960 and his master of arts degree in 1963. Trained as a computer expert and linguist, he initially worked as an applications programmer at IBM in London between 1962 and 1963 and as a systems programmer in 1964–65. Abandoning this career, he entered the academic world, and in 1969 he took a doctor of philosophy degree in literature from the University of Texas at Austin, with a thesis on Samuel Beckett, whom he often quotes as one of the main influences on his own writing. He then taught at the State University of New York, Buffalo, where he began writing his first work of fiction *(Dusklands)* in 1970. Returning to South Africa in 1972, Coetzee joined the faculty of the University of Cape Town, where in 1983 he was appointed professor of general literature. His inaugural lecture, entitled "Truth in Autobiography," was published in 1984.

Coetzee's literary career started in 1974 with the publication of *Dusklands*, two novellas on the attitudes and actions of the Americans in the Vietnam War and of Dutch settlers in eighteenth-century South Africa. He then published *In the Heart of the Country* (1977), filmed in 1986 as *Dust*, the same year that *Foe*, his rewriting of the Robinson Crusoe narrative, was published. *Waiting for the Barbarians* appeared in 1980, and *Life and Times of Michael K* in 1983. Very soon his novels started to receive international recognition: *In the Heart of the Country* was given the Central News Agency (CNA) Award, South Africa's premier literary prize; *Life and Times of Michael K* received the Booker Prize in 1983 and the

French Prix Etranger Fémina in 1985. *Waiting for the Barbarians* received the CNA Award, the Geoffrey Faber Memorial Prize, and the James Tait Black Memorial prize as well. *Age of Iron* (1990) won the 1990 Sunday Express Book of the Year Award; *The Master of Petersburg* (1994) was given the Irish Times International Fiction Prize for 1995. Coetzee received the Lannan Literary Award for Fiction in 1998, and the list of awards culminates with the Nobel Prize for Literature in 2003.

Coetzee is also the author of translations, linguistic studies, and literary criticism such as his collection of essays *White Writing: On the Culture of Letters in South Africa* (1988). He has published a collection of interviews and essays, *Doubling the Point* (1992), and a book of memoirs, *Boyhood: Scenes from Provincial Life* (1997). His novel *Disgrace*, published in 1999, is the tale of a dissatisfied university lecturer who, after being formally reprimanded for a sexual liaison with one of his students, abandons the academic world and joins his daughter on an isolated farm. *Disgrace* won the Booker Prize, thus making Coetzee the only author to have received this award twice.

MAJOR MULTICULTURAL THEMES

The long list of prizes received by Coetzee's novels throws light on the important link between his life in South Africa in the period of apartheid, his literary activity, and his international standing. Indeed, Coetzee has been hailed as both a national and an international literary master. In his own country, he managed to escape censorship, and his novels were never banned by the South African authorities, in part because the censors and their advisors read them as treatments of "universal" themes such as alienation (see McDonald, "'Not Undesirable': How J. M. Coetzee Escaped the Censor"). Interestingly, this generalized reading of Coetzee's works took place at the same time that foreign literary critics were interpreting him as representative of South African culture. These different forms of reception evidence his role as an author intimately connected with his own country, as a writer of contemporary postcolonial literature, and as the author of timeless tales about the human condition.

Coetzee's literary activity starts from a combination of South African experience and the tradition of the European novel, as well as from his background as a language and computer expert. The sign and the contact that communication entails are recurrent preoccupations and perhaps the most visible locations of his peculiar kind of multicultural writing. In his book of "constructed" memoirs, *Boyhood*, Coetzee examines the origins of his fascination with language(s), pointing out his bilingualism and the sense of being an outsider in two cultures (English and Afrikaans) at the same time. His first published work of fiction, *Dusklands*, provides an early example of his interest in the failure of communication and representation. The book comprises two different versions of the imperialist approach to otherness. The first centers on the Vietnam War, telling the story of Eugene Dawn, a psychological warfare expert working for the U.S. State Department, who is driven to murder by his involvement in a project to further U.S. chances of success in the conflict. Dawn's analysis of otherness is an obvious attempt to explain, control, and ultimately destroy an enemy force, yet this attempt brings destruction to himself and his world. Another kind of transcription of the contact with the other is offered by the second novella, narrating the tale of Jacobus Coetzee, an eighteenth-century Boer settler, who undertakes a journey north of the Cape in an attempt to make contact with the local peoples. He later returns to attack and torture these Hottentot tribes because he feels that they have thwarted his imperial project and humiliated him. Contacts with the other are invariably fraught with divides and gaps, and these themes emerge in several of Coetzee's later works.

The idea of the empire and the frontier separating it from the other is nowhere better explained than in *Waiting for the Barbarians*, in which contact with a nameless and faceless "barbarian" enemy is endlessly delayed. The protagonist, the magistrate of a frontier town in an anonymous empire, and other officials constantly look for signs of otherness, of a menacingly hostile difference that, in fact, never materializes. The empire fights a war against invisible enemies, identified with the former inhabitants of the land, while it is actually being eroded from within. In this sense, therefore, the barbarian may be interpreted as the haunting yet never materially available presence of the other. The book also presents, however, very physical images of the contact with otherness, especially the sufferings and tortures inflicted by the imperial authorities, a theme already evident in *Dusklands* and again used in *Foe*. In Coetzee's rewriting of the plot of Daniel Defoe's *Robinson Crusoe*, Friday has no tongue, an absence related to some form of physical violence that once more places the impossibility of contact and communication at center stage. In the novel, a female castaway, Susan Barton, is marooned on Cruso's island and finally succeeds in returning to Britain with him and his black servant Friday. Cruso dies during the voyage, and, once in London, Barton tries to get the writer Foe (Defoe) to write their story. Yet Friday's missing tongue prevents the complete reconstruction of the past and of the encounter between Cruso and Friday, and it is therefore symbolic of the inadequacy of language in establishing or retrieving a contact with otherness.

The difficulty of establishing links between racially different subjects is also one of the central themes of *In the Heart of the Country*, narrated in 266 fragments by Magda, a spinster living on an isolated South African farm with her despotic father. Oscillating between madness and sanity, the protagonist starts to imagine that she must kill her father in order to create relationships and to begin communicating with the other people on the farm, the black servants Hendrik and his wife, Klein-Anna. The murder, however, will have no effect, and Magda's attempt at breaching the gap with the two black servants will fail. The divides investigated by this complex novel are multiple, involving differences of sex, race, class, and family roles. The characters variously cross these gaps but ultimately are unable to bridge them completely by the creation of a communal language.

The idea of the difficulty inherent in establishing communication is also dealt with from a related, though less overtly multicultural, perspective in *Age of Iron*, in which Elizabeth Curren, a classics scholar slowly dying of cancer, writes letters to her daughter, who left South Africa to live in the United States. Here communication is attempted through the epistolary medium and is indicative of public and historical, not just private, implications because the reason for the daughter's emigration is the sociopolitical situation in South Africa; some critics have allegorically read the mother's death as a commentary on the slow death of South Africa's apartheid system.

The victim's point of view is given full scope in *Life and Times of Michael K*, the protagonist of which is both a Kafkaesque figure and a persecuted "Friday" character. Set in an imaginary war-torn South Africa of the future, the novel recounts Michael K's return to the countryside in an attempt to take his mother back to her native region. After his mother's death, he does not go back to the city but remains in the deserted country, finding peace in complete isolation and the absence of repressive systems, history, and civilization. Absence of communication then blooms into a brief idyll when Michael K starts growing fruit near a pool of water on a deserted farm. This interlude is soon brought to an end by the arrival of soldiers who, mistaking him for an enemy, take him back to the city and an internment camp.

The contrast between town and country is also relevant in *Disgrace*, the protagonist of which is, not by coincidence, a literature scholar who has had to recycle himself as a teacher of communication in the reconceived university system of the 1990s. This novel, too, revolves around a shift toward inland South Africa and the need for, the desire for, and the lack of contact. The narrative frequently compares the days of apartheid with a contemporary situation in which languages seem to be useless, and English, in particular, is revealed as a stiff, inadequate instrument of communication. The theme of intercultural contact also emerges in this novel through the relation between the protagonist's daughter, a farmer, and her black handyman, Petrus, who is slowly buying land near her farm and is therefore turning from servant to equal. Animated by the ideal of a new society, the woman tries to create bonds with the man, yet she will be raped by a group of black youths, known to her neighbor and possibly manipulated by him to frighten her away from her land. The crisis following the rape incident marks the end of the timid attempt at integration envisaged by the novel.

Overall, in Coetzee's fiction, the languages and the communication systems of the past are obsolete, whereas the new languages seem unable to create links between divided individuals and cultures. The sign as guarantee of interpersonal and intercultural contact is ineffective. Within this larger agenda, Coetzee's novels play with facts and inventions, oscillate between literalism and allegory, and reinvent cultural myths, such as the castaway (Robinson Crusoe), the frontier, and the desert. His writings confront and reelaborate the European literary tradition (especially Dante, Kafka, Defoe, and Dostoevsky) in an attempt to go beyond the British heritage and in order to overcome the limitations of postcolonial writing. Wary of embracing an exclusively political form of literature, Coetzee constantly seeks to question the generalized enthusiasm for politically self-conscious postcolonial fiction. By contrast, his works denote a form of political engagement tempered by ethical awareness, in the context of a search for new forms of expression of the dialectic of self and other, as well as for new modes of contact between individuals and cultures.

SURVEY OF CRITICISM

Critics have widely read Coetzee's works in the context of South African history, the apartheid system, and its historically located sociocultural divisions (David Attwell [1993] and Susan Gallagher [1991]). At the same time, his novels have been praised for their ability to overcome local issues, projecting them toward more general and universal thematics. His novels therefore have been read as representations of wider phenomena such as colonialism (Stephen Watson [1986]), the writing of otherness (Josephine Dodd [1987]), and empire and the dynamics of imperialism (Michael Moses [1993]). The links between his novels and their most immediate cultural context are constantly examined (Samuel Durrant [1999]), but Coetzee's works have also been the subject of theoretically informed, less openly historicist interpretations, such as Teresa Dovey's (1988) Lacanian readings and Gayatri Spivak's (1991) deconstructive analysis. Finally, several collections of essays have been devoted to Coetzee as one of the most outstanding and influential contemporary writers, gathering important recent critical commentary on his novels and the intellectual dimensions informing his extensive and consistent body of *engagée* literature (Graham Huggan and Stephen Watson [1996] and Michael Moses [1994]).

SELECTED BIBLIOGRAPHY

Works by Coetzee

Dusklands. Johannesburg: Ravan Press, 1974.
In the Heart of the Country. Johannesburg: Ravan Press; London: Secker and Warburg, 1977.
Waiting for the Barbarians. London: Secker and Warburg, 1980.
Life and Times of Michael K. London: Secker and Warburg, 1983.
Truth in Autobiography. Cape Town: University of Cape Town, 1984.
Foe. London: Secker and Warburg, 1986.
White Writing: On the Culture of Letters in South Africa. New Haven, Conn.: Yale University Press, 1988.
Age of Iron. London: Secker and Warburg, 1990.

Doubling the Point: Essays and Interviews. Cambridge, Mass.: Harvard University Press, 1992.

The Master of Petersburg. London: Secker and Warburg, 1994.

Giving Offense: Essays on Censorship. Chicago: University of Chicago Press, 1996.

Boyhood: Scenes from Provincial Life. London: Secker and Warburg, 1997.

Disgrace. London: Secker and Warburg, 1999.

Selected Studies of Coetzee

Attwell, David. *J. M. Coetzee: South Africa and the Politics of Writing.* Berkeley: University of California Press, 1993.

Dodd, Josephine. "Naming and Framing: Naturalization and Colonization in J. M. Coetzee's *In the Heart of the Country.*" *World Literature Written in English* 27 (1987): 153–61.

Dovey, Teresa. *The Novels of J. M. Coetzee: Lacanian Allegories.* Johannesburg: Ad Donker, 1988.

Durrant, Samuel. "Bearing Witness to Apartheid: J. M. Coetzee's Inconsolable Works of Mourning." *Contemporary Literature* 40 (1999): 430–63.

Gallagher, Susan Van Zanten. *A Story of South Africa: J. M. Coetzee's Fiction in Context.* Cambridge, Mass.: Harvard University Press, 1991.

Head, Dominic. *J. M. Coetzee.* Cambridge, England, and New York: Cambridge University Press, 1998.

Hoegberg, David. " 'Where Is Hope?': Coetzee's Rewriting of Dante in *The Age of Iron.*" *English in Africa* 25 (1998): 27–42.

Huggan, Graham, and Stephen Watson, eds. *Critical Perspectives on J. M. Coetzee.* London: Macmillan, 1996.

McDonald, Peter D. " 'Not Undesirable': How J. M. Coetzee Escaped the Censor." *Times Literary Supplement* (May 19, 2000): 14–15.

Moses, Michael Valdez. "The Mark of Empire: Writing, History, and Torture in Coetzee's *Waiting for the Barbarians.*" *Kenyon Review* 15 (1993): 115–27.

———. *The Writings of J. M. Coetzee.* Special issue, *South Atlantic Quarterly* 93, no. 1 (Winter 1994).

Penner, Dick. *Countries of the Mind: The Fiction of J. M. Coetzee.* New York: Greenwood Press, 1989.

Spivak, Gayatri Chakravorty. "Theory in the Margin: Coetzee's *Foe* Reading Defoe's *Crusoe/Roxana.*" In *Consequences of Theory: Selected Papers from the English Institute, 1987–88,* ed. Jonathan Arac and Barbara Johnson, 154–80. Baltimore: Johns Hopkins University Press, 1991.

Watson, Stephen. "Colonialism and the Novels of J. M. Coetzee." *Research in African Literatures* 17 (1986): 370–92. [Reprinted in Huggan, Graham, and Stephen Watson, eds. *Critical Perspectives on J. M. Coetzee.* London: Macmillan, 1996.]

MARYSE CONDÉ
(1937–)

Anne Mullen Hohl

BIOGRAPHY

A prolific multicultural author of novels, short stories, plays, and critical essays, Maryse Condé has been acclaimed worldwide, and her works have been translated into many languages. In the course of her studies and career, she has traveled, lived, and worked in numerous countries, including her homeland Guadeloupe, the Ivory Coast, Ghana, Guinea, Mali, Senegal, Jamaica, France, England, and the United States. All four of her children, whose father was Guinean, were born in African countries, and the characters and locales of her novels and stories are drawn from diverse peoples and cultures of Africa, the Caribbean, Europe, and the Americas.

She is the youngest child of middle-class Guadeloupean parents who refused to allow their children to socialize with poor blacks, mulattoes, or whites, leaving the bored Maryse to take refuge in the French literature of her father's library. Because Guadeloupe is a French Overseas Department, she received a French colonial education in which French was the language of instruction and the study of history and geography was focused on France. The concomitant lack of instruction in Guadeloupean affairs is a recurring theme in some of her works: *La civilisation du Bossale: Réflexions sur la littérature orale de la Guadeloupe et de la Martinique* (1978); *La vie scélérate* (1987), a fictional rendering of the history of generations of the Condé family; and *Traversée de la Mangrove: Roman* (1989). She has also been stimulated to educate the children of Guadeloupe by writing books for them, notably *Haïti chérie: Une histoire* (1991), that have both informed and delighted her younger readers and older ones as well.

Given the social constraints of her upbringing, Condé understandably considered her voyage to Paris at the age of 16 to study at the Lycée Fénélon to be one of freedom and liberation, but it also entailed the notion of permanent exile, or nomadism, a dominant theme in her experience and writing (e.g., *Hérémakhonon*, 1976; *Ségou: Roman*, vol. 1, *Les murailles de terre*, 1984, and vol. 2, *La terre en miettes*, 1985; and *Desirada: Roman*, 1997). At the lycée, she confronted virulent racism when one instructor continually pitted her against a Senegalese classmate, the school's only other black student. She also learned about African colonization and decolonization from a lycée schoolmate (whose father was a Marxist historian at the Sorbonne), who also introduced her to the writings of Aimé Césaire and Frantz Fanon. Condé subsequently enrolled at the Sorbonne, where she earned a *licence* in English and a *demi-licence* in classics.

In Paris, Condé's sense of liberation from her Guadeloupean upbringing was tempered by her feeling of alienation, another recurrent theme in her fiction (*Hérémakhonon* and *Une saison à Rihata: Roman*, 1981). This alienation was partially dissipated, however, during her student days at the Sorbonne when, through writers she met from Africa and other Caribbean islands, she discovered ways of being black that she had not known in Guadeloupe, and she acquired a lifelong interest in the black diaspora. Thus, her journey to Paris ultimately became a voyage of discovery of African cultures.

After a year of teaching in the Ivory Coast (1960), she rejoined her husband in Guinea in 1961. Her initial encounter with that culture was euphoric, resulting in her first novel, the brilliant *Hérémakhonon*. But political repression and the deterioration of her first marriage impelled her to leave Guinea in 1964. She moved with her children to Ghana, where she taught French, worked with teams of colleagues on textbooks for postcolonial Ghana, and met Kwame Nkrumah and other revolutionary leaders. Condé left Ghana for London with her children in 1966 to work at the BBC's foreign desk on programs in French beamed to Africa, for which she reviewed contemporary aspects of African culture. About two years later, she moved to Senegal, translating at first and later teaching at schools in Saint Louis and Kaolack, where she met the Englishman Richard Philcox, who later became her second husband. Before long, however, she concluded that Africa held no future for her. She returned to Paris in 1970, where she completed a thesis in comparative literature on stereotypical representation of blacks in West Indian literature, while also working for *Présence Africaine* and for *Radio France Internationale*. She held a series of positions as a university lecturer, teaching African and West Indian literature, and traveled periodically to the United States to lecture on Francophone literature. In 1978, she began her teaching in the United States at universities including Virginia and California-Berkeley. She is currently a professor of French and chair of the Center for Francophone Studies at Columbia University. The first woman to become a Puterbaugh Fellow at the University of Oklahoma, she is also the recipient of a Fulbright grant to teach in the United States, a Guggenheim Fellowship, the Grand Prix Littéraire de la Femme (1986), and the Prix de l'Académie Française (1988).

MAJOR MULTICULTURAL THEMES

At the core of Condé's multiculturalism, in both her scholarly writing and fiction, are exile, alienation, and slavery, the latter necessarily implying the brutal imposition of one or more foreign cultures on an original one. The violent nature of slavery is dramatically fictionalized in *Moi, Tituba, sorcière . . . noire de Salem: Roman* (1986), in which the first paragraph provides a striking metaphor for the rape of the Caribbean in the rape of Tituba's Ashanti mother, Abena, on the way to Barbados. Tituba, who becomes a slave to remain with the man she loves, John Indian, will end up in Salem in a totally foreign culture that rejects her Barbadian culture and healing powers and tries her as a witch.

Slavery is the subtext of *Hérémakhonon* and informs *Ségou*, a historical fiction of the Bambara civilization in the ancient kingdom of Mali that reveals the existence of slavery in precolonial Africa. The confrontation of the polytheistic animist civilization of the Bambaras with Islamic culture and religion effectively overwhelms the Bambara culture, easing the way for French colonization and the arrival of Christian missionaries. The toll of conflict, resistance, and ultimate accommodation extracted from the original Bambara culture by successive invasions of Islamic and French cultures has absorbed Condé's attention. In *Ségou*, she traces the lives of the descendants of Dousika Traoré, the founding father of a ruling Bambara family, whose son is sold into slavery and in the black diaspora is exiled as far away as Brazil. Just as Traoré's own slaves are exiled from their native cultures, so will his sons: Naba, as a slave, will be exiled and demeaned as the Other, and Tiékoro, as a convert to Islam, will also be treated as the Other.

For an Antillean, the journey back to Africa implies a search for origins lost through slavery and colonization. The quest for origins is at the heart of *Hérémakhonon*, in which the Guadeloupean protagonist, Véronica, seeks legitimacy in the arms of an African prince of authentic ancestry. Legitimacy is also a leitmotiv of Guadeloupean and Martinican tales. In *La civilisation du Bossale: Réflexions sur la littérature orale de la Guadeloupe et de la Martinique*, Condé shows how African riddles, tales, and proverbs that are transmitted by the "Bossale," or first generation of African slaves, constitute the basis of riddles, tales, and proverbs later translated into French in Guadeloupe and Martinique.

It has been said that Condé's search for African origins ends with *Ségou*. The preoccupation clearly endures, however, in her discussions of *Créolité*, or "creoleness"—cultural and linguistic mingling. She speaks of the different ways for a writer to be Creole, particularly in her 1993 interview with Françoise Pfaff *(Entretiens avec Maryse Condé)* and in her edited work *Penser la créolité* (coedited with Madeleine Cottenet-Hage, 1995), but she warns of the tendency of "creoleness" to reduce African origins to only one of many elements of Caribbean cultural heritage, thereby diminishing the significance of the sugarcane plantation culture and the history of slavery.

Just as Condé the writer has traveled through continents, so her characters come from cultures around the globe. In *Hérémakhonon*, the protagonist leaves Guadeloupe for Paris and Africa. The destiny of the Guadeloupean Marie-Hélène in *Une saison à Rihata* is played out in Africa. In *Ségou*, Naba ends up in Brazil, and his son Eucaristus goes to England to study for the ministry. *Moi, Tituba* takes place largely in the United States, but also in Barbados; *La vie scélérate* unfolds mainly in Guadeloupe but also develops in Jamaica, Panama, and the United States; *Desirada* and *Les derniers rois mages* (1992) are set in Guadeloupe and the United States; *Célanire Cou-coupé: Roman fantastique* (2000) in Guadeloupe and Africa; *La migration des coeurs: Roman* (1995) in Guadeloupe; and *La colonie du nouveau monde* (1993) largely in Colombia. *Traversée de la Mangrove* in principle is rooted in Guadeloupe, but the cast of characters is multicultural: Colombian, Cuban, East Indian, and Haitian. Similarly multicultural are the casts in Condé's short stories (e.g., *Pays-mêlé*, 1985, featuring the legendary Maroon Jamaican, Nanna-ya) and in her plays (e.g., *Pension les Alizés: Pièce en cinq tableaux*, 1988, with roles for a Haitian doctor and a Guadeloupean singer and dancer).

SURVEY OF CRITICISM

Three of Condé's numerous interviews are particularly valuable for their recording of the initial critical reception of her work and her struggle to combat and overcome misinterpretations: Françoise Pfaff's (1993); Vèvè Clark's (1989); and Emily Apter's (2001), in which *Hérémakhonon* is praised as both postmodern and diaspora literature before its time, although it initially received either little notice (in France) or condemnation (in Africa and the West Indies).

Leah Dianne Hewitt (1990) shows the connections between life, fiction, and the quest for ancestral African legitimacy in *Hérémakhonon*. Hewitt (1996) also explores the iconoclastic aspect of Condé's writing and her interest in cosmopolitan cross-sections of multiethnic societies: the cultural intertwining of the individual Antillean islands and the rest of the world, whether influenced by past shared cultures or by the multicultural characteristic of postmodern societies. Françoise Lionnet (1996) describes the linguistic *métissage* involved in the creative use of French to represent the plural ethnic and linguistic character of Creole cultures and sees *Traversée de la Mangrove* as undoing the old colonial and postcolonial dichotomies.

Christopher Miller (1996) notes that Condé debunks the myth of the return of the diaspora to Africa in *Hérémakhonon* and *Une saison à Rihata*, and he shows how her vision of Africa becomes increasingly historicized and politicized in the latter novel, laying the foundation for her historical saga *Ségou*, which, together with *Moi, Tituba*, demonstrates a reworking through history of the dispersed strands of the black diaspora.

Arlette M. Smith (1989) delineates the theme of exile in Condé's work and its concomitant alienation and shows how the metaphor of the (lost) mother substitutes the mother for the motherland, an idea expertly developed by Simone A. James Alexander (2001). As Condé's characters are condemned to perpetual wandering, so Condé herself concludes that nomadism is the ideal modus vivendi for the creativity of a writer who needs to feel at home but is at home nowhere—in the same way that the author's language must always in some sense be that of an outsider—a *langue étrangère*.

SELECTED BIBLIOGRAPHY

Works by Condé

Hérémakhonon. Paris: Union Générale d'Editions, 1976. Reprinted as *En attendant le bonheur (Hérémakhonon): Roman*. Paris: Seghers, 1988. [*Heremakhonon: A Novel*. Trans. Richard Philcox. Washington, D.C.: Three Continents Press, 1982.]

La civilisation du Bossale: Réflexions sur la littérature orale de la Guadeloupe et de la Martinique. Paris: L'Harmattan, 1978.

Une saison à Rihata: Roman. Paris: Robert Laffont, 1981. [*A Season in Rihata*. Trans. Richard Philcox. London: Heinemann, 1988.]

Ségou: Roman. Vol. 1, *Les murailles de terre*. Paris: Robert Laffont, 1984. [*Segu*. Trans. Barbara Bray. New York: Viking Penguin, 1987; New York: Ballantine, 1988.]

Ségou. Vol. 2, *La terre en miettes*. Paris: Robert Laffont, 1985. [*The Children of Segu*. Trans. Linda Coverdale. New York: Viking Penguin, 1989; New York: Ballantine, 1990.]

Pays-mêlé; suivi de Nanna-ya. Paris: Hatier, 1985.

Moi, Tituba, sorcière . . . noire de Salem: Roman. Paris: Mercure de France, 1986. [*I, Tituba, Black Witch of Salem*. Trans. Richard Philcox. Charlottesville: University Press of Virginia, 1992.]

La vie scélérate. Paris: Seghers, 1987. [*Tree of Life*. Trans. Victoria Reiter. New York: Ballantine, 1992.]

Pension les Alizés: Pièce en cinq tableaux. Paris: Mercure de France, 1988. [*The Tropical Breeze Hotel*. Trans. Barbara Brewster Lewis and Catherine Temerson. In *Plays by Women: An International Anthology*, book 2, 113–64. New York: Ubu Repertory Theater, 1994.]

Traversée de la Mangrove: Roman. Paris: Mercure de France, 1989. [*Crossing the Mangrove*. Trans. Richard Philcox. New York: Anchor Books/Doubleday, 1995.]

Haïti chérie: Une histoire. Paris: Bayard, 1991.

Les derniers rois mages: Roman. Paris: Mercure de France, 1992.

La colonie du nouveau monde: Roman. Paris: Robert Laffont, 1993.

"Order, Disorder, Freedom, and the West Indian Writer." *Yale French Studies* 83, no. 2 (1993): 121–35.

La migration des coeurs: Roman. Paris: Robert Laffont, 1995.

Penser la créolité. Ed. Maryse Condé and Madeleine Cottenet-Hage. Paris: Karthala, 1995.

Desirada: Roman. Paris: Robert Laffont, 1997.

Célanire Cou-coupé: Roman fantastique. Paris: Robert Laffont, 2000.

La belle Créole: Roman. Paris: Mercure de France, 2001.

Selected Studies of Condé

Alexander, Simone A. James. *Mother Imagery in the Novels of Afro-Caribbean Women*. Columbia: University of Missouri Press, 2001.

Apter, Emily. *Crossover Texts/Creole Tongues: A Conversation with Maryse Condé*. Durham, N.C.: Duke University Press, 2001.

Clark, Vèvè. "Developing Diaspora Literacy: Allusion in Maryse Condé's *Hérémakhonon*." In *Out of the Kumbla: Caribbean Women and Literature*, ed. Carole Boyce Davies and Elaine Savory Fido, 303–19. Trenton, N.J.: Africa World Press, 1990.

———. "Je me suis réconciliée avec mon île: Une interview de Maryse Condé / I Have Made Peace with My Island: An Interview with Maryse Condé." *Callaloo* 12, no. 1 (1989): 86–132.

Hewitt, Leah Dianne. "Meditations of Identity through the Atlantic Triangle: Maryse Condé's *Hérémakhonon*." In *Autobiographical Tightropes: Simone de Beauvoir, Nathalie Sarraute, Marguerite Duras, Monique Wittig, and Maryse Condé*, 159–90. Lincoln: University of Nebraska Press, 1990.

———. "Recontres explosives: Les intersections culturelles de Maryse Condé." In *L'oeuvre de Maryse Condé*, 45–56. Actes du Colloque sur l'oeuvre de Maryse Condé, organisé par le Salon du Livre de la ville de Point-à-Pitre (Guadeloupe), March 14–18, 1995. Paris: L'Harmattan, 1996.

Lionnet, Françoise. *Autobiographical Voices: Race, Gender, Self-Portraiture*. Ithaca, N.Y.: Cornell University Press, 1989.

———. " 'Logiques métisses': Cultural Appropriation and Postcolonial Representations." In *Postcolonial Subjects: Francophone Women Writers*, ed. Mary Jean Green, Karen Gould, Micheline Rice-Maximin, and Keith L. Walker, 321–43. Minneapolis: University of Minnesota Press, 1996.

Miller, Christopher. "After Negation: Africa in Two Novels by Maryse Condé." In *Postcolonial Subjects: Francophone Women Writers*, ed. Mary-Jean Green, Karen Gould, Micheline Rice-Maximin, and Keith L. Walker, 173–85. Minneapolis: University of Minnesota Press, 1996.

Ngate, Jonathan. "Maryse Condé and Africa: The Making of a Recalcitrant Daughter?" *A Current Bibliography on African Affairs* 19, no. 1 (1986–87): 5–20.

Pfaff, Françoise. *Entretiens avec Maryse Condé*. Paris: Karthala, 1993. [*Conversations with Maryse Condé*. Trans. Françoise Pfaff. Lincoln: University of Nebraska Press, 1996.]

Smith, Arlette M. "The Semiotics of Exile in Maryse Condé's Fictional Works." *French Review* 62, no. 1 (1989): 50–58.

JORGE DE SENA
(1919–1978)

António Fournier

BIOGRAPHY

A deep love-hate relationship bound Jorge de Sena to Portugal and Portugal to him. When for political reasons (he had participated in the so-called Conspiraçao da Sé, the failed coup against the dictatorship of António de Oliveira Salazar) he fled his country in 1959 and went to Brazil in voluntary exile, he left behind a series of defining ideas.

An only son without childhood friends, the young Jorge was encouraged to read from the age of three by his mother and especially by his maternal grandmother, without his father's knowledge. By the age of 10, he had already devoured an enormous number of books, including French ones. His father, a captain in the merchant navy, wanted his son to take up the same career; accordingly, the 18-year-old Jorge had his first experience abroad on the school ship *Sagres*, visiting the Canary Islands, Cabo Verde, São Tomé, Principe, and also Angola and Brazil, all places found again in his short stories *Os grão-capitães: Una sequencia de contos* (1976). But he abandoned his career after a disappointing experience on the ship.

Influenced by the music of Claude Debussy and by the poems of the Portuguese poet Teixeira de Pascoães, de Sena had begun writing poems at the age of 16, producing thereafter several volumes of published poetry. He also published a series of short stories, *Novas andanças do Demónio*, in 1960, but he had started very early to experiment with narrative techniques inspired by medieval legends, fairytales, fiction for young readers, comic strips, and motion-picture narration.

He had studied civil engineering in Porto in 1944 and had collaborated in the planning of Lisbon's landmark "April 25th" suspension bridge.

Even then he was already known for his intellectual and political work in the humanities and in the anti-Fascist movement, for his own poetry as well as his translations of other poets, for his contributions as theater and literary critic to the pages of the journals *Diario Popular* and *O Comércio do Porto*, and for his lectures around the country.

After his first captivating visit to England in 1952, he regularly visited both the United Kingdom and Portugal on his European tours (every year from 1971 to 1977). His *História geral da literatura inglesa* (1963) and the various monographs he wrote on William Shakespeare, T. S. Eliot, and on the English novel testify to his deep interest in English culture. In exile in Brazil, he taught English literature as a university professor.

Although he became a naturalized citizen of his adopted country in 1963, he went into exile once again for political reasons (Brazil fell under a rightist military dictatorship in 1964), this time to the United States, where he taught first at the University of Wisconsin (1965) and then at the University of California in Santa Barbara (1970). His home in Santa Barbara rapidly became a gateway for visiting Portuguese intellectuals and a temple of studies where his American students could further their interests and deepen their intellectual relationship with their professor even off campus. His American academic career finally offered the conditions that allowed him to dedicate himself to the world of letters.

He was fascinated, too, by Spanish culture, as shown in various comparative essays and poems and also in the unfinished novel *Sinais de fogo: Romance*, published posthumously in 1978, which may be seen as both private and public testimony on Fascist Portugal at the beginning of the Spanish civil war. In the last period of his life, he turned his attention to Italy, forming a friendship with the Italian poet Carlo Vittorio Cattaneo, who translated de Sena's *Exorcismos* (1972) into Italian in 1974 and was instrumental in having the Etna-Taormina, Sicily's international prize for poetry, awarded to de Sena in 1977.

De Sena spent the last 19 years of his life in exile, visiting Portugal in 1968 (when, before leaving the country, he was briefly arrested by the Portuguese political police at the Spanish border); and in 1971 (at the time of the deceptively called *primavera marcelista* during the premiership of Marcello Caetano, 1968–74). Yearly pilgrimages followed, but he never really returned to his home country, not even after the democratic revolution of April 1974, when he must have wished to do so. Instead, from abroad, he continued raising his provocative voice to express his visceral resentment of the provincialism of so many Portuguese intellectuals (*O reino da estupidez*, 1961, *Peregrinatio ad loca infecta*, 1969, and *Exorcismos* are intentionally iconoclastic books). He must have fed hatreds and rivalries in Portugal. Having himself won international prestige by openly, ironically, and uncompassionately refusing intellectual mediocrity, he created around himself the aura of a prodigal son. Perhaps this is the reason why it was not possible to realize the conditions for a final return to his country and acceptance in Portugal's universities as an eminently qualified professor.

He wrote his essays, fiction, poems, and plays in the Portuguese language, with the memory of Portugal as the homeland and bitterness in his heart, as we see in the poem that symbolizes his condition of exile, "Em Creta com o Minotauro" (in *Poesia III*, 1978). Although in some way foreignized, his writing always creates a virtual Portuguese reader, as demonstrated by the fact that he never chose to write in English and by the fact that his books continued to be published in Portugal, although he lived in exile. Even in absentia, Jorge de Sena cast an intellectual shadow that loomed large in Portuguese literature, and in that respect it is as if he had never left the country.

He died of cancer at the age of 58; his tomb is in the Calvary cemetery of Santa Barbara, California.

MAJOR MULTICULTURAL THEMES

The taste for adventure and the compulsive wanderings that mark de Sena's obviously autobiographical works have already prompted the question whether exile was not really his deep desire and above all a pretext to abandon his unsophisticated country.

His literary universe is multifaceted. A self-taught, pluralistic, and multicultural writer, de Sena mixed different territories of thought, arts, and letters, which is even more remarkable in the light of Portugal's isolation and backwardness at the time. This is shown also by the different intersemiotic processes that he began as a scientific, cosmogonic, and metaphysical codex (see Torres, *O código científico-cosmogónico-metafísico de "Perseguição," 1942, de Jorge de Sena*)—the fruit of his scientific studies and visible in the poems of *Perseguição* (1942), as well as in the dialogue between poetry and music that always attracted him (*Arte de música, trinta e duas metamorfoses musicais e um prelúdio, seguidos de um pot-pourri*, 1968), or in the varied *ekphrasis* of aesthetic objects from the world of painting and architecture, synthesized in his poetry and best exemplified in some of the poems of *Metamorfoses, seguidas de Quatro sonetes a Afrodite Anadiómena* (1963). But he was also clearly influenced by the works of philosophers such as Baruch Spinoza, Georg Wilhelm Friedrich Hegel, Immanuel Kant, Plato, Plotinus, René Descartes, Blaise Pascal, Gottfried Wilhelm Leibnitz, and Miguel de Unamuno. The amplitude of his cultural interests is shown by his innumerable translations, especially from English, but also of the Greek poet Constantine Cavafy, whom he introduced to Portuguese readers. He also translated works by André Malraux, Bertolt Brecht, Molière, Eugene O'Neill, Edgar Allan Poe, Graham Greene, Ernest Hemingway, William Faulkner, and, above all, Emily Dickinson and the English verse of the Portuguese poet Fernando Pessoa. Mention also must be made of the ambitious (sometimes referred to as megalomaniac) two-volume anthology de Sena compiled under the title *Poesia de vinte e seis séculos: Antologia* (vol. 1, *De Arquíloco a Calderón*, and vol. 2, *De Bashō a Nietzsche*, 1971–72), in which are gathered, in his translations, the classical poets of the entire world.

Though de Sena loved the literatures of many countries, it must be emphasized that much of what he wrote should be considered as a dialogue with another Portuguese poet—one who had known, well before him, the bitter taste of exile, a poet with whom he identified and on whose poetry he modeled his own lyric voice: Luís Vaz de Camões, Portugal's greatest poet, the author of the epic *Os Lusíadas* (1572). One of de Sena's lifelong dreams had been to know all the places where traces of a previous Portuguese presence could be found. Surely one of his most moving visits (1972) must have been to Mozambique, where Camões spent two years of his tormented life and where de Sena was inspired to write the beautiful poem "Camões na Ilha de Moçambique" (1973). Camões's work inspired more than 20 of de Sena's poems as well as his short story "Super flumina Babylonis" (1973), based on a well-known sonnet by the sixteenth-century poet. Quite strikingly, moreover, in de Sena's 1962 pseudo interview with Camões published in the newspaper *Estado de S. Paulo* and in a speech ("Discurso da Guarda") pronounced at Guarda (Portugal) during Camões celebrations in 1977, it was difficult to discern whether de Sena was speaking about Camões, the poet exiled and forgotten by his contemporaries, or about himself.

SURVEY OF CRITICISM

The first volume of studies dedicated to Jorge de Sena, edited by Eugénio Lisboa, appeared in Portugal in 1984; it brings together unpublished interviews and old articles. The following year, the Italian journal *Quaderni portoghesi* published a monographic issue on de Sena's work, edited by Luciana Stegagno Picchio (1985). The twentieth anniversary of de Sena's death (1998) triggered new interest in him, although to date few monographic studies have been devoted to his work. Helder Macedo (1999) reminds us that today, almost 25 years after his death, "the studies on Jorge de Sena have entered a healthy adolescence" (135).

The alleged hermeticism of de Sena's early production caused perplexities in many Portuguese literary critics of the 1940s who were still under the influence of symbolist and romantic models of the nineteenth century. But his intellectual and ironic poems (most likely from T. S. Eliot's influence), more conceptual than philosophical, more intelligent than sensual, and openly critical of the idea of sentiment as a poetical matrix, today occupy a privileged place in the canon of Portuguese letters. Eduardo Lourenço (1985) refers to de Sena's poems as "provocação ética" (26); Fàtima Morna (1985) detects signs of experimentalism and surrealistic influences; Luís Adriano Carlos (1983) discusses the testimonial aspect of de Sena's poetry that includes the "mythic dimension of emigration and exile" (248). Nikita Talan (1996) studies the religious-metaphysical dimension of his poems, and Paula Gândara (1999) and Francisco Cota Fagundes (1999) discuss the theme of exile, the former seeking its signs in the texture of his poems, and the latter analyzing the return from exile. Óscar Lopes (1986) concentrates on the "art of music" in de Sena, and Fernanda Conrado (2000) studies *ekphrasis* in his poetic production.

In the United States, a group of his former students created the Jorge de Sena Center for Portuguese Studies, which is very active in Santa Barbara today. *Studies on Jorge de Sena*, the published papers of a 1979 colloquium in memory of de Sena, edited by Harvey L. Sharrer and Frederick G. Williams (1981), focuses on his oeuvre and its place in Portuguese literature.

SELECTED BIBLIOGRAPHY

Works by de Sena

Perseguição: Poemas. Lisbon: Edições Cadernos de Poesia, 1942.

Novas andanças do Demónio. Lisbon: Estúdios Cor, 1960.

O reino da estupidez. Lisbon: Livraria Morais, 1961.

História geral da literatura inglesa. São Paolo: Cultrix, 1963. Revised ed. published as *A literatura inglêsa; ensaio de interpretaçâo e de história.* Ed. Mécia de Sena. Lisbon: Cotoria, 1989.

Metamorfoses, seguidas de Quatro sonetos a Afrodite Anadiómena, e com um postfácio e notas do autor. Lisbon: Livraria Morais, 1963. [*Metamorphoses.* Trans. Francisco Cota Fagundes and James Houlihan. Providence, R.I.: Copper Beech Press, 1991.]

Novas andanças do Demónio. Lisbon: Portugaia, 1966.

Arte de música, trinta e duas metamorfoses musicais e um préludio, seguidos de um potpourri. Lisbon: Livraria Morais, 1968.

Peregrinatio ad loca infecta. Lisbon: Portugália, 1969.

90 e mais quatro poemas de Constantino Cavafy. Trans. and ed. Jorge de Sena. Porto: Inova, 1970.

Poesia de vinte e seis séculos: Antologia. Vol. 1, *De Arquíloco a Calderón;* vol. 2, *De Bashō a Nietzsche.* Trans. and ed. Jorge de Sena. Porto: Inova, 1971–72.

Exorcismos. Lisbon: Moraes, 1972. [*Esorcismi.* Trans. and ed. Carlo Vittorio Cattaneo. Milan: Accademia, 1974.]

"Super flumina Babylonis" (1973). In *Antigas e Novas andanças do Demónio,* by Jorge de Sena, 179–92. Lisbon: Edições 70, 1978.

Camões dirige-se aos seus contemporâneos: E outros textos. Porto: Inova, 1973. [Includes "Camões na Ilha de Moçambique" and "Super flumina Babylonis."]

Poemas ingleses de Fernando Pessoa. Trans. and ed. Jorge de Sena. Lisbon: Edições Ática, 1974.

Os grão-capitães: Uma sequencia de contos. Lisbon: Edições 70, 1976.

Sobre esta praia: Oito meditaçôes á beira do Pacífico. Porto: Inova, 1977. [*Over This Shore: Eight Meditations on the Coast of the Pacific.* Trans. Jonathan Griffin. Santa Barbara, Calif.: Mudborn Press, 1979.

Poesia III. Lisbon: Livraria Morais, 1978.

Sinais de fogo: Romance. Lisbon: Edições 70, 1978.

80 poemas de Emily Dickinson. Trans. and ed. Jorge de Sena. Lisbon: Edições 70, 1979.

Selected Studies of de Sena

Carlos, Luís Adriano. "A escrita da emigração e a emigração da escrita na poesia de Jorge de Sena." *Nova Renascença* (Lisbon) 11 (1983): 248–56.

————. *Fenomenologia do discurso poético. Ensaio sobre Jorge de Sena.* Porto: Campo das Letras, 1999.

————. "O testemunho de Jorge de Sena." *Romântica* 7 (1999): 59–72.

Conrado, Fernanda. "*Ekphrasis* em Jorge de Sena." In *Para emergir nascemos: Estudos em rememoração de Jorge de Sena*, ed. Francisco Cota Fagundes and Paula Gândara, 293–309. Lisbon: Salamandra, 2000.

Fagundes, Francisco Cota. "O retorno do exilado: Subsídios para o estudo do drama humano na pessoa de Jorge de Sena." In *Jorge de Sena em rotas entrecruzadas*, ed. Gilda Santos, 103–16. Lisbon: Cosmos, 1999.

Gândara, Paula. "Jorge de Sena, ou para o exílio na palavra." In *Jorge de Sena em rotas entrecruzadas*, ed. Gilda Santos, 275–99. Lisbon: Cosmos, 1999.

Lisboa, Eugénio, ed. *Estudos sobre Jorge de Sena.* Lisbon: Imprensa Nacional-Casa da Moeda, 1984.

Lopes, Óscar. *Uma arte da música e outros ensaios.* Porto: Oficina Musical, 1986.

Lourenço, Eduardo. "Poesia e poética de Jorge de Sena." *Quaderni Portoghesi* 13–14 (1985): 23–33.

Lourenço, Jorge Fazenda. *O essencial sobre Jorge de Sena.* Lisbon: Imprensa Nacional-Casa da Moeda, 1987.

————. *A poesia de Jorge de Sena: Testemunho, metamorfose, peregrinação.* Paris: Centre Culturel Calouste Gulbenkian, 1998.

Macedo, Helder. "De amor e de poesia e de ter pátria." In *Jorge de Sena em rotas entrecruzadas*, ed. Gilda Santos, 133–43. Lisbon: Cosmos, 1999.

Miranda, José da Costa. "Jorge de Sena e a cultura italiana." In *Studi in memoria di Erilde Melillo Reali*, 141–47. Naples: Istituto Universitario Orientale, 1989.

Morna, Fátima, ed. *Poesia de Jorge de Sena.* Lisbon: Comunicação, 1985.

Quaderni portoghesi 13–14 (1985). Special issue dedicated to Jorge de Sena, ed. Luciana Stegagno Picchio.

Sharrer, Harvey L., and Frederick G. Williams, eds. *Studies on Jorge de Sena.* Proceedings of "Colloquium in Memory of Jorge de Sena," University of California, Santa Barbara, April 6–7, 1979. Santa Barbara: Jorge de Sena Center for Portuguese Studies, University of California, in association with Bandanna Books, 1981.

Talan, Nikita. "A problemática metafísico religiosa na poesia de Jorge de Sena." *Studia Românica et Anglica Zagrabiensia* (Zagreb) 41 (1996): 145–85.

Torres, Alexandre Pinheiro Torres. *O código científico-cosmogónico-metafísico de "Perseguição," 1942, de Jorge de Sena.* Lisbon: Moraes, 1980.

MARGUERITE DURAS
(1914–1996)

Lucille Frackman Becker

BIOGRAPHY

Marguerite Duras was born Marguerite Donnadieu in Gia Dinh in the suburbs of Saigon in French Indochina in 1914, the youngest child of Emile and Marie Donnadieu, two French school teachers on assignment in Indochina. She later abandoned the patronymic Donnadieu and adopted the pen name Duras, the name of a village in southwestern France where her father once owned property. When her father died from amoebic dysentery, the four-year-old Marguerite moved with her mother and two brothers to a house outside Saigon. Details about her childhood can be found in the autobiographical novel *Un barrage contre le Pacifique* of 1950.

Marguerite's early years were shadowed by the family's difficult financial problems and by the resentment she felt toward her older brother, who received the major share of their mother's love. But her hatred for her older brother was not founded exclusively on her mother's preference for him; she also detested him because he was a thief and a gambler. He stole from the poor native boys to buy opium and from their mother to pay his gambling debts. When he was young, he even tried to prostitute his sister. Marguerite's hatred for him was counterbalanced by her love for her younger brother. Some recent criticism has postulated that the madness and alienation of Duras's heroines in the major portion of her work result from what she ultimately acknowledged to have been an incestuous passion for this younger brother.

Her widowed mother gave both French and piano lessons and played the piano at the Eden cinema for 10 years. By rigid economizing, she was able to set aside money to buy a land grant in Cambodia from the French colonial government. Unfortunately, she was unaware of the corruption in the awarding of land grants and found herself with an uncultivable tract of land that was inundated by the Pacific Ocean every year. In a fruitless effort to hold back the floodwaters that devastated her rice paddies, she borrowed money to build a series of dams, which in the end were undermined by hordes of sea crabs that ate away at the sea wall, driving her into bankruptcy and bouts of madness.

During her childhood and adolescence, Duras spoke fluent Vietnamese and lived like an Asian child, listening, observing, and absorbing everything around her. All of the themes of her future work emanated from her experiences in a family of poor white settlers, isolated by color from the natives and by economic status from the French colonials—surrounded, on the one hand, by the savage jungle, the Mekong River, the ubiquitous odor of leprosy, and the desperate, unspeakable misery of the native population, and, on the other hand, by the luxurious residences and tennis clubs of the wealthy white community.

A second explicitly autobiographical novel, *L'amant* (Prix Goncourt, 1984), recounts the events of her last two years in Indochina. Motivated by a desperate desire to flee from unbearable poverty, an unstable mother, and a despicable older brother, she became at the age of 15 the mistress of a Chinese multimillionaire whom she met on a ferryboat crossing the Mekong River. It is this crossing of the river that constitutes the leitmotif of the novel; it symbolizes not only the passage from childhood to adulthood, but also the crossing of the barrier that separated the colonizers from the colonized. Duras considered this crossing to be the decisive event in her life. Although it led to the ostracization of her eccentric family by the French community, it provided the money for her liberation.

At the age of 17, Duras left Indochina for France, armed with a store of images, characters, and themes for her future work. She received *licences* in law and politics at the Sorbonne and worked for the Ministry of Colonial Affairs, where, paradoxically, her work was geared to perpetuating a colonial system she deplored. In 1939, she married the writer Robert Antelme, with whom she joined the French Resistance during the German occupation. In *La douleur*, published in 1985, Duras wrote about Antelme's arrest and deportation, his rescue by François Mitterand from Dachau, where he lay among the dead and the dying, and his slow return to life. Antelme's book *L'espèce humaine* of 1947 is considered the only real masterpiece written about the concentration camps.

After the Liberation, Duras joined the French Communist Party but left it in 1950 following the Prague uprising. A lifelong commitment to the disinherited, motivated by the poverty and suffering she had seen and experienced in Indochina, led her to militate against the Algerian War. She supported the student revolt of May 1968 and the feminist movement for which it had provided impetus. Although Duras always emphasized the freeing of her women characters from a stultifying social and domestic environment, she had certain reservations about aspects of the feminist movement that she found restrictive.

Fully engaged in all of the political and social events of the century, living an unconventional life, and debilitated by alcoholism, Duras never stopped writing, from her first novel, *Les impudents* of 1943, to her last novel, *L'amant de la Chine du Nord* of 1991, five years before her death. But her work was not limited to fiction; she wrote also for the theater and the cinema, often using the same plot in the three media. Some of her screenplays are adaptations of her own novels and short stories; others are translated into both theater and film at the same time. Her very last work, *C'est tout*, with its premonitory title, was published one year before her death in Paris in 1996.

MAJOR MULTICULTURAL THEMES

Marguerite Duras's oeuvre must of necessity be considered in terms of multiculturalism because it springs from her experiences in French Indochina during the formative first 17 years of her life. These experiences are at the heart of the anticolonialism first set forth in *Barrage contre le Pacifique*, where Duras shows the corruption, institutionalized graft, and violence of the colonial administration.

Recurring personae in her oeuvre are avatars of people she encountered in her youth in Indochina, among them a poor beggar woman who haunts Calcutta and who forms part of the native background of misery in *Le vice-consul* (1966) and *India Song* (1973). "The blind beggar woman who abandons her child came to our house in Cochin-China," Duras wrote, "and she returns in almost all of my books. She came with her baby, a little two-year-old girl who looked as if she were six months old, and who was full of worms. I adopted her, my mother gave her to me. She died, we could not save her. That was extremely traumatic for me, I was twelve years old" (quoted in Mariani, *Territoires du féminin avec Marguerite Duras*, 142).

Another archetypal figure, a world apart from the poor beggar woman, was Elizabeth Striedter, wife of the chief colonial administrator, who would appear under the name of Anne-Marie Stretter in *Le vice-consul* and *India Song*. Anne-Marie Stretter is devoured by the same ennui as the other idle colonial wives, but, unlike them, she refuses to conform to the rules and customs and openly deceives her husband with many lovers, one of whom kills himself when she leaves him.

Duras crosses multiple cultural boundaries in her oeuvre. The theme of miscegenation, echoing her own experiences with her Chinese lover, runs through her work; in *Hiroshima mon amour* (1960), for example, we find a love affair between a French woman and Japanese lover.

SURVEY OF CRITICISM

Laura Adler, in her biographical study *Marguerite Duras* (1998), writes that Duras identified herself with her work to such a great extent that she was not able to distinguish between autobiographical fact and fiction. Adler attempts to determine which of the different versions Duras gave of her life, particularly of her early years in Indochina, was true. For example, although Adler confirms the fact that the teenage Duras had an affair with a wealthy Chinese man in colonial Vietnam, she adds that it was not so much a love affair as prostitution, with Duras's mother acting as procurer. Lucile F. Becker, in a chapter devoted to the work of Duras in *Twentieth Century French Women Novelists* (1989), writes that in *Barrage contre le Pacifique* Duras depicts the emotional havoc that a woman destroyed by a corrupt colonial environment wreaks upon her children. Alain Vircondelet, in his comprehensive biography *Duras* (1991), states that nostalgia for the lost world of an exotic childhood permeates Duras's work. She wrote but one book, that of a childhood immersed in the scent of tamarind and cinnamon trees. It was that fantastic world with its dramatic contrasts and violent images that provided the material for her oeuvre.

SELECTED BIBLIOGRAPHY

Works by Duras

Un barrage contre le Pacifique. Paris: Gallimard, 1950.
Le marin de Gibraltar; Roman. Paris: Gallimard, 1952.
Dix heures et demie du soir en été. Paris: Gallimard, 1960.
Hiroshima mon amour [film script]. Paris: Gallimard, 1960.
Le vice-consul. Paris: Gallimard, 1966.
India Song [film script]. Paris: Gallimard, 1973.
L'éden cinéma [theater script]. Paris: Mercure de France, 1977.
L'amant. Paris: Editions de Minuit, 1984.
L'amant de la Chine du Nord. Paris: Gallimard, 1991.
C'est tout. Paris: Editions P.O.L. 2000, 1995.

Selected Studies of Duras

Adler, Laure. *Marguerite Duras*. Paris: Gallimard, 1998.
Armal, Aliette. *Marguerite Duras et l'autobiographie*. Talence: Le Castor Astral, 1990.
Becker, Lucille Frackman. *Twentieth Century French Women Novelists*, 119–35. Boston: Twayne, 1989.
Carlier, Christophe. *Marguerite Duras, Alain Resnais*, Hiroshima mon amour. Paris: Presses Universitaires de France, 1994.
Lebelley, Frédérique. *Duras, ou, Le poids d'une plume*. Paris: Grasset, 1994.
Ligot, Marie-Thérèse. Un barrage contre le Pacifique *de Marguerite Duras*. Paris: Gallimard, 1992.

Mariani, Marcelle. *Territoires du féminin avec Marguerite Duras.* Paris: Minuit, 1977.

Pierrot, Jean. *Marguerite Duras.* Paris: J. Corti, 1986.

Schuster, Marilyn R. *Marguerite Duras Revisited.* New York: Twayne, 1993.

Vircondelet, Alain. *Duras: Biographie.* Paris: François Bourin, 1991.

LAWRENCE DURRELL
(1912–1990)

Arianna Maiorani

BIOGRAPHY

Born in northern India on February 27, 1912, Lawrence George Durrell is one of the outstanding figures in the history of the twentieth-century Western experimental novel. Despite his Anglo-Irish origins, his Indian childhood influenced both his life and his art. After the death of his father when he was 11, young Lawrence and his family returned to England. This was the beginning of a very difficult time for him: he was repelled by the English lifestyle and felt almost alienated in his mother country. After having attended numerous schools from 1923 to 1928, each time trying to resist the regimentation imposed by the English education system of the time, he finally failed university exams and decided to become a writer. The year 1935 was a notable one in Durrell's life: having read Henry Miller's *Tropic of Cancer* (1934), he wrote a letter of praise to the writer, thus beginning a long correspondence and a 45-year friendship based on common interests in literature, art, and the East. In the same year, Durrell moved with his family (including his 10-year-old brother, Gerald, who was to become a writer and broadcaster) and his first wife to Corfu, Greece, to escape from England and to concentrate on writing. After publishing two not very brilliant novels, he wrote his first major work, *The Black Book: An Agon* (1938), much influenced by Miller. When Durrell, his wife, and his daughter were forced to leave Greece in 1941, they settled in Cairo, Egypt, where the couple separated. Durrell moved to Alexandria in 1942, where, while serving as a press attaché in the British Information Office, he was able to study the life of a city that was at the time an important crossroads of East and West. In

Alexandria, he met his second wife, the model for the character of Justine in *The Alexandria Quartet*. Permitted to return to Greece in 1945, he spent two years in Rhodes, where he worked as director of public relations for the Dodecanese Islands. Subsequently he directed the British Council Institute in Cordoba, Argentina (1947–48), then moved to Belgrade, Yugoslavia, where he worked as press attaché (1949–52) and where his second daughter was born. During his stay in Belgrade, he gathered material to write another of his major works, *White Eagles over Serbia*, published in 1957. Having bought a house in 1952 in Cyprus, where he wanted to concentrate again on writing, he earned a living there as an English literature teacher but soon returned to diplomatic service (1954–57) as director of public relations for the British government during the Cypriot revolution. An account of this bitter and even dangerous period of his life is given in *Bitter Lemons* (1957). While in Cyprus, he also started working on his masterpiece, *The Alexandria Quartet*, whose four books—*Justine, Balthazar, Mountolive,* and *Clea*—were published between 1957 and 1960 and earned him great international success. Forced to leave Cyprus, Durrell finally settled in Sommières, France, where he produced many other novels, continued writing poetry, plays, and essays, and married two more times. His final years were painfully marked by the suicide of his second daughter in 1985. The last work he published was *Caesar's Vast Ghost: Aspects of Provence* (1990); he died on November 7, 1990.

MAJOR MULTICULTURAL THEMES

Lawrence Durrell's figure in the world of English literature is a very peculiar one, both for his personality and for his artistic achievements. He himself, both as an individual and as an artist, can be considered a sort of multicultural "product": almost paradoxically, the years he spent in India as a child and the different world he experienced in that "exotic" colony of the British Empire made him always feel like a stranger in England. The exotic and multicultural settings of his major works are not only the literary reproduction of the places he really visited and lived in, but also the perfect set for the psychological dramas he created in order to analyze the relationship between reality and fiction, the difference between living reality and writing about it, and the nature of identity and its mutability in time and space. These exotic settings distanced Durrell the artist from the country he did not feel as his own.

In *Prospero's Cell, A Guide to the Landscape and Manners of the Island of Corcyra* (1945), Durrell's first travel book, the protagonist tries to change his life and discover the different aspects of his identity through travel. In *Bitter Lemons* (1957), another major travel book, Durrell directly presents his dangerous experience in Nicosia during the Cypriot revolution, when he was caught between multiethnic warring factions. Many of these themes are also present in other travel books, essays, and poetic and dramatic productions, and most of them may also be traced in his long and rich correspondence with Henry Miller, *The Durrell-Miller Letters: 1935–80* (1988).

Many of Durrell's major works deal with multicultural themes, which he weaves into existential and artistic questions. The protagonist of *The Black Book: An Agon* struggles to escape England and its lifestyle and flees to Greece: the novel clearly reveals strong autobiographical elements. In *White Eagles over Serbia*, another Britisher is sent on a dangerous military mission that takes him into the mountains of Yugoslavia: through long and impressive descriptions of foreign landscapes, the protagonist raises questions of culture and identity.

Many multicultural themes are present in *The Alexandria Quartet:* in these four novels, set in the crossroads city of Alexandria from the years just before to the years just after the end of World War II, the same story is narrated by different characters and from different points of view. Many philosophical questions are raised about the nature of reality, the poetic object of narrative, the importance of an exotic experience, and the encounter with otherness for the construction of an artist's identity. Through this cycle of novels (in which he often quotes Constantine Cavafy, the Greek poet who lived most of his life in Alexandria), Durrell tries to define what he calls "heraldic reality": a sort of deeper reality where, beyond space and time, every single existence is part of a superior unifying entity. This concept clearly reveals his multicultural education and the strong influence of Buddhism on his thought and art. He also focuses on many of these themes and questions in *The Avignon Quintet* (1974, 1978, 1982, 1983, and 1985).

SURVEY OF CRITICISM

Lawrence Durrell's works always had mixed and controversial reception during his lifetime, especially in England; critics were often ambivalent about them, even though the commercial success of some of his major novels was striking. If *The Alexandria Quartet* (from which a film adaptation of *Justine* was also made) was unanimously greeted, both by critics and readers, as a masterpiece warranting the granting of the Nobel Prize for Literature to the author, *The Black Book: An Agon*, first published in Paris in 1938, notwithstanding T. S. Eliot's praise, did not appear in England until 1973. *The Avignon Quintet* also received mixed criticism and did not achieve the same commercial success as *The Alexandria Quartet*, although the two cycles of novels have much in common.

Since the second half of the 1980s, however, interest in Durrell's narrative experimentalism and his multiculturalism has progressively increased among critics. G. S. Fraser (1968) and John A. Weigel ([1965] 1989) offer comprehensive critical surveys of Durrell's works and themes, and

Alan Warren Friedman (1970) provides a detailed study of *The Alexandria Quartet* that also focuses on descriptions and metaphors relevant to the Egyptian city. Richard Pine (1994), in his study of "mindscape," gives an interesting perspective on Durrell's use of his personal experience of travel. Donald P. Kaczvinsky (1997) studies Durrell's novels through the traveling character's search for wholeness in foreign countries and cultures; Gordon Bowker (1997) writes a biography of Durrell discussing his multicultural and travel experience both as a man and as an artist. Ian S. MacNiven's (1998) quite comprehensive biography focuses on the writer's many travels and friends (Henry Miller, Anaïs Nin, Alfred Perles, T. S. Eliot) and their influence on his work, as well as his ambivalent feelings toward Egypt and the influence of those feelings on *The Alexandria Quartet*.

SELECTED BIBLIOGRAPHY

Works by Durrell

The Black Book: An Agon. Paris: Obelisk Press, 1938.
Prospero's Cell, A Guide to the Landscape and Manners of the Island of Corcyra. London: Faber and Faber, 1945.
White Eagles over Serbia. London: Faber and Faber, 1957.
Bitter Lemons. London: Faber and Faber, 1957.
The Alexandria Quartet: Justine (1957), *Balthazar* (1958), *Mountolive* (1958), *Clea* (1960). London: Faber and Faber, 1962.
Spirit of Place: Letters and Essays on Travel. London: Faber and Faber, 1969.
Collected Poems, 1931–1974. Ed. James A. Brigham. London: Faber and Faber, 1980.
Durrell, Lawrence, and Henry Miller. *The Durrell-Miller Letters, 1935–80.* Ed. Ian S. MacNiven. London: Faber and Faber, 1988.
Caesar's Vast Ghost: Aspects of Provence. New York: Arcade, 1990.
The Avignon Quintet: Monsieur, or The Prince of Darkness (1974), *Livia, or Buried Alive* (1978), *Constance, or Solitary Practices* (1982), *Sebastian, or Ruling Passions* (1983), *Quinx, or The Ripper's Tale: A Novel* (1985). London: Faber and Faber, 1992.

Selected Studies of Durrell

Begnal, Michael H., ed. *On Miracle Ground: Essays on the Fiction of Lawrence Durrell.* Lewisburg, Pa. Bucknell University Press; London: Associated University Presses, 1990.
Bowker, Gordon. *Through the Dark Labyrinth: A Biography of Lawrence Durrell.* New York: St. Martin's Press, 1997.
Fraser, G. S. *Lawrence Durrell: A Critical Study.* London: Faber and Faber, 1968.
Friedman, Alan Warren. *Lawrence Durrell, and* The Alexandria Quartet: *Art for Love's Sake.* Norman: University of Oklahoma Press, 1970.
———, ed. *Critical Essays on Lawrence Durrell.* Boston, Mass.: G. K. Hall, 1987.

Kaczvinsky, Donald P. *Lawrence Durrell's Major Novels.* Selinsgrove, Pa.: Susquehanna University Press; London: Associated University Presses, 1997.

MacNiven, Ian S. *Lawrence Durrell: A Biography.* London: Faber and Faber, 1998.

Pine, Richard. *Lawrence Durrell: The Mindscape.* New York: St. Martin's Press, 1994.

Rowan Raper, Julius, Melody L. Enscore, and Paige Matthey Bynum, eds. *Lawrence Durrell: Comprehending the Whole.* Columbia: University of Missouri Press, 1995.

Weigel, John A. *Lawrence Durrell* (1965). Rev. ed. Boston: Twayne, 1989.

UMBERTO ECO
(1932–)

Giuseppe Gargiulo

BIOGRAPHY

Semiotics, a science and art primarily concerned with the interpretation of signs and symbols, is the field in which Umberto Eco has gained worldwide recognition as a man of science, a highly regarded literary artist, a philosopher of language, a novelist, and a scholar of the mass media.

Born in 1932 at Alessandria in Italy's Piedmont region, Eco spoke fluent English and French from childhood. Later he would introduce to Italy the analytic philosophy of the American Charles Sanders Peirce and the interdisciplinary orientation of the French structuralists Roland Barthes, Algirdas Julius Greimas, Claude Bremond, and Claude Lévi-Strauss.

An avid reader of literary works and philosophical treatises, he earned his laureate in philosophy at Turin in 1954 with a thesis on the aesthetics of Thomas Aquinas. Until 1959, he worked at the Italian radio-television network (RAI), at the same time forging rapidly ahead in a teaching career that has taken him from the Universities of Turin (1956–64) and Milan (1964–65) to Milan Polytechnic (1969–71) and the University of Bologna, where he obtained at the age of 39 the Chair of Semiotics that he still holds. Throughout these years, he was also very active in developing the new discipline of semiotics in specialized periodicals (as an editor of *Il Verri;* a founder of *Marcatré, Quindici,* and *Alfabeta;* and the director of *Versus*) and in publishing several major scholarly articles. He has served as president of both the International Association of Semiotics Studies and the Associazione Italiana di Studi Semiotici e Cognitivi.

Since 1980, he has gained still wider recognition with four internationally acclaimed novels embodying some of the concepts developed in his scientific work.

MAJOR MULTICULTURAL THEMES

The consistent object of Eco's work as semiologist and novelist has been the elucidation of signs interpreted from external reality and reproduced in thought, in written and oral discourse, and in every act of communication, verbal or other. Such has been his dominant concern in a series of theoretical works translated throughout the world: *Opera aperta: Forma e indeterminazione nelle poetiche contemporanee* (1962), on the multiple interpretations of a text as a system capable of containing and communicating multiple meanings; *Apocalittici e integrati* (1965), demonstrating the possibility of a sophisticated reading of an American comic strip and of other types of popular writing; *La struttura assente* (1968), which draws primary attention to semiotics and structuralism in organizing the meanings of a text, over and beyond any rationalistically abstract schematisms intended to describe it; *Trattato di semiotica generale* (1975), a rethinking and analytical definition of the theory of signs as a methodology of communication, from Aristotle to Charles Sanders Peirce; *Lector in fabula: La cooperazione interpretativa nei testi narrativi* (1979), in which the comprehension of a text is reorganized as a *macchina pigra* (lazy machine) explored in its levels of meaning with the reader's interpretive cooperation; *Semiotica e filosofia del linguaggio* (1984), which probes the notions of dictionary, encyclopedia, and sign as symbol in the language; and three further works—*Sugli specchi* (1985), *I limiti dell'interpretazione* (1990), and *Kant e l'ornitorinco* (1997)—that return to the themes of sign, interpretation, encyclopedia, and the possible world of narrative texts in seeking a definition that takes account of the observations and research of the wider scientific community.

The mere enumeration of these titles highlights Eco's penchant for discovering unforeseen perspectives and intriguing new relationships in a subject matter that in itself is familiar. This quality is even more noticeable in the four novels that embody the bulk of his literary contribution to date. Acknowledging no boundaries of time or place in examining the ways in which human beings communicate with one another, Eco here perhaps comes closest to what is traditionally thought of as a multicultural outlook. Distinctive in his individual multicultural approach, however, is what may be called a chronological, rather than a spatial, geographic or cultural perspective per se. With an imagination ranging widely over and beyond the terrestrial globe, he effectively uses a species of time travel in which a given geographical or linguistic culture is subjected to reexamination from different points of view and at different stages of its evolution. Each of his fictions involves a distinctive, shifting focus in which we discover unsuspected links between our own age and one or more historical epochs.

Il nome della rosa (1980), Eco's first narrative experiment, was the winner of the two most prestigious Italian literary prizes (Strega and Viareggio) and has been translated into more than 16 languages. On the surface, it is a kind of medieval detective story, a rigorously academic novel linked together in cinematic scenarios. A philosopher-monk with the mind of a Sherlock Holmes visits a monastery, in company with a young novice, for the purpose of solving a series of crimes, the mysterious deaths of certain monks who have come in contact with a manuscript codex of Aristotle's *Poetics*. The events of the story are revealed in a deductive process that, like Dante's *Divine Comedy*, can be understood on various levels but is rich in suggestive links to our own time: the cloister library with its precious contents is destroyed by fire, survived only by a very imperfect manuscript and by the young novice who lives to tell the tale. But this bare outline conveys little of the richness of insight and allusion, of Eco's virtuosity as a medievalist, a linguistic philosopher and semiologist, and an erudite bibliophile. This palimpsest narration—historical and bookish at the same time—evokes Jorge Luis Borges's labyrinthine library and links Eco to other metahistorical contemporary narrators such as Carlos Fuentes, José Saramago, Milorad Paviç, John Hawkes, Robert Coover, John Barth, Thomas Pynchon, and Salman Rushdie.

Eco's second novel, *Il pendolo di Foucault* (1988), also is dominated by the Middle Ages, the starting point for Western consciousness of the classical, philosophical, and religious cultures of the Latin and Germanic worlds rubbing shoulders, despite practical and ideological difficulties, with the Eastern world—the Hebrew, Arab, and Persian cultures. The title of the novel is a reference to the 200-foot experimental pendulum demonstrated in 1851 by the French physicist J. B. L. Foucault. The central scene this time is the Parisian monastery of Saint Martin-des-Champs, surviving in our day as the Musée des sciences et des techniques. Four venturesome young men in present-day Paris undertake to carry out a project originally conceived by the medieval Knights Templars—the control of a mystical source of power, the most potent the world has ever known. This audacious scheme, involving the concoction of a map to be placed beneath Foucault's pendulum, costs the four conspirators their lives. The narrative that moves to this apocalyptic climax is a mixture of a detective story, an introduction to physics and philosophy, and an amusing analysis of the folly and wisdom that, like a final revelation, embrace the entire history of humanity.

L'isola del giorno prima (1994) can be described as a historico-scientific travel tale that unfolds in 1643 in the South Pacific somewhere beyond the International Date Line. A grounded phantom ship serves the protagonist as a floating library and museum of seventeenth-century knowledge, incorporating both the philosophic outlook of the prescientific era and the sensibility of the baroque age. Never without a pedagogical aim, Eco also defies literary tradition by inserting in the central section of this compelling novel a long, excessively erudite encyclopedic compendium on the seventeenth-century philosophy of cognition.

With *Baudolino* (2000), Eco offers a new display of virtuosity in a medieval setting, this time in the twelfth-century reign of the Emperor Frederick Barbarossa. The peasant-born Baudolino, like Eco a native of Piedmont, has been adopted by the emperor as the result of a chance meeting and narrates his life to a Byzantine historian during a siege of Constantinople. The intelligent but frivolous youth had been sent to Paris to obtain the best possible education but had spent the greater part of his time in dissipation. In a romance in multiform variations, a kaleidoscope of exhilarating linguistic inventions, the magician-like Eco dominates his subject matter as a register of the fantastic, the gothic, and the adventurous, narrating from time to time, through the 40 chapters of the novel, the origins of relics, impossible loves, picaresque voyages, ferocious battles, stories of hate and friendship, and curious anecdotes.

Through these books, it has become evident that Eco the novelist is directly complementary to Eco the essayist. As he himself has said of his dual roles as scholar and creative writer, there is a fundamental difference between the two genres. A narrative text puts on the table a knot, an enigma, and exhibits all its complex ligature rather than disentangling it. The scientific text, in contrast, confronts a problem—the knot—and does everything to bring it to a unitary solution because the very object of a scientific work is to untie the knot. The object of a work of fiction, on the other hand, is to safeguard the oscillation between light and shadow, to preserve a density of ambiguity while maintaining the deep conviction that there *is* no unitary solution.

Animated and enlivened by such paradoxes, Eco's intellectual personality has done much to regain world attention for Italian fiction and to direct the attention of the intellectual community to the role played by the reader's mental universe in dealing with any given text. His rich and reticular encyclopedic culture and his analyses of Western literary texts from the Middle Ages to our day establish him as an archetype of the global thinker who joins past and present and lucidly directs our attention to the unfamiliar problems of the future.

As a man of culture, Eco negates the stereotype of the conventional savant, immured among books and meditating on the highest systems of things and the world. On the contrary, he demonstrates that one can know, read, love, and live through thousands of books, including very rare ones with mysterious and secret contents, but one can also read, with the same rigor and passion, other texts no less dense with significance: the output of computers and the Internet, cartoons and Western films, and popular romances hitherto disdained by "serious" critics. Eco represents an authentic novelty in the Italian literary universe, not only because he has claimed a vocation to cosmopolitanism, even to cultural globalization, but also because, as a philosopher of language and a "narratologist," he has used his familiarity with the functioning of narrative mechanisms—from highbrow to popular literature and the mass media, in particular television—to decode the complex cultural phenomena of contemporary society.

SURVEY OF CRITICISM

The vast critical bibliography on Eco takes into consideration the various aspects of his literary production—semiotic, artistic, philosophical, aesthetic, and mass-medial. Peter Bondanella (1997), in the light of the notion of *opera aperta* (open work), demonstrates the intellectual links connecting the diverse genres that Eco adopts. Roberto Cotroneo (1995) points out the process of observation and verification, in narrative form, of ambiguities in the interpretation of signs. Sven Ekblad (1994) draws a parallel between Dante's descent into the mystery of mind and soul in the realm of the dead and Eco's library exploration-voyage in search of evil in order to reach the palingenesis of good in *Il nome della rosa*. JoAnn Cannon (1989) discusses how the intellectual choices that link Eco to the important Italian writers of philosophical tales, such as Italo Calvino, Leonardo Sciascia, and Luigi Erba, are decisive in understanding the creative context in which the author of *Il nome della rosa* moves. But, as Manfred Moser (1986) demonstrates, Eco also must be regarded as one of the most significant European or planetary authors of the twentieth and twenty-first centuries, similar to Robert Musil and Elias Canetti.

SELECTED BIBLIOGRAPHY

Works by Eco

Opera aperta: Forma e indeterminazione nelle poetiche contemporanee. Milan: Bompiani, 1962; rev. ed., 1972. [*The Open Work*. Trans. Anna Cancogni. Cambridge, Mass.: Harvard University Press, 1989.]

Apocalittici e integrati. Milan: Bompiani, 1965; rev. ed., 1977.

Le poetiche di Joyce. Milan: Bompiani, 1965. [*The Aesthetics of Chaosmos: The Middle Ages of James Joyce*. Trans. Ellen Esrock. Cambridge, Mass.: Harvard University Press, 1982.]

La struttura assente. Milan: Bompiani, 1968.

Trattato di semiotica generale. Milan: Bompiani, 1975. [*A Theory of Semiotics*. Bloomington: Indiana University Press, 1976.]

Lector in fabula: La cooperazione interpretativa nei testi narrativi. Milan: Bompiani, 1979. [*The Role of the Reader: Explorations in the Semiotics of Texts*. Bloomington: Indiana University Press: 1979].

Il nome della rosa. Milan: Bompiani, 1980. [*The Name of the Rose*. Trans. William Weaver. San Diego: Harcourt Brace Jovanovich, 1983.]

Semiotica e filosofia del linguaggio. Turin: G. Einaudi, 1984. [*Semiotics and the Philosophy of Language.* Bloomington: Indiana University Press, 1984.]

Sugli specchi e altri saggi. Milan: Bompiani, 1985.

Il pendolo di Foucault. Milan: Bompiani, 1988. [*Foucault's Pendulum.* Trans. William Weaver. San Diego: Harcourt Brace Jovanovich, 1989.]

I limiti dell'interpretazione. Milan: Bompiani, 1990. [*The Limits of Interpretation.* Bloomington: Indiana University Press, 1990.]

La ricerca della lingua perfetta nella cultura europea. Bari, Italy: Laterza, 1993. [*The Search for the Perfect Language.* Trans. James Fentress. Oxford, England, and Cambridge, Mass.: Blackwell, 1995.]

L'isola del giorno prima. Milan: Bompiani, 1994. [*The Island of the Day Before.* Trans. William Weaver. New York: Harcourt Brace, 1995.]

Kant e l'ornitorinco. Milan: Bompiani, 1997. [*Kant and the Platypus: Essays on Language and Cognition.* Trans. Alastair McEwen. London: Secker and Warburg, 1999.]

Baudolino. Milan: Bompiani, 2000. [*Baudolino.* Trans. William Weaver. New York: Harcourt, 2002].

Selected Studies of Eco

Bondanella, Peter. *Umberto Eco and the Open Text: Semiotics, Fiction, Popular Culture.* Cambridge, England, and New York: Cambridge University Press, 1997.

Cannon, JoAnn. *Postmodern Italian Fiction: The Crisis of Reason in Calvino, Eco, Sciascia, Malerba.* Rutherford, N.J.: Fairleigh Dickinson University Press; London: Associated University Presses, 1989.

Cotroneo, Roberto. *La diffidenza come sistema: Saggio sulla narrativa di Umberto Eco.* Milan: Anabasi, 1995.

Ekblad, Sven. *Studi sui sottofondi strutturali nel "Nome della rosa" di Umberto Eco.* Lund, Sweden: Lund University Press, 1994.

Moser, Manfred. *Musil, Canetti, Eco, Calvino: Die überholte Philosophie.* Vienna: Verband der Wissenschaftlichen Gesellschaften Osterreichs, 1986.

GUNNAR EKELÖF
(1907–1968)

Ross Shideler

BIOGRAPHY

Gunnar Ekelöf identified himself as an outsider from an early age, an identification that influenced the rest of his life in and out of Sweden. Deeply
attached to his father, who became insane and died before Gunnar was 10,
Ekelöf resented his cold, aristocratic mother, who quickly remarried and
often left her son in the care of servants and relatives. Nonetheless, he was
able to travel to France and Germany in his teens. Having studied Greek,
Latin, and modern languages in high school, and inspired by the Sufi mystic Ibn 'Arabi, he went to London's School of Oriental Languages for a
summer (1926). He returned to Sweden, entered Uppsala University to
study Persian and Sanskrit, but did not complete his degree because he
decided to go to Paris to study music (1929–30)—a seminal period for his
lifelong interest in France. Still in his twenties, Ekelöf lost his inheritance
in a falling stock market, and from then on he earned his living as a poet,
translator, and art and literary critic. He published an anthology of translations of French poets in 1934. Although critics reading his first volume of
poetry, *sent på jorden* (1932), claimed he was a surrealist, he felt that Robert
Desnos was the only member of that group to influence him. More
inspired by Arthur Rimbaud's prose and poetry, Ekelöf intended to produce a volume of translations of and commentary on Rimbaud's work, but
only his translation of "Une saison en enfer" appeared in print (1935). His
many years of work on Rimbaud's poetry and prose was edited and published posthumously by Reidar Ekner in 1972.

During most of his life, Ekelöf lived in Sweden, but he frequently traveled abroad, primarily to France, Italy, Greece, and Turkey. His interests

and work, however, were driven by his love of languages and his interest in ancient and modern writers. From French, he translated novels by Marcel Proust and André Gide and poetry by Guillaume Apollinaire, Robert Desnos, and Stéphane Mallarmé. He also translated Chinese poets from French, Petronius from Latin, T. S. Eliot from English, and Nelly Sachs from German. In the long poem *En Mölna-Elegi: Metamorfoser* (1960), written over a 20-year period, he uses passages of Latin and Greek. His literary and philosophical interests ranged from the Indian poet Rabindranath Tagore and Sufi poets from the Middle East to nineteenth- and twentieth-century French and English poets, and from ancient and medieval European writers to Asian and South Asian Taoist and Buddhist thinkers. A brilliant essayist, he produced several volumes of prose, including essays on many of these authors. During his lifetime, Ekelöf published some 24 volumes, 15 of which were poetry, with the rest being collections of essays and translations. He is considered the major voice of lyric modernism in Swedish literature, and several of his poetry volumes, with their extraordinary range of styles, had a major impact on Swedish and Scandinavian poetry. He became a member of the Swedish Academy in 1958 and received an honorary doctorate from the University of Uppsala in the same year. The three volumes of poetry known as the "Dîwan trilogy" (1966–67) crowned his career.

MAJOR MULTICULTURAL THEMES

Ekelöf's entire literary production can be seen from the outsider perspective prominent in his debut volume, *sent på jorden*, labeled by critics as surrealist. Also apparent in that volume are the Eastern and Middle Eastern mysticism to which his personal experiences and literary studies led him, as well as his sense of isolation and psychological disorientation, expressed in poetic imagery of dreams and the unconscious. Rimbaud's famous search to become a *voyant* (seer), with its emphasis on the disorienting revitalization of the senses, served as the motto for Ekelöf's second volume, *Dedikation* (1934). His fourth volume, *Färjesång* (1941), established him as a major poet. His biographer, Carl Olov Sommar, refers to Ekelöf's own division of his early development into three phases: the high school years influenced by ancient India and Ibn 'Arabi, the debut years of 1929 to 1932 experienced in the dark tones of Igor Stravinsky, and the years from 1933 to 1938 influenced by the connection with Rimbaud and surrealism as well as by Ekelöf's own Nordic roots and their nature romanticism (*Gunnar Ekelöf: En biografi*, 200–201).

Even while translating André Malraux's novel *L'espoir*, Ekelöf wrote his breakthrough volume, *Färjesång*, with its Buddhist and antidualistic themes. Critics saw in this volume T. S. Eliot's style, and the question of Eliot's influence on Ekelöf has been debated since then even though Ekelöf denied any influence. Though Ekelöf hated fascism, his desire to see beyond good and evil contributed to his interest in Taoism, a theme apparent in *Non serviam* (1945). Deriving from his interest in Eastern and Middle Eastern philosophies such as Sufism, Buddhism, and Taoism, the creation and dissolution of oppositions became a central theme throughout Ekelöf's poetry. The poem "Gymnosofisten" in *Non serviam* takes its title from a sect of ancient Hindu philosophers who practiced asceticism. The next poem in that volume, "Absentia animi," one of Ekelöf's most famous, offers a meditation on antidualism, on presence and absence pursued into meaninglessness and beyond. Anders Olsson defines this mysticism as Ekelöf's *via negativa*—"a continual attempt to give expression to the experience of negativity in mystical terms" (*Ekelöfs nej*, 279), and he relates it to Ekelöf's studies and his sense of social alienation.

Several volumes continued Ekelöf's mixture of the poetic and the antipoetic, and many poems reflect his knowledge of the Mediterranean, but his "Dîwan trilogy" established him as one of the greatest twentieth-century Swedish poets. He had been visiting Italy and Greece off and on and began studying ancient Byzantine culture seriously in 1962. He and his wife went to Istanbul in 1965, where he saw in a small chapel a deteriorating portrait of a madonna that inspired him. Returning to his hotel room, he wrote seventeen poems in one night (Sommar, *Gunnar Ekelöf: En biografi*, 560). These poems and those that followed were published as the *Dîwan över fursten av Emgión, tolkad av Gunnar Ekelöf* (1965). *Sagan om Fatumeh* appeared in 1966 after visits to Greece and France; and *Vägvisare till underjorden* in 1967 after Ekelöf traveled to Tunisia despite serious illness. The three volumes tell the stories of a Byzantine prince, imprisoned and tortured in A.D. 1070, who is trying to return to his Kurdish home, and of a young prostitute, Fatumeh, who serves as his guide and beloved. The third volume seems to be a mystical journey to the underworld, with death as its dominant theme.

SURVEY OF CRITICISM

Reidar Ekner has edited eight published volumes of Ekelöf's poetry and prose (*Skrifter*, 1991–93) and has written a number of essays (1967) discussing the often exotic sources of many of Ekelöf's poems. Carl Olov Sommar's biography (1989) offers insightful discussions of Ekelöf's fascination with various cultures. Pär Hellström (1976) emphasizes the role of Chinese thought and Taoism in volumes such as *Färjesång* and *Strountes* (1955). Bengt Landgren (1971) argues that Ekelöf created his own way out of his sense of isolation through his study of "Indian Atman-Brahman speculation, the doctrine of Sufic mysticism on the divine immanence, [and] Spinoza's concept of God" (363). Landgren also studies the significance of Rimbaud and Breton for Ekelöf (chap. 4).

Leif Sjöberg (1973), an outstanding translator and critic, published in English the first major discussion of *A Mölna Elegy*. Ross Shideler's 1973 volume serves as an introduction to major themes in Ekelöf's poetry and prose. Several critics, such as Conradin Perner (1974), have commented on Mallarmé's significance for Ekelöf, and Erik G. Thygesen (1985) lucidly discusses Ekelöf's broad cultural and intellectual interests as well as the Eliot-Ekelöf debate. Anders Olsson (1983, 1997) has written two rich thematic studies, and, most recently, Anders Mortensen (2000) has produced an extensive study of tradition and originality in Ekelöf.

SELECTED BIBLIOGRAPHY

Works by Ekelöf

sent på jorden. Stockholm: Spektrum, 1932.

fransk surrealism. Stockholm: Spektrum, 1933.

Dedikation. Stockholm: Bonnier, 1934.

Färjesång. Stockholm: Bonnier, 1941.

Non serviam. Stockholm: Bonnier, 1945.

Strountes. Stockholm: Bonnier, 1955.

En Mölna-Elegi: Metamorfoser. Stockholm: Bonnier, 1960. [*A Mölna Elegy*. Trans. Muriel Rukeyser and Leif Sjöberg. Greensboro. N.C.: Unicorn Press, 1984.]

Dîwan över fursten av Emgión, tolkad av Gunnar Ekelöf. Stockholm: Bonnier, 1965.

Sagan om Fatumeh. Stockholm: Bonnier, 1966.

Vägvisare till underjorden. Stockholm: Bonnier, 1967. [*Guide to the Underworld: Gunnar Ekelöf*. Trans. Rika Lesser. Amherst: University of Massachusetts Press, 1980.]

Selected Poems. Trans. Muriel Rukeyser and Leif Sjöberg. New York: Twayne, 1967.

I Do Best Alone at Night: Poems. Trans. Robert Bly, with Christina Paulston. Washington, D.C.: Charioteer Press, 1968.

Selected Poems. Trans. W. H. Auden and Leif Sjöberg. Harmondsworth, England, and Baltimore, Md.: Penguin, 1971.

Arthur Rimbaud: Lyrik och prosa. Ed. Reidar Ekner. Uddevalla, Sweden: Forum Pocket, 1972.

Friends, You Drank Some Darkness: Three Swedish Poets, Harry Martinson, Gunnar Ekelöf, and Tomas Tranströmer. Ed. and trans. Robert Bly. Boston: Beacon Press, 1975.

Songs of Something Else: Selected Poems of Gunnar Ekelöf. Trans. Leonard Nathan and James Larson. Princeton, N.J.: Princeton University Press, 1982.

Skrifter. 8 vols. Ed. Reidar Ekner. Stockholm: Bonnier, 1991–93.

Modus Vivendi: Selected Prose. Ed. and trans. Erik Thygesen. Norwich, England: Norvik Press, 1996.

Selected Studies of Ekelöf

Ekner, Reidar. *I den havandes liv: Atta kapitel om Gunnar Ekelöfs lyrik*. Stockholm: Bonnier, 1967.

Hellström, Pär. *Livskänsla och självutplåning: Studier kring framväxten av Gunnar Ekelöfs Strountes diktning*. Uppsala, Sweden: Litteraturvetenskapliga institutionen vid Uppsala universitet, 1976.

Landgren, Bengt. *Ensamheten, döden och drömmarna: Studier över ett motivkomplex i Gunnar Ekelöfs diktning.* Stockholm: Läromedelsförlaget, 1971.

———. *Den poetiska världen: Strukturanalystiska studier i den unge Gunnar Ekelöfs lyrik.* Stockholm: Almqvist and Wiksell International, 1982.

Mortensen, Anders. *Tradition och originalitet hos Gunnar Ekelöf.* Stockholm: Brutus Östlings Bokförlag Symposion, 2000.

Olsson, Anders. *Ekelöfs nej.* Stockholm: Bonnier, 1983.

———. *Gunnar Ekelöf.* Stockholm: Natur och Kultur, 1997.

Perner, Conradin. *Gunnar Ekelöfs Nacht am Horizont und seine Begegnung mit Stéphane Mallarmé.* Basel and Stuttgart: Helbing and Lichtenhahn, 1974.

Shideler, Ross. *Voices under the Ground: Themes and Images in the Early Poetry of Gunnar Ekelöf.* Berkeley: University of California Press, 1973.

Sjöberg, Leif. *A Reader's Guide to Gunnar Ekelöf's "A Mölna Elegy."* New York: Twayne, 1973.

Sommar, Carl Olov. *Gunnar Ekelöf: En biografi.* Stockholm: Bonnier, 1989.

Thygesen, Erik G. *Gunnar Ekelöf's Open-Form Poem "A Mölna Elegy."* Stockholm: Almqvist and Wiksell International, 1985.

MIRCEA ELIADE
(1907–1986)

Luisa Valmarin

BIOGRAPHY

As the twentieth century's most prominent and widely respected interpreter of the history of world religions, Mircea Eliade transcended
national and linguistic limitations to become a multicultural author par
excellence, a writer of notable achievement on both the scholarly and the
literary and imaginative planes. Born and educated in Bucharest, Romania, he achieved the laureate in 1928 with a thesis on Italian philosophy
from Marsilio Ficino to Giordano Bruno, the result in part of two visits
to Italy and of contact with leading Italian writers. The Italian Renaissance was of utmost importance in Eliade's intellectual development,
which also featured youthful experimentation with imaginative writing in
the form of fantastic or autobiographical novels (never finished).

A major change of emphasis in Eliade's thinking followed his successful
application for a fellowship to study at Calcutta, India, under Suren-
dranah Dasgupta, a leading authority on Indian philosophy. Aided by a
grant from the local maharajah, Eliade spent three years in India
(1928–31) studying Sanskrit, philosophy, and yoga and finishing his doctoral dissertation, notwithstanding a breach with Dasgupta over his
attentions to Dasgupta's daughter. Back at the University of Bucharest,
the still youthful Eliade completed his doctorate, was named an assistant
in the faculty of letters and philosophy, gave a course on the problem of
evil in Indian philosophy, and inaugurated a period of intensive scholarly
and literary activity that made him an outstanding figure on the Romanian cultural scene. Among several novels and other prose works published in the early 1930s were two autobiographical romances, *Isabel și*

apele diavolului (1930), written in India, and the more celebrated *Maitreyi* (1933), a melancholy but gripping love tale based on the author's own unhappy love affair—a work that sets before our eyes a real clash of civilizations.

Following the outbreak of World War II, Eliade was named Romanian cultural attaché in London (1940) and later cultural attaché at Lisbon (1941–44). By the end of the war, he was well on the way to becoming a world-acknowledged writer and scholar, and he did not again set foot in his own country, which had succumbed to totalitarian rule. Based in Paris during the postwar years, he concentrated on university teaching and the publication of such now well-known scholarly works as *Techniques du yoga* (1948), *Traité d'histoire des religions* (1948), *Le mythe de l'éternel retour: Archétypes et répétition* (1949), and, in the early 1950s, *Le chamanisme et les techniques archaïques de l'extase* (1951), *Images et symboles: Essais sur le symbolisme magico-religieux* (1952), and *Le yoga: Immortalité et liberté* (1954). Emphasizing his standing as a world scholar, he was invited to the University of Chicago in 1956 as professor of the history of religions. Continuing the pace of his production as author of novels, short stories, and memoirs, he served as editor in chief of *The Encyclopedia of Religions* (1987) and accomplished a major synthesis of his studies of myths and religious beliefs in the three-volume *Histoire des croyances et des idées religieuses* (1976–83). He died in Chicago in 1986.

MAJOR MULTICULTURAL THEMES

Eliade's biography shows clearly how the intertwining of cultural and mythical-religious strands in his scholarly output identifies him with humanity as a whole rather than with any particular people or civilization. This distinctive trait appeared even in early youth in his studies of the Italian Renaissance. The fundamental influences in his intellectual development, however, were India and its philosophy. The traces of what has been called his "exceptional existential experience" in that country (Bălu, introduction to *Maitreyi. La țigănci*, vii) are found both in his major scholarly treatises and in numerous autobiographical works, especially in the volume of travel reminiscences *India* (1934); in *Șantier* (1935), which contains other romanticized fragments of the Indian experience; and, above all, in the novel *Maitreyi*, which has been lauded as "a romance of absolute love, but also of cognition, of initiation, of revelation of the sacred" (Roșca, "*Maitreyi*," 18). Even after apparently freeing himself of his Indian obsession with the 1934 novel *Lumina ce se stinge*, Eliade produced another pair of novels (*Secretul doctorului Honigberger* and *Nopți la Serampore*, 1940) with Indian backgrounds and with a startling disregard for Western notions about the fixity of time and place.

It has been pointed out that Eliade originally entered literature with the determination, typical of the post–World War I generation, of seeking a new definition of the human being and, above all, a new relationship between human and history (Simion, "M. Eliade," 289). From this orientation arose both his interest in the diary as a literary form and the aesthetic of the novel based on authentic facts. In his scholarly writing, Eliade pursued his early interest in Oriental religions and Indian philosophy, while in such broader studies as the *Traité d'histoire des religions, Le mythe de l'éternel retour,* and *Images et symboles: Essais sur le symbolisme magico-religieux* he developed the theory of the so-called "rejection of history" as cause and end of religious production, and he singled out a metahistorical sacrality posited by the various religions in the "mythic period" before historical time. Although all of his studies are basically devoted to intercultural religious thematics, it is in his great work of synthesis, the *Histoire des croyances et des idées religieuses,* that he traced a chronological profile of the manifestations of the sacred and, with it, an analysis of the creative moments of the different religious traditions. Also deserving mention in this context is the volume *De Zamolxis à Gengis-Khan* (1970), a comparative study on the religions and folklore of Dacia and central Europe, presenting the essential elements of the religion of the ancient Getae and Daci peoples and the most important mythological and folklorist traditions of the Romanians.

SURVEY OF CRITICISM

The introductory studies of Dumitru Micu and Sorin Alexandrescu to the volumes appearing in 1969, *Maitreyi* and *La ţigănci şi alte popvestiri,* respectively, emphasize the dominant features of the Indian cycle in the prose of Eliade, with numerous detailed references to his scientific interests in the field of philosophy and the history of religions. Similarly, Virgil Ierunca (1978), analyzing Eliade's entire literary output, emphasizes the way in which the fantastic element of certain narratives arises directly from his investigations of tantra and yoga. William A. Coates (1978) also focuses on Eliade's fantastic literature, showing how he lends credibility to extraordinary events by introducing into a realistic narrative various supernatural themes that, in the Indian cycle, are clearly related to his philosophical interests. The monograph by Ioan P. Culianu (1995), spiritual heir of Eliade until his sudden tragic death, draws a full portrait of the scholar on the scientific level; despite its omission of the literary aspect, this study remains extraordinarily useful in understanding Eliade's literary work with its many references to the world of myths and particularly to Oriental philosophy. Marin Mincu and Roberto Scagno (1987) highlight in their edited volume the catalyzing role of the Italian Renaissance in Eliade's intellectual formation. Nicolae Manolescu (1981) analyzes *Maitreyi* in the context of Eliade's novelistic production, concluding that it is the only one of his novels that still conveys "the definite impression of a chef-d'oeuvre" (200). Eugen Simion (2000) has written a good general account of Eliade as a prose writer, placing the Indian cycle in the context of the author's work as a whole. Lionel-Decebal Roşca (2001) examines *Maitreyi* on the literary plane of novelistic construction and on the plane of myth and philosophy.

SELECTED BIBLIOGRAPHY

Works by Eliade

Isabel şi apele diavolului. Bucharest: Ciornei, 1930.
Maitreyi. Bucharest: Cultura Nationala, 1933. [*Maitreyi. Nuntă în cer* (1939). Ed. Dumitru Micu. Bucharest: Pentru Literatură, 1969. *Maitreyi. La ţigănci* (1963). Ed. Ion Bălu. Bucharest: Albatros, 1994.]
India. Bucharest: Cugetarea, 1934.
Lumina ce se stinge. Bucharest: Cartea Romaneasca, 1934.
Şantier. Bucharest: Cugetarea, 1935.
Secretul doctorului Honigberger. Bucharest: Socec, 1940. [Includes *Nopţi la Serampore.*]
Techniques du yoga. Paris: Gallimard, 1948.
Traité d'histoire des religions. Paris: Payot, 1948.
Le mythe de l'éternel retour: Archétypes et répétition. Paris: Gallimard, 1949.
Le chamanisme et les techniques archaïques de l'extase. Paris: Payot, 1951.
Images et symboles: Essais sur le symbolisme magico-religieux. Paris: Gallimard, 1952.
Le yoga: Immortalité et liberté. Paris: Payot, 1954.
La ţigănci (1963) *şi alte popvestiri.* Ed. and introduction by Sorin Alexandrescu. Bucharest: Pentru Literatură, 1969. [Includes *Secretul doctorului Honigberger* and *Nopţi la Serampore.*]
De Zamolxis à Gengis-Khan: Études comparatives sur les religions et le folklore de la Dacie et de l'Europe orientale. Paris: Payot, 1970.
Histoire des croyances et des idées religieuses. 3 vols. Paris: Payot, 1976–83.
Contribuţii la filosofia Renaşterii. [*Itinerar italian.*] Ed. Constantin Popescu-Cadem. Preface by Zoe Dumitrescu-Buşulenga. Colecţia "Capricorn." Bucharest: Supliment anual al *Revistei de Istorie şi Teorie Literară*, 1984.
The Encyclopedia of Religions. Ed. Mircea Eliade. New York: Macmillan, 1987.
M. Eliade e l'Italia. Ed. Marin Mincu and Roberto Scagno. Milan: Jaca Books, 1987. (Italian translation of pages 24–70 of *Contributii la filosofia Renasterii.* [*Itinerar italian.*])

Selected Studies of Eliade

Coates, William A. "Littérature phantastique, métaphysique et occulte." In *Cahier de l'Herne, Mircea Eliade*, ed. C. Tacou, 325–35. Paris: L'Herne, 1978.
Culianu, Ioan P. *Mircea Eliade.* Bucharest: Nemira, 1995.
Ierunca, Virgil. "L'oeuvre littéraire." In *Cahier de l'Herne, Mircea Eliade*, ed. C. Tacou, 217–47. Paris: L'Herne, 1978.
Manolescu, Nicolae. "Jocurile Maitreyiei." In *Arca lui Noe: Eseu despre romanul românesc*, 2: 188–219. Bucharest: Minerva, 1981.
Roşca, Lionel-Decebal. *"Maitreyi."* In *Dicţionar analitic de opere literare româneşti*, ed. Ion Pop, 3: 16–19. Cluj-Napoca, Romania: Casa Cartii de Stiinta, 2001.

Simion, Eugen. "M. Eliade." In *Dicţionarul esenţial al scriitorilor români*, ed. Mircea Zaciu, Marian Papahagi, and Aurel Sasu, 3: 288–92. Bucharest: Albatros, 2000.

HANS MAGNUS ENZENSBERGER
(1929–)

Ingeborg Baumgartner

BIOGRAPHY

Poet, essayist, dramatist, novelist, critic, editor, and translator, Hans Magnus Enzensberger has contributed to almost every genre in literature and journalism. His immense oeuvre reflects an active, incisive, engaged mind, one that welcomes controversy and champions the underdog. Born the eldest of four sons in Kaufbeuren in the East Allgäu mountains of Germany, Enzensberger spent his childhood in Nuremberg, became a member of the Volkssturm, which conscripted all males aged 16 to 60 as decreed by Adolf Hitler on April 18, 1944, and finished secondary school in Nördlingen. Having studied literature, languages, and philosophy at universities in Freiburg, Hamburg, and Paris, he graduated in 1955 from Erlangen University with a doctoral dissertation on the poetry of Clemens Brentano (1778–1842). After a start as radio program editor in Stuttgart, where he gained an influential mentor in the person of Alfred Andersch (1914–80), the editor and novelist who, together with Hans Werner Richter, founded in 1947 the German organization of writers known as Gruppe '47.

Enzensberger traveled widely in the United States and Mexico before settling in Stranda, Norway (1957–59). Known early on as "an angry young man" (Wieland, *Der Zorn altert, die Ironie ist unsterblich: Über Hans Magnus Enzensberger,* 13), he first excelled in the lyrical genre. His collections of poetry *verteidigung der wölfe* (1957) and *landessprache: Gedichte* (1960) display a gift with words, sound combinations, and striking metaphors that couch themes of anger and even despair. These themes change to resignation in his third volume, *Gedichte: Die Entstehung eines*

Gedichts (1962) and give way to themes of death in *blindenschrift* (1964). Noteworthy in the latter volume are poems containing numerous motifs from the landscape of Norway (Falkenstein, *Hans Magnus Enzensberger,* 42), whereas the radio plays *Das babylonische Riff: Wachträume und Vexierbilder aus New York* and *Dunkle Herrschaft, tiefer Bajou* (both 1957) contain impressions of his first trip to the United States. A Villa Massimo grant for a sabbatical year in Rome (1959–60) inspired Enzensberger's astute comparison of life in the Federal Republic of Germany and in Italy (Lau, *Hans Magnus Enzensberger: Ein öffentliches Leben,* 104 ff.). Also at this time, he brought out one of his most original publications, *Museum der modernen Poesie* (1960), an anthology of 362 poems in 16 different languages, side by side with their German translations. This "Chrestomathie" (Falkenstein, *Hans Magnus Enzensberger,* 14) launched Enzensberger as a promoter of international literature that could also serve as models for the new generation of German writers. Though continuing his residence in Norway, he worked as reader and editor for Suhrkamp Verlag in Frankfurt, publishing essays on the media. He traveled to the Soviet Union in 1963.

The year 1965 marked important changes in his life. Having completed a guest lectureship at the university in Frankfurt (1964–65), he journeyed to Latin America, subsequently settling in Berlin. Here he founded and edited (1965–75) the influential journal *Kursbuch*, a vehicle for his essays on cultural criticism and political activism, engaging in discussion such intellectuals as Hannah Arendt, Jürgen Habermas, and Herbert Marcuse. Volume 15, devoted exclusively to Cuba, in particular aroused controversy. In 1968, Enzensberger was named a fellow at the Center for Advanced Studies at Wesleyan University in Connecticut, an award he abandoned to resume travels to the Far East and eventually to Cuba, where he stayed, intermittently, from 1968 to 1969. Following these journeys, he delved into experimental works. *Das Verhör von Habana* (1970) is a montage of excerpts and authentic depositions from interrogations of Cuban prisoners at the Bay of Pigs invasion. *El cimarrón: Biographie des geflohenen Sklaven Esteban Montejo Rezital für 4 Musiker,* based on Enzensberger's translations of the diary by Esteban Montejos, an escaped Cuban slave, was set to music by Hans Werner Henze and premiered at the Aldeburgh Festival as *El cimarrón: Rezital für vier Musiker* (1970). Material collected for a film on the Spanish anarchist Buenaventura Durruti inspired the documentary novel *Der kurze Sommer der Anarchie: Buenaventura Durrutis Leben und Tod* (1972).

Enzensberger lived in New York from 1974 to 1975, publishing in 1975 *Mausoleum: Siebenunddreißig Balladen aus der Geschichte des Fortschritts,* a collection of ballads about historical figures, artists, and scientists (e.g., René Descartes, Denis Diderot, Carolus Linnaeus, Sir Isaac Newton, and Francisco José de Goya) that subsequently engendered *Der Menschenfeind* (1979); *Diderots Schatten. Unterhaltungen. Szenen: Essays* (1994);

and *Voltaires Neffe: Eine Fälschung in Diderots Manier* (1996). An epic poem begun in the 1960s, *Der Untergang der Titanic: Eine Komödie* (1978), gives further testimony to Enzensberger's increasing resignation and disillusionment about progress.

Having moved to Munich in 1979, he founded the journal *TransAtlantik* in 1980 together with Gaston Salvatore. In the following decades, publications in a variety of genres appeared in quick succession: poetry collections (*Die Furie des Verschwindens: Gedichte*, 1980; *Zukunftsmusik*, 1991; *Kiosk: Neue Gedichte*, 1995; and *Leichter als Luft: Moralische Gedichte*, 1999); essays (*Politische Brosamen*, 1982; *Ach Europa! Wahrnehmung aus sieben Ländern. Mit einem Epilog aus dem Jahre 2006*, 1987; *Mittelmaß und Wahn: Gesammelte Zerstreuungen*, 1988; *Die Große Wanderung. Dreiunddreißig Markierungen. Mit einer Fußnote "Über einige Besonderheiten bei der Menschenjagd,"* 1992; *Aussichten auf den Bürgerkrieg*, 1993; and *Zickzack: Aufsätze*, 1997); and children's literature (*Der Zahlenteufel: Ein Kopfkissenbuch für alle, die Angst der Mathematik haben*, 1997). Enzensberger's numerous accomplishments were rewarded with the Georg Büchner Prize (1963), the Etna-Taormina Prize and the Nuremberg Cultural Prize (1967), the International Prize for Poetry (1980), the Pasolini Prize (1982), the Heinrich Böll Prize of the City of Cologne (1985), and the Bavarian Academy of Fine Arts Award (1987), among others.

MAJOR MULTICULTURAL THEMES

Enzensberger's life is governed by multicultural experiences. His extensive travels, longtime residence in foreign countries, fluency in at least eight languages, intimacy with world literature, and familiarity with foreign print journalism testify to a boundless capacity for absorbing and processing information. Furthermore, an insatiable curiosity about people, their history and political institutions, and a visceral drive to communicate explain why Enzensberger is regarded as a multicultural ambassador. Jörg Lau calls him "Dichter und umtriebiger, omnipräsenter Mann der Öffentlichkeit" (poet and peripatetic, omnipresent man of the public domain) (*Hans Magnus Enzensberger*, 70). Not surprisingly, Enzensberger's entire oeuvre is replete with references to life in foreign countries. Over the years, he has paid more attention to some countries than to others: the United States, for example, is singled out relentlessly, witness Enzensberger's essay "Wie ich fünfzig Jahre lang versuchte, Amerika zu entdecken" (How I tried to discover America for fifty years) (in Wieland, *Der Zorn altert*, 96–111). Cuba received special treatment, and Spain and its revolution aroused interest because of Enzensberger's opposition to fascism. More recently, interest in the French Enlightenment and questions about the notion of progress in Western culture dominate, as evidenced by *Mausoleum: Siebenunddreißig Balladen aus der Geschichte des Fortschritts*.

Multiculturalism informs Enzensberger's poetry, plays, and novels as they display a rich font of metaphors, subject matter, and techniques (e.g., *blindenschrift, Mausoleum, Untergang der Titanic, Das Verhör von Habana, Der kurze Sommer der Anarchie*). In his essays and documentaries, multiculturalism gives rise to polemics and sustained historical and cultural analysis (*Ach Europa!, Die Grosse Wanderung, Diderots Schatten*). Enzensberger's contribution to children's literature, notably his edition of *Allerleirauh: Viele schöne Kinderreime* (1961), testifies to his openness to different cultures. Multiculturalism is reflected in his translations of poetry, plays, and essays, for they show him as a mediator of cultures (e.g., his editions of *Museum der modernen Poesie* and *Der Weg ins Freie: Fünf Lebensläufe*, 1975). His breadth of interests and the masterful way he conveys these interests in appropriate genres attest to his receptive mind and creative spirit. The critic Gert Mattenklott asserts that Enzensberger possesses "an active, natural reflex to cross borders, an impatience with the borders themselves, independent of who erected them and why" ("Enzensberger's Iterology in the Century of Migrations," 7).

SURVEY OF CRITICISM

Soon after Hans Magnus Enzensberger published his first volume of poetry, enthusiastic reaction, both positive and negative, set in and has not subsided since. Henning Falkenstein's (1977) brief, succinct introduction with its generic organization provides helpful insights to Enzensberger's work. Reinhold Grimm (1984) lauds Enzensberger for being "the most innovative and stimulating, indeed most important, literary promoter and critical mediator of his whole generation" (*Texturen*, 13). Charlotte Melin's doctoral dissertation (1983) surveys Enzensberger's relationship to the United States, and K. Stuart Parkes (1986) focuses on political themes. The latest study by Jörg Lau (1999) excels in constructing the contexts of Enzensberger's work.

SELECTED BIBLIOGRAPHY

Works by Enzensberger

verteidigung der wölfe. Frankfurt am Main: Suhrkamp, 1957.
Das babylonische Riff: Wachträume und Vexierbilder aus New York. Hörbild, Germany: Süddeutscher Rundfunk, 1957.
Dunkle Herrschaft, tiefer Bajou. Hörspiel, Germany: Hessischer Rundfunk, 1957.
Museum der modernen Poesie. Ed. Hans Magnus Enzensberger. Frankfurt am Main: Suhrkamp, 1960.
landessprache: Gedichte. Frankfurt am Main: Suhrkamp, 1960.
Das Kursbuch. [Journal edited by Hans Magnus Enzensberger, Berlin, 20 vols., 1960–69.]
Allerleirauh: Viele schöne Kinderreime. Ed. Hans Magnus Enzensberger. Frankfurt am Main: Suhrkamp, 1961.

Gedichte: Die Entstehung eines Gedichts. Frankfurt am Main: Suhrkamp, 1962.

blindenschrift. Frankfurt am Main: Suhrkamp, 1964.

Das Verhör von Habana. Frankfurt am Main: Suhrkamp, 1970.

El cimarrón: Biographie des geflohenen Sklaven Esteban Montejo Rezital für vier Musiker. Music by Hans Werner Henze. Hörbild, Germany: Süddeutscher Rundfunk, 1970.

Der kurze Sommer der Anarchie: Buenaventura Durrutis Leben und Tod. Roman. Frankfurt am Main: Suhrkamp, 1972.

Mausoleum: Siebenunddreißig Balladen aus der Geschichte des Fortschritts. Frankfurt am Main: Suhrkamp, 1975.

Der Weg ins Freie: Fünf Lebensläufe. Ed. Hans Magnus Enzensberger. Frankfurt am Main: Suhrkamp, 1975.

Der Untergang der Titanic: Eine Komödie. Frankfurt am Main: Suhrkamp, 1978.

Der Menschenfeind. Notes to the original production at Freie Volksbühne, Berlin, December 1979; broadcast on Zweites Deutsches Fernsehen, 1980.

Die Furie des Verschwindens: Gedichte. Frankfurt am Main: Suhrkamp, 1980.

TransAtlantik. [Journal edited by Hans Magnus Enzensberger and Gaston Salvatore, München, 1980–1982.]

Politische Brosamen. Frankfurt am Main: Suhrkamp, 1982.

Ach Europa! Wahrnehmungen aus sieben Ländern. Mit einem Epilog aus dem Jahre 2006. Frankfurt am Main: Suhrkamp, 1987.

Mittelmaß und Wahn: Gesammelte Zerstreuungen. Frankfurt am Main: Suhrkamp, 1988.

Zukunftsmusik. Frankfurt am Main: Suhrkamp, 1991.

Die Große Wanderung. Dreiunddreißig Markierungen. Mit einer Fußnote "Über einige Besonderheiten bei der Menschenjagd." Frankfurt am Main: Suhrkamp, 1992.

Aussichten auf den Bürgerkrieg. Frankfurt am Main: Suhrkamp, 1993.

Diderots Schatten. Unterhaltungen. Szenen: Essays. Frankfurt am Main: Suhrkamp, 1994.

Kiosk: Neue Gedichte. Frankfurt am Main: Suhrkamp, 1995.

Voltaires Neffe: Eine Fälschung in Diderots Manier. Frankfurt am Main: Suhrkamp, 1996.

Zickzack: Aufsätze. Frankfurt am Main: Suhrkamp, 1997.

Der Zahlenteufel: Ein Kopfkissenbuch für alle, die Angst vor der Mathematik haben. Munich: Carl Hanser, 1997.

Leichter als Luft: Moralische Gedichte. Frankfurt am Main: Suhrkamp, 1999.

Selected Studies of Enzensberger

Dietschreit, Frank, and Barbara Heinze-Dietschreit. *Hans Magnus Enzensberger.* Stuttgart: J. B. Metzlersche, 1986.

Falkenstein, Henning. *Hans Magnus Enzensberger.* Berlin: Colloquium, 1977.

Fischer, Gerhard, ed. *Debating Enzensberger: "Great Migration" and "Civil War."* Tübingen: Stauffenburg, 1996.

Grimm, Reinhold. *Texturen: Essays und anderes zu Hans Magnus Enzensberger.* New York: Peter Lang, 1984.

———, ed. *Hans Magnus Enzensberger.* Frankfurt am Main: Suhrkamp, 1984.

Lau, Jörg. *Hans Magnus Enzensberger: Ein öffentliches Leben.* Berlin: Alexander Fest, 1999.

Mattenklott, Gert. "Enzensberger's Iterology in the Century of Migrations." In *Debating Enzensberger: "Great Migration" and "Civil War,"* ed. Gerhard Fischer, 3–11. Tübingen: Stauffenburg, 1996.

Melin, Charlotte Ann. "Hans Magnus Enzensberger and America: A Study of His Activities as a Poet, Translator, and Editor." Ph.D. diss., University of Michigan, 1983.

Parkes, K. Stuart. *Writers and Politics in West Germany.* New York: St. Martin's Press, 1986.

Schickel, Joachim, ed. *Über Hans Magnus Enzensberger.* Frankfurt am Main: Suhrkamp, 1970.

Wieland, Rainer, ed. *Der Zorn altert, die Ironie ist unsterblich: Über Hans Magnus Enzensberger.* Frankfurt am Main: Suhrkamp, 1999.

ORIANA FALLACI
(1930–)

Lee Baginski

BIOGRAPHY

Born in Florence, Italy, Oriana Fallaci has literally covered the world in her reporting and her novels. She grew up learning from her parents, Tosca and Eduardo, as well as from her uncle Bruno, a prolific writer, that books were treasures. Influenced by Jack London's works, Oriana from the age of nine had the desire to travel, to see, and to interpret the world. In her schooling, she translated Latin and Greek, was exposed to classical literature, and read Shakespeare and other world literature along with the expected Italian authors. Growing up in Fascist Italy under Mussolini's dictatorship also influenced her life and her convictions. In Italy, she and her father were both part of the underground resistance against the Nazis, and, after the Allied victory, she was given an honorable discharge at the age of only 14. At 16, she began her career as a reporter in Florence.

Fallaci indeed wished to follow in the footsteps of her uncle and to become a writer. However, she at first pursued medical studies that she financed through her work at a newspaper, but then opted for journalism after only one year as a medical student. As a reporter for *Il Mattino dell'Italia Centrale*, she interviewed major American celebrities who often visited Florence; later, when writing for *Europeo*, she was sent to the United States to interview celebrities. She was fascinated by Marilyn Monroe in particular but never had the opportunity to interview her, despite numerous attempts. These early interviews became her introduction to Hollywood and the basis of her book on the tinseltown elite (*I sette peccati di Hollywood*, 1958). She later revisited this topic in *Gli antipatici* (1963) by interviewing the likes of Sammy Davis Jr., Mary Hemingway, Hugh Hefner, Alfred Hitchcock, Dean Martin, and H. Rap Brown.

As a young journalist, Fallaci covered British topics, Iranian politics, and celebrated French authors such as Jean-Paul Sartre and Simone de Beauvoir. In the late 1960s and early 1970s, she interviewed many of the most significant political leaders in the world, including Henry Kissinger, King Hussein of Jordan, Nguyen Van Thieu, Indira Gandhi, Golda Meir, and Yasir Arafat; some of these interviews were published in *Intervista con la storia* (1974). Her diverse interests also led her to the interviews with U.S. astronauts recounted in *Se il sole muore* (1965).

In 1967, Fallaci went to Vietnam, where she spent eight years as a war correspondent. During this time, she interviewed soldiers of both sides as well as Vietcong prisoners and sympathizers. At the time, she admired the National Liberation Front fighters for their courageous struggle for national unity. Her anti–South Vietnamese sentiments earned her much criticism in the United States and Europe, but Fallaci held her own against her detractors. Her years in Vietnam were the raw material for many articles and a book, *Niente e così sia* (1969).

Her travels and her work virtually encompass the globe. As a reporter and writer, she journeyed to Mexico City; covered the assassination of Martin Luther King Jr. in Memphis; studied women in India, Pakistan, Hong Kong, and Hawaii; and interviewed the Dalai Lama and Haile Selassie. In *Il sesso inutile: Viaggio intorno alla donna* (1961), she tells the often tragic stories of the women she met as she traveled the world.

Fallaci chose to become a full-time novelist in 1973. While writing her novel *Lettera a un bambino mai nato* (1975), she met and interviewed Alekos Panagoulis, the man who became the love of her life and with whom she was living in Athens when she completed her novel. Their first encounter is preserved and recorded in the final chapter of *Intervista con la storia*. A member of the Greek resistance to the Colonels' junta, Panagoulis was killed in May 1976 in a suspicious car accident. For her next novel, *Un uomo* (1979), Fallaci investigated the facts of Panagoulis's death.

Material for the novel *Insciallah* (1990) ("as God wills," in Arabic) came in part as a result of her interview in 1982 with then-general Ariel Sharon after Israel's invasion of Lebanon. She had traveled to Beirut to see the devastating losses, finding herself most affected by the children among the casualties.

Fallaci now resides primarily in New York. Her firsthand knowledge of New York as an inhabitant was born out of interest in the freedom and rights of women and others who have preceded her as immigrants to the United States. At home in New York on September 11, 2001, she emerged from semiretirement (forced on her by cancer therapy) to write a scathing and controversial attack on extremist Islamic fundamentalists and their kamikaze terrorist envoys (*La rabbia e l'orgoglio*, 2001).

As a journalist, Fallaci became an ethnographer who was as much participant as observer. Her first impressions and detailed descriptions of the surroundings where the interviews took place added meaning about the subject as well as about Fallaci herself. Her political and human conscience speaks in dramatic asides in a function akin to that of the Greek chorus bemoaning and enlightening humankind on the upcoming onslaughts of fate.

MAJOR MULTICULTURAL THEMES

Whether acting in the role of journalist, novelist, historian, or humanitarian in covering the policies, politics, and peoples of the world, Fallaci emphasizes justice, injustice, freedom, equality, war, abuse of power, and death in her work.

In *Penelope alla guerra* (1962), the young female virgin leaves Italy for New York, where the Statue of Liberty represents the freedom that all deserve. Like Fallaci, the protagonist is a writer and independent woman who struggles in her relationships but ultimately is able to survive in the masculine world by becoming as strong-willed as a man. The inequality of the sexes and the power that male-dominant cultures wield over the women who are born into them is addressed in *Il sesso inutile: Viaggio attorno alla donna:* "From one end of the world to the other women are living in a wrong way, whether they are segregated like animals in a zoo, looking at . . . people from behind a sheet that envelops them as a shroud envelops a corpse, or whether they are unleashed like ambitious warriors, winning medals in shooting contests with men. And I didn't know whether I'd felt the most grief for the little bride in Karachi or for the ugly soldier girl in Ankara" (*The Useless Sex*, 183). Fallaci's inability to save the women from their unhappiness overwhelms her; she ends her book believing that nothing will change for these women for a very long time: "The great refrain that is stirring women all over the world is called Emancipation and Progress. . . . And in my wanderings I had followed the march of women revolving around an abysmal utterly stupid unhappiness" (183).

War is the grim background to many of Fallaci's works. In *Niente e così sia*, she asserts her message on war: "I'm here to understand life, to find out what a man thinks about and what he's looking for when he kills another man who would kill him in his turn. I'm here to prove something I believe: that war is useless and stupid, bestial proof of the idiocy of the human race" (*Nothing and So Be It*, 9). Space travel and war also do not mix according to Fallaci: "Come to think of it, man's a pretty ridiculous animal. He's so intelligent, yet he keeps settling everything with force. He goes to the moon and then fights in Vietnam" (174).

The related theme of death recurs throughout Fallaci's works. Nothing is more tragic to her than the death of an innocent child. She brings the themes of war and death together in her works *Niente e così sia* and in

Insciallah, as in this description: "Children two or three years old dangled from the beams of the exploded rooms like chickens hanging from a butcher's hooks. Newborns squashed or cut into, mothers struck down in the useless gesture of protecting them" (*Inshallah*, 40). She perceives war as especially senseless and cruel when those who have no part in the cruelties die brutally and unnecessarily. She also treats the courage to face death in her interviews with the astronauts featured in *Se il sole muore* and in *Un uomo*.

Fallaci also addresses power and the abuse of power in her interviews and her novels. In the preface to *Intervista con la storia*, she writes, "I cannot exclude the idea that our existence is decided by a few people, by their dreams and caprices, their initiative and will. Those few who through ideas, discoveries, revolutions, wars, or some quite simple gesture—the killing of a tyrant—change the course of events and the destiny of the majority" (*Interview with History*, 10).

All human beings, however, must fight against oppression and for freedom: "But the tragic side of the human condition seems to me precisely that of needing an authority to govern, a chief. One can never know where a chief's power begins and ends; the only sure thing is that you cannot control him and that he kills your freedom. Worse: he is the bitterest demonstration that absolute freedom does not exist, has never existed, cannot exist" (*Interview with History*, 13). Speaking out is always preferable to silence and is a testimony to those who use the "miracle" of their own lives for humanity: "I have always looked on disobedience toward the oppressive as the only way to use the miracle of having been born. I have always looked on the silence of those who do not react or who indeed applaud as the real death of a woman or a man" (*Interview with History*, 13).

Pessimism and hope are achingly intertwined in all of Fallaci's works. Although the struggles for power often lead to war and violence, hope that humankind will be resourceful enough to dig deep beneath the dark surface to extract the simple joy of living is an ever-present theme in both Fallaci's fiction and her real life.

SURVEY OF CRITICISM

Santo Aricò (1998) analyzes the connections between Fallaci's life and her work in order to explain the dramatic combination of self and reality, making Fallaci a myth, an enigma of grand proportions. In an earlier writing, Aricò (1986) explains how Fallaci's ruthless attacks made the interviewees defensive, causing them to stumble and to tell more than expected. John Gatt-Rutter (1996) analyzes her work thematically, breaking his book into sections such as "Reports from Other Worlds" and "Woman's Body." His analysis centers on multicultural experiences, the voices of others, and the language of freedom.

SELECTED BIBLIOGRAPHY

Works by Fallaci

I sette peccati di Hollywood. Preface by Orson Welles. Milan: Longanesi, 1958.

Il sesso inutile: Viaggio intorno alla donna. Milan: Rizzoli, 1961. [*The Useless Sex.* Trans. Pamela Swinglehurst. New York: Horizon Press, 1964.]

Penelope alla guerra. Milan: Rizzoli, 1962. [*Penelope at War.* Trans. Pamela Swinglehurst. London: Michael Joseph, 1966.]

Gli antipatici. Milan: Rizzoli, 1963. [*The Egotists: Sixteen Surprising Interviews.* Trans. Mihaly Csiksaentmihalyi, Oriana Fallaci, and Pamela Swinglehurst. Chicago: Henry Regnery, 1968.]

Se il sole muore. Milan: Rizzoli, 1965. [*If the Sun Dies.* Trans. Pamela Swinglehurst. New York: Atheneum House, 1966.]

Niente e così sia. Milan: Rizzoli, 1969. [*Nothing and So Be It.* Trans. Isabel Quigly. Garden City, N.Y.: Doubleday, 1972.]

Intervista con la storia. Milan: Rizzoli, 1974. [*Interview with History.* Trans. John Shepley. New York: Liveright, 1976.]

Lettera a un bambino mai nato. Milan: Rizzoli, 1975. [*Letter to a Child Never Born.* Trans. John Shepley. New York: Simon and Schuster, 1976.]

Un uomo. Milan: Rizzoli, 1979. [*A Man.* Trans. William Weaver. New York: Simon and Schuster, 1980.]

Insciallah. Milan: Rizzoli, 1990. [*Inshallah.* Trans. Oriana Fallaci from a translation by James Marcus. New York: Doubleday, 1992.]

La rabbia e l'orgoglio. Florence: Rizzoli, 2001. [*Oriana Fallaci: Anger and Pride.* Trans. Chris Newman and Paola Newman. Available at: http://www.fallaci.blogspot.com, 1–18.]

Selected Studies of Fallaci

Aricò, Santo L. "Breaking the Ice. An In-Depth Look at Oriana Fallaci's Interview Techniques." *Journalism Quarterly* (Autumn 1986): 587–93.

———. *Oriana Fallaci: The Woman and the Myth.* Carbondale: Southern Illinois University Press, 1998.

Gatt-Rutter, John. *Oriana Fallaci: The Rhetoric of Freedom.* Oxford, England, and Washington, D.C.: Berg, 1996.

FRANTZ FANON
(1925–1961)

Clément Mbom

BIOGRAPHY

Born on July 20, 1925 in Fort-de-France, capital of Martinique, Frantz Fanon became one of the most illustrious descendants of Africans deported to the New World. He actually lived his life on three continents: the Americas (Martinique), where he was born; Europe (France), where he continued his education; and Africa (Algeria), his adopted country.

His education was a blend of French and Caribbean. He completed high school at sixteen. By the 1940s, his family, like others of French Caribbean society, continued the trend of assimilation until Aimé Césaire, a high school teacher later considered subversive, brought about a radical transformation in attitude among blacks, as adumbrated in his *Cahier d'un retour au pays natal* (1939). He taught his readers and disciples to be conscious of their status and their future and to be capable of taking responsibility for their actions and thoughts. Instilling a sense of pride in the younger generation, Césaire, as noted by Fanon in *Les damnés de la terre* (1961), encouraged them to think that *black is beautiful*.

During World War II (1939–45), Fanon proved his mettle as a French soldier in France. He returned to Martinique, registered at the Lyceum Schoelsher (specializing in philosophy), and as a wounded and decorated veteran, received a scholarship in 1946 to study medicine in France. Drawn to philosophy and literature, he enrolled in the classes of Jean Lacroix and Maurice Merleau-Ponty. Among his favorite authors were Kierkegaard, Nietzsche, Hegel, Marx, Lenin, Husserl, Heidegger, and Sartre. He began publishing a typewritten newspaper, *Tam Tam*, for students of color, and became an assiduous reader of *Présence Africaine*, a magazine created by Alioune Diop in 1947. Fanon completed his medical studies in 1951.

When he returned to Martinique for a short stay, he performed autopsies. After exhuming the body of a woman who had died three months earlier, he discovered that the corrupt doctor on the case had falsified her death certificate, hiding the fact that her husband had beaten her to death. Upon Fanon's return to France, he met a young French intellectual, Marie-Josèphe Dublé, whom he married in 1952 after completing his university studies. A son, Olivier, was born to the couple. (Olivier presently works at the Algerian Embassy in Paris.)

Fanon's *Peau noire, masques blancs* (1952), a subtle analysis of the alienation phenomenon—between the colonized and the colonist, and its consequences on the evolution of humankind—points to his increasing interest and reputation as revolutionary and as creative writer. Césaire's influence on Fanon cannot be overemphasized, the former encouraging the latter to write some still unpublished Greek-style plays: *Les mains parallèles*, a tragedy in four acts with a prologue; *L'oeil se noie*; and *Conspiration*. Three barely legible pages of one of these works were exhibited at the International Frantz Fanon Memorial in Fort-de-France (March 31–April 3, 1982).

Fanon spent a few months in Europe, hoping all the while that Leopold Sédar Senghor would help him obtain a position at a hospital in Senegal. His hopes were not realized. Fanon went to Algeria instead, where he became chief of Blida's psychiatric hospital. "If psychiatry is the medical technique destined to prevent humankind from being permanently estranged from his environment," he declared, "then the Arab is not only permanently alienated from his country, but lives in a state of absolute depersonalization" (*Pour la révolution africaine: écrits politiques*, 50).

He participated in the first Congress of Black Writers and Artists organized at the Sorbonne in Paris (September 19–22, 1956). As a member of Martinique's delegation, he defined racism and culture and exposed their respective influences on the colonial environment in his communication "Racism and Culture." "The spasmodic and rigid culture of the occupant has finally opened itself up to the now-liberated colonized person. The two struggling cultures are mutually enriching. . . . Universality resides in the thought that once colonial status is irreversibly abolished, the reciprocal relativism of different cultures will be honored" ("Racism and Culture" in *Présence Africaine*, 1956, 131). The moderate tone of Fanon's loudly applauded speech was intentional and based on his wish to return to Algeria to participate in anticolonial activities. Nonetheless, he was expelled from Algeria in 1956, establishing himself in Paris, then returning to Martinique, then going back to Africa, settling briefly in Tunis, where he continued to serve the Algerian fight for its independence from France.

As a member of the Algerian delegation to the Pan-African Congress of Accra (December 1958), he delivered a speech and met several important African leaders: Kwame N'Krumah, president of Ghana; Patrice Lumumba, delegate of the Congolese National Movement; Félix Moumié, president of the Union of Cameroon People; and a number of other African revolutionaries. Fanon envisioned the possibility of transplanting the ideas and methods used by Algerian revolutionaries to the Pan-African struggle at large.

At the second Congress of Black Writers and Artists that was held in Rome (March 26–April 1, 1959), Fanon's speech, "Reciprocal Foundation of National Culture and the Liberation Struggle," traced the impact of the Algerian war on the progress of colonized countries (in *Présence Africaine*, special issue 24–25, février–mai 1959, 82–89). He was now convinced that only via the struggle for liberation could national cultures be maintained. During this second meeting of black writers and artists his influence skyrocketed.

In 1959 and 1960, he participated as Algerian delegate in a conference for Peace and Security in Accra and in an Afro-Asiatic Conference at Conakry, with the hope of integrating the Algerian Revolution into the African liberation movement. He envisioned the formation of a front against French colonizers in southern Algeria, near the border of Mali. Despite the demands he made of Modibo Kéita, Mali's chief of state, his project failed. Nonetheless, he continued to pursue his verbal struggle for the liberation of Algeria, blaming the French for the evils perpetrated there and revealing that a large segment of the French population favored the Algerian freedom fighters.

Now living at the border of Morocco and Algeria, Fanon organized medical services and a political staff of the National Liberation Army. During one of his many trips to and from Tunisia, Algeria, and Morocco, he was the victim of a suspicious car accident. He was hospitalized in Rome, where he barely escaped two assassination attempts, but completed *L'an V de la révolution algérienne* (1959), reflections on the Algerian war and its consequences on both the Algerians and the French. By 1961, Fanon was already suffering from leukemia, and was admitted to a clinic in Moscow. After his release, he returned to Tunis. He was not selected as ambassador to Cuba, a position he sought wanting to return to the Caribbean. He wrote *Les damnés de la terre* as an exceptional contribution to the struggle between the colonizers and the colonized, for which Jean-Paul Sartre wrote the preface.

Later in 1961 he arrived in the United States where he was admitted to a hospital in Washington D.C. He died on December 6, 1961 at the age of thirty-six. His fourth book, *Pour la révolution africaine: écrits politiques* (1964), consists of a posthumous compilation of articles drawn from *Esprit*, *Temps Modernes*, *Résistance Algérienne*, and *El Moudjahid*, realized by Fanon's wife, family, friends, and editor.

MAJOR MULTICULTURAL THEMES

The multicultural themes elaborated in Fanon's books—*Peau noire, masques blancs, L'an V de la révolution algérienne,* and *Pour la révolution algérienne: écrits politiques*—are related to the type of multiculturalism drawn from his firsthand experiences in America, Europe, and Africa. *Les damnés de la terre* more specifically treats the notion of culture and national culture. His writings are centered on three dichotomies: slavery / freedom, colonization / decolonization, and oppression / freedom. Other significant topics are incorporated into these themes: colonialism, violence, revolution, alienation, racism, freedom, minorities, classes, language, politics, and economic conditions. Improving the lot of humankind was at the root of the Fanonian universe.

Men and women have the right, Fanon believed, to assume their destiny as individuals, rather than allowing themselves to be oppressed by any person or group. They must learn to fight back and to rise above their status as the wretched of the earth and to become masters instead.

SURVEY OF CRITICISM

Djeghloul Abdelkader structures his pertinent unpublished thesis (1971–72) on a study of Fanon's seminal work, *Les damnés de la terre*—the work that must be analyzed in depth for a true understanding of the steps leading to Fanon's development as a revolutionary. David Caute's work (1970) traces Marxist influence on Fanon's spiritual itinerary. Although Marxists and Fanon shared socialist and humanitarian concerns, their approaches to these philosophical ideologies were different. Fanon hypothesized about issues, but he differed from Marxists about how the issues were to be resolved. Both Marxists and Fanon, however, believed in freeing the oppressed from the oppressor.

Irene Grendzier (1973) has written one of the most important works on our revolutionary author. Her seminal study explores Fanon's books, his introspections, and his awareness of the socioeconomic and psychological aspects of the origin of racism.

Clément Mbom (1985) points to Fanon's role as prophet and hero in his own time. His all-consuming struggle to transform the wretched into masters of the earth is detailed.

Fanon: A Critical Reader (1996, 1999, 2000) is edited by Lewis R. Gordon. A group of authors contributed to this volume, considered the fifth stage in Fanon's multidisciplinary studies and thought. Alice Cherki (2000), who worked with Fanon in Algeria and Tunisia, adds a different dimension to her biographical study. A Fanon promoter, she sees him as a generous but concessionless individual, whose life, while tragic, was always dominated by the hope of humankind's well-being.

SELECTED BIBLIOGRAPHY

Works by Fanon

Peau noire, masques blancs. Paris: Seuil, 1952.

"Racism and Culture." *Présence Africaine* numéro spécial 8–10 (juin–novembre 1956): 122–31.

L'an V de la révolution algérienne. Paris: F. Maspéro, 1959. 3rd ed. Paris: F. Maspéro, 1962.

"Reciprocal Foundation of National Culture and the Liberation Struggle." *Présence Africaine* numéro spécial 24–25 (février–mai 1959): 82–89.

Les damnés de la terre. Preface Jean-Paul Sartre. 2nd ed. Paris: F. Maspéro, 1961. [*The Wretched of the Earth.* Trans. Constance Farrington. Preface Jean-Paul Sartre. New York: Grove Press, 1963. London: MacGibbon and Kee, 1965.]

Pour la révolution africaine: écrits politiques. Paris: F. Maspéro, 1964.

Fanon: A Critical Reader. Ed. Lewis R. Gordon. Trans. Lewis R. Gordon, T. Denean Sharpley-Whiting, and Renée T. White. Oxford and Cambridge: Blackwell, 1996, 1999, 2000.

Related Work:

Césaire, Aimé. *Cahier d'un retour au pays natal* (1939). Paris: Présence Africaine, 1956, 1960, 1971.

Selected Studies of Fanon

Caute, David. *Frantz Fanon.* New York: Viking Press, 1970. [Trans. G. Dunaud. Paris: Seghers, 1971.]

Cherki, Alice. *Frantz Fanon, Portrait.* Paris: Seuil, 2000.

Djeghloul Abdelkader. "Franz Fanon: l'ambiguité d'une idéologie tiers-mondiste." Paris: Thesis, University of Paris V, 1971–72.

Gordon, Lewis R., ed. *Fanon: A Critical Reader.* Oxford: Blackwell, 1996, 1999, 2000.

Grendzier, Irene. *Frantz Fanon: A Critical Study.* New York: Pantheon Books, 1973.

Macey, David. *Frantz Fanon: A Biography.* New York: Picador USA, 2001.

Mbom, Clément. *Frantz Fanon, Aujourd'hui et Demain.* Paris: Editions Nathan, 1985.

Seibert, Renate. *L'Oeuvre de Frantz Fanon. Colonialisme et aliénation dans l'oeuvre de Frantz Fanon.* Trans. from the German by Roger Dangeville. Paris: Maspéro, 1970.

JOHN FOWLES
(1926–)

A. L. Rogers II

BIOGRAPHY

John Fowles—naturalist, philosopher, poet, and novelist—is often considered one of the more important writers since the Second World War because he has succeeded both in being popular and in being esteemed by literary scholars, a feat accomplished by only a small few. Fowles has lived exclusively in his native England since 1966, but his years living abroad in France and Greece and his interest in French literature and thought have had a tremendous impact on his work.

Born in Leigh-on-Sea, Essex, to middle-class parents, Fowles entered the Bedford School near London in 1939, where he studied French and German literature with intensity and depth. After serving in the Royal Marines from 1944–47, he returned to the study of German and especially French literature, now at New College at Oxford. Moving to France in 1950, he taught English literature for a year at the University of Poitiers. He spent the following two years teaching English at the Anargyrios and Korgialenios School on the Greek island of Spetsai in the Aegean Sea. Here he wrote the "Greek Poems" included in his *Poems* (1973), and here he met Elizabeth Whitton, whom he later married.

Though he started writing *The Magus* first, *The Collector* (1963) was Fowles's first published novel, and its popular success enabled him to give up teaching and become a full-time writer. *The Collector* was followed by *The Aristos: A Self-Portrait in Ideas* (1964), a series of philosophical notes conveying the existentialist beliefs formed initially from Fowles's reading of Jean-Paul Sartre and Albert Camus. The experimental novel *The Magus*, set in the fictitious Greek island of Phraxos (clearly Spetsai), was completed after twelve years of sporadic work and published in 1965. *The French Lieutenant's Woman* (1969), generally considered Fowles's most important novel, is also experimental in its complex blending of nine-teenth- and twentieth-century perspectives and in its self-conscious test-ing of the boundaries of conventional fiction with multiple endings from which the reader is invited to choose. *Daniel Martin* (1977), the most autobiographical of Fowles's novels, is set partly in the United States. The inspiration for this novel came from his impressions of Hollywood during a 1969 trip to arrange the adaptation of *The French Lieutenant's Woman* for film. *Mantissa* (1982), which is even more self-consciously metafictional than *The French Lieutenant's Woman*, and *A Maggot* (1985), an historical novel about an unsolved mystery in the 1730s, complete the canon of his novels.

In 1988 Fowles suffered a stroke that apparently ended his career as a novelist, though he has continued to write critical and philosophical non-fiction, as well as works on nature. The most notable of his nonfiction writings are brought together in the 1998 collection, *Wormholes: Essays and Occasional Writings*. Fowles currently resides in Lyme Regis, a seaside resort and fishing town in Dorsetshire, England, where he has lived since 1966.

MAJOR MULTICULTURAL THEMES

Fowles once said, "I don't want to be an English writer; I want to be a European one, what I call a mega-European (Europe plus America plus Russia plus wherever else the culture is essentially European) . . . I don't even want to be English. English is my language, but I am a mega-Euro-pean" ("I Write Therefore I Am," in *Wormholes: Essays and Occasional Writings*, 10). If Fowles is indeed a "mega-European" writer, the tran-scendence of his Englishness began with his studies in French literature, but his career as a writer was born in Spetsai.

His initial reaction to Greek culture was hostile, but in his experience with what he calls the "wild Greece" of remote and lovely hills, he came to have an intense and abiding love of Greece. He writes: "I remain deeply attached to that difficult, devious, and hospitable, sometimes monstrous yet almost always charming people, the Greeks, and have long said that in fact I have three homelands: my own England (not Britain), France, and Greece" ("Behind *The Magus*,"in *Wormholes: Essays and Occa-sional Writings*, 58). Fowles clearly conveys this deep attachment in the Greek section of his *Poems* and in *The Magus*. The most important of his Greek experiences was a euphoric, epiphanic insight he felt during soli-tary treks in the Spetsai hills, as described in "Behind *The Magus*": "an intense, as in a prolonged lightning flash, realizing of what I was; which was also a shadowing . . . of what I should or must become"—namely, a literary artist (63). Fowles exiled himself from Greece after his return to

England in 1952, because he feared that he would be disappointed in returning to the scene of such powerful, mystical experiences in later years. In fact, when he did return to Spetsai in 1996, he felt a "kind of almost unexpected sanction—that I hadn't been wrong to have lived for so many years dreaming both *of* and imaginatively *in* that exquisite landscape" ("Greece," in *Wormholes: Essays and Occasional Writings*, 72). As he says in the poem "Shepherd," in Spetsai he found and cherished "a silence in which a man could sing" (*Poems*, 11).

France holds an equally special and even more extensive attraction and influence over Fowles: the impact of French literature and philosophical thought, more particularly, was profound and lasting. First and foremost, the existentialist preoccupation with the individual's freedom of action and values in an apparently purposeless world that figures so prominently in *The Aristos: A Self-Portrait in Ideas, The Collector, The Magus*, and *The French Lieutenant's Woman* is clearly rooted in Sartre and Camus. More narrowly, Fowles acknowledges Henri Alain-Fournier's *Le Grand Meaulnes* as a vital influence in *The Magus* and in his later work. Sarah Woodruff, from *The French Lieutenant's Woman*, is based upon Claire de Durfourt's heroine in *Ourika*, a nineteenth-century French novel Fowles translated for publication in 1977. He also acknowledges the enduring impact of the medieval French romances he studied at Oxford. The quest motif from the French and Celtic romances is especially prominent in *The Magus, Daniel Martin*, and the collection of stories *The Ebony Tower* (1974). It is certainly worthy of note that Fowles included in *The Ebony Tower* his own translation of Marie de France's twelfth-century romance *Eliduc*, and that two of the volume's four original stories are set in France.

Despite his time in France and despite his extensive reading of French literature, including the several works he himself translated from French into English, Fowles explains in "A Modern Writer's France" that he considers it impossible to understand truly and absolutely any cultures other than one's own. He says of his own reading of French that he may understand the text "in every semantic and grammatical sense; but because I am not born French, nor bilingual, a final understanding—indeed, *the* final understanding—is forever beyond me" (in *Wormholes: Essays and Occasional Writings*, 45). Between all cultures, Fowles says, there are always "ghosts" of what we experience in our multicultural interactions but can never fully *know*. However, for him this "ghost of never completely knowing is, I believe, the quintessential part of any true and lasting love, whether between persons or between nations" ("Modern Writer's France," 46). Fowles clearly has a true and lasting love for France. He has visited the country almost yearly since the mid-1960s, taking care to avoid the cities and museums and to immerse himself in the countryside itself and the remote and tiny villages far from the beaten tourist paths. He has not written of France in his fiction beyond the two stories in *The Ebony Tower*, but he has said that he feels less than whole if he spends too much time away from "his" France. Through its literature, especially, and also through the "richness of freedoms" he sees in the French, Fowles considers himself "formed deeply" by the French culture. Imagining what he would be if he did not read French, "however imperfectly," if he "did not know its culture, however erratically, [and] did not know its nature and its landscapes, however partially," Fowles says, "I should be half what I am; half in pleasure, half in experience, half in truth" ("Modern Writer's France," 55). Indeed, John Fowles without the profound influence of French thought and literature would not at all be the John Fowles we know.

SURVEY OF CRITICISM

Robert Huffaker (1980) offers valuable discussion of Fowles's time in France and Greece and of the influence these experiences had upon his life and work. James Aubrey (1991) provides an equally valuable biographical essay and critical survey of Fowles's fiction and nonfiction writings. A Greek friend of Fowles, Kirki Kephalea, has written about Fowles's Greek experience in *E Ellenike Empeiria* (1996). Thomas Foster (1994) is especially helpful in negotiating the sometimes unsettling complexities of Fowles's fiction. There are several valuable articles on Fowles's narrative technique, existentialism, and reliance on the quest motif in Ellen Pifer's collection of critical essays (1986). Perhaps the most thorough discussion of Fowles's existentialism in the early novels is offered by James Acheson (1998) in the Modern Novelists series.

SELECTED BIBLIOGRAPHY

Works by Fowles

The Collector. Boston: Little, Brown, 1963.
The Aristos: A Self-Portrait in Ideas. Boston: Little, Brown, 1964, revised 1970.
The Magus. Boston: Little, Brown, 1965, revised 1977.
The French Lieutenant's Woman. Boston: Little, Brown, 1969.
Poems. New York: Ecco Press, 1973.
The Ebony Tower. Boston: Little, Brown, 1974.
Daniel Martin. Boston: Little, Brown, 1977.
Mantissa. Boston: Little, Brown, 1982.
A Maggot. Boston: Little, Brown, 1985.
Wormholes: Essays and Occasional Writings. Ed. Jan Relf. New York: Holt, 1998.

Selected Studies of Fowles

Acheson, James. *John Fowles.* Modern Novelists series. New York: St. Martin's Press, 1998.
Aubrey, James R. *John Fowles: A Reference Companion.* New York: Greenwood Press, 1991.

Foster, Thomas C. *Understanding John Fowles.* Columbia: University of South Carolina Press, 1994.

Huffaker, Robert. *John Fowles.* Twayne's English Authors Series. Boston: Twayne, 1980.

Kephalea, Kirki. *E Ellenike Empeiria.* Athens: Olkos, 1996.

Pifer, Ellen, ed. *Critical Essays on John Fowles.* Boston: G. K. Hall, 1986.

MAX FRISCH
(1911–1991)

Max E. Noordhoorn

BIOGRAPHY

The death of his architect-novelist-playwright father interrupted Max Rudolf Frisch's university studies of German literature (1931–33) in Zurich, his birthplace. He became a journalist, visited the Balkans (1934–36), then completed a course in architecture at the Technical University of Zurich (1936–41), doing his military service (1939–45) as a cannoneer and border guard. His first published diary, *Blätter aus dem Brotsack* (1940), is nonpolitical and provides no insight into the war that at that time was convulsing the world outside Switzerland's borders.

Frisch revisited the Balkans in 1948, traveling also to Berlin, Prague, and Warsaw and forming an acquaintance with Bertolt Brecht, the left-wing German writer who powerfully influenced his literary work. Visiting the United States and Mexico in 1951–52, Frisch closed the architectural office that he had established twelve years earlier and entered upon the career of a freelance journalist and author, revisiting the United States and Mexico in 1952, traveling to Cuba in 1956, and visiting several Arab countries in 1957. Living in Rome from 1960 to 1965, he later settled in the Ticino region of Switzerland, traveling to Poland and the Soviet Union in 1966; to Japan in 1959; to the United States for the third visit in 1970; and to China with the German Chancellor Helmut Schmidt in 1975.

This cosmopolitan experience, and the broad perspective of Frisch's mature writings, assure his place among the major multicultural writers of the twentieth century. His numerous plays and novels and his journalistic essays and diaries treating many of the same themes—all relating in some way to the predicament of the individual in an increasingly mechanized and bureaucratized society—contributed to an international reputation marked by numerous prizes and academic distinctions.

Although his output declined sharply in the last years of his life, he had by then become one of the world's most highly regarded authors. He died in the Ticino region of Switzerland on April 4, 1991.

MAJOR MULTICULTURAL THEMES

Because of his extensive and abiding interests in international politics, literature, and travel, one may truly regard Frisch as a multicultural observer and commentator even though the accidents of birth and residence led to his writing exclusively in the German language. His extensive travels abroad are reflected in the experiences of his foremost protagonists, particularly in *Homo Faber: Ein Bericht* (1957) and *Stiller, Roman* (1954). These characters, like the author himself, are struggling to escape what Frisch sees as the stifling limitations of Swiss society. Though his writings during the period of Nazi ascendancy in Germany remained noticeably apolitical, Frisch displayed an openly liberal and pacifist tendency after 1945, without identifying himself with any one particular party. As a Swiss national of cosmopolitan outlook, he tried to view political events within a larger European and world context and to expose what he saw as the provincialism, self-centeredness, and myopia of his countrymen.

Frisch's dramas, revolving around the difficult situations faced by complicated and questioning individuals in modern society, show a great variety of form and range, from farce and comedy to parable play, historical melodrama, and tragedy. Several of them show the influence of Bertolt Brecht whom he had known in Zurich, although he does not commit himself to a specific ideology as the latter had done.

Frisch's first major play, *Nun singen sie wieder: Versuch eines Requiems* (1945), influenced by Thornton Wilder and consisting of surrealistic scenes set in the afterlife, hinges on the prejudices of characters from opposing sides in World War II. A contrasting departure from the political and historical is presented in *Santa Cruz: Eine Romanze* (1946) that explores a marital relationship and introduces the author's lifelong concern with the delicate structure of one's own identity.

Two historical melodramas followed. *Die Chinesische Mauer: Eine Farce* (1946) explores the disproportion between humans' enormous intellectual and limited moral capacities. The Great Wall of China, designed to halt the inevitable passage of time, symbolizes the limitation of man's perception in deluding himself that building barriers prevents contagion by the outside world. The rather bleak parable play, *Als der Krieg zu Ende war* (1949), develops the main idea that appears also in the *Tagebuch 1946–1949* (1950), that of not making a graven image unto oneself. Set in

Berlin of 1945, the play depicts a German woman falling in love with a Russian officer, evading the danger to their relationship that would arise from having a common language with its inherent clichés and preconceptions.

Frisch's next parable play, *Graf Öderland: Ein Spiel in zehn Bildern* (1951), managed to maintain its topicality in depicting the terrorist, anarchic fantasies of a respectable government prosecutor whose alienation from middle-class society, in real life and in dream sequences, results in his metamorphosis into an urban terrorist.

In *Don Juan; oder, die Liebe zur Geometrie* (1953), a comedy in five acts, Don Juan is depicted as a lover of geometry cast by society's preconceptions into the philanderer's role. Again the stereotypical image replaces the true identity.

Among Frisch's best-known major plays, the black comedy, *Biedermann und die Brandstifter; ein Lehrstück ohne Lehre*, was produced initially as a radio play (1953) and later as a theater piece (1958). Its weak protagonist allows two arsonists to infiltrate and destroy his home. His attitude has been likened to the Germans' acceptance of Hitler's initially legal seizure of power, and also to the perceived irresponsibility of governments in overestimating the deterrent effect of nuclear armaments and overlooking their other and more dangerous characteristics. *Andorra: Stück in zwoelf Bildern* (1961) also appeared as a radio play before being adapted to the stage. Like *Don Juan*, it is a pessimistic depiction of contemporary society, in which humans, wittingly or unwittingly, contribute to their own downfall or that of others. The theme of hiding one's identity behind a mask returns here in a different form: the image of the stereotypical Jew is imposed upon a young man who accepts this false identity and dies as a result of anti-Semitic persecution by his fellow humans.

Of Frisch's last two major plays, *Biografie: Ein Spiel* (1967) is an experimental drama in which the protagonist is given the chance to go back over his life and change it. It turns out, however, that his freedom of action is limited owing to his own shortcomings, and he is doomed to repeat his failed life. *Triptychon: Drei szenische Bilder* (1978) treats the themes of transience and death. Language, shown in the past as obfuscating and distorting reality, has become so rigid in its use of clichés as to be wholly ineffectual in witnessing to humans' deepest concerns. The first of the three thematically-linked panels shows a group of mourners whose linguistic use is inadequate to cope with death and the hereafter. The second presents the dead slowly being overtaken by silence upon entering Hades, and the third shows a man who tries in vain to recall his dead mistress from the underworld. The ironic, secular use of what had originally been a religious form underscores the absence of a valid religious dimension in modern life.

Frisch's first ventures into fiction had been a novel under the title *J'adore ce qui me brûle, oder Die Schwierigen* (1943); and *Bin oder Die Reise nach Peking* (1945), that featured a dialogue between the hero and his alter ego. The author's use of surrealist techniques, together with the perceived necessity of having to flee in order to remain free, link these early prose works to the later ones. In the latter, variations of the themes treated in the dramas are played out.

The theme of concealed or lost identity—the discovery or flight from one's real self, hidden by stereotypes of one's own or others' making—dominates Frisch's three major novels: *Stiller*, *Homo Faber: Ein Bericht*, and *Mein Name sei Gantenbein: Roman* (1964). Stiller, in the eponymous novel, is a sculptor who, in a rather unbelievable plot, has taken on another's identity in order to escape his failure as an artist and husband, but is forced to face his true self in a painful process of self-discovery. In *Homo Faber*, the engineer Walter Faber, alienated from his true self because of his obsession with professional concerns to the detriment of his emotional life, inadvertently causes the death of a young woman with whom he has become involved and who, against all odds, turns out to be his illegitimate daughter by a former mistress. Confronted by this disconcerting discovery, Faber ultimately comes to terms with his human shortcomings and begins to appreciate the validity of realities beyond the sphere of technology. *Mein Name sei Gantenbein* has an extremely complex plot in which several characters assume different identities to discover the best mode of living before living it and thereby avoiding fate.

Of interest to many admirers of Frisch are also his two published diaries, *Tagebuch 1946–1949* (1950) and *Tagebuch 1966–1971* (1972), that possess an almost objective, documentary quality. The earlier book deals mainly with conditions in postwar Europe, observations on life and art, and ideas and sketches for later works. Prominent in the successor volume are political events in Europe, the ramifications of the Vietnam war, and literary concerns, including the newly prominent themes of aging and death. Also political in emphasis are *Wilhelm Tell für die Schule* (1971) and *Dienstbüchlein* (1974). The former presents Tell as a stupid murderer and the Swiss as backward conservatives; the second depicts the petrified class system of the Swiss army and the lack of political idealism and understanding of Nazism on the part of the Swiss public. Both works were of course severely criticized in Frisch's native land.

The successful and rather serene story, *Montauk: Eine Erzhählung* (1975), takes up the same themes of aging and death that recur in a more pessimistic form in *Triptychon*. An aging writer, Max, and a much younger American woman spend a pleasant weekend near Montauk, Long Island. Somewhat autobiographic in nature, the tale allows the writer to reflect upon his relationships with women—wives, mistress and daughter—and come to terms with aging and approaching death. The darker side of this same subject matter is pursued in *Mensch erscheint im Holozän: Eine Erzhählung* (1979), in which a man in his seventies, living in the isolation of a valley in the Ticino, totally cut off from civilization, ruminates on nature and humankind and comes to the conclusion that in the grand scheme of things, humans may be just a passing fancy and amount to very little.

Frisch never seemed to be able to resolve the issues he himself raised to his own satisfaction. It may be precisely this search for alternatives that keeps his work alive and the readers interested in revisiting this controversial artist.

SURVEY OF CRITICISM

The first major work on Frisch in English by Ulrich Weisstein (1967) is still an excellent introduction. Also of note are Hans Bänziger's work (1971) on *Frisch and Duerrenmatt*, Gerhard F. Probst's and Jay F. Bodine's edited *Perspectives on Max Frisch* (1982), and Wulf Koepke's general study (1991) that appeared in the year of the author's death. Solid introductions to both the novels and the plays are provided by Michael Butler (1976 and 1985).

SELECTED BIBLIOGRAPHY

Works by Frisch

Die Chinesische Mauer: Eine Farce (1946). [*The Chinese Wall*. Trans. James L. Rosenberg. Intr. Harold Clurman. New York: Hill & Wang, 1961.]

Tagebuch 1946–1949 (1950). [*Sketchbook 1946–1949*. Trans. Geoffrey Skelton. New York: Harcourt Brace Jovanovich, 1977.]

Stiller, Roman. Frankfurt am Main: Suhrkamp, 1954. [*I'm Not Stiller*. Trans. Michael Bullock. London and New York: Abelard-Schuman, 1958.]

Homo Faber: Ein Bericht. Frankfurt am Main: Suhrkamp, 1957. [*Homo Faber: A Report*. Trans. Michael Bullock. London and New York: Abelard-Schuman, 1959.]

Biedermann und die Brandstifter; ein Lehrstück ohne Lehre. Frankfurt am Main: Suhrkamp, 1958. [*The Fire Raisers: A Morality without a Moral*. With an Afterpiece. Trans. Michael Bullock. London: Methuen, 1962.]

Andorra: Stück in zwölf Bildern. Frankfurt am Main: Suhrkamp, 1961. [*Andorra: A Play in Twelve Scenes*. Trans. Michael Bullock. New York: Hill & Wang, 1964.]

Mein Name sei Gantenbein: Roman. Frankfurt am Main: Suhrkamp, 1964. [*A Wilderness of Mirrors. A Novel*. Trans. Michael Bullock. London: Methuen, 1965.]

Biografie: Ein Spiel. Frankfurt am Main: Suhrkamp, 1967. [*Biography: A Game*. Trans. Michael Bullock. New York: Hill & Wang, 1969.]

Tagebuch 1966–1971. Frankfurt am Main: Suhrkamp, 1972. [*Sketchbook 1966–1971*. Trans. Geoffrey Skelton. New York: Harcourt Brace Jovanovich, 1974.]

Montauk: Eine Erzähhlung. Frankfurt am Main: Suhrkamp, 1975. [*Montauk*. Trans. Geoffrey Skelton. New York: Harcourt Brace Jovanovich, 1976.]

Gesammelte Werke in zeitlicher Folge. 6 vols. Eds. Hans Mayer and Walter Schmitz. Frankfurt am Main: Suhrkamp, 1976.

Triptychon: Drei szenische Bilder. Frankfurt am Main: Suhrkamp, 1978. [*Triptych: Three Scenic Panels.* Trans. Geoffrey Skelton. New York: Harcourt Brace Jovanovich, 1981.]

Mensch erscheint im Holozän: Eine Erzhählung. Frankfurt am Main: Suhrkamp, 1979. [*Man in the Holocene: A Story.* Trans. Geoffrey Skelton. New York: Harcourt Brace Jovanovich, 1980.]

Stücke. 2 vols. Frankfurt am Main: Suhrkamp, 1962.

Selected Studies of Frisch

Bänziger, Hans. *Frisch und Dürrenmatt* (1960). 6th ed. Bern: Francke, 1971.

Butler, Michael. *The Novels of Max Frisch.* London: Oswald Wolff Ltd, 1976.

———. *The Plays of Max Frisch.* Houndmills, Basingstoke, Hampshire and London: Macmillan, 1985.

Jurgensen, Manfred. *Max Frisch. Die Dramen* (1968). 2nd ed. Bern: Francke, 1976.

———. *Max Frisch. Die Romane. Interpretationem* (1972). 2nd ed. Bern and Munich: Francke, 1976.

———, ed. *Frisch: Kritik, Thesen, Analysen.* Bern: Francke, 1977.

Kieser, Rolf. *Max Frisch. Das literarische Tagebuch.* Frauenfeld/Stuttgart: Huber, 1975.

Knapp, Gerhard P., ed. *Max Frisch. Aspekte des Prosawerkes.* Bern/Las Vegas: Peter Lang, 1978.

———. *Max Frisch. Aspekte des Bühnenwerks.* Bern/Las Vegas: Peter Lang, 1979.

Koepke, Wulf. *Understanding Max Frisch.* Columbia: University of South Carolina Press, 1991.

Pender, Malcolm. *Max Frisch: His Work and Its Swiss Background.* Stuttgart: Hans-Dieter Heinz, 1979.

Probst, Gerhard F. and Jay F. Bodine, eds. *Perspectives on Max Frisch.* Lexington: The University of Kentucky Press, 1982.

Schmitz, Walter. *Max Frisch: Das Spätwerk (1962–1982): Eine Einführung.* Tübingen: A. Francke, 1985.

———. *Max Frisch: Das Werk (1931–1961). Studien zu Traditionen und Traditionsverarbeitung.* Bern/New York: Peter Lang, 1985.

Steinmetz, Horst. *Max Frisch: Tagebuch, Drama, Roman.* Göttingen: Vandenhoeck & Ruprecht, 1973.

Stephan, Alexander. *Max Frisch.* Munich: C. H. Beck, 1983.

Weisstein, Ulrich. *Max Frisch.* New York: Twayne, 1967.

GAO XINGJIAN
(1940–)

M. Cristina Pisciotta

BIOGRAPHY

Recipient of the 2000 Nobel Prize for Literature, playwright, theatre director—but also novelist, literary and theatrical critic, and painter—Gao Xingjian is one of the most significant intellectuals of modern China. He was born into an intellectual family in Jiangxi Province in 1940. In secondary school, he happened to read an extract from the memoirs of Ilya Ehrenburg in which the author told of his life in Paris at the beginning of the 1920s. For Gao it was a flash of illumination, and from that moment on, French culture for him would always exist side by side with the Chinese. "The open-air cafés . . . the grand boulevards . . . the women in high heels . . . the France of that period," he says today, "gave me a sense of freedom that was exuberant and even a bit decadent" (interview with Jean-Luc Douin and Raphaëlle Rérolle, 35).

Gaining a diploma in French at Peking's Institute of Foreign Languages in 1962, he worked for some years as a translator at the Foreign Language Publishing House, translating Eugène Ionesco, Samuel Beckett, Jacques Prévert, Henri Michaux, Francis Ponge, Georges Perec, and others. Exiled to the country upon the outbreak of the Cultural Revolution, he returned after the fall of the Gang of Four in 1976 and began to publish his own work in 1978. Distribution of his 1981 essays *Xiandai xiaoshuo jiqiao chutan* and *Dangdai Zhongguo wenku jingdu* was blocked shortly after publication (they were later republished), but the essays precipitated a far-reaching debate in China on the theme of Modernism and Realism that opened the way to a new phase of cultural evolution. During the same period, his first theatrical work, *Juedui xinhao* (1982), signaled the birth of the Little Theater Movement within the so-called new research theater (*tansuoju*), of which the Chinese consider Gao to be the pioneer and true protagonist. *Juedui xinhao* was presented on a raised platform with no backdrop save for simple metal scaffolding meant to suggest conventional scenery, thus doing away with the illusion of four walls created by the proscenium and generally breaking with the whole mise-en-scène of the naturalistic tradition. With the audience seated around the stage and on the floor, the production also broke the barrier between actors and audience in the traditional theater. Strong lights and innovative sound effects accompanied a style of recitation completely unlike that of Konstantin Stanislavsky, to which the public was accustomed. Discussion sessions with the audience, the critics, and the actors after the performance also contributed to the enormous success of the production. The following year, *Chezhan* (1983) confirmed Gao's popularity: paired with *Waiting for Godot,* the work is seen by Chinese and Western critics as the beginning of the theater of the absurd (*huangtangju*) in China. Profoundly influenced in all his work by French surrealism in counterpoint with the Chinese traditional theater, Gao has managed to effect a wonderful synthesis. His research theater, strongly opposed by the authorities, has broadened the range of expression permitted to Chinese dramatists, setting them apart from the stereotyped characterizations of the realistic school and linking them with contemporary European culture. It has also encouraged the public to seek in its own cultural heritage those so-called national forms that could be assimilated into contemporary art. Thus what Gao calls the "modern theater-opera" has been born, and it has succeeded in projecting Chinese theater onto the international scene. The themes are highly sensitive: the absurdly long wait for a better society, mass paralysis in the face of an uncertain future, persecution of the individual in the name of the rules of collective life, the Tienanmen massacre. The works that followed *Chezhan—Xiandai shezi xi,* 1984; *Dubai,* 1985; *Yeren,* 1985; *Bi an,* 1986; *Ming Cheng,* 1987; *Shanhaijing Zhuan,* 1989—have a more mythological character, embracing a reconstruction of the ritualism related to the sources of popular culture. Yet the performances are immediately blocked by the Chinese authorities. Accused of "spiritual pollution" by the authorities in their campaign against politico-cultural deviations, Gao experienced difficult times and, during a 1988 lecture tour in Europe, decided to stop in Paris, where he continues to live as a political refugee with the support of the French Ministry of Culture and Communications. In 1992 he was made a Chevalier of the Order of Arts and Letters. His theater pieces produced in France are often written first in French and only afterward in Chinese: *Taowang,* 1989; *Au bord de la vie (Shengsijie),* 1991; *Dialoguer/interloquer (Dui hua yu fanhua),* 1992; *Le somnambule (Yeyoushen),* 1993; and *Quatre quatuors pour un week-end (Zhoumo sichongzou),* 1995.

In its entirety, the theatrical output of Gao Xingjian is voluminous: 25 comedies (10 of which, however, were destroyed during the Cultural Revolution) and a book of essays on the theater. One part of his work experiments with the techniques of symbolism, expressionism, and the stream of consciousness, often intermingled together; another explores more thoroughly the implications of the theater of the absurd. In more recent years there has been a progressive trend in Gao's work toward liberation of the theater from its excessive dependence on language and toward a beefing up of the multiple elements of *total* theater and, above all, toward an intensified search for inner truth: a theater that seeks to visualize what lies within. At the same time there is an attempt to incorporate certain elements of the traditional theater, such as the techniques of martial arts, masks, acrobatics, and mime. The influence of French surrealism remains strong. Gao's theatrical works have been translated into many languages and performed in the United States, France, Australia, Canada, Taiwan, Hong Kong, Germany, Italy, and England.

Though Gao's popularity stems from his activity as playwright and director, his narrative work must not be forgotten and in recent years has become ever more significant: *Gei wo laoye mai yugan* (1989), *Lingshan* (1990), *Au plus près du réel: dialogues sur l'écriture (1994–1997)* (1997), *Yigeren de Shengjing* (1999). These works intermingle essay and narrative, historical anecdote and literary research in an extraordinary mosaic of words, documents, and images. With a lyricism fraught with rage, Gao passes from daily life to the interior world and philosophic speculation. He oscillates between a lamentable past (ideological reeducation, cultural repression) and an exile's peaceful present (life in France, the deepening contact with French culture).

Memory is transformed into a violent and anguished denunciation of the Chinese totalitarian system. In his search for the sources of the old China and for the magic of a fabled Orient, Gao is on the road to a mysterious mountain, an ideal symbol and potential refuge from what Taoists and Buddhists call the "world of dust" (world of reality).

MAJOR MULTICULTURAL THEMES

French culture has been very significant for all modern Chinese writers. In the 1920s, French writers such as Rousseau, Voltaire, Balzac, Zola, and Hugo were translated, disseminated, and greatly loved. Then the penetration of Western culture was halted until the end of the Cultural Revolution. At the end of the 1970s, China once more felt the thirst for knowledge of European tradition, and many French works came into circulation in new translations. For Gao, living in this tormented period, Chinese education interacted with French culture in significant ways, recognizable in his entire literary output.

His first literary essay (1981) precipitated a clash between the realist tendency and the incipient modernist movement of avant-garde literature; it is based on the theories of the French structuralist school and made Gao, in the eyes of the authorities, a dangerous element who had undergone "noxious influences."

As a translator of Eugène Ionesco, Jean Genet, and Samuel Beckett, Gao builds upon his experience of the works, theories, and techniques of French surrealism and at the same time incorporates elements of traditional Chinese theater and themes relevant to the social reality and most burning questions of modern China. An example of this original synthesis is his popular absurdist piece *Chezhan* that in its techniques and themes is very reminiscent of *Waiting for Godot*. In a Peking suburb the characters arrive at a bus stop one by one from the orchestra in order to go to the city. Differing in age, sex, occupation, and personality, they are society in miniature. The buses go by without stopping; the conversation of the characters shows that time is passing without anything happening. Eventually, ten years have passed—the years of the Cultural Revolution—and suddenly they all realize that nothing written is posted at the stop, and therefore it is no longer a bus stop and perhaps has not been one for some time. The play is an allegory of the mass paralysis that the Chinese people experience as they face an uncertain future. Like *Waiting for Godot*, this work uses the concepts of confusion of time, senseless waiting, and the entirely uneventful passage of days. In *Juedui xinhao*, another work of the same period, one sees echoes of Antonin Artaud, whose theater and ideas have often inspired Gao. In Gao's latest theatrical pieces, written in French, the settings are changed to essentially Parisian environments, and the viewpoint is more individualized and internalized.

Yigeren de Shengjing, written in France from 1996 to 1998, interweaves memories of childhood in China and the violence of the Cultural Revolution with the life of an exile in France. Every memory, every testimony, every reflection is saturated with references to specifically French landscapes and Parisian daily life and culture. Here the protagonist is almost Gao himself—a man who has been able to harmonize Chinese and French culture in a rich and complex manner, and who seeks in this synthesis the means of breaking away from the violence of reality and, through literature, giving a powerful testimony: that of a solitary man who has chosen exile to maintain his intellectual freedom.

If *Yigeren de Shengjing* seems the obvious outgrowth of his multiculturalism, *Au plus près du réel* brings us into immediate contact with Gao's assimilation of the two cultures. The dialogue between a French writer (Denis Bourgeois) and a Chinese writer (Gao Xingjian) confronts the problems of writing, the role of the writer, and the relationship between literature and politics, between art and life. The points of contact and divergence between the Chinese and the French perspective are thus brought out and juxtaposed.

In the essay, "Le chinois moderne et l'écriture littéraire" (1998), Gao offers further exposition on his ideas about literary language, an investigation that naturally varies according to whether one is writing in Chinese or French. In a very technical manner, Gao analyzes the elements that seem to him most important in the search for "words, sounds and flavors" (80). Sonority, musicality, and essentiality appear as the fundamental characteristics of his literary writing, and he explains to us how to render them in both Chinese and in French. He adds, moreover, that in passing from French to Chinese and vice versa, he never resorts to translation, which he finds unthinkable in view of the enormous structural differences between the two languages; instead, he rewrites his work in the second language.

Multiculturalism is also evident in Gao's poetical work, unfortunately little published or studied, which makes constant references on the one hand to French surrealist poetry, and on the other to traditional Taoist poetry.

Nor should we forget the writer's essays on French literature, which reveal his talent for acute critical analysis. For example, his study of Jacques Prévert as a modernist-populist poet, published in *Zhongguo Qingnian Bao*, December 12, 1982, aroused great interest in China.

SURVEY OF CRITICISM

In his translation and critical study of the theatrical works of Gao Xingjian, Gilbert C. F. Fong (1999) discusses the theories and the literary production of the great playwright, dwelling particularly on his biographical details, his personal characteristics, and his dual cultural formation.

Henry Y. H. Zhao (2000), by contrast, explains the nature of the experimentalism in Gao's theatrical output, analyzing the various phases in the evolution of his work. With reference to the cultural synthesis in Gao's work, Zhao suggests that Gao is more influenced by Zen thought than by French culture in terms of esthetics, language, and themes. Barmé (1983), Ma Sen (1989), and Tam Kwok-kan (1990) study the relationship between Gao's theater of the absurd and the European (particularly the French) models and call attention to substantial differences. The most frequent comparison is between *Chezhan* (Gao Xingjian) and *Waiting for Godot* (Samuel Beckett). According to Ma Sen, Beckett's work is much more ambiguous and loaded with diverse meanings. The emphasis is on waiting, but not necessarily as a waste of time. In contrast, *Chezhan* is much more concrete: the people are waiting for a promised society, but the bus that brings it goes by without stopping. Gao seems to believe not that the goal of a better society is illusory, but that certain means of attaining this goal are a failure. To explain this more clearly, Gao makes the characters become narrators. For example, director Ma says, "Waiting in itself doesn't matter. What matters is that you must have a clear idea in the first place about what you are waiting for in the queue. If you just stand in the queue and keep waiting in vain for half a lifetime, aren't you making a big joke of yourself?" (Ma, 46). In fact, both Ma Sen and the Chinese critics see the work as a clear, direct, strong critique of a real society, and go so far as to say of Gao that "beneath the label of the absurd there beats the heart of a realist" (Ma, 147).

Two other comparative studies that highlight Gao's multiculturalism, taking his play *Yeren* as the point of departure for a broader inquiry, are those of Chen Xiaomei (1992) and Monica Basting (1988). Mabel Lee (1997) and Lodén Torbjörn (1993) are concerned, by contrast, with showing that Gao's narrative structure is derived from the Chinese tradition (a mélange of different genres, such as history, anecdote, autobiography, etc.), while his themes and language are influenced more by his twofold literary education.

Finally, for a general idea of Gao Xingjian's position in contemporary French culture, one should read at least the two articles of French Sinologists Alain Peyraube (1995) and Jacques Pimpaneau (1993).

SELECTED BIBLIOGRAPHY

Works by Gao

"Puleiweier shi yi ge mincui zhuyide xiandaipai de faguo shiren." *Zhongguo Qingnian Bao* (December 12, 1982).
Xiandai xiaoshuo jiqiao chutan. Guangzhou: Huacheng Chubanshe, 1984.
Gao Xingjian Xijuji. Beijing: Zhongguo Xiju Chubanshe, 1985. [Includes *Juedui xinhao, Chezhan, Yeren, Xiandai shezi xi,* and *Dubai.*]
Gei wo laoye mai yugan. Taipei: Lianhe Wenxue Chubanshe, 1989. [*Une canne à pêche pour mon grand-père.* La Tour d'Aigues: Editions de l'aube, 1997.]
Lingshan. Taipei: Lianjing chuban shiye gongsi, 1990. [*La montagne de l'âme.* La Tour d'Aigues: Editions de l'aube, 1995; *Soul Mountain.* Trans. Mabel Lee. New York: HarperCollins, 2000.]
Au bord de la vie (1991). Morlanwelz, Belgium: Editions Lansman, 1993.
Dialoguer/interloquer. Morlanwelz, Belgium: Editions Lansman, 1992.
Le somnambule. Morlanwelz, Belgium: Editions Lansman, 1993. [*Yeyoushen.* In *Qingxiang* 7 (1996): 12–62.]
Gao Xingjian Xiju Liu Zhong. Taipei: Dijiao Chubanshe, 1995. [Includes *Bi an, Ming Cheng, Shanhaijing Zhuan, Taowang, Shengsijie,* and *Dui hua yu fanhua.*]
Quatre quatuors pour un week-end (1995). Morlanwelz, Belgium: Editions Lansman, 1998.
Meiyou zhuyi. Hong Kong: Tianti Tushu Gongsi, 1996.
Cheung, Martha P. Y. and Jane C. C. Lai, eds. *An Oxford Anthology of Contemporary Chinese Drama,* 149–83. Hong Kong and New York: Oxford University Press, 1997.
Gao Xingjian and Denis Bourgeois. *Au plus près du réel: dialogues sur l'écriture (1994–1997).* La Tour d'Aigues: Editions de l'aube, 1997.

"Le chinois moderne et l'écriture littéraire." In *Littérature chinoise: Etat des lieux et mode d'emploi*, 75–93. Actes du Colloque organisé par le groupe de recherche sur l'Extrême-Orient contemporain (GREOC) de l'Université de Provence. Ed. Noël Dutrait. Aix-en-Provence: Publications de l'Université de Provence, 1998.

Dangdai Zhongguo wenku jingdu. Hong Kong: Mingbao Chubanshe, 1999.

Gilbert C. F. Fong, ed. and trans. *The Other Shore: Plays by Gao Xingjian.* Hong Kong: Chinese University of Hong Kong Press, 1999.

Yigeren de Shengjing. Taipei: Lianjing chuban shiye gongsi, 1999. [*Le livre d'un homme seul.* La Tour d'Aigues: Editions de l'aube, 2000.]

"En littérature, je chasse les mots comme des sons." Interview with Jean-Luc Douin and Raphaëlle Rérolle. *Le Monde* (October 14, 2000): 35.

"The Case for Literature." The 2001 Nobel lecture (December 7, 2000). *World Literature Today* 75 (Winter 2001): 5–11.

Selected Studies of Gao

Barmé, Geremie. "A Touch of Absurd." *Renditions* 19, no. 20 (1983): 373–79.

Basting, Monica. "Tradition und Avantgarde in Gao Xingjian's Theaterstück *Die Wilden.*" In *Yeren.* Bochum, Germany: Studienvert Brockmeyer, 1988.

Chen Xiaomei. "*A Wildman* between Two Cultures: Some Paradigmatic Remarks on Influence Studies." *Comparative Literature Studies* 29, no. 4 (1992).

Lee, Mabel. "Gao Xingjian's *Lingshan/Soul Mountain*, Modernism and Chinese Writer." *Heat* 4, Sydney (1997): 128–43.

Ma Sen. "The Theater of the Absurd in Mainland China: Gao Xingjian's *The Bus Stop.*" *Issues & Studies: A Journal of China Studies and International Affairs* 25, no. 8 (August 1989): 138–48.

Peyraube, Alain. "Voyage au bout de la Chine." *Le Monde*, December 16, 1995, V.

Pimpaneau, Jacques. "Gao Xingjian, auteur dramatique." *Le Rond Point janvier* (1993).

Tam Kwok-kan. "Drama of Dilemma: Waiting as Form and Motif in *The Bus Stop* and *Waiting for Godot.*" In *Studies in Chinese-Western Comparative Drama*, 23–45. Ed. Yun-Tong Luk. Hong Kong: The Chinese University Press, 1990.

Tay, William. "Avant-garde Theater in Post-Mao China: *The Bus-stop* by Gao Xingjian." In H. Goldblatt, ed. *Worlds Apart*, 111–119. New York: M. E. Sharpe, 1990.

Torbjörn, Lodén. "World Literature with Chinese Characteristic: On a Novel by Gao Xingjian." Stockholm University, *The Stockholm Journal of East Asian Studies* 4 (1993): 17–39.

Xu Guorong. *Gao Xingjian xiju yanjiu.* Beijing: Zhongguo Xiju Chubanshe, 1989.

Zhao, Henry Y. H. *Towards a Modern Zen Theatre: Gao Xingjian and Chinese Theatre Experimentalism.* London: School of Oriental and African Studies, University of London, 2000.

Zou Jiping. "Gao Xingjian and Chinese Experimental Theatre." Ph.D. diss., University of Illinois, 1994.

ÉDOUARD GLISSANT
(1928–)

Kaiama L. Glover

BIOGRAPHY

The Martinican writer Édouard Glissant was born in the hillside village of Sainte-Marie, a rural area in which cultural traditions from Martinique's pre-Columbian and African past persist to this day. Very shortly after his birth, however, his mother moved with her five children to urban Lamentin, the most important industrial zone in Martinique. Glissant's father, a hard-working plantation manager, was left behind, but Édouard frequently went to visit with him over school holidays. During these visits, he regularly accompanied his father on trips throughout Martinique, thus coming to know well the agricultural life of the island countryside. His relationship with his father was an ambivalent one. While he claims to have admired the way his father often stood up for himself with respect to his white employers, Glissant also admits to having felt disappointment at his father's complete lack of political consciousness and willingness to participate in, without challenging, the colonial status quo. Glissant recalls being aware, from a very young age, of the various ways in which Martinicans were consistently encouraged to admire France and all things French at the expense of their own cultural heritage. Indeed, from primary school in Lamentin to the prestigious Lycée Schoelcher in Fort-de-France, which he attended from 1939 through 1945, a blatant francophilia and elitist conception of French culture dominated the educational system. Never were students taught anything of the history, geography, or culture of Martinique, and speaking Creole in class was strictly forbidden. Glissant's innate refusal to accept such cultural hierarchization eventually became the principal motivation behind his creative and theoretical enterprise.

In 1945, as a member of the short-lived student group, *Franc-Jeu*, Glissant made his first foray into social activism. Concerned primarily with cultural issues, and peripherally involved in Aimé Césaire's election campaign, this group of young people sought to define an independent Martinican cultural identity, one that might resist French domination without falling into the trap of blind Afrocentrism. During this period, Glissant discovered the writings of the French surrealists as well as the philosophical works of Karl Marx and Georg Wilhelm Friedrich Hegel. He also made his first serious attempts at writing poetry. A year later, at the age of 18, he received a scholarship and left for Paris to pursue his education. He enrolled in a program of study at the Sorbonne but dropped out almost immediately in order to prepare his first collection of poems, *Un champ d'îles* (1953). He later returned to his studies at the Sorbonne where he earned degrees in both ethnology and philosophy. This accomplished, he definitively abandoned academics and devoted himself exclusively to writing.

Glissant's arrival in Europe corresponded with a very tumultuous time in France's history, on both a literary and political level. It was the time of the New Novel, a movement that called for a rethinking of art's role in society and an interrogation of such notions as authority, universality, and humanism. Politically, France's colonial power was being challenged throughout Africa and Asia. Living as he did in a residence populated mainly by Antilleans, Glissant came into contact with social theorist and activist Frantz Fanon, and became increasingly involved in worldwide struggles for independence. He participated in the *Présence Africaine* group, a social and literary cornerstone of the Pan-African intellectual community that publishes works of literature and organizes conferences worldwide. Together with his friend Paul Niger, Glissant founded in 1959 the *Front Antillo-Guyanais*, a sociopolitical group that called for the decolonization of France's Caribbean departments and their assumption of a regional identity. The group was disbanded by President Charles De Gaulle in 1961, and Glissant's revolutionary stance made him such a high-profile character that he was actually forbidden to leave France.

The period of his initial stay in France was also one of intense literary production. Between 1953 and 1964, he published several books of poetry (*Un champ d'îles*, 1953; *La terre inquiète*, 1954; *Les Indes: poème de l'une et l'autre terre*, 1956; *Le sel noir*, 1959; *Le sang rivé*, 1961), novels (*La lézarde*, 1958; *Le quatrième siècle*, 1964), an essay (*Soleil de la conscience*, 1956), and a play (*Monsieur Toussaint*, 1961). These were the years in which he began to articulate clearly his political and aesthetic philosophies.

In 1965, the travel ban was lifted and Glissant returned to Martinique. Since then, he has divided his time between France, the Caribbean, and the United States, making him a true product of the interrelating, multi-cultural world he describes in his work.

MAJOR MULTICULTURAL THEMES

The multicultural aspects of Glissant's work are detectable in his manipulation of a number of related concepts that not only serve as the basis for his own literary endeavor, but have also become essential to all modern-day postcolonial Francophone criticism. Among these notions, the concepts of opacity, relation, exile, and wandering are perhaps the most interesting in a multicultural context. For, indeed, whether voluntarily embraced or externally imposed, it is this experience of exile that enabled Glissant to develop the fundamental notions of opacity and relation. Any scholar of Glissant's work must therefore seek to determine in what manner and to what extent the author's wanderings have informed, and continue to inform, his literary adventure.

Although Glissant has produced only one text that specifically recounts his experiences in France, *Soleil de la conscience*, one might argue that the thematic foundations of his entire body of work are in many ways a response to the "alienating otherness" (Dash, 45), which he first felt as a student in Paris. Glissant's feelings of isolation and difference actually helped him to gain a better sense of his individuality and to recognize those aspects of his identity that were directly connected to the fact of his Martinican-ness. In effect, he lived his Parisian exile as a voyage of self-discovery. He found confirmation of this perspective in the works of French writers Victor Segalen, Paul Claudel and Michel Leiris, all of whom regarded their encounters with foreign cultures as opportunities for personal enlightenment.

Glissant's somewhat painful and destabilizing contact with Franco-European culture, a culture that he was ostensibly expected to embrace as his own, made apparent the links between landscape, climate, and identity construction. He realized that the orderly and structured quality of France's physical environment, as well as the cyclical regularity of its seasons, was reflected in the overall mentality of its citizens: "the periodic return of the seasons is well suited to teaching moderation," he explains in *Soleil de la conscience* (12). By the same token, the relative chaos of the Martinican landscape and the irrelevance of notions of seasonality exercise a significant, and particular, influence on the Caribbean individual. Viewing Martinique from the perspective of exile, Glissant saw the only way to enter into a "relation" with France was to embrace his "opacity"—his impenetrable difference—as a Martinican. Convinced that "every being first comes to his consciousness of the world from the perspective of his own world" (*Soleil de la conscience*, 18), Glissant denounced the danger of universalizing humanism and insisted on the value of cultural specificity. His desire to affirm Martinican culture, independent of the

Occidental monolith, led to Glissant's very Caribbean early creative expression. Avoiding the anticolonialist polemics and Afrocentric militantism that, in the wake of Sartre's concept of *engagement* and Césaire's *négritude*, characterized much of the literature produced by black intellectuals in Paris at the time, Glissant explored the imaginative space of the Caribbean. Images of the earth and the sea recur throughout the works of this period; notions of itinerancy and interrelation are offered as alternatives to imperialism and domination. Glissant's reflections on the early history of the Caribbean resist a simple condemnation of European imperialism. Rather, they poeticize the Western encounter with the New World as the source of countless cultural transformations, the repercussions of which Glissant felt most intensely as a young Martinican exile in Paris in the 1950s.

Paris for Glissant was indeed the spatial catalyst for an intellectual trajectory (Coutinho Mendes, "*Soleil de la conscience:* entre le regard du fils et la vision de l'étranger," 38). It was in Paris that Glissant first came to understand foreignness as an inherently relative concept— a realization that, from the perspective of the Antillean individual, France itself might legitimately be considered *outre-mer* (referring to the fact that Martinique is officially one of France's overseas departments—a "Département Outre-Mer" [DOM]). Glissant understood that "no longer will there be any culture without all cultures, no longer any one civilization to be the metropolis of others" (Édouard Glissant, *Soleil de la conscience*, 11). His experiences in exile facilitated the theoretical and literary formulation of what would eventually become his theory of *Antillanité* (Caribbean-ness) and the attendant *poétique de la relation* (poetics of relation). The open-ended, pluralistic vision of culture inherent in these concepts provides the backdrop for and principal subject matter of his 1993 novel, *Tout-monde*. Through a recounting of the psychological journeys of two young exiled Martinicans wandering throughout the European continent, the seasoned author-theorist Glissant revisits the multicultural intentions he first articulated as a student in Paris almost four decades earlier: "Wherever I go, I will feel solidarity with that 'little piece of earth' [Martinique] . . . and at the same time, I cannot deny that one whole part of me, at once the driest and the softest, is here in Paris" (Édouard Glissant, *Soleil de la conscience*, 54).

SURVEY OF CRITICISM

Very little criticism focuses exclusively on the influential significance of Glissant's Parisian experience to his literary endeavors. However, nearly all Glissantian theorists are concerned with those aspects of his theoretical and aesthetic philosophy that were first conceived during this period of exile in France. In the introduction to his 1982 work, Daniel Radford offers a concise presentation of Glissant's biography, successfully linking specific events with the author's literary production. Ana Paula Coutinho Mendes (1992) addresses issues of alienation and identity formation in her analysis of *Soleil de la conscience*. J. Michael Dash (1995) provides important biographical information on Glissant as well as chronologically organized analyses of his various works. Dash specifically comments on the impact of Glissant's first sojourn in Paris on his subsequent literary production. Chapter 1, "Contexts," and chapter 2, "The Poetic Intention," are particularly useful for a discussion of Glissant's multiculturalism.

SELECTED BIBLIOGRAPHY

Works by Glissant

Un champ d'îles. Paris: Dragon, 1953.
La terre inquiète. Paris: Dragon, 1954.
Les Indes: Poème de l'une et l'autre terre. Paris: Seuil, 1956.
Soleil de la conscience. Paris: Falaize, 1956; Paris: Seuil, 1960; Paris: Gallimard, 1997.
La lézarde. Paris: Seuil, 1958.
Le sel noir. Paris: Seuil, 1959.
Le sang rivé. Paris: Présence Africaine, 1961.
Monsieur Toussaint (1961). Fort-de-France: Acoma, 1978.
Le quatrième siècle. Paris: Seuil, 1964.
Poèmes: Un champ d'îles; La terre inquiète; Les Indes. Paris: Seuil, 1965.
Malemort. Paris: Editions du Seuil, 1975.
Tout-monde. Paris: Gallimard, 1993.
Sartorius: Le roman des Batoutos. Paris: Gallimard, 1999.

Selected Studies of Glissant

Coutinho Mendes, Ana Paula. "*Soleil de la conscience:* entre le regard du fils et la vision de l'étranger." In *Horizons d'Édouard Glissant.* Ed. Yves-Alain Favre and Antonio Ferreira de Brito, 37–48. Biarritz: J&D Editions, 1992.
Dash, J. Michael. *Édouard Glissant.* Cambridge, England, and New York: Cambridge University Press, 1995.
Radford, Daniel. *Édouard Glissant.* Paris: Seghers, 1982.

MICHEL GOELDLIN
(1934–)

Nadine Dormoy

BIOGRAPHY

Born in Lausanne, Switzerland, to a Swiss father of German-Swiss origin and an American-born mother, Michel Goeldlin had two nationalities at birth. Since childhood, he has vacationed regularly in the Adirondacks in upper New York state, where he remembers walking in the woods with Albert Einstein. As a teenager, he considered becoming a pilot, a physician, or a newsman. He experienced these vocations in his life and explored them in his writings.

After classical Latin studies in Switzerland, Goeldlin joined the family business (farm-produce industry and trade) that provided him many opportunities for travel across Europe and the United States. In 1959, he married Jolanda "Yucki" Zur Muhlen, his Dutch childhood sweetheart. In 1968, he decided to leave the business world and become a full-time writer. He produced two apprenticeship novels, one unpublished, the other rewritten much later (*Panne de cerveau*, 1997), but his third novel, *Les sentiers obliques* (1972), met with instant success. That same year he was awarded the Swiss Budry Prize for an unpublished short story, "La mutation," which was later integrated into *L'espace d'un homme* (1989, 61–75). A short time later he spent several weeks in Wyoming, after reading about a human tragedy in a Swiss newspaper: a man died on a highway in his car that had run out of fuel. After waiting eleven hours for help, the man eventually died of exposure, ignored by all passersby. This was the starting point of *Le vent meurt à midi* (1976), a best-seller later translated into German and Russian.

Returning once more to the familiar Adirondack Mountains near Lake Placid in 1975, he wrote *A l'ouest de Lake Placid* (1979), a novel in which the magnificent and endangered forest constitutes the main theme of the book.

In 1980 and 1982, the Goeldlins decided to explore the Sahara Desert. Goeldlin was particularly impressed with the austere landscape and the frugal-but-proud population that dwells within. He then imagined the story of a Tuareg family who refuses the transformations brought about by the exploitation of the oil wells in the region. This story is told in *Les moissons du désert* (1984). Here, characters and scenery are fully intertwined with overwhelming effect.

In 1988 and 1989, Goeldlin and his wife were accredited by the International Committee of the Red Cross to carry out missions in El Salvador, Angola, and Cambodian refugee camps. The result was *La planète des victimes* (1990), a fictionalized documentary which received the Alpes-Jura Prize from the Association des écrivains de langue française (ADELF, Association of French language writers).

In 1992, the Goeldlins joined the crew of a Hercules C-130 and flew 10,000 miles through the Canadian northwest territories, up to the magnetic north and the 80th parallel. His meeting with the Inuit tribes inspired the next book, *Péril au Nunavut* (1998). It tells of the difficult birth of a new Canadian province and the plight of a forgotten population, whose culture and lifestyle are threatened by the prospectors of a $300 billion reserve of gold, diamonds, and oil.

Goeldlin and his wife, a professional photographer, embarked on a cargo ship in 1998 for a journey around the world. This resulted in the creation of an illustrated logbook entitled *Chemins d'écume* (2001), which details four months of their trip.

MAJOR MULTICULTURAL THEMES

Although considered a novelist from *Suisse romande* (French-speaking Switzerland), there is little trace of Switzerland in Goeldlin's work, save the fact that he writes in French. His innumerable travels through five continents, his bicultural upbringing, and his taste for exotic peoples and locations make him a true citizen of the world. His is a profoundly universal spirit, and his method of work is so independent of literary currents, schools, or ideological groups that he remains an individualist, no doubt more in the American tradition than in the European. A self-made man in literature, he developed a very personal approach to writing. To him, much of the work is done beforehand: it consists in choosing a topic, gathering documentation, examining the location, speaking with the people, putting himself "in situation," and in the end producing books much as others produce films. He is also a hardworking artisan who concentrates much of his effort on style—the artistic form he will give to the episodes he has first imagined, then fully lived and actually experienced in situ. This writing technique was perfectly illustrated when he spent several weeks in Wyoming, discovering and reflecting on today's Far West, while writing one of his most accomplished novels, *Le vent meurt à midi*. In fact, Goeldlin is forever in search of situations that will help demonstrate how the human psyche works in conditions of extreme stress. Each of his novels, different as it may be from the others, is one piece of the puzzle of life that he is trying to compose. In *Les moissons du désert*, as in many other instances, he strikes a contrast between the true nature of man and the necessities of industrial development. This constant dichotomy is again brought to the foreground in *La planète des victimes*, the object of, among other things, a UNESCO exhibit.

The desire to penetrate the secrets of nature and wilderness, in people as well as places, is the true reason for Goeldlin's wanderings. In his autobiographical *L'espace d'un homme*, he writes: "Certain people know the planet only from the sedentary point of view, as earthlings; others only hear its music or see its visual aspects; still others are fascinated by financial and commercial activities. I am lucky to be able to try everything, to immerse myself in one milieu or another, to stroll as I please, to adapt and to share, always curious about people and situations, about large horizons as well as microcosms animating a blade of grass" (55, trans. Michel Goeldlin).

From the icy snows of Canada to the burning sands of the Sahara, Goeldlin is in search of original images, themes, settings, and characters, constantly trying to uncover the mystery of the planet—and of himself.

SURVEY OF CRITICISM

In her biography of Goeldlin (1995), Martine L. Jacquot demonstrates that "the key to all his novels is the facing of a fundamental choice, the workings of a deep psychological transformation," regardless of the characters involved (23, trans. Michel Goeldlin). Henri-D. Paratte, in his foreword to Jacquot's work, analyzes the characteristics of Swiss literature and finds the authors from *Suisse romande* to be victims of their enclosure inside the Alps. This isolation fuels their need to escape and to settle elsewhere. Such is the case of Goeldlin who "is torn between several worlds: America on his mother's side, Europe on his father's side, then a Dutch wife born in Java." Paratte adds: "his writing is at the junction of the powerful symbolism that the best European novelists know how to integrate into their works, and the will to remain in touch with the realism that was always the strength of American novelists, from Dos Passos or Hemingway to Mario Puzo or Mailer. . . . This novelist, like all great novelists, is above all an explorer of human beings" (12–13, trans. Michel Goeldlin).

SELECTED BIBLIOGRAPHY

Works by Goeldlin

Les sentiers obliques. Lausanne: Bertil Galland, 1972.

Le vent meurt à midi. Vevey: Bertil Galland, 1976. [*Wildstille gegen Mittag.* German trans. Pierre Imhasly. Cologne and Zurich: Benziger, 1977; *Vietier umiraiet v poldien.* Russian trans. E. Ivanova-Anninskaia and N. Popova. Moscow: Kstatie, 1997.]

A l'ouest de Lake Placid: Roman. Lausanne: Bertil Galland, 1979; Vevey: Editions de l'Aire, 1987.

Les moissons du désert. Lausanne: Editions de l'Aire, 1984.

L'espace d'un homme. Geneva: Zoé, 1989.

La planète des victimes. Lausanne and Boulogne: Editions de l'Aire; Editions du Griot, 1990.

Panne de cerveau. Vevey: Editions de l'Aire, 1997.

Péril au Nunavut. Montreal: Libre Expression, 1998. [*Coeur de neige.* Vevey: Editions de l'Aire, 1999.]

Chemins d'écume. Paris: Indo, 2001.

Sculpteur de nuages. Paris: Carnot, 2002.

Selected Studies of Goeldlin

Blanche, Martine. "Michel Goeldlin. *Coeur de neige.*" *Europe Plurilingue* (Paris) (May 2000): 213.

Capré, Raymond. "Le drame planétaire." *Écriture* (Lausanne) 40 (1992): 295–97.

Dictionnaire des littératures (1968). 4 vols. Ed. Philippe van Tieghem and Pierre Josserand, 1: 636. Paris: Presses Universitaires de France, 1984.

Duméry, Sophie. "Michel Goeldlin, *La planète des victimes.*" *Europe Plurilingue* (Paris) (May 1991): 146.

Jacquot, Martine L. *Michel Goeldlin, espace du réel, cheminements de création.* Foreword Henri-D. Paratte. Collection Aux Portes du Monde. Nova Scotia, Canada: Editions du Grand Pré, 1995.

JUAN GOYTISOLO
(1931–)

Arianna Maiorani

BIOGRAPHY

Juan Goytisolo was born in Barcelona of a Catalan mother, Julia Gay, and a father of Basque origin. During the Spanish Civil War his family lived in a Catalonian mountain village; when Juan was seven his mother was killed in Barcelona during a Nationalist air raid. He spent the rest of his childhood with his father, an anti-Communist loyal to Franco who was imprisoned by the Republicans, and his brothers, José Augustín, who became a poet, and Luis, also a future novelist. When Juan was eight he was molested by his maternal grandfather. Though it must have been a traumatic experience, Goytisolo has always claimed that this episode never influenced his subsequent sexual development and choices.

After a Jesuit education, he escaped from his Catholic middle-class environment, attending the University of Madrid and the University of Barcelona, where he studied law. His first novel, *Juegos de manos* (1954), was a success; meanwhile, in Barcelona he frequented slums and brothels in search of female prostitutes and men with whom to satisfy his homosexual tendencies, rejecting lovers from his own social class. This was a way of declaring his disdain for the bourgeois morality of his upbringing and for what he defined as the tradition of female passivity.

Goytisolo went to Paris in self-imposed exile in 1956. There he worked as a reader for the French publisher Gallimard and fell under the influence of the *nouveau roman* and experimental narrative techniques. He also met other Spanish writers who became his friends and whom he helped, such as Carlos Fuentes, Manuel Puig, and Guillermo Cabrera Infante. A supporter of the Cuban revolution, Goytisolo, accompanied by Cabrera Infante, visited the island after having discovered that his Basque great-grandfather had made his fortune in the local slave trade.

In Paris Goytisolo also wrote literary criticism and articles and worked as a journalist for *L'Observateur*, *L'Express*, and *El País*. He met his future wife, Monique Lange, who worked as a secretary in a translation agency and later became a novelist. (Notwithstanding his acknowledged homosexuality, Goytisolo always declared that the only love of his life was his wife; the couple's relationship, thanks to extraordinary mutual acceptance, lasted until Lange's death in 1996, although she did reveal some of her problems in her novel *Les poissons-chats*.) Thanks to her, Goytisolo met Albert Camus, Jean Genet (who became a mentor for him), Ernest Hemingway, Jean-Paul Sartre, and Simone de Beauvoir.

During the Algerian war (1954–1962), Goytisolo and Lange became supporters of the Algerian independence movement and actively protested against the crackdowns on Africans in Paris.

Between 1966 and 1975 Goytisolo wrote his famous autobiographical trilogy of novels: *Señas de identidad* (1966), *Reivindicación del Conde don Julián* (1970), and *Juan sin tierra* (1975). The first two were both published in Mexico, for all of Goytisolo's books were banned from Spain and their publication prohibited until after General Franco's death. The author considers these three novels as his first adult works, written after he had finally confessed his homosexuality. After the publication of the first book of the trilogy he disowned all his previous works as pertaining to a conventional tradition that was no longer his own.

His increasing activity as a journalist revolved mostly around conflicts and war and the relationship between Islamic and Christian cultures. His point of view was that of a self-exile who saw the refusal of multiculturalism as a form of fascism and the cause of sociopolitical conflicts throughout the world. His journalism was a continuing denunciation of every form of fascism, racism, and the "false morality" of post-Franco Spain; he defended not only contemporary immigrant minorities living in Spain (and in Europe) but also those who had suffered the same kind of discrimination in the Spain of past centuries.

Goytisolo now lives in Marrakesh, Morocco, where he strives to preserve those places he considers the source of an ancient and rich multicultural oral tradition, such as the Xemaá-El-Fná square and the old cafés that he sees as "international centres of culture."

MAJOR MULTICULTURAL THEMES

Multiculturalism is for Juan Goytisolo the real nature of every living and lively culture in the world. It is the source of a culture's richness and development, the recognition of its past, the force of its present and the only hope for its future. Multiculturalism is also linked to freedom, both political and moral (and sexual as well). It is the fundamental, universal value of human beings, a guiding concept that everyone should make a basic principle of life. Goytisolo uses multiculturalism to criticize and undermine the "official" culture of post-Franco Spain, a country he believes has no memory of its multicultural heritage, a country where multiculturalism (generated by Arab, Jewish, and Christian ancient cultures) should be considered the most important contribution to the creation and development of European culture.

Much of his work—both journalistic and fictional—focuses on multicultural themes. His autobiographical trilogy deals with the Moorish element of Spanish culture and celebrates its multicultural nature; the books also attack the role of Spain as a barrier between the Catholic and Islamic worlds and the purism that led to a centuries-long denial of the presence of Arabic elements in Spanish culture and language. In the 78 short chapters of *Paisajes después de la batalla* (1982), Goytisolo deals mainly with political issues. The story imagines that suddenly, in an area of Paris where immigrants have become predominant, all the writing in Roman script is suddenly replaced by Arabic. The central problem is the impossibility of communication caused by refusing the multicultural. *Crónicas Sarracinas* (1982) is a collection of essays and articles that deal principally with travelers' perceptions of foreign countries. *Coto vedado* (1985) and *En los reinos de taifa* (1986) are two volumes of memoirs in which he exposes his life and ideas: the first starts from his childhood and the Spanish civil war and traces his growth; the second is based on specific episodes of his life during the 1960s and early 1970s. In *Las virtudes del pájaro solitario* (1988), inspired by the figure of St. John of the Cross, he links the expulsion of Jews and Muslims from ancient Spain to the modern ideologies of ethnic, cultural, and blood purity. In *La cuarentena* (1991) the narrator accompanies a dead friend in a journey toward eternity, mixing Western and Eastern cultural traditions (Dante and Islamic figures, among others, appear in the novel). In *La saga de los Marx* (1993) Goytisolo imagines Karl Marx and his family living in our times and contemplating all of our contemporary political, social and cultural problems. *Paisajes de guerra con Chechenia al fondo* (1996) is a collection of short pieces previously published in various journals, in which Goytisolo narrates his experiences in areas troubled by the varying roles of Islam. *Las semanas del jardín* (1997) is the story of an imaginary poet, a friend of Federico García Lorca called Eusebio, who is arrested by Spanish Fascists in 1936, imprisoned in a military psychiatric center, and escapes physically and symbolically to North Africa. Goytisolo imagines here that the story is written by a reader's circle (the subtitle "*Un círculo de lectores*") of 28 members (28 is also the number of characters in the Arabic alphabet) acting as an "invented author," questioning the concept of authorship.

SURVEY OF CRITICISM

Criticism of Goytisolo's work centers mainly on his experimental writing techniques (cf. Manuel Ruiz Lagos and Alberto Manuel Ruiz Campos, 1995); on his dissidence with respect to Spanish and European official cultural and literary tradition (cf. Claudia Schaefer-Rodríguez, 1984; Bradley S. Epps, 1996; and Alison Margaret Kennedy, 1996); and on his homosexual tendencies. Some critics, such as Abigail Lee Six (1990), Manuel Ruiz Lagos (1992), Marta Gómez Mata and César Silió Cervera (1994), and Emmanuel Le Vagueresse (2000), have also focused their analysis on his mixing of narrative experimentalism, the African oral tradition, and some of his favorite multicultural issues. Abdelatif Ben Salem's (1996) edition of essays concentrates mostly on Goytisolo's experience as a traveler. Luce López Baralt (1985) considers Goytisolo's works the ultimate result of a cultural tradition of Islamic origin traceable in Spanish literature. Miguel Dalmau (1999) has studied the work of Juan, José Augustín, and Luis Goytisolo as a unique, multifaceted Spanish literary phenomenon, while some critics are attracted mainly by the techniques and multicultural themes that Goytisolo displays in his trilogy (Christian Meerts, 1972; Michael Ugarte, 1982; and Ksenija Fallend, 1998).

SELECTED BIBLIOGRAPHY

Works by Goytisolo

Juegos de manos. Barcelona: Destino, 1954. [*The Young Assassins.* Trans. John Rust. New York: Knopf, 1959.]

Señas de identidad. Mexico City: Joaquín Mortiz, 1966. [*Marks of Identity.* Trans. Gregory Rabassa. New York: Grove Press, 1969.]

Reivindicación del Conde don Julián. Mexico City: Joaquín Mortiz, 1970. [*Count Julian.* Trans. Helen R. Lane. New York: Viking Press, 1974.]

Juan sin tierra. Barcelona: Seix Barral, 1975. [*Juan the Landless.* Trans. Helen R. Lane. New York: Viking Press, 1977.]

Obras completas. 2 vols. Ed. Pere Gimferrer. Madrid: Aguilar, 1977.

Makbara. Barcelona: Seix Barral, 1980. [*Makbara.* Trans. Helen R. Lane. New York: Seaver, 1981.]

Crónicas Sarracinas. Barcelona: Ibérica de Ediciones y Publicaciones, 1982. [*Saracen Chronicles: A Selection of Literary Essays.* Trans. Helen R. Lane. London: Quartet, 1992.]

Paisajes después de la batalla. Barcelona: Montesinos, 1982. [*Landscapes after the Battle.* Trans. Helen Lane. New York: Seaver, 1987.]

Coto vedado. Barcelona: Seix Barral, 1985. [*Forbidden Territory: The Memoirs of Juan Goytisolo (1931–1956).* Trans. Peter Bush. London and New York: Quartet, 1989.]

En los reinos de taifa. Barcelona: Seix Barral, 1986. [*Realms of Strife: The Memoirs of Juan Goytisolo (1957–1982).* Trans. Peter Bush. San Francisco: North Point Press, 1990.]

Las virtudes del pájaro solitario. Barcelona: Seix Barral, 1988. [*The Virtues of the Solitary Bird.* Trans. Helen R. Lane. London: Serpent's Tail, 1991.]

La cuarentena. Madrid: Mondadori, 1991. [*Quarantine.* Trans. Peter Bush. Normal, Ill.: Dalkey Archive, 1994.]

La saga de los Marx. Barcelona: Mondadori, 1993. [*The Marx Family Saga.* Trans. Peter Bush. London and Boston: Faber, 1996.]

Paisajes de guerra con Chechenia al fondo. Madrid: El País/Aguilar, 1996. [*Landscapes of War: From Sarajevo to Chechnya.* Trans. Peter Bush. San Francisco: City Lights, 2000.]

Las semanas del jardín. Un círculo de lectores. Madrid: Santillana, 1997. [*The Garden of Secrets, As Written Down by Juan Goytisolo.* Trans. Peter Bush. London: Serpent's Tail, 2000.]

Selected Studies of Goytisolo

Ben Salem, Abdelatif, ed. *Juan Goytisolo, ou, Les paysages d'un flâneur.* Paris: Fayard, 1996.

Dalmau, Miguel. *Los Goytisolo.* Barcelona: Anagrama, 1999.

Epps, Bradley S. *Significant Violence. Oppression and Resistance in the Narratives of Juan Goytisolo, 1970–1990.* Oxford: Clarendon Press, and New York: Oxford University Press, 1996.

Fallend, Ksenija. *Prefigurar el porvenir: tiempo en la novela y su reflejo en la trilogía de Álvaro Mendiola de Juan Goytisolo.* Frankfurt am Main: Peter Lang, 1998.

Gómez Mata, Marta and César Silió Cervera. *Oralidad y polifonía en la obra de Juan Goytisolo.* Madrid: Jucar, 1994.

Kennedy, Alison Margaret. *Dissidence and the Spanish Literary Tradition in the Later Novels of Juan Goytisolo, 1970–1988.* Oxford: University of Oxford, 1996.

Le Vagueresse, Emmanuel. *Juan Goytisolo: écriture et marginalité.* Paris: Harmattan, 2000.

López Baralt, Luce. *Huellas del Islam en la literatura española: De Juan Ruiz a Juan Goytisolo.* Madrid: Hiperión, 1985.

Meerts, Christian. *Technique et vision dans "Señas de identidad" de J. Goytisolo.* Frankfurt am Main: Vittorio Klostermann, 1972.

Ruiz Campos, Alberto Manuel. *Estructuras literarias en la nueva narrativa de Juan Goytisolo.* Almería: Instituto de Estudios Almerienses, 1996.

Ruiz Lagos, Manuel. *Retrato de Juan Goytisolo.* Barcelona: Círculo de Lectores: Galaxia Gutenberg, 1993.

———. *Sur y modernidad. Estudios literarios sobre Juan Goytisolo: Las virtudes del pájaro solitario.* Sevilla: Don Quijote, 1992.

Ruiz Lagos, Manuel and Alberto Manuel Ruiz Campos. *Juan Goytisolo. El centro y el método.* Alcalá de Guadaira: Editorial Guadalmena, 1995.

Schaefer-Rodríguez, Claudia. *Juan Goytisolo: del "realismo crítico" a la utopía.* Madrid: José Porrúa Turanzas, 1984.

Six, Abigail Lee. *Juan Goytisolo: The Case for Chaos.* New Haven: Yale University Press, 1990.

Ugarte, Michael. *Trilogy of Treason. An Intertextual Study of Juan Goytisolo.* Columbia: University of Missouri Press, 1982.

JORIE GRAHAM
(1950–)

Deborah Phelps

BIOGRAPHY

It may be said that Jorie Graham has lived a charmed poet's life: romantic childhood in Italy, student days in Paris of the 1960s, a glamorous marriage into a famous publishing family, then a glittering career of prizes, academic posts, and praise for her difficult, often obscure, poetry. Although she has lived in the United States for most of her life, her poetry continues to reference the European perspectives and tastes of her expatriate youth.

Graham was born in New York City on May 9, 1950, but grew up in Rome where her father, William Pepper, worked as a foreign correspondent for *Newsweek*. Her mother, Beverly, was a sculptor and socialite who held parties at which the young Jorie would be introduced to a glittering array of social, political, and artistic celebrities, including the Italian *dolce vita* filmmakers Federico Fellini and Michelangelo Antonioni (who employed her as a researcher for his film *Zabriskie Point*). While studying philosophy at the Sorbonne, Graham was arrested for participating in the student demonstrations of May 1968 and was expelled from the country by the French government.

She returned to New York in 1969 to enroll in New York University's film school, where she studied under director Martin Scorsese and renewed her antiwar activities with Students for a Democratic Society (SDS), participating in demonstrations in New York and Washington, D.C. However, these interests palled after she attended a lecture on T. S. Eliot and fell in love with modern poetry. After a brief early marriage, she wed childhood friend William Graham, son of *Washington Post* publisher Katherine Graham. The couple lived in Mrs. Graham's Washington, D.C. home during the turbulent Watergate era, then moved to Los Angeles where William Graham worked as an attorney.

Despite her new marriage and plans for motherhood, Graham was discontented. She had continued her interest in poetry since her years at New York University and yearned for a more structured environment in which to study and write. In 1976 she enrolled in the University of Iowa Writer's Workshop, commuting between Iowa City and Los Angeles, until the stress of this arrangement led to her divorce from William Graham. She earned a master's degree in fine arts from the University of Iowa in 1978, by which time she had married fellow student and poet James Galvin and her poetry began to appear in major literary journals.

Graham was hired as a professor of poetry at Iowa in 1983 after publishing two celebrated collections of poetry, *Hybrids of Plants and Ghosts* (1980) and *Erosion* (1983). From 1995 to 2000, she headed the poetry department at the Iowa Writer's Workshop, imprinting the program with her taste for modernist, nonconfessional narrative poetry and becoming famous for both her flamboyant teaching and sartorial style.

Her publications have garnered significant awards; she has been the recipient of a John D. and Catherine T. MacArthur Fellowship (the so-called genius grant), the Morton Darwen Zabel Award from the American Academy and Institute of Arts and Letters, and has been named a Chancellor of the Academy of American Poets. In 1996 she was awarded the Pulitzer Prize for *The Dream of the Unified Field: Selected Poems 1974–1994* (1995). After her marriage to Galvin ended in 1999, she served as the first female Boyleston Professor of Rhetoric and Oratory at Harvard University. She returned to the faculty at the Iowa Writer's Workshop in 2001; her latest collection of poetry is entitled *Never: Poems* (2002).

MAJOR MULTICULTURAL THEMES

One of Graham's early poems contains the names in three languages for the tree facing her window: "*castagno,*" "*chassagne,*" and "chestnut." She defines herself through the nations these three names evoke: Italy represents her heart, her childhood family life; France, her teenage years when she was "anarchic, though well bred" ("I was Taught Three," in *Hybrids of Plants and of Ghosts*, 7); and America, the region of her adult career as a poet—a new self forged through hard work. Graham's poetry frequently revisits the places of her European past by invoking memory, then widening the poem's scope to mix the personal with global history.

In "The Hiding Place" (in *Region of Unlikeness*, 61–62) Graham remembers her days as a political activist in Paris. In her typical stream of consciousness, she brings the excitement and terror of that time to the reader while at the same time attempting to make sense of it to her adult self. Through reliving the danger she experienced, Graham melds the beliefs she had youthfully professed with her present position as a poet. The title poem "Region of Unlikeness" returns Graham to the Europe of the 1960s in a dream she first confuses with reality. Her dream self wanders through a cold flat while below her window armed counterterrorist police—her enemy—relax in a cafe. Here Graham puzzles the true nature of reality: is it the black and white dream or the sharp awakening in the dark bedroom?

Poems about art, particularly paintings, are arguably Graham's most successful in discussing the complex issues of history, memory, and individual cognition. In the collection *Erosion*, she takes the reader into the world of the painting or the artist in attempts to discover and share what was actually being experienced at that time. In "Scirocco," she visits Keats's house in Rome and relates seeing what he saw and through this, feeling what he felt. "San Sepolcro" enters Piero della Francesca's painting of the Virgin Mary. But more striking than the subject is Graham's confident recognition of the Italy the painting evokes; she tells the reader: "I can take you there" ("San Sepolcro," in *Erosion*, 2). Graham takes us into another, more somber world in "At Luca Signorelli's Resurrection of the Body" wherein she reveals that the painting's exquisite detail of Christ's resurrection was achieved through the painter's sorrowful dissection of his dead son's body.

The Holocaust is perhaps the most difficult event of modern times to depict in poetry. Graham has been criticized (à la Sylvia Plath) for relating it to personal turmoil. In two poems, however, the Holocaust is effectively set against the unobtrusive backdrop of the poet's experience. "Two Paintings by Gustav Klimt" centers on Graham's visit to Klimt's hometown, an idyllic landscape of beech forest. Graham explores the ironic contrast between Klimt's joyously erotic art and the enduring beauty of the place later notorious as Buchenwald, a Nazi death camp. In "History" Graham begins in the present with a Holocaust-denier's questions, shifts to scenes of wartime torture and violent death, and ends with the question of how to teach our children about a past we ourselves cannot fully understand.

SURVEY OF CRITICISM

From the time of her earliest publications, critics have noted the high seriousness of Graham's work and have consistently placed her in the pantheon of major contemporary American poets. Poet Mark Strand told the *New Yorker* in 1997 that he believed Graham to be a genius (Stephen Schiff, 60). But by far Graham's most influential champion has been Harvard professor and critic Helen Vendler, who likened Graham to Yeats in her book *The Breaking of Style: Hopkins, Heaney, Graham* (1995).

Vendler and others have praised Graham's refusal to write the sort of lyric, postconfessional poem that has become the standard in contemporary American poetry. Instead, she has developed a poetic that explores philosophy, history, art, and the mystery of individual cognition in a detached, almost disembodied style. Vendler has claimed that Graham's rejection of lyricism for difficult, experimental work harkens back to the High Modernist style of Eliot, Yeats, and Stevens.

However, this divergence from convention has also led to critical approbation. Graham has been criticized for being too obscure, too difficult. In a review of *The End of Beauty*, critic Adam Kirsch (2000) wrote that Graham's poetry assumed too much of her audience, that her wide-ranging knowledge of philosophical theory left less well-read readers unable to comprehend her message. He attacked her penchant for erratic line placement, the substitution of algebraic x's and y's for major images, and dashes ending poems as needlessly opaque.

Others have criticized Graham more personally. Fellow poet Richard Howard has suggested that Graham's work has been overshadowed by her celebrity in the hothouse poetry community, giving it a reputation for high art that it may not command (Stephen Schiff, ,62). Her courting of influential friends like Vendler has also engendered (mostly anonymous) sniping from other poets suspicious of Graham's swift rise to the top. Despite these negative voices, Graham continues to inhabit a realm of critical and commercial success shared by very few contemporary American poets.

SELECTED BIBLIOGRAPHY

Works by Graham

Hybrids of Plants and of Ghosts. Princeton: Princeton University Press, 1980.
Erosion. Princeton: Princeton University Press, 1983.
The End of Beauty. New York: Ecco Press, 1987.
Region of Unlikeness. New York: Ecco Press, 1991.
Materialism: Poems. Hopewell, N.J.: Ecco Press, 1993.
The Dream of the Unified Field: Selected Poems 1974–1994. Hopewell, N.J.: Ecco Press, 1995.
The Errancy: Poems. Hopewell, N.J.: Ecco Press, 1997.
Swarm: Poems. New York: Ecco Press, 2000.
Never: Poems. New York: Ecco Press, 2002.

Selected Studies of Graham

Kirsch, Adam. "The End of Beauty." *The New Republic* (March 13, 2000). Available at http://www.thenewrepublic.com/031300/kirsch031300.html.
Schiff, Stephen. "Big Poetry." *New Yorker* (July 14, 1997): 60–67.
Vendler, Helen. *The Breaking of Style: Hopkins, Heaney, Graham.* Cambridge, Mass.: Harvard University Press, 1995.
———. *The Given and the Made: Strategies of Poetic Redefinition.* Cambridge, Mass.: Harvard University Press, 1995.

GÜNTER GRASS
(1927–)

Robert E. Clark

BIOGRAPHY

Günter Grass grew up in a household of both Slavic and German cultures in Danzig (Gdansk), a city that has been forcibly claimed by both Germany and Poland. His birthplace is the setting of his major novels, and its history as a pawn in the clash of cultures is an important theme. Grass's father owned a grocery store; his mother's background was Kashubian—a Slavic group distinguished from Poles by both language and culture. Intellectually daring, Grass is also multitalented—a printmaker, sculptor, poet, playwright, ballet composer—but his greatest popular and critical successes have come as a novelist. Crossing freely between media, he has brought all of his artistic interests into his texts, including illustrating his works and sometimes even creating the jacket-art. His peripatetic life (as a young soldier, hand-laborer, speechwriter, and a lionized as well as much-attacked author), like the variety of his talents, seems to have helped him depict a broad swath of German culture across the country's history.

His early education was at Danzig *volksschule* and *gymnasium*. After World War II, he studied painting and sculpture at the Düsseldorf Academy of Art and the State Academy of Fine Arts in Berlin. But his wartime experience provided the background for his earliest fiction. He joined the Hitler Youth in the 1930s, was drafted into the army at 16, was wounded in battle in 1945, and spent the rest of that year as a prisoner at Marienbad, Czechoslovakia. After his release he worked as a farm laborer, a potash miner, and a stonecutter's apprentice.

He then moved to Berlin, where he played drums and washboard with a jazz band and wrote poetry before leaving for Paris in 1956. There he began his first novel, *Die Blechtrommel* (1959); it became an international sensation, causing an uproar in Germany for its depiction of the Nazis as an integral part of that culture, not a historical anomaly. Grass, the nation's first major author after the war, was suddenly seen internationally as a spokesman for the wartime generation of Germans.

Die Blechtrommel is part of a "Danzig trilogy," with *Katz und Maus: eine Novelle* (1961), about marginal middle-class Danzig youth culture from 1939 to 1944, and *Hundejahre* (1963). The latter focuses on Nazi crimes—and the postwar reintegration of former Nazis into the German mainstream. Grass eventually came to consider *Hundejahre* the weakest part of the trilogy.

He became a prolific and influential political essayist in the early 1960s and has remained one ever since. He was also a ghostwriter for Willy Brandt (Chancellor 1969–74). Grass believes Brandt's Social Democrats brought to German politics vision and opportunity that were subsequently betrayed. *Aus dem Tagebuch einer Schnecke* (1972) is a memoir of Grass's travels on the campaign trail, but also contains a fictional story about a collector of snails who takes refuge from the Nazis with a Kashubian woman who wishes to assimilate to German culture. (A sampling of his political writings should include *Der Burger und seine Stimme: Reden, Aufsatze, Kommentare*, 1974; *Deutscher Lastenausgleich*, 1990; and his political correspondence with the Japanese writer Ōe Kenzaburō (Nobel Prize for Literature, 1994), *Gestern, vor 50 Jahren: ein deutsch-japanischer Briefwechsel*, 1995.) After writing a number of minor plays, including *Die Plebejer proben den Aufstand* (1966, featuring Bertolt Brecht as a character more preoccupied with artistic questions than with East Berlin workers), and the novel *Ortlich betaubt* (1969), Grass took up the causes of the youth movements of the 1970s, particularly feminism and ecology, in fiction as well as in political activities.

Grass next explored the mythic realm of early human matriarchy in *Der Butt: Roman* (1977). In that novel, the talking fish from the Grimm brothers' "The Fisherman and his Wife" has its say. The action moves from prehistory to the Danzig shipyards of the late 1970s. But Grass writes as a fabulist more in Aesop's tradition than in the Grimms'. For throughout his works the despised and the freakish—snails, rats, the child-sized adult protagonist of *Die Blechtrommel*—speak moral truths to savage and corrupt modern cultures.

Grass's fiction of the 1980s and the 1990s has been less critically successful internationally. *Die Rattin* (1986) is consistent with his comic view of humanity. The narrator receives as a gift a female rat; the beast demonstrates in a series of tales that rodents will rule the world. Two widows in *Unkenrufe: eine Erzählung* (1992), one a German art historian and the other a Polish restorer, go into the macabre business of returning the remains of exiled Germans to Danzig after the war.

Grass lived in India in 1986 and 1987, and that experience is behind *Zunge Zeigen* (1988). Throughout the 1990s he remained prominent in political and cultural debate. *Ein weites Feld: Roman* (1995) covers the years of German reunification (1989–91)—the first fiction by a major German writer centered on that issue. The novel includes the character Ludwig Hoftaller, a spy convincingly free of scruples, equally happy working for the Gestapo or the Stasi. The risible German critic Marcel Reich-Ranicki posed for a well-known picture on the cover of *Der Speigel* tearing *Ein weites Feld* in two, an image corresponding to his violent reaction to the work as a critic.

The Nobel Prize for Literature awarded to Grass in 1999 added to his luster as an elder statesman of German letters. Yet his Nobel acceptance speech and irreverent interviews make clear that he has not relinquished his role of provocateur.

MAJOR MULTICULTURAL THEMES

Culture, to Grass, is the result of battles between cultures, and these battles are brutal, even horrific, as in the rise of the Third Reich. His writing and life are emblematic of the writer caught geographically, politically, and historically in cultural conflict. The opposition between factions is stark: Pole or German, Nazi or Jew, resister of fascism or casual collaborator. Although Grass's characters make compromises—to assimilate or to try to transform themselves—they are forced to make clear choices between evident evil and a much more dubious good. Oskar, the narrator of *Die Blechtrommel*, tries to opt out of the choices: at age three he "decides" not to grow (apart from a prodigious sexual organ) and not to communicate except by playing his tin drum or with glass-shattering screams. But this only puts Oskar in the hands of a succession of groups. This opposition—between those who choose a reasonable if perhaps bizarre detachment and those who become fanatics—is the fundamental division in Grass's vision of culture. His later characters cross back and forth over real or metaphorical walls between reason and various kinds of fury. A reasoned rejection of fanaticism—by way of compassion for workers, fairness toward women, and respect for the productive power of the earth—has always informed Grass's political fiction and writings.

The gravity of Grass's insight is tragic; greed, brutality, and lies are always near the surface of politics. He is nonetheless delightfully comic, the inventor of a German strain of magical realism that shares with Latin American fiction "boom" of the 1960s–1970s an interest in obsessive behavior and freakishness. Yet Grass has a more European than American view of nature and magic. His landscape is not a jungle that swallows cities and industries, as it is for Gabriel García Márquez. He does not see sex as a primordial urge that trumps culture. For Grass violence, not sex, leads to truly unnatural acts. In his magic realm animals truly possess wisdom, cities show stubborn resilience, and women's sexuality nurtures life as their maternal impulses protect it. Although Grass does not believe that nature provides metaphors for human freedom as did Jean-Jacques Rousseau, he does hold that the political order can learn from animals and natural processes.

His characters are perennial refugees and exiles, often caught between cultures from birth (cf. *Im Krebsgang*, 2002). Grass is perhaps the most eloquent contemporary author writing about the fortunes of refugees living in European and developed countries.

SURVEY OF CRITICISM

As Grass is both a major novelist and political commentator, in the United States much attention has gone to the question of the intersection of the cultures of art and politics (Michael Hollington, 1980; Alan Frank Keele, 1988; Philip Brady, Timothy McFarland, and John J. White, eds., 1990). Grass's own meditations on the question are rewarding, but non-German readers will need guidance in understanding his of-the-moment interventions in German political debates.

In recent years the relationship between Grass's fiction and his talents as a visual artist has been explored more thoroughly (Klaus-Jurgen Roehm, 1992; Ann L. Mason, 1974; Julian Preece, 2001). Again, Grass's own comments on his work, like his essays about other writers, are insightful and of high quality. Delving into Germany's fraught history has led Grass to compassionate ways to understand other cultures: from his political advocacy for Turkish laborers in Germany today, to his persisting sympathy for ancient Slavic groups in one-time Pomerania, to his fascination with Indian myth and legend (see Ervin C. Brody, 1996; Patricia Merivale, 1995; Rudolf Bader, 1984).

SELECTED BIBLIOGRAPHY

Works by Grass

Die Blechtrommel. Neuwied am Rhein: Luchterhand, 1959. [*The Tin Drum.* Trans. Ralph Manheim. New York: Pantheon, 1962.]

Katz und Maus: eine Novelle. Neuwied: Luchterhand, 1961. [*Cat and Mouse.* Trans. Ralph Manheim. New York: Harcourt, Brace and World, 1963.]

Hundejahre. Neuwied am Rhein: Luchterhand, 1963. [*Dog Years.* Trans. Ralph Manheim. New York: Harcourt, Brace and World, 1965.]

Die Plebejer proben den Aufstand. Neuwied: Luchterhand, 1966. [*The Plebians Rehearse the Uprising: A German Tragedy.* Trans. Ralph Manheim. New York: Harcourt, Brace and World, 1966.]

Örtlich betaubt. Neuwied am Rhein: Luchterhand, 1969. [*Local Anaesthetic.* Trans. Ralph Manheim. New York: Harcourt, Brace and World, 1970.]

Theaterspiele (Collected Plays) Neuwied: Luchterhand, 1970.

Aus dem Tagebuch einer Schnecke. Neuwied: Luchterhand, 1972. [*From the Diary of a Snail.* Trans. Ralph Manheim. New York: Harcourt Brace Jovanovich, 1973.]

Der Burger und seine Stimme: Reden, Aufsatze, Kommentare. Neuwied: Luchterhand, 1974.

Der Butt: Roman. Darmstadt and Neuwied: Luchterhand, 1977. [*The Flounder.* Trans. Ralph Manheim. New York: Harcourt Brace Jovanovich, 1978.]

Die Rattin. Darmstadt: Luchterhand, 1986. [*The Rat.* Trans. Ralph Manheim. San Diego: Harcourt Brace Jovanovich, 1987.]

The Danzig Trilogy [*The Tin Drum, Cat and Mouse, Dog Years*]. Trans. Ralph Manheim. San Diego: Harcourt Brace Jovanovich; and New York: Pantheon, 1987.

Zunge Zeigen. Darmstadt: Luchterhand Literaturverlag, 1988. [*Show Your Tongue.* Trans. John E. Woods. San Diego: Harcourt Brace Jovanovich, 1989.]

Deutscher Lastenausgleich (1990). [*Two States—One Nation?.* Trans. Krishna Winston and A. S. Wensinger. San Diego: Harcourt Brace Jovanovich, 1990.]

Unkenrufe: eine Erzählung. Göttingen: Steidl, 1992. [*The Call of the Toad.* Trans. Ralph Manheim. New York: Harcourt Brace Jovanovich, 1992.]

Ein weites Feld: Roman. Göttingen: Steidl, 1995. [*Too Far Afield.* Trans. Krishna Winston. New York: Harcourt Brace, 2000.]

Gestern, vor 50 Jahren: ein deutsch-japanischer Briefwechsel. Göttingen: Steidl, 1995.

Günter Grass and Pierre Bourdieu dialogue (1999), reprinted in *New Left Review* (March-April 2002): 10–21.

Im Krebsgang: eine Novelle. Göttingen: Steidl, 2002.

Selected Studies of Grass

Bader, Rudolf. "Indian Tin Drum." *International Fiction Review* 11, no. 2 (Summer 1984): 75–83.

Brady, Philip, Timothy McFarland, and John J. White, eds. *Gunter Grass's Der Butt: Sexual Politics and the Male Myth of History.* Oxford: Clarendon Press, 1990.

Brody, Ervin C. "The Polish-German Conflict in Gunter Grass's Danzig: Pan Kishot in *The Tin Drum.*" *The Polish Review* 41, no. 1 (1996): 79–107.

Hayman, Ronald. *Günter Grass.* London and New York: Methuen, 1985.

Hollington, Michael. *Günter Grass, the Writer in a Pluralist Society.* London and Boston: M. Boyars, 1980.

Keele, Alan Frank. *Understanding Günter Grass.* Columbia: University of South Carolina Press, 1988.

Lawson, Richard H. *Günter Grass.* New York: F. Ungar, 1985.

Mason, Ann L. *The Skeptical Muse: A Study of Günter Grass's Conception of the Artist.* Frankfurt am Main: Peter Lang, 1974.

Merivale, Patricia. "Saleem Fathered by Oskar: *Midnight's Children*, Magic Realism, and *The Tin Drum.*" In *Magical Realism: Theory, History, Community.* Ed. Lois Parkinson Zamora and Wendy B. Paris, 323–51. Durham, N.C.: Duke University Press, 1995.

Mews, Siegfried, ed. *The Fisherman and his Wife: Günter Grass's* The Flounder *in Critical Perspective.* New York: AMS Press, 1983.

Neuhaus, Volker. *Günter Grass* (1979). Stuttgart: Metzler, 1993.

O'Neill, Patrick, ed. *Critical Essays on Günter Grass.* Boston: G.K. Hall, 1987.

Pelster, Theodor. *Günter Grass.* Stuttgart: Reclam, 1999.

Preece, Julian. *The Life and Work of Günter Grass: Literature, History, Politics.* Houndsmills, Basingstoke, U.K. and New York: Palgrave, 2001.

Reddick, John. *The "Danzig Trilogy" of Günter Grass: A Study of* The Tin Drum, Cat and Mouse, *and* Dog Years. New York: Harcourt Brace Jovanovich, 1975.

Roehm, Klaus-Jurgen. *Polyphonie und Improvisation: zur offenen Form in Gunter Grass'* Die Rattin. New York: Peter Lang, 1992.

ROMESH GUNESEKERA
(1954–)

Maria Antonietta Saracino

BIOGRAPHY

Not much biographical information about Romesh Gunesekera has been made available, but sources agree that he was born in Sri Lanka, where he grew up speaking both English and Sinhala. He also lived for some time in the Philippines until he moved to England, where he spent his formative years. At the University of Liverpool he studied English and Philosophy. Throughout the years he has won several awards, including the Liverpool College Poetry Prize in 1972, the Rathbone Prize in Philosophy in 1976, and first prize in the Peterloo Open Poetry Competition in 1988. He has been a writer-in-residence in Copenhagen, Singapore, Hong Kong, and Southampton. He presently lives in London as a writer and poet, but travels widely.

His first collection of stories, *Monkfish Moon* (1992), was shortlisted for several awards including the Commonwealth Writers and David Hingham prizes, was named a *New York Times* notable book for 1993, and won the Yorkshire Post Best First Work prize (1995). His first novel, *Reef* (1994), like *Monfish Moon*, was widely acclaimed; it was shortlisted for the Booker Prize as well as for the Guardian Fiction Prize. In the United States, the writer was nominated for a New Voice Award.

His short stories have been widely anthologized in *Granta*, *Paris Review*, *New Writing*, *London Magazine*, and several other journals; they have also been broadcast by BBC Radio, BBC World Service, and Radiotelevisione Italiana (RAI). His work has been translated into several languages, including Italian, French, Spanish, German, Dutch, and

Hebrew. Gunesekera was awarded one of the prestigious Italian literary prizes, the Premio Mondello Five Continents, in 1997.

His second novel, *The Sandglass* (1998), was also highly praised and hailed as one of the six most interesting books of that year. Gunesekera received the inaugural BBC Asia Award for Achievement in Writing and Literature in 1998.

MAJOR MULTICULTURAL THEMES

Gunesekera's main achievement from the point of view of multiculturalism seems to be the author's ability to weave together—in fairly slim texts, unlike the bulky standards of most writers from the Indian subcontinent—themes of memory and exile, of past history and postcolonial upheaval, of contemporary London and postwar Sri Lanka. His literary language is a rich mixture of two different cultural traditions. A child of two worlds, he incorporates into his English texts a number of Sinhalese expressions coming from his mother language; he manages to do so as if it were natural and did not require explanation. At the very beginning of his novel *Reef*, for example, the reader comes upon words such as *kolla*, *rathmal*, *cadjan*, or *seeni-sambol*, for which no translation or explanation is given. Still, these words become familiar as the reader progresses through the story, and in a way they become part of a shared vocabulary.

Similarly, Gunesekera makes reference to great works of Western literature. Most of *Reef* unfolds in Asia, but the novel contains allusions to Shakespeare's *The Tempest*, beginning with the title itself and the opening quotation ("Of his bones are coral made"). He also makes reference to Western mythology. The novel describes the childhood and adolescence of Triton, now a London restaurant-owner from Sri Lanka. After burning down a roof in his schoolyard, he runs away and becomes a servant to Mr. Salgado, a wealthy marine biologist. He grows up, moves to England, and becomes a chef, while his country of origin undergoes a period of violent political upheaval: "All over the globe revolutions erupted, dominoes tottered and guerrilla war came of age," says Triton; "the world's first woman prime minister—Mrs. Bandaranaike—lost her spectacular premiership on our small island, and I learned the art of good housekeeping. Sam-Li, at number five, showed me how to stir-fry and turn a spring onion into a floating flower. Next door, Dr. Balasingham's young son, Ravi, obsessed by the American Wild West, educated me in the history of the Apaches in his father's backyard" (*Reef*, 55).

Narrations in many ways are rooted in both Asian and European culture. *The Sandglass* is set in London, but it retraces the history of two feuding families—the Ducals and the Vatunases—and their changing fortunes in postcolonial Sri Lanka. The novel moves back and forth between these two worlds in a kind of narrative meditation on history—

past and present—and the concepts of time and death. The story opens with Prins Duca arriving in London from Sri Lanka, for his mother Pearl's funeral. He grieves, but at the same time is full of unanswered questions about the family's past, such as the mystery of his father's accidental death forty years earlier. Central to this intricate novel is the story of a piece of property, a house called Arcadia, bought by the Ducal family in 1948. It is located not only in one of the most desirable parts of Colombo, the capital, but also, unfortunately, on the border of the land of the other feuding family, the Vatunas.

England and Sri Lanka are also the setting of the short stories of *Monkfish Moon*. We meet people returning to Sri Lanka, the land of their birth, after years of working and living abroad, as do Ray and Siri-Ray's houseboy in the story "A House in the Country"; or, conversely, people relocating themselves in London, as in "Batik," with Nalini, a Sinhalese, and her husband Tiru, a Tamil, fleeing from the increasing violence at home.

SURVEY OF CRITICISM

Critic Neloufer de Mel (1993) sees the nine short stories of *Monkfish Moon* as primarily about reconnection. People return to Sri Lanka after years of living abroad; estranged brothers and husbands and wives reunite. But such reconnections are often bittersweet and fragile. During the time spent away people and places have changed. Sri Lanka is no longer the idyllic place of childhood; rather there is violence in the air. "What Gunesekera deftly deals with is the fact that the land of one's childhood always haunts the exile. The memories, the nostalgia it provokes, the possibilities or impossibilities of return, its political and ideological battles become central to the identity of the exile abroad" (de Mel, 54). Far from representing a place for investment, the country of childhood is often portrayed in these stories as a battleground where notions of violence, decay, and estrangement make that longed-for reconnection to one's own past history often impossible. So the pearl-fisher's paradise, the original Garden of Eden (that is how Leonard Woolf saw Ceylon when he visited it in 1910 on a bicycle as a government agent) is nothing like the torn and bleeding setting of Gunesekera's novels. Rather, as South African critic Stephen Gray (1995) points out, "For Gunesekera's hero the situation is the exact reverse: the U.K. is where he may rest safely. A tropical island in the shape of a teardrop, then" (81). The greatest achievement, in Gray's words, rests with Gunesekera's use of English in *Reef,* as here "we are subtly reminded of our debt to the Orient, for verbal trading was never only one way. Salgado's *bungalow* has a *veranda,* he has Triton keep his *banyan* in an *almirah,* he orders a small carriage of *plantain,* which he has carried in a *gunnysack* . . . When in England Triton bumps into a new arrival from that 'sea of pearls' who nervously blurts at him: 'English only little', we realize the extent of verbal treasure this one still needs to recuperate so as to defend himself" (81).

In her review-article of *The Sandglass*, Gunesekera's most recent work to date, critic Paula Burnett (1999) sees the novel as being about memory, a retrospective fiction "driven by a concern for the present and future which asks how the past has got us *here*. . . . 'Sandglass' suggests an hourglass, and the theme of time, but sand, heated, becomes glass. This is history as crucible, the trial by ordeal which can generate the new and beautiful" (84–85).

SELECTED BIBLIOGRAPHY

Works by Gunesekera

Monkfish Moon. London: Penguin in association with Granta, 1992.
Reef. London: Granta, 1994.
The Sandglass. New Delhi: Viking, 1998.
"The Emporium of the Durians" (short story). *Wasafiri* 29 (Spring 1999): 62–64.
"Appetite" (a poem). *Wasafiri* 21 (Spring 1995): 65.
"The Lover" (short story). In *New Writing* 5. Ed. Christopher Hope and Peter Porter, 329–33. London: Vintage, 1996.

Selected Studies of Gunesekera

Burnett, Paula. "The Sandglass" (review-article). *Wasafiri* 29 (Spring 1999): 84–86.
de Mel, Neloufer. "Monkfish Moon" (review-article). *Wasafiri* 17 (Spring 1993): 54–55.
Gray, Stephen. "Best of Black British" (review-article of *Reef*). *Wasafiri* 21 (Spring 1995): 81–82.

STRATIS HAVIARAS
(1935–)

Bruce Merry

BIOGRAPHY

Born in Nea Kios, Greece, Haviaras published three slim volumes of verse in Greek, *I kyria me tin pyxida: piimata* (1963), *Verolino* (1965), and *I nychta tou Zilopodarou* (1967), before emigrating in 1967 to the United States, where he earned a college degree in 1973 and has been associated with Harvard University since that time. He has been curator of the Poetry and Farnsworth Rooms in the Harvard College Library for over 26 years. A collection of verse titled *Nekrofaneia* appeared in 1972; two years later he participated in a "Poets-in-the-Schools" program and in 1979 he gave personal readings at the St. Mark's Poetry Project in East Village, New York, involving his audiences in live commentary on the texts. His eclectic edition of six taped hours of readings by American poets from their own work, entitled *The Poet's Voice* (1978), includes T. S. Eliot, Ezra Pound, Marianne Moore, William Carlos Williams, Wallace Stevens, Robert Frost, W. H. Auden, Robinson Jeffers, Theodore Roethke, Randall Jarrell, John Berryman, Robert Lowell, and Sylvia Plath. Haviaras produced an edition of *Thirty-Five Post-War Greek Poets* (1972) as part of the privately printed journal that he edits, *Arion's Dolphin*. In his novel *When the Tree Sings* (1979) about a southern Greek coastal village caught up in the German occupation, emigration, and death have the same connotation. Privation, separation, migration, and exile hover threateningly; any belief in a better future is pitted against stark reality. This is the subject of works in other southern European languages as well. In 1983 Haviaras met the Italian novelist Italo Calvino, who was on a literary visit to Harvard. Calvino, like Haviaras, had told the story of the Italian rural resistance from the perspective of a 10-year-old boy in the novel *Il sentiero dei nidi di ragno* (1947). The Italian poet, novelist, and translator Cesare Pavese had also narrated the Resistance from the viewpoint of a young boy in *La luna e i falò* (1950). Calvino and Pavese were included in the harvest of international writing entitled *Ploughshares* (1986), edited by Haviaras, and in which he drew special attention to the mastery of language and alluded to the simplicity and difficulty of putting worldwide themes into a local language.

MAJOR MULTICULTURAL THEMES

The Greek title of *When the Tree Sings—Otan tragoudousan ta dendra: mythistorima*—is in the plural form and the past tense, and colors the text with the notion of a fleeting event. The title of the English original is both more permanent and more fabled. This editorial tactic was picked out for particular praise by the anonymous reviewer in *Choice* magazine (1979), on the grounds that it resisted the best-seller, or "eye-riveting" (1172), title that might have cornered the potential market for wartime horror and wartime atrocity. Instead, Haviaras adopted the enigmatic parable of trees that issue a rustling music when a human is going to meet death. The novel takes the bantering monologue of a thoughtful boy, first seen playing with his Turkish shadow puppet theater, and turns it into a universal war narrative. A rebel who insists on being called "Kanenas" ("No-man," like the Homeric Odysseus who put out the Cyclops's eye with a red-hot stake) asks the boy and his pals to make a big kite. The rebels, fighting up and down the hills against the occupying German administration, will use the kite to drag mines under German storage ships in the harbor. When the Greek rebel leader is killed, his widow takes over, and she prefers to be called "Antromachi" ("Man-battle") rather than Andromeda. When the war is finished, the Allies fly over and bomb the rebel stronghold. The Greek winners are shown losing the peace. But as always in war, who knows the truth, and is not every child an orphan?

The Heroic Age starts with a grandparent's pitiful declaration that "the heroic years" are those when a child is too young to fight for an army, but too old to ignore the catastrophe. The book tells of fearful hunger and extreme cold in Greece, and of children turned into rebel fighters in the mountains, fainting with deprivation, living in tunnels, or hiding in fields and cemeteries from murderers, Royalists, and postwar roundups. A group of these starving children leave home to wander in any direction except south, until they reach the Grammos mountains. Here they take part in a struggle to defend an imagined socialist utopia, because Bulgaria and Albania have closed their borders. Some expect the International Socialist Brigades to come and reinforce their position, but evidently these brigades do not exist. In the second part of his novel, Haviaras turns to the difficult theme of "Peace and Reformation." The rebels are strafed by American napalm. Their quarters are blown up. Their sick and their nurses are crushed. They are tried and taken by ship to detention on a waterless island, where they escape into rolls of barbed wire just to have something to do. Food is minimal, and conditions are Spartan; but when the government changes, they become entitled to release as laborers in nearby island communities. There is no solution for child rebels in this engrossing study: they are punished for nude swimming on peacetime beaches or asked to spy on hotel guests. One boy refuses to take the oath and accept his freedom. Nothing more is heard of the heroic struggle on the Grammos mountains. At the time, Europe was on the brink of the package holiday and the refrigerator in every home.

SURVEY OF CRITICISM

Kostas Myrsiades (1974) considers *Nekrofaneia* to be a crucial step in the recovery of the author's selfhood and identity, shattered in the aftermath of World War II and the German occupation of the Aegean. The verse is purposefully fragmented in order to express the deracination of a boy deprived of parents and driven into manual labor for survival. With *The Heroic Age*, according to Rosaly De-Maios Roffman (1984), there was an enormous artistic challenge in pushing so much adventure and pathos into the framework of a chronicle, but the reader can hardly avoid being moved by the presentation of historical events which "obviously have their roots in truth" (1144). The reader is also struck by the number of people who, during times of war, die in camps run by their own side. DGR (1984) sees the sequence of events in *The Heroic Age* as so relentless and grievous that any release from such devastation "would be better" (1152). Judy Cooke (1980) considers the suffering and horror of war in *When the Tree Sings* harder to stomach because the conflict is quite dramatically represented and the writing is poetically imaginative—and the Greek countryside is so beautiful. John Mellors (1980), also discussing *When the Tree Sings*, isolates the power of the new words and phrases— "death camps" and "gas chambers"—that come into the local vocabulary in the early 1940s. This critic picks out Haviaras's special skill in substantiating the pain, for adolescents, of "growing up in a time of famine" (31).

SELECTED BIBLIOGRAPHY

Works by Haviaras

I kyria me tin pyxida: piimata. Privately printed, 1963.
Verolino. Athens: Ekdot, 1965.
I nychta tou Zilopodarou. Privately printed, 1967.
Nekrofaneia. Athens: Kedros, 1972.
Crossing the River Twice (Poems). Cleveland: Cleveland State University Poetry Center, 1976.

Haviaras, Stratis, ed. *The Poet's Voice*. Cambridge, Mass.: Harvard University Press, 1978.

When the Tree Sings. New York: Simon and Schuster, 1979; London: Sidgwick and Jackson, 1979. [*Otan tragoudousan ta dendra: mythistorima*. Athens: Ermis, 1980.]

The Heroic Age. New York: Simon and Schuster, 1984. [*Ta eroika chronia*. Trans. Nestoras Chounos. Athens: Charlenik Hellas, 1985.]

Stratis Haviaras, ed. *Ploughshares*, issue of *International Writing* 11, no. 4 (Winter 1986) [includes Haviaras's "Advertisement," 11–14].

Millennial Afterlives: A Retrospective. Aurora, N.Y.: Wells College Press, 2000.

Selected Studies of Haviaras

Cooke, Judy. "Bull's Eye." *New Statesman* 100 (October 10, 1980): 23–24.

De-Maios Roffman, Rosaly. "Haviaras, Stratis. *When the Tree Sings*." *Library Journal* 104 (June 1, 1979): 1277–78.

———. "Haviaras, Stratis. *The Heroic Age*." *Library Journal* 109 (June 1, 1984): 1144.

DGR. "Haviaras, Stratis. *The Heroic Age*." *Booklist* 80 (April 15, 1984): 1152.

Du Plessix Gray, Francine. "Germans in Greece." *New York Times Book Review* (June 24, 1979): 14–15.

Georgakas, Dan. "An Interview with Stratis Haviaras." *Journal of the Hellenic Diaspora* 8, no. 4 (Winter 1981): 73–82.

"Haviaras, Stratis. *Crossing the River Twice*." *Choice* 14, no. 8 (October 1977): 1048.

"Haviaras, Stratis. *When the Tree Sings*." *Choice* 16, no. 9 (November 1979): 1172.

Kalogeros, Yiorgos D. "*When the Tree Sings*: Magic Realism and the Carnivalesque in a Greek-American Narrative." *International Fiction Review* 16, no. 1 (Winter 1989): 32–38.

Locker, Frances C., ed. "Stratis Haviaras." *Contemporary Authors* 105: 113–14. Detroit: Gale Research Company, 1982.

Maguire, Gregory. "Stratis Haviaras. *The Heroic Age*." *The Horn Book Magazine* 60, no. 4 (August 1984): 503–504.

Mellors, John. "Shouting Souls." *The Listener* 103, no. 2643 (January 3, 1980): 30–31.

Myrsiades, Kostas. "*Nekrofania*." *Books Abroad* 48, no. 1 (Winter 1974): 195–96.

Related Works

Calvino, Italo. *Il sentiero dei nidi di ragno*. Torino: Einaudi, 1947.

Pavese, Cesare. *La luna e i falò*. Torino: Einaudi, 1950.

BESSIE HEAD
(1937–1986)
Maria Antonietta Saracino

BIOGRAPHY

"I was born on the sixth of July, 1937, in the Pietermaritzburg Mental Hospital, in South Africa" Bessie Head wrote in one of her autobiographical notes. "The reason for my peculiar birthplace was that my mother was white, and she had acquired me from a black man. She was judged insane, and committed to the mental hospital while pregnant. Her name was Bessie Emery and I consider it the only honour South African officials ever did me—naming me after this unknown, lovely, and unpredictable woman" (quoted in Craig MacKenzie, *Bessie Head. An Introduction*, 3). One might say that Bessie Head's beginning, a story that seems to echo in many ways South Africa's troubled past, is a multiculturalism written on the body. As the daughter of a wealthy white woman and her family's black stable boy, Bessie was immediately given up for adoption to a white family by authorities who believed that she was white. But soon the adoptive family returned Bessie because they believed she looked strange. She was then adopted by a mixed race couple that was classified as colored and lived in the poorest part of the city. For a few years she believed herself to be their child. But when she reached the age of six, she learned about her true origins.

After finishing high school and a teacher-training course, Bessie Head worked as a teacher and also as a journalist for *Drum*, a South African magazine. She married and had a child, but the marriage soon ended in divorce. In an attempt to escape from the cruelty and madness of South African society, Head applied for a passport in 1963 to take up a teaching post in the neighboring state of Botswana. The request was refused.

Thus, with her small son, she left South Africa with an exit permit that at the time did not allow readmittance into the country. When she arrived in Botswana, she was able to teach for a while at a primary school in Serowe, but soon found herself unemployed.

Upon her arrival in Botswana, Bessie Head was an exile from South Africa as well as from meaningful human relationships, a refugee who could not claim the nationality of any country, and a lonely woman of mixed race, haunted by an unresolved past. "I have not a single known relative on earth, no long and ancient family tree to refer to," she wrote, "no links with heredity or a sense of having inherited a temperament, a certain emotional instability or the shape of a fingernail from a grandmother or great-grandmother. I have always been just me, with no frame of reference to anything beyond myself" (*A Woman Alone: Autobiographical Writings*, 3). Loneliness and rejection remained her painful legacy for the rest of her life and deeply influenced her writing.

Despite her difficult beginning, Head settled in Botswana and learned to love the country and its people. She became a well-known writer and was quickly acclaimed as the finest woman novelist in Africa. As a possible result, she was granted Botswanan citizenship in 1979. Until her premature death at the age of 49, she lived and worked in Serowe, producing a handful of remarkable novels, a collection of short stories, a study of Botswanan oral history (the first of its kind to have been written by an African), and many autobiographical writings (which have been published posthumously in recent years).

MAJOR MULTICULTURAL THEMES

The unusual circumstances of Bessie Head's life—her belonging to the first generation of South African children of biracial origin, her concern with the problems of mental instability and the experience of exile, her search for identity—are themes reflected in her novels, each in some way autobiographical. The first of them, *When Rain Clouds Gather* (1968), was written upon the suggestion of an American editor who had asked her to write a novel about Botswana. The story revolves around a black South African political activist in flight from his country who moves to Botswana, possibly because (like Head herself) he too "simply wanted a country to love, and chose the first at hand" (*When Rain Clouds Gather*, 17). But the novel also deals with the theme of racial conflict and the struggle to establish cooperative farming in Botswana. In *Maru* (1971), her second novel, Head explores the theme of racial oppression and abuse within the Botswanan culture through the story of a Masarwa girl of the lowest caste brought up by a white missionary's wife—a story that also is a powerful indictment of racial prejudice.

A Question of Power (1974) is a strongly autobiographical narrative. Here the central character, Elizabeth, experiences a nervous breakdown as a consequence of racial prejudice and is committed to an asylum. Like Head herself, the protagonist, having suddenly been told her origins, undergoes an identity crisis as a child of two races, as well as of two worlds. "I know myself to be cut off from all tribal past and custom," Head wrote, "not because I wish it, but because I am here, just here, in the middle of nowhere, being nothing and nothing. . . . Who am I? What am I? In past and present, the answer lies in Africa. . . . How can I discover the meaning and purpose of my country if I do not first discover the meaning and purpose of my own life?" (*The Cardinals, With Meditations and Stories*, 149).

In her country of exile, with its quiet rhythm of daily life and its continuity with the past, Head found some peace of mind. Botswana soon proved to be that quiet backwater she had been searching for throughout her life. It was perhaps this frame of mind that moved her towards an entirely new and in many ways experimental form of writing. She decided to explore the lives of the Tswana people living in Serowe. *Serowe, Village of the Rain Wind* (1981) is an unusual community-oriented book, the outcome of a collection of interviews intended to convey a real sense of the villagers' lives and customs that had never before found their way into literature. Using the help of a translator, as she did not speak any of the local languages, Head managed to weave together the fragments of a history that was never recorded in writing before and otherwise doomed to disappear—a history she defines as "precariously oral" (*Serowe, Village of the Rain Wind*, xii).

Some of the narratives recorded over the years for *Serowe* inspired Head to write a book of short stories called *The Collector of Treasures, and Other Botswana Village Tales* (1977). The two books are in many ways complementary, as each of them represents a different portrait of the same village. But while Serowe is clearly intended as a documentary reportage, a book based on oral history, *The Collector of Treasures* is history shaped into fiction at its highest and most moving degree. *Serowe* may be considered her grateful tribute to her adoptive country, as she humbly acknowledged: "It was by chance that I came to live in this village. I have lived most of my life in shattered little bits. Somehow, here, the shattered bits began to grow together. There is a sense of wovenness, a wholeness in life here; a feeling of how strange and beautiful life can be—just living" (*Serowe, Village of the Rain Wind*, x). In *The Collector of Treasures*, she feels free to portray the other side of the coin as well, especially in reference to the difficult lives of the village women subjected to social and moral prejudices deeply embedded in their male-dominated society.

SURVEY OF CRITICISM

Scholars and critics of Bessie Head's work unanimously praise the author's capacity to give high narrative voice to the unendurable, as imbedded in the pre-independence South African society of her time. In Charles

Sarvan Ponnuthurai's words (1987), "human beings sometimes have to endure the unendurable: Bessie Head writes of the human capacity to endure 'the excruciating'" ("Bessie Head: *A Question of Power* and Identity," 82). Indeed, the situation in South Africa was excruciating, where the simple joys of life were denied to nonwhites. For Sophia O. Ogwunde (2000), Bessie Head is an exile who writes eloquently about everything from which she has been exiled ("An Exile Writing on Home," 65). For Cecil Abrahams (1990), Bessie Head's approach to the South African problem arises from within the soul of man. She understands that racists are not free as "they simply imprison their souls in their own cobweb of hatred" (*Bessie Head and Literature in South Africa*, 10). Craig MacKenzie (1989), in his introductory work to Bessie Head, emphasizes the writer's lifelong struggle to acquire a sense of identity and a sense of self-worth.

SELECTED BIBLIOGRAPHY

Works by Head

When Rain Clouds Gather (1968). London: Victor Gollancz, 1969.

Maru. London: Victor Gollancz, 1971.

A Question of Power. London: Heinemann, 1974.

The Collector of Treasures, and Other Botswana Village Tales. London: Heinemann, 1977.

Serowe, Village of the Rain Wind. London: Heinemann, 1981.

A Bewitched Crossroad. An African Saga. Johannesburg: Ad Donker, 1984.

Tales of Tenderness and Power. Johannesburg: Ad Donker, 1989.

A Woman Alone: Autobiographical Writings. Ed. Craig MacKenzie. Oxford: Heinemann, 1990.

A Gesture of Belonging: Letters From Bessie Head, 1965–1979. Ed. Randolph Vigne. London: Heinemann, 1991.

The Cardinals, With Meditations and Stories. Ed. M. J. Daymond. Cape Town: David Philip, 1993.

Selected Studies of Head

Abrahams, Cecil, ed. *Bessie Head and Literature in South Africa.* Trenton, N.J.: Africa World Press, 1990.

Eilersen Stead, Gillian. *Bessie Head: Thunder Behind Her Ears: Her Life and Writing.* London: James Currey, 1996.

MacKenzie, Craig. *Bessie Head. An Introduction.* Grahamstown, South Africa: National English Literary Museum, 1989.

Ogwunde, Sophia O. "An Exile Writing on Home: Protest & Commitment in the Works of Bessie Head." *Exile & African Literature Today* 22 (2000): 64–76.

Saracino, Maria Antonietta, "Se Shahrazàd avesse avuto una sorella." In *Introduzione a Bessie Head, La donna dei tesori,* vii-xix. Roma: Edizioni Lavoro, 1987.

Sarvan Ponnuthurai, Charles. "Bessie Head: *A Question of Power* and Identity." *Women in African Literature Today* 15 (1987): 82–88.

GEORGES HENEIN
(1914–1973)

Cristina Boidard Boisson

BIOGRAPHY

Few readers of the French magazine *L'Express* would have known that the articles signed by Georges Henein up until July 1973 were written by an Egyptian author who had introduced surrealistic postulates into Cairo society and had become a contributor to the magazine because of financial difficulties. Henein belonged to the surrealist movement from 1936 to 1948, first because he accepted its theories, and second, inasmuch as it favored free art and literature, he believed it might lead to greater freedom in Egyptian society.

Even fewer readers would have suspected that Henein's background had afforded him a genuine knowledge of various cultures, of which he was an important exponent. The stage was set for his multicultural interests by the diplomatic missions in Madrid, Rome, and Paris of his father, Sadik Pacha Henein, a Copt, and his mother's family, of Italian origin. Both parents belonged to the Cairo Francophone cultural élite that promoted an Egyptian literature written in French. Young Georges spoke Italian first, then French, Arabic, and English. After studying law in Paris, he spent every spring and summer there, thus affording this "flâneur des deux mondes" (stroller between two worlds) (Alexandrian, 67) a solid knowledge of both Oriental and Occidental cultures, which affected positively his social dimension and literary production.

In Paris, his appreciation of French culture increased as he made contact with literary and artistic vanguard movements, such as surrealism, that suited his rebellious nature. The surrealist movement proclaimed the supremacy of freedom at all levels, sparking Henein to explode old prejudices by expressing his personal ideas. Many of the youthful works of this second-generation surrealist—virulent articles or theater pieces—were aimed at provoking reactions in the Cairo society that he wanted to prepare for surrealism and freedom.

In Paris he became an active member of the surrealist movement and a friend of its founder, André Breton. Simultaneously he organized prosurrealism activities in Cairo, published poems and pamphlets about political events, and meditated on what the writer's commitment should be in matters such as politics. His alternate stays in Cairo and Paris were interrupted by World War II, a circumstance he employed to organize a proper surrealist group, a sort of literary *résistance* in Cairo. After the war, he resumed his temporary stays in Paris; in Egypt, however, he was considered a dangerous intellectual by the Nasser regime. Therefore, he went into exile in 1962, traveling from Greece to Italy and finally to Paris, where he died in 1973.

MAJOR MULTICULTURAL THEMES

One of Henein's multicultural characteristics is the adoption of French for his major works and for his correspondence, although he used the Arabic language to popularize his work. He always believed in the permeability of cultures, especially between the Middle East and the Occident. He saw in surrealism a literary movement that stood above nations and cultures; its international characteristics provided it with a multicultural essence. If in his surrealistic poems and short stories he naturally blends Occidental and Oriental culture, it is in his essays, *Deux effigies* (1953, 1978), that different cultures interact, thanks to Henein's intermixture of Occidental and Oriental subjects, characters, towns, civilizations, and concepts. He had a special interest in characters who lived on the border of diverse worlds and cultures—multicultural characters such as those we see in *Deux effigies* (1978): Julian the Apostate in "Julien l'Apostat ou le snobisme métaphysique" (15–28) or Alexander the Great in "Le Règne qui est au-delà de la destruction" (29–41). He analyzes Byzantium as an exponent and symbol of the struggle between Occidental rigor and Oriental opulence in "Un luxe de combat" (43–52). He writes also about Søren Kierkegaard in "Désert et Impiété" (53–63), about Franz Kafka in "L'Homme est un sémaphore démodé" (65–78), about surrealist poetry in "La voix du poète a tout chanté hormis l'indifférence" (93–107), and about the German romantic authors considered as presurrealists in "Voyageur Albinois, mordant à sa lumière . . . " (131–39). Particularly interesting are his study, in "Le geste et son ombre" (109–22), of the relationship between Occidental and Oriental literatures, as well as his analysis of Arabian poetry and Arabian literary issues.

His experience of living in a culture different from the one in which he grew up permeates all his works but seems present mainly in his journal, in his correspondence with French writer Henri Calet, and in his essays and numerous articles. In them he offers his views on Oriental and Occidental civilizations, on Egypt and France, on political life in general, and on world issues such as the bombing of Hiroshima. His analysis of the Egyptian situation mix with increasingly severe judgments of France and Europe, especially in the political field. In many letters to Henri Calet, he communicates his suffering because of what he considered the French *Front Populaire*'s betrayal of the Spanish Republicans during the Spanish civil war. If comparison favored France and Occidental culture in the first part of Henein's life, disenchantment set in later on. With the same lucidity as earlier, he rejected the excesses of some surrealist strategies, and his rupture with André Breton took place in 1948.

A major aspect of Henein's multiculturalism was his vision of the function of the writer considered as a cultural mediator between different cultures and different cultural levels. The writer serves as a bridge as well as a bicultural or multicultural analyst and polemicist. Henein himself was convinced of the importance of multiculturalism at all levels, not only within international organizations such as UNESCO, but also among individuals of diverse cultures.

SURVEY OF CRITICISM

Sarane Alexandrian (1981) has introduced Henein to a larger public in his volume *Georges Henein*, but a critical survey had been issued in Cairo the year after Henein's death: *Hommage à Georges Henein, dernier cahier de littérature appliquée* (1974). Some of these texts were published again in *Georges Henein, Hommages, Études* (1981) along with new and interesting viewpoints on Henein's multiculturalism.

Cristina Boidard Boisson (1993) contrasts Henein's works with surrealist postulates, and refers to the multicultural aspects of the author's biography, while in her articles (1992, 1994, 1999) she studies other multicultural dimensions of his works. Marc Kober (1996) centered on Henein's short stories in his doctoral dissertation, and Henein is one of the literary figures studied in Kober's edited volume (1999) on Egyptian authors writing in French.

SELECTED BIBLIOGRAPHY

Works by Henein

L'incompatible. Cairo: La Part du Sable, 1949.
Deux effigies. Cairo: La Part du Sable, 1953; Geneva: Puyraimond, 1978.
La force de saluer. Paris: Éditions de la Différence, 1977.
Le signe le plus obscur. Paris and Geneva: Éditions de la Présence/Puyraimond, 1977.
Notes sur un pays inutile. Geneva: Puyraimond, 1978; new edition, revised and completed, Paris: Le Tout sur le Tout, 1982 [includes the short stories pub

lished in *Un temps de petite fille*. Paris: Éditions de Minuit, 1947; and *Le seuil interdit*. Paris: Mercure de France, 1956, with new texts.]
L'esprit frappeur, Carnets 1940–1973. Paris: Encre, 1980.

Selected Studies of Henein

Alexandrian, Sarane. *Georges Henein*. Paris: Seghers, 1981.
Boidard Boisson, Cristina. "Georges Henein ou le courage d'être surréaliste en Égypte." *Francofonía* 1: 17–37. Cádiz: Servicio de Publicaciones de la Universidad de Cádiz, 1992.
———. *Georges Henein y el Surrealismo* (doctoral diss., 1991). Cádiz: Servicio de Publicaciones de la Universidad de Cádiz (microfichas), 1993.
———. "Georges Henein: un cas de double appartenance culturelle." *Actas del VII coloquio Asociación de Profesores de Filología Francesa de la Universidad Española* (APFFUE), Vol. I, 111–17. Cádiz: Servicio de Publicaciones de la Universidad de Cádiz, 1999.
——— "La poésie de Georges Henein." In *Entre Nil et sable. Écrivains d'Égypte d'expression française (1920–1960)*. Ed. Marc Kober. Paris: Centre National de Documentation Pédagogique, 1999.
———. "L'image de la France chez les Surréalistes Égyptiens à travers l'oeuvre de Georges Henein." *Francofonía* 3: 21–32. Cádiz: Servicio de Publicaciones de la Universidad de Cádiz, 1994.
Bornier, Evelyne M. "Le sens de la vie selon Georges Henein." In *Entre Nil et sable. Écrivains d'Égypte d'expression française (1920–1960)*. Ed. Marc Kober, 161–66. Paris: Centre National de Documentation Pédagogique, 1999.
Fargues, Nicolas. *Incidences d'un parcours consenti de Georges Henein de 1933 à 1973*. Mémoire de Diplôme d'Études Approfondies. Paris: Paris IV Sorbonne, 1995.
———. "Les mots contre soi." In *Entre Nil et sable: Écrivains d'Égypte d'expression française (1920–1960)*. Ed. Marc Kober, 153–60. Paris: Centre National de Documentation Pédagogique, 1999.
Georges Henein, Hommages, Études. Paris: Le Pont de l'Epée, no. 71–72, 1981.
Hommage à Georges Henein, dernier cahier de littérature appliquée. Cairo: La Part du sable, 1974.
Kober, Marc. *Éloge de la ténuité – les récits de Georges Henein* (doctoral diss., Paris-III Sorbonne Nouvelle, 1996).
———. "Bienvenue à Elseneur! Shakespeare dans l'oeuvre de Georges Henein." In *Entre Nil et sable. Écrivains d'Égypte d'expression française (1920–1960)*. Ed. Marc Kober, 135–41. Paris: Centre National de Documentation Pédagogique, 1999.

EUGÈNE IONESCO
(1909–1994)

Gisèle Féal

BIOGRAPHY

In his early years, Eugène Ionesco—Eugen Ionescu in Romanian—was a man with two countries. He was born in Romania of a French mother and a Romanian father. His family moved to Paris when he was one, and he lived there with his mother until age 13. His father, who had returned to Bucharest several years earlier without informing his family, demanded his children in 1922. So Eugène went to Bucharest and lived there until 1938. As a child, he experienced school in Paris and the countryside where his mother, to protect him and his sister from the bombs of World War I, entrusted her children to a farmer in Mayenne. Later Eugène learned Romanian and attended high school in Bucharest. Here he discovered the poetry of Tristan Tzara, a Romanian-born poet who had become a leading figure in the French surrealist movement.

Ionesco completed a bachelor's degree and became a teacher of French in the Romanian capital. In the early thirties he published articles of literary criticism, a booklet of poems, and a controversial book, aggressively entitled the negative *Nu* (1934), in which he derided various established writers and denounced the vanity of literature.

His creative activities began in one country and culminated in another. In 1938, he received a grant to prepare a thesis in Paris; the thesis did not materialize, but he sent "Letters from Paris" to Romanian journals. When he went back to Romania, he was horrified by the rise of fascism. With difficulty he returned to France in 1942. There the creation of *La cantatrice chauve* in 1950 marked his debut as a French playwright. Significantly, the outline of the play had been written several years earlier in

Romanian; it was inspired by a manual for learning English called *English without Professor*. The play was appreciated only by a select few who saw it as a surrealist work, but it introduced Ionesco into the Parisian literary circles.

The 1950s were years of intense creative activity. Ionesco's principal plays were *La leçon*, *Les chaises*, *Amédée*, *Victimes du devoir*, and *Rhinocéros*. *Rhinocéros* was inspired by the rise of fascism in Romania but it could be applied to any form of fanaticism and it rapidly became an international success. It was the first of Ionesco's plays performed in Bucharest (1964). In the 1960s, Ionesco's dramatic production, represented by *Le piéton de l'air*, *Le roi se meurt*, and the four episodes of *La soif et la faim*, was complemented by journals on the theater, politics, and personal experiences. In 1971, Ionesco was admitted to the venerable Académie française, a surprising accomplishment for the man who had written *Nu*. His last plays, *L'homme aux valises* (1975) and *Voyages chez les morts: Thèmes et variations* (1981), conceal intimate experiences under a complex system of images. In 1978, a conference on Ionesco's work was organized at the International Cultural Center of Cerisy-la-Salle in France; in 1995, the French Institute of Bucharest offered a similar event.

Besides writing short stories and novels, journals, articles, prefaces, and film scenarios, Ionesco also experimented with lithographs. But his fame rests on his plays. *La cantatrice chauve* and *La leçon* have run without interruption in the Théâtre de la Huchette since 1957. His works, initially labeled as avant-garde, have been translated and presented in more than thirty languages; they are classics of the twentieth century.

MAJOR MULTICULTURAL THEMES

The theater that was created in Paris in the early 1950s, later known as the Theater of the Absurd, broke new ground. It has frequently been noted that three of its major representatives—Arthur Adamov, Samuel Beckett, and Eugène Ionesco—wrote in French but were born in countries other than France. It has also been argued that their bilingualism distanced them from the language they used in their literary work and helped them find the incongruities it contained. The idea cannot be proven. However, in his interview with Claude Bonnefoy, Ionesco pointed to his double cultural experience as the source of his skepticism. After being taught in France that French was the most beautiful language in the world and the French people the most courageous, he learned in Bucharest that Romanian was the most beautiful language in the world and the Romanian people the most courageous. The result was that he changed the patriotic play he had written around age eleven into a comic one. In a similar manner, after the success of *Rhinocéros*, he refused any rapprochement with the French intelligentsia, whose positions were to a large extent on the left, and repeatedly declared himself apolitical.

He also mistrusted language. *La cantatrice chauve* introduced the results of this mistrust through the use of a language made of commonplace sentences, cliches, word associations, sound associations, and other plays on words, all of them spoken in a rhythm that could accelerate and produce verbal flights void of sense. For the following 30 years of his career, Ionesco experimented with meaningless language. In his last play, *Voyages chez les morts*, he intuited that such language is caused either by an exclusive reliance on rationality or, at the opposite end, by a predominance of raw emotions.

The image of the foreigner and the theme of the journey emerged slowly in Ionesco's plays. The character Amédée, from the play of the same title, seems to have lived all his life in Paris; but his last name—like that of his creator—is foreign: Buccinioni. Bérenger, in *Le piéton de l'air*, is a French writer vacationing in England; he surprises the British with his exuberant behavior. Jean, in *La soif et la faim*, is the explorer of vast spaces, unnamed because his physical journey is also an examination of himself and the human condition. As indicated by their titles, the theme of the journey invades the last two plays: *L'Homme aux valises* and *Voyages chez les morts*. The journey of the man with bags is a return to childhood; but the mythical elements of the play make him a modern equivalent of the ancient heroes in search of themselves. In *Voyages chez les morts*, the search for an identity continues. It takes the form of a visit to the two sides of the protagonist's family: the maternal and the paternal. From the playwright's perspective, these are his French and his Romanian ancestry. The two clans are opposed: the maternal side lives wretchedly; the paternal clan is rich and lives in luxury. This contrast leads to a final scene in which the maternal grandmother, like a Fury, defeats each and every member of the other clan. The scene is an expression of Ionesco's resentment against his father; it could also be the image of an internal conflict: between the two cultures that Ionesco carried within.

SURVEY OF CRITICISM

Gisèle Féal's study (2001) focuses on Ionesco's dreamlike plays. She brings to light five major themes—language, the search for the unconscious, sexuality, the mother, and paternity—and traces the writer's psychological evolution from *La cantatrice chauve* to *Voyages chez les morts*. Marie-France Ionesco, Norbert Dodille, and Gabriel Liiceanu (1996) have gathered Ionesco texts presented at the French Institute Conference in Bucharest, while André Coutin (1995) gives us an interview with Ionesco, in which the writer reiterates that an artist should not be limited by political commitment and needs a total freedom of expression. Ecaterina Cleynen-Serghiev (1993) studies Ionesco's literary beginnings in Bucharest: his attempts at poetry and the vehemence he cultivated in his literary criticism; she comments on the writer's bicultural background.

Nancy Lane (1994) charts first the early absurdist works, then the mature humanism of the Bérenger cycle and finally the intensely personal phase of the last plays. Rosette C. Lamont (1993) reveals the dramatist as profoundly marked by his experience with war and the occupation; she shows that the power of his plays resides in his synthesis of the political, the psychological, and the metaphysical.

SELECTED BIBLIOGRAPHY

Work in Romanian

Nu. Bucharest: Vremea, 1934. Trans. into French by Marie-France Ionesco as *Non*. Paris: Gallimard, 1986.

Plays

Théâtre I: La cantatrice chauve, La leçon, Jacques ou La soumission, Les chaises, Victimes du devoir, Amédée ou comment s'en débarrasser. Paris: Gallimard, 1954.

Théâtre III: Rhinocéros, Le piéton de l'air, Délire à deux, Le tableau, Scène à quatre, Les salutations, La colère. Paris: Gallimard, 1963.

Théâtre IV: Le roi se meurt, La soif et la faim, La lacune, Le salon de l'automobile, L'oeuf dur, Le jeune homme à marier, Apprendre à marcher. Paris: Gallimard, 1966.

L'homme aux valises suivi de *Ce formidable bordel!*. Paris: Gallimard, 1975.

Théâtre VII: Voyages chez les morts: Thèmes et variations. Paris: Gallimard, 1981.

Théâtre complet. Ed. Emmanuel Jacquart. Paris: Gallimard, La Pléiade, 1991.

Ruptures de silence: Rencontres avec André Coutin. Paris: Mercure de France, 1995.

Lectures de Ionesco. Ed. Marie-France Ionesco, Nobert Dodille and Gabriel Liiceanu. Paris: L'Harmattan, 1996.

In English

Four Plays. The Bald Soprano, The Lesson, Jack or the Submission, The Chairs. Trans. Donald M. Allen. New York: Grove, 1958.

Amédée, The New Tenant, Victims of Duty. Trans. Donald Watson. New York: Grove, 1958.

Rhinoceros, and Other Plays. Trans. Derek Prouse. New York: Grove, 1960.

A Stroll in the Air, Frenzy for Two, or More. Trans. Donald Watson. New York: Grove, 1965.

Hunger and Thirst, and Other Plays. Trans. Donald Watson. New York: Grove, 1968.

Man with Bags: A Play. Trans. Marie-France Ionesco, adapted by Israel Horovitz. New York: Grove, 1977.

Journeys Among the Dead. Trans. Barbara Wright. New York: Riverrun, 1985.

Selected Studies of Ionesco in French

Cleynen-Serghiev, Ecaterina. *La jeunesse littéraire d'Eugène Ionesco*. Paris: Presses Universitaires de France, 1993.

Féal, Gisèle. *Ionesco. Un théâtre onirique*. Paris: Imago, 2001.

Vernois, Paul. *La dynamique théâtrale d'Eugène Ionesco.* 2nd ed. Paris: Klincksieck, 1991.

In English

Bonnefoy, Claude. *Conversations with Eugène Ionesco.* Trans. Jan Dawson. New York: Holt, Rinehart and Winston, 1971.

Gaensbauer, Deborah B. *Eugène Ionesco Revisited.* New York: Twayne, 1996.

Lane, Nancy. *Understanding Eugène Ionesco.* Columbia: University of South Carolina Press, 1994.

Lamont, Rosette C. *Ionesco's Imperatives: The Politics of Culture.* Ann Arbor: University of Michigan Press, 1993.

PAULA JACQUES
(1949–)

Susan D. Cohen

BIOGRAPHY

Born in Cairo in 1949, Paula Jacques (née Abadi) was uprooted from her native land in 1958, along with many thousands of Jewish Egyptians forced to depart by circumstances that had steadily deteriorated for Egyptian Jews since the creation of the state of Israel in 1948. She experienced a radical sense of dislocation on a kibbutz in Israel, where her widowed mother sent her while she and several of her similarly widowed sisters, in the classical situation of stateless persons, attempted to find work and lodgings in Paris. Her father's death in Cairo near the end of 1955 became associated with the death of her Jewish life in Egypt, and with what she experienced as abandonment by her mother. She rejected the three years spent on the kibbutz with horror, not only because of the wrenching violence of the events that brought her there, but also due to its extreme foreignness.

Jacques considers herself the product of a multicultural environment. In Cairo, she spoke Arabic with her grandmothers, who, though illiterate like many of their generation, were connected to ancient culture and the culture of the poor. Her family communicated in Arabic with the lower classes. Some Jews chose to send their children to Arabic-speaking schools. Her immediate milieu, however, was informed by French culture and the French language, which she spoke at home, in school, and with friends of the same middle class as her family, whatever religion they professed. The Egyptian middle and upper classes generally scorned Arabic, which the king himself spoke poorly. The cultivated and the wealthy did study English, the language in which business was conducted, but preferred French to the detested idiom of the British occupiers.

For reasons of family, cultural identification, language, and the habits of urban life, the sudden, solitary removal to an Israeli kibbutz constituted far more of a shock than France would have, had it been Paula's initial country of exile. Rather than weave it into the fabric of her cultural plurality, the child rejected it, at least on the conscious level. When aged 12 she joined her mother in Paris. Like all adolescents she had but one aim: to resemble other teenagers. She never thought about her "Jewish past" (Jacques, unpublished interview with Susan D. Cohen). She participated in all the movements of the 1960s, from the 1968 revolts to feminism.

Although Paula lacked formal higher education and training upon her arrival in France, she possessed great intelligence and energy. After beginning by working in a theater, she forged a successful career in radio journalism. She wrote for newspapers as well. Her first book, *Lumière de l'oeil* (1980), a small masterpiece, was universally hailed. She received the Fémina Prize for *Déborah et les anges dissipés: Roman* (1991), and *Les femmes avec leur amour: Roman* (1997) won the prestigious German Liberatur prize for the best novel of the year by a woman.

At the age of 17 Paula Abadi wed, and has retained Jacques, her married name. It has particular resonance for her, since Jacques was her beloved father's given name and the name she used for the protagonist's father in her first novel.

The concept of multiculturalism is essential for her, inasmuch as it constructed her very person (Jacques, unpublished interview with Susan D. Cohen). It shapes all her fiction, and her journalism centers on it. "Cosmopolitan," her weekly two-hour radio program on France Inter, consistently addresses cultural mixing, multiculturalism, and diversity throughout the world, especially in those areas "mixed" with French presence. If, on the one hand, Paula Jacques has few actual memories of her life in Egypt, on the other, writing fiction lifted the "veil" that fell over that past with exile and a certain assimilation (Jacques, unpublished interview with Susan D. Cohen). Writing effects her return to Egypt, to her and her family's past, and to the past of her people there. It awakens her sense of connectedness to Jews.

Having already published six novels, she now is working on a seventh. It will evoke what does not appear in her other texts: the painful period, for her parents' generation, of starting over, stateless and poor, in France; the adjustments required of her own generation; the advantages afforded it. She attributes the absence of these themes so far to the amnesia incurred by the shock of her father's death, separation from her mother and her home, exile in Israel, and so on. Revived by the gesture of writing, her memory was so fascinated and galvanized by the richness of Jewish life in Egypt that priority went to exploring that first, by telling its stories. Now she has begun to address stories of the arrival in France.

MAJOR MULTICULTURAL THEMES

All of Jacques' novels are structured on alternation between France and Egypt, and describe, variously, the collapse of Jewish-Egyptian society. As Isaac Bashevis Singer does for the disappearing Yiddish world in New York, Jacques concentrates on a vanished world, the destroyed world of Egyptian Jews. A multicultural situation, thematic and dynamic, defined that world as it does Jacques' novels.

The theme of how to situate identity, common to all of Jacques' texts, is prominent in *Les femmes avec leur amour* (1997). At the very moment the twelve-year-old female protagonist's dawning sexuality destabilizes her because of ambient representations of menstrual blood as defilement, she finds herself forced to ponder the question of her social identity as well, for Jacques set the book in 1956, the year of the Suez war that was followed by mass expulsions and departures. History forces her to wonder who she is, why the Jews get classified together with the English foreigners of whom Egypt must rid itself, which misrepresentations of Jews are concocted, which are brandished as their mirror image, and so forth. The politically aware suffered enormous discomfort. Some Jews adopted Egyptian nationalism, considering Egypt their country and themselves Egyptian above all, and espoused Arabic as their language. However, Jews had never been granted equal status in Egypt despite their 2,000-year presence in a country they had helped make. Egyptian nationalism merged into Islamic, Arab nationalism. Many Jews opted for Western culture, so that they became "caught between the bark and the tree," as her village sheikh phrases it to the sympathetic Arab governess in *Lumière de l'oeil*, which contains similar themes . Islamification, the lack of citizenship, and the creation of the state of Israel made it impossible for Jews not to perceive that they were being associated with the foreigners, and subsequently with the Israelis, with whom ever latent anti-Semitism was all too ready to amalgamate them, despite examples of Jewish Egyptian support of Egyptian war efforts.

In *Lumière de l'oeil*, a woman narrator's depictions of the life of her family in Cairo, with the focus on herself as a little girl, show how being female inflects the dialectics of belonging and exclusion, and how it intersects with the issue of language as the key mediation of individual and cultural identity. After the expulsion from the group, the individual asserts her identity, through conversations with her mother and an act of cultural and linguistic retrieval that is the novel itself.

Language constitutes a key element of multiculturalism and identity. The Egyptian Jews spoke a French full of flourishes, rich in imagery, and grammatically correct, for they had attended French schools. Jacques writes a French in which one can hear Arabic underneath. It contains literal translations of Arabic expressions ("lumière de l'oeil" is one). It has an Eastern theatricality of speech, and discursive practices such as never approaching problems directly, love of speaking and of joking. Different from the less flowery French of the North African Jews, the French of the Egyptian Jews is more comparable to the speech in the works of Albert Cohen, the Greek-Swiss writer who treats questions of displacement, language, and European anti-Semitism.

Another recurrent topos is that of life stories and tales told by various characters, such as the black Muslim maid, a beloved, rebellious figure in *Les femmes avec leur amour*. She recounts her life of poverty and the abuses of patriarchy, racism, and class. Further perspectives in the texts are represented by the stories of an illiterate grandmother, workers, Arab governesses, female relatives who convey and object to their inferior status as women, and other people of various generations. The theme of the Muslim-Jewish interaction and symbiosis in everyday life in Egypt, as described by Bernard Lewis in *The Jews of Islam*, appears in many of her texts.

The theme of love of Egypt permeates all of Jacques' fiction. Memory embellishes the past of the generation of exiled adults. Those who had to start over, ladies who became maids when struggling in Paris, represent life in Cairo as a lost paradise. This connects to the theme of elderly Jews clinging to their native land, refusing to leave, and ending up mad or eeking out a suspicious living by their wits as in *Déborah et les anges dissipés* and *L'héritage de tante Carlotta: Roman* (1987). In *Un baiser froid comme la lune: Roman* (1983) Alexandria replaces Cairo as beloved home of a working-class father and his daughter, who, expelled after 1956, aspire to French citizenship: he in order to obtain some sense of belonging that a passport would afford him, and she in order to become an independent woman and a writer.

Jacques' gift is that she conveys the warmth, poignancy, and underlying anxiousness of Jewish life in Egypt before its demise with great humor and life, and with the discretion afforded by the use of the third person in all her novels. Her work depicts the pleasant and precarious life of an entire community that lived connected to their Muslim and Christian fellow Egyptians, but was soon destroyed abruptly and irrevocably.

SURVEY OF CRITICISM

Susan D. Cohen's articles (1994, 1996) are the only critical pieces available, aside from press reviews. Cohen contextualizes Jacques' *Lumière de l'oeil* historically and socially. Through the stories and storytelling of an extended Jewish Egyptian family, Paula Jacques demonstrates the acute double bind in which Egyptian Jews found themselves in an Islamified Egypt in the 1950s.

SELECTED BIBLIOGRAPHY

Works by Jacques

Lumière de l'oeil. Paris: Mercure de France, 1980.

Un baiser froid comme la lune: Roman. Paris: Mercure de France, 1983.
L'héritage de tante Carlotta: Roman. Paris: Mercure de France, 1987.
Déborah et les anges dissipés: Roman. Paris: Mercure de France, 1991.
La descente au paradis: Roman. Paris: Mercure de France, 1995.
Les femmes avec leur amour: Roman. Paris: Mercure de France, 1997.
Unpublished interview with Susan D. Cohen, Paris, July 30, 2001.

Historical sources

Hassoun, Jacques, ed. *Juifs du Nil: textes.* Paris: Le Sycomore, 1981.
Kramer, Gudrun. *The Jews in Modern Egypt, 1914–1952.* Seattle: University of Washington Press, 1989.
Landau, Jacob M. *Jews in Nineteenth-Century Egypt.* New York: New York University Press, 1969.
Lewis, Bernard. *The Jews of Islam.* Princeton, N.J.: Princeton University Press, 1984.
al-Sayyid-Marsot, Afaf Lutfi. *A Short History of Modern Egypt.* Cambridge, England, and New York: Cambridge University Press, 1985.

Study of Jacques

Cohen, Susan D. "Cultural Mixing, Exile, and Femininity in Paula Jacques' *Lumière de l'oeil.*" *French Review* 67, no.5 (April 1994): 840–53. (Reprinted, translated by the author into French with the title "Mixage Culturel, Exil et Féminité dans *Lumière de l'oeil* de Paula Jacques," in *La voix migrante au féminin en France et au Canada.* Ed. Lucie Lequin et Maïr Verthuy, 115–29. Paris: L'Harmattan, 1996; and, in a shorter version, in *Actes du Colloque: La France des années 1980: le roman,* 126–38. Saratoga, Calif.: ANMA Libri, 1994.)

NIKOS KAZANTZAKIS
(1883–1957)

Bruce Merry

BIOGRAPHY

Born at Herakleion, Kazantzakis liked to say that he was first a Cretan, then a Greek. He translated up to fifty books into Greek, including works of Homer, Dante, and Goethe. He wrote nine screenplays, travel essays, an autobiography, school textbooks, a history of Russian literature, contributions to encyclopedias, hundreds of periodical articles, and an (unpublished) French-Greek dictionary. He produced 30 novels, plays, and philosophical books, alongside his life's work: *Odússeia* (1938). He studied law in Athens (1902–06), then took a trip to Italy promised by his father as a reward for graduation. In 1907 he was in Paris, attending lectures at the Collège de France by Henri Bergson, whose *Le Rire* (1900) he translated in 1911. He wrote a thesis, "Frederick Nietzsche and the Philosophy of Justice and Government," which he published in Crete, where he returned in 1909. At Athens in 1910, Kazantzakis was among 36 intellectuals who founded the Educational Society to reform Greek schools by introducing demotic, vernacular language. He married Galateia Alexiou in 1911, and together they entered a competition for elementary school textbooks written in demotic language. He used the cash prize (for a primer and five teaching manuals) to finance his subsequent travels, including a journey in the footsteps of Nietzsche in Switzerland.

A volunteer in the Balkan Wars, he served in the office of the prime minister, Eleftherios Venizelos. The Ministry of Social Welfare sent him to organize the repatriation of Greeks subject to ethnic persecution in the Caucasus, and in 1919 he went to Paris to report on his assignment to

Venizelos, then a delegate at the Versailles Peace Conference. In January 1920 we find Kazantzakis "personally superintending the resettlement of the refugees in the orphanages of Macedonia and the abandoned villages of Thrace" (Bien, 1989, 103). When Venizelos was defeated in the elections of 1920, Kazantzakis was disappointed and embittered. He left Greece and thereafter spent most of his life abroad. His philosophical essay *Askitikí* (1927) had been composed between Vienna and Berlin (1922–23). In 1927, he published a travel book in Alexandria (Egypt), including an interview with the Italian dictator Mussolini (whom Kazantzakis at first admired). He went to China and Japan from February to May 1935, on assignment for the Athenian newspaper *Acropolis*. The trip was also designed to collect new fauna and flora for descriptions in his *Odússeia*. Kazantzakis died in the south of France in 1957 and was buried in Crete.

MAJOR MULTICULTURAL THEMES

In the early 1920s, Kazantzakis traveled inside Germany and soaked up the atmosphere of postwar Communism. In 1924, he joined a group of left-wing insurgents on Crete, and was arrested for his activities. In the late 1920s, he made three visits to the Soviet Union. Despite his Marxist sympathies, he was condemned by the Greek Communist Party and rejected by Resistance forces as a cadre in May 1941. He wrote a novel in French about the Soviet Union, *Moscou a crié*, changing the title to *Toda-Raba* (1929), after an African magician. Another novel, published in French as *Le jardin des rochers* (1936), concerns a European traveler caught in the war between China and Japan in the 1930s. The novel *Ófis kaì kríno* (1906) is in decadent diary form, in the manner of Swinburne, Oscar Wilde, or D'Annunzio, foregrounding a youth who kills himself with his beloved in a flower-strewn chamber. Kazantzakis's play *Ximeróni* concerns a married woman's love for her brother-in-law, in 1906 a daring subject. His play *Hristós* (1928) created further controversy, with its counterpoint of Buddhist and Christian ideas. A charge of sacrilege was filed with the Athens Public Prosecutor's office in 1930. The plays *Mélissa* (1937) and *Ioulianòs o Parabátis* (1939) did not reach theater production. *Protomástoras* (1909), based on the demotic song "The Bridge of Arta," also failed to gain a production, with its folkloric motif of a woman immured in her husband's masonry. The aftermath of the Greek civil war seemed to locate Kazantzakis outside prevailing ideology. In 1941, he completed a new play, *Boúdas*, and by 1945 he had emerged as a major writer in Greece and beyond.

He continued to support himself with journalism and by describing his ever-widening travels. In Greece, he became the popular author of a modern *synaxarion* (biography of a saint), *Bíos kaì politeía toû Aléxi Zórmpa* (1946). Later translated as *Zorba the Greek*, the novel was based on a larger-than-life, plebeian illiterate. This Macedonian Zorba and "the Boss," Kazantzakis himself, were involved in a mine project (1916–1917). Zorba's personality reflects the trauma of the German occupation: a famine caused the loss of nearly half a million lives, in winter 1941, when Kazantzakis was writing *Zorba* and at times stayed in bed to conserve energy. *Hristòs xanastaurónetai* (1948) is set in the year of the Asia Minor catastrophe (1922), when Turks crushed a Greek expeditionary force advancing into central Anatolia. The novel describes an Anatolian village that rehearses a performance of the Last Passion. In this alien setting, Greek refugees are persecuted by their Turkish masters, and by fellow-Greeks from a neighboring village. The novel *O Kapetàn Mihális* (1950) is set in Crete and transforms the author's father, actually a seed merchant, into an irredentist hero in the Cretan insurrections of 1889 and 1897–99. Certain passages in this novel led the Holy Synod of the Greek Orthodox Church to accuse Kazantzakis of blasphemy. *O Teleftaíos pirasmós* (1950–1951) creates an iconoclastic hero out of Judas, invited by Jesus to betray Him so the Son of God may consummate his mission by being crucified. Because of this novel (which the Vatican placed on the Index), Kazantzakis was excommunicated by the Greek Orthodox Church. In 1953, he finished *O Ftohoúlis toû Theoû*, the fictional biography of Saint Francis. His last published novel, *Oi Aderfofádes* (written in 1949) tells the story of a priest trapped between Royalist and Communist forces in the civil war. In those years of growing success and prestige, Kazantzakis lived on the southern coast of France, in a kind of temperamental exile from Greece.

SURVEY OF CRITICISM

C.-D. Gounelas (1998) notes the allusive subtlety of Kazantzakis's plays *Hristós* and *Boúdas*, the former using duplication and apparition, like Greek icons, in order to "construct a universally attainable image of Christ" (323). In *Boúdas*, Gounelas sees the Chinese village setting as a dream, a symbol of "the mind's illusory contrivance" (326). Critics emphasize the Herculean nature of the Greek writer's literary labors (cf. George Pappageotes, 1972), fostering the idea that Kazantzakis translated Dante's *Divina Commedia* in forty-five days (1932) and part I of Goethe's *Faust* in twelve (1936). The text of Kazantzakis's *Odússeia*, with its 33,333 lines, has been seen as a monument of our age. The poetic achievement of Kazantzakis is prodigious (cf. David Ricks, 19–35)—the creation of a new epic, in a new epic meter (the 17-syllable line), with a new demotic vocabulary. Peter Bien (1988) points out that Kazantzakis abandoned the novel form more or less completely for 30 years. He came back to it only "begrudgingly," when international recognition as a writer appeared to depend on fiction. Roderick Beaton (1994) concedes Kazantzakis's fascination with the apparent titans of literature (Bergson,

Nietzsche) and of the world (Buddha, Jesus) (117), but plays down the weighty comparisons with Homer, Dante, or Lenin.

SELECTED BIBLIOGRAPHY

Works by Kazantzakis

Ófis kaì kríno (1906). [*Serpent and Lily: A Novella.* Trans. Theodora Vasils. Berkeley: University of California Press, 1980.]

Hristós. Athens: Stochastes, 1928.

Toda Raba (1929). Trans. [from the French] Amy Mims. New York: Simon and Schuster, 1964.

Le jardin des rochers (1936). [*The Rock Garden.* Trans. Richard Howard. New York: Simon and Schuster, 1963.]

Odússeia (1938). [*The Odyssey: A Modern Sequel.* Trans. Kimon Friar. New York: Simon and Schuster, 1958.]

Boúdas. (1941). [*Buddha.* Trans. Kimon Friar and Athena Dallis-Damis. San Diego, Calif.: Avant Books, 1983.]

Bíos kaì politeía toû Aléxi Zórmpa (1946). [*Zorba the Greek.* Trans. Carl Wildman. London: John Lehmann, 1952.]

Hristòs xanastaurónetai (1948). [*Christ Recrucified.* Trans. Jonathan Griffin. New York: Simon and Schuster, 1953.]

Oi Aderfofádes (1949). [*The Fratricides.* Trans. Athena Gianakas Dallas. New York: Simon and Schuster, 1964.]

O Kapetàn Mihális (1950). [*Freedom or Death: A Novel.* Trans. Jonathan Griffin. New York: Simon and Schuster, 1956.]

O Teleftaíos pirasmós (1950–1951). [*The Last Temptation of Christ.* Ed. and trans. P. A. Bien. New York: Simon and Schuster, 1961.]

O Ftohoúlis toû Theoû (1953). [*Saint Francis: A Novel.* Trans. P. A. Bien. New York: Simon and Schuster, 1962.]

Taxidéfontas: Á Italía, Aíuptos, Siná, Ierosólima, Kúpros katà tò 1927. Athens: Ekdoseis E. Kazantzaki, 1965. [*Journeying; Vol. I, Travels in Italy, Egypt, Sinai, Jerusalem and Cyprus.* Trans. Themi and Theodora Vasils. Boston: Little, Brown, 1975.]

Selected Studies of Kazantzakis

Antonakes, Michael. "Christ, Kazantzakis, and Controversy in Greece." In *Modern Greek Studies Yearbook* 6 (1990): 331–43.

Beaton, Roderick. *An Introduction to Modern Greek Literature.* Oxford: Clarendon Press, 1994.

Bien, Peter. "Kazantzákis' Attitude towards Prose Fiction." In *The Greek Novel: AD 1–1985.* Ed. Roderick Beaton, 81–89. London: Croom Helm, 1988.

———. *Nikos Kazantzakis: Novelist.* Bristol: Bristol Classical Press, 1989.

Dombrowski, Daniel A. *Kazantzakis and God.* Albany: State University of New York Press, 1997.

Gounelas, C.-D. "The Concept of Resemblance in Kazantzakis's Tragedies *Christ* and *Buddha.*" In special issue "Nikos Kazantzakis," *Journal of Modern Greek Studies* 16, no. 2 (Oct. 1998): 313–30.

Pappageotes, George C. *The Story of Modern Greek Literature. (From the 10th Century A.D. to the Present).* New York: Athens Press, 1972.

Ricks, David. *The Shade of Homer: A Study in Modern Greek Poetry.* Cambridge: Cambridge University Press, 1989.

JAMAICA KINCAID
(1949–)

Deborah Phelps

BIOGRAPHY

Jamaica Kincaid's writing, while not strictly autobiographical, is always infused with her strong emotions about her bleak childhood origins in the colonial British West Indies. Kincaid was born Elaine Potter Richardson in St. Johns, Antigua. Her father, a carpenter, was largely absent from the family. Raised by her mother in a society circumscribed by poverty and patriarchy, Kincaid attended a government school and worked in the home to care for her three younger brothers. At 17, frustrated with the limits on her life in Antigua, she traveled to New York, where she worked first as an au pair and then as a secretary and model while earning her high school diploma. She briefly attended Franconia College in New Hampshire on a scholarship before returning to New York, where she began to write articles for *The Village Voice* and *Ingenue* under the name Jamaica Kincaid. These articles attracted the attention of *New Yorker* editor William Shawn, who hired Kincaid as a columnist for the "Talk of the Town" section of the magazine. In 1978 *The New Yorker* published her first short story, "Girl." Subsequent *New Yorker* fiction led to the publication in 1983 of her first book, *At the Bottom of the River.* This collection of short stories set in her childhood Antigua won the Morton Dauwen Zabel Award of the American Academy and Institute of Arts and Letters and was nominated for a PEN/Faulkner Award. Kincaid published her first novel, *Annie John,* to critical acclaim in 1985.

Although known primarily for her novels, Kincaid has also garnered critical attention for her nonfiction. *A Small Place* (1988) is a decidedly unsentimental portrait of Antigua, triggered by the writer's first visit to the island after its independence from British rule. *My Brother* (1997) discusses the tragedy of AIDS in the third world Caribbean in terms of the experience of Kincaid's youngest brother who was stricken with and later died of the disease. On the lighter side, Kincaid has translated her life-long love of plants into a book, *My Garden* (1999).

In 1995, she resigned her staff position at *The New Yorker* when it came under new editorial management. She is married to the composer Allen Shawn (son of the late *New Yorker* editor) with whom she has two children. She lives in Bennington, Vermont, and has held visiting faculty positions at several universities including Bennington College and Harvard.

MAJOR MULTICULTURAL THEMES

All of Kincaid's work discusses the problems of colonialism. Her novels and short stories feature female protagonists from the Caribbean whose bitter anger over their restricted lives causes them to retreat emotionally from others. The heroines of *Annie John* and *Lucy* (1990) flee their impoverished homes for opportunity abroad, only to find themselves employed as au pairs, or "servants," as Kincaid calls them. Xuela in *The Autobiography of My Mother* (1994) remains on the island, dispassionately living from man to man while inwardly raging against her powerlessness. At the core of these characters' anger—and Kincaid's—is the history of Antigua itself. A British colony while Kincaid lived there, Antigua achieved independence in 1981, but remains part of the British Commonwealth. She consistently describes Antigua as a corrupt, poverty-riven island where the people are made small-minded and self-loathing under the racist, patriarchal British rule. Kincaid stresses in *A Small Place* and *My Brother* that independence did little to improve the lot of Antiguans—they remain as poor and politically impotent as ever.

In the novels, colonialism's bitter legacy is highlighted in Kincaid's recurrent theme of difficult mother-daughter relationships. Both Annie John and Lucy suffer in adolescence when their mothers inexplicably grow distant from them. Xuela's stunted emotions in *The Autobiography of My Mother* derive from never knowing the mother who died in childbirth. Kincaid has explained in interviews that her relationship with her own mother became unloving after the birth of her brothers and remains cool to this day. The critic Leslie Garis claims that "Kincaid has never gotten over the betrayal she felt when she began to suffer from her mother's emotional remoteness" ("Through West Indian Eyes," 70). The uncaring, yet ironclad hold mothers have over daughters in Kincaid's fiction mimics the larger bond of British colonial rule over Antiguans. The hectoring, imperious voice of the mother in "Girl" is the only one so privileged; the daughter remains submissively silent. Like the soul-killing effects of colonialism on its subjects, the inadequacies of their primary relationship leaves the daughters' emotional lives forever poisoned.

SURVEY OF CRITICISM

Kincaid's work has been generally well received. Critics routinely admire her simple, yet elegant narrative style. Derek Walcott has noted in reference to *Lucy* that her sentences seem to be "discovering themselves" as they are written (cited in Garis, 80). Jaime Manrique (1999) wrote that Kincaid's *My Garden* was her "most companionable book" because it was largely devoid of the author's "misanthropic flare-ups," but he felt that Kincaid's "dashing style" can "sometimes be too precious" in the context of gardening.

Critics have been less complimentary to the tone Kincaid wields in her writings on colonialism. They lament her heroines' resolute cold-heartedness. The ruthlessly amoral Xuela in *The Autobiography of My Mother* was nearly universally condemned by reviewers, who tended to see the novel as autobiographical. But the slim volume on Antigua, *A Small Place*, has engendered the strongest critical reaction. Robert Gottlieb, Kincaid's editor at *The New Yorker*, refused to publish it in excerpt, as was his habit with her longer works, due to the essay's anger toward the white, privileged first world. Isabel Fonseca (1992) criticized its "shapelessness" and "savage tone" (Draper, 1172).

Kincaid does, however, have influential fans among other writers and scholars. Susan Sontag described her rage as "poignant because it's so truthful" (cited in Garis, 41). Henry Louis Gates, Jr. stated that Kincaid excels at presenting a black world that is not circumscribed by race; that, like Toni Morrison, she cannot be contained by the label "black novelist" (cited in Garis, 44). In her monograph, Diane Simmons (1994) praises Kincaid's work, angry tone included, because of its stringently unsentimental description of the tremendous damage done to "paradise" by colonialism and its latter-day incarnation, tourism.

SELECTED BIBLIOGRAPHY

Works by Kincaid

At the Bottom of the River. New York: Farrar, Straus, and Giroux, 1983.
Annie John. New York: Farrar, Straus, and Giroux, 1985.
A Small Place. New York: Farrar, Straus, and Giroux, 1988.
Lucy. New York: Farrar, Straus, and Giroux, 1990.
The Autobiography of My Mother. New York: Farrar, Straus, and Giroux, 1994.
My Brother. New York: Farrar, Straus, and Giroux, 1997.
My Garden. New York: Farrar, Straus, and Giroux, 1999.
Talk Stories. New York: Farrar, Straus, and Giroux, 2001.
Mr. Potter. New York: Farrar, Straus, and Giroux, 2002.

Selected Studies of Kincaid

Bloom, Harold, ed. *Jamaica Kincaid*. Philadelphia: Chelsea House, 1998.

Bonetti, Kay. "An Interview with Jamaica Kincaid." *Missouri Review* 15 (1993): 325–40.

Draper, James P., ed. *Black Literature Criticism: Excerpts from Criticism of the Most Significant Works of Black Authors over the Past 200 Years.* 3 vols., 2: 1164–78. Detroit: Gale Research, 1992.

Ferguson, Moira. *Colonialism and Gender Relations from Mary Wollstonecraft to Jamaica Kincaid: East Caribbean Connections.* New York: Columbia University Press, 1993.

———. *Jamaica Kincaid: Where the Land Meets the Body.* Charlottesville: University of Virginia Press, 1994.

Garis, Leslie. "Through West Indian Eyes." *New York Times Magazine* (October 7, 1990): 42–44, 70, 78, 80, 91.

Lindfors, Bernth, and Reinhard Sander, eds. *Twentieth-Century Caribbean and Black African Writers, Third Series,* 131–39. Detroit: Gale Research, 1996.

MacDonald-Smythe, Antonia. *Making Homes in the West/Indies: Constructions of Subjectivity in the Writings of Michelle Cliff and Jamaica Kincaid.* London: Routledge, 2001.

Manrique, Jaime. Review of *My Garden.* Available at http://www.salon.com/books/review/1999/12/20/kincaid/index. html.

Nelson, Emmanuel S., ed. *Contemporary African-American Novelists: A Bio-Bibliographic Critical Sourcebook,* 260–65. Westport: Greenwood Press, 1999.

Parvisini-Gebert, Lizabeth. *Jamaica Kincaid: A Critical Companion.* Westport: Greenwood Press, 1999.

Parvisini-Gebert, Lizabeth and Olga Torres-Seda, eds. *Caribbean Women Novelists: An Annotated Critical Bibliography.* Westport: Greenwood Press, 1993.

Simmons, Diane. *Jamaica Kincaid.* New York: Twayne, 1994.

ARTHUR KOESTLER
(1905–1983)

Stuart Knee

BIOGRAPHY

Nominated on three occasions for the Nobel Prize and the 1968 recipient of Copenhagen University's Sonning Prize for outstanding contributions to literature and European culture, Arthur Koestler defined modernist preoccupations with fragmented sensibilities and anticipated global, post-modern tendencies to cross cultures, integrate knowledge, and dissolve intellectual boundaries. As journalist, political analyst, Revisionist Zionist, and natural philosopher, he produced some of the most penetrating prose of his generation. In 1998, the Modern Library Association poll of the 100 best novels of the twentieth century ranked Koestler's *Darkness at Noon* (1940) eighth. If creativity is the product of unresolved personal tensions, then Arthur Koestler was a genius.

Secular but not assimilated, Koestler was born in Budapest, the only child of Central European Jewish parents. While he was ambivalent toward them, he always kept in touch with them even in maturity and, in telling public and private ways, adopted their personality traits. Like his father, he was enthralled by certain ideas that became enthusiasms and, like his mother, he was self-centered, capricious, domineering, and often callous. Sometimes well-off and sometimes needy, the Koestler family sought business opportunities in Budapest and Vienna during and after World War I; eventually Arthur was sent to a small boarding school at Baden, near Vienna.

He matriculated at but never graduated from a Viennese technical university, where he concentrated in engineering and physics. After having joined Unitas, a Jewish student fraternity committed to the Zionist enterprise, he left for Palestine and tramped around the country for most of 1926, doing odd jobs and briefly living on a kibbutz. Truthfully, he liked the realities of day-to-day existence and the earthiness of the pioneers a lot less than the romantic ideal that initially motivated him to live there. Interestingly, that is the way he would always feel about the people and the land, even when he returned as foreign correspondent and celebrated author to cover the final years of the British mandate and the birth of the state of Israel.

Politics projected Koestler upon history's center stage and kept him there for a generation. A position as executive secretary to the World Union of Zionist Revisionists did not materialize. However, upon his 1927 return to Europe, friends referred him to the prestigious Berlin-based Ullstein newspapers, where he was employed for about five years. Based in Jerusalem, Paris, and Berlin, he rose from reporter to editor but, in December 1931, he made a momentous decision that would alter the contour of his career: he joined the Communist Party.

Given the profound nature of interwar liberal drift and the specter of fascism, this option was not particularly unusual for a sensitive Jewish mind, especially if it was rooted in the past of Middle Europe, where anti-Semitism and a Jewish self-perception of otherness was endemic. In the mid-1930s, Koestler was living in Paris as a Hungarian expatriate, serving the German Communist Party in exile as a talented conduit for Stalinist propaganda by composing articles favorable to that ideology while working steadily on his first novel. With a British newspaper credential acting as a cover for his Communist affiliation, he traveled to Spain three times in a brief period to probe the civil war. He offered vivid accounts of General Franco's collusion with the Nazis before he was imprisoned in Seville from February to May 1937.

As a result of this traumatic episode, a disillusioning tour he had taken through the famine-wracked Soviet Union in 1932, the suppression of Trotskyite dissent within the Communist Party, the expedient nature of Stalinist dogma, and the Great Purge with Moscow show trials of 1934–38, Koestler resigned from the Party in April 1938. Thereafter, he was as zealous an anti- as he was a pro-Communist. As night descended upon Europe, he escaped from occupied France and, by 1941, found asylum in England. There, he related his odyssey entirely in English (a third language) in *Scum of the Earth* (1941); he had previously used Hungarian in *Gladiátors* (1939) and then German in *Sonnenfinsternis* (1940). A few years hence, he further demonstrated his virtuosity by completing the French translation of *Promise and Fulfillment: Palestine 1917–1949* (1949).

Until 1955, he carried his anti-Stalinist crusade from England back to France, to America, and then to Berlin, where he was a guiding spirit for the 1950 Congress for Cultural Freedom. Thereafter he tired of his involvement, despite the fact that it had made him as acclaimed as George Orwell, Simone de Beauvoir, Jean Paul Sartre, Albert Camus, and the Andrés: Gide and Malraux. He spent the rest of his life—28 years—addressing what he claimed was the tyranny of physical science and behaviorism. While shifting from idea to idea, country to country, and residence to residence, he fathered an illegitimate daughter whom he chose never to meet, had an infinite number of liaisons, and was married three times. The last of these, to his former secretary Cynthia Jefferies, ended on March 1, 1983, when he and his wife committed suicide.

MAJOR MULTICULTURAL THEMES

A triad of tyrannies defined Arthur Koestler's multiculturalism. The first of these was the tyranny of his Jewish identity which he never entirely relinquished, despite the fact that he muted the issue in the 1950s and 1960s; the second was the tyranny of Stalinism which he confronted from 1932–55 in a series of autobiographical, journalistic and fictional works. As a body, they are metaphorically powerful, apocalyptic, grim and depressing. To read them is to touch prophetic flames too searing for the tenderhearted. The third is the world of natural science, seemingly divorced from the first two in content but not in intent: to Koestler, the empiric, behaviorist, positivist, reductionist physical universe was a tyranny as profound as those he revealed in ethnicity and politics. According to him, this ultimate tyranny was hardest to uproot since it defined an unassailable nineteenth- and twentieth-century orthodoxy. Between 1955 and 1983, his massive output of monographs, essays, and articles spoke for a new form of science, inclusive of that which is observed but whose essence is not necessarily quantifiable. These phenomena, he opined, which were as legitimate as those of the Newtonian machine and the behaviorism of B. F. Skinner, were unconscious, intuitive, and bisociative, that is to say existing on two or more mental planes which somehow intersected to create patterns in the brain.

Always at war with his Jewish identity, Koestler approached it from a secular perspective in *Arrival and Departure* (1943), *Thieves in the Night: Chronicle of an Experiment* (1946), *Promise and Fulfillment: Palestine 1917–1949*, and *The Thirteenth Tribe: The Khazar Empire and its Heritage* (1976). The first two are novels, the third is history, and the fourth is speculative. He covers the Holocaust, Jewish nationalism, and genetic Judaism. Discounting the Hebrew language as primitive, Jewish ceremonialism as tribal, and ethnic Judaism as an irrelevant extrusion of a dead past, he called for Zionist militancy and nation-building to end Jewish homelessness and solve the so-called Jewish question.

Stalinism was, he believed, a similar cage designed to crystallize and stultify personal identity. Imaginatively limned accounts of the Communist struggle in *L'Espagne ensanglantée* (1937) and the abortive utopian search of *Gladiátors* gave way to *Scum of the Earth*, a gritty record of his flight across two continents to escape the Nazi onslaught. *Sonnenfinster-*

nis, his classic, extends beyond its particular time and embraces the human condition at all times. Koestler's old revolutionary, under interrogation and inquisition, troubles us today with pertinent, contemporary queries that are his and our undoing: what are the connections between ends and means? morality and expedience? is history a science? are human beings predictable? what is the nature of salvation? is it attainable? Protagonist Nikolai Salmanovich Rubashov finds an answer in the hour of his execution by accepting individual responsibility for friends and lovers betrayed: it is Koestler's "oceanic feeling"(Cesarani, 175).

Before impersonal science destroyed the planet, Koestler as angry prophet made an attempt to reconcile the 500-year-old rupture between materialism and mysticism. Tiring of the Cold War, or perhaps his role in it as standard bearer, he challenged his final tyranny: the physical sciences and behaviorism. After his fashion, he sought a universe as orderly as that of the conventional scientists, but only on his terms. Stated most systematically in *The Sleepwalkers: A History of Man's Changing Vision of the Universe* (1959), *The Watershed: A Biography of Johannes Kepler* (1960), *The Trail of the Dinosaur and Other Essays* (1955), *Insight and Outlook: A Inquiry into the Common Foundations of Science, Art, and Social Ethics* (1949), *The Act of Creation* (1964), *The Ghost in the Machine* (1967), and *Bricks to Babel: A Selection from 50 Years of his Writings* (1981), Koestler urged a transcendent leap of creativity incorporating intuition, bisociation, inspiration, drugs, and paranormal activity, all of which would herald an improved civilization. Upon his death, he bequeathed about 750,000 British pounds to the founding of a Chair in Parapsychology at Edinburgh University.

SURVEY OF CRITICISM

Both of the recent, comprehensive Koestler biographies fall short of perfection, but for different reasons. Iain Hamilton's study (1982) has the virtue of a living subject who was interviewed but the vice of self-serving testimony. In short, should a biographer rely on a less than objective contextualization of events and motivation? Hamilton knew his limits and focused on the years 1940–70, a period with which he was most familiar.

By contrast, David Cesarani's research (1998) is impeccable but his presentation is less so. He made full use of the Koestler Archive at the Edinburgh University Library and evaluated primary materials from Moscow's Center for the Conservation of Historical Documentary Collections, Yale University's Edmund Wilson Correspondence at the Beinecke Rare Book and Manuscript Library, and London's Public Record Office. He also used the letters of Mamaine Paget, Koestler's second wife, edited by her twin sister Celia Goodman and published in 1985, as well as the revealing correspondence of Simone de Beauvoir to Nelson Algren between 1947 and 1964, published in 1998. The result is a unique, sometimes gripping psychobiography with certain shortcomings. It is socially and privately revealing albeit akin to hammer blows, relentless, perhaps too much so, to have the desired effect. It leaves readers shocked and numb; any laudatory conclusions drawn concerning Koestler's literary legacy that are, indeed, summarized in the author's conclusion are, to my mind, anticlimactic.

Some journal articles and scholarly periodicals have done a good job focusing on Koestler's diversity. For example, Emery E. George (1998) published a long essay comparing the literary merit of *Darkness at Noon* to that of *Hyperion,* an eighteenth-century novel by Friedrich Hölderlin, while certain symbolism in *Darkness at Noon* was the subject of Alexander George's (1994) article in *The North American Review.* Also, graphic designer Roy Behrens (1998) has only praise for Koestler's *The Act of Creation* which, he avers, taught him how to think creatively.

SELECTED BIBLIOGRAPHY

Works by Koestler

L'Espagne ensanglantée. Paris: Carrefour, 1937.
Sonnenfinsternis (1940). [*Darkness at Noon.* New York: Macmillan, 1941.]
Scum of the Earth. New York: Macmillan, 1941.
Arrival and Departure. New York: Macmillan, 1943.
Thieves in the Night: Chronicle of an Experiment. New York: Macmillan, 1946.
Insight and Outlook: An Inquiry into the Common Foundations of Science, Art, and Social Ethics. New York: Macmillan, 1949.
Promise and Fulfillment: Palestine 1917–1949. New York: Macmillan, 1949.
The Invisible Writing: An Autobiography. Boston: Beacon Press, 1954.
The Trail of the Dinosaur and Other Essays. New York: Macmillan, 1955.
Reflections on Hanging. New York: Macmillan, 1957.
The Sleepwalkers: A History of Man's Changing Vision of the Universe. New York: Macmillan, 1959.
The Watershed: A Biography of Johannes Kepler. Garden City, N.Y.: Anchor Books, 1960.
The Act of Creation (1964). London: Arkana, 1989.
The Ghost in the Machine. New York: Macmillan, 1967.
The Thirteenth Tribe: The Khazar Empire and its Heritage. New York: Random House, 1976.
Bricks to Babel: A Selection from 50 Years of his Writings. New York: Random House, 1981.
Arthur and Cynthia Koestler. *Stranger on the Square.* Ed. Harold Harris. New York: Random House, 1984.

Selected Studies of Koestler

Behrens, Roy R. "Encountering Koestler." *Print* 52 (September–October 1998): 38–41.

Cesarani, David. *Arthur Koestler: The Homeless Mind*. New York: The Free Press, 1999.

Crick Bernard. "Putting the Rat in Rational: Monster of Misogyny or Master of the Mind?" *The Independent* (London) (November 7, 1998): 15.

George, Alexander. "Inconsistency in 'Darkness at Noon': Slip or Tip?" *The North American Review* 279 (May–June 1994): 24–25.

George, Emery E. "'Hyperion' and 'Darkness at Noon': Resemblance with a Difference." *Journal of English and German Philology* 97 (January 1998): 51–68.

Gleason, Abbott. *Totalitarianism: The Inner Secret of the Cold War*. New York: Oxford University Press, 1995.

Hamilton Iain. *Koestler: A Biography*. New York: Macmillan, 1982.

Ingle, Stephen. "Politics and Literature: Means and Ends in Koestler." *Political Studies* 47, no. 2 (June 1999): 329–44.

Rogers, Ben. "A Rake's Progress Through Art, Religion and Women." *The Independent Sunday* (London) (November 15, 1998): 12.

Romano, Carlin. "The Life and Contradictions of Arthur Koestler." *Philadelphia Inquirer* (January 16, 2000): K01.

Scammel, Michael. "Arthur Koestler Resigns: A Discovery in the Moscow Archives." *The New Republic* 218 (May 4, 1998): 27–33.

Shaw, Brent D., ed. *Spartacus and the Slave Wars*. Boston: Bedford / St. Martin's, 2001.

Wullschlager, Jackie. "A Hideous Humanitarian." *Financial Times* (November 21, 1998): 6.

MILAN KUNDERA
(1929–)

Rolando Perez

BIOGRAPHY

Milan Kundera was born in Brno, Czechoslovakia, the son of Milanda and Ludvik Kundera. His father, a pianist and musicologist, was a student of the Czech composer, theorist, and collector of Slavic folk music, Leoš Janáček. Milan's early studies were devoted to music—a topic he has often written about and discussed in interviews, and a subject that has influenced the very structure of his novels. One of his early jobs was playing piano in a jazz ensemble in his hometown of Brno; he continued to study music, as well as film and drama, until graduation from The Academy of Music and Dramatic Arts (Prague) in 1956. His book of essays, *Les testaments trahis* (1993), is about music, literature, and the relationship between the two.

Since the writing of his first short story (in the collection, *Směšne lásky: Tři melancholické anekdoty*, 1963), and his first novel, *Žert* (1967), Kundera has maintained that he is a novelist above all, though he has written several essays and plays. "With the first short story of *Laughable Loves* [*Směšne lásky*] (I wrote it in 1959), I was certain of having 'found myself.' I became a prose writer, a novelist, and I am nothing else. Since then, my aesthetic has known no transformation; it evolves, to use your word, linearly" (quoted in Oppenheim, 11). But Kundera's own life has been less than linear.

Having begun his intellectual career in music, he turned to literature in the early 1950s. By the time he emigrated to France in 1975, he was already quite famous in Czechoslovakia. Though it is true that he was for many years a favorite of the Communist Party of Czechoslovakia, he remained openly critical of the shallowness and narrow-mindedness of socialist aesthetics to the very end, at times publishing articles in defense of the kind of avant-garde literature that was officially attacked by the Party. Jaromil, the unforgettable protagonist of *Život je jinde* (1973), is a lyrical poet who, in Faust-like fashion, ends up selling his soul to the Party in exchange for fame and recognition. He reports his girlfriend to the police, and she is unjustly imprisoned for many years. Jaromil acts in the name of the Party, in the name of poetry, in the name of a "romanticism" that ironically leads to the betrayal of the loved one.

Kundera had spoken at a gathering of the Fourth Czechoslovak Writers' Congress, calling for tolerance and freedom of speech and leveling a frontal attack against those who repress free expression. Within a mere four months of the speech, Czechoslovakia was invaded and occupied by the Soviet Union. Not long after that, Kundera was blacklisted and his works banned as subversive and counterrevolutionary. Granted permission to accept a teaching position at the University of Rennes in 1975, he moved to France. The Czechoslovakian government revoked his citizenship after the publication of *Kniha smíchu a zapomnění* (1979), Kundera's public "forgetting" of Czechoslovakia as an exile. He became a French citizen in 1980, and his four most recent books, originally written in French, *L'art du roman* (1986), *Les testaments trahis* (1993), *La lenteur* (1995), and *L'identité* (1997), bear witness to the influence of his adopted country. His latest novel, *La ignorancia* (2000), was first published in a Spanish translation, as Kundera wanted the book to be a tribute to Spanish intellectuals exiled in Paris during Franco's dictatorship.

MAJOR MULTICULTURAL THEMES

"For Kundera, the problem is not the impossibility of accumulating a past, but the horrific consequences of being forcibly severed from it . . . and thus the most terrifying prospect in life is the loss of this past through forgetting. This is Kundera's own dilemma as an exile, it is the dilemma of his native country whose customs were systematically destroyed through a process of 'organized forgetting' and replaced with official Soviet ideology" (Workman, 37).

If there is anything that is generally at the heart of all of Kundera's novels, it is history—the history of Czechoslovakia and the history of Central Europe. His most famous novel, or to be more precise, the novel that made him famous in the West, is *Nesnesitelná lehkost bytí* (1984)—made into a film directed by Phillip Kaufman in 1988. It narrates the story of a Czech couple who return home from exile in the West.

In the novel *Valčik na rozloučenou* (1976), translated as *La valse aux adieux* (1976), or *The Farewell Waltz* (1998), the following dialogue takes places between the character of Olga (a young woman) and Jakub (an older man), who have met to say goodbye. Kundera's dialogue is imbued with the kind of tension that anyone who has ever had to emigrate feels at the very last moment before leaving:

> "I can tell you I don't feel any love for my homeland. Is that bad of me?"
> "I don't know," said Jakub. "I really don't. As far as I'm concerned, I've been rather attached to this country."
> "Maybe it's bad of me," Olga went on, "but I don't feel tied to anything. What could I be attached to here?"
> "Even painful memories are ties that bind."
> "Bind us to what? To staying in a country where we were born? I don't understand how people can talk about freedom and not get that millstone off their necks. As if a tree were at home where it can't grow. A tree is at home wherever water percolates through the soil." (*The Farewell Waltz*, trans. Aaron Asher, 99)

The idea that one is not a citizen of a particular nation but of the world at large may belong more to what Kundera refers to as the "lyrical" than it does to social reality. For though there is much that unites the different peoples of the world, there is also a certain concrete specificity to any culture or religion that is not so easily transcended by mere wishful thinking. This "transcendental" view of culture may be easier to maintain, as Kundera wants to claim, by the more powerful, dominant nations—whose identity and political existence are free of threat from imperial forces—than by smaller nations whose fate is always in question, threatened by the same powers that support the "transcendental" view. It is in such a cultural nexus that a writer like Kundera finds himself, even after so many years of living in France. The concept of *a small nation*, he writes in *Les testaments trahis*, "is not quantitative; it describes a situation; a destiny: small nations haven't the comfortable sense of being there always, past and future" (*Testaments Betrayed*, trans. Linda Asher, 192). Thus, the citizen of a small country, always conscious of his precarious place in world politics, does not have the luxury of taking the same cultural and political stance toward his own country as does the citizen of a strong, powerful nation, who has no reason to fear the ostracism of his own countrymen. The citizens of a small nation "see their existence perpetually threatened or called into question: for their very existence is a question" (*Testaments Betrayed*, 192). Such a history overdetermines the intellectual's life with respect to his birthplace. "In the big family that is a small country, the artist is bound in multiple ways, by multiple cord," writes Kundera, thinking of his native Czech Republic. He continues: "When Nietzsche noisily savaged the German character, when Stendhal announced that he preferred Italy to his homeland, no German or French took offense; if a Greek or Czech dared to say the same thing, his family would curse him as a detestable traitor" (*Testaments Betrayed*, 193).

Moreover, writers of small nations, Kundera tells us, often have their work narrowly relegated to the literature of "nationhood"—that is, to a literature of "local color," while being denied the more fruitful and perhaps accurate "universal perspective." Writing about the Polish author Witold Gombrowicz, Kundera declares that "foreign commentators struggle to explain his work by discoursing on the Polish nobility, on the Polish Baroque, etc., etc. . . . they 'Polonize' him, 're-Polonize' him, push him back into the *small context* of the national. However, it is not familiarity with the Polish nobility but familiarity with the international modern novel (that is, the *large context*) that will bring us to understand the originality and, hence, the value of Gombrowicz's novels" (*Testaments Betrayed*, 193–94). But the writer of "minor literature" (to borrow a term from Gilles Deleuze) is hardly ever allowed to partake in the universal history of literature. His identity as a writer remains a national identity.

Now, what of immigrant artists, writers in exile who, like Samuel Beckett, Witold Gombrowicz, Vladimir Nabokov—and like Kundera—wrote both in the language of their adopted country and in their native language? What is interesting in Kundera is that though he has achieved the universal fame of the larger context, his writing embraces both French and Czech culture—albeit with a slight tinge of sadness over the loss of a past that, as he says, is unrecoverable. "Emigration is hard from the purely personal standpoint. . . . People generally think of the pain of nostalgia; but what is worse is the pain of estrangement: the process whereby what was intimate becomes foreign. . . . Only returning to the native land after a long absence can reveal the substantial strangeness of the world and of existence" (*Testaments Betrayed*, 94–95). This feeling of estrangement from one's birthplace can be experienced only by the exile for whom return was never an option. If Gombrowicz, writes Kundera, never returned to Poland, even when he had the opportunity to do so, it is precisely because he did not feel he could confront the sense of estrangement that would arise from such a visit. It was an existential choice or refusal rather than a political one: "incommunicable because too intimate. Incommunicable, also because too wounding for the others. Some things we can only leave unsaid" (*Testaments Betrayed*, 95). Unlike the archetypal Ulysses who after many years away from home finally returns to recover his rightful place in his native land, the political exile like Kundera is fated to die in some faraway land that had nothing to do either with his birthplace or the country to which he originally emigrated. "Vladimir Nabokov lived in Russia for twenty years, twenty-one in Europe (in England, Germany, and France), twenty years in America, sixteen in Switzerland. He adopted English as his writing language . . . He was unequivocal and insistent in proclaiming himself an American citizen and writer. His body lies at Montreux in Switzerland" (*Testaments Betrayed*, 95).

SURVEY OF CRITICISM

According to Ewa Thompson (1989), some writers—such as Kundera—have separated themselves from their "ethnic ghettos" as they have "forged a definition of that part of the world [Eastern Europe] that has become comprehensible to the home audience *and* to the audiences of the host countries" (505). In an interview given to Lois Oppenheim (1989), Kundera takes the following position on "Slavic culture": "There is, of course, a linguistic unity of the Slavic languages. But there doesn't exist any Slavic cultural unity. 'Slavic culture' doesn't exist . . . I'll never stop repeating that the only context that can reveal the meaning and value of a novelist's work is the context of the history of the European novel. . . . But I understand this adjective . . . not as a geographical term, but a 'spiritual' one which takes in both America and, for example, Israel" (10). When asked whether he would ever write a novel outside of the Czech sociohistorical context, given that he is "so at home in Paris," Kundera's response to Oppenheim was: "I lived in Czechoslovakia until I was forty-five. Given that my real career as a writer began when I was thirty, I can say that the larger part of my creative life is taking place in France. I am much more tied to France than is thought" (10).

Ivan Sanders (1991) reports that in the 1980s Kundera had his "books removed from Penguin Books' prestigious *Writers from The Other Europe* series" (109) in rejection of the limiting label.

SELECTED BIBLIOGRAPHY

Works by Kundera

Směšne lásky: Tři melancholické anekdoty. Prague: Československý spisovatel, 1963. [*Laughable Loves.* Trans. Suzanne Rappaport. New York: Knopf, 1974.]

Žert. Prague: Československý spisovatel, 1967. [*The Joke.* Trans. (from the Czech) Michael Henry Heim. New York: Harper and Row, 1982.]

Život je jinde (1973). [*La vie est ailleurs.* Trans. (into French) François Kérel. Paris: Gallimard, 1973; *Life is Elsewhere.* Trans. (from the Czech) Peter Kussi. New York: Knopf, 1974.]

Valčik na rozloučenou (1976). [*La valse aux adieux.* Trans. (into French) François Kérel. Paris: Gallimard, 1976; *The Farewell Party.* Trans. (from the Czech) Peter Kussi. New York: Knopf, 1976; *The Farewell Waltz.* Trans. (from the French) Aaron Asher. New York: HarperCollins, 1998.]

Kniha smíchu a zapomnění (1979). [*Le livre du rire et de l'oubli.* Trans. (into French) François Kérel. Paris: Gallimard, 1979; *The Book of Laughter and Forgetting.* Trans. (from the Czech) Michael Henry Heim. New York: A.A. Knopf, 1980.]

Nesnesitelná lehkost bytí (1984). [*L'insoutenable légèreté de l'être: Roman.* Trans. (into French) François Kérel. Paris: Gallimard, 1984; *The Unbearable Lightness of Being.* Trans. (from the Czech) Michael Henry Heim. New York: Harper and Row, 1984.]

L'art du roman: Essai. Paris: Gallimard, 1986. [*The Art of the Novel.* Trans. (from the French) Linda Asher. New York: Grove Press, 1988; reissued by Harper-Collins, 1993; revised edition published by HarperPerennial, 2000.]

Les testaments trahis. Paris: Gallimard, 1993. [*Testaments Betrayed: An Essay in Nine Parts.* Trans. (from the French) Linda Asher. New York: Harper-Collins, 1995.]

La lenteur: Roman. Paris: Gallimard, 1995. [*Slowness.* Trans. (from the French) Linda Asher. New York: Harper-Collins, 1996.]

L'identité: Roman. Paris: Gallimard, 1997. [*Identity.* Trans. (from the French) Linda Asher. New York: HarperFlamingo, 1998.]

La ignorancia. Trans. [from the French] Beatriz de Moura. Barcelona: Tusquets, 2000.

Interviews

Liehm, Antonin J. "Milan Kundera." Trans. Peter Kussi. In *The Politics of Culture* (1968). Ed. Antonin J. Liehm, 130–50. New York: Grove Press, 1972.

Oppenheim, Lois. "Clarifications, Elucidations: An Interview with Milan Kundera." *Review of Contemporary Fiction* 9 (Summer 1989): 7–11.

Selected Studies of Kundera

Adams, Vicki. "Milan Kundera: The Search for Self in a Post-modern World." In *Imagination, Emblems, and Expressions: Essays on Latin American, Caribbean, and Continental Culture and Identity.* Ed. Helen Ryan-Ranson, 233–46. Bowling Green, Ohio: Bowling Green State University Popular Press, 1993.

Czerwisnki, E. J. "Czesław Miłosz: The Persistence of Existence." *World Literature Today* 73, no. 4 (Autumn 1999): 669–71.

Donahue, Bruce. "Viewing the West from the East: Solzhenitzyn, Miłosz, and Kundera." *Comparative Literature Studies* 20 (Fall 1983): 247–60.

Jefferson, Ann. "Counterpoint and Forked Tongue: Milan Kundera and the Art of Exile." *Renaissance and Modern Studies* 34 (1991): 115–36.

Liehm, Antonin J. "Milan Kundera: Czech Writer." In *Czech Literature Since 1956: A Symposium.* Ed. William E. Harkins and Paul I. Trensky, 40–55. New York: Bohemica/Columbia University, 1980.

Misurella, Fred. "Not Silent, But in Exile and with Cunning." *Partisan Review* 52, no. 2 (1985): 87–98.

Peretz, Martin. "Mittel Europa." *The New Republic* 193 (August 26, 1985): 43.

Richterová, Sylvie. "La littérature tchèque en exil et le problème du polyglottisme." In *Les effets de l'émigration et l'exil dans les cultures tchèque et polonaise.* Ed. Hana Jechova and Helene Wlodarczyk, 49–60. Paris: Presses Universitaires de Paris-Sorbonne, 1987.

Sanders, Ivan. "Mr. Kundera, the European." *The Wilson Quarterly* 15 (Spring 1991): 102–109.

Thompson, Ewa M. "The Writer in Exile: The Good Years." *Slavic and East European Journal* 33 (Winter 1989): 499–515.

Workman, Mark E. "Folklore and the Literature of Exile." In *Folklore, Literature, and Cultural Theory: Collected Essays.* Ed. Cathy Lynn Press, 29–42. New York: Garland Publishing, Inc., 1995.

HANIF KUREISHI
(1954–)
Maria Antonietta Saracino

BIOGRAPHY

"I was born in London of an English mother and Pakistani father," writes
Hanif Kureishi in *The Rainbow Sign*, his autobiographical preface to *My
Beautiful Laundrette* (1986). "My father, who lives in London, came to
England from Bombay in 1947 to be educated by the old colonial power.
He married here and never went back to India. The rest of his large family, his brothers, their wives, his sisters, moved from Bombay to Karachi,
in Pakistan, after partition . . . From the start I tried to deny my Pakistani
self. I was ashamed. It was a curse and I wanted to be rid of it. I wanted to
be like everyone else" (9).

This unusual start worked inspirationally for Hanif Kureishi, whose
writing often reflects the racism and cultural clashes he experienced in the
first part of his life. At a fairly young age he decided that he wanted to be
a writer and began writing novels that were published when he was still a
teenager. He read philosophy at the University of London, King's College, worked as an usher for the Royal Court Theatre, and later supported
himself by writing pornography under the pseudonym "Antonia French."
It was the theater that launched Kureishi. His first play, *Soaking Up the
Heat* (1976), was produced at London's Theatre Upstairs; his second, *The
Mother Country*, won the Thames Television Playwright Award in 1980.
He became better known with his first play for the Royal Court Theatre,
Borderline (1981), a story of immigrants living in London, and a piece per-
formed by London's Royal Shakespeare Company, titled *Outskirts* (1982).

If theater gave Kureishi the initial start, it was cinema that made him
famous and garnered him a larger audience. During a period spent at his

uncle's house in Karachi in 1985, Kureishi wrote *My Beautiful Laundrette*, a screenplay about a young Pakistani immigrant who opens a laundromat in London with his gay white lover; he also sells drugs in order to make money to refurbish his laundry business. The script won several awards, including one for the best screenplay from the New York Film Critics Circle, and in 1986 was made into a film directed by Stephen Frears. Frears also directed *Sammy and Rosie Get Laid* (1987), which was scripted by Kureishi and also focuses on mixed-race relationships; it tells the story of a racially mixed couple living in London during the race riots.

The Black Album (1995) is set in London in 1989, the year of the fall of the Berlin wall, and also the year of the *fatwah:* it represents Kureishi's response to Salman Rushdie's *The Satanic Verses*. The novel centers upon the story of Shahid, a young immigrant who moves to London after the death of his father and finds himself caught between liberalism and fundamentalism.

The Buddha of Suburbia (1990), a semi-autobiographical novel, is about a young man, half-Indian and half-English, growing up in London. The novel, unanimously regarded as Kureishi's most engaging work, won the Booksellers Association of Great Britain and Ireland's Whitbread Book of the Year Award for a first novel and was later adapted by Kureishi himself for a television series. Kureishi wrote and directed *London Kills Me* (1991), a story of immigration in a world of drugs and gangs. The film *My Son the Fanatic* (1993), directed by Udayan Prasad, is based on a short story that originally appeared in *The New Yorker* and was later published in the collection *Love in a Blue Time* (1996). It deals with the life of a Punjabi immigrant whose son becomes engaged to the white daughter of a local police chief. In both *The Black Album* and some of the short stories of *Love in a Blue Time*, Kureishi attempts to tackle the rising issue of Islam among young generations of Asian immigrants in Britain.

MAJOR MULTICULTURAL THEMES

My Beautiful Laundrette was regarded by some as the definitive picture of life under Margaret Thatcher. It also gave a voice to the ethnic mix that had evolved in Britain during those years. With this work, Kureishi illuminated the presence of the immigrant Pakistani community, as well as that of other "black" or "brown" Asian communities, to an unprecedented degree. However, it was the widely acclaimed and successful *The Buddha of Suburbia* that drew attention to those very communities, whose countries of origin lie at the heart of the former British Empire, now living in the London suburbs and struggling to come to terms with their new cultural identity. "My name is Karim Amir," says the hero of *The Buddha of Suburbia*, "and I am an Englishman born and bred, almost. I am often considered to be a funny kind of Englishman, a new breed as it were, having emerged from two old histories. . . . Perhaps it is the odd mixture of continents and blood, of here and there, of belonging and not, that makes me restless and easily bored" (3). Conscious as they are of representing a "new" and "odd" sort of breed, Karim and his father Haroon start a sort of pilgrimage from the suburbs where they live to downtown London; and in so doing they are constantly reminded of their not being eligible to be considered authentic Englishmen. Even though the British Empire has collapsed, certain colonial attitudes have not, Kureishi seems to be saying. Karim—uncertain of his cultural or sexual identity, but sure of himself and of his moral values—rejects most of the second-rate options offered. Rebellious by nature, he tries to locate himself and achieve success in a white world without betraying his family and cultural background. London, the once mythicized center of colonial England, acts as a metaphorical center of authority.

SURVEY OF CRITICISM

Critic Seema Jena (1993) points out the extent to which immigrant writers such as Hanif Kureishi find themselves in the position of representing the marginalized immigrant community to the dominant one through their fiction—an act of representation that establishes a power relationship in which the marginalized are offered to the judgmental gaze of the white audience and are rendered vulnerable. Writing about "their own kind" puts minority writers in the spotlight in several ways: for instance, being pigeonholed and regarded as cultural or sociological representations. Writers like Hanif Kureishi, Jena maintains, "use the anti-hero as textual strategy to address issues such as the moral dilemma of immigrant writers as to how to both represent and not offend their communities; the position they assume as middlemen-interpreters-interacting between two cultures . . . and above all the means by which they try to impart the message of survival in spite of the hurdles that confront them" (3–4). Fawzia Afzal-Khan (1995) underlines how, in the genre of drama, Pakistani writers have not produced anything significant in English—with the sole exception of Kureishi, who is one of the few writers of Pakistani background to deal seriously and consistently with the issue of class in his work. In this, he has more in common with some of the earlier novelists and short-story writers who wrote socialist fiction (60). Critic Jamal Mahjoub (1998) writes enthusiastically about Kureishi, whom he defines as "confident, anarchic, irreverent and very funny . . . a voice clearly aimed at uncovering the hypocrisy and racism in British society without compromise" (51).

SELECTED BIBLIOGRAPHY

Works by Kureishi

Borderline. London: Eyre Methuen, 1981.

Outskirts (1982); *The King and Me; Tomorrow-today.* London: J. Calder, 1983.

My Beautiful Laundrette and *The Rainbow Sign* (film script with autobiographical essay). London: Faber and Faber, 1986.

Sammy and Rosie Get Laid (1987). Published as *Sammy and Rosie Get Laid: The Script and the Diary.* London: Faber and Faber, 1988.

The Buddha of Suburbia. London: Faber and Faber, 1990.

London Kills Me. London: Faber and Faber, 1991.

The Black Album. London: Faber and Faber, 1995.

Love in a Blue Time. Stories. London: Faber and Faber, 1997.

Selected Studies of Kureishi

Afzal-Khan, Fawzia. "Pakistani Writing in English: 1947 to the Present: A Survey." *Wasafiri* 21 (Spring 1995): 58–61.

Ball, John Clement. "The Semi-Detached Metropolis: Hanif Kureishi's London." ARIEL 27, no. 4 (October 1996): 7–27.

Jena, Seema. "The Anti-hero As a Narrative Strategy In Asian Immigrant Writing With Special Reference to *The Buddha of Suburbia.*" *Wasafiri* 17 (Spring 1993): 3–6.

Kaleta, Kenneth C. *Hanif Kureishi: Postcolonial Storyteller.* Austin: University of Texas Press, 1998.

Mahjoub, Jamal. "Love in a Blue Time" (review-article). *Wasafiri* 27 (Spring 1998): 51–52.

Wilholt, Claudia. "Hanif Kureishi: Postcolonial Storyteller" (review-article). *Wasafiri* 30 (Autumn 1999): 73–74.

LINDA LÊ
(1963–)

Mai Mouniama

BIOGRAPHY

Linda Lê was born on July 3, 1963 in Dalat (Vietnam) to a Vietnamese couple. Because her mother was sickly, Linda's father cared for her. He took her on picnics at the Cam-Ly waterfalls, on pedalos on lake Xuan Huong, and on walks around the lake of Sighs—all well-known sites in this city of temperate climate. Although the maternal family thought little of Linda's father, a strong bond developed between him and his daughter. He was a Catholic and taught her the Bible and the Lives of the Saints, which became her favorite reading material during her adolescent years. Even now, John of the Cross and Theresa of Avila (as well as mystical literature in general) continue to fascinate her "for their submission to God, their absolute rebellion, and their attraction toward self-denial" (quoted in Argand, "Entretien avec Linda Lê," 33). When Linda was six years old, her parents moved to Saigon. As the first displacement in her life, she considered the move a fall from paradise—a fall from the climate of fresh, cool air to one of scorching heat and from family harmony to disunity. During this time, as she witnessed her parents fighting, she learned what madness and death meant: her tragic vision of life was born.

With the taking of Saigon (1975), the long Vietnamese war finally came to an end and the Americans left. But for the South Vietnamese who rejected the new regime, the exodus began. Linda left Vietnam for France with her mother and three sisters while her father remained alone in Saigon. She attended the preparatory classes at the *lycée* Henri IV in Paris in 1981, but failed the competitive examination required to enter the Ecole Normale Supérieure. In 1987, she published her first novel, *Un si tendre vampire*, followed by *Fuir* in 1988. She later dismissed both works, to the point of deleting them from her bibliography, because she considered their style too neat and their language hyperpolished, as though the author were a newcomer who has to prove her mettle. With *Les Évangiles du crime* (1992), *Calomnies* (1993), and *Les dits d'un idiot* (1995), she discovered a style of her own. She jostles language, superposes voices, blends registers, juggles words and images: she is indeed an accomplished iconoclast who destroys and creates with a sense of rhythm and a taste for perpetual risk-taking.

In 1997, after learning of the death of her father whom she had not seen again after her departure from Vietnam, Linda went through a period of deep crisis that brought her to the brink of insanity and suicide. Echoes of this are evident in *Voix: Une crise* (1998), the second volume of a trilogy. The three volumes are devoted to the father figure, the first being *Les trois parques* (1997) and the last, *Lettre morte* (1999). *Lettre morte*, an elegy, explores her past and gives way to nostalgia, a feeling that she had repressed in her previous writings. In this last volume, imprecation, anathema, sarcasm, rebellion, and derision predominate: "What my father gave me, no man will ever give me. I shall live forever in the nostalgia of this love, my head resting on the heart of a dead man" (*Lettre morte*, 97). In 1999, she published a collection of prefaces and articles on 38 writers, including Marina Tsvetaeva, Natsume Soseki, Paul Nizon, Joseph Conrad, and others with whom she felt affinities and kinship. Exiles, expatriates, traitors to their languages or countries, all share the capacity to make her happy, or so it seems from the title under which she has grouped them: *Tu écriras sur le bonheur*, which clashes with the 10 (or so) titles that make up her work. Indeed we are dealing with an oeuvre strictly built and rigorously conducted, with no concessions, in silence and discretion.

MAJOR MULTICULTURAL THEMES

Her native land, which she had to leave under painful circumstances at the age of 14, although not named in her early texts, haunts the writings of Linda Lê. Her narrators are, for the most part, displaced people living their exiles in France as a curse: "the man who leaves his country is condemned to carry a goblin on his back to remind him of his betrayal" (*Fuir*, 53). Nonetheless, the native land represents in the imaginations of her characters neither a haven, nor a cultural anchor, nor a happy past to dream of: "I never loved my native land. I was already an exile in my own country" (*Fuir*, 15), declares the narrator, evoking North Vietnam as a hostile land, where village life is ruled by a narrow and primitive understanding of Confucianism; Saigon as a metropolis filled with slums, oozing sweat and poverty; and Vietnamese as insensitive people. Nor does the land that takes you in offer you any shelter; immigrants feel it as a secretly hostile mistress. They are wanderers, but with no taste for the poetry of bohemia, and for whom exile is definitive. "Let her cease believing that one day she will find a family, a country. Since the men in black have hunted out the Stranger, her native land has nothing to give her. She and I are wandering souls," soliloquizes the uncle, thinking of his niece "as an outsider writing in French" (*Calomnies*, 173). The acquisition of a new language increases the vertigo of exile in that it entails the loss of one's native idiom, which is experienced as a loss of identity, as a betrayal: "I cheapened myself by keeping company with those foreign words, I betrayed my country with scandalous voluptuousness. I cultivated the language of the occupier" (*Fuir*, 50). Exiles, amnesiacs, amputees, the blind, the countryless, the armless, the mad, and the suicidal beings that haunt Linda Lê's tales symbolize an original void.

Les trois parques ("They are three. Like Lear's three daughters. Like the three regions of Vietnam") was written after her father's death, when she was experiencing a "state of utter isolation" followed by "three months of stupor and confusion" (Linda Lê, quoted in Van Renterghem, "Le sabbat de Lady Lê," I). Vietnam's recent history is traced through the father's eyes. Immobile in his small blue house, for twenty years he has seen the events of the world unfold without playing any part in them. Just prior to the arrival of the black forest men, he had observed the strange comings and goings of the regime's rich and privileged crowding Vung Tau, only to embark speedily like thieves carrying off money and jewels. He returns to the same beach regularly to contemplate the sea that witnessed his three daughters being carried off. He reports the effect of reeducation on his friend, the priest-squealer, whose vocal cords were destroyed due to screaming out under the torture of the new masters of the country. In 1985, the old palaces near his shack were still standing, while the Saigonese were starving in front of the state-owned stores, queuing up for a handful of moldy rice. Ten years later, the setting changed in decor and discourse: the country opened up to a liberal economy and to the frenzy of consumerism. He sees the return of the enriched diaspora rivaling with the regime's parvenus to invest in concrete. Linda Lê ironically and ferociously lumps together the buildings that proliferate as well as the capitalistic or Communist profiteers under the same technical acid-like homophonic term saprophytes, the vegetal parasites that grow on decayed organic matter. Beyond the seas, the image of the escapees gathering together like clandestine groups plotting against "the fanatics of purity, assembly-line brain washers" and weeping over their martyred land around an exotic meal and alcoholic beverages, is both derisive and sardonic. Next to those group photographs we find individual portraits engraved in acid, like that of Lady Chacal, the hard, avid anti-Communist grandmother duped by a Fox wearing the uniform of the southern army, who passes himself for a representative of an association working for the regeneration of Vietnam. The weapon of irony, sarcasm, and imprecation, used as an art of keeping a distance, of setting up safeguards, becomes ineffective in the face of her father's death.

Voix: Une crise is the narration of the crisis generated by this death and the guilt feelings it engenders; it is the story of a persecution mania. It is the story of a desperate flight through the streets of Paris to escape the members of an omnipotent organization that spreads its network even into the nerves and the neurons of the author-narrator, forcing her into wandering and self-destructiveness: "The Organization's men are driving me out of Paris, I am a pariah. The Organization has given the city orders to turn away from me. She should go home" (*Voix*, 61). Thus, she returns to the land of her birth where she searches in vain for her father's house, the one with the blue shutters, but everything is in ruins and ashes, the river beds are dry, the trees are burnt out, the consonants mutilated, the vowels disemboweled. Obsessive visions of decapitated heads rolling along the streets or floating on the water, of plunged knives and daggers, of gunshots, barbed wire, packs of three-headed dogs, mass graves of birds crunching under foot, friends transformed into Grand Inquisitors; visions of relentless persecution and unending flight interweave at a lancinating, hammering, torturing pace. How can one not read this as the interiorization of a collective tragedy, the drama of a country doomed to woe and division?

The flight eventually concludes in a snow-covered landscape. White is the color of mourning for the Vietnamese. Peace returns with the acceptance of the loss. But the only possible haven is also the whiteness of the paper. Writing is the space that one creates, word after word, and conquers, sentence after sentence. Thanks to the international of the countryless, of the sounders of the abysses, of the surveyors of the infinite, Linda Lê can find a horizon with markers, lighthouses, and signposts. They lead the way through her texts. So does, for instance, Sola, the protagonist in *Les aubes*, in which one may recognize Ingeborg Bachmann, the burnt poet of Rome: "A writer is by definition a bad citizen. He follows only one imperative: the obligation to betray. He is a double agent in the pay of good and evil—lying in wait for darkness and light. Every writer dreams of being a traitor and an orphan—owing nothing to anyone, cutting clear, being a renegade forever" (Preface to Joseph Conrad's *Sextuor*, in *Tu écriras sur le bonheur*, 59).

SURVEY OF CRITICISM

Although Lê's writings are not widely known, critics nonetheless recognize her talent, referring to her as "an undaunted explorer of the dark zones of the mind" (Kéchichian, 2000, III), to her prose as "angry, bewitching" (Van Renterghem, 1997, I), to her "style [as] both precise and incantatory" and to her "universe [as] strange, violent, and refined" (Savigneau, 1999, IV).

SELECTED BIBLIOGRAPHY

Works by Lê

Un si tendre vampire: Roman. Paris: La Table Ronde, 1987.

Fuir: Roman. Paris: La Table Ronde, 1988.

Solo. Paris: La Table Ronde, 1989.

Les Évangiles du crime. Paris: Julliard, 1992.

Calomnies. Paris: Christian Bourgois, 1993.

Les dits d'un idiot. Paris: Christian Bourgois, 1995.

Les trois parques. Paris: Christian Bourgois, 1997.

Voix: Une crise. Paris: Christian Bourgois, 1998.

Lettre morte. Paris: Christian Bourgois, 1999.

Tu écriras sur le bonheur. Paris: Presses Universitaires de France, 1999.

Les aubes. Paris: Christian Bourgois, 2000.

Selected Studies of Lê

Argand, Catherine. "Entretien avec Linda Lê." *Lire* 274 (April 1999): 28–34.

Kéchichian, Patrick. "La voix des démons." *Le Monde des Livres* (September 18, 1998): IV.

———. "Envers de la corruption." *Le Monde des Livres* (September 29, 2000): III.

Rose, Sean James. "Les élégies de Lê." *Libération* (October 26, 2000): IV.

Savigneau, Josyane. "Linda Lê, au nom du père." *Le Monde des Livres* (May 7, 1999): IV.

Tison, Jean-Pierre. "Diabolique Linda Lê." *Lire* 236 (June 1995): 64–65.

———. "Les sortilèges de Linda Lê." *Lire* 260 (November 1997): 70–71.

Van Renterghem, Marion. "Le sabbat de Lady Lê." *Le Monde des Livres* (October 31, 1997): I.

JEAN-MARIE GUSTAVE LE CLÉZIO
(1940–)

Nadine Dormoy

BIOGRAPHY

Certainly the most ubiquitous of all major contemporary French authors, Le Clézio was born in Nice, his mother's native city, during World War II when his father was serving in the British army in Nigeria. The family originally came from Brittany, but Le Clézio's more immediate roots lie on the island of Mauritius, where a certain François Alexis Le Clézio had settled with his wife and daughter in 1798. The island at the time, a French possession called île de France, fell to the British in 1810 during the Napoleonic wars and was renamed île Maurice, or Mauritius, even as its citizens became British subjects. Although Le Clézio has never lived in Mauritius for more than a few months at a time, he considers himself both a Frenchman and a Mauritian.

He attended the local lycée, but his imagination carried him far beyond the gentle hills of the Côte d'Azur. Many of his short stories recapture the world of his childhood in the 1940s and 1950s, his early fascination with the sea, with ships, with children of mixed origins, and generally with people whose psyche bears witness to a life that is different. As an adolescent, he spent the years 1959–60 in Britain, where he attended the University of Bristol and taught school in Bath. His first novel, *Le procès-verbal* (1963) was accepted by the prestigious Parisian publishing house Gallimard and eventually received the Prix Renaudot, as well as excellent reviews from the press. Written in the dry, concise style of the then prevalent *nouveau roman*, it was visibly influenced by Albert Camus's *L'étranger* and Jean-Paul Sartre's *La nausée*. Through the marginal character of Adam Pollo, the young author pointed to the collective trauma of the Algerian war and at the same time heralded the rebel spirit of the 1960s. He is a vivid incarnation of the alienation that a whole generation felt in regard to society.

Always attracted to exotic destinations, Le Clézio traveled to Bangkok in 1966–67, lived in Panama among Emberra Indian tribes, and made several visits to the land of his ancestors, Mauritius and its dependency, the island of Rodrigues. Starting in 1967, he taught at the University of Mexico and also in the United States, in Albuquerque, New Mexico, where he still lives part of the year. Between 1969 and 1973, he has lived intermittently among the Mayas in Mexico and the Emberra Indians in Panama and has learned their dialect. Meanwhile, he has produced a variety of books—novels, essays, and short stories, which cannot easily be classified. Fiercely individualistic, keeping his distance from all major currents or literary schools, Le Clézio, himself a cultural mix whose works reflect the combined influence of the South Seas, Central and North America, France and Africa, stands in staunch defense of peoples of the developing countries. The beauty of his poetic prose is largely due to his multicultural experience of men and nature and his determination to find, through the life of traditional societies, the essence of humankind.

MAJOR MULTICULTURAL THEMES

In one of his most accomplished novels, *Le chercheur d'or* (1985), all of Le Clézio's major themes are fully developed. It opens with the narrator's mother reading aloud the Bible "with its red leather cover, a large golden sun, and the soft, slow voice of Mam" (*Le chercheur d'or*, 31). His father, by contrast, tells him about such legendary heroes as "Marco Polo in China, De Soto in America, Orellano, who followed the Amazon rivers, Gmelin who traveled through Siberia, Mungo Park, Stanley, Livingstone, Prjevalski. I listen to these stories, to the names of the lands, Africa, Tibet, the South islands: they are magical words, they are like the names of stars" (*Le chercheur d'or*, 48). The narrator in *Le chercheur d'or* is in fact the author's grandfather, who embarked on a quest to find a treasure buried by a pirate somewhere on Rodrigues island. The action starts in 1892, when the narrator is eight years old, and concludes in 1922. During that period, he takes part in World War I and makes several trips to Rodrigues in search of the hidden treasure. But the cache turns out to be empty and the treasure is never found. However, in the course of his quest, the narrator finds another more authentic treasure in the person of the enigmatic Ouma, a girl born of the water, the mountain, and the air. To him, this native girl is the living spirit that animates the cosmos: she reveals to him a treasure of eternal value, the force of life itself. But Le Clézio the adventurer has embarked on a different sort of voyage: his quest takes place through writing; the pen replaces the navigator's ship and has the magical power of reversing the course of time. The poet recaptures the legend of the mythical ship Argo on which Jason and the Argonauts sailed in search of the Golden Fleece. According to the *Odyssey*, the goddess Athena ultimately transformed the ship into a group of stars, a constellation commonly referred to as *the ship*. For Le Clézio, language is meant to make time and space rejoin. Here the author, in search of his grandfather who was also in pursuit of a myth, transforms the act of writing into a cosmic experience.

In the autobiographical sequel to *Le chercheur d'or*, entitled *Voyage à Rodrigues: Journal* (1986), the narrator-poet tells how his personal history drove him to search for truth "as far as the horizon where clouds begin" (110). This quest is a recurrent obsession for most of Le Clézio's characters. They are often old sea captains with lifelong experience sailing the seven seas in search of an impossible goal; or, by contrast, they are semi-literate adolescents, especially young girls, who live in close contact with nature, without communication with the civilized world. Le Clézio thus finds his way between old and new but always in defiance of the materialistic culture and the technology of Western culture. He is particularly concerned about the destruction of Indian culture in Mexico, publishing *Le déluge* (1966) and the essay *Le rêve mexicain, ou, La pensée interrompue* (1988). In another major novel, *Désert* (1980), we witness the conquest of Morocco by the French between 1909 and 1912. The Bedouin horsemen of the desert are annihilated by the troops of General Mangin during the famous—or infamous—battle of Agadir. In a parallel register, we follow the itinerary of Lalla, a young Bedouin girl who ends up a refugee in Marseilles. Lalla tries to adapt to a new culture and at first succeeds but finally decides to return to her homeland. Two distinct types of society, both destined to disappear, are examined and depicted with implacable realism: the desert tribes who refuse to accept any change in their nomadic way of life and, at the other end, across the Mediterranean, the new North African immigrants forced to live in the ghettos of Marseilles in humiliation and misery. Colonialism will in time die out, as did the Bedouin tribes, but misery will remain. To Le Clézio, uncovering the mystery of human nature makes the world forever fascinating.

SURVEY OF CRITICISM

Not much has been written on Le Clézio in English, except for a number of unpublished doctoral dissertations. The most accessible is "Jean-Marie Gustave Le Clézio, the Building of a Fictional World" by Kathleen White Reish (1973). Jennifer R. Waelti-Walters's 1977 book offers a serious and factual presentation of all the works published up to that date, but it is necessarily incomplete and lacks an overall view.

In French, a number of works have appeared recently: the University of Copenhagen has published Miriam Stendal Boulous's doctoral dissertation on Le Clézio (1999). Germaine Brée's 1990 volume is a most useful although not exhaustive presentation of Le Clézio's world. It includes a chronological list of novels, essays, and short stories up to the year 1990 and a brief outline of the major themes. Brée points out similarities to *Alice in Wonderland* in a title such as *Voyages de l'autre côté* (voyages on the other side of the mirror). She focuses on the poetic nature of Le Clézio's narrative style, citing the author himself for the definition of his goal: "to speak to you from far away, for a long, long time, with words that wouldn't just be words, but would lead up to Heaven, to space, to the sea" (*L'inconnu sur la terre*, 7).

Michelle Labbé's excellent work (1999) discusses Le Clézio's rejection of the traditional novel, his exceptionally rich imagination, and the diversity and above all the mystery of his characters. It is as though all of Le Clézio's writings were but a quest whose secret code is known only to himself. It is based on a subtle subversion of the relation between author, characters, and readers, as well as of the relation between language and reality. Monologue, dialogue, description, and analysis are intertwined in every Le Clézio book. The succession of discourse and silence along with the alternate use of different genres and narrative points of view contribute to a sense of being carried away elsewhere. Labbé's book provides a thorough analysis of a number of novels and discusses Le Clézio's transgression of narrative rules, the role of the characters, the importance of the time element, and the distortion of genres. It includes a bibliography and index.

Gérard de Cortanze (1999) sees Le Clézio's posture as partly a failure, in the sense that his attempt is constantly repeated again and again in a sort of permanent ritual that becomes stratified and rigid, much as in the case of Mallarmé's perennially frozen flight. This point of view is echoed by Jennifer R. Waelti-Walters (1981).

SELECTED BIBLIOGRAPHY

Works by Le Clézio

Le procès-verbal. Paris: Gallimard, 1963.
Le déluge. Paris: Gallimard, 1966.
Le livre des fuites. Paris: Gallimard, 1969.
Voyages de l'autre côté Paris: Gallimard, 1975.
L'inconnu sur la terre. Paris: Gallimard, 1978.
Mondo et autres histoires. Paris: Gallimard, 1978.
Désert. Paris: Gallimard, 1980.
La ronde et autres faits divers. Paris: Gallimard, 1982.
Le chercheur d'or. Paris: Gallimard, 1985.
Voyage à Rodrigues: Journal. Paris: Gallimard, 1986.
Le rêve mexicain, ou, La pensée interrompue. Paris: Gallimard, 1988.
Printemps et autres saisons: Nouvelles. Paris: Gallimard, 1989.
Étoile errante. Paris: Gallimard, 1992.

La fête chantée et autres essais de thème amérindian. Paris: Gallimard, 1997.
Hasard; suivi de, Angoli Mala: Romans. Paris: Gallimard, 1999.

Selected Studies of Le Clézio

Boulous, Miriam Stendal. *"Chemins pour une approche poétique du monde, le roman selon J.M.G. Le Clézio."* Doctoral diss., University of Copenhagen, 1999.

Brée, Germaine. *Le Monde Fabuleux de J.M.G. Le Clézio.* Amsterdam, Atlanta: Rodopi, 1990.

Cortanze, Gérard de. *Jean-Marie Gustave Le Clézio: Le nomade immobile.* Paris: Editions du Chêne, 1999.

Domange, Simone. *Le Clézio, ou, La quête du désert.* Paris: Imago, 1993.

Labbé, Michelle. *Le Clézio, L'écart romanesque.* Paris: L'Harmattan, 1999.

Reish, Kathleen White. "Jean-Marie Gustave Le Clézio, the Building of a Fictional World." Doctoral diss., University of Wisconsin (Madison), 1973.

Ridon, Jean-Xavier Didier. *Henri Michaux, J.M.G. Le Clézio: L'exil des mots.* Paris: Editions Kimé, 1995.

Scanno, Teresa di. *La vision du monde de Le Clézio: Cinq études sur l'oeuvre.* Paris: Nizet, 1983.

Waelti-Walters, Jennifer R. *Jean-Marie Gustave Le Clézio.* Boston: Twayne, 1977.

———. *Icare, ou L'évasion impossible: Étude psychomythique de l'oeuvre de J.M.G. Le Clézio.* Sherbrooke, Quebec: Naaman, 1981.

DORIS LESSING

(1919–)

Maria Antonietta Saracino

BIOGRAPHY

Multiculturalism is part and parcel of Doris Lessing's entire literary production as well as of her whole life experience. The most prolific of contemporary British writers and the recipient of more than twenty literary prizes and awards, Doris May Tayler was born in Kermanshah, Persia (now Iran), where her father, Alfred Cook Tayler—formerly a World War I army captain—worked as a bank clerk. The family moved to Southern Rhodesia (now Zimbabwe) in 1924 where they bought a large maize farm and hoped to start a new life. It was the period when farming in Rhodesia seemed to be a very profitable enterprise. More and more land was coming under cultivation in that part of the continent; the Africans had been moved off their lands and settled in reserves, thus providing labor for white farmers, including Doris's father. The family went out, she said later, "with very little money, a governess, a piano, clothes from Liberty's, visiting cards," and there they all sat "in an elongated thatched hut, while the farm did not succeed" (quoted in Drabble, 52).

Doris attended the Roman Catholic convent school in Salisbury (now Harare), leaving school at the age of 14 to serve first as a nursemaid and then as a telephone operator and clerk. At the age of 18, she worked in the Rhodesian parliament and helped to start a nonracist left-wing party in the country. Later she joined the Rhodesian Communist Party and entered into a second unsuccessful marriage, this time with the German political activist Gottfried Lessing, who later became the German ambassador to Uganda and was killed in 1979 during the revolt against then-president Idi Amin.

She moved to England in 1949 with the youngest of her three children and the manuscript of her first novel, *The Grass Is Singing*, which was published in 1950 and gained its author immediate success. Since then she has never ceased writing, producing a remarkable number of novels, short stories, personal narratives, plays, and poems exploring many areas, languages, and multicultural themes. *Five Short Stories* (1953), four of which are set in Southern Africa and focus on the problem of the division between blacks and whites, won the Somerset Maugham Award (1954) for the best work of fiction of that year by a writer under 35.

After a seven-year absence, Lessing returned to Southern Rhodesia in 1956 to revisit the country of her childhood. At the end of her trip—during which she had been under constant surveillance by the political police—her presence was declared undesirable in both Southern Rhodesia and South Africa. The experiences of this trip are narrated in her book *Going Home* (1957), partly a personal narrative, partly a travel notebook. It was only after Rhodesia gained independence in 1980 that she was able to return to that part of Africa. *African Laughter: Four Visits to Zimbabwe* (1992) describes her four visits to southern Africa between 1982 and 1992. Her autobiographical volume *Under My Skin* (1994) depicts her childhood in Zimbabwe, and *Walking in the Shade: Volume Two of My Autobiography* (1997) covers the years from 1959 to 1962. Also, one must not omit mentioning the many volumes of short stories and novellas, mostly set in Africa, and collected in *This Was the Old Chief's Country* (1951) and *The Sun between Their Feet* (1973).

Though a passionate Communist during her adolescence and early youth, in postwar years Lessing became increasingly disillusioned with the Communist movement, leaving it altogether in 1954. She became involved in the Afghan resistance movement through the aid organization Afghan Relief, visiting in 1986 the refugee camps in Pakistan and Afghanistan—an experience she deals with in *The Wind Blows Away Our Words, and Other Documents Relating to the Afghan Resistance* (1987). A politically minded believer in the need for human beings to retain an independent frame of mind in order to be able to fight all forms of oppression and discrimination, Lessing attempts to find an answer to a simple but disturbing question: why do human beings continue to make the same mistakes? (cf. her 1985 lectures in Canada published in the volume *Prisons We Choose to Live Inside*, 1987)

On December 31, 1999, in the United Kingdom's last Honours List before the end of the millennium, Doris Lessing was appointed a Companion of Honour, an exclusive order for those who have rendered "conspicuous national service." At the same time, consistent with her principles concerning imperialism, she declined the title of Dame of the British Empire. Her most recent novel to date is *The Sweetest Dream* (2001), published in Britain at the age of 83.

MAJOR MULTICULTURAL THEMES

The years spent in Africa influenced Lessing deeply as a woman and as a writer. "Africa belongs to the Africans," she wrote in 1956. "The sooner they take it back, the better. But a country also belongs to those who feel at home in it" (*Going Home*, 11). Undoubtedly she is one of "those," to the extent that ever since she left Africa, she has regarded herself as an exile from the continent. But living in a white-dominated colonial society has also meant the acquisition of a deep sense of social responsibility in the face of the problems of an agitated society, which are reflected in her works. "Because I was brought up in Southern Rhodesia, a part of my work has been set there and the salience of the colour clash has made it inevitable that those aspects which reflect the 'colour problem' should have overshadowed the rest" (*This Was the Old Chief's Country*, 7).

A considerable portion of her work specifically deals with Africa as Lessing knew it, and consequently, with the conflicts rooted in a society based on racial discrimination. When she began writing, there were very few novels about Africa, and this is perhaps why her first novel, *The Grass Is Singing*, and her first collections of short stories were soon labeled as stories specifically about the "colour problem," which is not how Doris Lessing saw them.

Short stories with African settings have appeared in all the collections she has published so far, including *The Habit of Loving* (1957), *A Man and Two Women: Stories* (1963), *The Black Madonna* (1966), and *The Story of a Non-Marrying Man, and Other Stories* (1972).

In *This Was the Old Chief's Country*, Africa is perceived through the sensibility of an alien colonist. Lessing's sense of setting is so vivid and immediate that Africa, with the wrongs of the white man towards the black man, takes on a much broader symbolic meaning. She writes that "while the cruelties of the white man towards the black man are among the heaviest counts in the indictment against humanity, color prejudice is not our original fault, but only one aspect of the atrophy of the imagination that prevents us from seeing ourselves in every creature that breathes under the sun" (*This Was the Old Chief's Country*, preface, 8).

The master-servant relationship that underlies the great majority of Lessing's short stories assumes central importance in *The Grass Is Singing*, a devastating study of the dream of living an easy European life against the harshness of the African ground. The story is the tragedy of two Europeans unsuited to the role of colonists and nevertheless forced—inasmuch as they live in a color-dominated society—to live up to the image their race has created for them. The whites' desperate struggle, ending in their defeat, to impose themselves on Africa mirrors the story of Lessing's own parents as narrated in her autobiographical *Under My Skin*.

SURVEY OF CRITICISM

Critics of Doris Lessing's works have tended to label her variously, according to the specific themes of her novels. She has been regarded as the most intensely committed of contemporary British authors to seek to reform society by active persuasion. Janet Todd (1989) criticizes her novels in the light of that commitment. Elaine Showalter (1977, 1982) praises her attempt to write honestly about women; few female novelists indeed have succeeded in demonstrating as she does what it is like to be a woman in a society whose values are relatively liberal. Many critics, including Margaret Drabble (1972), emphasize the pessimism that pervades Lessing's novels. Drabble sees her as "a prophet who prophesies the end of the world," a novelist used by now "to living on the edge of destruction" (50). Lessing has also been labeled as an experimental novelist, an ex-Communist political enthusiast, or an "inner-space" cultist with apocalyptic visions. As for her multicultural themes, she has been regarded as a writer concerned with the racial question. At the same time, arriving in England as she did from a place like Southern Rhodesia, her position within both mainstream and marginal British cultural formation was a revitalizing one, contributing to the reversal of a dominant set of literary conventions—Africa signifying the exotic and the marvelous (cf. Jenny Taylor, 1982).

SELECTED BIBLIOGRAPHY

Works by Lessing

The Grass Is Singing. London: Michael Joseph, 1950.
This Was the Old Chief's Country. London: Michael Joseph, 1951.
Five Short Stories. London: Grafton Books, 1953.
Going Home. London: Michael Joseph, 1957.
The Habit of Loving. London: MacGibbon and Kee, 1957.
A Man and Two Women: Stories. New York: Simon and Schuster, 1963.
The Black Madonna (1966). St. Albans: Panther, 1974.
The Story of a Non-Marrying Man, and Other Stories. London: Jonathan Cape, 1972.
The Sun between Their Feet. London: Michael Joseph, 1973.
Prisons We Choose to Live Inside (1985). London: Jonathan Cape, 1987.
The Wind Blows Away Our Words, and Other Documents Relating to the Afghan Resistance. London: Pan Books, 1987.
African Laughter: Four Visits to Zimbabwe. New York: HarperCollins, 1992.
Under My Skin. London: HarperCollins, 1994. [*Sotto la pelle.* Trans. Maria Antonietta Saracino. Milano: Feltrinelli, 1997.]
Walking in the Shade: Volume Two of My Autobiography. New York: HarperCollins, 1997.
The Sweetest Dream. London: Flamingo, 2001.

Selected Studies of Lessing

Drabble, Margaret. "Doris Lessing: Cassandra in a World Under Siege." *Ramparts* X, 8 (1972): 50–54.

Klein, Carole. *Doris Lessing: A Biography.* New York: Carroll and Graf, 2000.

Saracino, Maria Antonietta. "Debiti del cuore." Introduction to *L'erba canta*, 7–17. Milan: La Tartaruga, 1989.

———. "Ritratto di un'artista da gatta." Postface to *Gatti molto speciali*, 163–67. Milan: La Tartaruga, 1989.

Saxton, Ruth, and Jean Tobin, eds. *Woolf and Lessing: Breaking the Mold.* New York: St. Martin's Press, 1994.

Showalter, Elaine. *A Literature of Their Own: British Women Novelists from Brontë to Lessing.* Princeton, N.J.: Princeton University Press, 1977; rev. ed. London: Virago, 1982.

Sprague, Claire, ed. *In Pursuit of Doris Lessing: Nine Nations Reading.* New York: St. Martin's Press, 1990.

Taylor, Jenny. *Notebooks, Memoirs, Archives: Reading and Rereading Doris Lessing.* Boston: Routledge and Kegan Paul, 1982.

Todd, Janet, ed. *British Women Writers: A Critical Reference Guide.* New York: Continuum, 1989.

CARLO LEVI
(1902–1975)
Rolando Perez and Rosa Amatulli

BIOGRAPHY

Carlo Levi, son of Ercole (a merchant and painter) and Annetta Treves (the sister of Mussolini's political enemy, Claudio Treves), was born in Turin, Piedmont. He was Jewish on both sides of the family and the intellectuals who made up his circle were also Jewish—except for Piero Gobetti (below). From early on in life, Levi circulated in a world of intellectuals and political figures that included the political theorists Antonio Gramsci and Filippo Turati, the father of Italian socialism, both of whom he knew personally.

It was during his years as a medical student that, together with a group of other young intellectuals, he began to follow the ideas of the liberal-socialist, Piero Gobetti (Turin 1901–Paris 1926), who founded the political newspapers *Rivoluzione Liberale* and *Baretti*, to which Levi contributed articles.

In 1924 he obtained a medical degree from the University of Turin, but practiced medicine only briefly, during his later exile. More interested in letters than in science, he became a painter, a novelist, a journalist, a political activist, and a senator. After having founded the anti-Fascist Action Party in 1930, he became the head of the Piedmontese branch of Carlo Roselli's anti-Fascist movement, *Giustizia e Libertà* (Justice and Liberty)—the group to which Carlo Levi's namesake, Primo Levi, belonged when he was arrested and subsequently interned in Auschwitz.

Carlo Levi was arrested for anti-Fascist activities in 1934, and was confined to a year of exile in Lucania (also known as the region of Basilicata). He devoted his time to painting, writing, and providing medical assistance to the villagers of Gagliano who were plagued by an inadequate and backward health system. Levi's moving account of his year of banishment is contained in the neorealistic work *Cristo si è fermato a Eboli* (1945) that won the Arianna Mondadori del Corriere Lombardo Prize and made him famous.

At the end of his term of exile, he emigrated to Paris, returning to Italy in 1942. Having established himself in Florence, he took active part in the Resistance and once again was arrested. He was lucky, however, to be released in 1943 about a month and a half before the Nazi invasion of Italy. He went into hiding in Florence, where he remained until the liberation of Italy by the Allied forces. He became an editor (1944–45) of *Nazione del Popolo* (The People's Nation), an anti-Fascist journal, and then editor-in-chief (1945–46) of *Italia libera* (Free Italy), a left-wing newspaper. An entire room was dedicated to his paintings at the prestigious Biennale in Venice in 1954, thirty years after the first exhibit of his work. In the following years, numerous one-man shows of his artwork were held in both Europe and the United States.

Writer, activist, and *rofe* (Hebrew for healer), a word he used in *Cristo si è fermato a Eboli*, Levi died of pneumonia in Rome in 1975. He was a senator at the time, representing the peasants of Lucania whom he had known and written about some 30 years earlier.

MAJOR MULTICULTURAL THEMES

Cristo si è fermato a Eboli is an ethnographic document on peasant life in Italy's Mezzogiorno (literally *midday*, a name used for the south of Italy)—an archaic reality almost out of place and out of time. Levi's work is a sociological investigation characterized by historical inquiry and the personal experience of a man from the north who witnesses firsthand the remote and primitive countryside of Lucania.

As the author tells us, the peasants of Grassano (a village in the province of Matera, on the eastern side of Basilicata), when referring to themselves, often would say "Noi non siamo Cristiani" (We're not Christians): "Christ stopped short of here, at Eboli. 'Christian' in their way of speaking means 'human being,' and this almost proverbial phrase that I have so often heard them repeat may be no more than the expression of a hopeless inferiority. We're not Christians, we're not human beings; we're not thought of as men but simply as beasts, beasts of burden, or even less than beasts, mere creatures of the wild" (*Christ Stopped at Eboli: The Story of a Year*, 1–2).

With the intention of writing a "lengthy opus, a sort of twentieth-century summa" of politics, art, philosophy, religion, science, and social life (Baldassaro, 146), Levi began an unfinished essay later published as *Paura della libertà* (1946). The title (fear of freedom) evokes the primordial wish to emerge from a state of inorganic matter as an independent consciousness and be absorbed into what Levi called the *indistinto originario* (primordial chaos). In terms of political will, the desire to be absorbed into the primordial chaos is translated into submission of individual will to the Church or State. *Lo sacro* (the sacred) engendered terror because it put human beings in touch "with the primordial chaos that preexists human consciousness and out of which we are all born" (Baldassaro, 145). This Jungian philosophy of the sacred was the foundation of Levi's political philosophy and, more generally, of his overall worldview. What he found in the peasants of Lucania was a people who lived on the periphery of primordial chaos: beyond hope, beyond history, and beyond time. "Christ did stop at Eboli, where the road and the railway leave the coast of Salerno and turn into the desolate reaches of Lucania. Christ never came this far, nor did time, nor the individual soul, nor hope, nor the relation of cause to effect, nor reason, nor history. . . . The seasons pass today over the toil of the peasants, just as they did three thousand years before Christ; no message, human or divine, has reached this stubborn poverty" (*Christ Stopped at Eboli: The Story of a Year*, 1–2). Again politically speaking, Levi realized that nothing brought from the outside (e.g., from the north) would help in the emancipation of the peasants of Lucania. Because the outside world had no way of understanding this remote culture, all external political and economic solutions could lead only to disaster for the impoverished *contadini* (peasants) of Gagliano and Grassano. Levi saw the relationship "between city and country, center and margin, in terms analogous to that between first and third worlds" (Ward, 172). What the South needed was not internal colonization, or central government intervention, but free political space for self-determination. "The State can only be a group of autonomies, an organic federation. The unit or cell through which the peasants can take part in the complex life of the nation must be the autonomous or self-governing rural community. This is the only form of government which can solve in our time the three interdependent aspects of the problem of the south; which can allow the co-existence of two different civilizations. . . . But the autonomy or self-government of the community cannot exist without the autonomy of the factory, the school, and the city, of every form of social life. This is what I learned from a year of life underground" (*Christ Stopped at Eboli: The Story of a Year*, 259–60). This is what he longed for: entire communities and peoples that would rule themselves.

By the time Levi wrote *L'orologio* (1950), however, he had seen a great many of his ideals betrayed, co-opted, and crushed in the tentacles of official State power. What was even more disappointing was the fact that many who should have opposed the State ended up by endorsing and even adopting a set of values that was diametrically opposed to their best interests. Jolanda (a character in *L'orologio*), a lower-middle-class washerwoman, imagining herself of noble birth, unwittingly endorses the values that keep her in her own burdened condition.

Levi never stopped concerning himself with the oppressed, the voiceless, and the unrepresented in the theater of grand politics. Like many of his fellow writers and political activists in his Turin circle, he never renounced his vision of a better world. His Jewishness found expression in his political concerns and commitments: "When an Italian Jew wrote of the sufferings he or she had endured, it was not simply *as a Jew:* it was as someone giving testimony on behalf of all the victims of oppression, wherever and of whatever religious origin they might be" (Hughes, 65). This Italian-Jewish universal perspective reflects the view that Judaism was not a stopping point but a key into a universe in which all religions, all people came together, in the fullness of their humanity.

SURVEY OF CRITICISM

Most of the critical work on Carlo Levi focuses on *Cristo si è fermato a Eboli.* English readers know of him either through the book or the film of the same name. Yet, without a reading of *Paura della libertà* it is difficult to understand both *Cristo si è fermato a Eboli* and *L'orologio* in all their depth. *Paura della libertà* articulates the political and anthropological philosophy underpinning Levi's understanding of the life of the peasants in *Cristo si è fermato a Eboli* and the ideological struggles he depicts in *L'orologio* (cf. Baldassaro, "*Paura della libertà:* Carlo Levi's Unfinished Preface," 1995). David Ward's *Antifascisms* (1996) is an invaluable source for anyone wanting to know more about Levi's life and work both as a writer and as a man of action. R. D. Catani (1979) affirms that Levi's politics informed the subject of his literary work as well as his style.

The researcher looking for information on Levi's Jewish background will find that few books, either in English or in Italian, make any reference to his Jewish ancestry. It is true, as some writers have pointed, that he was so assimilated that for him his Jewishness was something he took for granted—an observation that has been made about Alberto Moravia as well. H. Stuart Hughes (1983) writes: "Carlo Levi was . . . five years older than Moravia; they were alike of the fully assimilated generation which grew up in the period between the waning of the old religiously based anti-Semitism and the advent of the new 'racial' variety. No more than Moravia was his youth colored by Jewish associations. Yet his ancestry . . . and the accidents of his existence threw him into closer contact with Jews than was true of the Roman novelist. Moreover, he made a far deeper ideological commitment" (Hughes, 65). Hughes makes interesting connections between Levi's Jewish background, his literary milieu, and his worldview.

SELECTED BIBLIOGRAPHY

Works by Levi

Cristo si è fermato a Eboli. Turin: Einaudi, 1945. [*Christ Stopped at Eboli: The Story of a Year.* Trans. Frances Frenaye. New York: Farrar, Straus, 1947; re-issue Time, Inc., 1964.]

Paura della libertà (1946). 2nd ed. Turin: Einaudi, 1948. [*Of Fear and Freedom.* Trans. Adolphe Gourevitch. New York: Farrar, Straus, 1950.]

L'orologio. Turin: Einaudi, 1950. [*The Watch.* Trans. John Farrar. London: Cassell, 1952; South Royalton, Vt.: Steerforth Press, 1999.]

Il futuro ha un cuore antico; viaggio nell' Unione Sovietica. Turin: Einaudi, 1956.

Le parole sono pietre: Tre giornate in Sicilia. Turin: Einaudi, 1956. [*Words Are Stones: Impressions of Sicily.* Trans. Angus Davidson. New York: Farrar, Straus and Cudahy, 1958.]

L'altro mondo è il Mezzogiorno. Ed. Leonardo Sacco. 2nd ed. Reggio Calabria: Casa del libro, 1980.

Selected Studies of Levi

Baldassaro, Lawrence. "*Paura della libertà:* Carlo Levi's Unfinished Preface." *Italica* 72, no. 2 (Summer 1995): 143–54.

Caretti, Lanfranco. *Testi del Novecento letterario italiano,* 1043–49. Milan: Mursia, 1995.

Catani, R.D. "Structure and Style As Fundamental Expression: The Works of Carlo Levi and Their Poetic Ideology." *Italica* 56, no. 2 (Summer 1979): 213–29.

Hughes, H. Stuart. "Two Captives Called Levi." In H. Stuart Hughes, *Prisoners of Hope: The Silver Age of the Italian Jews, 1924–1974,* 65–73. Cambridge, Mass.: Harvard University Press, 1983.

Miccinesi, Mario. *Invito alla lettura di Carlo Levi.* Milan: Mursia, 1973.

Napolillo, Vincenzo. *Carlo Levi: Dall'antifascismo al mito contadino.* Cosenza: Brenner, 1984.

Stille, Alexander. "Commitment and Betrayal: The Foas of Turin." In Alexander Stille, *Benevolence and Betrayal: Five Italian Jewish Families Under Fascism,* 99, 102, 121. New York: Summit Books, 1991.

Ward, David. "Carlo Levi: From Croce To Vico." In David Ward, *Antifascisms: Cultural Politics in Italy, 1943–46: Benedetto Croce and the Liberals, Carlo Levi and the "Actionists,"* 157–91. Madison, N.J.: Fairleigh Dickinson University Press, and London: Associated University Press, 1996.

PRIMO LEVI
(1919–1987)

Rolando Perez

BIOGRAPHY

Primo Levi was born in Turin, the son of an electric engineer who was an avid reader, interested in culture and the arts, and spoke several languages. It was in this highly intellectual and cultured milieu that Primo was raised. He received a classical education at Turin's *ginnasio-liceo* "D'Azeglio," where for a while he was a student of the poet and novelist Cesare Pavese. Levi then obtained from the University of Turin a degree in chemistry *maxima cum laude* but already with the words "*di razza ebraica*" (of the Jewish race) inscribed on his diploma as the result of the 1938 racial laws that, at least on paper, had been passed the year after he began his university studies.

Levi and most Italian Jews saw themselves as "Italians first, Jews second" (Segre, "Primo Levi, Witness of the Holocaust," 229). If the racial laws were a wake-up call, Italy's traditional tolerance, integration, and total acceptance of the Jews in the culture made it difficult for any middle-class Jew to see in the laws the signs of what was to come. Italian Jews had been part of the Italian government ever since the unification of Italy in 1860. In fact, Italy's first secretary general of the Ministry of Foreign Affairs was Jewish; and "Italy's first Jewish general served as an instructor to Victor Emmanuel III, and no less than fifty Jewish generals served in the Italian army during World War I" (Segre, "Primo Levi, Witness of the Holocaust," 229). What is even more surprising is that Jews held cabinet positions even "during the early years of Italy's love-hate relationship with the Fascist regime" (Patruno, *Understanding Primo Levi*, 1).

Levi's focus, it has been pointed out, was "almost entirely on Germany. About Italy, about Mussolini, about the racial laws, he has virtually nothing to say. In effect, he continues the standard view of Italian Fascism, as a lightweight regime and Mussolini as a dictator without the aura and authority of a Stalin, a Hitler, or a Churchill" (Segre, "Primo Levi, Witness of the Holocaust," 237). Elsewhere it has been pointed out that "under Fascism the number of Jewish university teachers continued to be disproportionately high, and so did the number of Jewish generals and admirals. Nor was the Fascist party by any means *judenrein* (free of Jews)" (Michaelis, *Mussolini and the Jews*, 53).

But by the summer of 1943, with the collapse of the Fascist government, Italy fell under the "Republic of Salò," a puppet of Germany. The laws of 1938 began to be enforced with the support and coercion of the German occupying forces, even against the will of the Fascists. In September of 1943, in protest against the German invasion, Levi joined the inexperienced partisan group *Giustizia e Libertà* (Justice and Freedom) in the region of Valle d'Aosta. His role as partisan was shortlived; for, as he tells us in *Se questo è un uomo* (1947), on December 13, 1943, at the age of 24, he, along with others, was arrested and sent to the internment camp in Carpi-Fossoli and thence to Auschwitz. He was a slave laborer in Auschwitz from February 1944 until January 1945, when the advancing Soviet army liberated the camp. In the years after the war, Levi was employed as a chemist at a factory near Turin, from which he retired in 1975 in order to continue to write on a full-time basis.

As a result of his experiences, he wrote *Se questo è un uomo* and *I sommersi e i salvati* (1986). *La tregua* (1963) is the story of his nine-month, seemingly interminable journey home to Italy after his release from Auschwitz. He also wrote a number of works of fiction, starting with *Storie naturali* (1966) and *Vizio di forma* (1971), followed by *La chiave a stella* (1978) and *Se non ora, quando?* (1981), two books of essays, *Il sistema periodico* (1975) and *L'altrui mestiere* (1985), and a collection of short stories, *Lilit e altri racconti* (1981).

Levi died on April 11, 1987, as a result of a fall from the building in which he lived—a death believed by some to have been a suicide.

MAJOR MULTICULTURAL THEMES

A horrific world, as he himself said—*created* Primo Levi. "I was turned into a Jew by others," was his comment in an interview with Edith Bruck in 1976. "Before Hitler I was a middle-class Italian boy. The experience of the Race Laws helped me to recognize the many threads that made up the Jewish tradition, a number that I could accept" (*The Voice of Memory: Interviews 1961–1987*, 262).

In his refusal to appeal to facile, negative emotions, Levi writes in a clear, precise and distant style that makes for the great impact of his work. His detachedness in describing the atrocities of Auschwitz has at times been criticized. Writing with the precision of a scientist, he wanted to tell his story of the Holocaust in a way that would "furnish documentation for a quiet study of certain aspects of the human mind" (*Survival in Auschwitz: The Nazi Assault on Humanity*, trans. Stuart Woolf, 9). Yet, if he saw the Holocaust as primarily a human tragedy, he also placed the history of the Italian Jews—and of his own family—at the very center of that tragedy and of its history, as is evidenced in *Il sistema periodico*, the book that many critics consider his best. In this work, the first chemical substance he describes is the inert gas, Argon. Inert gases, he writes, are "so satisfied with their condition, that they do not interfere in any chemical reaction with any other element, and for precisely this reason have gone unnoticed for centuries" (*The Periodic Table*, trans. Raymond Rosenthal, 3). He then likens his ancestors to such inert gases, not so much for being materially inert but rather, as he says, for being inert "in their inner spirits, inclined to disinterested speculation, witty discourses, elegant, sophisticated, and gratuitous discussion" (*The Periodic Table*, 4).

Here he traces the history of his ancestors to about the year 1500, when they arrived in Piedmont by way of Provence as a result of Spain's 1492 expulsion of the Jews under the Catholic kings. In time this small minority thrived in the silk industry, and though "they were never much loved or much hated [,] stories of unusual persecutions have not been handed down." However, he continues, "a wall of suspicion, of undefined hostility and mockery must have kept them substantially separated from the rest of the population" (*The Periodic Table*, 4). His own father, Levi reports, was often mocked by his classmates in anti-Semitic ways. The history of the silent, rare Argon, Levi equated with the history of the Italian Jews of the Piedmont region.

But what of the essence of the Jewish people? How was that determined? What is it that made one human being *essentially* Jewish as opposed to essentially Gentile? Describing Zinc as a substance that in its *pure* form could resist outside influence from other elements, and as a substance that in its *impure* form could give rise to other forms of life when mixed with other chemicals, Levi began to see himself more and more as the impure Zinc. "One could draw from this two conflicting philosophical conclusions: the praise of purity, which protects from evil like a coat of mail; the praise of impurity, which gives rise to changes, in other words, to life. . . . In order for the wheel to turn, for life to be lived, impurities are needed, and the impurities in the soil, too, as is known" (*The Periodic Table*, 33–34). He continues: "I am the impurity that makes the zinc react. . . . Impurity, certainly, since just during those months the publication of the magazine *Defense of the Race* had begun, and there was much talk about purity, and I began to be proud of being impure. In truth, until precisely those months it had not meant much to me that I was a Jew" (*The Periodic Table*, 35).

In an interview during which he was asked whether he felt that there existed today such a thing as a "Jewish culture of the Diaspora," Levi responded enthusiastically that the United States had become the center of Jewish culture of the Diaspora, and that as a result even Yiddish, once influenced by German, Hebrew, Russian, and Polish, and now influenced by English, was changing. "These are phenomenons that are gold-dust for linguists, because they can watch a truly hybrid language, the most hybrid in the world, surviving precisely because it is hybrid. The very idea of pure language is a folly. Think of how hybrid English is: Yiddish is even more so" (*The Voice of Memory: Interviews 1961–1987*, 268). The language of Zinc is Yiddish.

SURVEY OF CRITICISM

Because so much of what Levi says about Jewish culture is not to be found in the writings themselves, but in interviews, the reader interested in Levi's thought Jewish culture post-Holocaust does well to consult Marco Belpoliti and Robert Gordon's 2001 edition of the 1961–87 interviews, *The Voice of Memory*.

To the very end of his life, Levi maintained that the only way to speak of the Shoah was to do so rationally, with human calm, and without judgment. As Ariella Lang (1999) has pointed out, for Levi, hatred fostered irrationality, irrationality that led directly to "injustice" and to the camps (255). This is an attitude that some of his critics have found difficult, if not impossible, to accept. His descriptions of the infernal conditions of the concentration camps in such books as *Se questo è un uomo* and *I sommersi* have led some critics, including Risa Sodi (1990), to call him a modern-day Dante and to see, both in the quietness of the style and in the treatment of the subject matter, a literary relation to the Italian master. Lynn M. Gunzberg (1996) writes: "For Levi during his internment and later while he constructed his memoir, the most immediate and influential model was the first Canticle of Dante's *Divine Comedy*. . . . During his journey through Hell Levi meets a number of people from whom he gains insights necessary to turn the system to his advantage. As with that of Dante, Levi's story is told through a series of portraits which serve as milestones of his education in coping with the Lager" (13, 19). Both Dante and Levi emerged from the inferno with the mission to tell the story of the horror they had seen, felt, thought, and experienced in Hell.

Gerda Reeb (1995) and Massimo Lollini (1999) compare and contrast Levi's poetry thematically and stylistically to that of Paul Celan—testimonial poetry of the writer who must write in order to keep the memory of the offense alive in the name of all humanity.

SELECTED BIBLIOGRAPHY

Works by Levi

Se questo è un uomo. Turin: F. de Silva , 1947. [*If This Is a Man.* Trans. Stuart Woolf. New York: Orion Press, 1959; *Survival in Auschwitz: The Nazi Assault on Humanity.* Trans. Stuart Woolf. New York: Collier 1961 and 1993. The 1993 edition includes "A conversation with Primo Levi by Philip Roth".]

La tregua. Turin: Einaudi, 1963. [*The Truce.* Trans. Stuart Woolf. London: Bodley Head, 1965; *The Reawakening: A Liberated Prisoner's Long March Home Through East Europe* (1965). Trans. Stuart Woolf. New York: Simon and Schuster, 1995.]

Storie naturali [published under pseudonym Damiano Malabalia]. Turin: Einaudi, 1966. [*The Sixth Day and Other Tales* (includes *Storie naturali* and *Vizio di forma*). Trans. Raymond Rosenthal. New York: Summit Books, 1990.]

Vizio di forma. Turin: Einaudi, 1971. [*The Sixth Day and Other Tales* (includes *Storie naturali* and *Vizio di forma*. Trans. Raymond Rosenthal. New York: Summit Books, 1990.]

Il sistema periodico. Turin: Einaudi, 1975. [*The Periodic Table.* Trans. Raymond Rosenthal. New York: Schocken Books, 1984.]

La chiave a stella. Turin: Einaudi, 1978. [*The Monkey's Wrench.* Trans. William Weaver. New York: Summit Books, 1986; reprint New York: Viking/Penguin, 1995.]

La ricerca delle radici: Antologia personale. Turin: Einaudi, 1981.

Lilìt e altri racconti. Turin: Einaudi, 1981. [*Moments of Reprieve.* Trans. Ruth Feldman. New York: Summit Books, 1986; reprint New York: Viking/ Penguin, 1995.]

Se non ora, quando?. Turin: Einaudi, 1981. [*If Not Now, When?* Trans. William Weaver. New York: Summit Books, 1985; reprint New York: Viking/Penguin, 1995.]

L'altrui mestiere. Turin: Einaudi, 1985. [*Other People's Trades.* Trans. Raymond Rosenthal. New York: Summit Books, 1989.]

I sommersi e i salvati. Turin: Einaudi, 1986. [*The Drowned and the Saved.* Trans. Raymond Rosenthal. New York: Summit Books, 1988.]

Autoritratto di Primo Levi. Ed. Ferdinando Camon. Padua: Nord-Est, 1987. [*Conversations with Primo Levi.* Ed. Ferdinando Camon. Trans. John Shepley. Marlboro, Vt.: Marlboro Press, 1989.]

The Voice of Memory: Interviews 1961–1987. Ed. Marco Belpoliti and Robert Gordon. Trans. Robert Gordon. New York: New Press, 2001.

Selected Studies of Levi

Banner, Gillian. "Primo Levi." In *Holocaust Literature: Schulz, Levi, Spiegelman and the Memory of the Offence,* 87–130. London and Portland, Ore.: Vallentine Mitchell, 2000.

Cavaglion, Alberto. "Argon e la cultura ebraica piemontese." *Belfagor* 43, no. 5 (September 1988): 541–62.

Gunzberg, Lynn M. "Down Among the Dead Men: Levi and Dante in Hell." *Modern Language Studies* 46, no. 1 (Winter 1996): 10-28.

Hughes, H. Stuart. "Two Captives Called Levi." In *Prisoners of Hope: The Silver Age of the Italian Jews, 1924–1974*, 65–73. Cambridge, Mass.: Harvard University Press, 1983.

Knapp, Bettina L. "Levi's *Survival in Auschwitz:* Exile and the Death Machine." In Bettina L. Knapp, *Exile and the Writer: Exoteric and Esoteric Experiences: A Jungian Approach*, 151–71. University Park: Pennsylvania State University Press, 1991.

Lang, Ariella. "Reason as Revenge: Primo Levi And Writing The Holocaust." *Symposium* Vol. 52 (Winter 1999): 255–64.

Lollini, Massimo. "Perchè si scrive? Primo Levi e Paul Celan." *Rivista di Letterature Moderne e Comparate* 52, no. 2 (April-June 1999): 149–66.

Michaelis, Meir. *Mussolini and the Jews: German-Italian Relations and the Jewish Question in Italy, 1922–1945*. London: Clarendon Press, 1978.

Patruno, Nicholas. *Understanding Primo Levi*. Columbia: University of South Carolina Press, 1995.

Reeb, Gerda. "Ironies of the Language of Testimony: Primo Levi's Clarity and Paul Celan's Obscurity." *RLA: Romance Languages Annual* 7 (1995): 340–43.

Segre, Claudio. "Primo Levi, Witness of the Holocaust." In *Why Germany?: National Socialist Anti-Semitism and the European Context*. Ed. John Milfull, 227–40. Providence, R.I.: Berg, 1993.

Sodi, Risa. "An Interview with Primo Levi." *Partisan Review* 54, no. 3 (Summer 1987): 355–66.

———. *A Dante of Our Time: Primo Levi and Auschwitz*. New York: Peter Lang, 1990.

ARTUR LUNDKVIST
(1906–1991)

Susan Brantly

BIOGRAPHY

Artur Lundkvist, the author of over 80 books as well as scores of critical articles, indefatigably remained throughout his life what was called in the 1930s a "cultural laborer"—that is, an author allied with the working class. This was all the more remarkable considering that he was born on a small farm in northern Skåne to a family with no particular interest in literature. Lundkvist's grandniece, Kay Glans, has commented, "No Swedish author has probably ever come from such a limited environment and made himself so at home in the great wide world" (cited in Díaz, *Det okuvliga gräset*, 178). Despite a chronic lack of books and schooling, Lundkvist knew early that he wanted to be a writer. He submitted his first book manuscript to the Stockholm publishing house of Bonnier at the age of 16. He wrote poems for left-wing newspapers as well as book reviews. He starved rather than sell his precious typewriter. Lundkvist was predominantly an autodidact, originally by necessity and later by choice. He felt that educational institutions prevented students from thinking outside the boundaries of tradition.

In the 1930s, Lundkvist became perhaps the foremost proponent and practitioner of modernism in Sweden. In 1932, he made his first major journey, of which there would be many more. In his autobiographical work *Självporträtt av en drömmare med öppna ögon* (1966), he wrote, "All journeys are, for the most part, illusions that get shattered" (73). He traveled to Africa expecting a primitivist paradise, but was instead shocked by the ugly realities of colonialism. The book describing his journey came out the following year, *Negerkust* (1933). His travel books have made him an important cultural mediator in Sweden, helping to shape that country's attitudes towards developing nations.

He waited out the years of World War II, believing it to be a conflict between "bad and even worse." He was unlucky enough to be in Norway when the Germans invaded, and after arrest and interrogation was allowed to return to Sweden. The postwar years were among Lundkvist's most politically active. He was a primary spokesman for the "third viewpoint" debate. He and others felt that during the Cold War the world was being torn between the two forces of capitalism and dictatorial communism. He felt that Social Democratic Sweden was in the position to offer a third viewpoint on world events.

In the 1950s, Lundkvist traveled to India, the Soviet Union, China, and Latin America. As always, he reported on his travels in book form. He appeared to favor the Communist rule in China over that of the Soviet Union, and at the same time he sought to combat the tendency to demonize communist countries in the 1950s. He received the Lenin Prize in 1958. Thinking of himself as a "free socialist," he reflected that accepting the prize might seem to put him in the position of endorsing communism, while rejecting it would mean siding with capitalism. He solved his dilemma by accepting the prize and donating most of the money to a fund that would sponsor the translation of Swedish literature into other languages.

He became a member in 1968 of the Swedish Academy, in which he was a well-informed and strong participant in the selections of the Nobel Prize for Literature. He had introduced little-known writers to Sweden throughout his career, in addition to translating poetry and fiction. During his tenure, the Swedish Academy appeared both to favor innovative writers and to try to draw attention to unknown writers. Both of these preferences accorded with Lundkvist's already well-established tastes. The deliberations of the Swedish Academy are confidential, but it has long been rumored that Lundkvist blocked Jorge Luis Borges's nomination because of Borges's support of dictatorship. In general, Lundkvist warmly supported Latin American writers both through his translations and critical writing. Gabriel García Márquez in *Tärningkastet 8* (1981), a book in honor of Lundkvist's 75th birthday, characterized Lundkvist's advocacy of Latin American literature as follows: "This has made him, much against his will, into a distant and mysterious deity upon whom the fate of our literature in the world more or less depends" (65).

MAJOR MULTICULTURAL THEMES

Lundkvist was always interested in transgressing boundaries, be they the boundaries of genre, the limitations of idealism, or the lines drawn on maps. He savored the challenge that meeting new cultures poses to one's own sense of identity.

In his travel books, he does not pretend to leave his own cultural identity behind. His biases as a traveler are especially apparent in his books on developing countries. In *Negerkust*, he sees racial oppression as another form of class oppression and he predicts a revolution, especially in South Africa. He was a lifelong atheist and has no appreciation or sympathy for the spiritual life of India. In *Indiabrand* (1950), he complains of seeing sacred cows wandering freely among people who are starving. It is the material conditions of Indians that capture Lundkvist's attention; he sees their religion as a remnant of a dark and primitive past. His book on Latin America, *Vulkanisk kontinent. En resa i Sydamerika* (1957), translated into ten languages, stresses Latin America's potential. Quite conscious of the impossibility of capturing an entire continent in a book, Lundkvist himself saw Latin America as a vibrant, vital, developing area. He has a tendency to see developing countries, as the very phrase "developing countries" implies, as occupying a lower rung of the ladder of cultural evolution. European culture is the standard by which all other cultures are judged.

Lundkvist's fiction takes up themes inspired by his travels but plays with them freely. *Malinga* (1952) is a fictional travelogue that describes a dystopia. His traveler exclaims, "Out of the secure, blinding habits! Transform, revise yourself according to the reality of the world! And yet, remain embarrassingly like yourself amidst everything that is different" (122). The novel *Darunga* (1954) describes a Latin American revolution. In hindsight, it seems as though Lundkvist had predicted the revolution in Cuba that he endorsed in a foreword to a later edition of the novel. His poem *Agadir* (1961) has been translated into a number of languages and describes the 1960 earthquake in Morocco, which Lundkvist experienced firsthand.

Lundkvist turned to historical fiction in the 1970s in order to explore issues of cultural identity and nationalism. The novels *Himlens vilja. En forestallning am Djingis Khan* (1970), *Krigarens dikt: En sannolik framställning av Alexander den Stores handlingar och levnadsöden* (1976), and *Babylon, gudarnas sköka* (1981) deal with powerful rulers: Genghis Khan, Alexander the Great, and Nebuchadnezzar respectively, whose realms seem to be the culmination of civilization. Each of these rulers' empires contains the seeds of decay and will in turn be succeeded by other empires equally convinced of their lasting supremacy. This idea of the temporality of power undermines any nationalistic aspirations to lasting supremacy. *Tvivla, korsfarare! En sannolik berättelse* (1972) and *Utvandring till paradiset* (1979) demonstrate what happens to Swedish nationals who enter the wide world of tremendous diversity. Not surprisingly, their sense of national identity as Swedes becomes profoundly relativized. The Swedish way is only one of a myriad of ways of doing things. In seems as though, through these fictional venues, Lundkvist sought to come to terms with the biases he himself displayed in his travel writings from the 1950s.

SURVEY OF CRITICISM

The sheer bulk of Lundkvist's literary and critical production is enough to daunt any scholar. Most critics have focused on his poetry, and comparatively less attention has been paid to his fiction. The scope of these studies is more aesthetic than political, and they do not betray much of an interest in multicultural issues. Lundkvist's activities as a translator of foreign literature have received virtually no critical attention. Paul Lindbom (1991) and Kjell Espmark (1991) in their scholarly monographs have only made mention of Lundkvist's role as a presenter of foreign literature in Sweden.

Examining Lundkvist as a writer of travel books is almost virgin territory. Margarete Petersson's article (1989) has some critical things to say about Lundkvist's narrative posture in *Indiabrand*: "Lundkvist conjures an image of himself as a clear-eyed and alert traveler far above the confusion and torpor of India. He represents a different cultural level. He perceives his journeys to be not only movements in space, but also travels in time" (13). For Lundkvist, Africa is a continent at the stage of a child, and India is a country in deep cultural decline. Considering the strong impact of Lundkvist's travel books, those texts certainly deserve further study.

SELECTED BIBLIOGRAPHY

Works by Lundkvist

Negerkust. Stockholm: Bonnier, 1933.
Indiabrand. Stockholm: Bonnier, 1950.
Malinga. Stockholm: Bonnier, 1952.
Darunga. Stockholm: Bonnier, 1954.
Den förvandlade draken. En resa i Kina. Stockholm: Tidens, 1955.
Vulkanisk kontinent. En resa i Sydamerika. Stockholm: Tidens, 1957.
Agadir. En dikt. Stockholm: Bonnier, 1961.
Självporträtt av en drömmare med öppna ögon. Stockholm: Bonnier, 1966.
Himlens vilja. En forestallning am Djingis Khan. Stockholm: Bonnier, 1970.
Tvivla, korsfarare! En sannolik berättelse. Stockholm: Bonnier, 1972.
Krigarens dikt: En sannolik framställning av Alexander den Stores handlingar och levnadsöden. Stockholm: Bonnier, 1976.
Utvandring till paradiset. Stockholm: Bonnier, 1979.
Babylon, gudarnas sköka. Stockholm: Bonnier, 1981.

Selected Studies of Lundkvist

Brantly, Susan. "Artur Lundkvist." *A History of Swedish Literature.* Ed. Lars G. Warme, 353–56. Lincoln: University of Nebraska Press, 1996.
Díaz, René Vasquez, ed. *Det okuvliga gräset: En bok om Artur Lundkvist.* Stockholm: Bonnier, 1986.
Eriksson, Magnus. "The Formation of Artistic Identity: The Young Artur Lundkvist." *Scandinavian Studies* 66, no. 3 (Summer 1994): 382–99.

Espmark, Kjell. *Livsdyrkaren Artur Lundkvist: Studier i hans lyrik till och med Vit man.* Stockholm: Bonnier, 1964.

———. *The Nobel Prize in Literature: A Study of the Criteria behind the Choices.* Boston: G. K. Hall, 1991.

García Márquez, Gabriel. *Tärningkastet 8,* 64–66. Stockholm: Bonnier, 1981.

Lindblom, Paul. *Samtiden i ögat: En bok om Artur Lundkvist.* Stockholm: Tidens, 1991.

Nordberg, Carl-Eric. *Det skapande ögat: En färd genom Artur Lundkvists författarskap.* Stockholm: Bonnier, 1981.

Petersson, Margarete. "Betrakta er själva, europeer." *Horisont* 36, no. 1 (1989): 13–17.

Sondrup, Steven. "Artur Lundkvist and Knowledge for Man's Sake." *World Literature Today* 55, no. 2 (Spring 1981): 233–38.

ANDREI MAKINE
(1957?–)

Christopher W. Lemelin

BIOGRAPHY

Andrei Makine appeared on the literary stage only in 1995, when his fourth novel, *Le testament français*, won the Prix Médicis, the Prix Goncourt, and the Prix Lycée Goncourt. Before Makine, no author had won all three prestigious awards for the same work, and no author born outside of France had won the Prix Goncourt. Makine's multiculturalism is grounded in the simple fact that he is a Russian who lives in France and writes novels in French. His work is therefore both French and Russian, about both France and Russia, and represents an attempt to discover a personal multiculturalism and its liminal nature.

Biographical information for Makine is generally scant and sometimes contradictory. He was born in 1957 or 1958, but it is difficult to determine where he was born or grew up. Some sources say that he was born in Krasnoyarsk, Siberia; others that he was born in Penza, in European Russia. The details of his education are also unclear, though most sources say that he studied in Moscow. Makine probably traveled within the USSR before emigrating, but it is doubtful that he went abroad during those years. He left Russia for Paris in 1987, and it was then that he began his literary career. Since then he has published six novels, all written in French, but all of which utilize Russian themes or subject matter in addition to images of the West, primarily of France. Initially his first novels went unnoticed, but since the success of *Le testament français* (1995), which has appeared in over twenty-five languages, all but one of his novels have been reprinted and translated into English. Aside from the basic fact that Makine is a Russian who writes in French, it is difficult to assess the truth about his multicultural experience. It is tempting to see an autobiography in *Le testament français*, a coming-of-age story about a Russian boy whose grandmother is French and who eventually goes to Paris to become a writer. Some claim that Makine grew up in a similar multicultural environment, but when asked if he really had a French grandmother, he refuses to answer. Nevertheless, he admits there is something autobiographical in his novels and that he was fascinated by French culture at an early age. But he also says that his knowledge of France came only from reading the great works of literature (see Masson, "An Interview with Andrei Makine").

After *Le testament français* won its unprecedented triple crown, Makine was finally granted French citizenship in 1997, after 10 years of trying. The popularity of translations of that novel has given him the opportunity to travel internationally. He continues to live in Paris, though he has also recently built a small home in the coastal region of Landes in southwest France, which offers a landscape not unlike Russia's.

MAJOR MULTICULTURAL THEMES

Whether Makine's novels belong to the corpus of French literature or to that of Russian literature is debatable (see Tolstaya 1997, 4; Tolstaya 1998, 200, 209). Whatever the origins of Makine's multiculturalism—a French line in his genealogy or simply youthful curiosity—he goes beyond simple representation of foreign culture through the prism of Russia. His multiculturalism delves into the very essence of cultural difference, questioning its origins and its effects. Nearly all of his works portray life in the Soviet Union, often during the post-Stalinist era of his own childhood. He focuses on the ways Russian culture interacts with other cultures, how exposure to them changes the lives of his characters, and how Russia fits into the larger cultural landscape. In this, Makine continues a long tradition, the debate on the nature of Russia: Is Russia East or West?

His first novel, *La fille d'un héros de l'Union Soviétique* (1990), focuses on life in Soviet Russia and its interaction with the West. Olia, the daughter of the hero, trains at a foreign-language institute and has an affair with a visiting French athlete. She is saved from discipline by her father's status as a World War II hero, and begins a career as a translator and escort for foreign visitors. Olia becomes a symbol of a Russia "prostituted" to the West. When the democratizing efforts of perestroika arrive, they too are out of place. Russia remains an entity immiscible with the West (see Taras, 53–54). In *Confession d'un porte-drapeau déchu* (1992), Makine's Russian narrator lives in France, and the novel centers on the reminiscences of Kim and Arkadii, two émigré friends, about their childhoods in Leningrad. Makine also weaves in the recollections of the boys' fathers. Most important in *Confession* is the fact that Arkadii's family is Jewish, while Kim's is Russian Orthodox. The different perspectives form the most important multicultural aspect of the novel.

Makine's third and fourth novels, *Au temps du fleuve Amour* (1994) and *Le testament français*, are his most richly multicultural works and contain many similarities. Both are coming-of-age stories with young protagonists who create a fantasy of the West that significantly impacts their maturation. In *Au temps du fleuve Amour*, the West appears in the films of Jean-Paul Belmondo, the French James Bond. These films free the boys from their monotonous existence in a small Siberian town. In *Le testament français*, Alyosha's fascination with the West comes from listening to his grandmother's stories about growing up in Belle Époque France. The conflict Alyosha feels between his French and Russian heritages forms the crux of his maturation. In both novels the protagonists are caught between cultures, and in *Au temps du fleuve Amour*, Russia is likened to a pendulum swinging between West and East. Both novels also display a sensitivity to interlinguistic play. The title *Au temps du fleuve Amour* contains an untranslatable intercultural pun—the name of the Siberian river, *Amur*, sounds like the French *amour*, love. In *Le testament français*, language is the basis of Alyosha's reconstruction of his grandmother's France. He believes that secret French words give the women in faded photographs their elusive smiles. He marvels at the French names of dishes served to Nicholas II during a trip to Paris. He contemplates the strange words that label his grandmother's collection of rocks.

In *Le crime d'Olga Arbélina* (1998), Makine transplants a Dostoevskian mystery onto French soil, setting his psychological drama in a Russian émigré community near Paris. He focuses on the princess Olga's émigré life, and despite the inherent multiculturalism here, he deals less with these issues than with the psychology of the heroine. But like her creator, Olga is an outsider, lost somewhere between cultures. She belongs neither to the world of the French town nor to the world of the émigré community. Makine deftly incorporates this idea into a description of the temporal slippage between the French and Russian calendars.

Makine's latest novel, *Requiem pour l'Est*, was released in France in 2000, and appeared in English translation in 2001. Here, Makine both returns to the epic and tragic history of Soviet Russia and combines this theme with the narrator's romantic search for his identity in Africa, the Near East, and the Caucasus. Again, Makine's overarching multicultural theme deals with personal identity within, without, and between cultures.

SURVEY OF CRITICISM

While Makine's appearance has made a considerable impact in the contemporary press, his works have not fully been examined in critical works. The handful of scholarly articles has focused on *Le testament français*. One of the main themes that critics have considered is the connection between that work and Marcel Proust. Els Jongeneel (2000) directly compares *Le testament français* to Proust's *A la recherche du temps perdu*. The theme of memory—the "language of memory" or the "poetics of nostalgia"—plays a vital role. (Makine might also be seen as a disciple of another multicultural author, Russian Vladimir Nabokov; much in *Le testament français* recalls Nabokov's *Speak, Memory*.) Ray Taras (2000) focuses on political questions, but also discusses the writer's multiculturalism. Taras concludes that Makine is the author of the border text, simultaneously highlighting the importance of and "deterritorializing" the border between East and West.

Reviews of Makine's work have generally been laudatory, although Russian critics are less favorable than Western ones. Some reviewers, such as Tatyana Tolstaya, have delved more deeply into Makine's style and thematics. Tolstaya seems ambivalent in her assessment of Makine. In her 1997 review, she states that "Makine is French in his style [but] his themes are undeniably Russian" (4). In her later "Russkii chelovek na rendevu" (1998), she says that Makine is "Russian but not a Russian writer, and yet he isn't a Frenchman" (201). In the end she calls him a "philological half-breed" and a "cultural hybrid" (209), appellations that Makine, perhaps, would not deny.

SELECTED BIBLIOGRAPHY

Works by Makine

La fille d'un héros de l'Union Soviétique. Paris: Editions Robert Laffont, 1990.
Confession d'un porte-drapeau déchu. Paris: Gallimard, 1992. [*Confession of a Fallen Standard-Bearer*. Trans. Geoffrey Strachan. New York: Arcade, 2000.]
Au temps du fleuve Amour. Paris: Editions du Felin, 1994. [*Once upon the River Love*. Trans. Geoffrey Strachan. New York: Arcade, 1998.]
Le testament français. Paris: Mercure de France, 1995. [*Dreams of My Russian Summers*. Trans. Geoffrey Strachan. New York: Arcade, 1997.]
Le crime d'Olga Arbélina. Paris: Mercure de France, 1998. [*The Crime of Olga Arbyelina*. Trans. Geoffrey Strachan. New York: Arcade, 1999.]
Requiem pour l'Est. Paris: Mercure de France, 2000. [*Requiem for a Lost Empire*. Trans. Geoffrey Strachan. New York: Arcade, 2001.]

Selected Studies of Makine

Jongeneel, Els. "L'Histoire du côté de chez Proust: Andrei Makine, *Le testament français*; Mélanges offerts à Evert van der Starre." In *Histoire jeu science dans l'aire de la litterature*. Ed. Sjef Houpperman, Paul J. Smith, and Madeleine van Strien-Chardonneau. Amsterdam: Rodopi, 2000.
Knorr, Katherine. "Andrei Makine's Poetics of Nostalgia." *The New Criterion* 14, no. 7 (March 1996): 32–36.
Masson, Sophie. "An Interview with Andrei Makine." *Quadrant* 42, no. 11 (November 1998): 62–63.

Remier, Andrew. "The Russian Testaments of Andrei Makine." *Quadrant* 44, no. 7 (July 2000): 74–78.

Sankey, Margaret. "Between and across Cultures: The Language of Memory in Andrei Makine's *Le testament français;* Studies in Honor of Kenneth Raymond Dutton." In *Variété: Perspectives in French literature, Society and Culture.* Ed. Marie Ramsland, 293–303. Frankfurt am Main: Peter Lang, 1999.

Taras, Ray. "A la recherche du pays perdu: Andrei Makine's Russia." *East European Quarterly* 34, no. 1 (Spring 2000): 51–79.

Tolstaya, Tatyana. "Love Story." *New York Review of Books* (November 20, 1997): 4–5.

———. "Russkii chelovek na rendevu." *Znamia* 6 (1998): 200–209.

Zlobina, Maya. "V poiskakh utrachennykh mgnovenii." *Novyi mir* 10 (1996): 242–45.

CLAIRE MESSUD

(1966–)

Deborah Phelps

BIOGRAPHY

When Claire Messud speaks, audiences often have difficulty placing her origins. Her accent is transatlantic—perhaps Canadian, perhaps English. Her fiction also reflects a distinctly non-American character in its settings and sensibilities. In fact, Messud *is* an American, born in Connecticut, but she has spent the bulk of her life outside the United States. Her Canadian mother and French father moved the family frequently. Messud lived in Canada until age four, when she began her education at the Kambala School for Girls in Sydney, Australia, until 1975. She returned to North America to attend high school, graduated from Yale University in 1987, and then moved to England to pursue postgraduate work in English at Cambridge University. She lived in London working as a waitress and secretary before becoming a deputy editor at the *Guardian* newspaper. In 1993 she left journalism to write fiction full time. She published *When the World Was Steady* (1994) in England, to excellent notices for a first novel. After its American publication in 1996, the novel became a finalist for the prestigious PEN / Faulkner award (a British Booker prize nomination had to be retracted after a conflict of interest was discovered). Even greater acclaim followed the publication of *The Last Life* (1999) and, most recently, *Simple Tale. The Hunters: Two Short Novels* (2001).

Messud presently lives in the United States with her husband, the English writer James Wood. She has taught creative writing and literature as a visiting professor at several institutions, including Warren Wilson College, the University of the South, and the Johns Hopkins

University. For the academic year 2001–02, she was a member of the faculty at Amherst College. She also supports her writing through teaching fiction workshops at Sewanee Writers' Conference at the University of the South each summer. Her short fiction and book reviews continue to appear in major newspapers and literary journals. She has recently indicated in an interview that her next work will be a departure from her more multiculturally directed fiction: "My new novel is set in New York. That would be the first thing I've ever written set in this country" (quoted in Digon, "Messud Makes Her Mark").

MAJOR MULTICULTURAL THEMES

All of Messud's book-length fiction deals in some way with themes of multiculturalism, displacement, and exile. Her female protagonists struggle to preserve their equilibrium against the horrors of history, the peculiarities of family, and the problem of finding a personal and cultural identity in the late twentieth century.

The sisters of *When the World Was Steady* lose the security of their settled lives in middle age and journey, literally and emotionally, towards adaptation. Emmy, the younger sister, travels from Australia after a traumatic divorce, to Bali. Virginia, after suffering a series of personal devastations that lead her to question her faith, takes a trip from London back to the family home in Scotland with her mother. Both sisters have to come to terms with their lifelong beliefs in the security of home, place, and family ties after unexpected events dismantle them. In traveling from prosaic, safe city homes to wilder, romantic islands, the sisters learn to find comfort within the parameters of their new lives.

Sagesse La Basse, the fifteen-year-old heroine of *The Last Life*, has to recover a new life and identity for herself much earlier. Sagesse is the child of exiled parents: an American mother who chose to move to France, and a French-Algerian (or *pied-noir*) father who, because of postcolonial resentment, was forced from the family home in Algeria after the war for independence from France. Against the backdrops of historical dislocation, failed family dreams, and the reverberations of colonialism, Sagesse must grow up and find her own identity as a woman. The family's internal damage is brought to the surface when her grandfather commits a violent act, isolating Sagesse from her friends and splintering the family. She must determine who she is amidst a community that has failed, with the help of history, to make a place for themselves. Is Sagesse Algerian? French? American? Where is home? Ironically, the heroine and her family struggle with these questions of identity in the beautiful but tourist-driven environs of the Côte d'Azur. Sagesse, from a family of expatriates and from a place where no one is truly a native, ultimately decides to continue her family's escapist tradition and disguise herself in exile to America, itself a land of immigrants.

Messud's third book is a set of novellas. *A Simple Tale* is the story of Maria Poniatowski from the Ukraine, who has survived a German labor camp experience and finds a new life in Canada as a displaced person. The novella opens when Maria is elderly but still stubbornly clinging to her job as a cleaning woman, despite her son's insistence that she retire. When her last client becomes unable to run her own household, Maria must face another sort of displacement—life without the old comfort zones of work and family. Her husband has died; her successful son has married a woman Maria hates. As Maria recalls her old life of danger and exile, juxtaposed with the new settled life of old age, she must cope with her anxiety over feelings of redundancy and isolation.

The second novella, *The Hunters*, is quite different. The nameless narrator, an American academic unhappily living in a dingy section of London, is coping with a failed relationship by escaping into her research on death. Unlike the historical sweep of *A Simple Tale*, Messud centers on her isolated character's inner life, although the reader is not even sure of the gender. *The Hunters* is a story of psychological suspense. The narrator becomes obsessed with the goings-on of her neighbor Ridley Wandor, a caregiver for the elderly whose clients have been rapidly dying. The narrator begins spying on her neighbor and eventually comes to believe that Ridley is a murderer. Messud provides a Poe-like twist at the end of *The Hunters*, surprising both the narrator and the reader. The dislocation inherent in the appearance-verses-reality plot mirrors the narrator's emotional and cultural displacement. The subject of death looms large here as a place in which the narrator and the reader are both naive outsiders.

SURVEY OF CRITICISM

Criticism of Messud's fiction consists mainly of book reviews. Critics have especially noted her work for its meticulous attention to fine writing. Michiko Kakutani (1999) in the *New York Times* praises the "dense lyric prose" of *The Last Life*, and Eileen Murphy (1999) in the *Baltimore City Paper* calls Messud a writer of "belles lettres" fiction, one who deliberately goes against the popular trend of action-based novels. The *Ruminator Review*'s Rosellen Brown (1999), however, felt that Messud's style can be too "show-offy" and "challenging in syntax," forcing the reader to look up unfamiliar words. Kakutani also allows that Sagesse's adult voice in *The Last Life* "can sound wordy and pretentious." Candida Clark (1999) of the *New Statesman* took *The Last Life* to task for the awkward dualism of Sagesse's voices and for sounding "too much like memoir."

Although all of Messud's fiction has been generally well received, critics have singled out *The Last Life* and the novella *A Simple Tale* for special praise. *The Last Life*'s deft handling of history, culture, and family drama raises it above "the usual Bildungsroman to become a thoughtful meditation upon the uses of personal and public narrators" (Kakutani, "'The Last Life': A Girl's Life, in a Family Unhappy in Its Own Way").

John Ziebel (2001) of the *Las Vegas Mercury* felt that Messud's achievement in *A Simple Tale* was in her storyteller's integrity in presenting Maria's character fully formed, "avoiding even the hint of unearned empathy by romanticizing absolutely nothing." Ziebel noted that, of the two novellas, *A Simple Tale* and *The Hunters*, the former was the more polished. Tilly Ware (2002) of *The Guardian Unlimited Observer* also believed that *A Simple Tale* was superior to *The Hunters* and should have been published alone.

SELECTED BIBLIOGRAPHY

Works by Messud

When the World Was Steady. London: Granta, 1994.
The Last Life. New York: HarcourtBrace, 1999.
Simple Tale. The Hunters: Two Short Novels. New York: Harcourt, 2001.

Selected Studies of Messud

Brown, Rosellen. "Wise Daughter." *Ruminator Review*. Fall 1999. Available at http://www.ruminator.com/hmr/51/fiction/51_brown.html.

Clark, Candida. "Books: Novel of the Week: *The Last Life*." *New Statesman*. September 13, 1999. Available at http://www.newstatesman.co.uk/199909130053.html.

Digon, Rocio. "Messud Makes Her Mark." *Amherst Student Online*. Available at http://halogen.note.amherst.edu/~student/2000-2001/issue23/features/07.html.

Friedman, Paula. "The Meaning of Exile, the Magnitude of Home." *The Oregonian*. November 1, 1999. Available at http://www.oregonlive.com/books/99/11/bk991101_messud.html.

Jones, Maggie. "'The Last Life' by Claire Messud." *Salon.com*. September 3, 1999. Available at http://www.salon.com/books/review/1999/09/03/messud/html.

Kakutani, Michiko. "'The Last Life': A Girl's Life, in a Family Unhappy in Its Own Way." *New York Times*. August 10, 1999. Available at http://www.nytimes.com/books/99/08/08/daily/081099messud-book-review.html.

Murphy, Eileen. "*Steady* On: Messud Remains True to the Craft of Belles-Lettres." *Baltimore City Paper*. August 29–September 4, 1999. Available at http://www.citypaper.com/2001-08-29/books.html.

Ware, Tilly. "Mrs. Ellington's Cleaner Is Not What She Seems." *The Guardian Unlimited Observer*. March 3, 2002. Available at http://www.observer.co.uk/review/story/0,6903,660790.html.

Ziebel, John. "Books: Near Perfect Prose." *Las Vegas Mercury*. September 7, 2001. Available at http://www.lasvegasmercury.com/2001/MERC-Sep-07-Fri-2001/16872778.html.

MARCO MICONE
(1945–)

Betty Bednarski

BIOGRAPHY

Marco Micone, award-winning Quebec playwright, essayist, and literary translator, was born in 1945 in the village of Montelongo in the Molise region of southern Italy. He has lived in Montreal since 1958, and is today one of a growing number of immigrant writers whose maternal language is not French, but who have chosen to write in the official language of their adopted province, Quebec, stretching cultural bounds, indeed, changing the very notion of what constitutes *la littérature québécoise*. Micone writes exclusively about the immigrant experience and about the complex relationship between immigrant and host cultures in an already culturally divided Quebec. He first knew the ravages of emigration at the age of 6, when his father joined the economic exodus from Italy to Canada, leaving his wife and young sons behind. Seven years later, the father sent for the family, and the young Micone left the predominantly feminine universe of his childhood village, rediscovered paternal authority, and became an immigrant himself, at the age of 13.

In Montreal, denied entry to the neighborhood French school and educated, like the majority of immigrant children of his generation, in special English schools, Micone subsequently became fluent in French, which was for him the language of the street, and also of the working class and the cultural majority. In school, he was doubly marginalized: as an immigrant in a country foreign to him, and as part of an English-language milieu foreign to Quebec. It was nevertheless in grade school that he discovered *La petite poule d'eau*—in French—and became enchanted with the writing of Gabrielle Roy. He read widely and independently and came to know and admire the great works of Quebec literature. At Loyola College and McGill University, both anglophone institutions, he chose to study French literature and was able at the same time to pursue his interest in the French writing of Quebec. His 1971 master's thesis, written at McGill, was a study of the theatre of playwright Marcel Dubé.

Micone experienced his Road to Damascus in the early 1970s, as a teacher of Italian at a Montreal English-language college frequented by young people of Italian descent. Here, he discovered a generation speaking poor English, French, and Italian, as ignorant of their own culture as they were of the culture of Quebec, and inhabiting a kind of cultural no-man's-land. Micone began to reflect on the intersecting nature of the immigrant and Quebec Francophone identities. There was a need, he could see, to tell the immigrants more about themselves and, at the same time, to increase their knowledge of Francophone Quebec. It was equally urgent to raise Francophones' awareness of the immigrants in their midst. For his students, Micone developed a course on the history of Italian immigration and, in the Quebec media, he became known as a spokesperson for immigrants, a defender of their cause and an interpreter of their reality to Francophones. He has written penetrating analyses of what he calls *la culture immigrée* (immigrant culture), which he sees as a dominated and subaltern culture, "like the culture of women and the working classes" ("The Emigrated Word," 188), and as a culture in transition, destined to be modified and absorbed, living on in the host culture, which it will, in turn, radically change.

Micone is himself a sovereigntist, a supporter of political separation for Quebec, which he perceives as the only solution for the survival of Quebec Francophone culture and of the immigrant cultures that are becoming part of it. He is an outspoken critic of official Canadian multiculturalism (still popular among the conservative immigrant elites), because in his view it can only perpetuate the ghettoization and folklorization of immigrant culture. At the same time, he keeps a watchful eye on Quebec cultural politicians who pay lip-service to the province's policy of *transculturalisme*, more progressive, undoubtedly, than the Canadian model, stressing as it does the inevitable and desirable hybridization of cultures, but always in danger of being betrayed.

Micone has given dramatic expression to his ideas in a series of plays, which are strongly didactic and make extensive use of Brechtian distance techniques. His trilogy—*Gens du silence* (1982), *Addolorata* (1984) and *Déjà l'agonie* (1988)—was reworked as *Trilogia* in 1996, and a one-act play, "Babele," appeared in the crosscultural magazine *Vice-versa* in 1989. The trilogy shows several generations of Italo-Québécois struggling to cope with the effects of displacement and cultural marginalization in a context of family tensions, linguistic dysfunction, and uncertain identities. Micone can be credited with having created, almost overnight, the new phenomenon of Quebec immigrant theater in French. He is also the author of translations into French of plays from the English and Italian repertoires, plays by Shakespeare, Pirandello, Gozzi and above all Goldoni, all of which have been produced for Montreal audiences—another instance of his dynamic contribution to cultural exchange and to French language theater in Quebec. Besides his theatrical texts, Micone has published a controversial poem-manifesto, *Speak What* (1989), a subversive and parodic response to Michèle Lalonde's 1969 classic, *Speak White*, which he has rewritten from the immigrant perspective; and *Le figuier enchanté* (1992), a book combining first person narrative, essays, letters, and dialogue in an account of emigration-immigration that is lyrical, humorous, and polemical in turn.

MAJOR MULTICULTURAL THEMES

"If I hadn't emigrated, I would never have had to write," says the father of the narrator of *Le figuier enchanté*, who has overcome his illiteracy in order to write letters home (57).

Micone himself, unsure of his grasp of any one of his several languages, first began writing plays to prove to himself that he was capable of writing in French. For him, the act of writing is bound up inextricably with the immigrant experience. And emigration-immigration is the one great theme out of which all others flow. Micone writes of memory and of what has been "lost in translation": "As long as the words of my childhood evoke a world that the words of this place cannot express, I will remain an immigrant" (Epigraph, *Le figuier enchanté*). He writes *out of* the immigrant's fear of silence and at the same time *about* loss of language and linguistic insecurity. His Voiceless People (the title of one of his plays) struggle to overcome the silence that threatens to engulf them. That silence can grow, paradoxically, out of Babel's clamor. What his characters lack is the ability to speak a language—any language—adequately. They also lack the power that would allow them to speak with authority, and so break free from subordination—double subordination in the case of immigrant women and girls, whose plight he has foregrounded. But, for these people, to have a voice would above all mean to know their own story and be able to pass it on. In *Gens du silence*, Nancy writes plays in which immigrants can recognize themselves; and, like her creator, Micone, she writes them in French, so that within Quebec their forgotten story can at last be heard. Micone writes, then, of silence; and he himself breaks a silence. Through his poem *Speak What*, he issues an admonition, and at the same time an invitation and a challenge to a Quebec reluctant to move beyond the old dualism of French-English antagonisms. By engaging a Québécois poet in dialogue, Micone has forced his way into a conversation, claiming for the immigrant the status of cultural interlocutor.

SURVEY OF CRITICISM

Fulvio Caccia (1985) and Joseph Pivato (2000) comment on Micone's preoccupation with the theme of language (and silence) in the context of Italian Canadian immigrant writing, but like Sherry Simon (1985), and in particular Lise Gauvin (2000), they also make the connection between Micone's treatment of the theme and the hyper-awareness of language that has characterized so much Francophone writing in Quebec. All discuss the nature of the French language Micone has invented for his immigrant characters (who in real life would undoubtedly speak to each other in Italian or one of its dialects and be capable of only a very halting French): it is a nonrealistic and highly simplified form of standard French, with the ring of popular speech, and is suggestive of a trilingual environment. Several critics defend Micone's rewriting of Michèle Lalonde's *Speak White* (attacked in the press as plagiarism), which Gauvin sees as legitimate literary dialogue and, in spite of its irreverence, as acknowledgment of a Québécois classic. Pivato emphasizes Micone's feminist perspective, echoing Simon and Pierre L'Hérault. The latter place discussion of his work in the context of their analysis of *identity fictions* and their theorizing of cultural heterogeneity. With Monique LaRue (1988, preface, *Déjà l'agonie*), Gauvin, and Pivato, they stress the importance of his opening up of Quebec literature to the immigrant voice and the urgency of the questions his writing poses for Quebec. L'Hérault (1996) presents the figure of the child in *Déjà l'agonie* as an agent of transformation and acceptance, and, in the symbol of the enchanted fig tree, he sees a tree of life, bearing fruit—and progeny—in a new, culturally hybrid Quebec.

SELECTED BIBLIOGRAPHY

Works by Micone

Gens du silence. Montreal: Québec/Amérique, 1982.

Addolorata. Montreal: Guernica, 1984.

"The Emigrated Word." In *Interviews with the Phoenix: Interviews with Fifteen Italian-Québécois Artists.* Trans. Daniel Sloate. Ed. Fulvio Caccia, 186–94. Montreal: Guernica, 1985. (First published as "La Parole immigrée." In Fulvio Caccia, ed. *Sous le signe du Phénix.* Montreal: Guernica, 1985.)

Déjà l'agonie. Preface Monique LaRue. Montreal: Hexagone, 1988.

Two Plays: Voiceless People, Addolorata. English translation of *Gens du silence* and *Addolorata* by Maurizia Binda. Montreal: Guernica, 1988.

"Babele." In *Vice-versa* 26 (1989): 30–32.

"Speak What." In *Cahiers de théâtre, jeu* 50 (1989): 83–85.

Le figuier enchanté. Montreal: Boréal, 1992.

Beyond the Ruins. English translation of *Déjà l'agonie* by Jill MacDougall. Toronto: Guernica, 1995.

La culture immigrée comme dépassement des cultures ethniques. Occasional Paper 6. Eds. Richard Beach and Jeanne Kissner. Plattsburgh: State University of New York Press, 1996.

Trilogia: Gens du silence, Addolorata, Déjà l'agonie. Preface Pierre L' Hérault. Montreal: VLB Éditeur, 1996.

Selected Studies of Micone

Caccia, Fulvio. "The Italian Writer and Language." In *Contrasts: Comparative Essays on Italian Canadian Writing.* Ed. Joseph Pivato, 155–67. Montreal: Guernica, 1985.

Gauvin, Lise. "De 'Speak White' à 'Speak What': du côté des manifestes", and "L'écriture nomade." In Lise Gauvin, *Langagement,* 53–63 and 195–202. Montreal: Boréal, 2000.

L' Hérault, Pierre. "Voyage vers ici." *Spirale* 121 (1993): 6.

———. "Addolorata, Giovanni . . . et Jimmy." *Spirale* 148 (1996): 28.

Pivato, Joseph. "Five-fold Translation in the Theatre of Marco Micone." *Canadian Theatre Review* 104 (2000): 11–15.

Simon, Sherry. "Speaking with Authority: The Theatre of Marco Micone." *Canadian Literature* 106 (1985): 57–63.

CZESŁAW MIŁOSZ
(1911–)

Jerzy R. Krzyżanowski

BIOGRAPHY

"A writer living among people who speak a language different from his own," wrote Czesław Miłosz in his "Notes on Exile" (1976), "discovers after a while that he senses his native tongue in a new manner. It is not true that a long stay abroad leads to a withering of styles, even though the vivifying effect of everyday speech is lacking. What is true, however, is that new aspects and tonalities of his native tongue are discovered, for they stand out against the background of the language spoken in the new milieu" (283).

Born in the territory that used to be called "The Republic of Two Nations"—Poland and Lithuania—Czesław Miłosz studied at the Polish University of Wilno (today Vilnius, the capital of Lithuania). In the mid-1930s he made his mark as one of the young poets representing "the catastrophic" trend in Polish poetry. These poets were sensitive to the mood and the dramatic problems of a country located between Nazi Germany and Soviet Russia, the two neighboring powers that partitioned Poland in 1939. Miłosz, like most of his contemporaries, lived for four years in Nazi-occupied Poland; then, in 1945, he became a subject of the Communist regime imposed on that country. He reacted to the historic changes taking place in his own poetic way, registering events and impressions in poems that evoke such traumatic experiences as the destruction of the Warsaw ghetto ("Campo di Fiori," 1943, in *Ocalenie*, 40–42).

The postwar years turned out relatively well for Miłosz. He was appointed to a diplomatic post in Washington, D.C., and then to a similar position in Paris. His experience in foreign countries provided him with new perspectives and acquainted him better with Western cultures. During the rising political tension of the 1950s and the seemingly inevitable clash between West and East, Miłosz found himself in the center of the upcoming storm, and he made his choice.

His historical essay *Zniewolony umysł* (1953) was published in Paris by a Polish émigré publishing house, Instytut Literacki, two years after he officially announced his decision to defect and to stay permanently in the West. As one of the most penetrating studies of the intellectuals' corruption under communism, it became an international classic, translated into at least fourteen foreign languages, gaining the hitherto unknown author a worldwide reputation. After the initial success of his poetic treatise "Traktat poetycki" (1956–57), published in the Polish émigré monthly *Kultura* in Paris, he began producing an impressive number of collections of his poems and essays. While he was completely ignored by the Communist media in Poland, his fame in the West, and in the United States in particular, grew steadily, and by the end of the 1970s he was generally recognized as a major contemporary poet. Appointed professor of Slavic literatures at the University of California (Berkeley), he moved to the United States, where he became an active member of the writing community. Beginning in the 1960s, he continually published volumes of poems written in Polish but almost instantly translated into English, thus enriching both literatures. His growing fame won him the Neustadt Prize for Literature (1978) and eventually the Nobel Prize for Literature (1980), as well as many other honors and awards. The assimilation of a foreign poet into American society had been completed.

Once the Communist system had been abolished in Poland (1989), Miłosz's visits there became more and more frequent, and eventually he divided his time between Berkeley and Cracow, publishing almost exclusively in Poland. At the age of 90, he has put out three more collections of poetry and essays and contributes regularly to literary magazines and periodicals.

MAJOR MULTICULTURAL THEMES

Miłosz's return to his roots did not mean severing his ties with American culture—to the contrary, he enriched Polish letters not only with a number of translations from American literature, but also with themes of his American experience that are a permanent contribution to modern Polish poetry. His works provide a perfect example of a multicultural blend on many different levels of perception.

With his translations, Miłosz bridged the gap between two cultures with his own poetic taste in mind. He translated into Polish poems by his favorite American authors, Walt Whitman and Robinson Jeffers, among many others, as well as English poets such as T. S. Eliot and William

Blake. For American readers he translated or edited, or both, several collections of modern Polish poetry and wrote *The History of Polish Literature* (1969) in English.

Even before his American period, Miłosz wrote a number of prose works, beginning with the contemporary war novel *Zdobycie władzy* (1955) and the autobiographical novel *Dolina Issy* (1955). Based on reminiscences of his youth, *Dolina Issy* brought back memories of the land of his ancestors, the land that ceased to exist in its traditional form, wiped out by the torrents of history. The success of the novel prompted him to focus on more recent recollections of events that have shaped the modern world. His long autobiographical essay *Rodzinna Europa* (1959), is subtitled "A study of the inhabitants of Eastern Europe based on the author's life experiences."

The reflexive, philosophical character of Miłosz's poems renders perfectly well their main motif, a combination of nostalgia for the old and enchantment with the new land. Pondering fate and the human condition, he often returns to his "native realm," juxtaposing it with the open spaces of the San Francisco Bay, the Great Plains, and the Rocky Mountains. His poetry and essays focus more and more on transcendental, often religious themes, with questions that go beyond space and time—questions about the universal quest for the true meaning of life and an individual's place in the world. Referring to his own experience, he eventually asked: "Who am I now, years later, here on Grizzly Peak, in my study overlooking the Pacific?" And he continues: "One of the most serious and frustrating dilemmas resulting from prolonged residence abroad is having to repress the constantly intruding thought: How would this sound in English?" The answer is simple: "How glad I am now that I clung to my native language (for the simple reason that I was a Polish poet and could not have been otherwise)" (*Ziemia Ulro*, trans. Louis Iribarne, 12).

Miłosz's poems have been published in English translations almost simultaneously with their Polish originals and have become a living part of the American poetic scene. He has achieved the symbiosis of two cultures, two landscapes, two nations. His work crosses Polish and American cultural and linguistic boundaries.

SURVEY OF CRITICISM

The number of critical studies of Miłosz's work in Polish, English, and other languages continues to grow, and collections of critical essays can be found in special issues of numerous literary journals. Still valid, although slightly dated, is Rimma Volynska-Bogert's and Wojciech Zalewski's (1983) *Czesław Miłosz: An International Bibliography 1930–1980*. A penetrating insight into the poet's creative world is offered by Ewa Czarnecka and Aleksander Fiut (1987) in *Conversations with Czesław Miłosz* and by

Fiut's 1994 edition of *Czesława Miłosza autoportret przekorny*. More analytical in character and underscoring the multicultural character of Miłosz's poetry and prose are studies by Edward Możejko in his 1988 edition of *Between Anxiety and Hope: The Poetry and Writing of Czesław Miłosz*, and by Aleksander Fiut (1990).

Collections of critical essays can be found in special issues of literary journals devoted to Miłosz's works. Louis Iribarne (1999), in an article of an issue of *World Literature Today*, writes: "[T]he fact that a poet from the outer rim of Europe not only survived literary exile but was strengthened by it must be recorded as something of a phenomenon" (637). *Partisan Review* (Winter 1999) devoted an entire issue to the 1998 Miłosz International Festival, with poets from a number of countries discussing the poet's multiculturalism. In that issue, the American Robert Pinsky writes:

> This phenomenon—the importance of an Eastern European poet, and a poet who writes in a language never associated with great political, economic, or military power, for American poets younger than himself—has its own history. Intense engagement with Czesław Miłosz's poetry could be observed among young American poets before the 1980 Nobel Prize, before the days of Solidarity in Poland, before lines of Miłosz's were inscribed on a monument in Gdansk, before he was celebrated in a country where publication of his work and mention of his name were once forbidden. (145)

SELECTED BIBLIOGRAPHY

Works by Czesław Miłosz

Ocalenie. Warsaw: Czytelnik, 1945.

Zdobycie władzy. Paris: Instytut Literacki, 1955. [*The Seizure of Power*. Trans. Celina Wieniewska. New York: Criterion, 1955.]

Zniewolony umysł. Paris: Instytut Literacki, 1953. [*The Captive Mind*. Trans. Jane Zielenko. New York: Knopf, 1953.]

Dolina Issy. Paris: Instytut Literacki, 1955. [*The Issa Valley*. Trans. Louis Iribarne. New York: Farrar, Straus and Giroux, 1981.]

"Traktat poetycki." *Kultura* 6 (1956): 3–25; *Kultura* 1 (1957): 46–55.

Rodzinna Europa. Paris: Instytut Literacki, 1959. [*Native Realm: A Search for Self-Definition*. Trans. Catherine S. Leach. Garden City, N.Y.: Doubleday, 1968.]

The History of Polish Literature. London and New York: Macmillan, 1969.

Emperor of the Earth: Modes of Eccentric Vision. Berkeley: University of California Press, 1977.

"Notes on Exile." *Books Abroad* 50, no. 2 (Spring 1976): 283–84.

Ziemia Ulro. Paris: Instytut Literacki, 1977. [*The Land of Ulro*. Trans. Louis Iribarne. New York: Farrar, Straus and Giroux, 1984.]

Widzenia nad Zatoką San Francisco. Paris: Instytut Literacki, 1969. [*Visions from San Francisco Bay*. Trans. Richard Lourie. New York: Farrar, Straus and Giroux, 1982.]

Conversations with Czesław Miłosz. Ed. Ewa Czarnecka and Aleksander Fiut. Trans. Richard Lourie. San Diego, Calif.: Harcourt Brace Jovanovich, 1987.

The Collected Poems 1931–1987. Trans. Czesław Miłosz and various hands. New York: Ecco, 1988.

Between Anxiety and Hope: The Poetry and Writing of Czesław Miłosz. Ed. Edward Możejko. Edmonton, Canada: University of Alberta Press, 1988.

Czesława Miłosza autoportret przekorny. Ed. Aleksander Fiut. Kraków: Wydawnictwo Literackie, 1994.

To Begin Where I Am. Selected Essays. Ed. Bogdana Carpenter and Madeleine G. Levine. New York: Farrar, Straus and Giroux, 2001.

Selected Studies of Miłosz

Czarnecka, Ewa. *Podrózny swiata: rozmowy z Czesławem Miłoszem: komentarze.* New York: Bicentennial Publishing Corporation, 1983.

Fiut, Aleksander. *The Eternal Moment: The Poetry of Czesław Miłosz.* Trans. Theodisia S. Robertson. Berkeley: University of California Press, 1990.

Iribarne, Louis. "Lost in the 'Earth-Garden': The Exile of Czesław Miłosz." *World Literature Today* 73, no. 4 (Autumn 1999): 637–42.

Kwiatkowski, Jerzy, ed. *Poznawanie Miłosza: studia i szkice o twórczósci poety.* Kraków: Wydawnictwo Literackie, 1985.

Nathan, Leonard and Arthur Quinn. *The Poet's Work: An Introduction to Czesław Miłosz.* Cambridge: Harvard University Press, 1991.

Pinsky, Robert. "Introducing Czesław Miłosz to the audience at the Miłosz International Festival." *Partisan Review* 1 (Winter 1999): 145–47.

Riggan, William, ed. *World Literature Today* 73, no. 4 (Autumn 1999). Special issue devoted to Czesław Miłosz.

Volynska-Bogert, Rimma and Wojciech Zalewski. *Czesław Miłosz: An International Bibliography 1930–1980.* Ann Arbor: Department of Slavic Languages and Literatures, University of Michigan, 1983.

VILHELM MOBERG
(1898–1973)

Roger McKnight

BIOGRAPHY

The son of a humble militiaman, Vilhelm Moberg was above all a champion of the common people. He was born in the impoverished forest areas of the southern Swedish province of Småland, from which over 300,000 persons emigrated to North America between 1850 and 1930, seeking to escape famine and religious persecution. Moberg later recalled this area of long winters and uncertain agriculture as one in which books were rare, schools poor, and communications limited. From his childhood he remembered two major points of inspiration. One was the time-honored folk traditions of his home area. The other was the dream of America, where nearly his entire extended family had found new homes.

Driven by a youthful love of books, he emerged in the 1920s as one of the foremost proletarian writers in Sweden. During his career, which extended over fifty years, he produced 20 novels, 35 stage and radio dramas, 15 works of nonfiction, numerous essays, several autobiographical reminiscences, countless debate and travel articles, and a controversial (though unfinished) two-volume social history of Sweden. His career as a writer of fiction began only slowly, however. With barely five years of public schooling and several stints as a manual laborer behind him, Moberg enrolled, as a young man, at the Grimslöv adult high school only to have his education cut short by a nearly fatal bout of Spanish flu (1918). Thereafter he worked as a small-town journalist in southern Sweden. Unflagging in his energy, he set type and wrote articles by day and practiced the art of storytelling by night. His breakthroughs, both personal and professional, came in the 1920s. First was his marriage to Margareta Törnquist (1923), with whom he had five children and remained married until his death. Second came the publication of *Raskens, en soldatfamiljs historia* (1927), a novel depicting the lives of a professional militiaman's family.

Raskens established Moberg's reputation as a regional realist. It also gave him the economic freedom to move to Stockholm, where he and his family were to make their permanent home, even if he was there only sporadically in the 1950s. During the 1930s and 1940s, he continued developing his literary art, producing dramas, novels, and frequent essays on Swedish politics. Increasingly disillusioned with the machine age and urban life, he looked fondly in his writings back to rural Småland, where he saw (or imagined) a more pristine set of nonmaterialistic values. Initially a supporter of Social-Democratic reforms, Moberg also became critical of the party's failure to abolish the monarchy or dismantle the Swedish State Church. Ever the people's tribune, he was frequently embroiled in public debates over corruption in the bureaucracy, the national police force, and the royal house of Sweden.

In the late 1930s he held pacifist views regarding the threat of war. A trip to Finland during the Winter War of 1939 showed him firsthand the horrors of aggression, however. By the early 1940s he was a fearless critic of Nazism. This attitude resulted in his second masterpiece, the novel *Rid i natt!: Roman fra n varend 1650* (1941), a protest against dictatorship and foreign encroachment. With the filming of this novel, Moberg became a national celebrity among the general reading and viewing public, though he was often viewed with suspicion by established Swedish politicians, who carefully maintained a policy of wartime neutrality.

By war's end Moberg's thoughts increasingly drifted across the Atlantic. On one hand, he had tired of the Kingdom of Idyllia, as he ironically called Sweden. On the other, he dreamed of erecting a literary monument to his relatives who had settled in the United States. This dream turned what Moberg called a stay-at-home Swede into an inveterate traveler and an observer of America. Beginning in 1948, he crisscrossed America from New York to California, stopping frequently for historical research in Swedish settlements throughout the Midwest. By 1960 he had completed the renowned tetralogy of Emigrant Novels about Småland settlers in Minnesota, which established his international reputation. First envisioning personal fame and fortune in America, Moberg grew increasingly embittered at the conservative politics of his new land (especially the Joseph McCarthy communist hunts), and he returned to Sweden in 1955, admitting his attempt to become an American had failed and vowing to leave America out of his future plans.

Throughout the 1960s, Moberg remained a prolific writer. The novel *Din stund på jorden* (1963) attempted, in the life story of one aging immigrant, to bridge the psychological gap between the Old and New Worlds.

At the same time Moberg, from his bases in Sweden and various parts of Europe, spoke out against the American involvement in Vietnam. Though he claimed the opposite, he had long dreamed of a Nobel Prize for Literature, only to be denied it. As he aged, he had his wife, his work, and his love of the common people. While at work on his people's history of Sweden, he drowned in the sea near his home at Väddö, north of Stockholm.

MAJOR MULTICULTURAL THEMES

The Sweden of Moberg's youth and young manhood was a nation whose rulers emphasized unicultural concepts of one people, one language, and one religion. In the absence of significant racial or religious minorities, cultural debates thus often focused on class, regional, and generational differences. Those themes run through the writings of Moberg's pre-America period (before 1948). As a realistic portrayal, *Raskens* implicitly contrasts the habits of the rural folk to those of the propertied classes, who long had been the focus of Swedish letters. In Moberg's view, the ruling classes had given the commoners only the rudiments of education and no public voice as a conscious ploy to keep them as loyal, unquestioning subjects of the Crown. Thus *Raskens*, along with Moberg's so-called *allmogedramer* (peasant dramas) of the 1920s and 1930s, helped to bring into focus the cultural clash between the wealthy and working classes at a time when Social-Democratic reforms were gaining headway across Scandinavia.

Regional and generational themes are also present in Moberg's earlier works. His novels *Långt från landsvägen* (1929) and *De knutna händerna; skadespel i fem akter* (1930) deal with the struggles of the main character, Adolf from Ulvaskog, to keep his farm and family intact as his grown children abandon rural life and move to cities, where industry and urban life beckon. Unable to accept this generation gap or the introduction of new mechanized farming techniques, Adolf suffers a psychological breakdown, which results in his murdering his last child at home, rather than allowing her to move to Stockholm. Through the years Moberg was to present these themes of differing regional and generational cultures often and in various guises, most notably perhaps in his Knut Toring trilogy. *Sänkt sedebetyg* (1935), *Sömnlös* (1937), and *Giv oss jorden!* (1939) deal with Knut Toring, a son of the land who is transplanted into Stockholm, the same concrete jungle that had led one of Adolf from Ulvaskog's daughters into prostitution. The city has a deleterious psychological effect on Toring, who seeks to rebuild his life by returning to the countryside. Even there, however, modernity has already made intrusions with problematic results for the farming culture.

Moberg's works prior to the late 1940s depict a Swedish nation of differing cultures: working class versus upper class, rural versus urban, and the older versus the younger generation. Moberg found equally firm ground for multicultural theme-making in his Emigrant Novels. From the first volume *Utvandrarna* (1949) to the final *Sista brevet till Sverige* (1959), he developed themes reminiscent of those from his earlier works. Much of the thematic framework is based on irony. In emigrating, Moberg's protagonist Karl Oskar Nilsson ignores the feelings of his father and his wife Kristina that he is abandoning an ancient Swedish birthright. Karl Oskar argues that America is the land of material opportunity. His children will grow up to thank him for taking them there. However, just as he had left his own father behind in Sweden, Karl Oskar's children in Minnesota eventually marry into other ethnic groups and leave their aging father behind on his frontier farm. Thus the theme of children abandoning the traditions of their elders is repeated on American soil.

Racial or interethnic cultural themes also exist in the emigrant narrative. Oppressed and deprived of a public voice in the Old World, Karl Oskar and his group escape the tyranny of Sweden and find land that guarantees them future well-being in America. But the assertion that immigrants in America gained their prosperity by taking the land from its rightful owners, the Native Americans, is one that Karl Oskar is faced with accepting or rationalizing away. Implicit in this clash of cultural values is the idea that the humble immigrants from Europe, in their hunger for land, repeat Old World cycles of injustice against increasingly marginalized native minorities in America. Moberg also shows a sensitivity to gender roles in his Emigrant Novels. He delves into the psyche of the devout, homesick Kristina, while also showing the rapid transformation of the reviled prostitute Ulrika into a forward-looking, respected American woman.

Moberg published several nonfictional works reflecting his own American experiences. In *Den okända släkten* (1950) and the posthumous *Att upptäcka Amerika: 1948–49* (1995), he contrasted the material success of Swedish Americans to their intellectual narrowness. Likewise he was taken aback at the political conservativeness and religious intolerance of the Midwest, which he contrasted to the liberal attitudes of Europe and California, his favorite American state. In "Romanen om Utvandrarromanen" (1968) Moberg discussed at length his own failed attempt at assimilation in American society.

SURVEY OF CRITICISM

Though much has been written about Moberg's authorship, few in-depth analyses of his themes exist. Gunnar Eidevall (1974, 1976) provides a far-ranging examination of Moberg's literary methods. Magnus von Platen (1978) has given a thorough description of Moberg's early years and the growth of themes out of his youthful experiences. Philip

Holmes (1980), the most thorough English-language discussant, sees a biblical anchoring in Moberg, including an exodus theme in the Emigrant Novels. Some of the best material is in unpublished dissertations or articles. Roland Thorstensson (1974) has shown the grassroots nature of Moberg's drama, while Rochelle Wright (1975) has described the theme of America as "a shadow kingdom" in Moberg. Roger McKnight (1992, 1998) has discussed the ethnic and generational differences in the Emigrant Novels, including Moberg's depiction of the Dakota War of 1862.

SELECTED BIBLIOGRAPHY

Works by Moberg

Raskens, en soldatfamiljs historia (1927). Stockholm: Bonnier, 1983.

Långt från landsvägen (1929). Stockholm: Bonnier, 1946.

De knutna händerna; skadespel i fem akter. Stockholm: Bonnier, 1930.

Sänkt sedebetyg. Stockholm: Bonnier, 1935. [*Memory of Youth.* Trans. E. Björkman. New York: Simon and Schuster, 1937.]

Sömnlös. Stockholm: Bonnier, 1937.

Giv oss jorden! Stockholm: Bonnier, 1939. [*The Earth is Ours!* Trans. E. Björkman. New York: Simon and Schuster, 1940.]

Rid i natt! Roman fra n varend 1650. Stockholm: Bonnier, 1941. [*Ride This Night!* Trans. H. Alexander. New York: Doubleday and Doran, 1943.]

Utvandrarna: Roman. Stockholm: Bonnier, 1949. [*The Emigrants.* Trans. Gustaf Lannestock. St. Paul: Minnesota Historical Society, 1995.]

Den okända släkten. Stockholm: Bonnier, 1950. [*The Unknown Swedes.* Trans. and ed. Roger McKnight. Carbondale: Southern Illinois University Press, 1988.]

Invandrarna: Roman. Stockholm: Bonnier, 1952. [*Unto a Good Land.* Trans. Gustaf Lannestock. St. Paul: Minnesota Historical Society, 1995.]

Nybyggarna. Stockholm: Bonnier, 1956. [*The Settlers.* Trans. Gustaf Lannestock. St. Paul: Minnesota Historical Society, 1995.]

Sista brevet till Sverige. Stockholm: Bonnier, 1959. [*The Last Letter Home.* Trans. Gustaf Lannestock. St. Paul: Minnesota Historical Society, 1995.]

Din stund på jorden. Stockholm: Bonnier, 1963. [*A Time on Earth.* Trans. Naomi Walford. New York: Simon and Schuster; London: Heinemann, 1965.]

"Romanen om Utvandrarromanen," in *Berättelser ur min levnad.* Stockholm: Bonnier, 1968.

Att upptäcka Amerika: 1948–49. Ed. Gunnar Eidevall. Stockholm: Carlssons, 1995.

Selected Studies of Moberg

Delblanc, Sven. "Den omöjliga flykten." *Bonniers Litterära Magasin*, 62 (1973): 264–69.

Eidevall, Gunnar. *Vilhelm Mobergs emigrantepos. Studier i verkets tillkomsthistoria.* Stockholm: Norstedt, 1974.

———. *Berättaren Vilhelm Moberg.* Stockholm: Pan / Norstedt, 1976.

Holmes, Philip. *Vilhelm Moberg.* Boston: Twayne, 1980.

McKnight, Roger. "The New Columbus: Vilhelm Moberg Confronts American Society." *Scandinavian Studies* 64 (Summer 1992): 356–89.

———. "Vilhelm Moberg, the Emigrant Novels, and Their Changing Readers." *The Swedish-American Historical Quarterly* 49 (July 1998): 245–56.

Thorstensson, Roland. *Vilhelm Moberg, a Dramatist for the People*. Ph.D. diss., University of Washington, 1974.

von Platen, Magnus. *Den Unge Vilhelm Moberg*. Stockholm: Bonnier, 1978.

Wright, Rochelle. *Vilhelm Moberg's Image of America*. Ph.D. diss., University of Washington, 1975.

HENRY DE MONTHERLANT
(1895–1972)

Lucille Frackman Becker

BIOGRAPHY

Henry Millon de Montherlant was born in Paris on April 21, 1896. His father's family, which was said to have originated in Spain, had settled centuries before in Picardy on the northwestern coast of France. It was from his father that Montherlant inherited the serious, arrogant, somewhat taciturn side of his character. His belief in his Spanish ancestry may also account for the constant interest he showed in that land of violent contrasts and extreme temperaments. Spain provided the background for several of Montherlant's novels and plays. His mother, a granddaughter of Count Henry de Riancey, a nineteenth-century champion of the church and monarchy, transmitted to her son her zest for life and her gaiety. A strong influence was also exerted on Montherlant by his devout maternal grandmother, in whose home he lived until he was 27 years old. Pierre Sipriot writes in his biography, titled *Montherlant sans masque*, that it was to this pious noblewoman that Montherlant confided his homosexual adventures.

During the early years Montherlant spent at the *écoles* Janson de Sailly and Saint-Pierre in Neuilly, two important events influenced his artistic development. The first was his discovery of ancient Rome on reading Henryk Sienkiewicz's *Quo vadis?*, a book that stimulated his interest in classical antiquity with its love of beauty and frank sensuality. More than fifty years later, in the postface to his play *La guerre civile* (1965)—which takes place in the camps of Caesar and Pompey three weeks before the defeat of Pompey by Caesar at Pharsala—Montherlant stressed the primacy of classical antiquity in his work. The influence of classical studies counterbalanced his Catholic upbringing, producing throughout his life and work an alternation between pagan sensuality and Christian asceticism.

The second important influence of these early years was his introduction to bullfighting in Bayonne (in southwestern France) in 1909. His constant desire for new experiences led him to the bullring in Spain in an attempt to recapture there the "hours of poetry" he had lived in the sports stadium. He fought bulls on Spanish stock breeding ranches in 1923 and again in 1925, when he was severely wounded by a bull. In the same year, he wrote the lyrical, autobiographical novel *Les bestiaires* (1926), which celebrates the mysteries of the cult of bullfighting, a religious sacrifice inherited from the pagan cult of Mithra, the Sun God. Combined with the mystical aspects, the novel contains realistic and detailed descriptions of both the bullfight and its milieu. In Montherlant's later novel, *Le chaos et la nuit* (1963), set during the Spanish dictatorship of Franco, the focal point again is the bullfight, a microcosm of all human existence.

In 1911, Montherlant entered the *collège* Saint-Croix de Neuilly to prepare for his *baccalauréat*. His experiences there inspired the essays of *La relève du matin*, published at the author's expense in 1920; the play *La ville dont le prince est un enfant* (1951); and the novel *Les garçons* (1969). The years from 1912 to 1914, Montherlant's "worldly period," have been described by him as years of absolute mediocrity. His frequentation of society confirmed his distaste for the hypocrisy and banality of bourgeois existence. In 1917, after the death of his mother, Montherlant enlisted in the army, refusing a commission. Although assigned to limited service for reasons of ill health, he requested active duty, in the course of which he was wounded in the back by shell fragments. After his release from the hospital, he became an interpreter for the American army and remained with them until he was demobilized in September 1919. His wartime experiences are recounted in the autobiographical novel *Le songe* (1922).

Montherlant turned to sports after the war in an attempt to recapture the violent activity and virile comradeship of the war years. He explained that sports were war from which the horror had been removed, but where the philosophy remained the same—human is pitted against human and not against ideas. In 1924, he published the two volumes of *Les olympiques, Le paradis à l'ombre des épées* and *Les onze devant la porte dorée*, a series of stories, poems, essays, and a short one-act play dedicated to soccer and track. Sports represented for Montherlant an exclusive "order" that continued the orders of school and war.

After the death of his grandmother in 1925, Montherlant felt free to break all ties with France and devote himself solely to realizing his desires. His travels, which were to last for more than seven years, took him to Italy, Spain, and North Africa, with occasional short trips back to Paris. The literary result of these travels was the trilogy *Les voyageurs traqués* (*Aux fontaines du désir*, 1927; *La petite infante de Castille, historiette*, 1929; and *Un voyageur solitaire est un diable*, 1955), described by the author as a diary of the crisis in the life of a thirty-year-old man who stops to take stock of his life "midway between the crisis of adolescence and the one of old age" (*Mors et vita* [1946 ed.], 146). He also wrote a long novel in 1930, *La Rose de sable*, attacking the abuses of French colonialism in North Africa. He decided not to publish the work because he felt that it would be detrimental to French interests, but published the love story later, in 1954, under the title *L'histoire d'amour de "La Rose de sable."* After a few years, he realized that the life he was leading made him no happier than his former existence and in 1936 he returned definitively to Paris.

While his novel *Les célibataires* (1934) was awarded the Grand Prix de Littérature by the French Academy, the tetralogy *Les jeunes filles* (1936–39) is considered his major work of fiction. He turned to the theater in 1942 with the historical drama *La reine morte; ou, Comment on tue les femmes*, set in fourteenth-century Portugal. Among his most important plays with exotic locales are *Le maître de Santiago* (1947) and *Le cardinal d'Espagne* (1960), both set in sixteenth-century Spain, and *Malatesta* (1946), which takes place in Renaissance Italy.

When the war ended, Montherlant was censured by the National Committee of Writers, a Resistance organization, for articles written under the occupation in which he exalted the swastika, symbol of German virility and power. Nonetheless, 15 years later he was elected to the French Academy (1960). In 1972, fearing blindness, he emulated the Roman Petronius, whom he had first encountered as a youth in the pages of *Quo vadis?*, and committed suicide.

MAJOR MULTICULTURAL THEMES

In Montherlant's work, France is always placed in juxtaposition to another country that becomes more or less the symbol of all the virtues France lacks. The first and foremost of these pairs is that of France and Spain. The Spanish people incarnate, for Montherlant, the grandeur of the warrior's creed as opposed to the mediocrity of the "shopgirls' morality" infecting France. The Spanish are seigneurs, imbued with the principle of "useless service" that postulates action in full knowledge of the uselessness of such action; Don Quixote and Sancho Panza, the dreamer and the realist, are emblematic of the idealism that requires service and the realism that knows that this service is useless.

Spain, for Montherlant, was also the country of alternation between sensual pleasure and asceticism, an alternation that affirms the fundamental goodness of all things in nature and the necessity for humans to taste of every experience in order to find happiness. Life, in all of its manifestations, is a force that does not have to be justified, just lived to the fullest. Montherlant found in North Africa, as well as in Spain, a liberation of all the senses far from the rigid constraints of French morality. It was there, too, that he came in contact with colonialism, an evil that he attacked not only in *L'histoire d'amour de "La Rose de sable,"* but also in the play *Le cardinal d'Espagne*, in which the protagonist condemns the Spanish exploitation of the Indians in South America.

SURVEY OF CRITICISM

Lucille Frackman Becker, in her literary biography (1970), writes that the relationship between the French career officer in North Africa and his fifteen-year-old Arab mistress in *L'histoire d'amour de "La Rose de sable"* is symbolic not only of the subjugation of one race by another, but also of the relationship between conqueror and conquered inherent in the male-female relationship. In André Marisel's view (1966), Montherlant's distress at the plight of the native population in North Africa and his desire to go to the aid of the oppressed Arabs and Kabyles classify him as perhaps the first anticolonialist writer. The critic Jean Joubert (1959) writes that every period and every civilization has its own myths that permit it to breathe something other than the rarified air of reality. Among these myths, exoticism (particularly that of Spain) seems to have profoundly marked not only Montherlant, but also the entire period between the beginning of the nineteenth century and the middle of the twentieth. Pierre Sipriot (1982) explains that Africa, for Montherlant, as for Flaubert and Gide, was antiquity regained with its frank sensuality and emphasis on the inner life.

SELECTED BIBLIOGRAPHY

Works by Montherlant

La relève du matin. Paris: Société littéraire de France, 1920.

Le songe. Paris: Grasset, 1922.

Les olympiques: Le paradis à l'ombre des épées; Les onze devant la porte dorée (1924). 2nd ed. Paris: Grasset, 1938.

Les bestiaires. Paris: Gallimard, 1926.

Aux fontaines du désir. Paris: Grasset, 1927.

La petite infante de Castille, historiette. Paris: Grasset, 1929.

Mors et vita. Paris: Grasset, 1932; Paris: Gallimard, 1946.

Les célibataires. Paris: Grasset, 1934.

Les jeunes filles (tetralogy). *Les jeunes filles, Pitié pour les femmes.* Paris: Grasset, 1936. *Le démon du bien.* Paris: Grasset, 1937. *Les lépreuses.* Paris: Grasset, 1939.

La reine morte; ou, Comment on tue les femmes, drame en trois actes; suivi de Régner après sa mort, drame de Luis Velez de Guevara. Paris: Gallimard, 1942.

Malatesta; Pièce en quatre actes (1946). Paris: Gallimard, 1948.

Le maître de Santiago; Trois actes. Paris: Gallimard, 1947.

La ville dont le prince est un enfant; Trois actes. Paris: Gallimard, 1951.
L'histoire d'amour de "La Rose de sable": Roman. Paris: Plon, 1954.
Un voyageur solitaire est un diable. Monaco: Éditions du Rocher, 1955.
Le cardinal d'Espagne; Pièce en trois actes. Paris: Gallimard, 1960.
Le chaos et la nuit. Paris: Gallimard, 1963.
La guerre civile; Pièce en trois actes. Paris: Gallimard, 1965.
Les garçons. Paris: Gallimard, 1969.

Selected Studies of Montherlant

Becker, Lucille Frackman. *Henry de Montherlant: A Critical Biography.* Carbondale: Southern Illinois University Press, 1970.

Corgan, Margaret M. "The Spanish Vein in the Works of Henry de Montherlant." Dissertation Abstracts, Ann Arbor, Mich.: 1968.

Joubert, Jean. "Montherlant et la tauromachie." In *Montherlant vu par des jeunes de 17 à 27 ans.* Ed. Jean-Jacques Thierry, 39–51. Paris: La Table Ronde, 1959.

Lecerf, Emile. *Montherlant ou la guerre permanente.* Brussels: Éditions de la Toison d'Or, 1944.

Marisel, André. *Montherlant.* Paris: Éditions Universitaires, 1966.

Michel, Jacqueline. "*Le Cardinal d'Espagne:* Jeux et masques de la peur." *Revue de littératures française et comparée.* Pau, France (November 3, 1994): 175–80.

O'Flaherty, Patricia. "*La rose de sable:* une déclaration politique inspirée par l'amour." *Australian Journal of French Studies* 25, no. 3 (1988): 261–66.

Perruchot, Henri. *La haine des masques: Montherlant, Camus, Shaw.* Paris: La Table Ronde, 1955.

Sipriot, Pierre. *Montherlant sans masque.* Paris: Robert Laffont, 1982.

Sito-Alba, Manuel. *Montherlant et l'Espagne: Les sources hispaniques de "La reine morte."* Paris: C. Klincksieck, 1978.

VLADIMIR NABOKOV
(1899–1977)

Kristen Welsh

BIOGRAPHY

"I probably had the happiest childhood imaginable," Nabokov said in a 1971 interview filmed in Montreux, Switzerland (Interview with Kurt Hoffman and Jochen Richter, 1971). In addition to being happy, that childhood was multilingual, establishing the foundation for his artistic career. Using Russian, English, and French, Nabokov wrote 17 novels, as well as many short stories, poems, plays, reviews, critical essays, translations, chess problems, scientific papers on lepidoptera, and several versions of an autobiography. Selections from his correspondence have been published, and two volumes have been created from his university lectures. He translated Lewis Carroll's *Alice's Adventures in Wonderland* into Russian (1923) and Aleksandr Pushkin's *Evgenij Onegin* into English (1964). Nabokov also translated Nabokov, often working with his son, Dmitri, to *English* his Russian works.

Nabokov was born at his family's home in St. Petersburg. He grew up in the city and on his family's country estate, where he and his younger brother Sergei were looked after by an English nanny, a French governess, and finally a village schoolmaster who taught them to read and write in Russian. Nabokov enrolled in the progressive Tenishev school in St. Petersburg in 1911, finishing his graduation exams there against the backdrop of the October Revolution (1917). Shortly thereafter, his father, Vladimir Dmitrievich Nabokov, a member of the Constituent Assembly, sent his two eldest sons to the Crimea in order to protect them from conscription into the Bolshevik army. The rest of the family soon joined them. The Nabokovs then fled to London via Athens in April

1919. Vladimir matriculated at Trinity College, Cambridge, taking a degree in French and Russian in 1922. His studies were interrupted when his father was killed in Berlin while shielding his political foe, Pavel Miliukov, from an assassination attempt on March 28, 1922.

After Cambridge, Nabokov returned to Berlin, where he continued to write the poems and stories he had been publishing in the émigré press since 1920, supporting himself by tutoring and giving tennis lessons. He married Véra Slonim in 1925 and published his first novel, *Mashen'ka: Roman*, the following year. By the mid-1920s, the center of the Russian emigration had moved from Berlin to Paris. Nabokov, however, chose to stay in Berlin, in part because he felt that the daily use of French, a language he knew almost as a native, would threaten his Russian. Through the 1920s and 1930s, he built his reputation as one of the finest novelists among the Russian émigrés and engaged in intense polemics over the purpose and validity of Russian émigré literature and over his lifelong policy of political disengagement. Nabokov, his wife, and young son left Berlin for France in 1937, and in 1940 they were able to leave France for the United States. In 1938, he had completed *Dar,* his Russian masterpiece that, from 1937, had been published serially in the émigré paper *Sovremennye zapiski* (Paris). (A complete Russian version of the text appeared only in 1952). *The Real Life of Sebastian Knight*, completed in 1939 and published in 1941, marked his switch from Russian to English.

Nabokov worked at the Museum of Comparative Zoology at Harvard University, conducting research on lepidoptera (1941–46). He taught literature and Russian language at Wellesley College, Harvard University, and Cornell University (1941–59), retiring from teaching after the commercial success of *Lolita* (1955), which enabled him to move to Europe. He and his wife settled permanently in Montreux, Switzerland (1962), where he continued to write and to collect butterflies until his death in 1977.

MAJOR MULTICULTURAL THEMES

Nabokov's aristocratic, multilingual parents provided their children with a large, decidedly international library, and Nabokov loved English and American classics as a child. His exceptional education gave him a trilingual flexibility and an arsenal of cultural allusions that he cherished throughout his career. Asked during a 1971 interview about his ability to write in three languages, Nabokov identified its disadvantage as "the inability to keep up with their ever-changing slang" and its advantage as "the ability to render an exact nuance by shifting from the language I am now using to a brief burst of French or to a soft rustle of Russian" (Interview with Paul Sufrin, 1971, 184). In even his earliest works, these multicultural and multilingual aspects play an important role, whether Nabokov is portraying a boardinghouse full of Russian émigrés maladjusting to life in Berlin (*Mashen'ka: Roman*, 1926), or ending a story with a brilliant trilingual pun ("Lik," 1939). Like *Mashen'ka: Roman*, most of Nabokov's Russian novels feature Russian characters making their way through European exile. While these works use precise details to convey the poverty of émigré life, they are, above all, novels about memory, about time and displacement, and about the role of art in transcending mortal existence. In *Zashchita Luzhina* (1930), a Russian chess prodigy negotiates the parallel planes of his life and the chessboard, with starkly different results. *Podvig* (1932) follows another young émigré, Martin Edelweiss, who decides to slip secretly into Soviet Russia. *Priglashenie na kazn'* (1938), often read as a critique of totalitarianism as practiced under the Third Reich and in the Soviet state, had, according to Nabokov, much more to do with the history of the French Revolution. Ultimately, it is a story of individuality, integrity, and art. *Dar*, Nabokov's last novel written in Russian, follows a young émigré living in Berlin as he transforms himself from a poet overshadowed by his Russian past into a novelist who uses his Russian heritage to nourish a new literary form that is his alone.

Nabokov began his American period with *Bend Sinister* (1947), by which time he had already become a U.S. citizen (1945). Writing to his publisher about the first version of his autobiography, *Conclusive Evidence: A Memoir* (1951), Nabokov emphasized this latest multicultural transformation: "The new blurb [for the autobiography] seems very satisfactory. I only think that the fact that I am an American citizen and an American writer should have been stressed" (letter to Harper and Bros., 1950; cited in Boyd 1990, 3). *Lolita*, a novel that aroused controversy for its perceived obscene content, conveyed Nabokov's immersion in American culture better than any jacket blurb could. The novel was banned in France in 1956 at the request of the British government and was published in the United States only in 1958, where it promptly sold 100,000 copies. In this work, Humbert Humbert, a middle-aged European émigré, pursues twelve-year-old Dolores Haze through a maze of American motels, teen magazines, and his own confused typology of the nymphet. Nabokov filters the details of American life in the early 1950s—from Charlotte Haze's pink toilet cozy to the bizarre curriculum of a private girls' school—through the émigré's powerful lens, portraying America in a light at once sharply critical and deeply affectionate. *Pnin* (1957) chronicles the foibles of Professor Timofey Pnin, a Russian who teaches at a small American college. *Pale Fire* (1962) brings together characters of various national origins, intellectual abilities, and levels of sanity. After *Pnin*, *Pale Fire* represents a return to the metaliterary territory that is more typical of Nabokov's other novels. *Ada; or, Ardor: A Family Chronicle* (1969) describes the nearly lifelong, multinational, multilingual passion between Van Veen and Ada Veen, placing them within an environment that is not so much multicultural as multiterrestrial.

SURVEY OF CRITICISM

Many critics focus on Nabokov's multilingualism. Jerzy Durczak (1993) takes a broader approach. He examines multiculturalism in Nabokov's life from early childhood, the dearth of analysis of the exile's life within Nabokov's works (though he cites *Pnin* as an exception), and the constant separation between Nabokov and his new homelands. Durczak ultimately describes a multiculturalism that is, like so many elements of Nabokov's work, peculiarly Nabokovian; not only is Nabokov an outsider among exiles, he is a multicultural writer unlike any other.

Alfred Appel (1974) discusses the idiom of American popular culture, suggesting that Nabokov does not quite master it in early works from his American period, but that he excels in *Lolita* and in the later works set in America. Galya Diment (1993) analyzes Nabokov's autobiography, considering him alongside James Joyce, Marina Tsvetaeva, and Joseph Brodsky. She retreats from the analytic mode that emphasizes Nabokov's anglophilic childhood, suggesting instead that his use of English that Diment terms "a tongue of 'alienation'" (352) for his memoirs represents a critical step in providing the distance that enables Nabokov and other writers to create memorial from memory (357). Paul Giles (2000) writes about the structural and thematic resonance between *Lolita* and the American Studies movement, both of which came into being in the early 1950s. Discussing the "bizarre and paradoxical relationship" between the novel and the United States (66), Giles reads Nabokov against the background of American Transcendentalism and the cold war, suggesting that Humbert Humbert attempts "to aestheticize America" (50), while the novel itself both reflects and parodies American mythologies and their self-conscious restructuring in the postwar era (42).

SELECTED BIBLIOGRAPHY

Works by Nabokov

Ania v stranie chudes (1923). [*Alice's Adventures in Wonderland*, by Lewis Carroll. Trans. Vladimir Nabokov. New York: Dover, 1976.]

Mashen'ka: Roman (1926). [*Mary: A Novel*. Trans. Michael Glenny in collaboration with Vladimir Nabokov. New York: McGraw-Hill, 1970.]

Zashchita Luzhina (1930). [*The Defense: A Novel*. Trans. Michael Scammell in collaboration with Vladimir Nabokov. London: Weidenfeld and Nicolson, 1964.]

Podvig (1932). [*Glory: A Novel*. Trans. Dmitri Nabokov in collaboration with Vladimir Nabokov. New York: McGraw Hill, 1971.]

Dar (1937–1938). New York: Izdatel'stvo imeni Chekhova (Chekhov Publishing House), 1952. [*The Gift: A Novel*. Trans. Michael Scammell in collaboration with Vladimir Nabokov. New York: Putnam, 1963.]

Priglashenie na kazn' (1938). [*Invitation to a Beheading*. Trans. Dmitri Nabokov in collaboration with Vladimir Nabokov. New York: Putnam, 1959.]

"Lik." *Russkie zapiski* 14 (1939): 3–27. ["Lik." Trans. Dmitri Nabokov in collaboration with Vladimir Nabokov (1964). Repr. in *The Stories of Vladimir Nabokov*. New York: Alfred A. Knopf, 1995.]

The Real Life of Sebastian Knight. Norfolk, Conn.: New Directions, 1941.

Bend Sinister. New York: Henry Holt, 1947.

Conclusive Evidence: A Memoir. New York: Harper and Bros., 1951.

Lolita. New York: Putnam, 1955.

Pnin. Garden City, N.Y.: Doubleday, 1957.

Pale Fire. New York: Berkley, 1962.

Eugene Onegin: A Novel in Verse by Aleksandr Pushkin. Trans. With commentary by Vladimir Nabokov. Princeton, N.J.: Princeton University Press, 1964; rev. ed., 1975.

Speak, Memory: An Autobiography Revisited. New York: Putnam, 1966.

Ada; or, Ardor: A Family Chronicle. New York: Mc Graw-Hill, 1969.

Interview with Paul Sufrin, September 8, 1971, for *Swiss Broadcast*, European and Overseas Service. In Vladimir Nabokov, *Strong Opinions*, 183–84 (excerpts). New York: McGraw-Hill, 1973.

Interview with Kurt Hoffman and Jochen Richter, Montreux, Switzerland, September/October 1971. Broadcast by Bayerischer Rundfunk, München, Bayern III, May 26, 1972 and July 7, 1977.

Strong Opinions. New York: Mc Graw-Hill, 1973.

Lectures on Literature. Ed. Fredson Bowers. Intro. John Updike. New York: Harcourt Brace Jovanovich, 1980.

Lectures on Russian Literature. Ed. Fredson Bowers. New York: Harcourt Brace Jovanovich, 1981.

Selected Studies of Nabokov

Appel, Alfred, Jr. "The Road to Lolita, or the Americanization of an Émigré." *Journal of Modern Literature* 4, no. 1 (1974): 3–31.

Beaujour, Elizabeth Klosty. *Alien Tongues: Bilingual Russian Writers of the "First" Emigration*. Ithaca, N.Y.: Cornell University Press, 1989.

———. "Translation and Self-Translation." In *The Garland Companion to Vladimir Nabokov*. Ed. Vladimir Alexandrov, 714–24. New York: Garland Publishing, Inc., 1995.

Boyd, Brian. *Vladimir Nabokov: The Russian Years*. Princeton, N.J.: Princeton University Press, 1990.

———. *Vladimir Nabokov: The American Years*. Princeton, N.J.: Princeton University Press, 1991.

Diment, Galya. "English as Sanctuary: Nabokov's and Brodsky's Autobiographical Writings." *Slavic and East European Journal* 37, no. 3 (1993): 346–61.

———. "Vladimir Nabokov and the art of autobiography." In *Nabokov and His Fiction: New Perspectives*. Ed. Julian W. Connolly, 36–53. Cambridge: Cambridge University Press, 1999.

Durczak, Jerzy. "Nabokov's *Speak, Memory* as Multicultural Autobiography." *Lubelskie materialy neofilologiczne* 17 (1993): 15–28.

Foster, John Burt, Jr. *Nabokov's Art of Memory and European Modernism*. Princeton, N.J.: Princeton University Press, 1993.

Giles, Paul. "Virtual Eden: Lolita, Pornography, and the Perversions of American Studies." *Journal of American Studies* 34, no. 1 (2000): 41–66.

Grayson, Jane. *Nabokov Translated: A Comparison of Nabokov's Russian and English Prose.* Oxford: Oxford University Press, 1977.

Milbauer, Asher Z. *Transcending Exile: Conrad, Nabokov, I. B. Singer.* Miami: Florida International University Press, 1985.

Nassar, Joseph. "Transformations in Exile: The Multilingual Exploits of Nabokov's Pnin and Kinbote." *Visible Language* 27 (1993): 253–72.

Rosengrant, Judson. "Bilingual Style in Nabokov's Autobiography." *Style* 29, no. 1 (Spring 1995): 108–27.

V.S. NAIPAUL
(1932–)

Maria Antonietta Saracino

BIOGRAPHY

"My background is at once exceedingly simple and exceedingly confused," declared Sir V(idiadhar) S(urajprasad) Naipaul in his Nobel lecture of December 7, 2001. "I was born in Trinidad, a small island in the mouth of the great Orinoco river of Venezuela. So Trinidad is not strictly of South America, and not strictly of the Caribbean" (Nobel lecture, 2001).

A true child of many worlds, one of the most important voices in the history of contemporary literature in English, but also a controversial one, V. S. Naipaul was born on August 17, 1932, in Chaguanas, a village not far from Port of Spain, the capital city of Trinidad. His family was of Indian Brahmin origin, and of Nepalese origin on his father's side. His Hindu grandfather had emigrated to the Caribbean from west India as an indentured servant, as often occurred after 1880. People indentured themselves for five years to serve in the estates, at the end of which time they were given a small piece of land or a passage back to India.

His father, Seepersad Naipaul, was a correspondent for the *Trinidad Guardian*, with literary aspirations later inherited by the son, who received his education at Queen's Royal College, Port of Spain. He was awarded a Trinidad government scholarship in 1950 that allowed him to study literature at University College, Oxford, where he graduated in 1953. While at Oxford he met an English woman, Patricia Hale, whom he married in 1955. Naipaul started his career as a freelance writer for the British Broadcasting Corporation (BBC), hosting the program *Caribbean Voices*; he also has been a regular contributor to the literary journal

New Statesman. Since 1950, although traveling extensively, he has lived in England. *Miguel Street* (1959) was awarded the Somerset Maugham Award in 1961, the year in which he received a grant from the Trinidad government to travel to the Caribbean. The book represents a sort of farewell to Port of Spain; it pays homage to the colorful characters of his childhood, to those men and women whose lives he used to observe as a child, from the verandah of his house. "One day," Naipaul recalls in "Reading & Writing" (1999), "I began to see what my material might be: the city street from whose mixed life we had held aloof, and the country life before that, with the ways and manners of a remembered India. It seemed easy and obvious when it had been found; but it had taken me four years to see it. Almost at the same time came the language, the tone, the voice for that material. It was as if voice and matter and form were part of one another" (16). Since then he has published more than 12 works of fiction and 11 volumes of nonfiction, revolving mainly around the theme of the encounter between cultures, religions, and beliefs.

Naipaul is the recipient of many literary prizes in addition to the Nobel: the 1958 Llewellyn Rhys Memorial Prize for his first novel *The Mystic Masseur* (1957); the 1971 Booker Prize for *In A Free State*, three novellas about exile (1971); the T. S. Eliot Award for Creative Writing in 1986; and the first David Cohen British Literature Prize, for his lifetime work, in 1993. He holds honorary doctorates from various colleges and universities and was knighted by Queen Elizabeth II in 1990. After the death of his first wife in 1996, he married Nadira Alvi, a Pakistani journalist.

MAJOR MULTICULTURAL THEMES

Set in Trinidad, Naipaul's first novels focus on the encounter between different communities, as in *A House for Mr Biswas* (1961), regarded by many as one of his best works of fiction, in which the protagonist is modeled on the author's father. It is an imaginative account of the Indian experience in Trinidad, the author's birthplace but also the place in which, as a child, he had perceived himself as "surrounded by areas of darkness. . . . When I became a writer those areas of darkness around me as a child became my subjects" (Nobel lecture, 2001). A few years after the success of *A House for Mr Biswas*, Naipaul went to India, and his reaction was one of sheer disappointment. The country was far from the one that his forefathers had brought with them in their memories, the one that they could, as it were, "unroll like a carpet on the flat land" (Nobel lecture, 2001). The India he saw was a subject country, a place of poverty, the one from which his grandfather had had to escape in the late nineteenth century. "It was to this personal India that I went, when the time came. . . . But nothing had prepared me for the dereliction I saw. No other country I saw had so many layers of wretchedness, and few countries were as populous. I felt I was in a continent where, separate from the rest of the world, a mysterious calamity had occurred" ("The Writer and India," 14). Over the years, the many contrasting aspects of contemporary India became the subject of books such as *An Area of Darkness* (1964); *India: A Wounded Civilization* (1977); and *India: A Million Mutinies Now* (1990).

A narrator whose entire adult life had been spent in countries where he felt a stranger could not, as a writer, go beyond that experience. His sense of alienation and of responsibility as a postcolonial writer are the object of *The Mimic Men* (1967). The issues of colonialism and of the impact of emerging nationalism on the so-called Third World are given voice, with increasing pessimism, in *Guerrillas* (1975) and in *A Bend in the River* (1979), a novel set in Uganda, often compared to Joseph Conrad's *Heart of Darkness*. In his travel books, Naipaul has also dealt extensively with the theme of religious conflicts, as well as with that of Muslim fundamentalism in non-Arab countries such as Indonesia, Iran, Malaysia, and Pakistan in *Among the Believers: An Islamic Journey* (1981), and in *Beyond Belief. Islamic Excursions Among Converted Peoples* (1998).

SURVEY OF CRITICISM

Although generally in agreement about the exceptional literary qualities of Naipaul's work, scholars and critics nonetheless have at times disputed his pessimistic and, in their opinion, unfair portraits of the Indian and the Muslim worlds. Salman Rushdie (1997), in his introductory essay to an anthology of contemporary Indian writing, regrets the omission of V. S. Naipaul--though regarded as one of the most important voices in the history of modern literature—due to the fact that his harsh response to India in three nonfictional works had irritated too many Indian critics. In Rushdie's opinion, Naipaul's scorn of Indian traditions too often appears supercilious: his migrant ancestors' lost paradise never ceases to disappoint him. Consequently, says Rushdie, when Naipaul concludes that India is little more than a community of mimic men, "that the country's artistic life has stagnated, that 'creative urge' has 'failed' . . . then I fear we part company altogether" (Rushdie 1997, xxi). In two of Rushdie's earlier essays (1981 and 1987) published in his collection *Imaginary Homelands: Essays and Criticism* (1991), he had already expressed similar feelings of disappointment and annoyance at Naipaul's choice to consider himself a true British author. "Interestingly, and unlike most of his fellow-migrants," Rushdie wrote, "Naipaul has chosen to inhabit a pastoral England, an England of manor and stream. . . . So the new world begins to be seen for what it is, but at what a price! It's as if Naipaul expended so much of his energy on the effort of creating and comprehending his piece of Wiltshire that he had no strength left with which to make the characters breathe and move" (Rushdie 1987, 148–49).

Naipaul's description of four different Islamic countries and of their civilizations (in volumes such as *Among the Believers: An Islamic Journey* and its sequel *Beyond Belief: Islamic Excursions Among Converted Peoples*) elicited crushing criticism from the late Palestinian comparatist Edward Said (1998), a leading figure in the field of postcolonial studies. Said expressed his own disappointment and that of many of Naipaul's readers, writing that, for Naipaul, "The West is the World of knowledge, criticism, technical know-how and functioning institutions, Islam is its fearfully enraged and retarded dependent, awakening to a new, barely controlled power. The West provides Islam with good things from the outside, because 'the life that had come to Islam had not come from within.' Thus the existence of one billion Muslims is summed up in a phrase and dismissed. . . . The greater pity is," Said concluded bitterly, "that Naipaul's latest book on Islam will be considered a major interpretation of a great religion, and more Muslims will suffer and be insulted. And the gap between them and the West will increase and deepen" (Said, "An Intellectual Catastrophe").

SELECTED BIBLIOGRAPHY

Works by Naipaul

The Mystic Masseur. London: A. Deutsch, 1957.
Miguel Street. London: A. Deutsch, 1959.
A House for Mr Biswas. London: A. Deutsch, 1961.
The Middle Passage: Impressions of Five Societies—British, French and Dutch—in the West Indies and South America. London: A. Deutsch, 1962.
An Area of Darkness. London: A. Deutsch, 1964. New York: Macmillan, 1965.
The Mimic Men. London: Deutsch and New York: Macmillan, 1967.
In a Free State. London: Deutsch and New York: Knopf, 1971.
Guerrillas. London: Deutsch, 1975; New York: Vintage Books, 1980.
India: A Wounded Civilization. London: Deutsch and New York: Knopf, 1977.
A Bend in the River. London: Deutsch and New York: Knopf, 1979.
Among the Believers: An Islamic Journey. London: A. Deutsch, 1981.
India: A Million Mutinies Now. London: Heinemann, 1990. "Acceptance Speech of the First David Cohen British Literature Prize." *Wasafiri* 21 (1995): 7–8.
Beyond Belief: Islamic Excursions among the Converted Peoples. London: Little, Brown, 1998.
"Reading & Writing." *New York Review of Books* (February 18, 1999): 13–18.
"The Writer and India." *New York Review of Books* (March 4, 1999): 12–16.
Nobel Lecture, December 7, 2001. Available at www.nobel.se/literature/laureates/2001/naipaul-lecture-e.html.

Selected Studies of Naipaul

Khal, Sauvir. "Turning on V. S. Naipaul." *Wasafiri* 10 (Summer 1989): 21–22.
Levy, Judith. *V. S. Naipaul: Displacement and Autobiography.* New York: Garland, 1995.

Niven, Alastair. "V. S. Naipaul talks to Alastair Niven." *Wasafiri* 21 (Spring 1995): 5–6.

Rushdie, Salman. "Naipaul Among the Believers" (1981). In *Imaginary Homelands: Essays and Criticism*, 373–75. London: Granta, 1991.

———. "V. S. Naipaul" (1987). In *Imaginary Homelands: Essays and Criticism*, 148–51. London: Granta Books, 1991.

———. "Introduction." In *The Vintage Book of Indian Writing, 1947–1997*. Ed. Salman Rushdie and Elizabeth West, xix–xxi. London: Vintage, 1997.

Said, Edward. "An Intellectual Catastrophe." *Al-Ahram Weekly On-line* 389, August 6–12, 1998. Available at www.google.com.

Theroux, Paul. *Sir Vidia's Shadow: A Friendship Across Five Continents*. Boston: Houghton Mifflin, 1998.

Turner, Martin. "The Enigma of Arrival." *Wasafiri* 6/7 (Spring/Autumn 1987): 44.

PABLO NERUDA
(1904–1973)

James O. Pellicer

BIOGRAPHY

Pablo Neruda was born Ricardo Eliezer Neftali Reyes Basoalto in the town of Parral more than two hundred miles south of the Chilean capital, Santiago. Parral had little to offer financially or culturally. Neruda's mother died of tuberculosis one month after he was born; his father, a farmer, earned a meager income. Seeking a better life, the widower José del Carmen Reyes left his infant son with grandparents and traveled south to Temuco, about four hundred miles from Santiago. There pioneers had begun to clear the forest and disperse the Indians, with the help of Cornelio Saavedra Rodríguez, a military man who was an expert in cleansing territories via the convincing language of lethal weapons. Neruda's father found a job with the railroad: Germans, Americans, and other foreigners were following the heavy smoke of the steam locomotives bearing south. Soon after, a school was opened and José del Carmen Reyes brought his son to the frontier. He married Trinidad Candia, who was to be the child's beloved stepmother. Neruda grew up in a rugged environment replete with the smell of freshly cut wood, mountain rivers, and rain forests populated by a myriad of exotic insects and birds. This setting, together with the strong presence of the ocean, marked the future poet's soul. He experienced the roar of the South Pacific as "the loud pounding of a gigantic heart, the heartbeat of the universe" (*Memoirs*, trans. Hardie St. Martin, 16).

The untimely death of his mother left him with a sense of emptiness and a longing that later would be imprinted in his poetry. The definition of the human being, coined by the Spanish philosopher José Ortega y

Gasset, "I am me and my circumstances" (Ortega y Gasset, 51), admirably defines the man Neruda. Despite the variety of cultural realities to which he was exposed during his long life, he was always faithful to himself and to his land.

Neruda's faithfulness to the Chilean landscape by no means signified a cultural confinement. Chilean people have always felt they lived in a country too small, remote, and far distanced from cultural exchanges. As a result, Chile's intelligentsia, since the country's independence, yearned to invite important figures such as Domingo Faustino Sarmiento from Argentina, Andres Bello from Venezuela, Rubén Darío from Nicaragua, and so forth.

In 1921, the 17-year-old Neruda moved to the capital, where he taught French at the Teachers Institute. He had already published his first poems and had decided to change his surname in honor of Jan Neruda, the Czech poet known for his sardonic sketches. He took Pablo from Paolo Malatesta, Francesca da Rimini's unfortunate lover; he liked the sound of it. Pablo Neruda, then, formed a beautiful dactylic pentasyllabic verse. In "Ivresse," from his first published book *Crepusculario* (1923), he identified himself with Paolo: "Paolo's passion dances in my body" (http://www.poesia-castellana.com/neruda.html). Neruda's biographer Volodia Teitelboim believes that the poet did not take his name from the personage in Dante's *Divina commedia*, but rather from the play *Francesca da Rimini* (1901)—a play about the sensuous passion of lovers by Gabriele D'Annunzio, who was then influential in the Western world. Outbursts of love are evident in the many poems Neruda published in the early 1900s in newspapers and magazines. He translated into Spanish some poems by D'Annunzio, Walt Whitman, Rainer Maria Rilke, Marcel Schwob, and especially Anatole France, winner of the Nobel Prize in 1921, whose urbane skepticism and enlightened hedonism greatly pleased the young Neruda.

His many loves are described in his first published books, *Crepusculario* and his celebrated *Veinte poemas de amor y una canción desesperada* (1924) that sold one million copies by 1961. But soon, his romantic spirit felt the need to escape. The Chilean Foreign Office helped by naming him consul in various Far Eastern capitals. He returned to Chile in 1932 and soon after published *Residencia en la tierra 1925–1931* (1933). His readers missed the nostalgic clarity of his previous books. These new poems were written during his days in the mysterious East and his writing was marked by obscurity and fragmentation, a reflection of a disintegrated world. The critic Amado Alonso states that Neruda's writings at this time show no traces of positive religious thought, no indication of a divine force in the metaphysical sense. Only the title *Residencia en la tierra* would seem to allude to certain beliefs of Oriental religions (cf. Alonso, 35). Volodia Teitelboim, referring to readers who were dissatisfied with Neruda's book, says: "They did not understand that the poet who wrote in Chile is not the same who now writes in Rangoon or in Colombo. His reality has changed; his conscience evolved. Therefore, his poetry is now different, conditioned by the new environment and by the creative process of metamorphosis" (Teitelboim, 122).

After his return from the Orient, Neruda was appointed consul in Buenos Aires (1933), then he was transferred to Barcelona, Spain (1934). In the 1930s Buenos Aires was the largest metropolis in the Spanish-speaking world and a sort of cultural capital. There, Neruda met Federico García Lorca, who had come to present his play, *Yerma*. Neruda now mixed with the best Spanish writers, especially Ramón Gómez de la Serna, as well as Jorge Luis Borges from Argentina, and he began to be recognized. He was transferred again in 1935, this time to Madrid, where he found himself in the center of Europe's artistic and literary movements, inasmuch as Spain was enjoying an artistic revival. Finally free from the power of Rome, Europe was enjoying new ideological freedoms despite frenetic condemnations by the popes. Freedom of thought found its way into the Spanish language. Not for long, though: General Francisco Franco, in October of 1936, took over the insurgent movement that overthrew the elected Republican government. After a bloody and cruel civil war, and with the help of Hitler, the upper classes, and the endorsement of the Roman Church, Franco took over all of Spain and imposed a fascist dictatorship that lasted for the following 40 years. Dissidents were persecuted and killed, including Federico García Lorca. As a consequence, Neruda wrote in 1937 one of the best books ever written on the Spanish civil war, *España en el corazón* (1937, published in 1947 in *Tercera residencia 1935–1945*). He subsequently declared himself a communist and later officially joined the party. Forgetting his diplomatic capacity, he worked actively against the fascist regime and consequently was dismissed from his consular post.

Thereafter he worked actively in politics and poured out innumerable aggressively antifascist poems. In 1945 he was elected senator and at the same time won Chile's National Prize for Literature, which set in motion an international recognition of his merits and initiated his frequent travels for literary and political purposes. In 1948, his senatorial speech "I accuse" resulted in his impeachment and expulsion from the senate. The Chilean Supreme Court, at the instigation of the country's president, ordered his arrest. He went into hiding but persecution was so harsh that he had to leave the country secretly, crossing the Andes on horseback. In tight secrecy, he flew from Argentina to Paris, where he attended the First World Congress for Peace, thereby disclosing his whereabouts. In Moscow, he was honored by the Union of Soviet Writers. He also visited Poland and Hungary. In Mexico, he participated in the organization of the Latin American Congress of Partisans for Peace. By 1950, published translations of his works appeared in many countries of the world in various languages, and they continue to do so.

Neruda received the International Peace Prize in 1950, together with Pablo Picasso. Two years earlier, at the World Congress of Intellectuals gathered in Poland, Picasso had declared in the only speech he made in his life: "I have a friend who is one of the greatest poets of the world, he is Pablo Neruda . . . who has always been for the poor and the persecuted men, those who ask for justice and fight for it" (quoted in Teitelboim, 251).

In 1952, the order for his arrest was revoked and he returned to Chile where he was frenziedly active both literarily and politically. He received a series of distinctions, such as the publication of his *Complete Works* in 1957 and the honorary degree of Doctor of Letters from Oxford University in 1965. In September 1969 he was appointed candidate for the presidency of Chile by the Central Committee of the Communist Party, a candidacy he later resigned in order to facilitate the formation of the Popular Unity Party and permit Salvador Allende to become sole candidate. Allende became President of Chile in 1970 and appointed Neruda Ambassador to France, which was the summit of his diplomatic career.

Having received the Nobel Prize for Literature in 1971, Neruda decided to resign his position and return to Chile. He did so the following year and was welcomed in the National Stadium of Santiago, where he was acclaimed by huge crowds. On September 11, 1973, General Augusto Pinochet led a military coup d'état, established a bloody dictatorship, and assassinated every important figure in the Popular Unity Party, starting with President Allende himself. Pablo Neruda died in his house in Santiago crying, "They are killing them, they are killing them" (*Memoirs*, 364). His house in Valparaiso was vandalized and the one in Santiago, where his wake was held, was ransacked.

MAJOR MULTICULTURAL THEMES

The above biographical notes have been especially selected with the purpose of revealing the major cultural themes that enriched and influenced Neruda's writings.

In "I explain a few things," one of the most appealing poems in *España en el corazón*, the poet affirms the very Chilean quality that distinguishes all of his writing. Raising the question of why his poetry dwells on reality and neither on dreams nor on the forests and the great volcanoes of Chile, he answers by thrice emphasizing: "Come and see the blood on the streets!" (*Antología esencial*, 81). This very point reveals not only one but two of his major themes: the first, which pervades all of his poetry, is that of the aforementioned might of Chilean nature; the second, is that of his abhorrence of the generals, the upper classes, and priests. Although the latter theme was provoked by the coup d'état orchestrated by General Franco in Spain, it was present in his mind from his childhood and mentioned in his *Memoirs* with reference to Chilean expansion—the expansion of the frontier and the annihilation of the Indians by the military man with the help of lawyers and priests. Such an association of ideas strengthened Neruda's bond with communists and led to a deep sympathy for Russia and countries associated with communism. During 1949 and 1951, he traveled more than once to such faraway places as China and Mongolia. These extensive experiences enriched his poetry so that his work became appealing to cultures and peoples totally different from his own Western, Chilean origins.

SURVEY OF CRITICISM

The 1984 biography written by Neruda's close friend, Volodia Teitelboim, is profound and sensitive, but at times Teitelboim's writing becomes difficult because he prefers to abandon the chronological aspect of Neruda's poetic development in order to follow a thematic approach.

An excellent, and frequently reissued analytical study (1940, latest edition 1977) by Spanish poet and critic Amado Alonso, interprets Neruda's most intricate poems in depth. Emir Rodríguez Monegal and Enrico Mario Santí published a still very helpful book (1980) by collecting essays written by different specialists on Neruda, both Spanish and Hispanic American. This work offers an excellent bibliography as well. Eduardo Camacho Guizado (1978) studies each of Neruda's works individually. Margarita Aguirre (1964), who knew Neruda well, published a short biography of him in the "Genio y figura" series and, at the time of his death, *Las vidas de Pablo Neruda* (1973).

A specialized study (1976) of one of Neruda's most important works, *Canto general* (1950), is offered by Juan Villegas, professor of Spanish literature both in Chile and the United States. Villegas approaches Neruda's poetry as though it were a new literary theory showing the relationship between poetry and myth and myth and politics.

SELECTED BIBLIOGRAPHY

Works by Neruda

Crepusculario. Santiago: Claridad, 1923.

Veinte poemas de amor y una canción desesperada. Santiago: Nascimento, 1924.

Residencia en la tierra 1925–1931. Santiago: Nascimento, 1933.

Tercera residencia 1935–1945. Buenos Aires: Losada, 1947. [Includes *España en el corazón*, 1937.]

Canto general. Mexico City: Oceano, 1950.

Antología esencial, Pablo Neruda. Ed. Hernán Loyola. Buenos Aires: Losada, 1971.

Five Decades: A Selection (Poems 1925–1970). Ed. and trans. Ben Belitt. New York: Grove Press, 1974.

Confieso que he vivido: memorias (1974). [*Memoirs*. Trans. Hardie St. Martin. New York: Farrar, Straus and Giroux, 1977.]

Selected Studies of Neruda

Aguirre, Margarita. *Genio y figura de Pablo Neruda*. Buenos Aires: Editorial Universitaria de Buenos Aires, 1964.

———. *Las vidas de Pablo Neruda*. Santiago: Zig-Zag, 1967; Mexico City: Grijalbo, 1973.

Alonso, Amado. *Poesía y estilo de Pablo Neruda. Interpretación de una poesía hermética* (1940). 7th ed. Buenos Aires: Editorial Sudamericana, 1977.

Camacho Guizado, Eduardo. *Pablo Neruda. Naturaleza, historia, y poética*. Madrid: Sociedad General Española de Libreria, 1978.

Loyola, Hernán. *Ser y morir en Pablo Neruda*. Santiago: Editora Santiago, 1967.

Rodríguez Monegal, Emir. *El viajero inmóvil: Introducción a Pablo Neruda*. Buenos Aires: Losada, 1966.

——— and Enrico Mario Santí, eds. *Pablo Neruda*. Madrid: Taurus, 1980.

Silva Castro, Raúl. *Pablo Neruda*. Santiago: Editorial Universitaria, 1964.

Teitelboim, Volodia. *Neruda*. Madrid: Michay, 1984.

Villegas, Juan. *Estructuras miticas y arquetipos en el "Canto general" de Neruda*. Barcelona: Planeta, 1976.

Yurkievich, Saúl. *Fundadores de la nueva poesía latinoamericana: Vallejo, Huidobro, Borges, Neruda, Paz* (1971). 2nd ed. Barcelona: Barral, 1973.

Related Work

Ortega y Gasset, José. *Meditaciones del Quijote* (1914). 2nd ed. Madrid: Revista de Occidente, 1966.

EUGÈNE NICOLE
(1942–)

Sonia Assa

BIOGRAPHY

Geography was destiny for the writer and visual artist Eugène Nicole. He was born at St. Pierre, in the capital city of Saint Pierre and Miquelon, a 242-square-kilometer archipelago off the southern coast of Newfoundland, the only French territory now remaining in North America. These bleak, windswept islands crystallized in his writings as intensely visual time-space moments, and they were reborn in the exile's narrative trilogy. Nicole's condition of exile began in 1956. At the age of 14, there being no high school on the islands, he left his native land to pursue his studies in France. He attended a Catholic boarding school in the region of Vendée, where his childhood world vanished. He faced loneliness, the remoteness of his loved ones, and the rule of silence imposed by the institution. This painful separation may have reactivated the trauma he suffered at the age of 5 when his mother died, an experience of loss followed by his first exile: the family's abandoning of the maternal home to go to live with the paternal grandmother.

France, in a sense, remained forever foreign to Nicole; it was always the place outside, from which he looked in, fantasizing about the Americanness of his archipelago. Most importantly, he began the mental haunting of his island's capital, which he later transmuted into the matter of his books. Every night, from his school dormitory in the remote Vendée, he indefatigably retraced his daily peregrinations in St. Pierre and minutely reconstituted the landscapes of his childhood.

Nicole attended the University of Paris (1959–66), earning a double degree, in literature from the Sorbonne and in political science from the

Institut d'études politiques. These student years inaugurated an era of traveling back and forth between Paris and the islands, which Nicole would later name "the time of the shuttle" (*Le caillou de l'Enfant-Perdu*, 268).

His American experience began in 1966. After spending a year in Alaska, he enrolled at the International Creative Writing Center in Iowa, then taught at Princeton University. In 1970, he joined the Department of French at New York University, where he has been teaching ever since. New York City henceforth was the substitute pole for St. Pierre. After Paris, his American world became the third apex in a triangle of experience that magnified his vision through the lens of separation.

Author of a 1977 doctoral thesis that examined the semiotics of proper names in the novel, Nicole has published several articles on this topic. He has also published numerous articles and spoken at many conferences on Marcel Proust, as well as collaborating in the editorship of the Pléiade edition of Proust's *A la recherche du temps perdu* (4 volumes, 1987–89). To date, his narrative cycle comprises three novels: *L'oeuvre des mers* (1988, shortlisted for the Prix Médicis), *Les larmes de pierre* (1991), and *Le caillou de l'Enfant-Perdu* (1996). He is at work on the fourth volume of this saga centered on his native archipelago, which the narrator conjures up by means of an exact, meticulous, and wonder-struck memory. Large and minute events of the islands' history, their fauna and flora, local myths and personal memories, geology, philology and philately, all contribute to the evocation of a place derealized through distance and the magic of naming. From one book to the next, the child narrator grows into a young man; stories are taken up again and amplified or redistributed, with slight shifts in emphasis or perspective. An endearing cast of real life, fictional, and historical characters, introduced in the first novel, returns throughout the trilogy. Usually these characters appear fleetingly against a backdrop of sea-battered islands—the main protagonists.

Nicole has also pursued an active if mostly private career as a visual artist, exhibiting his works at the Galería Fúcares in Madrid, at the University of Bordeaux, and at New York University. Working in a variety of media—gouache, watercolors, acrylics, colored pencils, collages, and found objects that he calls *piétinés* (trampled-on)—he has produced a whimsical, brightly colored, and original oeuvre. He achieves a mosaic effect through the use of bits and pieces as compositional elements. There is a striking continuity between this artistic production, which proposes unconventional ways of seeing and emphasizes fragmentation, and his postmodern writing style.

Nicole was inducted into the French Order of Arts and Letters in February 2001, with the title of Chevalier.

MAJOR MULTICULTURAL THEMES

A wanderer on both shores of the Atlantic, Eugène Nicole has never ceased looking back, mentally surveying and pacing the landscape he left behind. His project has been to "tell" St. Pierre, and the stories are the stuff of the islands from the perspective of the exile who returns periodically and imperceptibly adjusts his point of view. Indeed, perspective and scale define his writing. He chooses to present St. Pierre of the notoriously overcast sky "sous son jour clair" (on a clear day or under a bright lighting) in *Le caillou de l'Enfant-Perdu* (203). He tells the story of his "first departure" as remembered during his "first return" (*L'oeuvre des mers*, 158; *Le caillou de l'Enfant-Perdu*, 12). He describes Lindbergh's flight over the islands through the eyes of Gabie, the confused and mildly deranged mother of a "lost child" (*L'oeuvre des mers*, 15; *Les larmes de pierre*, 96). With a meticulous memory served by an impeccable style and heightened by the consummate art of perceiving and naming minute bits of reality, Nicole conjures up a world whose very familiarity becomes exotic. Minuscule changes of position, such as the moving of a desk from one floor to another (*Les larmes de pierre*, 229), the grandmother's daily trips along the street from the Café du Nord to the "maison Jacquet" (*Les larmes de pierre*, 15), or the locking-up of summer houses at the end of the season (*Les larmes de pierre*, 229), take on the same ominous significance as the incursions of historical events into local life—be it Charles Lindbergh's flight, the first air service to the islands (*Les larmes de pierre*, 10), visits by the author René de Chateaubriand and the navigator and explorer Jacques Cartier (*L'oeuvre des mers*, 30–39), or the island's role in smuggling during the Prohibition years (*Les larmes de pierre*, 209). "Small scale and picturesque go together," says Miss Maple, the First Tourist, in *Les larmes de pierre* (106). Fragmented into myriad pebbles of reality seen under the intense light of distance and nostalgia, the islands grow, covering a symbolic space much wider than France or any part of the world outside.

In the trilogy's lyrical titles the islands are present as permanence and flow: the permanence of rock and stone and of the writer's work (*l'oeuvre, pierre, le caillou*); the ebb and flow of the sea, of human emotion, and human trajectories (*les mers, les larmes, l'enfant perdu*). The layering of meaning goes still further: *L'oeuvre des mers* is the archipelago "made by the seas," but it is also the name of the motion-picture theater where the narrator-as-child catches his first glimpse of France in the guise of two children who have lost their way in the woods (*L'oeuvre des mers*, 23–24). The *larmes de pierre* (tears of stone), the very tears of St. Pierre, are the *graves*, those fields of gravel on which the island's catch of cod once dried and where the little *graviers*, the child-laborers, cried their tears of cold and homesickness. Now the *graves* are to serve as a runway, so that the island's past, its very identity as the home of seafaring people, fishermen, and sailors, who depended on the salt-cod trade for their survival, will be both erased and engraved in this takeoff strip from which the narrator will depart (*Les larmes de pierre*, 176). The *Enfant-Perdu* is first of all a tiny island, hardly an island, part of the archipelago, a rock that would be lost if it were not named; it is also the narrator lost in the forbidding boarding school in remote France and the child-worker laboring far away from his home. Trajectories, shuttles, crossings, ways lost and found, and the magical and not altogether stationary nature of place names define home and exile in spatial as well as temporal terms. As a curator friend tells the narrator: "For you, then, history is geography" (*L'oeuvre des mers*, 95).

Memory is thus inflected by exile in Eugène Nicole's three novels. From the beginning, the islands cannot but be "told" from the perspective of the one who left, always to return, never to remain again—from the perspective of loss. Strong intertextual connections link these books to the *nouveau roman* marked by obsession with architectural space, absence, and photographic recording. But the narratives are also haunted by Proust, and by Mallarmé as well. *Les larmes de pierre* (191) presents the hallucinating episode of the *Théâtre de la Morte* (The Theater of the Dead Mother) or the *Théâtre du Froid* (The Theater of Cold) in which, in very Mallarmean terms, nothing takes place, but the place. Throughout the trilogy, the narrator "tells" a place that is the story. Shuttling travelers and concentric stories may weave maps or itineraries (Langlade or l'île Languette in *L'oeuvre des mers*, 169; the *route Iphigénie* in *Le caillou de l'Enfant-Perdu*, 70). They may evoke scenes frozen in memory: a frieze on the pier—the distraught family as burghers of Calais (*L'oeuvre des mers*, 158; *Le caillou de l'Enfant-Perdu*, 17); the mad high school teacher, his ear pressed to the earth, listening for long-gone Indian voices (*Le caillou de l'Enfant-Perdu*, 61); a guillotine execution that still haunts the public spaces (*L'oeuvre des mers*, 55). Always, the absent island wrapped in mist is the story. Nothing takes place but St. Pierre.

SURVEY OF CRITICISM

Chantal Thomas (1996) praises Eugène Nicole's art of perception and naming (952). She notes how his "*pursuit* of the islands does not aim at securing an external reality but rather at searching for an equivalence in the materiality of writing" (947). For those islands, which may appear as fixed points on a map from the objective point of view of a geographer, "are in fact the object of a quest for the narrator, the motive for a tireless reconstruction in the enigmatic light of passion" (948). Thomas further points out that "the fall into exile," having forced the narrator to constitute a "mental atlas" of his native archipelago as a way to appease his grief, constituted him as a writer (954).

SELECTED BIBLIOGRAPHY

Works by Nicole

L'oeuvre des mers: Roman. Paris: François Bourin, 1988. Paris: "Folio" Gallimard, 1990.
Les larmes de pierre: Roman. Paris: François Bourin, 1991. Paris: "Folio" Gallimard, 1993.
Le caillou de l'Enfant-Perdu: Roman (1996). Paris: Flammarion, 1998.

Study of Nicole

Thomas, Chantal. "Le dernier regard." *Critique* 594 (November 1996): 947–55.

BEN OKRI
(1959–)

Bill Wolf

BIOGRAPHY

Ben Okri was born to Grace and Silver Oghekenenshineke Okri, of the Urhobo people, in Minna, Nigeria, on March 15, 1959—20 months before Nigeria was granted independence from Great Britain on October 1, 1960. The two events in essence fused to give to the world a dozen books, published in the 1980s and 1990s, that peer deeply into precolonial, colonial, and postcolonial Nigeria; into the spirit world of Yoruba mythology rendered with fierce yet natural realism and loving sympathy; and, more significantly, into the hearts and minds of all people born into the universal wrap of sorrow and joy.

When Okri was 3, he joined his parents in England where his father was studying law. He began his own education at the John Donne Primary School in London, then returned to Africa in 1966 to continue his studies at the Urhobo College in Warri. His secondary education was completed in 1972, when he was 13. Admitted to Essex University, he returned to England in 1978 to study comparative literature. These were hard times for Okri, working at menial jobs and sleeping on floors; eventually, lack of funds forced him to leave the university without obtaining his degree. For seven years, he was a poetry editor for the London-based *West Africa Magazine*, and he was also employed as a broadcaster for the British Broadcasting System (BBC) World Service. During this time he wrote and continued to travel between England and Africa.

He won the Commonwealth Writers Prize for Africa in 1987 for his book of short stories, *Incidents at the Shrine* (1986), and in 1991 he was awarded the prestigious Booker Prize for his best-known work, *The Fam-*

ished Road. He was a visiting writer-in-residence at Trinity College, Cambridge, England, and has also been honored with the Order of the British Empire. Considering the tenure of the times and his creative and innovative spirit, it is not surprising to find Okri publishing poetry on-line. He writes in English and he remains a beloved major force in world literature; he offers a constant reminder and admonition to the West that Africa, with its vast accomplishments and potential, along with its dire problems and woes, *exists*—and that attention must be paid to it.

MAJOR MULTICULTURAL THEMES

It can be stated without exaggeration that Ben Okri is a quintessential multicultural writer. He infuses Yoruba mythology with magic realism; he blends empathetic tenderness for the impoverished of Nigeria and for Africa as a whole—a tenderness often mixed with impatience and frustration, with a disdainful, unmitigated anger against political corruption; and all of this is underscored by his use of Western literary traditions, which he modifies to suit his ends and to establish the phantasmagoric quality of his best work. The first two novels, *Flowers and Shadows* (1980) and *The Landscapes Within* (1981) are both cast in West African urban settings, in which squalor, despair, cruelty, depravity, and tyranny remain a constant backdrop. Characters try to come to grips with their basic needs, their cultural identity of both the past and the present, and their passions—obstructed and reduced, yet flaring up maddeningly and always somehow inappropriately. Although these books are about Africa in its fiery attempt to reshape and reclaim itself, they are primarily about the reshaping and reclamation of the hearts of his characters who are faced, as we all are, with the ineluctable challenges of life.

Two collections of short stories followed: *Incidents at the Shrine* (1986) and *Stars of the New Curfew* (1988). These show advancement in Okri's work, a maturity, a gathering and display of strength. Most of the stories are set in Nigeria, many tell of the Nigerian civil war, but others relate the adventures, usually adverse, of Nigerians living in London. Although harsh realism permeates the stories as they tell of beggars, prostitutes, the working poor, the sick, the lame, cruel soldiers, and corrupt officials, it is in these stories that Okri truly finds his power to delineate another world, the world of spirits and ancient gods. He convinces the reader of the reality of this nether world, and he seamlessly incorporates this reality into his characters' daily routine—thereby opening some doors long bolted, to admit the light of new speculation concerning some very basic assumptions held by Western pragmatists and skeptics everywhere.

Other work came before and after *The Famished Road*—stories, novels, and poetry—but it is this novel that has set Okri's reputation. Henry Louis Gates Jr. describes the book as "engagingly lyrical and intriguingly postmodern" ("Between the Living and the Unborn," 3). This long and generous story is told from the point of view of Azaro, an *abiku*. An *abiku*, as related in Yoruba mythology, lives "in the limited realm between the worlds of the living and the unborn" ("Between the Living and the Unborn," 3). His *abiku* kin relentlessly attempt to pull Azaro back into their world, both threatening him with pain and suffering and tempting him with otherworldly delights. An *abiku* is born and dies cyclically, always returning to aggrieve his mother. In *The Famished Road*, as in several of the short stories mentioned above, the spirit world coexists naturally with so-called normal reality. It is through Okri's skill that his readers believe in it all, and perhaps this makes it the ultimate multicultural statement—in the sense that it is an ethereal culture, or subculture, that is being portrayed, observed and accepted. But the book contains so much more than the supranatural. It becomes a wild, frolicking story of family ties and tensions, sometimes loving, sometimes tumultuous; it is a story of African politics and revolution, of the seemingly inexhaustible and unremitting problems of colonialism and postcolonialism; but above all, it is a story, both tragically and humorously told, of the indomitable spirit of people engaged in the grand and fantastic endeavor of life itself. This is Okri's power; this is what transcends the multiplicity of cultures that blanket our world and goes deeply to the heart of any reader anywhere.

SURVEY OF CRITICISM

As of this writing, criticism has been sparse. Okri was often interviewed throughout the 1990s: Carolyn Newton's "An Interview with Ben Okri" (1992) and the several pages of *The New Yorker* given over to Jonathan Wilson's interview, "A Very English Story" (1996), by way of example. Throughout these interviews, Okri discusses his literature, his growth as an artist, and Nigerian and world politics.

Both the *London Times* and the *New York Times* offer generally favorable reviews of the major works, among them Henry Louis Gates Jr.'s review of *The Famished Road* (1992), which places Okri in the context of both world and African literature. Gates' examination of the author's use of lore and myth in the novel is significant and useful. Not surprisingly, articles and reviews are also found in the various journals devoted to African literature, such as the *Southern African Review of Books*, *West Africa*, and the *African Accord*. No biographies are available at this time, and, so far, very few books on Okri exist. Brenda Cooper's 1998 volume is the best known. As the title suggests, Cooper examines Okri's use of magical realism, distinguishing it from that of Latin American authors and less cosmopolitan African writers. Cooper expresses along the way her views of contemporary Marxist opinion.

SELECTED BIBLIOGRAPHY

Works by Okri

Flowers and Shadows. London: Longman, 1980.
The Landscapes Within. Burnt Mill, Harlow, Essex: Longman, 1981.
Incidents at the Shrine: Short Stories. London: Heinemann, 1986.
Stars of the New Curfew (1988). New York: Viking, 1989.
The Famished Road. London: Jonathan Cape, 1991; New York: Doubleday, 1996.
An African Elegy. London: Jonathan Cape, 1992.
Songs of Enchantment. New York: Doubleday, 1993.

Selected Studies of Okri

Cooper, Brenda. "Out of the centre of my forehead, an eye opened: Ben Okri's *The Famished Road.*" In *Magical Realism in West African Fiction: Seeing with a Third Eye,* 67–114. London and New York: Routledge, 1998.

Cribb, T. J. "Transformations in the Fiction of Ben Okri." In *From Commonwealth to Post-Colonial.* Ed. Anna Rutherford, 145–50. Sydney: Dangaroo Press, 1992.

Gates, Henry Louis, Jr. "Between the Living and the Unborn." *New York Times Book Review* (June 28, 1992): 3, 20.

Newton, Carolyn. "An Interview with Ben Okri." *South African Literary Review* 2.3 (1992): 5–6.

Wilson, Jonathan. "A Very English Story." *The New Yorker* (March 6, 1996): 96–106.

MICHAEL ONDAATJE
(1943–)

Arianna Maiorani

BIOGRAPHY

Born in Colombo, Sri Lanka (formerly Ceylon), on September 12, 1943, Michael Ondaatje comes from a prominent family in Ceylon's colonial society. His father, Mervyn Ondaatje, after his turbulent youth became a plantation superintendent; his mother, Doris Gratiaen, who sometimes performed as a dancer inspired by Isadora Duncan's school, separated from her husband because of his alcoholism. After having begun his education in Ceylon, Michael moved to England with his mother in 1954 and continued his education in London. In 1962, he emigrated to Canada where he received the bachelor of arts degree from the University of Toronto (1965) and the master of arts degree from Queen's University in Kingston, Ontario (1967). Between 1967 and 1971, he taught at the University of Western Ontario in London, Canada; and in 1971 he became a member of the Department of English at Glendon College of York University in Toronto. Poet, editor, and author of several novels and critical works, his literary career is studded with numerous awards, such as the Ralph Gustafson Award, the Epstein Award, and the President's Medal of the University of Ontario; he has also won two Canadian Governor-General's Awards, the Canada-Australia Prize, and in 1992 was corecipient of the Booker Prize for his best-known work, *The English Patient: A Novel*.

MAJOR MULTICULTURAL THEMES

A member of a family with multicultural roots and raised in a multicultural society, Michael Ondaatje inevitably stems from his own background. Having spent much time in Sri Lanka and in Canada, he naturally considers himself a citizen of both countries. This feeling of double citizenship strongly influences his idea of "exotic," which is almost always present in his fiction. Exotic for Ondaatje is neither an Eastern country or place, nor a Western one; it is a country or place where his characters, Easterners as well as Westerners, feel far from home. This situation often arises in Ondaatje's works, and especially in his novels, in times of crisis and great change, in periods of struggle or war, when his characters, coming from different cultures and countries, meet and create a multicultural and multiform reality. The novel *Coming Through Slaughter* (1976) mixes both fictional and real events to tell the tale of Buddy Bolden, a jazz cornetist in New Orleans; here Ondaatje introduces another important and recurrent element of his narrative: music, a world where different cultures and languages mix and melt, and also a means to recall either homely or exotic memories and atmospheres.

Running in the Family (1982) is the story of the Ondaatje family in Ceylon, in which the author mixes different writing techniques (narration, description, conversation, poetry, and even photographs) and different narrating voices (the book contains stories told by relatives, friends, and old family acquaintances). Retracing the roots and the story of his European-Ceylonese family, as well as its both real and legendary history, he recreates the multicultural reality of Ceylonese colonial society before World War II in which his parents and grandparents lived. In doing so, he often quotes from or refers to several great classics of Western literature as well as purely Ceylonese poetry and traditions, sometimes turning to music. This multiform, multivocal book describes the world in which Ondaatje was born and spent his childhood, and the multicultural atmosphere he experienced while growing up, an element which is often present in his works. His Ceylon is a place where nature is gorgeous and powerful in all its elements. It is a place where the smell and colors of plants and flowers, the fury of floods, or the strength of sea currents can decide a person's destiny; a place where families of different origins and roots, coming from different countries, sometimes belonging to different ethnic groups, live together and mix, sharing or confronting their cultures and ways of life, following the fortunes of their land and the island's seasonal changes and cycles.

In the Skin of a Lion: A Novel (1987), set in Toronto during the 1930s, contains multiculturalism as an important theme. It is a story of people working and struggling in a town where Canadians and immigrants meet, sometimes mixing, sometimes not.

The complex structure of the novel *The English Patient*, whose film adaptation won nine Academy Awards in 1996, is based on four main characters whose stories and lives meet in an abandoned Italian villa at the end of World War II: Hana, a Canadian nurse, suffers from shell shock and has to overcome her father's death; Almasy, her only and last patient, is a severely burned man of presumably English nationality;

Hana's old friend Caravaggio is a Canadian spy and thief whose hands were maimed; and Kip is an Indian sapper trained in England. They all carry with them their cultures and experiences, their stories of love and grief, and the injuries, visible and invisible, that war has inflicted on them and from which they try to recover in different ways. Each is a foreigner in an exotic country. Italy is exotic for all of them because it is not home. Africa is the exotic land where Almasy, the Hungarian "Englishman," just before the beginning of war, attempts to delete the concepts of *nation* and *nationality*, where he tries to lose his past and present in the timeless desert and the history of its past civilizations, and where he lives the tragic love story that fascinates Hana and leads Caravaggio to discover his real identity. The entire Western world is exotic for Kip, who, trying at first to become part of a society (the English) he both admires and criticizes, definitely condemns the West and a war he no longer feels his own when the atomic bombs are dropped on Hiroshima and Nagasaki. The abandoned Italian villa is a sort of multicultural microcosm where East and West meet in a situation of historical crisis, where characters interact to overcome their personal crises, where their common experience ends after the critical episode of the atomic bomb. Ondaatje's allusions to the classics of Western literature and music serve as a means of introspection for his characters and their worlds.

The novel *Anil's Ghost* (2000) is set in Colombo, Sri Lanka, and is the story of a forensic anthropologist, Anil, who after having lived abroad for 15 years returns home to participate in a human-rights mission. Her task is to find, examine, and attempt to identify the bones of the missing persons who disappeared during the 16-year conflict between Sri Lanka's government and separatist forces. As Anil works on a skeleton, she begins to imagine the past life and experiences of the person it represents, to whose remains she tries to give a name. In an attempt to reconstruct the history of the Sri Lankan people and their country, she searches for the reasons and facts that led to the prolonged conflict on this once-multicultural island.

SURVEY OF CRITICISM

Criticism touching on Michael Ondaatje's multicultural element focuses mostly on his fiction, and particularly on his way of analyzing the relationship between his characters and history, the problem of identity, alterity, and culture, and on his use of different narrative techniques. After the release of the film adaptation of *The English Patient*, critics also dwelt on the differences between the book and the movie screenplay. His works have also been the object of some psychological analysis, centered on the personality of certain characters.

Leslie Mundwiler (1984) analyzes Ondaatje's works as a whole, focusing on the author's concept of history. Sam Solecki (1985) is the editor of a comprehensive anthology of essays, reviews, and interviews dealing with the major themes of Michael Ondaatje's fiction and poetry. Winfried Siemerling (1994) examines the works of Ondaatje among others in the light of how he deals with alterity and history and the relationship between author and hero, as well as his use of metaphors. Graham Huggan (1995) examines the exotic and ethnic elements specifically in *Running in the Family*, as does Smaro Kamboureli (1988), who focuses on the language the author uses in this biographical work.

SELECTED BIBLIOGRAPHY

Works by Ondaatje

Coming Through Slaughter. Toronto: House of Anansi; New York: W. W. Norton; New York: Avon, 1976.

There's a Trick with a Knife I'm Learning to Do: Poems 1963–1978. New York: Norton; Toronto: McClelland and Stewart, 1979.

Running in the Family. Toronto: McClelland and Stewart; New York: W. W. Norton, 1982.

In the Skin of a Lion. Toronto: McClelland and Stewart; New York: Knopf, 1987.

The English Patient: A Novel. Toronto: McClelland and Stewart; New York: Knopf, 1992.

Handwriting: Poems. Toronto: McClelland and Stewart, 1998; New York: Knopf, 1999.

Anil's Ghost. Toronto: McClelland and Stewart; New York: Knopf, 2000.

Selected Studies of Ondaatje

Barbour, Douglas. *Michael Ondaatje.* New York: Twayne, 1993.

Heble, Ajay. "Michael Ondaatje and the Problem of History." *Clio: A Journal of Literature, History, and the Philosophy of History* 19, no. 2 (1990): 97–110.

Huggan, Graham. "Exoticism and Ethnicity in Michael Ondaatje's *Running in the Family*." *Essays on Canadian Writing* 57 (1995): 49–70.

Kamboureli, Smaro. "The Alphabet of the Self: Generic and Other Slippages in Michael Ondaatje's *Running in the Family*." In *Reflections: Autobiography and Canadian Literature.* Ed. K. P. Stich, 79–91. Ottawa: University of Ottawa Press, 1988.

Mundwiler, Leslie. *Michael Ondaatje: Word, Image, Imagination.* Vancouver: Talonbooks, 1984.

Siemerling, Winfried. *Discoveries of the Other: Alterity in the Work of Leonard Cohen, Hubert Aquin, Michael Ondaatje, and Nicole Brossard.* Toronto: University of Toronto Press, 1994.

Solecki, Sam, ed. *Spider Blues: Essays on Michael Ondaatje.* Montreal: Véhicule Press, 1985.

IRIS ORIGO
(1902–1988)

Benedetta Origo

BIOGRAPHY

Iris Origo was born in England but lived at the intersection of several worlds, both in a literal sense and a temporal one. Her mother, Sybil Cuffe, came from an Anglo-Irish family, whose house in county Kilkenny where Iris loved to spend her summer holidays was completely burned down in the Anglo-Irish war. Her father, Bayard Cutting, a friend of Edith Wharton, was a brilliant young diplomat from a rich New York family. He died of consumption while traveling up the Nile in a houseboat when Iris was only seven. His widow then settled at the Villa Medici in Florence, acting on Bayard's wish that Iris should be brought up in a country where she did not belong, as nationalism had "brought so much unhappiness to the world" (Iris Origo, *Images and Shadows: Part of a Life*, 1998, 88). Here Sybil and Iris soon became part of the cosmopolitan and intellectual Anglo-Florentine milieu, which included Mary and Bernard Berenson and their circle, Harold Acton, Janet Ross, Edith Wharton, and many others. Iris's time was divided between Florence, her maternal grandparents in Ireland and London, the Cutting grandparents in Long Island and New York, and constant travels with her mother. Her studies were wide but solitary: languages, literature, music, and, above all, the classics, guided by a great Italian tutor recommended by Berenson, Solone Monti, who would shape the course of her intellectual development.

Her ambitions as a writer were deflected for a number of years by her marriage to Marchese Antonio Origo (1924). Together they bought a derelict but beautiful property, La Foce, in the Val d'Orcia in the Sienese region, and devoted their lives to creating a model estate, with a hospital, schools, and the use of modern farming methods. After the death of their only son, Gianni (1933), she dedicated more of her time to writing. Her first book was a biography of the melancholy, semicloistered, hunchbacked Italian poet, Giacomo Leopardi, whose genius, pain, and frustrated hopes found their outlet in poetry: *Leopardi, A Study in Solitude*, was originally written in 1935 for an English public who had never heard of him before. A second edition (1954) provided further information and documents, following the discovery in Italy of previously unknown material concerning the poet.

With the outbreak of World War II, Origo joined the prisoners-of-war office of the Italian Red Cross in Rome. When the war reached the Val d'Orcia, she returned there to join her husband in sheltering refugee children, helping Italian partisans, hiding escaped Allied prisoners, and protecting their own property and family. The last years of their experience is described in her book, *War in Val d'Orcia, 1943–1944: A Diary, by Iris Origo* (1947). During the war, she gave birth to two daughters, Benedetta (1940) and Donata (1943).

After the war, the Origos, facing the critical years of political and social change in Italy with the transformation of farming policies and the growth of communism, resisted the temptation to emigrate to the United States. Her grandparents' world, both in England and the United States, had also radically changed and then disappeared. Origo now dedicated herself to writing and research, and to the publication of her best-known books, including *The Last Attachment: The Story of Byron and Teresa Guiccioli as Told in Their Unpublished Letters and Other Family Papers* (1949); *The Merchant of Prato, Francesco di Marco Datini, 1335–1410* (1957), which brought her to the attention of scholars and historians and has been translated into many languages; and her own autobiography, *Images and Shadows: Part of a Life* (1970). She also devoted much time to public charitable activities, such as the Italian Red Cross and the International Social Service, and to private ones nearer home, including the running of her home for underprivileged children at La Foce and placing many of them in families for adoption. She is remembered with love and admiration still, and has become something of a legend in the Val d'Orcia.

She never lost touch with her English and American heritages, traveling frequently to both countries to visit friends and families. Although she was of frail constitution and accustomed to comfort, her passion for travel to distant lands, possibly equal to that of her mother, was tireless. She lectured in the United States at Smith College and Harvard University and held honorary doctorates from Smith College and Wheaton College. She was awarded the Isabella d'Este Medal for essays and historical studies in 1966. A Fellow of the Royal Society of Literature, she was named a Dame Commander, Order of the British Empire, in 1977. *Un'Amica. Ritratto di Elsa Dallolio* (1988) was her last book, and the only one she wrote directly in Italian. It evokes her friendship of over 20 years with Elsa Dallolio, a prominent figure in the liberal and literary panorama of postwar Italy. Origo died at La Foce, 12 years after her husband.

MAJOR MULTICULTURAL THEMES

The best way to understand Origo's thought and evolution is to read her own assessment of them in her autobiography *Images and Shadows: Part of a Life*, particularly those chapters dealing with "growing up and coming out" and "writing." The countries of her varied background—England, Ireland, the United States, Italy—as well as the different traditions, beliefs, and codes of behavior that each of these countries bequeathed to her (and to which she was expected to adapt instantly) eventually gave her a sense of belonging to the world rather than to a particular nation.

Though she looked, and perhaps felt, unmistakably Anglo-Saxon, her unusual upbringing had enabled her to absorb Italian culture and traditions to the marrow. Her marriage to an Italian and her plunge into Italian politics and agriculture completed her education. This helped her to write with rare insight and understanding about those Italian figures whose human or intellectual qualities particularly caught her imagination. Nationality, in any case, was never an issue in her evaluation of human character: it was the individual and the mind that interested her.

Her choice of subjects, as she herself admits, did not always coincide with "a personal liking . . . or even an especial interest" in her characters (*Images and Shadows*, 184). In the case of Lord Byron and the merchant Datini, she had happened to "stumble upon some irresistibly good material" (*Images and Shadows*, 184) that convinced her to write about them. The Byron "material" consisted of the unpublished correspondence between the English poet and the lovely young Contessa Teresa Guiccioli in Ravenna. Byron is seen here in an Italian setting and through contemporary Italian eyes, as he gets ever deeper into the labyrinth of Italian social and political life. The "material" also included letters from Percy Bysshe Shelley, Mary Shelley, Lady Marguerite Blessington, Alphonse de Lamartine, and others, as well as excerpts from contemporary Italian diaries and chronicles and from the archives of the Italian and Austrian police. The extraordinary treasure in the Francesco di Marco Datini archives in Prato (Florence), consisting of thousands of business and private letters, as well as ledgers and account books, all of them almost completely unstudied, convinced Origo that here was the *"chair humaine"* (*Images and Shadows*, 184) she had been seeking for a detailed and vivid picture of a fourteenth-century family in Tuscany.

Several essays, in both *A Measure of Love* (1957) and *A Need to Testify* (1984), include portraits that span two cultures, English and U.S., and Italian: the friendship between the Italian revolutionary patriot Giuseppe Mazzini and Thomas Carlyle during Mazzini's exile in London; the great historian and philosopher Gaetano Salvemini's 13-year exile as professor at Harvard University; the passionate love affair between the American actress Ruth Draper and the Italian antifascist Lauro de Bosis.

SURVEY OF CRITICISM

Caroline Moorehead's interesting book is the only existing biography (2000) of Iris Origo. It is in great part an account of her life, based on interviews with her family and a few friends who are still alive, and on letters and documents. A critical examination of Origo's work has yet to be undertaken. However, there exist various comprehensive articles and reviews of her books: Sergio Romano (1985) points out that Origo's themes—"chapters of a medieval and romantic Italy" (133)—belong traditionally to northern European writers (English, American, German) who have made Italy their literary country, as much as to Italians. In reviewing *A Need to Testify*, he suggests that these Italian portraits are offered as an homage to her adopted country, especially that of Gaetano Salvemini, who is perhaps even more respected in the Anglo-American cultural and political milieu than in his original Italian one. Harold Acton (1984) calls Origo "an inspired interpreter of Italian character and culture" (11) and comments on her style, so "exquisite—perhaps because she is bilingual" (11). Both Elizabeth Bowen (1947) and Piero Calamandrei (1949), in writing about her war diary, speculate on Origo's capacity to understand and sympathize with different mentalities and cultures due to her multicultural background as well as her own deep humanity.

In the opinion of Werner Stark (1957), *The Merchant of Prato, Francesco di Marco Datini, 1335–1410* sheds light on the problem of the origins of modern capitalism, which is generally attributed to the advent of Calvinism, as opposed to Catholicism's sense of sin (see the merchant's motto, "for God and profit," and his strong disapproval of usury). Both Ernesto Rossi (1959) and Luigi Einaudi in his foreword (1958) to *Il mercante di Prato* appreciate Origo's ability to enter into the spirit and mentality of the fourteenth century—its men and its economy, as seen through the life of a much-traveled merchant.

Tim Parks (2000) explores Origo's connection with Leopardi through her own understated but tragic and early contact with death, and acknowledges her "sterling work" (38) in sifting through a wealth of original sources, not the least of which was Leopardi's vast *Zibaldone* or day book. Unexplored material was often at the origin of Origo's biographies, as Harold Nicolson (1949) points out in his article reviewing Origo's account of Byron's last love affair. He declares that these papers "could not have found a more ideal editor, as Origo is bilingual, has spent most of her life in Italy, is a woman of letters and possesses a scholarly mind" (8). Clive Bell (1949) admits that "we see the poet from a new angle, through Italian eyes" (22).

SELECTED BIBLIOGRAPHY

Works by Origo

Leopardi, A Study in Solitude (1935). New York: Helen Marx, 1999.

War in Val d'Orcia, 1943–1944: A Diary, by Iris Origo (1947). Intro. Denis Mack Smith. Boston: David R. Godine, 1984.

The Last Attachment: The Story of Byron and Teresa Guiccioli as Told in Their Unpublished Letters and Other Family Papers (1949). New York: Helen Marx, 2000.

A Measure of Love. [Contains the essays "Allegra," "The Lady in the Gondola; A Portrait of Contessa Marina Benzon," "The Carlyles and the Ashburtons; A Victorian Friendship," "The Revolutionary and the Prophet; Mazzini in Cheyne Row," "The Mirage; A Portrait of Marie Lenéru."] London: Jonathan Cape, 1957.

The Merchant of Prato, Francesco di Marco Datini, 1335–1410 (1957). Foreword Barbara Tuchman. Boston: David R. Godine, 1986. [*Il Mercante di Prato.* Foreword Luigi Einaudi. Milan: Bompiani, 1958.]

The World of San Bernardino. New York: Harcourt, Brace and World, 1962.

Images and Shadows: Part of a Life (1970). London: John Murray, 1998, and Boston: David R. Godine, 1999.

A Need to Testify (1984). [Contains the essays "Biography: True and False," "Lauro De Bosis, Icarus," "Ruth Draper and Her Company of Characters," "Gaetano Salvemini: the Man Who Would Not Conform," "Ignazio Silone: A Study in Integrity."] New York: Helen Marx, 2000.

Un'Amica. Ritratto di Elsa Dallolio. Preface Geno Pampaloni. Florence: Passigli, 1988.

Selected Studies of Origo

Acton, Harold. "Bearing Witness. A Need to Testify: Four Portraits by Iris Origo." *Books and Bookmen* (April 1984): 11–12.

Ajello, Nello. "Iris Origo. La gentildonna partigiana tra le colline della Val d'Orcia." *La Repubblica* (July 14, 2002): 31.

Bell, Clive. "Byron and the Guiccioli." *The Spectator* (September 16, 1949): 22–23.

Bowen, Elizabeth. "War in Val d'Orcia." *Tatler* (February 12, 1947): 39.

Calamandrei, Piero. "Iris Origo, 'War in Val d'Orcia'." *Il Ponte* (October 1949): 1302–5.

Gentile, Panfilo. "La musa di carne." *Il Mondo* (February 25, 1950): 103–4.

Moorehead, Caroline. *Iris Origo: Marchesa of Val d'Orcia.* London: John Murray, 2000.

Nicolson, Harold. "Byron in Italy." *The Observer* (September 11,1949): 8.

Parks, Tim. "In Love with Leopardi." *New York Review of Books* (March 23, 2000): 38–40.

Romano, Sergio. "Un ritratto anglo-americano di Salvemini." *Lingua e letteratura* 4 (1985): 133–41.

———. *La Toscana Conquistata di Iris e Antonio Origo.* Rome: Elefante, 1989.

Rossi, Ernesto. "Il Mercante di Prato." *Il Mondo* (February 3, 1959): 11–12.

Rossi Doria, Manlio. "Immagini senza vernice." *L'Indice* 3 (1985): 18.

Stark, Werner. "For God and Gain. On the 'Merchant of Prato' by Iris Origo." *The Listener* (May 30, 1957): 879.

OCTAVIO PAZ
(1914–1998)

James O. Pellicer

BIOGRAPHY

Octavio Paz was born in Mixcoac, a suburb of Mexico City, on March 31, 1914. His father and grandfather were both men of letters, and the boy felt encouraged to continue his studies, which he did at the National University. Although he never graduated, he took courses in law and literature. In 1931, at the age of 17, he started to publish poems in a local literary magazine, *Barandal*. Two years later, he completed his first book of poetry, *Luna silvestre* (1933). Following in the steps of his father, a writer for the revolutionary agrarian leader Emiliano Zapata, Paz sided with the left and traveled to Spain to work for the republican Spanish government threatened by the fascist insurgent movement. By 1937, he had met important international figures who were in Spain working for the same cause: André Malraux, André Gide, and Ilja Ehrenburg. The position of these men of letters, sufficiently close to the left but independent of Russian Marxism, also contributed to Paz's political thought. His second book, *Bajo tu claro sombra y otros poemas sobre España* (1937), reflects on his experiences with these three writers, whose influence he recognized.

Upon his return to Mexico from Spain, Paz wrote for several magazines: *El popular*, *Taller*, and *Laurel*—which resulted in the publication of books of poetry such as *Raíz del hombre* (1937), *Entre la piedra y la flor* (1941), and *A la orilla del mundo* (1942). Having won a Guggenheim Fellowship in 1944, he went to study at the University of California at Berkeley. He remained in the United States for two years and began writing one of his most important collections of essays, *El laberinto de la soledad* (1950), dealing with issues related to Mexican identity.

Returning to Mexico, he entered the Department of Foreign Affairs and in 1945 was sent to Paris where he met André Breton and the surrealist artists and writers, as well as Albert Camus and European and Hispanic American intellectuals, all of whom helped shape his cultural and political position. Thanks to these relationships, he abandoned his Marxist stance and began forming his own philosophy of life. Attracted by the mysterious Orient, he took a one-year trip to India and Japan—a journey that was to have enormous influence in his life.

Back in Mexico, thanks to a fellowship (1953) from the Colegio de México and under Breton's influence, Paz published *El arco y la lira* (1956) in which he attempted to establish his "Ars Poetica." His increasing fame allowed him to approach the writers Carlos Fuentes and Emmanuel Carballo and to contribute to their literary journal *Revista mexicana de literatura*. He also launched a series of publications that further enhanced his literary reputation: *Libertad bajo palabra* (1949), *Aguila o Sol* (1951), *Semillas para un himno* (1954), *Piedra de Sol* (1957), *La estación violenta* (1958), *Salamandra* (1962), and *Solo a dos voces* (1973). He was appointed Mexican ambassador to India in 1962, a position he occupied until 1968 when he resigned in protest against the government's bloody suppression of the students' demonstrations during the Olympic Games in Mexico City.

Returning once again to his native land, he cofounded the literary magazine *Plural* and published *Ladera Este* in 1969. In *Postdata* (1970), he concluded that Mexico's dominant political party had failed to keep in touch with the common people, one of the basic principles on which the party had been founded. In *El mono gramático* (1971), Paz gave voice to philosophical reflections in poetic prose. During 1971 and 1972, he was invited to deliver the Charles Eliot Norton Lectures at Harvard University; he then published *Los hijos del limo* (1974), a study of poetry from Romanticism to the avant-garde and in 1976 he created the journal *Vuelta*, which was dedicated to art and politics. In *El ogro filantrópico* (1979), he continued his political reflections. One of his most important publications at this time was *Sor Juana Inés de la Cruz o las trampas de la fe* (1982), a biography of the famous seventeenth-century Mexican nun and writer. Harvard University awarded him an honorary doctorate in 1980, and the following year he received Spain's most important literary award, the Premio Cervantes. He won the American Neustadt International Prize for Literature in 1982, and in 1990 the Nobel Prize for Literature. In 1998, the faculty of social sciences at the University of Chile dedicated the week of May 11–17 to study Paz's legacy and concluded, "Paz, a man demanding of himself and others, . . . has been capable of intertwining varied interests in but a single voice. . . . In addition to poetry, he searched other cultural heritages, feeding his own writings and in so doing understanding the world. If his poetry fills the void of being, his essays may be experienced as probings into the most diverse and profound aspects of our time" (http://rehue.csociales.uchile.cl/rehuehome/facultad/publicaciones/autores/paz-a.htm [page 2]).

Paz died of cancer at 84 years of age in Mexico City, in the arms of his wife, María José Tramini, whom he had met and married in India in 1964.

MAJOR MULTICULTURAL THEMES

Many of Paz's sources contributing to the expansion of his world of ideas were due to his grandfather's wisdom. Additional influences may be attributed to his father's profound Mexicanism and to the European thinkers he met in Spain. Perhaps the best way to review his writings from the point of view of multiculturalism is to reconsider his Nobel lecture of December 8, 1990, "In Search of the Present," in which he referred to a concept in some way already mentioned by Simón Bolívar at the outcome of Spanish American independence: that Spanish Americans are characterized by "the coexistence of different civilizations and different pasts" (http://www.nobel.se/literature/laureates/1990/paz-lecture.html [page 2], trans. Anthony Stanton).

Paz referred to himself as a poet and declared that his case was neither unique nor exceptional. "From the symbolist period, all modern poets have chased after that magnetic and elusive figure [modernity] that fascinates them." He then traced this pursuit for modernity back to Baudelaire, "who was the first" to discover that modernity "is nothing but time that crumbles in one's hand" (http://www.nobel.se/literature/laureates/1990/paz-lecture.html [page 2], trans. Anthony Stanton). Paz added that there was more than this to modernity. For him, the Mexican Revolution was not the expression of a utopian ideology, "but rather the explosion of a reality that had been historically and psychologically repressed" (http://www.nobel.se/literature/laureates/1990/paz-lecture.html [page 2], trans. Anthony Stanton). In addition to this enormous native-Mexican presence that modified his Baudelairean search for modernity, the impact of his Oriental experience had been decisive in forming not only his thought but also his way of thinking. In reference to this impact, the critic José Quiroga writes: "Paz's first encounter with Asia occurs in 1951, one year after he had published the first edition of *The Labyrinth of Solitude*, his thorough exploration of Mexican myth, history, and politics" (Quiroga, *Understanding Octavio Paz*, 123).

The critic Luis Pulido Ritter underlines that the first result produced by the Oriental impact on Paz was not only a theme but, more importantly, "a different way to feel life; a change that allowed him to understand the other while bringing him to see more in depth his own Occidental reality" (Pulido Ritter, 2). As was customary in the Western tradition, Paz's first view of the Orient fell within the parameters of religion. Pulido Ritter continues by saying that religion was for many modern philosophers just one variant to explain certain processes, but for Paz this variant is unique and absolute. "Orient is religion. This is to say that the only way to decipher the Oriental mind is through religion" (5). To a great extent, Paz studied in *Ladera Este*, in *Conjunciones y disyunciones* (1991) and in *Los hijos del limo* the relationships between Hinduism and Buddhism and then with Islamism. Obviously he made an immediate comparison between Oriental and European history. The process of secularization in the Occident removed control of life away from the priest. Sciences, medicine, astronomy, philosophy, art, and even morality and life itself were snatched from the domain of the Inquisition. But now the Occidentals destroy themselves in violent contradiction, while the Orientals grow sclerotized. He himself tried to find an answer to both contradiction and sclerosis. Contrarily to Pope Pius IX's solemn condemnation of faith in the future and in progress (*Quanta Cura* and the papal syllabus of errors of December 8, 1864, propositions 5 and 80), Paz sees an exit from the dilemma through the concept of modernity: "History's sun is the future, and Progress is the name of this movement towards the future.... Modernity is the spearhead of historical movement, the incarnation of evolution or revolution, the two faces of progress, ... thanks to the dual action of science and technology applied to the realm of nature and to the use of her immense resources" (http://www.nobel.se/literature/laureates/1990/paz-lecture.html [page 6], trans. Anthony Stanton).

SURVEY OF CRITICISM

Lloyd Mallan was the first English-language translator of Paz's poetry in "A Little Anthology of Young Mexican Poets" published in London in *New Directions* 9 (1947). Soon thereafter, Paz edited a French edition of Mexican poetry under the title *Anthologie de la poésie méxicaine* (1952), with a presentation by Paz himself and an introductory note by Paul Claudel. *Piedra de Sol* was Paz's first complete book of verse to be published in English; Muriel Rukeyser translated it as *Sun Stone* (1962). From then on, every year witnessed a translation as well as a new book by Paz.

The first study of his work is Claire Céa's (1965), while Carlos H. Magis (1978) was the first to attempt to deepen analysis of the surrealists' influence on Paz's poetry. Enrico Mario Santí published in 1988 *Primeras letras (1931–1943)*, a 415-page book that gathers Paz's earliest publications and contains an introductory note by Paz himself as well as an excellent introduction in which Santí studies Paz's association with the Marxists first, and then with the surrealists.

In 1985, Hugo J. Verani, the compiler of the best critical bibliography (1983) of Paz's works, published *Pasión crítica*, 12 interviews with Paz by well-known writers. Verani's introduction justifies the book's title; critical inquiry was Paz's dominating passion.

Unpretentious yet very helpful is José Quiroga's *Understanding Octavio Paz* (1999), which studies key works by Paz and a few very important themes in his poetry, such as "A poetics of East and West" and "A poetics of Space."

Revista Iberoamericana dedicated a special number to the author in January-March 1971 and occasionally publishes enlightening articles on different aspects of Paz's work, for example, "Octavio Paz y España" (October–December 1987), in which Peter G. Earle studies Paz's early relationships in Spain. The July–December 1989 issue presents an interview by Manuel Ulacia in which Paz speaks on poetry, painting, and music, and mainly on Mexico's fame as a country of illustrious painters.

SELECTED BIBLIOGRAPHY

Works by Paz

Luna silvestre. Mexico City: Fábula, 1933.

Bajo tu clara sombra y otros poemas sobre España. Valencia: Ediciones Españolas, 1937.

Raíz del hombre. Mexico City: Simbad, 1937.

Entre la piedra y la flor. Mexico City: Nueva Voz, 1941.

A la orilla del mundo. Mexico City: Ars, 1942.

Libertad bajo palabra. Mexico City: Fondo de Cultura Económico, 1949.

El laberinto de la soledad. Mexico City: Cuadernos Americanos, 1950.

Aguila o Sol (1951). Mexico City: Fondo de Cultura Económico, 1959.

————, ed. *Anthologie de la poésie mexicaine*. Intro. Paul Claudel. Paris: Nagel, 1952.

Semillas para un himno. Mexico City: Fondo de Cultura Económico, 1954.

El arco y la lira. Mexico City: Fondo de Cultura Económico, 1956.

Piedra de Sol. Mexico City: Fondo de Cultura Económico, 1957. [*Sun Stone*. Trans. Muriel Rukeyser. London: New Directions, 1962.]

La estación violenta. Mexico City: Fondo de Cultura Económico, 1958.

Salamandra. Mexico City: Joaquín Mortiz, 1962.

Conjunciones y disyunciones. Mexico City: Joaquín Mortiz, 1969; Barcelona: Seix Barral, 1991.

Ladera Este. Mexico City: Joaquín Mortiz, 1969.

Postdata. Mexico City: Siglo XXI, 1970.

El mono gramático (1971). Barcelona: Seix Barral, 1974.

Solo a dos voces. Barcelona: Lumen, 1973.

Los hijos del limo. Barcelona: Seix Barral, 1974.

El ogro filantrópico. Mexico City: Joaquín Mortiz, 1979.

Sor Juana Inés de la Cruz o las trampas de la fe. Mexico City: Fondo de la Cultura Económico, 1982.

Pasión crítica (Interviews). Ed. and intro. Hugo J. Verani. Barcelona: Seix Barral, 1985.

Primeras letras (1931–1943). Ed. and Intro. Enrico Mario Santí. Barcelona: Seix Barral, 1988.

Nobel lecture (1990). Available at http://www.nobel.se/literature/laureates/ 1990/paz-lecture.html (9 pages, trans. Anthony Stanton).

Selective Studies of Paz

Céa, Claire. *Octavio Paz; Étude*. Paris: Seghers, 1965.
Chantikian, Kosrof, ed. *Octavio Paz. Homage to the Poet*. San Francisco: Kosmos, 1980.
Cuadernos Hispanoamericanos. Nos. 343–45 (1979). Homenaje a Octavio Paz.
Earle, Peter G. "Octavio Paz y España." *Revista Iberoamericana* 141 (October–December 1987): 945–53.
Flores, Angel, ed. *Aproximaciones a Octavio Paz*. Mexico City: Joaquín Mortiz, 1974.
Gimferrer, Pere, ed. *Octavio Paz*. Madrid: Taurus, 1982.
Lemaitre, Monique. *Octavio Paz: poesia y poética*. Mexico City: Universidad Nacional Autónoma de Mexico City, 1976.
Magis, Carlos H. *La poesía hermética de Octavio Paz*. Mexico City: El Colegio de México, 1978.
Pulido Ritter, Luis. "La imagen del Oriente en Octavio Paz." *Revista Panameña de cultura MAGA* (September–December 1998). Available at http://www.utp.ac.pa/revistas/imagen_oriente.html (Trans. James O. Pellicer).
Quiroga, José. *Understanding Octavio Paz*. Columbia: University of South Carolina Press, 1999.
Revista Iberoamericana 37:74 (January–March 1971). Homenaje a Octavio Paz.
Rodríguez Padrón, Jorge. *Octavio Paz*. Madrid: Júcar, 1975.
Ulacia, Manuel. "Poesía, pintura, música. Conversación con Octavio Paz." *Revista Iberoamericana* 148–49 (July–December 1989): 615–36.
Verani, Hugo J. *Octavio Paz: Bibliografía crítica*. Mexico City: Universidad Nacional Autónoma de México, 1983.

e-Bibliography

http://www.nobel.se/literature/laureates/1990/paz-lecture.html
http://www.jornada.unam.mx/1997/dic97/971214/semb
http://almaz.com/nobel/literature/1990a.html
http://www.ur.mx/division/chepe/homepage/letras/PAZ.htm
http://www.ensayo.rom.uga.edu/filosofos/mexico/paz/biblio-de.htm
http://www.columbia.edu/~gmo9/poetry/paz/paz-bio.html
http://www.fundacionpaz.org.mx/main.htm
http://rehue.csociales.uchile.cl/rehuehome/facultad/publicaciones/autores/paz-a.htm
http://www.ekeko.rep.net.pe/IAL/vm/bec/etexts/quanta.htm

PEPETELA
(1941–)

Maria Grazia Orsi

BIOGRAPHY

Artur Carlos Mauricio Pestana dos Santos is the registered name of the
Angolan writer better known as Pepetela, a word that means "eyelashes"
in the Ambundan language and corresponds to the Portuguese *pestana*.
Pepetela was born into a commercial family in Benguela in the center of
Angola's coastline. His father was Portuguese, his mother Brazilian. Up
to the age of 17, he remained in this ethnically mixed port city, but
moved to Lisbon in 1958, enrolling in the Superior Technical Institute
but subsequently transferring to the study of history in the Faculty of
Letters. He was seen less often in the halls of the university than in those
of the *Casa dos Estudiantes do Império* (CEI—Empire Students' House),
the cultural center and meeting place of young African students. Here he
took an active part in debates on the political-social status of the Portuguese colonies and in plans for the achievement of national unity in
African countries. From these discussions there emerged a number of
revolutionary militants who were to play a decisive part in the wars of liberation from Portuguese colonialism. Armed struggle for independence
in Angola began in 1961, and Pepetela in the following year escaped to
France to avoid military service in Portugal. He lived in the Belleville
quarter of Paris and worked in the Desfossés printing office. Six months
later, he was in Algeria, drawn by the dreams and utopias that were taking shape in that country. Enrolling in sociology courses at the University of Algiers, he threw himself into the political campaign for Angolan
independence, officially becoming a militant of the *Movimento Popolar de
Libertação de Angola* (MPLA—Popular Movement for Angolan Libera-

tion) which fought for the construction of a multiracial Angolan nation. Here he founded the *Centro de Estudos Angolanos* (Center for Angolan Studies) and collaborated with the Angolan writers Costa Andrade and Henrique Abranches on the compilation for the MPLA of a history of Angola (*História de Angola*) and in 1965 a manual to teach reading and writing (*Manual de Alfabetização*). After having spent six years in Algeria and obtaining his degree in sociology, he returned to Angola in 1969 as a guerrilla combatant of the national liberation movement on the northern Cabinda front. During the five years of armed struggle against the Portuguese army, Commander Pepetela (a pseudonym he acquired in the guerrilla struggle and used also in his literary activity) was occupied in finishing his first two novels: *Muana Puó* (written in 1969; published in 1978) and *Mayombe: Romance* (written in 1971; published in 1980). In 1972, he transferred to the eastern front in the guerrilla war, leading a group of seven men. In 1973, he was cultural secretary of the MPLA, and in 1974 he set up the first MPLA delegation in Luanda, the Angolan capital. Following Angola's proclamation of independence on November 11, 1975, Pepetela was involved in the center of the country, at Cuanza Sul, fighting not the Portuguese but the rival nationalist movement, the *União Nacional para a Independência Total de Angola* (UNITA—National Union for the Total Independence of Angola). A grave case of hepatitis caused Pepetela to lay down his arms and become deputy minister of education in the newly independent government, a post he occupied until 1982. Having since then abandoned all political offices, he has served as president of the *União dos Escritores Angolanos* (UEA—Union of Angolan Writers) and now teaches sociology in the school of architecture of Agostinho Neto University in Luanda. In 1997, he was awarded the Camões Prize for the entire body of his work.

MAJOR MULTICULTURAL THEMES

Pepetela's literary work is a reflection on the historical events that brought Angola to independence, and on a country lacerated by civil war and the incurable corruption of the ruling political class. His life experience as a full participant in the liberation struggle and the construction of a multiethnic country is joined with a tireless exploration of the past to find the meaning of the present and a hope for a better future. The integration of history in literary creation and the utilization and reinterpretation of the myths and symbols of the Angolan oral tradition constitute an underlying strategy to which the author constantly reverts in his effort to affirm a national, cultural, and political identity.

Pepetela wrote his first novel, *Muana Puó*, while still in Algeria at the end of the 1960s. It is the story of a mysterious mask, which is founded on a myth in the oral tradition of the Lunda and Tchokwe cultures of eastern Angola. Muana Puó is an oval mask, divided into two parts by a forbidden mountain. Transgression of the rule by the protagonists becomes a metaphor for the possibility of critically changing the world without fleeing from it. The utopia of an ideal country as here described is realized in the desire to construct a real country based on a solid democracy and on respect for the differences among the numerous ethnic groups residing in Angolan territory. Pepetela's second novel, *Mayombe: Romance*, is the fruit of the author's direct participation in the guerrilla war on the northern Cabinda front. Written initially as a military communiqué, it gradually acquires the form of a critical narrative aimed at the MPLA itself, at local tribalism, and at corruption and power. *As Aventuras de Ngunga* (written in 1973; published in 1976) is the story of an adolescent, Ngunga, and his militancy in the national liberation struggle. Written for use as a textbook in the schools of the zones liberated by the MPLA, it constitutes an authentic bildungsroman in which the political ideals of the movement to which Pepetela belonged are commingled with the oral traditions of the country.

The first of Pepetela's writings to see the light after independence was a brief theatrical work, *A Corda: Peça num acto e doze cenas* (written in 1976; published in 1978), in which a tug-of-war was represented with the Angolans on one side and the South African invaders and the adherents of the UNITA movement on the other. Thereafter followed another theater piece, *A Revolta da Casa dos Ídolos: Teatro* (written in 1979; published in 1980). It brings to the stage an incident at the beginning of the colonial period in the sixteenth century: a popular revolt against the Portuguese fathers and their allies, the Manicongos (chiefs of the Kingdom of the Congo), who prohibited the animist worship of idols and fetishes.

Yaka: Romance (1984), a novel whose idea originated in 1975 on the battlefield at Benguela while waiting at night for the enemy, is a saga of 100 years of Angolan history, told through the development and vicissitudes of a family of Portuguese colonists arriving in the nineteenth century. The novel ends with the conquest of a new identity on the part of a settler who finds himself living in a historical-social reality greatly modified by the advent of independence. Pepetela merges African and European myths to create an osmosis of the Hellenic and Angolan cultures: Yaka is the statue that does not speak, the guardian of a secret like the sphinx in the myth of Oedipus. Alexandre, the first of the Semedo family of Portuguese settlers to be born in Angola, at the end of his life fathoms the statue's secret: only death can bring complete awareness—just as the answer to the riddle that the sphinx puts to Oedipus consists in self-knowledge that is attainable only at the very last stage of life.

In a subsequent work, *Lueji: O Nascimento dum Império* (1989), past and present are joined in determining the destinies of two women, Lueji and Lu. In the first part of the novel, Pepetela reconsiders the antique legend of Lueji and the creation of the Lunda Empire in northeast Angola. In the second part, at a distance of 400 years, Lu, a young ballerina of

Lunda descent, tries to reconstruct the myth of the foundation of the Lunda Empire for a dance performance. The book as a whole thus offers an analysis of the consolidation of power in an African kingdom and at the same time is a reflection on the cultural identity of a country in transition.

In 1991, while in Berlin, Pepetela wrote the novel *A Geração da Utopia: Romance* (1992), covering 30 years of Angolan history (1961–91) from the beginning of the armed struggle to the eve of the first elections. It describes the end of the utopias and dreams of a generation of young intellectuals committed to the creation of a democratic state. In *O Desejo de Kianda* (1995) and in *Parábola do Cágado Velho* (1996), Pepetela delineates the new historical-social reality of Angola in the postindependence period. Amid the loss of traditional values and the spreading ills of modern society, he seeks to rethink and recast the national cultural identity in the hope that the recovery and reevaluation of a mythic and ancestral past will provide the key to an understanding of the present.

SURVEY OF CRITICISM

Ana Mafalda Leite (1996) sees in *Yaka* the allegory of the union between Europe and Africa as a possible "brotherhood of cultures and the fusion of 'imaginaries' " (116). In her 1997 article, she points out the confluence in Pepetela's novels of European cultural elements with those of the African oral tradition. The result of this symbiosis is the realization of a mythic dream, or the construction of a nation on a multiethnic social basis (10).

Maria Teresa Gil Mendes da Silva (1985) sees in Pepetela's work a continuing search for the origins of the Angolan people and the determination to construct an Angolan nation that in its formative phase "must take account of the five centuries of Portuguese presence, of the existence of the mulattos and whites who feel themselves to be profoundly Angolan, since they have completely severed their ties with the mother country and are ready to make their own contribution to the birth of an independent Angola" (435).

Rodrigues da Silva (1995) writes concerning the origin of Pepetela's family that "the maternal grandparents were Portuguese (or Brazilian), but mixed (Gypsy, Indian); this explains the skin color of the writer, which at first seemed to me neither white nor black, but mulatto, as I had wished in order to justify in the body the imaginary figure which he conveyed in his books—books that owe as much to African mythology as they are subsidiary to European culture, all of it the fruit of an itinerary that in the intervals of travel within Angola touched also Lisbon, Paris, Berlin, and many other places" (14).

Inocência Mata (2001), in stressing the multicultural character of Benguela observes that "Pepetela has been confronted since infancy with two realities, two philosophies, two traditions, two ways of life, from which there results a culture made up of confluences, one whose roots are found in African and European, especially Portuguese civilization" (167).

SELECTED BIBLIOGRAPHY

Work by Pepetela

Muana Puó (1969). Lisbon: Edições 70 and Luanda: União dos Escritores Angolanos, 1978.

Mayombe: Romance (1971). Lisbon: Edições 70 and Luanda: União dos Escritores Angolanos, 1980.

As Aventuras de Ngunga (1973). Lisbon: Edições 70 and Luanda: União dos Escritores Angolanos, 1976.

A Corda: Peça num acto e doze cenas. (1976). Luanda: União dos Escritores Angolanos, 1978.

A Revolta da Casa dos Ídolos: Teatro. Lisbon: Edições 70 and Luanda: União dos Escritores Angolanos, 1980.

Yaka: Romance. São Paulo: Ática, 1984.

Lueji: O Nascimento dum Império. Luanda: União dos Escritores Angolanos, 1989.

A Geração da Utopia: Romance. Lisbon: Dom Quixote, 1992.

O Desejo de Kianda. Lisbon: Dom Quixote, 1995.

Parábola do Cágado Velho. Lisbon: Dom Quixote, 1996.

Selected Studies of Pepetela

Alegre, Manuel. "Muana Puó: ou talvez o nosso rosto." *Jornal de Letras, Artes e Ideias* (Lisbon) (March 29, 1995): 19–20.

Drndarska, Dea and Ange-Severin Malanda. *Pepetela et l'écriture du mythe et de l'histoire.* Paris: L'Harmattan, 2000.

Guardão, Maria João. "Pepetela e a guerrilha da escrita." *Jornal de Letras, Artes e Ideias* (Lisbon) (October 4, 1988): 7.

Leite, Ana Mafalda. "Angola." In *The Post-Colonial Literature of Lusophone Africa.* Ed. Patrick Chabal, 115–23. London: Hurst, 1996.

———. "O desconstrutor de mitos." *Jornal de Letras, Artes e Ideias* (Lisbon) (May 7, 1997): 10.

Mata, Inocência. "Pepetela: um escritor (ainda) em busca da utopia—Alguns lugares da obra de Pepetela." In *Silêncios e Falas de uma Voz inquieta*, 166–208. Lisbon: Mar Além, 2001.

Perassi, Emilia. "Incontro con lo scrittore angolano Pepetela." *Africa America Asia Australia* (Rome) 2 (June–December 1987): 67–79.

———. "Due culture: angolana e portoghese." *Uomini e libri* (Milan) 124 (September–October 1988): 50–54.

Portugal, Salinas Francisco. "*Yaka*: a Viagem e a Esfinge no Universo do Colono." In *Atti del Convegno Internazionale "Il Portogallo e i mari: un incontro tra culture." Napoli, 15–17 Dicembre 1994.* Ed. M. Luisa Cusati, vol. I, 161–69. Naples: Liguori, 1997.

Silva, Maria Teresa Gil Mendes da. "O Mayombe na produção de Pepetela." *Annali dell'Istituto Universitario Orientale di Napoli*, Sezione Romanza 27, no. 2 (July 1985): 419–35.

Silva, Rodrigues da. "Da Utopia à Amargura." *Jornal de Letras, Artes e Ideias* (Lisbon) (March 29, 1995): 14–16.

Torres, Alexandre Pinheiro. "*Yaka* ou o calcanhar da Aquiles." In *Literaturas Africanas de Língua Portuguesa*. Ed. Manuel Ferreira, 197–203. Lisbon: Fundação Calouste Gulbenkian, 1987.

ELISABETH PLESSEN
(1944–)

Ingeborg Baumgartner

BIOGRAPHY

Born and raised in Neustadt in Schleswig-Holstein, the northernmost state of the Federal Republic of Germany, Elisabeth Charlotte Marguerite Augusta, Countess of Plessen, was educated in private schools before she became a student of literature, philosophy, and history at universities in Berlin and Paris. Keenly aware of the student movement in the late 1960s, Plessen developed a pronounced social conscience that affected her view of her family background, raising doubts about the status of nobility and concern about her father's attitude toward the politics of the Third Reich. Her dissertation on contemporary epic in the border area between fiction and nonfiction (*Fakten und Erfindungen-zeitgenössische Epik im Grenzgebiet von fiction und nonfiction*) earned her a doctorate in Berlin in 1971. It explores novels that deal with the relationship between fiction and fact and stands out because even in this work Plessen focuses on non-German writers (Per Olov Enquist and Truman Capote). Subsequently she embarked on travels to Egypt, Tunisia, Morocco, the West Indies, South America, and the Soviet Union, and in later years she visited Australia, Central America, and the United States.

Having first settled in Berlin, Plessen moved to Munich, and later to Hamburg, eventually establishing residence in Vecoli (Italy). As a freelance writer, she has produced a variety of genres: poetry, essays, radio plays, short stories, novellas, and novels. Furthermore, she has established herself as a translator of plays by Anton Chekhov, Henrik Ibsen, and William Shakespeare (especially). In 1974 Plessen, along with Michael Mann, edited Katia Mann's memoirs, *Meine ungeschriebenen*

Memoiren. Two years later Plessen's first novel, *Mitteilung an den Adel: Roman* (1976), appeared, for which she received the Kritiker Preis für Literatur. The novel introduced a series of *Tochtergraphien,* as the protagonist, Augusta, "tries to come to terms with a father who is a rich landowner and nobleman in Northern Germany" (Moffit, 55). In this novel Plessen displays a unique, kaleidoscopic structure, stressing "the importance of creativity through which the individually perceived fragments of reality can form a relevant picture of the world" (Kraft and Marshall, 158). Shifting focus from the autobiographical to the biographical, Plessen's second novel, *Kohlhaas: Roman* (1979), relates the story of the sixteenth-century rebel. Again using the fragmentary time / space kaleidoscope technique (cf. Kraft and Marshall, 163), Plessen juxtaposes imaginary dialogues with personal recollections and historical events with anachronisms, in order to arrive closer to the historical truth.

No doubt as a consequence of extended travels, notably to the United States, and of establishing residence in Italy, Plessen expands attention to international settings and casts characters to include multicultural themes in fiction. For example, her first collection of narratives, *Zu machen, dass ein gebraten Huhn aus der Schüssel laufe* (1981), features many stories set in the United States, while her novel *Stella Polare: Roman* (1984) tells of a female German writer who lives with a Polish-German dentist-novelist in Italy. The anthology *Lady Spaghetti: Erzählungen* (1992), as the title suggests, contains stories set in Italy. Plessen's latest novel, *Der Knick: Roman* (1997), deals with a journalist and an actress dependent on medication, who move effortlessly between Germany and Austria, peppering their dialogues with phrases from English and French. Plessen's association with the stage director Peter Zadek, who dedicates his autobiography to her and calls her "*mehr ein Zuhause als Vecoli*" (more of a home than Vecoli, Zadek, 81), has inspired her numerous translations of plays. But also in her introduction to *Auf ein Neues Vor und zurück in Beziehungen* (1987), an anthology of texts by an international roster of poets and writers, she demonstrates breadth of knowledge in world literature. These love stories by writers of different social levels, from different countries, and different times, sing in multifarious voices on the same theme.

MAJOR MULTICULTURAL THEMES

Indeed, multifarious voices may be taken as the overriding theme of Plessen's work from the 1980s. The anthology *Zu machen, dass ein gebraten Huhn aus der Schüssel laufe* contains stories with titles such as "Reisegepäck" (travel luggage) or "Grenzüberschreitungen" (border crossings), announcing departures from her native land to explore life elsewhere. Thus, in some of these stories, characters originate from Switzerland, Czechoslovakia, Great Britain, Romania, the United States, or Nicaragua. Plessen meets them at parties, on the street, in galleries, or in hotels, documenting behavior that contrasts with her own upbringing and tradition, such as preparing eggplant relish or throwing a pomegranate out of the window. A number of narratives target America's popular culture (e.g. the love for sending greeting cards on any occasion) or mock the American propensity for addressing people by the first initials of their names. Notably in depictions of life in the United States, a penchant for caricature and satire obtrude. In one story, a German language professor in California, "*so weit ab vom Schuß*" (so uninvolved, *Zu machen, dass ein gebraten Huhn aus der Schüssel laufe*, 74), who possesses only "ninety volumes," is considered "unserious . . . in the discipline she was teaching" (*Zu machen*, 75). Moved by the obituary for Alfred Andersch, the narrator experiences grief in the midst of an overpowering, lifeless landscape (cf. *Zu machen*, 79). In the last and longest story of this anthology, the narrator describes in a matter-of-fact tone her frustrations with bureaucracy, the deleterious effects of tropical weather, and the abject poverty she witnesses as she and her companion Peter undertake the treacherous drive from Costa Rica to Managua, Nicaragua, then to Léon.

Plessen's tone softens when depicting Italy and its people, succumbing to the soothing landscape, tempered climate, and noble architecture of Tuscany. Her third novel, *Stella Polare*, begins: "Das Haus lag in den Hügeln oberhalb Luccas" (The house was located in the hills above Lucca, *Stella Polare*, 7); its stunning beauty mesmerizes the owner Max Fischer and his partner, the narrator Luise von Kai. A dentist and writer, Max reached his goal after an odyssey "die in Warschau begann, um ihn während des Krieges durch polnische Dörfer und danach via Israel nach Deutschland und in dieses Haus zu bringen" (which began in Warsaw, to take him during the war through Polish villages, after that via Israel to Germany and into this house, *Stella Polare*, 127). Luise, too, finds refuge in this paradise of a place: "gab es einen schöneren Fleck auf der Erde?" (was there a more beautiful spot on this earth?, *Stella Polare*, 126). Here they are joined by widely traveled, international, polyglot guests to celebrate Christmas and the New Year. Not hermetically sealed off from surrounding communities, this extended family frequents the local bar Stella Polare, shops in Lucca, visits the nearby coast, and enjoys warm relationships with their indigenous neighbors. Especially in Erina Petruzzi, the native Italian housekeeper and cook, Plessen created a sympathetic figure with depth and feeling. While stories in *Lady Spaghetti* are set in France, Israel, Austria, or Germany, and the narrator carries on an imaginary dialogue with Anton Chekhov, most of the tales take place in Italy. All narratives display the confidence and ease with which Plessen traverses countries, creating characters rooted in their native soil but also given to adventures when visiting foreign places. In the title story, Hansjürgen Jasper symbolizes travel-savvy everyman. At 21 he vacations in

Italy, falling in love with a waitress he nicknames Lady Spaghetti. Thirty years later, now an experienced traveler, he comes back as a successful businessman to return the gift he had received from her. Plessen's attitude to Italy is characterized by her fascination with the everyday activities of ordinary people dealing with ordinary problems. Familiar with languages, Plessen's narrators speak in the vernacular, suggesting that boundaries between cultures have become fluid and surmountable.

SURVEY OF CRITICISM

At this time, Plessen's work has not been examined with respect to themes of multiculturalism. The most recent criticism by Gisela Moffit (1993) focuses on father/daughter relationships, while Germany's past and the role of aristocracy in the Third Reich are assessed by Sandra Frieden (1982). The rebellious opposition to corrupt government or conflict between the individual and the establishment are the subjects of study by Helga Kraft and Harry Marshall (1985).

SELECTED BIBLIOGRAPHY

Works by Plessen

Mitteilung an den Adel: Roman. Cologne and Zurich: Benzinger, 1976.
Kohlhaas: Roman. Cologne and Zurich: Benzinger, 1979.
Zu machen, dass ein gebraten Huhn aus der Schüssel laufe: Geschichten. Cologne and Zurich: Benzinger, 1981.
"Hedwig Dohm." In *Frauen Porträts aus zwei Jahrhunderten.* Ed. Hans Jürgen Schultz, 128–41. Stuttgart: Kreuz, 1982.
Stella Polare: Roman. Frankfurt am Main: S. Fischer, 1984.
"'Du hast Frühling um mich gemacht': Clara Wieck und Robert Schumann." In *Liebespaare.* Ed. Hans Jürgen Schultz, 199–224. Stuttgart: Kreuz, 1989.
Lady Spaghetti: Erzählungen. Frankfurt am Main: S. Fischer, 1992.
Der Knick: Roman. Zurich: Nagel and Kimche, 1997.
Editions:
Mann, Katia. *Meine ungeschriebenen Memoiren.* Ed. Elisabeth Plessen and Michael Mann. Frankfurt am Main: S. Fischer, 1974. [*Unwritten Memories.* Trans. Hunter Hannum and Hildegarde Hannum. New York: Knopf, 1975.]
Plessen, Elisabeth, ed. *Auf ein Neues Vor und zurück in Beziehungen.* Hamburg: Rowohlt Taschenbuch Verlag, 1987.

Selected Studies of Plessen

Bagley, Petra M. "The Death of the Father—the Start of a Story: Bereavement in Elisabeth Plessen, Brigitte Schwaiger, and Jutta Schutting." *New German Studies* 16 (1990–91): 21–38.
Frieden, Sandra. "'Selbstgespräche': Elisabeth Plessen's *Mitteilung an den Adel.*" *Seminar* 18 (1982): 271–86.

Helbling, Robert E. "'Kohlhaas'-Metamorphosen." In *Sprache und Literatur, Festschrift für Arval L. Streadbeck zum 65. Geburtstag.* Ed. Gerhard P. Knapp and Wolff A. von Schmidt, 65–74. Bern, Frankfurt am Main: Peter Lang, 1981.

Kiefer, Rumjana. *Kleists Erzählungen in der Literatur der Gegenwart: Ein Beitrag zur Geschichte der Intertextualitat am Beispiel von Texten.* St. Ingbert: W. J. Röhrig, 1994.

Kraft, Helga and Harry Marshall. "Elisabeth Plessen's Discourse with the Past: Two Historical Novels from the 1970s." *Monatshefte* 77 (1985): 157–70.

Moffit, Gisela. *Bonds and Bondage: Daughter-Father Relationships in the Father Memoirs of German-Speaking Women Writers of the 1970s.* New York: Peter Lang, 1993.

Zadek, Peter. *My Way. Eine Autobiographie 1926–1969.* Cologne: Kiepenheuer and Witsch, 1998.

JEAN RHYS
(1890–1979)

Giovanna Silvani

BIOGRAPHY

Jean Rhys was born Ella Gwendolen Rees Williams in Roseau, Dominica, one of the Leeward Islands in the Antilles. Her father, William Rhys Williams, was a Welsh doctor who had migrated to the West Indies; her mother, née Minna Lockhart, came from a Creole family that had settled many years earlier in the British-owned islands. In 1907, Jean went to England with an aunt (the model for Anna Morgan's rasping Aunt Hester in *Voyage in the Dark*, 1934) to study acting at the Royal Academy of Dramatic Arts, but her father's death the following year, which cut off her allowance, ended her schooling. Adrift in an alien culture, she toured the English provinces as a chorus girl and then worked as a model. In 1910, she had an affair with Launcelot Hugh Smith, 20 years her senior, who left her in 1912 (the story is told in *Voyage in the Dark*). In 1912, she went to Holland to marry Jean Lenglet, a Dutch-French poet and journalist. Roaming the Continent, the ill-fated couple lived impecuniously in Paris, Vienna, and Budapest. The failure of her marriage led to an affair with Ford Madox Ford, who also sponsored her first work of fiction, a collection of short stories entitled *The Left Bank and Other Stories*, published in 1927 in Britain and the United States. Tilden Smith became her literary agent and her second husband in 1934, after her divorce from Lenglet. Although artistically fertile, her haphazard expatriate years were full of stress; the same sorrows riding the marooned characters of *The Left Bank* also rode their creator. She returned to England and settled in Cornwall with her husband until his death in 1945. In 1928, *Postures* (later retitled *Quartet*) was published in

Britain, followed by *After Leaving Mr. Mackenzie* (1931) and *Voyage in the Dark*. Rhys visited Dominica with Tilden Smith in 1936 and the following year, during a visit to Paris, she started writing *Good Morning, Midnight*, which appeared in 1939.

In 1947, she married her second husband's cousin, the poet and retired naval officer Max Hamer, who was imprisoned for minor fraud in 1950. When he was released in 1952, the couple moved to Cornwall. The combination of World War II and the failure to win readers silenced Rhys's pen in the 1940s and 1950s. Ending her retirement in the country was the decision of the BBC's Third Programme to dramatize *Good Morning, Midnight*. In the same year, she signed a contract with the publisher André Deutsch for the novel which was to become *Wide Sargasso Sea*, the story of Edward Rochester's mad West Indian wife in Charlotte Brontë's *Jane Eyre* (1847). The book came out in 1966, winning the W. H. Smith Prize. In the same year, Hamer died. After the success of *Wide Sargasso Sea*, Rhys's previous novels *Voyage in the Dark* and *Good Morning, Midnight* were reissued in 1967, *Quartet* in 1971, and *After Leaving Mr. Mackenzie* in 1969. In 1968, she published *Tigers are Better-Looking*, a collection of short stories including some from *The Left Bank*. In 1975, *My Day*, a collection of three autobiographical pieces, was published in the United States; in 1976, *Sleep It Off, Lady*, a collection of short stories, came out in Britain and the United States. Jean Rhys died in 1979; her autobiography, *Smile, Please: An Unfinished Autobiography* was published posthumously, shortly after her death.

MAJOR MULTICULTURAL THEMES

Both *Wide Sargasso Sea* and its predecessors take root in Jean Rhys's private experience. Disguised and rearranged, the materials of her life pulsate through her novels. She shares many of her heroines' experiences: Anna Morgan's letdown on first arriving in London from the West Indies and her short turn as a chorus girl in *Voyage in the Dark*; Marya Zelli's marriage to a penniless Continental in *Quartet*; Sasha Jansen's brief modeling career in *Good Morning, Midnight*; and Julia Martin's lonely exile in *After Leaving Mr. Mackenzie*. Sadness runs through both her work and life. Her novels begin like epilogues or postscripts to conventional love stories, but the girl in Jean Rhys's works does not get the man: the novels specialize in the loser, the outcast. The three constants in the world of Rhys's heroines are fear, loneliness, and lack of money. Rebellion and moral self-examination never occur: the Rhys heroine lacks the self-respect to believe she deserves something better, while indifference and fatalism are evident in her casual attitude towards sex, and her readiness to rely on men and to subjugate herself.

If in her early novels Jean Rhys dramatizes the problem of being a woman in between wars in London and Paris, her portrayal of the nineteenth-century Creole, Antoinette Cosway, in *Wide Sargasso Sea*, shows women to be mistreated and exiled in the last century as well. In all her novels, silenced "foreign" and female voices, inhabiting marginalized and usually urban social spaces, speak and signify their lives in ways that have profoundly disturbed the novels' readers. Perhaps the best way to examine the powerful yet disconcerting effects of Rhys's fiction is to understand more fully the nature of the in-between spaces it explores. They are the spaces of colonial and sexual exile: the streets of London in 1914, where a young Creole woman attempts to support herself; the bars of Paris in 1937, where a somewhat older woman of vague nationality attempts to improvise an identity; and the rooming houses in either city that both shelter and isolate most of Rhys's solitary protagonists.

Reading Rhys's fiction as West Indian literature suggests also a cultural and historical context outside the strictly European, offering possibilities for interpretation that go beyond the psychological. One of the most relevant aspects is the tension between the two spaces or contexts of Rhys's writing—the West Indian colonial context and the modernist European—as it is inscribed in terms of sex/gender relations in her novels. The Caribbean cultures that emerge fully in *Wide Sargasso Sea* shift the moral ground of critical judgment by presenting an alternative to European concepts of character and identity. The experience of colonial exile reveals much about Jean Rhys's fiction and its place at the intersection of several kinds of modernism. One of these modernist crosscurrents is that of an emerging West Indian literature that develops from a strong sense of its own place in the Caribbean and of its plural histories and cultures. Like other West Indian writers of the pre- and post–World War I generation, Jean Rhys left the Caribbean island of her birth for Europe. However, unlike her fellow exiles (such as Claude McKay and V. S. Naipaul), as a woman she experienced a specifically female form of alienation and sexual vulnerability.

In *Wide Sargasso Sea*, the young blacks call Antoinette "white cockroach" and "white nigger," epithets for the Euro-Creole woman who bears the brunt of guilt for the history of slavery and the cruelties committed by her ancestors. In some ways, white Creoles experience a double dose of a quintessential aspect of the Caribbean experience, the marginality of living between two cultures. This is what happened to Jean Rhys; this is most clearly what happened to the heroine of *Wide Sargasso Sea*, Antoinette.

In Charlotte Brontë's novel *Jane Eyre*, Edward Rochester's marriage to a West Indian woman, Bertha Mason, is seen only through Rochester's English eyes, who tells Jane the story of their unhappy marriage. Bertha's point of view is never given; she is never allowed to speak; the reader sees her only in her insane state, confined like a beast to the attic of Rochester's ancestral home. In *Wide Sargasso Sea*, Jean Rhys provides a twentieth-century response to Brontë's novel in which the colonies and colonialism play a very reduced role: the West Indies are depicted merely as a place where an Englishman can travel, find a wealthy wife, and attempt to mend his ailing fortune, or where a young impoverished woman can find a miraculous reprieve from straitened circumstances (Jane's Madeiran inheritance). Rhys was indignant at the portrayal of Bertha—one who, like herself, had been brought to England from the Caribbean—and wanted to give this shadowy and frightening creature the opportunity to tell her story, to establish herself as a human being, and to discredit Rochester's dominant—male, European—discourse.

SURVEY OF CRITICISM

Veronica Gregg (1995) reads Rhys in relation to the work of Caribbean historians, providing a context for her discussion of Rhys's fictional portrayal of race, gender, and class. Gregg rightly argues that intertextuality is a crucial element in Rhys's writings, especially in the context of her subversive rewriting of *Jane Eyre*. Ileana Rodriguez's analysis (1994) of a group of Caribbean fictions also firmly locates Rhys as a Caribbean writer; her reading, like Gregg's, is strongly affiliated with a specific body of theory, in this case the role of neopositivism and Marxism in the transitions to modernity in various Caribbean and Latin American contexts. Helen Carr's discussion of Rhys (1996) begins with three chapters that summarize Rhys's relation to a variety of literary and cultural currents: Carr identifies in her work a feminized, ex-colonial modernism, and claims that Rhys moves closer to postmodernism than any other of her contemporaries because she writes from a position of marginality and dislocation and employs multiple voices and "fragmentary, shifting collages" (26). Malcolm and Malcolm (1996) have filled a gap in Rhys studies by offering an analysis of the place and nature of the short stories, and their volume is structured in two sections given over to brief commentary on Rhys's letters and extracts.

SELECTED BIBLIOGRAPHY

Works by Jean Rhys

The Left Bank and Other Stories. Preface Ford Madox Ford. London: Jonathan Cape, 1927.

Postures. London: Chatto and Windus, 1928; printed as *Quartet*. New York: Harper and Row, 1957.

After Leaving Mr. Mackenzie. London: Jonathan Cape, 1931.

Voyage in the Dark. London: Constable, 1934.

Good Morning, Midnight (1939). London: André Deutsch, 1967.

Wide Sargasso Sea. London: André Deutsch, 1966.

Tigers Are Better-Looking. London: André Deutsch, 1968.

My Day: 3 Pieces. New York: Frank Hallman, 1975.

Sleep It Off, Lady: Stories. London: André Deutsch, 1976.

Smile, Please: An Unfinished Autobiography. London: André Deutsch, 1979.

Correspondence: Jean Rhys Letters, 1931–1966. Ed. Francis Wyndham and Diana Melly. London: André Deutsch, 1984.

Selected Studies of Jean Rhys

Brathwaite, Edward Kamau. *Contradictory Omens: Cultural Diversity and Integration in the Caribbean.* Mona, Jamaica: Savacou, 1974.

Campbell, Elaine. "From Dominica to Devonshire: A Memento of Jean Rhys." *Kunapipi* 1 (1979): 6–22.

Carr, Helen. *Jean Rhys.* Plymouth, U.K.: Northcote House, 1996.

Gering, August. "The Celtic Creole in Jean Rhys's *Wide Sargasso Sea.*" *Jean Rhys Review* 11 (1999): 35–61.

Gregg, Veronica. *Jean Rhys's Historical Imagination: Reading and Writing the Creole.* Chapel Hill: University of North Carolina Press, 1995.

Hulme, Peter. "The Place of *Wide Sargasso Sea.*" *Wasafiri: Journal of Caribbean, African, Asian, and Associated Literature and Film* 20 (Autumn 1994): 5–11.

Lewis, Andrea. "Immigrants, Prostitutes, and Chorus Girls: National Identity in the Early Novels of Jean Rhys." *Journal of Commonwealth and Postcolonial Studies* 6 (Spring 1999): 82–95.

Luengo, Anthony E. "*Wide Sargasso Sea* and the Gothic Mode." *World Literature Written in English* 15 (1976): 239–45.

Malcolm, Cheryl Alexander, and David Malcolm. *Jean Rhys: A Study of the Short Fiction.* New York: Twayne, 1996.

Morrel, A. C. "The World of Jean Rhys's Short Stories." *World Literature Written in English* 18 (1979): 235–44.

Nixon, Nicola. "*Wide Sargasso Sea* and Jean Rhys's Interrogation of the 'Nature Wholly Alien' in *Jane Eyre.*" *Essays in Literature* 21 (1994): 267–84.

Porter, Dennis. "Of Heroines and Victims: Jean Rhys and *Jane Eyre.*" *The Massachusetts Review* 17 (1976): 540–51.

Rodriguez, Ileana. *House/Garden/Nation: Space, Gender and Ethnicity in Post-colonial Latin American Literatures by Women.* Trans. Robert Carr and Ileana Rodriguez. Durham: Duke University Press, 1994.

Rosenberg, Leah R. "Mother and Country: Implications of Rhys's Construction of Exile." *Macomere: Journal of the Association of Caribbean Women Writers and Scholars* 1 (1998): 161–69.

Sarvan, Charles. "Flight, Entrapment, and Madness in Jean Rhys's *Wide Sargasso Sea.*" *International Fiction Review* 26 (1999): 58–65.

Savory, Elaine. "Recent Locations on the Map of Rhys Studies: A Review Essay." *Jean Rhys Review* 9 (1998): 44–49.

Sternlicht, Sanford. *Jean Rhys.* New York: Twayne, 1997.

Tarozzi, Bianca. *La forma vincente: I romanzi di Jean Rhys.* Verona: Arsenale, 1984.

Thomas, Clara. "Mr. Rochester's First Marriage: *Wide Sargasso Sea* by Jean Rhys." *World Literature Written in English* 17 (1978): 342–57.

Thum, Angela M. "*Wide Sargasso Sea*: A Rereading of Colonialism." *Michigan Academician* 3 (1998): 147–62.

Tiffin, Helen. "Mirror and Mask: Colonial Motifs in the Novels of Jean Rhys." *World Literature Written in English* 17 (1978): 328–41.

Van Neck-Yoder, Hilda. "Colonial Desires, Silence, and Metonymy: 'All Things Considered' in *Wide Sargasso Sea.*" *Texas Studies in Literature and Language* 40 (1998): 184–208.

Wickramagamage, Carmen. "An/Other Side to Antoinette/Bertha: Reading 'Race' into *Wide Sargasso Sea.*" *Journal of Commonwealth Literature* 35 (2000): 27–42.

Wolfe, Peter. *Jean Rhys.* Boston: Twayne, 1980.

RI KAISEI (YI HOE-SŎNG, ALSO TRANSCRIBED AS LEE HWE-SONG)
(1935–)

Maria Teresa Orsi

BIOGRAPHY

As a leading representative of the group of Korean writers who had been resident in Japan for one or two generations and emerged on the literary scene around the 1970s, Ri Kaisei shares with the others of the group the same marginality in relation to the traditional culture and a resistance to any form of homogenization.

The son of Koreans who entered Japan in search of work during the period of Japanese occupation of Korea, Ri Kaisei was born in 1935 at Maoka (now Khmolsk) on the island of Sakhalin, which at that time was Japanese territory. Compelled to leave his homeland following its annexation to the Soviet Union after World War II, he remains bound to the island through an intense emotional relationship in which nostalgia for his childhood years is interwoven with the exhausting search for a personal identity as a Korean in Japan—and, paradoxically, as a "Japanese" in Sakhalin, which for him has suddenly become foreign ground.

The ambiguous Japanese policy that during the war years combined overtly discriminatory features with an external and mystifying concept of integration under the banner of slogans such as "universal brotherhood" or "fusion between Koreans and Japanese," did not fail to evoke some initial response on the part of the then-very-youthful Ri, who thought briefly of identifying himself with that generation of Sons of the Emperor who were ready to contribute in all ways to the victory of Japan, their native land. (Korean residents in Japan were granted Japanese nationality, which, however, was revoked in 1952.)

The end of the war, and of the Japanese occupation of Korea, confronted Ri with the painful necessity of choosing a personal identity—a necessity that, in fact, had dogged him throughout the years of secondary school and university. Such a choice was now made even more difficult, on the one hand, by political developments that promptly quashed any hope of returning to a Korea that to him still remained basically a foreign country, and, on the other, by the persistence even in postwar Japan of a form of discrimination against ethnic minorities, fed by the myth of a nonexistent racial homogeneity that the new Japan seemed unwilling to renounce and that was subtly encouraged by mass media and some political quarters. Finally, the choice was made even more agonizing by an awareness that, though born and raised in Japan, he remained legally a foreigner, like others in his situation, and was registered as such in the appropriate immigration bureau. It was not until 1982 that the government granted the status of permanent residents to Koreans who had lived in Japan in the period before the end of the Pacific war, and to their children; while the same right was extended in 1991 to third-generation Korean residents in Japan.

In 1947, after the end of the war and the annexation of Sakhalin by the Soviet Union, Ri's family moved first to the nearby island of Hokkaidō, in the north of Japan, afterward proceeding farther south to a refugee camp in the island of Kyūshū, and, finally, again moving northward to Sapporo. Complicating this precarious existence were difficult personal events: the death of his mother a few months before the end of the war, the second marriage of his father to a woman who was to represent the one positive element of cohesion and security in a family that was otherwise in a process of complete dissolution, continuing quarrels with his father, and economic difficulties. In 1955, after a last domestic conflict, Ri Kaisei left Sapporo for Tokyo, where he enrolled in Russian language courses at Waseda University, supporting himself through a series of precarious jobs. The years at the university also marked the beginning of a social and political commitment which would bring him closer to the other Korean groups involved in the struggle against the various forms of discrimination. At the same period came also the decision to learn his "own mother tongue"—a positive experience that brought with it the sensation of happiness of one who finds again something that had been lost, and that increases at the same pace as the number of new words learned. Yet when Ri, after his graduation and first beginnings as a journalist and author of critical essays, decided to begin writing short stories and novels, he chose to write in Japanese. In 1969, his story *Mata futatabi no michi* won the prize for new writers awarded by the periodical *Gunzō*, connected with the powerful Kōdansha publishing house. The decision of the jury hinged especially on the language, which, while respecting within limits the conventions of literary Japanese, tended at the same time toward very personal solutions, in a tension that went well beyond a pure aesthetic choice to include also a clear political standpoint.

There followed *Kayako no tame ni* (1970), perhaps Ri's best-known work—a kind of bildungsroman that is not without a certain sentimental strain in which autobiographical elements are incorporated in a fore-doomed romance between a young Korean resident in Japan and a Japanese girl brought up in a Korean family. It is just this Korean family that, paradoxically, shares the existing prejudices and mistrust and opposes the marriage by all available means. The story develops through a series of flashbacks in which the protagonist relives his childhood and his sense of foreignness in the very country in which he has been born and grown up.

Kinuta o utsu onna (1972) won the prestigious Akutagawa Prize, awarded for the first time to a "foreign" writer. Since then, the author has regularly published new works in which, while continuing in substance to explore the key themes of all his oeuvre, he presents them each time from a different angle, now dwelling upon autobiographical events, now emphasizing the political aspect, and now abandoning himself to the always-illusory hope for a Korea that has been reunified and is capable of surmounting political and ideological barriers: *Mihatenu yume* (1979), *Saharin e no tabi* (1983), *Hyakunen no tabibitotachi* (1994).

MAJOR MULTICULTURAL THEMES

In a 1972 essay, whose title is clearly derived from a work of George Orwell, *Kita de are minami de are wa ga sokoku* (My Country, North or South), Ri writes: "Japanese is for me a foreign language . . . but, when I think of writing a novel, I observe, not without bitterness, that I can use no other language. I am obliged to realize that it is not a language I have chosen, but the only one in which I can express myself" (in *Warera Seishun no tojō nite*, 1994, 332). The search for an individual cultural identity—which is continually being brought into doubt—is reflected also in the choice, dating from his secondary school years, of using for his own name the Korean version Yi Hoe-Sŏng, rather than Ri Kaisei, which would be more familiar to any Japanese reader of his novels. Cultural identity remains one of the key themes of the writer's production, in which the autobiographical element, often evident and admitted, is broadened into a more comprehensive, global and political vision, but is intermixed as well with cultural and literary references that transcend the geographical limits of Japan and extend to the continental area and the omnipresent heritage of Chinese culture. Thus *Kinuta o utsu onna* revolves around the image of the dead mother, whose memory is recalled by the words of the narrator's grandmother as she describes the figure of a decisive, headstrong woman who has left home at 18 to go and seek work in Japan—"that Japan which, after robbing us of our country, has robbed us also of our daughter" (*Kinuta o utsu onna*, 1977, 24), as the old lady bitterly points out. Her daughter's continued struggles with her husband, her affectionate but brusque and forthright character, and the bitterness of a life of privation are collated in her silent and tenacious figure, intent on beating fabrics methodically to make them more malleable and lustrous. The potency of the image transcends the limits of pure description and attains a broader, symbolic dimension because the *kinuta* (which appears also in the title)—the wooden mallet used to give fabrics pliancy and brightness—is a topos in Chinese classical literature, found regularly in poetry and romance. Linked to languishing lyrics lamenting the separation of lovers or spouses, the sound of the mallet in Ri's novel becomes an emblem not only of the solitude of the mother, but also of the difficult situation of the minority to which she belongs.

Mihatenu yume by contrast is a long and ambitious novel in which the most recent history of the relations between Japan and the two Koreas plays an important part, interwoven with the "unrealizable" hope of a unification in which Koreans of the mother country collaborate with Korean residents in Japan. *Hyakunen no tabibitotachi*, finally, whose scene is the island of Sakhalin two years after the arrival of the Soviet armed forces and whose subject is the flight of some Korean families seeking refuge in Japan, has been compared to an epic symphony that interweaves diverse themes—nationality and ethnicity, historical heritage, interpersonal relations—in which, as the title (Pilgrims of a Hundred Years) suggests, the "pilgrims" seem to carry on their shoulders the weight of one hundred years of history.

SURVEY OF CRITICISM

The principal critical essays on Ri Kaisei are in Japanese. An important reference source, even though not updated, is the catalog *Ri Kaisei chosaku mokurokokō—Sankō bunken mokurokukō (1988)*, edited by Kawarasaki Naoko. Other works—like *Shigen no hikari: zainichi Chōsenjin bungakuron* (1979) by Isogai Haruyoshi and *"Zainichi" to iu konkyo* (1983) by Ikeda Seiji—examine the production of Ri Kaisei as part of a broader study on Korean writers residing in Japan. In addition, the principal novels published in Japan are followed by abundant critical comments and by an account of the author's life and personality.

SELECTED BIBLIOGRAPHY

Works by Ri

Mata futatabi no michi. Tokyo: Kōdansha, 1969.
Kayako no tame ni. Tokyo: Shinchōsha, 1970; Tokyo, Shinchō bunko, 1975.
Kinuta o utsu onna (1972). Tokyo: Bungei shunjū, 1977.
Mihatenu yume. Tokyo: Kōdansha, 1979.
Saharin e no tabi. Tokyo: Kōdansha, 1983.

Hyakunen no tabibitotachi. Tokyo: Shinchōsha, 1994.
Warera seishun no tojō nite (1973). Postface Iguchi Tokio. Tokyo: Kōdansha, 1994.

Selected Studies of Ri

Ikeda [Takeda] Seiji. *"Zainichi" to iu konkyo: Ri Kaisei, Kin Sekihan, Kin Kakuei.* Tokyo: Kokubunsha, 1983.

Isogai Haruyoshi [Jiro]. *Shigen no hikari: zainichi Chōsenjin bungakuron.* Tokyo: Sōjūsha, 1979.

Kawarasaki Naoko. *Ri Kaisei chosaku mokurokokō—Sankō bunken mokurokukō.* Tokyo: Fuji joshi daigaku kokubungaku zasshi, 1988.

SALMAN RUSHDIE
(1947–)

Alessandro Monti

BIOGRAPHY

Salman Rushdie was born in Bombay about two months before the independence of India. His parents were well-off Muslims and from an early age he partook of a composite heritage in which the fantastic world of the *Arabian Nights* and British culture (his father was from Cambridge) gave rise to an inebriating mix. However, at home his mother spoke Urdu (the language of the Indian Muslims) and refused to use English, a language (she said) that made her mouth feel tired. These early seeds, sown as they were in the rich soil of cosmopolitan Bombay, eventually germinated into the too exuberant style of the narrator, who was successively influenced by Western magical realism and by the German and Italian writers Günter Grass and Italo Calvino. Ovid's *Metamorphoses*, Laurence Sterne, and Rabelais also constituted powerful sources of inspiration.

At the beginning of the 1960s Rushdie left the sheltered John Cotton Boy's High School in Bombay (snapshots of this period are found in *Midnight's Children*, 1980) for the rough and snobbish atmosphere of Rugby, where he was first confronted with racial hostility. In the meantime his family had moved to Pakistan and after Rugby he joined them grudgingly, leaving for Cambridge (King's College) in 1965. Of an undistinguished academic career we may remember his active participation in the stage activities of the Footlights Club and a history paper entitled "Muhammed, Islam and the Rise of the Caliph." While researching this paper he found mention of the so-called Satanic Verses falsely inspired in the Prophet by the devil himself.

Rushdie's first novel *Grimus* (1975) was a false start. A science-fiction extravaganza, it was received with biting coldness. The following year he married an upper-class young English woman, Clarissa Luard, and left for India after 10 years of absence, in search of material for a comprehensive novel. *Midnight's Children*, a skillful blending of Eastern and Western voices, with its first person narrative voice inspired by *Tristam Shandy* and its fluidity of discourse reminiscent of the *Arabian Nights*, was awarded the prestigious Booker Prize (1981). Now a successful man, Rushdie started writing for *The Guardian* and his sharp criticism made many enemies, including Mrs. Thatcher and V. S. Naipaul.

Further embitterment was caused by the racial tension in England, with the ensuing Brixton riots among the fascists of the National Front and the Eastern or African migrants. Rushdie's sister was beaten up by an unpunished white gang. *Shame* (1983) reflects the heavy atmosphere of those troubled years, with its deep analysis of the shameful roots of violence. In 1987 he went to India again and found the country riddled by Hindu, Muslim, and Sikh communalisms, which seemed to contradict his words expressing hope and optimism in the conclusion of *Midnight's Children* apropos of the rational Indian generation born in 1947. After this trip he started writing *The Satanic Verses*, published in 1988. In the meantime he divorced from Clarissa and then married the American-born writer Marianne Wiggings, who left him during his long period of forced concealment from the world.

Western critics were baffled by the Muslim sections of *The Satanic Verses*, and a shocked India banned the novel on October 5, 1988. In an interview prior to the public circulation of the book, Rushdie remarked that it would be absurd to think that a book could cause riots, observing that it would be a strange view of the world. Yet, in England, angry Muslim migrants burnt the book in the streets, an act soon imitated by the Muslim communities all over the world. The climax was reached by the *fatwa* (a decree sentencing the writer to death) pronounced by the Iranian Ayatollah Khomeini on February 14, 1989, Saint Valentine's Day. Rushdie disappeared to lead an underground life. The compulsory isolation and forced silence of his life in hiding found a moving outlet in *Haroun and the Sea of Stories* (1990), a collection of 12 stories for his young son. The book narrates the war that opposes the forces of Darkness and Silence to the creative world of the storyteller. *Imaginary Homelands: Essays and Criticism* (1991) may be considered the definitive version of his beliefs and views, particularly on the debated issue of his cultural affiliations and of his identity as a postcolonial writer.

Rushdie's life, both public and private, has percolated gradually into an acceptable routine of normality. His literary output in the last decade includes *The Moor's Last Sigh* (1995), *The Ground beneath her Feet: A Novel* (1999) and the recent *Fury: A Novel* (2001), a dark comedy prophetically set in New York. The cover of the book shows a photograph of the Empire State Building capped by a black and fiery bursting cloud. One more work worth mentioning is the collection of short stories *East, West* (1994).

MAJOR MULTICULTURAL THEMES

If we claim Salman Rushdie for multiculturalism we should consider two major themes: the dissonance of time and space in his fictional strategies (with subsequent effects of timelessness and problematic belonging) and the structural devices that prefigure a state of being in-between the world of reality and the world of fantasy. Rushdie himself speaks of a "tangential" angle of vision, a perspective that reminds one of the processes of hybridization and of the postmodernist thrust towards decentralization. However, more clues are possible. In *Fantasy: The Literature of Subversion*, Rosemary Jackson defines as fantastic a marvelous narrative that has a potential relation to the real (22). In *Shame* Rushdie echoes this very definition: "there are two countries, real and fictional, occupying the same space, or almost the same space. My story, my fictional country exists, like myself, at a slight angle to reality" (29).

To me, this deflected angle coincides with discursive clauses of estranged displacement in style and in the dubitative representation of history and its human agencies. Rather than glossing the issue of multiculturalism in Rushdie as a mere instance of moving across borders, I would speak of a disturbed linearity in genealogies, either in the sharp deconstruction of post-independent India featured in *Midnight's Children*, or in the unnegotiated mongrelization of identities and religious script in *The Satanic Verses*. In these novels (and in *Shame* as well) such techniques of oblique representation emphasize disagreement and suggest an everlasting position of challenge. I would then posit a version of multiculturalism that construes sequences in between the discourse of history and its fictionalized allegory. For instance, in *Midnight's Children*, this radical reshuffling of values interfaces verbatim pages from Stanley Wolpert's *The New History of India* (1977) with their chutnification brought about by Saleem's grotesque adventures.

The gargantuan burst that concludes the novel deploys a deep distrust in any possible vision of consonance. This deconstitution of values comes to the surface again in *The Satanic Verses* and in *The Moor's Last Sigh*. According to the critic Homi K. Bhabha, Rushdie introduces hybridity in *The Satanic Verses* by misnaming the authority of the sacred word. He thereby translates what is untranslatable and taints with the ambiguous mark of high hybridity a text that should be ascriptive (Bhabha, *The Location of Culture*, 225). Then, we should consider carefully how hybridity activates unsettling effects of "disjunctive temporality" (Bhabha, *The Location of Culture*, 225), such as witnessed by the grim Muslim response to *The Satanic Verses*, one that denies any dislocation and relocation of culture. Perhaps we should refer to another statement by Bhabha, who further defines hybridity as an unfinished zone of border that gathers undeveloped and retroactively diasporic lives (Bhabha, 139).

The Moor's Last Sigh projects the carnivalesque representation of multi-layered identities into a forlorn and distanced metaphor of regretted loss and exile, whose baroque symbol is represented by the final destruction of Bombay, a city that in *Imaginary Homelands: Essays and Criticism* stands for multiculturalism and cosmopolitan identity. In *The Ground beneath her Feet*, myth constitutes the true backdrop for ubiquity and parallel realms of existence: a mirror image without the flexibility of form that we find in *Midnight's Children* and in *The Satanic Verses*.

SURVEY OF CRITICISM

Biographical studies focus on the *fatwa* affair. Postcolonial criticism offers more valuable insights into such seminal issues as migration and marginality, hybridity (Bhabha, 1994) and nationhood (Aijaz, 1992), transitional identities, and Bakhtinian parody (Fludernik, 1998). Indian critics emphasize Rushdie's procedure and techniques of oral telling, with particular reference to the reinterpretation of the recent history of the Indian subcontinent. Gender critique is only marginally interested in Rushdie. Aijaz (1992) observes, however, that the oppositional politics sustained by the writer do not contemplate female resistance as an instance of regenerative reaction.

Rushdie's multiculturalism is viewed by Aijaz in terms of grotesque representation of the world: in other words, the writer's postcolonial stance seems to percolate into the deconstructed chaos of postmodernism.

SELECTED BIBLIOGRAPHY

Works by Rushdie

Grimus: A Novel. London: Alfred A. Knopf, 1975.
Midnight's Children. London: Jonathan Cape, 1980.
Shame. London: Jonathan Cape, 1983.
The Satanic Verses. London: Viking, 1988.
Haroun and the Sea of Stories. London: Granta, 1990.
Imaginary Homelands: Essays and Criticism. London: Granta, 1991.
East, West. London: Jonathan Cape, 1994.
The Moor's Last Sigh. London: Jonathan Cape, 1995.
The Ground beneath her Feet: A Novel. New York: Henry Holt, 1999.
Fury: A Novel. New York: Random House; and London: Jonathan Cape, 2001.

Selected Studies of Rushdie

Aijaz Ahmad. *In Theory: Classes, Nations, Literatures.* New Delhi: Oxford University Press, 1992.

Bhabha, Homi K. *The Location of Culture*. London and New York: Routledge, 1994.

Brennan, Timothy. *Salman Rushdie and the Third World: Myths of the Nation*. Houndmills, Basingstoke, Hampshire: Macmillan, 1989.

Cundy, Catherine. *Salman Rushdie*. Manchester: Manchester University Press, 1996.

Fletcher, M. D., ed. *Reading Rushdie: Perspectives on the Fiction of Salman Rushdie*. Amsterdam and Atlanta, Ga.: Rodopi, 1994.

Fludernik, Monika, ed. *Hybridity and Postcolonialism: Twentieth-Century Indian Literature*. Tübingen: Stauffenburg, 1998.

Harrison, James. *Salman Rushdie*. New York: Twayne, 1992.

Mongia, Padmini, ed. *Contemporary Postcolonial Theory: A Reader* (1996). New Delhi: Oxford University Press, 1997.

Parameswaran, Uma, ed. *The Perforated Sheet: Essays on Salman Rushdie's Art*. New Delhi: Affiliated East-West Press, 1988.

Petersson, Margareta. *Unending Metamorphoses: Myth, Satire and Religion in Salman Rushdie's Novels*. Lund (Sweden): Lund University Press, 1996.

Punter, David. *Postcolonial Imaginings: Fictions of a New World Order*. Edinburgh: Edinburgh University Press, 2000.

Ruthven, Malise. *A Satanic Affair: Salman Rushdie and the Rage of Islam* (1990). London: The Hogarth Press, 1991 (revised and updated edition).

Suleri, Sara. *The Rhetoric of British India*. Chicago: Chicago University Press, 1992.

Weatherby, W. J. *Salman Rushdie: Sentenced to Death*. New York: Carroll and Graf, 1990.

Wolpert, Stanley. *A New History of India*. New York: Oxford University Press, 1977.

Other Work

Jackson, Rosemary. *Fantasy, the Literature of Subversion*. London and New York: Methuen, 1981.

CARL SAGAN
(1934–1996)

Richard Sussman

BIOGRAPHY

Carl Sagan was born in Brooklyn, New York City. His childhood interest in science and science fiction led him to study physics at the University of Chicago, and even while a student he gave a series of public lectures on the subject of astronomy. As these early lectures showed, Sagan was unusually adroit at explaining arcane principles of science. His son Dorian once commented on his father's preternatural ability to speak in polished and complete paragraphs. This facility, augmented by a personal, easygoing manner and a well-developed sense of humor, is on display in *The Cosmic Connection. An Extraterrestrial Perspective* (1973), Sagan's first best-selling book, the central thesis of which is the connectedness of life on earth with the rest of the material universe.

For a number of years after receiving his Ph.D. Sagan pursued planetary astronomy, the subject of his dissertation, at several universities. By the late 1960s, however, especially after his coauthorship with I. S. Shklovskii of *Intelligent Life in the Universe* (1966), he had become increasingly interested in the search for life beyond the earth, specifically the search for extraterrestrial intelligence (SETI), and exobiology. Over the last two millennia the notion of life on other worlds has had supporters (e.g., Kant, Bruno, Kepler) and deniers (chiefly major religions and, more recently, most scientists). Without evidence, early supporters simply argued for the notion based on analogy with the earth. After Giovanni Schiaparelli's discovery in the nineteenth century of what was believed (and has since been disproved) to be canals on Mars *(canali)*, the astronomer Percival Lowell (1855–1916) claimed that such canals had been constructed by a race of intelligent beings. Such speculations, going far beyond the evidence, made SETI an object of ridicule, even if they provided impetus for the rebirth of science fiction in the twentieth century.

In 1979, Sagan and several others laid plans to found the Planetary Society with the mission of providing political support and funding for SETI and for space research. Membership rapidly grew to one hundred thousand members, and, with such a substantial constituency, Sagan was successful in his appearances before government officials in gaining funding. In 1982 the filmmaker Steven Spielberg, after meeting Sagan, agreed to fund the Planetary Society's Project META (Mega-channel Extraterrestrial Assay). Sagan spent most of his professional career at Cornell University. He was married three times, and all three wives were notable. Lynn Margulis is a renowned biologist. Linda Salzman, an artist, helped design the plaque that was carried into deep space on Pioneer 10. Ann Druyan helped coauthor several of Sagan's books and was involved in the production of the film *Contact* and the television series *Cosmos*.

MULTICULTURAL THEMES

Sagan's publications include more than a dozen books and over six hundred scientific articles, but it is in his extremely popular writing for the general public (*Cosmos*, 1980, is the best-selling English-language science book of all time) that he addresses two parallel but related multicultural themes, the terrestrial and the extraterrestrial. In both, Sagan seeks to bring in the outsider, the disenfranchised Other, into what is often criticized as being the dominant conversation.

Throughout the body of his work Sagan was ever mindful of the contributions of women, minorities, and persons from non-Western societies. It was he who all but resurrected Hypatia (370–415 C.E.), the first major female mathematician, from the shadows of ancient history. He knew Hypatia as an important scholar, but he also recognized her symbolic value: as a young woman she was the acknowledged leader of the Neoplatonists centered in Alexandria, renowned for her intellect and her teaching skills, but she came into conflict with the local Christian hierarchy who regarded learning and science as pagan irreligion. Her torture and murder by followers of Bishop Cyril elicits the following sardonic comment from Sagan: "Her remains were burned, her works obliterated, her name forgotten. Cyril was made a saint" (*Cosmos*, 336).

At the same time, Sagan was wholly mainstream and traditionalist in his scientific and cultural views. Unlike some postmodern critics, who see science as an agent of the powerful who would use the scientific way of knowing as a means of oppressing the disenfranchised, Sagan believed that science and other subjects of a liberal education led to personal empowerment and to an unbiased acceptance of alien beings and alien ideas. Sagan's admiration for the ancient city of Alexandria and the library it contained reflects this belief. "Alexandria was the greatest city the Western world had ever seen. People of all nations came there to live, to trade, to learn. . . . Greeks, Egyptians, Arabs, Syrians, Hebrews, Persians, Nubians, Phoenicians, Italians, Gauls, and Iberians exchanged merchandise and ideas" (*Cosmos*, 334). Moreover, it was in Alexandria, "during the six hundred years beginning around 300 B.C.E. that human beings . . . began the intellectual adventure that has led us to the shores of space" (*Cosmos*, 18). The death of Hypatia, a martyr to intellectual freedom, coincides with the sharp decline of Alexandria as a major city and, as Sagan notes, with the onset of the Dark Ages. Testimony to his strong feelings on the subject, Sagan named his fourth child and only daughter Alexandra.

Sagan was an enemy of chauvinism at all levels, fond of noting that we are not much different from them. In books written decades apart he introduces us to the Kung, Bushmen of the Kalahari desert in Botswana, whose creation story (cf. *Cosmos*, 172), while differing in detail, is no different in kind from the Western (Ptolemaic) view that prevailed for more than a millennium (cf. *Billions and Billions: Thoughts on Life and Death at the Brink of the Millennium*, 36–7).

But beyond such standard Enlightenment thinking, Sagan buttressed his arguments for inclusion on his knowledge of the physical constitution of the universe. To emphasize the connection that all living forms in the universe have with each other, Sagan was fond of noting how we are all "star stuff" (*The Cosmic Connection. An Extraterrestrial Perspective*, 255, 258; *Cosmos*, 233). The original universe was composed solely of loose subatomic particles and hydrogen and helium gases. None of the heavier elements, such as carbon and calcium, existed except in minuscule amounts. These elements were produced only in the interiors of stars in the end stages of their existence. Thus, all of the calcium, iron, oxygen, and so on that living beings require were produced in the interiors of now defunct stars, so that most of our body weight is composed of materials manufactured in some distant part of the universe aeons ago. For Sagan, all living creatures "are, in the most profound sense, children of the Cosmos" (*Cosmos*, 242).

His scientific and social convictions come together in his one work of fiction, *Contact: A Novel* (1985), in which the radio astronomer Eleanor Arroway, a character loosely modeled on Sagan himself, finds that she has a coherent signal from the vicinity of the star Vega, 26 light years distant from Earth. When the message from Vega is decoded, it contains plans for a device that will allow a team to travel to that distant star. The device is built at colossal expense and the voyage is begun. For witnesses on the ground, the device never takes off, but Arroway believes that she has been able to travel the 26 light years by passing through a space-time wormhole and that, while on this journey, she has met with her long-deceased father. On her return, however, she has no physical evidence. Sagan, who was insistent on the accuracy of the science in his science fiction, thereby avoided the issue of depicting aliens: since aliens would have evolved in environments radically different from our own, we can not even remotely guess their characteristics. (As an advisor to Stanley Kubrick during the making of the film *2001: A Space Odyssey*, Sagan also recommended not portraying the aliens). But with the development of better instrumentation as a result of World War II (cf. *Cosmic Connection. An Extraterrestrial Perspective*, 194), there has been an increase in data about our solar system, and Sagan was confident that he or someone after him would find life elsewhere in the universe because of improved radio electronics and better equipment. He also believed that any society sufficiently advanced to overcome the colossal technical difficulties of communicating with another civilization several (or several thousand or even million) light years distant would have overcome the problems of war, violence, political domination, or exploitation that plague humanity at its present stage of development. "I can imagine that they [aliens] are motivated by benevolence; that during their emerging phases they were themselves helped along by . . . messages [from other alien civilizations]" (*Cosmic Connection. An Extraterrestrial Perspective*, 219; cf. *Contact: A Novel*, 119; cf. *Pale Blue Dot: A Vision of the Human Future in Space*, 353, 372).

Sagan regularly took issue with the Judeo-Christian-Muslim tradition (and with other similar traditions) that held the chauvinistic view that the universe was created for the benefit of humans. Our sun is only one of about two hundred billion stars in the Milky Way, while this galaxy is itself only one of several hundred billion galaxies in the known universe (see ch. 10 in *Cosmos* and ch. 4 in *Pale Blue Dot: A Vision of the Human Future in Space*). Sagan was aware of the way in which chauvinism develops in pretechnical societies with limited knowledge of the world beyond their borders. The feeling of singularity that develops in physical and cultural isolation acts as a wellspring of ill will and prejudice. At one level we overcome this insularity by education and exposure to those beyond our own kind. At another level, we break down parochialism by demonstrating that none of us is very special, that our position in the universe is hardly privileged: our planet is a pale blue dot.

For Sagan there were no aliens, only distant neighbors we have not yet met and to whom he would extend the hand of friendship. In a scene in *Contact: A Novel*, the Soviet physicist Lunacharsky toasts, "Every village is a planet," to which Ellie Arroway responds, "And every planet a village" (*Contact: A Novel*, 115).

The chapters in many of Sagan's popular books are headed by epigrams drawn from every realm of human thought: Strabo's *Geography*, the Old Testament, Chuang Tzu, the Koran, Vincent Van Gogh, Ptolemaic Egypt, Aztec chronicles, and Eskimo creation myths, to name a few.

Sagan believed that each culture had something valuable to add to the great conversation. Yet while a lifelong champion of the Other, Sagan makes little mention of identity politics. In his view women and others who have been excluded are benefited not by segregation, self-imposed or otherwise, but by contact.

SURVEY OF CRITICISM

Sagan's celebrity, and his regular appearances on best-seller lists and on television, caused no small amount of professional jealousy. Keay Davidson (1999) reveals that when Sagan was due to receive tenure at Harvard University, among those who blackballed him was Harold Urey, Nobel Prize-winning chemist and exobiologist, who was concerned that the nature of Sagan's notoriety was detracting from the seriousness of the field of exobiology (cf. Davidson, 202–4). To some, Sagan's work in exobiology was a waste of effort and facilities. William Poundstone (1999) quotes Harvard astronomer David Layzer's remark, reflective of the views of a number of distinguished scientists: "Its [exobiology's] speculations cannot be confirmed by observations or experiments and so it is not a science; it has no data. It only sounds like science" (Poundstone, 107).

SELECTED BIBLIOGRAPHY

Works by Carl Sagan

I. S. Shklovskii and Carl Sagan. *Intelligent Life in the Universe.* Trans. from the Russian *Vselennaia, zhizn, razum* by Paula Fern. San Francisco: Holden-Day, 1966.

The Cosmic Connection. An Extraterrestrial Perspective. Garden City, N.Y.: Anchor Press, 1973.

Cosmos. New York: Random House, 1980.

Contact: A Novel. New York: Simon and Schuster, 1985.

Carl Sagan and Ann Druyan. *Shadows of Forgotten Ancestors: A Search for Who We Are.* New York: Random House, 1992.

Pale Blue Dot: A Vision of the Human Future in Space. New York: Random House, 1994.

Billions and Billions: Thoughts on Life and Death at the Brink of the Millennium. New York: Random House, 1997.

Selected Studies of Sagan

Davidson, Keay. *Carl Sagan: A Life.* New York: John Wiley and Sons, 1999.

Poundstone, William. *Carl Sagan: A Life in the Cosmos.* New York: Henry Holt, 1999.

SAID
(1947–)

Thomas Baginski

BIOGRAPHY

The Iranian-born author Said is an award-winning poet, historian, and political activist who has emerged as one of the preeminent exile voices against the two modern Iranian dictatorships. Constant fear of assassination, the fate of some of his closest friends in the antifundamentalist opposition, has caused Said to publish only under his first name, a common one in the Muslim world. The poet's literary acclaim and his long-time chairmanship of the international aid organization Writers in Prison were instrumental in his election as president of the German PEN (Poets, Essayists, Novelists) in May 2000, with the overwhelming support of Germany's artistic and intellectual elite. For the first time in PEN's history, a non-German citizen and member of an ethnic and religious minority group holds its highest office. It is an ironic twist of fate, yet telling for the changing nature of German society, that an Iranian immigrant poet, sometimes dubbed the German Salman Rushdie, has become one of the internationally most recognized and influential representatives and spokesmen of Germany's modern literature and culture.

Exiled by the late Shah Reza Pahlavi's authoritarian regime in 1965, the 17-year-old dissident fled his birthplace Teheran and found political refuge in Munich. After the fall of the Pahlavi monarchy in January 1979, Said returned to his native country full of hope that Iran's presumed democratization would be founded upon the rationalistic principles of Western enlightenment. After Ayatollah Khomeini seized power in the Islamic Fundamentalist Revolution and officially proclaimed the Islamic Republic of Iran in February 1979, however, Said witnessed firsthand the wave of executions of political dissidents, artists, so-called immoral women and men, and Iran's religious and ethnic minorities. Among the tortured and murdered were many of his friends, which led the poet to write acerbically in deep dismay: "The dictators trade places; the terror remains the same. For the first time I am allowed to cast my vote—for the Islamic Republic or for nothing at all!" (*Wo ich sterbe, ist meine Fremde: Gedichte*, 32). Openly despising and actively opposing the oppressive, religious dictatorship of the mullahs and their reign of terror, Said was forced into exile for the second time. For nearly 40 years he has lived in political asylum in Munich. From that vantage point he has chronicled the crimes committed in his home country and the suffering of his people, has lobbied for the right of free speech, and has untiringly worked for the liberation of writers and journalists who are persecuted, tortured, and imprisoned by totalitarian regimes around the world.

Landschaften einer fernen Mutter (2001) is the riveting autobiographical story of Said's alienation from his mother. His parents' divorce was already final during his mother's pregnancy, and a few days after his birth he was forcibly taken away from her. Once only, for the duration of a single afternoon, the 12-year-old Said was permitted to visit her. Three decades later, at the age of 43, he had the opportunity of seeing her for a second and, as it turned out, the very last time in his life. He traveled to Toronto, Canada, where his mother had already arrived from Teheran. He describes this meeting and his chaotic feelings that ranged from yearning and hope to anger and profound sadness. It becomes hauntingly clear that Said's first exile had already begun at birth. He is the existential stranger: a man without a country, a son without a mother.

Said writes his works directly in German, which is not his native language. His choice of the German language rather than his native Persian as his literary medium stems from his intent to reach the German public. He tries to enlighten that audience not only about the political conditions in Iran and its rich intellectual and artistic traditions—suppressed under the rule of the imams—but also about the plight of foreigners in the German host society. Moreover, the German language allows him to enter into dialogue with the politically and culturally unintegrated, multinational, and multiracial minority communities in Germany.

MAJOR MULTICULTURAL THEMES

German and Iranian themes appear side by side in Said's writings. His book *Es war einmal eine Blume, die hatte keine Farbe* (1998) thematically represents the forced expulsion from his native land, the subsequent loss of personal, cultural, and political identity and sense of belonging, the forced migration to a new world, and the search for (and eventual reconstruction of) a new identity in a foreign land. Here, and throughout his entire work, Said challenges Germans to rethink their essentialist notions of German nationhood as a homogeneous racial, cultural, and religious entity. A profound humanism rooted in the humanistic tradition of the French Enlightenment undergirds Said's utopian vision of Germany's society of the future—a vision of ethnic and cultural pluralism, of cultural synthesis, and mutual recognition and acceptance.

Wo ich sterbe, ist meine Fremde (1987) is a collection of poems about Teheran and the author's hurried return to exile in Germany only a few weeks after the Islamic Revolution. In terse, unadorned and direct style, these poems speak of the impossibility of ever returning home after decades in exile. Said comes to the painful recognition that existentially he is forever precluded from returning home, because reclaiming the space once called home inevitably entails the impossible task of reclaiming lost time.

The acclaimed *Der lange Arm der Mullahs: Notizen aus meinem Exil* (1995) is a hybrid poetic construct consisting of poetry, letters, political commentary, eyewitness reports, imagined conversations with dead friends, censored news items, never-before-published political information and statistical reports, and personal reflections in diary form. The work provides a look at both daily life in exile in Germany and life in Iran under Islamic rule. On the one hand, Said examines the daily trauma of exile by exploring the émigré's feelings of loneliness and isolation in the German host culture, the poet's painful sense of powerlessness to bring about political change through art, the constant paranoia of being a potential murder victim as a result of a religious *fatwa* issued by Moslem clerics, and the deep-seated sense of suspicion and distrust even among the closest of friends. On the other hand, Said paints a portrait of the radicalization of Iranian society under Islamic rule. In highly charged rhetoric, the poet chronicles the ubiquitousness and unspeakability of terror: religiously inspired carnage; state-sponsored spectacular public executions; worldwide calls for assassinations in the name of God, as in the case of Salman Rushdie; the oppression of women and girls; the starvation of large segments of the population; the persecution of artists; the intolerance of all others; and the mass destruction of classical and modern Iranian art and culture. Yet, in their suffering, the victims are shown by Said to retain a silent yet unbroken spirit of humanism and humanitarianism. Moreover, Said presents a trenchant critique of the capitalist culture of the West that has turned a blind eye to these atrocities and thereby has become an accomplice through its silence, if not through passive collaboration. By far the most important theme in this book is the idea of memory against ideologically induced amnesia. Where barbarism spreads, Said believes, the poet must speak out. His writings are primarily a struggle against forgetting. It is his conviction that the writer is called upon to be the moral conscience of his time and to preserve social and cultural memory in exile. Thus, Said considers himself to be the voice of all victims persecuted and silenced. He offers a living voice of memory and his poetry safeguards remembrance not only of the trauma of life in foreign exile but also of the ongoing sufferings of the victims in his homeland.

SURVEY OF CRITICISM

Until 1980, Said and the other writers of national and ethnic minority groups residing in Germany could not reach the general German reading public, since German publishing houses, newspapers, and the media—often in deliberate disregard—excluded their literary works and art from publication. In the mid-1980s, the editorial team *Südwind Literatur* was founded by five foreign writers: the Italians Gino (Carmine) Chiellino and Franco Biondi, the Syrians Rafik Schami and Suleman Taufiq, and the Lebanese Jusuf Naoum. Financially and editorially independent from the German literary and media establishment, the editors published, for the first time, the German-language writings of minorities living and working in Germany. The establishment's wall of silence erected by German publishing houses against foreign writers and artists eventually collapsed, and Said's literary voice was among the first to be heard. While leading newspapers nowadays regularly publish reviews of his latest books, literary critics have yet to embark on a serious critical investigation of his multifaceted writings. In like fashion, the German-language writings of exiled writers of other national origins, who are creating a rich tradition of exilic literatures produced on German soil, have yet to be discovered by critics.

SELECTED BIBLIOGRAPHY

Works by Said

Liebesgedichte von Said (1981). 4th ed. Munich: Peter Kirchheim, 1989.

Ich und der Schah—Die Beichte des Ayatollah: Hörspiele. Hamburg: perspol-verlag, 1987.

Wo ich sterbe, ist meine Fremde: Gedichte (1987). 4th ed. Munich: Peter Kirchheim, 1994.

"Die erste und für mich wichtigste Gemeinsamkeit ist die Sprache: Said im Gespräch mit Gino Chiellino." In Gino Chiellino, *Die Reise hält an. Ausländische Künstler in der Bundesrepublik*, 76–88. Munich: C. H. Beck, 1988.

Dann schreie ich, bis Stille ist: Gedichte. Tübingen: Heliopolis, 1990.

Selbstbildnis für eine ferne Mutter. Munich: Peter Kirchheim, 1992.

Der lange Arm der Mullahs: Notizen aus meinem Exil. Munich: C. H. Beck, 1995.

Es war einmal eine Blume, die hatte keine Farbe. Gossau: Neugebauer, 1998.

Sei Nacht zu mir: Liebesgedichte. Munich: C. H. Beck, 1998.

Dieses Tier, das es nicht gibt: Ein Bestiarium. Munich: C. H. Beck, 1999.

Landschaften einer fernen Mutter. Munich: C. H. Beck, 2001.

Selected Studies of Said

Baginski, Thomas. "Von Mullahs und Deutschen: Annäherung an das Werk des iranischen Exillyrikers Said." *German Quarterly* 74, no. 1 (2001): 21–35.

Freund, Wieland. "Das erste Exil: Mann ohne Land, Sohn ohne Mutter—Der iranische Lyriker und deutsche PEN-Präsident Said." *Die Welt* 59 (March 10, 2001): 2.

Müller, Herta. "Es möge deine letzte Trauer sein: Notizen und Gedichte des iranischen Exilautors Said." *Die Zeit* 50 (August 11, 1995): 40.

JEAN-PAUL SARTRE
(1905–1980)

Sandra Teroni

BIOGRAPHY

Having lost his father almost at birth, Jean-Paul Sartre was brought up by his mother, first at Meudon and later in Paris, in the house of his maternal grandfather, Charles Schweitzer (an uncle of Albert Schweitzer). Schweitzer was a member of a Protestant family of Alsatian origin, a professor of German, and author of scholastic manuals for the teaching of foreign languages. Of his solitary childhood distinguished by a precocious, chaotic, and pervasive relationship with reading and writing, Sartre later painted a ruthless portrait in *Les Mots* (1964), the satirical account of the birth of his vocation for letters.

The trauma of his mother's remarriage at the height of his adolescence was aggravated by the family's removal to La Rochelle, where his new stepfather was in charge of the naval dockyards. Escape from what Sartre recalled as the worst years of his life brought a return to Paris, magazine publication of his first short stories, independence from his family, a distinctive record at the École Normale Supérieure, the award of an *agrégation* in philosophy, and the meeting in 1929 with his lifelong companion, Simone de Beauvoir.

As a professor at the lycée of Le Havre during the 1930s, Sartre, writer and philosopher, aspired to be a combination of Stendhal and Baruch Spinoza in seeking a form for the essay on contingency that became the novel *La nausée* (1938), and pursued the fascinating discovery of phenomenology. During this time, he also began to indulge his passion for travel—to Spain, Morocco, London, Italy, Germany (where, at the French Institute in Berlin, he studied the phenomenology of Edmund Husserl in depth), Norway, and Greece.

At the outbreak of World War II, he was initially assigned to the meteorological services in Alsace. There he spent his days reading and writing and achieving, in a confrontation with history and the other, a profound reexamination of himself and his cultural foundations—the new record of which was posthumously published under the title *Carnets de la drôle de guerre: septembre 1939-mars 1940* (1995). Taken prisoner in 1940, he was interned for a time in the German Stalag XII D at Trier, from which he managed to escape by masquerading as a civilian. Following his return to Paris in March 1941 and an unsuccessful attempt to organize with Maurice Merleau-Ponty, Simone de Beauvoir, and others an intellectual resistance group called Socialisme et Liberté, he returned to the only form of resistance available to him: writing. After completing his design of a phenomenological ontology (*L'être et le néant: Essai d'ontologie phénoménologique*, 1943), he had recourse to the rewriting of a myth, that of Orestes, as an appeal to liberty and to resistance against the invader (*Les mouches*, 1943); in addition, he carried forward the writing of the novelistic cycle *Les chemins de la liberté* (1945–49); became interested in designing motion picture scenarios; collaborated in the clandestine *Lettres françaises* and *Combat;* and planned the review that later became *Les Temps modernes.*

Sartre represented *Combat* in the delegation of journalists invited to Washington, D.C. by the Office of War Information in January 1945. The following year he undertook a lecture tour in the United States and then in Italy, the country where he was to form the most numerous friendly, intellectual, and political relationships, and the only one to have inspired him literarily (*Dépaysement*, 1936, and the incomplete *La reine Albemarle ou le dernier touriste*, fragments published postuhumously, 1991). In the 1950s and 1960s, the moral authority he enjoyed made Sartre a symbol, "a voice of France, a countervoice, whose least word has an unequaled resonance" (Bernard-Henri Lévy, *Le siècle de Sartre*, 33). His voice and photographic image reverberated from Latin America, Africa, the USSR, Japan, and China, where he was received as the official representative of France and invited to ascend the tribune of honor for the ceremonies on the anniversary of the revolution; from Cuba, where he was warmly received by Fidel Castro and Che Guevara; from Brazil, where his passionate defense of the cause of Algerian independence transformed a lecture into an open-air demonstration in honor of the Algerian National Liberation Front (FLN); and from Egypt and Israel, where he attempted without success to promote a *rapprochement* of the two countries' left-wing elements.

Sartre declined, with characteristic intransigeance, the 1964 Nobel Prize for Literature. He died in Paris on April 15, 1980.

MAJOR MULTICULTURAL THEMES

Sartre became the symbolical representative of an internationalist current sustained more than once by European literature. Accompanying his physical presence, his political and emotional participation in the great cataclysms of history was a complex of theoretical problems with strong moral implications involving the relationship with the other—the forms that this assumes in both interpersonal and social relations, and a tenacious aspiration to grasp the world as a synthetic reality, every fragment of which carries the totality within itself. Even as far back as *La nausée*, Sartre made his characters change our view of the world and ourselves in order to lay bare the reassuring function of the mental grids within which we live our being-in-the-world—being in time, being in language. The *Carnets de la drôle de guerre: septembre 1939-mars 1940* bear witness to a lucid awareness that consciousness of self and consciousness of the other proceed conjointly, thus establishing the basis of that phenomenology of the effect produced on the ego by the presence of the other that is the central problem of *L'être et le néant: Essai d'ontologie phénoménologique*, and is echoed also in the *Réflexions sur la question juive* (1946). Such writings bear witness also to that need for conversion to an uncomplicit reflection that sustains his unfinished undertaking on ethics, *Cahiers pour une morale*, published in 1983.

Notwithstanding his categorical tone and trenchant judgments, Sartre was a man of dialogue, fascinated by the grafting of his own discourse onto that of another, committed to the search for the conditions of reciprocity. During his imprisonment, his encounter with Catholic culture led to the creation of a theatrical piece, *Bariona* (published in 1967), a reinterpretation of the Nativity in Roman-occupied Palestine—a subject deliberately chosen to bring about the broadest union of believers and nonbelievers in resistance to the oppressors. After the war, despite the violent attacks directed against him by the Communists, Sartre tried to start a critical dialogue with Marxist culture by way of a theoretical reflection (cf. *Critique de la raison dialectique*, 1960). Similarly, he sought to explore a European third way with the *Rassemblement Démocratique Révolutionnaire* (cf. *Entretiens sur la politique*, with David Rousset and Gérard Rosenthal, 1949); and to counterpoise the demands of politics and ethics in the screenplay *L'engrenage* (1948) and the drama *Les mains sales* (1948). Then, from May 1968 until his death, he attempted to carry on a dialogue with the New Left on the relationship of ethics and revolution and on the subject of revolutionary strategies (*On a raison de se révolter*, with Pierre Victor and Philippe Gavi, 1974). Finally, a kindred dialogistic attitude characterizes the singular psychoanalytic biographies of Charles Baudelaire, Stéphane Mallarmé, Jean Genet, and Gustave Flaubert; the scenario for John Ford's film about Sigmund Freud; the essays on Alexander Calder, Alberto Giacometti, Tintoretto, André Masson, and Søren Kierkegaard (that offers him the occasion to elaborate the notion of singular universal); and the article-portraits of André Gide, Maurice Merleau-Ponty, Albert Camus, Paul Nizan, and Patrice Lumumba.

As with many writers of his generation, the United States for Sartre was above all a cultural myth, nurtured in its infancy by comic-strip characters, from Buffalo Bill to Nick Carter; then by the cinema, jazz, the novels of William Faulkner, John Dos Passos, Ernest Hemingway, John Steinbeck, and Erskine Caldwell, with their revolution in narrative techniques. Sartre the writer was especially sensitive to this myth until the attention of Sartre the intellectual was turned to the economic structure, the organizational consensus, the inequalities and colonial character of the United States, ending with a resolute political condemnation that culminated in the denunciation—by the presidency of the Russell Tribunal—of war crimes in Vietnam. In the novel that established him as a writer, *La nausée*, a ragtime heard on a disk left by U.S. soldiers in La Rochelle, with music by a Jewish composer sung by a Negress, is given the function of representing an alternative temporality to the sickening continuum of existence.

Sartre brings into focus the diverse European and American perspectives, fully aware of the cultural conditioning that weighs upon our perception of the world, and hence of the necessity of quitting the European parameters in order to see the other and to see our own reality better. These problems, too, are already present in the *Carnets de la drôle de guerre*, after *La nausée* had already liquidated the mythology of exoticism and adventure associated with travel.

The encounter with American reality also signals the entry of a problematics of liberation that, introduced with some reports on the conditions of blacks in the most opulent of white societies, and with the theater piece written on his return from his second sojourn in the United States, *La putain respectueuse* (1946), develops rapidly into a sympathetic reflection on the status of anticolonial struggles. A text written to salute the birth of the review *Présence africaine* (1947) denounces the false conscience of the French, who are colonizers but are proud of the civil customs they practice in their own country; looks forward to a salutary grafting of African culture onto "our old ceremonious culture . . . embarrassed in its traditions and etiquette" (quoted in Michel Contat and Michel Rybalka, ed., *Les écrits de Sartre*, 687); and sketches a line of thought that will be amply developed in *Orphée noir*, the preface to the *Anthologie de la nouvelle poésie nègre et malgache de langue française* edited by Léopold Sedar Senghor (1948). Sartre reflected on the loss of identity caused by the use of the oppressor's language even to verbalize one's own revolt, the subjugating power exercised in language, and the destructive character of the dissolution of the prose medium effected by colonized blacks. Then, while opposition to the war in Algeria was becoming more widespread, taking up one of Frantz Fanon's basic theses in the preface to *Les damnés de la terre* (1961), Sartre upholds the need for "performing a striptease of our humanism" ("*Les damnés de la terre*," in *Situations, V,* "Colonialisme et néo-colonialisme," 186), of a humanism that, while it does not impede enslavement and massacres, is based on the category of the universal in order to protect the subject in true confrontation with reality.

SURVEY OF CRITICISM

The attention given Sartre's work from a multicultural standpoint has been somewhat late in arrival and limited in quantity. His reflections on the colonial question are studied by Azzedine Haddour (2000), who places the subject in a wider context and in historical perspective. Henri Meschonnic (1984) offers an analysis of the reflections on Jewish identity in the context of Sartrian anthropology.

Interest in Sartre's relationship with Italy is increasing, Gerald Prince's 1984 essay pointing the way. The volume *Sartre e l'Italia* (1987), edited by Ornella Pompeo Faracovi and Sandra Teroni, offers the first overall view of Sartre's relations with Italian culture and the Italian left. Attention is given to intertextuality in two studies by Sandra Teroni (1990 and 1998) analyzing Sartre's pages devoted to Venice and Rome, respectively.

Sartre's relations with U.S. culture and society are focused on in an essay by Gilbert Pestureau (1986) and have become the object of an exhaustive study by Eleanor Ann Fulton (1991).

SELECTED BIBLIOGRAPHY

Works by Sartre

Dépaysement (1936). In *Oeuvres romanesques*. Ed. Michel Contat and Michel Rybalka, with Geneviève Idt and George H. Bauer, 1537–57. Paris: Gallimard, 1981.

La nausée (1938). In *Oeuvres romanesques*. Ed. Michel Contat and Michel Rybalka, with Geneviève Idt and George H. Bauer, 1–210. Paris: Gallimard, 1981.

Les mouches (drame en trois actes). Paris: Gallimard, 1943.

L'être et le néant: Essai d'ontologie phénoménologique. Paris: Gallimard, 1943.

Les chemins de la liberté. 3 vols. Paris: Gallimard, 1945–1949.

Réflexions sur la question juive (1946). Paris: Gallimard, 1962.

La putain respectueuse (1946). Paris: Nagel, 1948.

"Nick's Bar, New York City." *America (Cahiers France-Amérique-Latinité)* 5 (1947) in *Les écrits de Sartre*. Ed. Michel Contat and Michel Rybalka, 680–82. Paris: Gallimard, 1970.

"Présence noire." *Présence africaine* 1 (November–December 1947). In *Les écrits de Sartre*. Ed. Michel Contat and Michel Rybalka, 685–87. Paris: Gallimard, 1970.

Orphée noir. Preface to Léopold Sedar Senghor's *Anthologie de la nouvelle poésie nègre et malgache de langue française* (1948). In Jean-Paul Sartre, *Situations, III*, 229–86. Paris: Gallimard, 1976.

L'engrenage. [Scénario]. Paris: Nagel, 1948.

Les mains sales (pièce en sept tableaux). Paris: Gallimard: 1948.

Situations, III (1949). "Lendemains de guerre." Paris: Gallimard, 1976.

Entretiens sur la politique, with David Rousset and Gérard Rosenthal. Paris: Gallimard, 1949.

"Préface." Preface to *Les Pays Nordiques* of *Les Guides Nagel*, dir. Gilbert R. Martineau. Paris, Geneva, New York: Nagel, 1952.

Critique de la raison dialectique (précédé de Questions de méthode). Paris: Gallimard, 1960.

Sartre on Cuba (includes 13 articles published in *France-Soir*, June 28–July 15, 1960, under title "Ouragan sur le sucre"). No translator indicated. New York: Ballantine Books, 1961.

"Préface." Preface to Frantz Fanon, *Les damnés de la terre*, 2nd ed. Paris: F. Maspéro, 1961. (Also in *Situations, V*, "Colonialisme et néo-colonialisme," 67–93. Paris: Gallimard, 1964.

Les mots. Paris: Gallimard, 1964.

Situations, V. "Colonialisme et néo-colonialisme." Paris: Gallimard, 1964.

Bariona. Paris: E. Marescot: 1967.

Les écrits de Sartre. Ed. Michel Contat and Michel Rybalka. Paris: Gallimard, 1970.

On a raison de se révolter, discussions with Philippe Gavi and Pierre Victor. Paris: Gallimard, 1974.

Cahiers pour une morale. Paris: Gallimard, 1983.

Carnets de la drôle de guerre: septembre 1939-mars 1940 (1983). New edition, ed. Arlette Elkaïm-Sartre. Paris: Gallimard, 1995.

Selected Studies of Sartre

Haddour, Azzedine. *Colonialism and Ethics of Difference: From Sartre to Saïd.* London: Pluto Press, 2000.

Fulton, Eleanor Ann. *Sartre in America, 1945–1963.* Ph.D. dissertation, University of Madison–Wisconsin, 1991.

Lévy, Bernard-Henri. *Le siècle de Sartre.* Paris: Grasset, 2000.

Meschonnic, Henri. "Sartre et la question juive." *Etudes sartriennes* 1, 123–54. Nanterre: Centre de sémiotique textuelle, 1984.

Pageaux, Daniel-Henri. "Sartre, les Juifs, les Noirs . . . et les Autres." *Portulan 2. Mémoire juive, mémoire nègre*, 249–72. Châteauneuf-le-Rouge, Bouches du Rhône: Vent des îles, 1998.

Pestureau, Gilbert. "Sartre et les Etats-Unis." *Etudes sartriennes* 2–3, 301–8. Nanterre: Centre de sémiotique textuelle, 1986.

Pompeo Faracovi, Ornella and Sandra Teroni, ed. *Sartre e l'Italia.* Livorno: Belforte, 1987.

Prince, Gerald. "Dépaysement de Sartre ou les déboires d'un touriste." *French Review* 58, no. 2 (1984): 255–59.

Teroni, Sandra. "Venise: la ville et le fantasme." *Les Temps Modernes* 531–33 (October–December 1990): 760–74.

————. "Passeggiate romane dell'ultimo turista." In *Roma nella letteratura francese del Novecento*. Ed. L. Norci Cagiano and Valeria Pompejano Natoli, 165–80. Rome: Aracne, 1998.

Tobner, Odile. "Les intellectuels français et l'Afrique, II: Dans le champs philosophique—Sartre." *Peuples Noirs—Peuples Africains* 17 (September–October 1980): 11–29.

GEORGES SCHEHADÉ
(1905–1989)

Michèle Ratsaby

BIOGRAPHY

Georges Schehadé is one of the best-known French language poets and playwrights of Lebanon. He was born in 1905 in Alexandria, Egypt, the son of a Christian Lebanese family who had left Beirut several years earlier. Moving away from heavy Ottoman domination in Lebanon, they had gone to cosmopolitan Alexandria, open to the influence of Europe and the world. Schehadé spent his first 15 years there, surrounded by all kinds from all places, who lived and worked together in harmony.

Although living in countries of Arabic culture, first in Egypt, then in Lebanon, the Schehadé children spoke French at home and in the religious schools where they received their education. French is the only language ever used by Georges Schehadé in his poems and plays. In 1986 he was awarded the Grand Prix de la francophonie by the Académie française. Although he himself always felt Lebanese and refused to adopt French nationality, he did not consider himself a specifically Lebanese writer and the name of his country never appears throughout his works. To write was for him to escape reality by creating a borderless world of his own.

His father having lost his fortune in 1921, the family moved back to Lebanon where Georges, after graduating from the Collège du Sacré-Coeur, one of Beirut's leading private schools, went to study law at the Université Saint-Joseph of Beirut, affiliated with the Lyons Law School. Here he started writing and publishing his first poems and plays, such as *Le Père Eusèbe* (1920), a comedy written when he was sixteen; *Etincelles* (1926); and *La chevelure de Bérénice* (1926), a collection of poems written between 1924 and 1926. These first works were still naive, influenced by

French Romantics like Alphonse de Lamartine. But together with a group of friends also interested in modern French literature, he soon discovered Jean Cocteau, Max Jacob, Paul Eluard, and the surrealist movement.

From 1930, he published in the literary review *Commerce* more poems that were admired by the French poets Saint-John Perse and Paul Eluard, who loved his enigmatic ambiguous verses: "Every day I read and reread your poems. Thank you for having written them. With you, suddenly, poetry becomes new. . . . Your poems bring me a deep view, a true melody that I had forgotten" (cited in Danielle Baglione *Georges Schehadé, poète des deux rives, 1905–1989*, 86).

From 1933, Schehadé traveled to Italy, Poland, and Paris, where he met Max Jacob, Jules Supervielle, and Saint-John Perse. In 1939 he wrote his most famous play, *Monsieur Bob'le*, the story of a mysterious character, a dreamer loved by everybody he meets and who seems to purify all things around him. In 1951, *Monsieur Bob'le* was successfully played in Paris at the Théâtre de la Huchette under the direction of Georges Vitaly.

After having safely spent the war in Beirut as general secretary of the Ecole Supérieure des Lettres, he moved to Paris in 1949. There he continued to write poetry and poetic dramas such as *La soirée des proverbes; Trois actes* (1954); *Histoire de Vasco: Pièce en six tableaux* (1956), performed the same year in Zurich under the direction of Jean-Louis Barrault; *Les Violettes: Comédie en onze tableaux avec des chansonettes* (1960); and *L'émigré de Brisbane: Pièce en neuf tableaux* (1965). In 1958 he also wrote the scenario and dialogues of the film *Goha* that received the International Critics' Prize at the 1958 Cannes Festival. In Paris he met and befriended the writer Julien Gracq, the surrealist artists André Breton and Max Ernst, and the actor Jean-Louis Barrault, who loved the poetic qualities of his plays and who in 1954 produced *La soirée des proverbes* at the Petit Théâtre Marigny. In the 1950s, Schehadé also participated in literary meetings with surrealists such as Samuel Beckett, Eugene Ionesco, and Jacques Audiberti.

From this time his literary fame grew steadily; his plays were performed in many Parisian théâtres: La Huchette, Marigny, Sarah-Bernhardt, the Odéon, and even at the Comédie-Française (*L'émigré de Brisbane* was presented there in 1967). Other European stages as well—the Schauspielhaus in Zurich, the Schiller theater of Berlin, and the Royal Dramatic Theater of Stockholm—saw presentations of his plays. In 1976 he was chosen to be a member of the jury at the Cannes Festival, and in 1977 the Georges Pompidou Center in Paris dedicated a special evening to his life and works. He died in Paris in 1989.

MAJOR MULTICULTURAL THEMES

Georges Schehadé has been called "poète des deux rives" (the poet of two shores, Baglione, *Georges Schéhadé, poète des deux rives, 1905–1989*), and the originality of his works is often attributed to the blending of his Oriental emotional roots with the sober precision of his French vocabulary. His writings, which seem to lie on the border between the two cultures that nurtured him, are imaginary Oriental fairy tales, told in a concise and perfect French language: "Lucky Georges who combines the gifts of the best Arabic storytellers with the gifts of the purest of French poets" (Jules Supervielle, "Georges Schehadé et l'histoire de Vasco," *Cahiers de la Compagnie Madeleine Renaud-J.L.Barrault*, 3).

Unlike any other French playwright of his time, Schehadé composed his dramas using the language of his poems, effortless and limpid, as if written in a free world of dreams. First of all he is a poet and his plays seem to be the continuation of his verses: simple stories, with strange and extravagant characters living in some indefinable imaginary places, like Paola Scala, the ideal little village of *Monsieur Bob'le*, where "happiness is a very ordinary event" (*Monsieur Bob'le*, 22). His heroes are always leaving for faraway places, a nameless island, a mountain, or some lost paradise. A poet of exile, he describes constant departures, but without any tension or conflict and the action always flows smoothly to an often melancholy conclusion.

SURVEY OF CRITICISM

Schehadé's work has been admired by many artists of his time for the originality of its poetic qualities. Saint John-Perse, in a letter cited in Danielle Baglione's book (1999), wrote to him in 1949: "Give in, always give in to this voice of your own . . . Your strength resides in this human wisdom which you maybe owe to the Orient" (121). Baglione adds: "Contemporary French poetry doesn't have any magician that can be compared to Schehadé . . . and the world has been metamorphosed through the poet's words. It fluctuates, floats, and becomes illuminated" (151). The image of the transparency of water is often used to describe his language. In an article about Schehadé's *Monsieur Bob'le* published in *Combat* (September 2, 1951), Thierry Maulnier writes: "The play flows like a transparent and secret spring" (Baglione, 133). Jean-Louis Barrault (1956), in the program he wrote for the play *Histoire de Vasco*, expresses his admiration for Schehadé's work: "I totally love Vasco, for its deep meaning, for its winged form, for its atmosphere at the same time foolish and tragic, for the deep beauty of its language" (3). For Martin Esslin (1993) Schehadé is a member of the "poetic avant-garde" (921), a literary group that relies on fantasy and dream reality and uses lyrical speech in plays that are in effect poems.

SELECTED BIBLIOGRAPHY

Works by Schehadé

Monsieur Bob'le. Paris: Gallimard, 1951.

La soirée des proverbes; Trois actes. Paris: Gallimard, 1954.

Histoire de Vasco: Pièce en six tableaux. Paris: Gallimard, 1956.

Les violettes: Comédie en onze tableaux avec des chansonettes. Paris: Gallimard, 1960.

Le voyage: Pièce en huit tableaux. Paris: Gallimard, 1961.

L'émigré de Brisbane: Pièce en neuf tableaux. Paris: Gallimard, 1965.

Les poésies. Suivi de "Portrait de Jules" et de "Récit de l'an zéro." Preface Gaetan Picon. Paris: Gallimard, 1969.

L'écolier sultan. Suivi de "Rodogune Sinne." Paris: Gallimard, 1973.

L'habit fait le prince; Pantomime inspirée (si l'on veut) d'une nouvelle de Gottfried Keller: "Kleider machen Leute." Paris: Gallimard, 1973.

Anthologie du vers unique. Paris: Ramsay, 1977.

Le nageur d'un seul amour. Paris: Gallimard, 1985.

Poésie VII. Beirut: Dar an-Nahar, 1998.

Selected Studies of Schehadé

Baglione, Danielle. *Georges Schehadé, poète des deux rives, 1905–1989.* Paris: Éditions de l'IMEC; Beirut: Dar an-Nahar, 1999.

Esslin, Martin. "From the Theatre of the Absurd." In *The HBJ Anthology of Drama.* Ed. W. B. Worthen, 918–21. Fort Worth: Harcourt Brace Jovanovich College Publishers, 1993.

Michel, Jacqueline. *Le pays sans nom: Dhotel, Supervielle, Schehadé.* Paris: Lettres Modernes, 1989.

Saba-Jazzar, Diah. *Introduction au théâtre de Georges Schehadé.* Beirut: Dar an-Nahar, 1999.

Supervielle, Jules. "*Georges Schehadé et l'histoire de Vasco.*" *Cahiers de la Compagnie Madeleine Renaud-Jean Louis Barrault* 17 (September 1956): 2–26.

W. G. (WINFRIED GEORG) SEBALD
(1944–2001)

Elizabeth Powers

BIOGRAPHY

W. G. Sebald was born in 1944 in the Bavarian Alps, in the village of Wertach im Allgäu, but it was only in 1950, when his family moved to Sonthofen, a town nineteen kilometers distant, that he first encountered remains of the physical destruction caused by World War II. He began his university studies in German literature at the University of Freiburg in 1963, and continued his education in Switzerland. After receiving the Licence des Lettres in 1966, he went in the same year to Manchester, England. The period in Manchester, during which he was a lecturer in German at the university, is indirectly chronicled in *Die Ausgewanderten: Vier lange Erzählungen* (1992), in which Sebald mentions that, until 1966, he had "never been more than five-six hours by train from home" (219). In 1970 he began teaching at the University of East Anglia in Norwich. He received his Ph.D. in 1973 from the University of Hamburg with a dissertation on Arnold Döblin, but, aside from interruptions for travel, continued to live in England. He had been a professor of German and European literature for many years at the university in Norwich when he died as the result of an automobile accident in December 2001.

Sebald's death put an untimely end to the literary career of an internationally acclaimed writer who, many critics believed, would one day be rewarded with a Nobel Prize for Literature. Following early scholarly writings on German and Austrian writers, he published in 1988 *Nach der Natur: Ein Elementargedicht*, a slender volume of three prose poems that mixed historical subjects (e.g., the German Renaissance painter Matthias Grünewald) and autobiographical reflections. In its mixture of history and biography, *Nach der Natur* is a preface to Sebald's succeeding works, and it also introduces characteristic formal elements of that oeuvre: a highly poeticized language of often voluminous sentence length, which bestows gravity and stateliness on its subjects, and a painstaking attention to place and setting as well as to the details of art works and other products of human labor. These two elements, which harness a great fund of literary and historical research, reflect Sebald's academic grounding. The photographs that accompany *Nach der Natur*, by Thomas Becker, also presage a distinctive element of succeeding works, namely, the insertion of photographs and other illustrative material into the narrative flow that substantiate the real, lived nature of the subject. The result is what one reviewer has called "a hybrid genre . . . a mixture of fact and fiction, illustrated by small blurry photographs which may, or may not, be photographs of the places and people in the stories" (Annan, "Ghosts," 29).

The belletristic works for which Sebald gained an international reputation were produced while the author was living in England, beginning in 1990 with *Schwindel. Gefühle*. Missing from these works are the concerns that animated writers in his native country in the 1990s, including the nature of a unified Germany or contemporary sexual politics. Sebald's quasi-documentary style, however, links him with the politically engaged German writing of the 1960s. In documentary literature (or theater, as some of the most notable examples are in that genre, e.g., Rolf Hochhuth's 1963 play *Der Stellvertreter*), literary and factual material are mixed with little distinction between the two. Similarly, in Sebald's works a first-person narrator (who may or may not be Sebald the writer) constructs, with a patient and, indeed, lawyerly accumulation of detail, what might be called a dossier concerning the alienation of the modern self from traditional sources of culture and identity.

MAJOR MULTICULTURAL THEMES

For Sebald, culture itself has been fractionated in the modern world, leaving us all deracinated and decultured. Thus, marginal existences, whether of exiles or other displaced persons, are a constant in his works. For instance, among the presiding ghosts in *Schwindel. Gefühle* are the exile Dante Alighieri and Franz Kafka's wandering hunter, Gracchus. In this work Sebald initiates his use of the convention of the *promeneur solitaire*, an unattached male traveler whose peregrinations produce the feelings of vertigo to which the title alludes. In *Die Ausgewanderten* (1992), it is the subjects of the four poeticized biographies who suffer from alienation and have removed themselves from everyday reality. The unstated subtext is the Holocaust: three of the stories in *Die Ausgewanderten* concern Jews who escaped it but were thereby severed from their connection with traditional sources of identity.

Such marginalization is a long ongoing process, the result of destructive events of the past two centuries, including the massive colonial and architectural ventures of the nineteenth century described in *Die Ringe des Saturn: Eine englische Wallfahrt* (1995) and in *Austerlitz* (2001). The former work, a first-person account of a walking tour through the English county of Suffolk, mixes reports of the present-day state of things with archival and historical material concerning earlier inhabitants, occupations, habitats, and life cycles of this coastal region. As the journey proceeds, every town gives evidence of some earlier, mostly nineteenth-century, splendor that has now fallen into ruin. A large swath of destruction is shown as emanating from one English county, ranging from the exploitation of Africa to the Taipeng rebellion in China.

Austerlitz has a similar scope. The title reminds us of the site of a great military engagement, an outcome of Napoleon's grandiose campaign to remake the world according to the ideals of the Enlightenment. But it is also the name of the man who is the subject of the work, who as a child on the eve of World War II was separated from his Jewish parents in Prague and grew up in England. His present-day amnesia suggests the way our historical memory is being eradicated by the process of modernization, leaving us at a loss as to who we are. Loss of memory is also the theme of *Luftkrieg und Literatur: mit einem Essay zu Alfred Andersch* (1999). According to Sebald the avoidance by German writers of the subject of the Allied aerial bombardment of Germany during World War II remains "a shameful family secret"; yet "the loss of the heavy historical burden" that the fires represented was a welcome one since the ability to forget this horrible chapter has allowed Germans to build an affluent modern society. "Unconsciousness," he writes, quoting Hans Magnus Enzensberger, "is the precondition of their [economic] success" (18–20).

Underlying Sebald's works are a critique of capitalism and a lament for what he sees as the destruction of the natural world. In *Die Ringe des Saturn* it is evident that the destruction is no longer a local event but a global one. The incorporated literary and archival material evokes all that has been lost. Thus, Sebald's works blend, sometimes literally, sometimes in highly poeticized form, passages and motifs from literary, biographical, or historical works (of influence here are Adalbert Stifter, Jorge Luis Borges, and Joseph Eichendorff). In constructing the memoirs of the exiles portrayed in *Die Ausgewanderten* or in *Austerlitz*, Sebald relies on letters or documents purportedly written by the person in question. Whether these documents are authentic is secondary to the purpose of giving existence to what has otherwise been forgotten or lost. For Sebald, texts do not support the postmodern notion of human constructedness but rather serve to render an authentic, lived life. The result is the reclamation of culture that has been lost.

A comment made by the author in *Luftkrieg und Literatur* offers a personal view of the modern lack of rootedness and loss of memory his works portray. Feelings of home ("Heimatgefühle"), Sebald writes, are not elicited by the German landscape of meadows and mountain pastures, which were typical of the village of his birth. It was instead the images of destruction that he encountered in Sonthofen, the ruins of bombed buildings, that represented "the more powerful, higher reality of my first years" (83). On his return 30 years later, also described in *Schwindel. Gefühle*, a self-service store occupied the space on which the ruins had stood, its walls covered with advertisements for victuals.

SURVEY OF CRITICISM

Critics concur that a unifying theme of Sebald's work is that of the outsider. Michael Butler (1998), for instance, speaks of the eccentric figures who "live their imaginative lives at a tangent to social reality" (10). In this connection, Gabriel Annan (1997) quarrels with the English translation of "The Emigrants" for *Die Ausgewanderten:* the French word *dépaysés* would better describe the subjects of this work, referring to men without the sense of purpose implied by the word "emigrant" (29).

Sebald, who is not a Jew, has received sympathetic response for his treatment of Jewish subjects, though, as Annan writes, not even *Die Ausgewanderten* is really "Holocaust literature." Instead, "Sebald's affection and pity for Jews is part of a general sorrow for the dead" (29). Richard Eder (2000) comments in a similar vein on *Die Ringe des Saturn:* "The Holocaust, lethally radiating in every temporal direction, contaminates in its foreshadowings and rememberings all human chronicles, not just those of the Jews" (E8). Yet, as Michiko Kakutani (2001) points out in connection with *Austerlitz*, "the Holocaust remains a chasm in the historical continuum, robbing [Sebald's characters] of a sense of continuity" (E42).

In reviewing *Austerlitz*, Daniel Mendelsohn (2001) remarked on Sebald's "obsession with the burdens of remembrance and guilt" (70). Likewise, Susan Sontag (2000) has drawn attention to the "acts of remembering" that Sebald's works enact (3), while Eder (2000) has spoken of Sebald as "memory's Einstein" (E8). But Sontag stresses Sebald's avoidance of romantic myth-making: while the photos in the books "are an exquisite index of the pastness of the past" (4), the past itself is unrecoverable. Erhard Schütz (1999) has taken issue with Sebald's interpretation of the absence of postwar German literature on the subject of the Allied bombardment. Calling *Luftkrieg* an epilogue (*Nachstück*) to Daniel Goldhagen's book concerning the collective responsibility of Germans for the crimes of the Nazis, Schütz proposes that the experience of the attacks was not a collective but rather an individual one (15).

SELECTED BIBLIOGRAPHY

Works by Sebald

Nach der Natur: Ein Elementargedicht. Nördlingen: Greno, 1988.

Schwindel. Gefühle. Frankfurt am Main: Vito von Eichborn, 1990.

Die Ausgewanderten: Vier lange Erzählungen. Frankfurt am Main: Vito von Eichborn, 1992.

Die Ringe des Saturn: Eine englische Wallfahrt. Frankfurt am Main: Vito von Eichborn, 1995.

Logis in einem Landhaus: über Gottfrid Keller, Johann Peter Hebel, Robert Walser und andere. Munich: Carl Hanser, 1998.

Luftkrieg und Literatur: mit einem Essay zu Alfred Andersch. Munich: Carl Hanser, 1999.

Austerlitz. Munich: Carl Hanser, 2001.

Selected Studies of Sebald

Aciman, André. "In the Crevasse." *Commentary* (June 1997): 61–64.

Annan, Gabriele. "Ghosts." *New York Review of Books* (September 25, 1997): 29–30.

Butler, Michael. "The Human Cost of Exile." *Times* (London) *Literary Supplement* (October 2, 1998): 10.

Eder, Richard. "Exploring a Present That Is Invaded by the Past." *New York Times* (May 23, 2000): E8.

———. "Excavating a Life." *New York Times Book Review* (October 28, 2001): 10.

Falcke, Eberhard. "Mords-Erinnerungen." Reprinted from *Die Zeit* (Hamburg), November 27, 1992, in *Deutsche Literatur 1992: Jahresüberblick.* Ed. Franz Josef Görtz, Volker Hage, and Uwe Wittstock, 263–67. Stuttgart: Reclam, 1993.

Kakutani, Michiko. "In a No Man's Land of Memories and Loss." *New York Times* (October 26, 2001): E42.

Lewis, Tess. "W. G. Sebald: The Past Is Another Country." *The New Criterion* (December 2001): 85–90.

Mendelsohn, Daniel. "Foreign Correspondents." *New York* (October 8, 2001): 70–72.

Ozick, Cynthia. "The Posthumous Sublime." In *Quarrel and Quandary* 26–41. New York: Alfred A. Knopf, 2000.

Scholz, Christian. "'Aber das Geschriebene ist ja kein wahres Dokument': Ein Gespräch mit dem Schriftsteller W. G. Sebald über Literatur und Photographie." *Neue Zürcher Zeitung* (February 26/27, 2000): 51–52.

Schütz, Erhard. "Kollektive Verstocktheiten: Von metaphysischer Vaterlandsverzweiflung und moralischem Herkunftsekel: W. G. Sebalds jetzt in Buchform vorliegende Ausführungen zum Luftkrieg und den Versäumnissen der Literatur als Nachstück zu Goldhagen." *Tageszeitung* (Berlin), (March 31, 1999): 15.

Sontag, Susan. "A Mind in Mourning." *Times* (London) *Literary Supplement* (February 25, 2000): 3–4.

Steinfeld, Thomas. "Die Wünschelrute in der Tasche eines Nibelungen: Der Kopfbahnhof der literarischen Welt heißt 'Austerlitz.'" *Frankfurter Allgemeine Zeitung* (March 3, 2001): 18.

LUIS SEPÚLVEDA
(1949–)

Arianna Maiorani

BIOGRAPHY

Luis Sepúlveda was born in Ovalle, Chile, into a politically engaged family. His paternal grandfather, a Spanish anarchist, had chosen South America for his exile. Sepúlveda himself was a political militant for many years. He began writing with contributions to his high school journal, after which he worked as a professional journalist. He also wrote for radio programs and studied as a theatrical director. He claimed that his artistic and literary activities of those years were intimately linked with his political engagement. In 1964 he joined the Juventud Comunista of Chile, a Communist youth organization. He published his first collection of short stories in 1969 and in the same year won a scholarship for the University of Lomonosov in Moscow. After a few months, he left both the University and the Juventud Comunista and decided to leave his parents' home. He worked as a theater director from 1970 to 1971, and in 1973 joined the socialist party that supported Salvador Allende, becoming a member of his personal guard. After Pinochet's *golpe*, Sepúlveda was imprisoned for three years and tortured. In 1976 the German section of Amnesty International began a campaign for his release. Having become too popular to be eliminated or even to be held in prison, he was placed under house arrest, only to resume his clandestine militant activities. He was then condemned to life imprisonment; but again, thanks to the intervention of Amnesty International and in accordance with the general law decree 504, his sentence was commuted to exile.

He left Santiago in 1977 with a visa for Sweden but at a stopover in Buenos Aires decided to remain in Argentina for a while. He began traveling through South America, never interrupting his writing. During this period he lived for seven months with the Shuar Indios in the Amazon forest: he became one of them without being one of them, learning to love and live in the natural environment without exploiting it. This unique experience inspired one of his most famous novels, *Un viejo que leía novelas de amor* (1989). In 1979 he went to Nicaragua but because of political frictions and disappointments he decided to leave South America for Europe. He settled in Hamburg, Germany, and during the 1980s he joined Greenpeace teams on several ecological missions throughout the world, thus becoming one of the most prominent correspondents for the German press. His experiences with Greenpeace inspired the novel *Mundo del fin del mundo* (1989), an indictment of indiscriminate exploitation of the planet. After having lived between Hamburg and Paris and having reached international fame (he was awarded several international prizes, such as the Tigre Juan prize), he settled in Asturias, Spain, where he writes for readers of all ages, as he loves to say.

MAJOR MULTICULTURAL THEMES

Sepúlveda considers himself a Latin American and a writer without a homeland. He is a member of a new generation of Latin-American authors who shun the "magic realism" tradition, who do not belong to a single place, and who write according to the ideal of a multicultural literature. When interviewed, Sepúlveda often says that since the 1960s Europe has lost its power to produce narrative; that European writers often mistake the act of *writing* literature for the act of *writing about* literature. Latin-American writers, according to him, are the real heirs of European literary tradition, having brought back to Europe the kind of purely narrative literature that readers were looking for.

Having been born and raised in a family of both European and South American origins, and having traveled all over the world, he insists that the real solution to conflicts must be a multicultural one. This includes ecology and biology, in order to build a new relationship between human civilization and the planet, and to find new ways of cooperating with nature instead of exploiting it. In this sense, multiculturalism can be considered the major theme of his more important works.

Un viejo que leía novelas de amor, inspired by Sepúlveda's experience of life in the Amazonian forest with the Shuar Indios, is the story of an old man, Antonio José Bolívar, who after a difficult life retires to a village at the border of the forest to enjoy the romantic love novels he has managed to collect. But when the "white men" undertake an indiscriminate hunt for a *tigrillo* (a typical feline of the area), thereby enraging the female, who begins to kill people, Bolívar must return to the forest to reestablish the natural equilibrium disturbed by the ignorance and greed of humans who will never understand nature's laws. The Amazon forest and its inhabitants (humans and animals) can be read as a metaphor for a multicultural way of life, an almost ideal world in which every creature takes advantage of the environment without exploiting it and learns from all the others the importance and richness of diversity, and the white "civilized" men, who are unable to understand and respect all this, represent the world dominated by greed and commercial interest.

Mundo del fin del mundo tells the partly autobiographical story of a Chilean journalist who investigates and protests against whale hunters: it is also the story of human beings of different countries and cultures who travel and fight together to preserve a world that is a treasure for all and contains a universal magic. *Patagonia Express: apuntes de viaje* (1995) is a travel book full of legends, stories, and reflections about Sepúlveda's journey through Patagonia and Tierra del Fuego. The book is a multicultural and multifaceted picture of a land in which different peoples and countries met and melded. The author had intended to make this journey with Bruce Chatwin himself, but at the time could not go back to his own country because of his militant past.

La frontera extraviada (1994), another strongly biographical novel, is the story of a Chilean former political prisoner who, after years of jail and torture, travels through South America trying to find a continuity between his past and his present and those of the countries he visits, and finally goes to Spain to find his roots in a small Andalusian village. Many of the short stories contained in Sepúlveda's collections, such as *Desencuentros* (1997) and *Historias marginales* (2000), are based on multicultural issues and autobiographical episodes (like those of the Russian women pilots called the White Roses of Stalingrad, and of Professor Carlos Gálvez, a Chilean socialist). Characters from different countries meet and create special situations in stories of places where "culture" is a word of different roots. They realize that the only real culture is world culture and that the only real homeland is Earth, which can be preserved only by taking a multicultural view of all its creatures.

Even in his thriller stories Sepúlveda uses characters who come from different parts of the world and interact on an international set, as in *Nombre de torero* (1994), *Diario de un killer sentimental* (1998), and *Yacaré* (1998). *Historia de una gaviota y del gato que le enseñó a volar* (1996) is a children's book that can be read as a metaphor for a multicultural solution to our world's problems: it is the story of a cat, Zorba (modeled on the author's own cat), who finds the egg of a seagull that has died of pollution. Zorba cares for the egg until a small seagull is born; the cat and his friends raise the seagull and even teach her to fly, while all the animals of the story teach men how differences can be used to produce fruitful collaboration and a deeper respect for the environment.

SURVEY OF CRITICISM

During the 1990s, Luis Sepúlveda achieved considerable fame in Europe both as a committed writer and as a political-ecological activist. His books are mostly appreciated in Italy, where he is also editor of "La frontiera scomparsa," a special series by authors who have experienced the cultural frontiers of the world and who are often Latin-American. Actually, criticism of his literary work consists of a few short essays, international reviews and many interviews (mainly Italian).

Pino Cacucci (1996), a writer and a friend of Sepúlveda, writes about the author's work and life in an informal interview. Ilide Carmignani (1996), Sepúlveda's Italian translator, calls his work "militant writing," considering his ideological and ecological commitment and his way of looking for magic in reality. Adele Galeotta Cajati (1999) analyzes the way *Historia de una gaviota y del gato que le enseñó a volar* was transformed into an animated film directed by Enzo d'Alò and produced by Cecchi Gori. Juan D. Cid Hidalgo (1998) and C. Heymann (1997) focus on the meaning of reading in *Un viejo que leía novelas de amor*. Clara Camplani (1998) analyzes Sepúlveda's career and growing fame, while Andrew Graham-Yooll (1994) studies his role as a member of a new generation of Latin-American writers. Angiola Codacci-Pisanelli (1997) makes a comparison between Sepúlveda's and Jorge Amado's children's books; Betti Filippini's 1995 interview offers an interesting comparison between the new generation of Latin-American writers who want to show the magic of reality, and the preceding "magic realism" generation; Claudio Tognato (1997) presents an interesting portrait of Sepúlveda and his literary production, while Leonetta Bentivoglio (1997), Renato Minore (1997), Aldo Garzia (1996), Matteo Collura (1993), Fabrizio Carbone (1993), Miguel Angel Quemain (1993), Cristóbal Sárrias (1997), Guillermo Altares (1993), and M. Schneider (1993) all review and interview the author, focusing on many aspects of his work, life, and political commitment.

SELECTED BIBLIOGRAPHY

Works by Sepúlveda

Un viejo que leía novelas de amor. Madrid: Jucar, 1989.
Mundo del fin del mundo (1989). Barcelona: Tusquets, 1994.
Nombre de torero. Barcelona: Tusquets, 1994.
Patagonia Express: Apuntes de viaje. Barcelona: Tusquets, 1995.
La frontera extraviada (1994). *La frontiera scomparsa.* Trans. Ilide Carmignani. Parma: Guanda, 1996.
Historia de una gaviota y del gato que le enseñó a volar. Barcelona: Tusquets, 1996.
Desencuentros. Barcelona: Tusquets, 1997.
Diario de un killer sentimental: Seguido de Yacaré. Barcelona: Tusquets, 1998.
Historias marginales. Barcelona: Seix Barral, 2000.

Selected Studies of Sepúlveda

Altares, Guillermo. "Sepúlveda, Luis: *El viejo que leía novelas de amor.*" *El Urogallo* 85 (1993): 69–70.

Bentivoglio, Leonetta. "La mia vita dal mitra alla penna." *La Repubblica* (July 18, 1997): 36–37.

Cacucci, Pino. In "Il cileno errante." *Camminando: Incontri di un viandante*, 25–34. Milan: Feltrinelli, 1996.

Cajati, Adele Galeotta. "Storia di un gatto e di una gabbanella che volarono da un libro ad un film." *Annali dell'Istituto Universitario Orientale di Napoli, Sezione Romanza*, 41:2 (1999) 495–502.

Camplani, Clara. "Il 'fenomeno' Luis Sepúlveda." *Rassegna Iberistica* 63 (1998): 43–45.

Carbone, Fabrizio. "Il vecchio e la giungla: un romanzo sull'Amazzonia." *Linea d'Ombra* 86 (1993): 21–22.

Carmignani, Ilide. "Dal realismo magico alla magia della realtà." *Linea d'Ombra* 118 (1996): 32–34.

Cid Hidalgo, Juan D. "El acto de 'leer' en *Un viejo que leía novelas de amor*: aproximación a Luis Sepúlveda." *Atenea: revista de ciencia, arte y literatura de la Universidad de Concepción* 477 (1998): 241–47.

Codacci-Pisanelli, Angiola. "È arrivato prima Amado." *L'Espresso* 15 (1997): 113.

Collura, Matteo. "Contro i predatori dell'Amazzonia. Un romanzo la salverà." *Corriere della Sera* (June 4, 1993): 31.

Filippini, Betti. "Garcia Marquez è magico, io guardo la realtà." *Il Giorno* (January 25, 1995): 18.

Garzia, Aldo. "Vincere 'l'olvido.'" *Il Manifesto* (June 11, 1996): 25.

Graham-Yooll, Andrew. "Light at the end of the tunnel: The New Writers of Latin America." *The Antioch Review* 52, no. 4 (1994): 566–79.

Heymann, C. "Les chemins de lecture dans *Un viejo que leía novelas de amor.*" *Les langues Néo-latines* 91, no. 300 (1997): 141–62.

Minore, Renato. "Cambiare il mondo è ancora possibile." *Il Messaggero* (July 18, 1997): 19.

Quemain, Miguel Angel. "No soy un escritor cileno. Entrevista con Luis Sepúlveda." *Quimera. Revista de Literatura* 121 (1993): 20–24.

Sárrias, Cristóbal. "Sepúlveda, Luis. *Desencuentros.*" *Reseña Madrid* 285 (1997): 32.

Schneider, M. "La grâce de Luis Sepúlveda." *Espaces Latino-américains* 99 (1993): 33.

Tognato, Claudio. "L'esploratore cileno." *Il Manifesto* (July 16, 1997): 20–21.

ISAAC BASHEVIS SINGER
(1904–1991)

Michèle Ratsaby

BIOGRAPHY

Isaac Bashevis Singer, the storyteller novelist and journalist who won the Nobel Prize for Literature in 1978, was born in Radzymin, a small town in eastern Poland. He grew up during World War I in a poor Jewish neighborhood of Warsaw, where his father, a Hassidic rabbi, supervised a *beth din*, a rabbinical court that Singer described in his 1956 book *Majn Tatn's Bes-din shtub*. Singer received a traditional Jewish education, and even enrolled in 1920 in the Rabbinical Seminary of Warsaw to become a rabbi. But two years later he rebelled against his strict upbringing and left school to work as a proofreader, a journalist and a translator for the *Literarische Bleter*, a prestigious Yiddish weekly that was edited by his secular older brother, Isaac Joshua Singer.

Singer's earliest short stories, written in Yiddish, were produced while he was working as a journalist. His first novel *Sotn in Goraj* (1935) takes place in the seventeenth century, after pogroms by Bohdan Chmielnicki and his Cossacks on the Jewish population of Poland. The story, written in a mediaeval style imitative of some old Yiddish Book of Chronicles, treats some of Singer's favorite themes: the conflict between tradition and mysticism in the Jewish religion, the knowledge of good and evil, and the existence of free will. The novel is about the appearance of a false Messiah, Sabbatai Zvi, the mass hysteria that develops around him, and the disappointment of those who wanted to believe in his powers. Even before the horrors of the Holocaust, Singer was troubled by the question of how and why such terrible things happened: were the Jews of Goray ripe for Messianism because they needed to understand their recent sufferings and was their traditional religion inadequate to help them?

Singer emigrated to the United States in 1935, leaving behind his first wife Rachel and a son, who later both fled to Palestine. He settled in New York and began working for *Forverts* (*Jewish Daily Forward*), a Yiddish newspaper for new immigrants, publishing short stories or chapters of novels for more than 40 years under the name Isaac Warshofsky. Later he took his mother's name Batsheba and made Bashevis his pen name for his serious literary works. He was greatly influenced by his older brother, who continued publishing after emigrating to the United States and was already a successful Yiddish writer in the 1930s. When the brother died unexpectedly in 1944, Singer, already depressed by the loss of his former world in the Holocaust, felt abandoned and stopped writing for seven years. But after his first collection of stories *Gimpl tam un andere dertseylungen* (1956) was published in English in 1957, his public expanded. He became well-known and loved by general American readers, thanks to the translations of his works, often in collaboration with distinguished translators such as Irving Howe, Cecil Hemley, and Saul Bellow. After two decades of poverty and obscurity, Singer gained fame and prosperity. He published 45 volumes of short stories, novels, children's tales, and memoirs and continued writing until his death in 1991. He wrote about the past world of European Hassidic Jews; about the temptations of the devil and the dangers of the flesh in *Der Gentelman fun Krakaw* (1957); about religious doubt and sexual desire in *Der Kunstnmakher fun Lublin: roman* (1959); the laughable vanity of intellectuals in *Der Spinoza fun Markt Strass* (1961); and the decline of Polish Jewry in the nineteenth century in his long novels, *Die Familje Moshkat* (1950) and *Der Hoyf* (1952). Above all, he kept alive in his stories the world of the *shtetl*, the East European Jewish village, a world that disappeared after 1945.

MAJOR MULTICULTURAL THEMES

Isaac Bashevis Singer devoted his life to writing about a culture that was brutally destroyed during World War II in a language also on the verge of extinction. With his 1964 election to the National Institute of Arts and Letters, he became the only American member to write in a language other than English. Yiddish, the language of his childhood, has its origins in the European Middle Ages. The language is built on the different cultures with which the Jewish people came into contact. Although Singer's literary world, rich in intricate situations, universal human problems, and vibrant characters, had been initially created for his Jewish readers, it grew to be loved by the general public. Some stories are centuries-old memories and dreams. Ghosts, demons, and other supernatural powers mingle with humans, usually making them miserable. Other stories are semiautobiographical sketches, describing the vanished world of prewar Warsaw, such as *Majn Tatn's Bes-din shtub* (1956). A few novels treat of contemporary questions, as in *Sonim, geshikhte fun a libe* (1970) or *Shotns baym Hodson*, published posthumously in 1998. In *Sonim, geshikhte fun a libe*, one of his most famous books, a Holocaust survivor, who remarried after the war and lives in Brooklyn, finds out that his first wife survived and is coming to America. After catastrophic experiences, he has to deal also with his loss of faith. *Shotns baym Hodson*, set in the late 1940s, traces the destinies of a group of refugees in the aftermath of the Holocaust, searching for answers to life's questions.

Behind its colorful folklore, Singer's world is realistic, and his impassioned tales bring universal human conditions to life. His themes are universal, describing passions, spiritual dilemmas, lust, and power. In the short story "Feuyer" (in *Der Shpiegl un andere dertseylungen*, 1975), Singer vividly describes the evil of jealousy in the deathbed confession of a man obsessed by guilt for having been all his life jealous of his brother. *Der Kunstnmakher fun Lublin* narrates the life of a Jewish Don Juan who ends up as an ascetic.

His characters are real—tragic, grotesque, base, spiritual, or wise—and always deeply human. Some of them, like Gimpel the fool or Jacob in *Knekht* (1961), become eternal figures of world literature. Singer also wrote children's stories, many of them set in Chelm, an imaginary town housing many funny fools, where the magic beyond everyday life is always present.

In many interviews, Singer claimed to be surprised by the success of his works. But, as Christopher Lehmann-Haupt mentioned in his November 6, 1978 *New York Times* article "Nobel Prize to I.B. Singer," Singer's stories are for everyone: "As for his appeal, one needs only note that any writer who can command a following in such disparate publications as the *Jewish Daily Forward*, *The New Yorker*, and *Playboy*, can scarcely be accused of cultural parochialism" (55).

SURVEY OF CRITICISM

Ruth Wisse (1971), describing Singer's hero Gimpel in "Der Shpiegl," stresses how Singer links the character's innocence to historical reality, to "the refusal of the majority of the Jews to face reality when they were herded into ghettos, concentration camps and finally gas chambers" (64). Edward Alexander (1980) compares the novel *Der Hoyf*, which depicts the disintegration of Polish Jewry during the late nineteenth century, to the major works of the French, English, and Russian literatures of the same period. But Singer was aware that "this European destruction was accompanied by the beginning of a new culture, French, English or Russian. The Jews of nineteenth-century Poland did not have this choice. Their loss of unity in religion meant the loss of Jewish identity itself" (84). Alexander also admires Singer's original way of using his memories in his short stories: "Within his limits, Singer is a genius. He has total command of his imagined world; he is original in his use both of traditional Jewish materials and his modernist attitude towards them . . . and he is a master of Yiddish prose" (111). Irving Howe's introductory essay to *Selected Short Stories of Isaac Bashevis Singer* (1966) stresses the uniqueness of Singer's writing "about the destroyed world of Eastern European Jews as if it were still alive. . . . Singer's ultimate concern is not with the collective experience of a chosen or martyred people but with the enigmas of personal fate" (xix).

SELECTED BIBLIOGRAPHY

Works by Singer

Sotn in Goraj (1935). [*Satan in Goray*. Trans. Jacob Sloan. New York: Noonday Press, 1955.]

Die Familje Moshkat (1950). [*The Family Moskat*. Trans. A. H. Gross. New York: Knopf, 1950.]

Der Hoyf (1952). [*The Manor*. Trans. Elaine Gottlieb and Joseph Singer. New York: Farrar, Straus and Giroux, 1967; *The Estate*. Trans. Joseph Singer, Elaine Gottlieb and Elisabeth Shub. New York: Farrar, Straus and Giroux, 1969.]

Gimpl tam un andere dertseylungen (1956). [*Gimpel the Fool, and Other Stories*. Trans. I. B. Singer, Martha Glicklich, Elaine Gottlieb, and Norman Guterman. New York: Noonday Press, 1957.]

Majn Tatn's Bes-din shtub (1956). [*In My Father's Court*. Trans. C. Kleinerman-Goldstein. New York: Farrar, Straus and Giroux, 1966.]

Der Gentelman fun Krakaw (1957). [*The Gentleman from Cracow*. Trans. Martha Glicklich and Elaine Gottlieb. New York: Limited Edition Club, 1979.]

Der Kunstnmakher fun Lublin: roman (1959). [*The Magician of Lublin*. Trans. Elaine Gottlieb and Joseph Singer. New York: Noonday Press, 1960.]

Der Spinoza fun Markt Strass (1961). [*The Spinoza of Market Street*. Trans. Martha Glicklich. Philadelphia, Pa.: Jewish Publication Society of America, 1961.]

Knekht (1961). [*The Slave. A Novel*. Trans. I. B. Singer and Cecil Hemley. New York: Farrar, Straus and Giroux, 1962.]

Short Friday, and Other Stories. New York: Farrar, Straus and Giroux, 1964.

Sonim, geshikhte fun a libe (1970). [*Enemies, A Love Story*. Trans. Aliza Shevrin and Elisabeth Shub. New York: Farrar, Straus and Giroux, 1972.]

Der Shpiegl un andere dertseylungen. Jerusalem: Jerusalem University Press, 1975.

Shosha (1974). [*Shosha*. Trans. Joseph Singer. New York: Farrar, Straus and Giroux, 1978.]

Kenig fun di felder. [*The King of the Fields*. Trans. Isaac Bashevis Singer. New York: Farrar, Straus and Giroux, 1988.]

Shoym. [*Scum*. Trans. Rosaline Dukalsky Schwartz. New York: Farrar, Straus and Giroux, 1991.]

Isaac Bashevis Singer: Conversations. Ed. Grace Farrell. Jackson: University Press of Mississippi, 1992.

Tsertifikat. [*The Certificate*. Trans. Leonard Wolf. New York: Farrar, Straus and Giroux, 1992.]

Meshuge. [*Meshugah*. Trans. Isaac Bashevis Singer and Nili Wachtel. New York: Farrar, Straus and Giroux, 1994.]

Shotns baym Hodson. [*Shadows on the Hudson*. Trans. Joseph Sherman. New York: Farrar, Straus and Giroux, 1998.]

More Stories from My Father's Court. Trans. Curt Leviant. New York: Farrar,
Straus and Giroux, 2000.

Selected Studies of Singer

Alexander, Edward. *Isaac Bashevis Singer.* Boston: Twayne, 1980.

Farrell, Grace. *Critical Essays on Isaac Bashevis Singer.* New York: Hall, 1996.

Feldman, Irving. "The Shtetl World." *Kenyon Review* 24 (Winter 1962): 173–77.

Friedman, Lawrence S. *Understanding Isaac Bashevis Singer.* Columbia: University of South Carolina Press, 1988.

Howe, Irving. Introduction to *Selected Short Stories of Isaac Bashevis Singer.* New York: The Modern Library, 1966.

Lehmann-Haupt, Christopher. "Nobel Prize to I. B. Singer." *New York Times* (November 6, 1978): 55.

Malin, Irving. *Critical Views of Isaac Bashevis Singer.* New York: New York University Press, 1969.

Wisse, Ruth. *The Schlemiel as Modern Hero.* Chicago: University of Chicago Press, 1971.

ALEKSANDR ISAYEVICH SOLZHENITSYN
(1918–)

A. L. Rogers II

BIOGRAPHY

Two decades of forced exile from his native Russia—years spent mainly in the United States—certainly make Aleksandr Solzhenitsyn a multicultural writer, and given his outspoken championing of individual rights in the face of systematic oppression, it is no surprise that multicultural themes abound in his work. But in all his writings, even those addressed to his Western audience, Solzhenitsyn focuses persistently on his homeland. He is truly a *Russophile:* his deep, abiding passion throughout a half century of writing has been his love of his native land and its people.

Born in Kislovodsk (north Caucasus) to a father who died before his birth and a mother of genteel ancestry, Solzhenitsyn grew up in Rostov on the lower Don. He received degrees in mathematics and physics from Rostov University. After induction into the Red Army in October 1941 as a driver of horse-drawn wagons, he became an artillery officer in 1942 and served with distinction as a battery commander until his arrest in February 1945 for criticizing Stalin in private letters. He was sentenced to eight years' labor. Initially assigned to a construction camp, Solzhenitsyn was transferred after one year to the Marfino Prison for communications scientists described in *V'kruge pervom* (1968). In 1950 he was transferred again, to a camp for political prisoners in Ekibastuz, Kazakhstan, where he was a bricklayer, as described in *Odin dyen' Ivana Denisovicha* (1962). Upon release in 1953, Solzhenitsyn was ordered into internal exile in Kok-Terek, Kazakhstan, where he taught mathematics and began writing the stories he had been unable to write in the camps.

Odin dyen' Ivana Denisovicha was published only with the personal approval of Soviet premier Nikita Khrushchev, as part of an ill-fated official attempt to condemn the criminal excesses of Joseph Stalin—excesses described at length in *Arkhipelag Gulag, 1918–56: Op'bit khudozhestvennovo issledovaniia* (1973–1975). Solzhenitsyn became an overnight sensation worldwide after the publication of *Ivana Denisovicha*, but his increasingly outspoken views limited his publications to only a handful of shorter works in the Soviet Union. When his exile in Kazakhstan was rescinded, Solzhenitsyn married and moved to Ryazan', southeast of Moscow, where he wrote diligently, taking care to conceal his work from the KGB, who became increasingly interested in him after Khrushchev's downfall in October 1964. In the coming years several of his works were published in the form of *samizdat* (underground publication, sometimes distributed only in typewritten copies made with carbon paper) and in the West—most notably *V'kruge pervom* and *Rakovyi korpus* (1968), the latter based on his own experiences in cancer treatment at Tashkent (the capital of Uzbekistan). On the strength of his publications abroad, Solzhenitsyn won the Nobel Prize for Literature in 1970, and in 1971 *Avgust chetyrnadtsotovo* was published in the West, the first in a cycle of novels describing the genesis of the Soviet state during the World War I years. Constantly at odds with the Soviet regime from the time of *Ivana Denisovicha* forward, Solzhenitsyn was expelled from the Writers' Union in 1969, and following French publication of *Arkhipelag Gulag* in 1973, he was arrested and deported to West Germany in February 1974.

He settled in Zurich, but was unprepared for constant attention from the Western press; after an initial round of interviews he withdrew from Swiss society and immersed himself in his writing. The seclusion ended with a trip to Stockholm for a belated acceptance of his Nobel Prize, and then travel in Europe, Canada, and the United States. A brief return to Zurich in 1975 was followed by visits to England and Spain, and in July 1976 he moved to Cavendish, Vermont, where he found the climate reminiscent of his home in Russia. Excepting occasional travels for lectures and interviews, he remained in relative isolation in Vermont for 18 years, writing mainly nonfiction warning the West of the dangers of communism. Solzhenitsyn's highly polemical nonfiction generated hostility in the West, where his scathing criticism of Western politics and culture led many to consider him a religious zealot and political reactionary (views later shared by many in the "New Russia" as well).

Mikhail Gorbachev restored Solzhenitsyn's Soviet citizenship in 1990, but only after the fall of the Soviet Union did Solzhenitsyn return to live in Russia, in May 1994. Even into his eighties he is still active in calling for needed reforms in his native land, but his popularity has dwindled in recent years both in Russia and abroad, the general consensus being that his stature as a great Russian writer has been sorely diminished by his abandonment of fiction in favor of stridently polemical writings.

MAJOR MULTICULTURAL THEMES

In his fiction, Solzhenitsyn's consistent aim has always been to expose the truth about the Soviet Union, from its birth during World War I through its maturity under Stalin. His nonfiction writings focus mainly on the dangers of communism to both East and West. In a commencement address at Harvard University in 1978 (published as *A World Split Apart*), he condemned the West for its passive and even cowardly acceptance of the spread of communism worldwide with the *détente* policy of the 1970s, a theme he expands upon in *The Mortal Danger: How Misconceptions about Russia Imperil America* (published originally in English, 1980). Solzhenitsyn saw the United States, particularly, as weakened by gross materialism and mindless preoccupation with inane and decadent popular culture, and he urged the West to avoid ultimate ruin by learning from the sufferings of the Soviets.

Sometimes lost in the concentration on Solzhenitsyn's writing about Soviet excesses is his pointed insistence on the value of multiculturalism. In his Nobel lecture, delivered in absentia in 1970, he states that one of the primary functions of literature is defining and preserving national and cultural identity as "the living memory of a nation," while at the same time bridging the gaps between different peoples and cultures and celebrating their differences as the "wealth of humanity" (trans. F. D. Reeve, 19). *Odin dyen' Ivana Denisovicha, Rakovyi korpus, V'kruge pervom*, and *Arkhipelag Gulag* establish that the Soviet prisons and camps were indeed a melting pot of the more than one hundred ethnicities and nationalities contained within the Soviet Union. In his reflections on how to revitalize Russia, *Kak nam obustroit' Rossiiu?: Posil'nye soobrazheniia* (1990), Solzhenitsyn sees the tensions between these many peoples in Russia as one of the greatest problems facing the postcommunist Russian state. Emphatically, he argues for the preservation and affirmation of unique national characteristics in language, culture, and religion even for the "smaller" ethnic groups in Russia. One of the greatest Soviet evils for Solzhenitsyn is that the smallest ethnic groups within the Soviet Union—the "Nenets, Permyak, Evenki, Mansi, Khakas" and many other cultures—were driven to the brink of extinction. "Every people," he says in *Kak nam obustroit' Rossiiu?*, "even the very smallest, represents a unique facet of God's design" (trans. Alexis Klimoff, 21). Above all Solzhenitsyn is distressed at the decline of the "Great Russian" culture devastated by the loss of tens of millions in war, state-sanctioned execution and brutal imprisonment, and by the system of agricultural collectivization that destroyed the life of the Russian village, the heart of the Russian people as a whole, in Solzhenitsyn's view. Naturally, he has been harshly critical of the "Westernizing" influence that has been rampant in Russia since the fall of the Soviet Union.

SURVEY OF CRITICISM

Though it extends only through the early 1980s, Michael Scammell's is still the most definitive biography (1984). D. M. Thomas's (1998) is overly sympathetic at times and indulges in flights of novelistic fancy, but offers significant coverage of Solzhenitsyn's second decade in the United States and first years upon returning to Russia. The articles collected in *Solzhenitsyn at Harvard* (1980) offer a range of perspectives on the author's controversial condemnation of the West, as do many of the items in John B. Dunlop's, Richard S. Haugh's and Michael Nicholson's edition of *Solzhenitsyn in Exile* (1985). Both David Rowley's (1997) and Michael Confino's (1991) articles consider the author's perception of the Russian people as distinct from other cultures. Rowley analyzes the author's significant contribution to the dissolution of the Soviet empire and offers a synthesis of his ideal Russian state. Confino examines Solzhenitsyn's impact on emerging Russian nationalist groups, with particular attention to his views of both Western and Russian history and the West's culpability in dealings with Russia throughout the twentieth century.

SELECTED BIBLIOGRAPHY

Works by Solzhenitsyn

Odin dyen' Ivana Denisovicha. Novy Mir, November 20, 1962. [*One Day in the Life of Ivan Denisovich*. Trans. Ralph Parker. New York: Dutton, 1963.]
V'kruge pervom (1968). [*The First Circle*. Trans. Thomas P. Whitney. New York: Harper and Row, 1968.]
Rakovyi korpus (1968). [*Cancer Ward*. Trans. Rebecca Frank. New York: Dial Press, 1968.]
Nobel Lecture: Nobelevskaya lektsiya po literatur (1970) (Russian and English texts). Trans. F. D. Reeve. New York: Farrar, Straus and Giroux, 1972.
Avgust chetyrnadtsotovo (1971). [*August 1914*. Trans. Michael Glenny. London: Bodley Head; and New York: Farrar, Straus and Giroux, 1972.]
Arkhipelag Gulag, 1918–56: Op'bit khudozhestvennovo issledovaniia (1973–75). [*The Gulag Archipelago, 1918–1956: An Experiment in Literary Investigation*. 3 vols. Trans. Thomas P. Whitney. New York: Harper and Row, 1974–78.]
Warning to the West (1975–1976). (Collection of speeches given in Russian, published first in translation.) Trans. Harris L. Coulter and Nataly Martin. New York: Farrar, Straus and Giroux, 1976.
A World Split Apart: Commencement Address Delivered at Harvard University June 8, 1978 (read in Russian, translated on the spot, published first in English). Trans. Irina Ilovayskaya Alberti. New York: Harper and Row, 1978.
The Mortal Danger: How Misconceptions about Russia Imperil America (published originally in English). Trans. Michael Nicholson and Alexis Klimoff. New York: Harper and Row, 1980.
Kak nam obustroit' Rossiiu?: posil'nye soobrazheniia. Komsomolskaya Pravda; and *Literaturnaya Gazeta*, September 1990. [*Rebuilding Russia: Reflections and Tenta-*

tive Proposals. Trans. and annot. Alexis Klimoff. New York: Farrar, Straus and Giroux, 1991.]

"'*Russkii vopros' k kontsu XX veka.*" *Novy Mir* 7 (1994): 135–76. [*The Russian Question: At the End of the Twentieth Century.* Trans. and annot. Yermolai Solzhenitsyn. New York: Farrar, Straus and Giroux, 1995.]

Selected Studies of Solzhenitsyn

Confino, Michael. "Solzhenitsyn, the West, and the New Russian Nationalism." *Journal of Contemporary History* 26 (1991): 611–36.

Dunlop, John B., Richard S. Haugh, and Michael Nicholson, eds. *Solzhenitsyn in Exile: Critical Essays and Documentary Materials.* Stanford, Cal.: Hoover Institution, 1985.

Rowley, David G. "Aleksandr Solzhenitsyn and Russian Nationalism." *Journal of Contemporary History* 32 (1997): 321–37.

Scammell, Michael. *Solzhenitsyn: A Biography.* New York: Norton, 1984.

Solzhenitsyn at Harvard: The Address, Twelve Early Responses, and Six Later Reflections. Ed. Ronald Berman. Washington, D.C.: Ethics and Public Policy Center, 1980.

Thomas, D. M. *Alexander Solzhenitsyn: A Century in His Life.* New York: St. Martin's Press, 1998.

MURIEL SPARK
(1918–)

Marina MacKay

BIOGRAPHY

Muriel Spark was born Muriel Sarah Camberg in Edinburgh, Scotland, in 1918, the daughter of an English mother and a Scottish-Jewish father. She was educated in Edinburgh and subsequently traveled to Southern Rhodesia (now Zimbabwe) with her new husband Sydney Oswald Spark in August 1937. The marriage was not a happy one, largely because of the mental health problems of S. O. S. (as Spark refers to her husband in her autobiographical writing). She took her young son Robin home to Britain via South Africa in 1944, and she found employment at Woburn Abbey. Britain was then in the final year of its war with Germany, and Spark's occupation involved writing black propaganda for German radio broadcasts, a job that she revisited in her novel *The Hothouse by the East River* (1973), in which the protagonists (by now dead, in a typically morbid Spark twist) recount, from their New York City home, their wartime activities for the British government. For this novel, Spark utilized her years spent in the United States; she had lived in New York City between 1962 and 1965. Before going to New York, she had spent two months of the previous year in Israel, gathering material for what became *The Mandelbaum Gate* (1965), a novel in which a gentile Jewish woman, now converted to Roman Catholicism, illicitly traces her Middle Eastern cultural heritage.

When not traveling, Spark spent most of the late forties, fifties, and early sixties in London, where she wrote poetry, journalism, and criticism. In the late forties, she edited *Poetry Review*, although her unpopular modernist tastes meant that she eventually left this post somewhat acrimoniously. In 1954, she was received into the Roman Catholic Church, as she discusses in her essay "My Conversion." Her autobiography, *Curriculum Vitae* (1992), tells of her life in Edinburgh, Africa, and London, and is especially disarming on the collapse of her relationship with the Poetry Society. Although apparently settled in London, it was in Italy that Spark finally made her home, and many of her novels are set there: *The Public Image* (1968), *The Driver's Seat* (1970), *The Takeover* (1976), and *Territorial Rights* (1979). She moved to Rome in 1966 and lives in Italy still. Notwithstanding her multicultural status, she was made a Dame of the British Empire in 1993.

MULTICULTURAL THEMES

Although Spark has consistently referred to herself as a Scottish writer and is appropriated as such in studies of Scottish fiction, her novels and short stories reflect both her youthful travels and her expatriation in Italy. Many of her early short stories concern her experiences of Africa as a young bride from a sheltered Scottish background. These African stories can almost be divided in half: some are supernatural, while the others are about human violence. In "The Portobello Road," violence and the supernatural are united: the murdered narrator recounts her meetings in Africa with her eventual killer, whom she threatens to expose as a bigamist (he is ashamed to confess the existence of his first wife, an African). Likewise, in "The Seraph and the Zambesi," a fierce fire is started in order to destroy an angel who has appeared in a remote African settlement. In this story, we are dryly told of how "European residents are often irresistibly prompted to speak Kitchen Kaffir to anything strange" (Spark, *Collected Stories I*, 118), as if to suggest that the colonizing peoples associate any type of threat or disturbance with native activity. "Bang-bang You're Dead" and "The Curtain Blown by the Breeze" tell of white colonials degenerating into states of murderous conflict, where shooting affairs are commonplace because of the strain imposed by living in the wild. Indeed, in "The Pawnbroker's Wife," the title character seems to be going mad, inventing stories to enrich her bleak life in South Africa. "The Go-Away Bird" deals at greater length with explicitly racial issues, telling as it does of the guilty interdependence of colonizer and colonized, and of the relationship between South Africans of British descent and the old country. The search for ancestry is an important component of the plot of *The Mandelbaum Gate*. In this novel, the heroine finds out how dangerous racial and cultural identifications can be: Barbara Vaughan, with a Jewish mother and English father (the opposite of Spark herself), finds herself at the trial of Adolf Eichmann in Jerusalem in 1961.

Although *The Hothouse by the East River* is set in New York, its only comment on American culture is pointedly satirical: Elsa and her husband, extraordinary (and dead) as they are, are no stranger than the natives of the city. *The Abbess of Crewe* (1974) is likewise satirical: although set in an English convent, it takes its plot from the Watergate scandal that forced President Nixon from public office. Witty as the American novels are, Italy has perhaps provided richer imaginative fuel for Spark. She indeed seems to mock her own love of Italy in her most famous novel, *The Prime of Miss Jean Brodie* (1961), in which the most memorable of Edinburgh spinsters extols to her young pupils the virtues of Italy: ancient Rome, Giotto, and Mussolini alike. Here, Spark appears to be using Italy as an illustration of the dangers of romanticizing foreign cultures: to embrace Italy's magnificent cultural life and glorious history may, but need not, entail the acceptance of its occasional political atrocities. In *The Takeover*, Spark likewise undercuts bogus mythologizing of Italy through the fraudulent Hubert Mallindaine's attempts to claim Diana the huntress as his ancestor. Lise in *The Driver's Seat* goes to Italy to seek out not the expected conventional romance, but her own murderer. Modern Italy gets dealt with rather harshly in *The Public Image* and *Territorial Rights*, in which la dolce vita is demonstrated to be a sham consolatory myth.

Spark's most recent novel, *Aiding and Abetting* (2000), has a very comic multicultural take on mythologies, dealing as it does with the travels across Europe of two characters in search of the real Lord Lucan, almost a proverbially elusive figure in British culture after his disappearance following the suspicious murder of his children's nanny, and the attempted murder of his estranged wife. Spark's Lucan eludes capture in Europe, but ends up dead, eaten by African cannibals, as though his author equates British mythologizing of Lucan with other peculiar tribal beliefs. The death of Lucan offers relief from the threat of exposure to the novel's other fraud: Beate Pappenheim, a bogus stigmatic (also based on a real-life person). Notwithstanding her own Roman Catholic beliefs, Spark uses the Beate plot to link the comical aspects of Roman Catholic superstition (Beate's career as a stigmatic has been a lucrative one) to the excesses of cannibalistic beliefs.

SURVEY OF CRITICISM

Alan Bold's study (1986) of Spark's fiction up until the early eighties is a short, insightful account of the influences on her work. He places emphasis not only on poetic (rather than prose) influences, but also on the effects of Spark's conversion to Catholicism. He shows convincingly how Spark refuses to use her work as an apology for either her religion or her coreligionists, and his discussion of how, for Spark, "intrigue . . . is an international affair" (108), is compelling. Allan Massie's earlier, landmark book (1979) about Spark's fiction perhaps predictably foregrounds her status as a major Scottish writer; he argues that only her novels set in

Edinburgh and Kensington reflect in any realistic sense their locations. New York and Italy are, he contends, treated only as symbolic locales by Spark. Although Massie emphasizes Spark's Scottishness, he makes the interesting case that Spark is culturally marginalized; he links the otherness of her Scottish nationality to her outsider status as a Jew and a Catholic convert. Peter Kemp's monograph on Spark (1974) is also influential and persuasive. His discussion of political, national, and religious schisms in his account of *The Mandelbaum Gate* is particularly compelling, as is his description of how Spark's novels show an ambivalent fascination with English class distinctions, at odds with her Scottish upbringing. As its title suggests, Ruth Whittaker's study emphasizes the relationships between fictional form and Roman Catholic belief in Spark's novels, and identifies a "tension . . . between feeling and form" (17) in her work.

SELECTED BIBLIOGRAPHY

Works by Spark

The Prime of Miss Jean Brodie. London: Macmillan, 1961.
The Mandelbaum Gate. London: Macmillan, 1965.
Collected Stories I. London, Melbourne, Toronto: Macmillan, 1967. [Contains "The Portobello Road"; "Bang-bang You're Dead"; "The Seraph and the Zambesi"; "The Pawnbroker's Wife"; "The Curtain Blown by the Breeze"; "The Go-Away Bird."]
The Public Image. London: Macmillan, 1968.
The Driver's Seat. London: Macmillan, 1970.
The Hothouse by the East River. London: Macmillan, 1973.
The Abbess of Crewe. London: Macmillan, 1974.
The Takeover. London: Macmillan, 1976.
Territorial Rights. London: Macmillan, 1979.
Curriculum Vitae: Autobiography. London: Constable, 1992.
Aiding and Abetting. London and New York: Viking, 2000.

Selected Studies of Spark

Bold, Alan. *Muriel Spark*. London, New York: Methuen, 1986.
Kemp, Peter. *Muriel Spark*. London: Elek, 1974.
Massie, Allan. *Muriel Spark*. Edinburgh: Ramsay Head Press, 1979.
Whittaker, Ruth. *The Faith and Fiction of Muriel Spark*. London: Macmillan, 1982.

SUGA ATSUKO
(1929–1998)

Giorgio Amitrano

BIOGRAPHY

Suga Atsuko's activity as a writer spans just under a decade. Although she had been involved in literary work since her youth, she did not make her debut as an author until she was 61. When her first book, *Mirano kiri no fūkei*, was published in 1990, she was immediately recognized as an outstanding writer. From that moment, she worked intensely for a few years, publishing several books until her death from cancer in 1998 at the age of 69.

Mirano kiri no fūkei, a book of memories of her Italian years, impressed critics and writers as a fully mature work. The prizes the book received, the Kodansha essei shō, awarded to works of nonfiction, and the Joryū bungaku shō, for works of fiction, illustrate the impossibility of assigning the work to a specific genre. In fact, in all of Suga's books, it would be hard to separate the objective recording of facts from the subjective filter that makes the narrative fade imperceptibly into the realm of novel.

Suga's interest in the language and culture of foreign countries started when she was still a child. She was born in 1929 into a wealthy family of Ashiya, a residential town in the Hyōgo Prefecture, in the Kansai area (the region of Osaka, Kyoto, and Kobe). Her upper-middle-class background is reminiscent of the society described in Tanizaki Jun'ichirō's masterpiece *Sasame yuki:* a rich bourgeoisie more faithful to their traditions than Tokyoites, but open to the suggestions of the West. When she was seven, her family moved to Tokyo, where she studied in the Sacred Heart girls' school, learning English and French from nuns who were native speakers. After the war, she graduated from Sacred Heart University in Tokyo, majoring in English literature.

When she left Japan to spend a year in Paris studying comparative literature in 1953, young Oriental women studying abroad were so rare that the event was reported in local newspapers. A few years later, in 1958, she returned to Europe, this time to Italy, where she studied at the Regina Mundi University in Rome. During this stay, she became acquainted with a group of Catholic intellectuals based in Milan and was so impressed with their ideas and work that she moved to Milan to join in their activities. The group used to gather in a bookshop run by Giuseppe Ricca called Corsia dei Servi after the name of the street where it was located. Besides being a bookseller and a small publisher, Ricca did voluntary social work, as did other members of the group. Suga, who had already converted to Catholicism and who read Simone Weil and Antoine de Saint-Exupéry with the same passion, found a perfect match in Ricca, a poet and Catholic philanthropist whom she married. For a few years they shared their work and ideals, but Giuseppe Ricca died suddenly in 1967.

Although Suga had always enjoyed her independent life abroad, with the death of her husband she suddenly felt alienated. Ricca had been the prime mover of the Corsia dei Servi group, and without his quiet charisma, it slowly collapsed. In 1971, Suga decided to return to Japan, but not wanting to rely on her family's money, she took on several part-time teaching jobs and did voluntary social work for the homeless. At the beginning of the 1980s, as her social position became more secure (she obtained a post as an associate professor at Sophia University, Tokyo, teaching Japanese literature and world literature), she resumed her various literary activities. In 1985, she started writing essays on her Italian experience for a literary magazine which were later published under the title *Mirano kiri no fūkei*. The success of the book, which was widely read and earned high praise from the critics, turned Suga Atsuko into a protagonist of the literary scene almost overnight. Her activity in the last years of her life was intense, almost frantic, as one realizes from the edition of her complete works, published posthumously. These nine volumes of impressive bulk contain writings produced in less than nine years, following her debut in 1990: memoirs, essays, book and film reviews, translations of poetry, and so forth. Even the briefest, most occasional articles for daily newspapers reflect her particular cultural syncretism, in which barriers are overcome through respect of cultural identities and acknowledgment of differences.

MAJOR MULTICULTURAL THEMES

Suga Atsuko was a multicultural writer par excellence, her inspiration coming almost entirely from comparisons among different cultures. She lectured in Japanese, English, Italian, and French, and although she spoke all these languages fluently, she had a particular bond with Italy and its culture. During her Italian years, and especially after her marriage, she adapted almost mimetically to the new environment. She mastered Italian—a language relatively new to her—so perfectly that she became a leading translator of Japanese literature into Italian, introducing for the first time to Italian readers works of Tanizaki Jun'ichirō, Kawabata Yasunari, Ishikawa Jun, and others. She suffered a culture shock when, after the death of her husband, she returned to her country. Having lived abroad for a long time, she did not seem to belong to Japanese society any longer. But slowly she began to look at Japanese culture (and her own past) with different eyes, through the filter of her experience abroad. Learning how to integrate Europe and Japan, she found her real literary persona. In *Mirano kiri no fūkei* she poured out the memories, feelings, and impressions that she had kept pent up within herself for so long. The theme is her life in Italy, but her evocation of the years she spent there is often intermingled with memories of Japan.

Other books followed at a steady pace, evoking places, characters, and scenes crossing all barriers of time and culture. They won her many readers in Japan. It was as if she was able to express a deeply felt need among the Japanese to go beyond the limits of a stifling national identity. But rather than expressing a contemporary tendency to globalization, Suga seems to express an aspiration to universality of an exquisitely literary nature.

In *Yurusunāru no kutsu* (1996), Suga retraces Marguerite Yourcenar's steps from Flanders to France, then to Italy and to Maine, seeing Yourcenar's life through the prism of her own life story and journeys through Europe. In doing so she builds a jigsaw puzzle of memories, flashbacks, and associations, where the lives of two women who had never met become amalgamated, each one complementing the other.

SURVEY OF CRITICISM

Nishiguchi Tetsu and Kimura Yumiko's edited volume (1998) of studies of Suga Atsuko contains notable contributions from critics and writers, including Yoshimoto Banana, Ikezawa Natsuki, and Antonio Tabucchi. Suga has sometimes been defined "a writers' writer," because her literary qualities seem to have stronger appeal for writers than for critics.

A special issue of the literary magazine *Bungakukai* was dedicated to Suga Atsuko in 1999. Again we find an essay by Ikezawa Natsuki, along with an analysis of Suga's posthumous *Toki no kakeratachi* (1998) by the critic Matsuyama Iwao. Matsuyama is also the author of an extremely detailed chronology of Suga's life, included in the eighth volume of her complete works. Each volume of the complete works includes essays on different aspects of Suga's life and work by critics and writers. Also recommended are the *geppō*, slim pamphlets appended to each volume, which include other contributions on the writer.

A series of illustrated volumes on "Suga's cities" by the writer-photographer Ōtake Akiko is currently being published. The first two volumes (2001) feature Venice and Milan.

SELECTED BIBLIOGRAPHY

Works by Suga

Mirano kiri no fūkei. Tokyo: Hakusuisha, 1990.
Yurusunāru no kutsu. Tokyo: Kawade shobo, 1996.
Toki no kakeratachi. Tokyo: Misuzu shobo, 1998.
Suga Atsuko zenshū. 9 vols. Ed. Maruya Saiichi, Ikezawa Natsuki, Matsuyama Iwao. Tokyo: Kawade shobo, 2000–2001.

Selected Studies of Suga

Nishiguchi Tetsu and Kimura Yumiko, eds. *Suga Atsuko: Kiri no mukō ni (Tsuitō tokushū).* Tokyo: Kawade shobo, November 1998.
"Suga Atsuko no sekai." Special issue of *Bungakukai* (May 1999): 233–87.
Ōtake Akiko. *Suga Atsuko no Mirano.* Tokyo: Kawade shobo, 2001.
———. *Suga Atsuko no Venezia.* Tokyo: Kawade shobo, 2001.

ANTONIO TABUCCHI
(1943–)

Bruno Ferraro

BIOGRAPHY

Antonio Tabucchi was born in Pisa and resides in the nearby town of Vecchiano. His studies at the University of Pisa in Portuguese literature (decided upon after a chance reading of one of Fernando Pessoa's poems during a stay in Paris) resulted in the publication of his theses on the Portuguese surrealist poets (1971) and on the postwar Portuguese theater (1976). With his wife, Maria José de Lancastre, he is responsible for the Italian translation and publication of Pessoa's works and, more recently, for having introduced to Italian readers the Portuguese novelist Antonio Lobo Antunes (b. 1942). Tabucchi holds the chair of Portuguese literature at the University of Siena.

A writer who has seen translation into more than thirty languages, Tabucchi has published since 1975, novels, short stories, plays, and a variety of newspaper articles. He was the winner of the French Prix Médicis Étranger in 1987 and in 1994 was awarded all of the most prestigious Italian literary prizes for his novel *Sostiene Pereira: una testimonianza.* (A film version of the novel with Marcello Mastroianni in the main role has received world acclaim.) His love for Portugal and the Portuguese people has won him official recognition from the president of the Portuguese Republic, Mário Soares, who in 1989 conferred on Tabucchi the title of Comendador da Ordem do Infante Dom Henrique. In France, the title of Officier des Arts et des Lettres was conferred on him in 1996 .

More recently, Tabucchi has been responsible, along with a number of illustrious writers and intellectuals (Octavio Paz, Günter Grass, and

Salman Rushdie, to mention a few), for the establishment of the International Parliament of Writers, whose purpose is to set up an organization to protect, almost physically, writers and intellectuals threatened with death or who are persecuted or imprisoned in their countries, and to provide them with a safe haven in various parts of the world. Tabucchi's involvement in civil issues and social affairs is marked in Italy by his active participation in the legal debate over the complex political homicide affair centered on the former leader of the rebel group Lotta Continua (Continuous Struggle), Adriano Sofri, who is now serving a 22-year sentence in a Pisa jail. Tabucchi has also made efforts to draw public attention to the pitiful condition of gypsies in various parts of Italy by publishing a pamphlet and a series of thought-provoking articles on the subject.

MAJOR MULTICULTURAL THEMES

With his discovery of Pessoa's works and the stimuli received during his first trips to Portugal in the 1960s, Tabucchi stored in his literary baggage elements pertaining to the literature and the culture of the country which keep resurfacing in most of his works. In the title piece "Il gioco del rovescio" of his first collection of short stories (1981), Tabucchi introduced Pessoa, whose works are used as a password by the characters, with the following words: "Pessoa is a genius because he understood the reversal of real and imagined things. His poetry is a *juego del revés* (backwards game)" (*Il gioco del rovescio*, trans. *Letter from Casablanca: Stories*, 107). The "backwards game" is a literary instrument peculiar to the works of Pessoa and to his heteronyms, and it is used to express existential doubts and fragments of life which are impossible to convey otherwise: it is closely connected to the elements of the unresolved, the double, the "other," the oneiric. It is through the mechanism of dreams that Tabucchi's characters have the chance to meet in the same story, on the same narrative plane, on the same stage; it is through dreams that the notion of the fantastic—in the sense of what cannot be resolved within realistic parameters—can activate a dialogue, justify a situation, convey a mood. It is through the fantastic that a character can explore the reverse side of a situation. While in "Il gioco del rovescio" the visual stimulus is provided by Velasquez's complex painting *Las Meninas*, in *Requiem: Un'allucinazione* (1992)—the most Portuguese of his novels—Tabucchi's narrator is enthralled by Bosch's triptych *The Temptation of Saint Anthony* which he views at the Museum of Ancient Art in Lisbon and from which he seeks answers to his many existential queries. The hallucinatory atmosphere created by the torrid summer day in Lisbon and the reappearance of Pessoa dictate the mood of what is a homage to Portugal and its people. Tabucchi wrote the text in the language of the country that has adopted him. The oneiric element that characterizes the ending of "Il gioco del rovescio" allows for the surreal, the absurd, and the unsubstantial to coexist with the real; this creates an atmosphere in which spatial and temporal limitations no longer exist and in which ghosts and people sit at the same table and partake of the specialties of Portuguese cuisine, just as in *Requiem: Un'allucinazione*. It is the "backwards game" that allows Tabucchi to introduce the themes of the quest, the journey and the search; these are themes well worked by so many classical and modern authors but not so adroitly as by Tabucchi in a number of his works.

Presented in a lattice pattern, through which runs a *fil rouge*, the themes are central to his first major success, *Notturno indiano* (1984), in which the trip to India is inextricably linked to Portugal since the narrator travels from Madras to the former Portuguese possession of Goa in search of his "other-than-himself." Elsewhere—in *Donna di Porto Pim* (1983) and in *I volatili del Beato Angelico* (1987)—Tabucchi reiterates his interest not only in matters dealing with Portugal but also with its territories, in this case the Azores. In *Gli ultimi tre giorni di Fernando Pessoa* (1994), he pays his last respects to Pessoa by imagining how the writer spent the last three days of his life taking leave of the characters he had created in his fiction.

The search for identity and for self-realization is the driving force behind *Sostiene Pereira*, the story of the obese journalist who breaks away from a life tied to the past and to habit in order to assert himself and denounce Salazar's criminal dictatorship. Set in Lisbon in 1938, the novel was written by Tabucchi during 1993 at a moment when he sensed the resurgence in Europe of extreme nationalism and terrorism (as in the former Yugoslavia), and a wave of xenophobia and racism. *Sostiene Pereira: una testimonianza*, set in the immediate past, is an indictment of all oppressive and violent regimes; a preview of this theme was already to be found in the short story "Notte, mare e distanza" in the collection *L'angelo nero* (1991). Similarly, *La testa perduta di Damasceno Monteiro* (1997), the last of Tabucchi's novels set in Portugal, is an indictment of police brutality and of the collusion between the police and the criminal world.

SURVEY OF CRITICISM

All of Tabucchi's critics refer to some degree to the Portuguese element in his works since it is inextricably woven into his narrative, whether this touches upon literary, social, or historical situations. Specific themes are highlighted in *Antonio Tabucchi: A Collection of Essays* (1997), edited by Bruno Ferraro and Nicole Prunster, which provides the best overview of Tabucchi's production. The best and most up-to-date commentaries on individual works are by Giovanni Tessitore (1999) on *Requiem: Un'allucinazione*, by Anna Dolfi (1996) in her introduction to *Notturno indiano*, and by Manuele Bertone (2000) on *La testa perduta di*

Damasceno Monteiro. Carlos Gumpert's published interview with Tabucchi (1995) contains the author's views on his poetics as well as a variety of other subjects.

SELECTED BIBLIOGRAPHY

Works by Tabucchi

Il gioco del rovescio. Milano: Il Saggiatore, 1981. [*Letter from Casablanca: Stories.* Trans. Janice M. Thresher. New York: New Directions, 1986.]

Donna di Porto Pim. Palermo: Sellerio, 1983. [*The Woman of Porto Pim.* In *Vanishing Point; The Woman of Porto Pim; The Flying Creatures of Fra Angelico*, 85–176. Trans. Tim Parks. London: Chatto and Windus, 1991.]

Notturno indiano. Palermo: Sellerio, 1984. Intro. and notes Anna Dolfi. Torino: Società Editrice Internazionale, 1996. [*Indian Nocturne.* Trans. Tim Parks. London: Vintage, 1991.]

Piccoli equivoci senza importanza. Milano: Feltrinelli, 1985. [*Little Misunderstandings of No Importance.* Trans. Frances Frenaye. New York: New Directions, 1987.]

I volatili del Beato Angelico. Palermo: Sellerio, 1987. [*The Flying Creatures of Fra Angelico.* In *Vanishing Point; The Woman of Porto Pim; The Flying Creatures of Fra Angelico*, 177–257. Trans. Tim Parks. London, Chatto and Windus, 1991.]

L'angelo nero. Milan: Feltrinelli, 1991.

Requiem: Un'allucinazione. Milan: Feltrinelli, 1992. [*Requiem.* Trans. Margaret J. Costa. London: Harvill, 1994.]

Gli ultimi tre giorni di Fernando Pessoa. Palermo: Sellerio, 1994.

Sostiene Pereira: una testimonianza. Milan: Feltrinelli, 1994 [*Pereira Declares: A Testimony.* Trans. Patrick Creagh. New York: New Directions, 1995.]

Conversaciones con Antonio Tabucchi. Interview by Carlos Gumpert. Barcelona: Anagrama, 1995.

La testa perduta di Damasceno Monteiro. Milan: Feltrinelli, 1997.

Selected Studies of Tabucchi

Arvigo, Tiziana. "La figura di fondo: il problema dell'opera d'arte nella narrativa di Antonio Tabucchi." *Resine* 65–66 (1995): 11–18.

Bertone, Manuela. "Antonio Tabucchi istruisce il caso Damasceno Monteiro." *Novecento* 23 (2000): 109–25.

Brizio, Flavia. "La narrativa postmoderna di Antonio Tabucchi." *Filologia antica e moderna* 4 (1993): 249–66.

Budor, Dominique. "Antonio Tabucchi ou la création *traversière.* In *Dire la création: La culture italienne entre "poetique" et "poïétique."* Ed. Dominique Budor, 219–29. Lille: Presses Universitaires, 1994.

Ferraro, Bruno and Nicole Prunster, ed. *Antonio Tabucchi: A Collection of Essays.* In monographic number of the journal of Italian Studies *Spunti e Ricerche* 12 (1997), 225 pages. Melbourne, Australia.

Ferraro, Bruno. "Antonio Tabucchi's 'Returned Gaze': Art, Fiction, and Reality". In *—una veritade ascosa sotto bella menzogna—: zur italienischen Erzähllit-*

eratur der Gegenwart. Ed. Hans Felten and David Nelting, 31–41. Frankfurt am Main: Peter Lang, 2000.

Giordano, Alberto. "*Sostiene Pereira.*" *La Pagina* 15 (1994): 53–57.

Jansen, Monica. "Tabucchi: Molteplicità e rovescio." In *Piccole finzioni con importanza. Valori nella narrativa italiana contemporanea.* Ed. Nathalie Roelens and Inge Lanslots, 421–29. Ravenna: Longo, 1993.

Lepschy, Laura. "Filling the Gaps: Dreams in the Narrative Fiction of Antonio Tabucchi." *Romance Studies* 18 (1991): 55–64.

———. "Antonio Tabucchi: Splinters of Existence": In *The New Italian Novel.* Ed. Zygmunt Baransky and Lino Pertile, 200–218. Edinburgh: Edinburgh University Press, 1993.

Tessitore, Giovanni. "*In limine scripturae. Requiem di Antonio Tabucchi.*" *Critica letteraria* 103 (1999): 363–93.

TAWADA YŌKO
(1960–)

Maria Gioia Vienna

BIOGRAPHY

Born in Tokyo as the daughter of an intellectual whose love for books led him to establish his own small publishing house, Tawada Yōko grew up surrounded by books and since childhood has felt deep bonds with literature. Frustrated by school life and the impossibility of protesting effectively against it, she began writing short stories as her own "fashion of resistance" (quoted in Itakura Kimie, 31). She intensely perceived and was fascinated by the strength of words that can elicit all kinds of reactions from human beings—a leitmotiv in her literary production.

After studies in Russian literature and graduation from Waseda University, having been offered a two-year job as trainee with a German book exporter, she moved to Hamburg in 1982, where she has lived ever since. In Germany, she obtained the equivalent of a master's degree at Hamburg University in 1990. The experience of living in a foreign country and facing each day a culture so different from her own led to keener sensitivity to Japanese language and culture and a desire to experiment with the German and Japanese languages as well as with different literary styles and genres. The result of this adventure is a colorful, unique writing supported by a vivid imagination that often brings unexpected solutions in the plots.

Tawada's first published book was a bilingual collection of poetry and prose in Japanese and German entitled *Nur da wo du bist da ist nichts* (1987). In accordance with respective tradition, to read the Japanese original, one opens the book from the back, while to read the German translation by Peter Pörtner, one opens it from the front, so that the two texts follow two separate paths. This preannounced theme of the impossibility of word-for-word translation proved to be of the utmost importance for Tawada.

Her first novel was *Das Bad* (1989), published only in German, from the original Japanese text; once again this early work already presented features that are found again and again in her work. A first-person narration, *Das Bad* is a mixture of imagination and autobiographical suggestions. As in many of the author's other works, the protagonist is a Japanese woman who lives in Germany—in a surrealistic setting.

The first work that Tawada wrote directly in German, without the help of anyone's translation, is *Wo Europa anfängt* (1991), a collection of essays—in mixed prose and poetry—on the theme of travel. Based on memories of her first trip to Europe made via the Trans-Siberian Railway, the title essay is a long, first-person narration by a Japanese woman. Her travel report is interpolated with memories of her childhood, comments on cultural differences between Europe and Japan, and references to Japanese and Western folktales.

The short story "Kakato o nakushite" (1991) was written and published directly in Japanese, without German translation. The narration spans five days in the life of the protagonist, a mail-order bride freshly arrived in some European town, who never has occasion to converse face-to-face with her new husband, though he does join her at night when she is asleep and leaves money at her bedside. The people with whom she tries to communicate seem to be the arrogant product of a self-professedly "superior" culture, definitely group-oriented, and full of prejudices. The plot resolves itself strangely in a kind of hallucinatory atmosphere as we are led to suspect that the husband was a squid, echoing those folktales, Japanese as well as European, in which a girl marries a beast without knowing it just to discover the real nature of the bridegroom by breaking a taboo. Tawada transports an old tradition into the contemporary world and everyday life in a detached, objective, and cynical style reminiscent, especially in the end, of features of fantastic literature.

Other short stories published in Japanese in the literary magazine *Gunzō* are "Sannin Kankei" (1991), which takes place in Japan, and "Perusona" (1992), whose setting is Hamburg. Especially interesting is the latter, again the story of a young Japanese student who experiences a new life in a foreign country. But this time, the themes of being observed as a stranger and the observation of a new culture, the growing feelings of racial discrimination toward non-Germans, and so forth, are conveyed by the metaphor of the Japanese Nō theater mask.

Recognized as one of Japan's most talented contemporary authors, Tawada was awarded the coveted Akutagawa Prize for the story "Inu muko iri" (1992). In a new reinterpretation of the folktale motif of marriage outside the species (the title means "the bridegroom was a dog"), the male protagonist, Taro, is a big man around 30 with pronounced doglike tendencies whose relationship with the beautiful Kitamura Mitsuko—erotic and absurd at the same time—is described by Tawada with subtle irony.

Making her debut as a theater author with *Die Kranichmaske, die bei Nacht strahlt* (1993), Tawada offers a complex work revolving around a number of themes that she again approaches in later essays, such as the inner meaning of the mask, the language of the dead, and so forth. Over the years, she has returned to the theater and to other performing arts such as radio plays or poetry readings accompanied by live music as expressions of her deep interest in the impact on audiences of spoken words, even when not translated into a language understandable to the public.

In *Arufabetto no kizuguchi* (1993), a sort of essay about translation and the translatability of a text, the first-person narrator is a translator who, during her work translating from German into Japanese, notices (once again) the surprising results obtained in attempting to transfer a meaning into another language. A provocative work, it clearly demonstrates Tawada's strong mixture of fantasy and reality and her skill in rereading, in a totally unconventional way or in unexpected metaphors, a variety of traditional European cultural motifs.

An essay (1996) in German in *Talisman*, whose title "Im Bauch des Gotthards" means "In Gotthard's Womb," takes on a different guise when translated into Japanese by Tawada herself under the title "Gottoharuto-tetsudō," meaning "Gotthard Railway." Midway between essay and travel journal, it becomes a kind of short story, and even the meanings of the metaphors change. Similarly, *Kitsunetsuki* (1998) presents a number of texts translated by the author from the German version into a renewed Japanese one.

Also in *Talisman* appeared the essay "Eigentlich darf man es niemandem sagen, aber Europa gibt es nicht," a sharp reading of a typical, hypercritical European pose: "You can criticize it [Europe], but in no case can you say that it doesn't exist. It is even difficult to criticize it, because it does so continuously and with such speed and such skill that nobody else can do it as well" (5th edition, 47–48). Ironical but never aggressive, this kind of comment only proves the intense relation that Tawada shares with Europe. As an acknowledgment of this deep understanding of her acquired new culture, she was awarded in 1996 the Adelbert von Chamisso Prize which Germany offers to foreign writers who contribute to German culture.

Tawada continues to publish novels, short stories, and essays, even while delivering lectures in various universities around the world. Some of her works have been translated and published in France, Holland, Poland, Hungary, the Czech Republic, and the United States.

MAJOR MULTICULTURAL THEMES

Critic Theodore Goossen asks: "Can Yōko Tawada's works in German be regarded as 'Japanese Literature?' The question, I feel, is more than technical. Certainly, a Japanese writer who writes in a foreign language for a non-Japanese audience can be seen as working within the context of her or his adopted culture. . . . At the same time, it is obviously ludicrous for us to separate the German and the Japanese streams within Tawada's writing as if we were dealing with two separate authors. In a real sense, therefore, what her dual career underlines is the absurdity of any monolithic, prescriptive definition of 'national literature' " (Theodore Goossen, "The Bridegroom was a Dog: Book review," 18–19).

Tawada's works belong to a complex and conspicuous stream of contemporary Japanese literature of the 1990s, whose framework has broadened notably thanks to the contribution of authors of growing relevance who are Okinawan or Korean-Japanese, or even Japanese who have established bonds with other non-Japanese communities.

Confrontation with a foreign culture has had dramatic significance for Tawada Yōko. In the essay "Erzähler ohne Seelen" she writes: "At the time of my first coming to Europe via Trans-Siberian Railway I lost my soul. When I went back by train, my soul was still traveling to Europe. I never managed to grasp it again. When I came back to Europe, it was going to Japan. After that, [it flew] back and forth so many times that I haven't the slightest idea where my soul is" (in *Talisman*, 5th edition, 21–22). It seems impossible, therefore, to determine her cultural and national identity in any traditional way; her entire oeuvre deals with the implicit or explicit quest for a sense of belonging to a specific, well-defined world.

Her multicultural point of view is fundamentally represented by her search for a new language strong enough to overcome the so-called mother tongue. "I was struck how much a work seems to mature in the process of translation, moving away from its author and taking on a new life of its own. . . . I felt that the process of creating a work was not complete until it had been translated into German," she writes in "Literary Discovery through Translation" (21). When she began writing fiction in German as well as in Japanese, the style was perceived by the author herself as being unmistakably influenced by previous German translations of her works. She has also become aware that the difference between her writing style in Japanese and in German emerges all the more distinctly when the works are translated into the common language of English.

What interests Tawada most are the holes of a language that one perceives only when one looks at it from the outside, trying to express oneself by using words that have a very different meaning and structure compared to one's mother tongue. Literature springs exactly from these holes, and the writer, as a kind of medium, in a concept expressed by other authors as well, fixes on the paper in written form a still nonexistent text that is waiting to be heard and understood by the artist.

The consciousness of a double extraneousness to both her new language and her mother tongue causes Tawada Yōko to reconsider the whole way of seeing the world around her; she somehow becomes much more aware of what plays a fundamental role in judging reality. Her aim, then, ceases to be speaking German like a native, or speaking a refined Japanese, but rather to widen the sense of language to a very general and deeper analysis of the world that surrounds her. She rediscovers many elements of Asiatic culture that today have a place of great importance in her works, thanks to her experience of European culture.

In her recent *Opium für Ovid: ein Kopfkissenbuch von 22 Frauen* (2000), she draws 22 portraits of women whose names are taken from Ovid's *Metamorphoses* inasmuch as her characters show all the same physical and spiritual frailties that the Latin poet had perceived in human beings.

SURVEY OF CRITICISM

Criticism and essays about Tawada's work are written mainly in Japanese and German. Japanese literary magazines follow her writing activity with great interest; we will cite here only the essay by Wada Tadahiko (1997) that offers a number of samples of Tawada's various works and focuses on the most recurring themes. Criticism in German is also very rich; we will mention only the useful piece by Albrecht Kloepfer and Miho Matsunaga (2000). Bio-bibliographical information about the author may be obtained from Sachiko Schierbeck (1994), who looks at Tawada's writing from the perspective and in the context of contemporary gender literature.

SELECTED BIBLIOGRAPHY

Works by Tawada

Nur da wo du bist da ist nichts (bilingual text). Trans. Peter Pörtner. Tübingen: Konkursbuchverlag C. Gehrke, 1987.

Das Bad. Trans. Peter Pörtner. Tübingen: Konkursbuchverlag C. Gehrke, 1989.

Wo Europa anfängt. Partly translated by Peter Pörtner. Tübingen: Konkursbuchverlag C. Gehrke, 1991.

"Kakato o nakushite." In *Gunzō* (June 1991): 6–35. ["Missing Heels." Trans. Margaret Mitsutani. In Tawada Yōko, *The Bridegroom Was a Dog*, 63–128. Tokyo: Kōdansha International, 1998.]

"Sannin Kankei." In *Gunzō* (December 1991): 64–105.

"Perusona." In *Gunzō* (June 1992): 168–202.

"Inu muko iri." In *Gunzō* (December 1992): 6–33. ["The Bridegroom Was a Dog." Trans. John Munroe. In *Japanese Literature Today* 19 (1994): 17–39. Trans. Margaret Mitsutani. In Tawada Yōko, *The Bridegroom Was a Dog*, 7–62. Tokyo: Kōdansha International, 1998.]

Arufabetto no kizuguchi. Tokyo: Kawadeshobō Shinsha, 1993.

Die Kranichmaske, die bei Nacht strahlt. Tübingen: Konkursbuchverlag C. Gehrke, 1993.

"Gottoharuto-tetsudō." In *Gunzō* (November 1995): 50–68. ["Gotthard Railway." Trans. Margaret Mitsutani. In Tawada Yōko, *The Bridegroom Was a Dog*, 129–65. Tokyo: Kōdansha International, 1998.]

Talisman. With translations by Peter Pörtner. Tübingen: Konkursbuchverlag C. Gehrke, 1996 (5th ed. 2000).

"Im Bauch des Gotthards." In Tawada Yōko, *Talisman*, 5th edition, 93–99. Tübingen: Konkursbuchverlag C. Gehrke, 1996.

"Eigentlich darf man es niemandem sagen, aber Europa gibt es nicht." In Tawada Yōko, *Talisman*, 5th ed., 45–51. Tübingen: Konkursbuchverlag C. Gehrke, 1996.

Kitsunetsuki. Tokyo: Shinshokan, 1998.

Opium für Ovid: ein Kopfkissenbuch von 22 Frauen. Tübingen: Konkursbuchverlag C. Gehrke, 2000.

"Erzähler ohne Seelen." In Tawada Yōko, *Talisman*, 5th ed., 16–27. Tübingen: Konkursbuchverlag C. Gehrke, 1996.

"Literary Discovery through Translation." In *Japanese Book News* 32 (Winter 2000): 22. (No translator indicated.)

Selected Studies of Tawada

Goossen, Theodore. "The Bridegroom Was a Dog: Book Review." In *The Japan Foundation Newsletter* 26, nos. 5–6 (April 1999): 18–19.

Itakura Kimie. "Profile: Novelist Wins on Double Wordplay." *International Herald Tribune—The Asahi Shimbun* (Tokyo) (October 27–28, 2001): 31.

Kloepfer, Albrecht, and Miho Matsunaga. "Tawada Yōko." In *Kritisches Lexikon zur deutschsprachigen Gegenwartsliteratur*, 1–18. Munich: KLG, 2000.

Schierbeck, Sachiko. "Tawada Yōko." In Sachiko Schierbeck, *Japanese Women Novelists. 104 Biographies 1900–1993*, 332–34. Copenhagen: Museum Tusculanum Press, 1994.

Wada Tadahiko. "Tawada Yōko ron." *Bungakukai* (February 1997): 212–23.

TZVETAN TODOROV
(1939–)

Jeanine Parisier Plottel

BIOGRAPHY

Tzvetan Todorov was born in Sofia, Bulgaria, at the outbreak of World War II. By the age of 24 he had earned a degree in literature from a Bulgarian university. In 1963 Todorov moved to Paris, where he studied under Roland Barthes, who directed Todorov's doctoral thesis on a structural approach to the fantastic. Todorov's early research and writings were devoted to semiotics, structuralism, and philosophy of language, and he became a prominent figure in Paris culture. Today, he is a widely respected intellectual, and leading universities throughout the world have invited him to lecture and teach. His principal institutional affiliation is with the Centre National de la Recherche Scientifique in Paris, which has sponsored his research for many years.

A turning point in Todorov's intellectual orientation took place in the late 1970s, when the focus of his scholarship changed from the formal language and structural aspects of symbolism and hermeneutics to topics with a political and moral dimension. In 1979 he resigned from *Poétique*, the journal he had founded with Gérard Genette in 1970, to turn his scrutiny toward cultural issues.

MAJOR MULTICULTURAL THEMES

Todorov traced his profound attentiveness to cultural pluralism to his childhood and adolescence in Bulgaria, a poor country with a totalitarian political system and other characteristics of developing countries. His experience as an immigrant in France made him aware that his sense of exile from the dominant culture had a universal dimension. *La Conquête de l'Amérique: La question de l'autre* (1982) deals with the Spanish conquest of Mexico in the sixteenth century and the ensuing clash of cultures. *Nous et les autres: La réflexion française sur la diversité humaine* (1989) handles the same issue, but draws on a different subject: French thinkers of the Enlightenment who attempted to place diversity of cultures within a framework that valued individual characteristics and maintained universal values.

Pursuing this line of thinking by trailing a chronological "great chain of being," Todorov was led to the twentieth century and to masterful studies of the effects of totalitarianism, communism, and Nazism. *Face à l'extrême* (1991) examines and compares tragic conditions of life in Nazi concentration camps and Soviet gulags. Such material may be familiar to readers of Arthur Koestler and Aleksandr Solzhenitsyn, but this is probably not the case with Todorov's studies dealing specifically with Bulgaria.

The controversy surrounding the fate of Bulgarian Jews, most of whom were alive when the Soviet army entered Bulgaria in September 1944, is the theme of *La fragilité du bien: Le sauvetage des Juifs bulgares* (1999). The accounting of the balance sheet underlying the survival of Jewish persons is subtle. At the outbreak of World War II, Bulgaria was supposedly neutral, but its anti-Jewish legislation was among the harshest in Europe. It helped Hitler fight his Yugoslav military campaign, and the reward was a number of territories, including Thrace and Macedonia. The government granted residents of these regions Bulgarian nationality, but made an exception for Jews. In March 1943, 11,000 of these Thracian and Macedonian Jews were handed over to the Nazis, who deported them to various camps, including Auschwitz and Treblinka, where all but a small handful were exterminated.

The Bulgarian Orthodox State Church led street demonstrations in protest, and the Jews of Bulgaria itself were spared the fate of their neighbors. Vice-chairman of the National Assembly Dimitur Peshev, whom Israel eventually recognized to be a "Righteous Gentile," asked his fellow deputies to refuse handing over the Jews to the Germans and to sign a statement stating it would be contrary to their country's honor to do so. Stefan, the Metropolitan of Sofia known for his pro-Allied sympathies, invited Bulgaria's Chief Rabbi, Asher Hananel, to live in his house. After the war, with the Communist takeover, 20 of the deputies who had signed the statement were sentenced to death. Peshev and most of the others were punished with prison terms, the Communists in this instance proving to be no less evil than the Nazis. Todorov passionately believes that in the realm of evil, the two totalitarian systems mirror each other.

The twentieth-century legacy of good and evil is the subject of the author's key study *Mémoire du mal, tentation du bien: Enquête sur le siècle* (2000). He has chosen to describe the biography and intellectual stance of several figures whose lives were dominated by Nazi, communist, or both totalitarianisms: Vassili Grossman, Margaret Buber-Neumann, David Rousset, Primo Levi, Romain Gary, and Germaine Tillon. His argument is that the humanity of these women and men asserts itself through rejection of heroism, victimhood, and sainthood. Gray, not black or white, constitutes their moral landscape insofar as they remain human.

An important theme is that democracies are duplicitous when they justify their use of power in the name of morality and the common good. Examples include the two atomic bombs that resulted in Japanese surrender and the 1999 military intervention in Kosovo labeled "punitive expedition." The goal of concluding the war and punishing its perpetrators had an ethical dimension (i.e., the greater good), but this was hardly an excuse for killing innocent Japanese civilians. Dropping the atomic bombs on Japan was immoral. Likewise, Todorov believes that the situation in Kosovo did not justify bombing Serbia.

We may question the political aptness of these instances. We can argue for instance that the atomic bombs avoided the planned invasion of Japan, an invasion that would have killed even more persons on both sides. Todorov rejects this rationale and any other justification offered by Americans who sought to justify using the bombs in 1945.

In the spirit of recognizing the gray areas of morality, democratic countries shun whenever possible actions in which human lives are taken as a means to an end. When dealing with the hypocrisy at the heart of democracies' pursuit of righteousness, Winston Churchill's famous statement comes to mind: "Many forms of Government have been tried and will be tried in this world of sin and woe. No one pretends that democracy is perfect or all-wise. Indeed, it has been said that democracy is the worst form of Government except all those other forms that have been tried from time to time" (*Winston S. Churchill. His Complete Speeches 1897–1963*, ed. Robert Rhodes James, vol. 7, 7566).

SURVEY OF CRITICISM

Although Todorov himself has an impressive bibliography, there are very few secondary sources. Jean Verrier (1995) traces Todorov's evolution from his initial pursuit of formalist and structuralist conceits to his subsequent concern with multicultural issues. The historian István Deák has written two excellent studies of Todorov's books in the *New York Review of Books:* "Memories of Hell" (1997) and "Heroes and Victims" (2001).

SELECTED BIBLIOGRAPHY

Works by Todorov

La Conquête de l'Amérique: La question de l'autre. Paris: Seuil, 1982. [*The Conquest of America: The Question of the Other.* Trans. Richard Howard. New York: Harper and Row, 1984; Norman: University of Oklahoma Press, 1999.]

Nous et les autres: La réflexion française sur la diversité humaine. Paris: Seuil, 1989. [*On Human Diversity: Nationalism, Racism and Exoticism in French Thought.* Trans. Catherine Porter. Cambridge, Mass.: Harvard University Press, 1993.]

Face à l'extrême. Paris: Seuil, 1991. [*Facing the Extreme: Moral Life in the Concentration Camps.* Trans. Arthur Denner and Abigail Pollak. New York: Metropolitan Books, 1996.]

La fragilité du bien: Le sauvetage des Juifs bulgares. Paris: Albin Michel, 1999. [*The Fragility of Goodness: Why Bulgaria's Jews Survived the Holocaust. A Collection of Texts.* Trans. Arthur Denner. Princeton, N.J.: Princeton University Press, 2001.]

Mémoire du mal, tentation du bien: Enquête sur le siècle. Paris: Robert Laffont, 2000.

Selected Studies of Todorov

Deák, István. "Memories of Hell." *New York Review of Books* (June 26, 1997): 38–43.

———. "Heroes and Victims." *New York Review of Books* (May 31, 2001): 51–56.

Verrier, Jean. *Tzvetan Todorov: Du formalisme russe aux morales de l'histoire.* Paris: Bertrand-Lacoste, 1995.

Related work

James, Robert Rhodes, ed. *Winston S. Churchill. His Complete Speeches 1897–1963.* Vol. 7 (1945–1949). New York: Chelsea House and R. R. Bowker, 1974.

TATYANA TOLSTAYA

(1951–)

Elena Dúzs

BIOGRAPHY

Tatyana Nikitichna Tolstaya was born in Russia on May 3, 1951, to one of the most distinguished literary families. She is the great-grandniece of Lev Tolstoy, and the granddaughter of the well-known Soviet writer Alexey Tolstoy (best known for his trilogy about the Revolution, *Khozhdenie po mukam*, 1943) and his wife, the poet Natalya Krandiyevskaya. Tolstaya's maternal grandfather, Mikhail Lozinsky, was a distinguished translator of literature. His skillful translations of Dante and Shakespeare are still read in Russia.

Tolstaya grew up in Leningrad (now St. Petersburg), where she later studied Latin and Greek at Leningrad State University (1968–74). After graduating and marrying Andrej Lebedev, she relocated to Moscow, where she worked as a junior editor in the Division of Oriental Literature at the Nauka publishing house (1974–1983).

Partially due to her discontent, as a reader, with the quality of publications in current Soviet literary journals, Tolstaya began writing at the age of 31. Her first short story appeared in 1983 in the journal *Avrora*. It was soon followed by the publication of several stories in a variety of literary journals. Four years after her literary debut, she published her first collection of stories, entitled "*Na zolotom kryl'tse sideli . . .*": *Rasskazy* (1987). Its 65,000 copies sold out within hours.

Tolstaya's arrival on the Soviet literary scene was timely. As a result of the expanded political and cultural freedoms, Soviet periodicals of the late 1980s were dominated by social and political concerns. In contrast, her own writings possessed an appreciable aesthetic value, rather than a strong ideological or moral message. Readers and critics alike welcomed her work, which was evocative of the past, free of the usual Soviet feel, and distinctive in its complexity, allusiveness, and abundant irony. By 1987, she was considered one of the most original writers in contemporary Russian literature.

Since 1988, she has divided her time between the United States and Russia, teaching courses in creative writing and Russian literature at various American universities and colleges. She has also become known within liberal academic and journalist circles in the United States for her commentaries on various aspects of American and Russian culture (in the *New York Review of Books*, *The New Republic*, *The Wilson Quarterly*, and other journals and newspapers). Two of her short story collections have been translated into English and her writings have been included in various literary anthologies.

During the second half of the 1990s, Tolstaya published little new prose; however, the year 2000 saw the publication of her most significant work to date, an anti-utopian novel entitled *Kys*. Conceived in the year of the Chernobyl catastrophe and set in historic Moscow some 300 years after an explosion that had enormously devastating consequences, the novel describes a disfigured world populated by mutant people. Her novel draws greatly from Russian literary tradition, including its social strand, evoking such diverse Russian prose writers as Nikolay Gogol, Andrei Bely, Aleksej Remizov, Andrei Platonov, Evgeny Zamyatin, Mikhail Bulgakov, Vladimir Nabokov, and even Aleksandr Solzhenitsyn, whom Tolstaya had criticized in the past for using literature as a didactic tool. *Kys* is written in an ornate language that intricately combines the author's neologisms with elements of Russian folklore and Soviet slang. While it serves as an affirmation of Russian literary tradition, Tolstaya's novel also offers a whimsical allegory of Russia's past, present, and future, and provides an original interpretation of the role of literature and culture in Russian society.

MAJOR MULTICULTURAL THEMES

In her analysis of American society, Tolstaya is most often critical, like many other Russian intellectuals. Her harshest criticisms are usually directed towards the prevalence of what she considers ideological trends (especially feminism) in academic and mainstream circles in the United States. At the same time, in her analysis of Russian culture, she has often taken an unsympathetic, almost Russophobic stance.

Although indicative of her semi-émigré status, Tolstaya's awareness of different cultural points of view, her penchant for foreign perspectives, and her confrontational mode (as expressed by the public persona in her essays) have roots in her poetics. The elements of her poetics include the device of distancing from the object of portrayal, the use of double or multiple voices, and a proclivity to challenge conventions. Tolstaya the public persona thus exploits her semi-émigré status as she extends her narrative into life.

Her interest in alienation and culture clash harks back to the beginning of her writing career. The most common characters of her stories are misfits and unfortunates—lonely, unattractive, lethargic, infantile, old, confused people who live sheltered lives, unable to escape their isolation and join in the normality of existence. In Tolstaya's works, normality almost always transpires as an imaginary state, while the misery of alienated life is revealed as the ordinary human condition. Culture clash invariably emerges as a conflict between aristocratic and plebeian worlds, revealing Tolstaya's adherence to romantic sensibility. In her prose and essays, an artist or a cultured individual carries out the noble mission of guarding culture in the face of the triumphing banality of the plebeian world. This banality subsists in the form of stifling conventions, fashionable trends, prejudices, and bad taste. In order to shield oneself from its aggressive manifestations, the guardian of culture must use his gift of irony, while his creative powers allow him to transform the banal by incorporating it into the sphere of art (hence, by both poeticizing and distancing it).

SURVEY OF CRITICISM

The Explosive World of Tatyana Tolstaya's Fiction (1996) is the most comprehensive study of Tolstaya's short stories to date. The author, Helena Goscilo, has situated herself as the utmost authority on the subject. She has also authored a number of articles dealing with various aspects of Tolstaya's prose. In her book, Goscilo offers a number of constructive and complementary perspectives on Tolstaya's fiction. She undertakes a thorough analysis of Tolstaya's presentation of characters, which is mediated through the use of irony and double—or multiple—voicing, and examines her reliance on Russian cultural tradition, from fairy tales and urban folklore to Aleksandr Pushkin, Nikolay Gogol, Mikhail Lermontov, and symbolist poetry. Goscilo's study looks at Tolstaya's ambivalent treatment of such themes as childhood, art, and time; it also analyzes her use of tropes and establishes the commonality of her fictional writings and journalism. Goscilo then undertakes a feminist reading of Tolstaya's texts, thus demonstrating that, contrary to Tolstaya's assertion, her fiction readily lends itself to such a reading. Goscilo thus arrives at the conclusion that, despite the seeming prevalence of her skepticism of traditional values, Tolstaya ultimately adheres to the principles of Western humanism.

In her *Voices of Russian Literature* (1999), British scholar Sally Laird suggests that the moral imperative in Tolstaya's writing lies in the significance of remembering. She also links Tolstaya's depiction of unfortunates both with Russian literary tradition's concern for small, underprivileged people, and with Russian skepticism about the possibility or necessity to change one's course of life. Laird praises Tolstaya's prose for its sensual quality: its reliance on the senses for depicting the phenomenal world and its linguistic richness.

Svetlana Boym (1993) discusses Tolstaya's ambivalence in her treatment of the banal, revealing Tolstaya's particular attraction to the phenomenon. In fervently denouncing banality, she establishes links with Nikolay Gogol, Andrei Bely, and Vladimir Nabokov who found authorial pleasure in depicting the banal. Boyd argues, however, that flashes of high culture do not fully illuminate Tolstaya's fictional world and that folklore, particularly urban, remains her major subtext.

SELECTED BIBLIOGRAPHY

Works by Tolstaya

"Na zolotom kryl'tse sideli." In *Avrora* 8 (Leningrad) (1983): 94–101.
"Na zolotom kryl'tse sideli . . . ": Rasskazy. Moscow: "Molodaia gvardiia," 1987. [*On the Golden Porch.* Trans. Antonina W. Bouis. New York: Knopf, 1989.]
Sleepwalker in a Fog (originally published in English; includes short stories published in various literary journals in Russia). Trans. Jamey Gambrell. New York: Knopf: London: Virago, 1992.
Three Stories/ Tri rasskaza. Ed. S. Dalton-Brown. London: Bristol Classical Press, 1996.
Sestry (collection of essays by Tatyana Tolstaya and of stories by Natalya Tolstaya). Moscow: Izdatelskii dom "Podkova," 1998.
Kys: Roman. Moscow: Podkova, 2000.

Selected Studies of Tolstaya

Boym, Svetlana. "The Poetics of Banality: Tat'iana Tolstaia, Lana Gogoberidze, and Larisa Zvezdochetova." In *Fruits of Her Plume: Essays on Contemporary Russian Women's Culture.* Ed. Helena Goscilo, 59–94. Armonk, N.Y.: M. E. Sharpe, 1993.
Dalton-Brown, S. "A Map of the Human Heart: Tatyana Tolstaya's Topographies." *Essays in Poetics* 21 (1996): 1–18.
Goscilo, Helena, ed. *Fruits of Her Plume: Essays on Contemporary Russian Women's Culture.* Armonk, N.Y.: M. E. Sharpe, 1993.
Goscilo, Helena. "Perspective in Tatyana Tolstaya's Wonderland of Art." *World Literature Today* 67, no. 1 (Winter 1993): 80–90.
———. *The Explosive World of Tatyana N. Tolstaya's Fiction.* Armonk, N.Y.: M. E. Sharpe, 1996.
Greber, Erika. "Carnivalization of the Short Story: Tatyana Tolstaya's The Poet and the Muse." *Essays in Poetics* 21 (1996): 50–78.
Laird, Sally. In *Voices of Russian Literature: Interviews with Ten Contemporary Writers,* 95–117. Oxford and New York: Oxford University Press, 1999.

LEON (MARCUS) URIS
(1924–)

A. L. Rogers II

BIOGRAPHY

Over a career spanning five decades, Leon Uris has enjoyed phenomenal popularity, with five of his twelve novels classified as number-one best-sellers by the *New York Times*. While the shortcomings in his prose, characterization, and political outlook have been well noted, Uris certainly ranks among the more important multicultural writers since World War II. His books explore a number of the defining cultural conflicts of the twentieth century: the Nazis' attempted extermination of the Jews, the volatile clash between Arabs and Israelis in the Middle East, and the long-running battle between the British and Irish in Ireland, most notably. Millions of readers have learned the history behind these major intercultural conflicts from Uris's fiction.

Born in 1924 in Baltimore, Maryland, to Jewish parents of Polish descent, Uris left high school in 1942 to enlist in the U.S. Marine Corps. He trained in New Zealand and fought at Tarawa (Gilbert Islands) and Guadalcanal (Solomon Islands), experiences he translated into his first novel, *Battle Cry* (1953). Following *The Angry Hills* (1955), a spy thriller based on the journal of an uncle who served in the Palestinian Brigade in Greece, came the immensely popular *Exodus* (1958), which describes the birth of modern Israel (Uris's stay in Israel also led to *Exodus Revisited* [1959], a travel book with photographs by Dimitrios Harissiadis). In gathering information for *Exodus*, Uris traveled extensively throughout Israel, Poland, Italy, Denmark, Cyprus, and Iran, finally taking up residence in Herzlia, Israel, in 1956. An episode in *Exodus* portraying the

Jewish resistance in the Warsaw ghetto was expanded to book length in *Mila 18* (1961), requiring another extended trip to Poland for research.

When war broke out between Israel and Egypt in 1956, he went into the Sinai as a newspaper correspondent. (These experiences in the Sinai would be revisited three decades later in *Mitla Pass* [1988].)

Armageddon (1964) explores Cold War hostilities in postwar Berlin, and the thriller *Topaz* (1967), based on factual documents Uris received during his 1964 residence in Mexico, depicts Soviet infiltration of Charles de Gaulle's French government. With *QB VII* (1970), Uris returned to Jewish themes, this time with factual basis in a libel suit brought against him for identifying a German doctor in *Exodus* who performed experimental surgery on concentration camp inmates during the Holocaust. While in London in 1968, Uris became interested in the "troubles" in Northern Ireland, and the seed was sown for his two "Irish" novels, *Trinity* (1976) and *Redemption* (1995).

During 1969 and 1970, Uris traveled in Israel and Europe researching the history of Russian Jews, with stops also in Cyprus, Turkey, Afghanistan, Pakistan, and New Zealand. With his third wife, Jill, a professional photographer, he moved to Dublin in the early 1970s, and jointly they published *Ireland: A Terrible Beauty. The Story of Ireland Today* (1975), a travel book with a pointedly republican slant on Irish history. *Trinity*, a novel of Ireland from the 1840s through 1916, followed. From Ireland, Uris moved to Aspen, Colorado, but in 1978 he returned to Israel to gather information for *The Haj* (1984), a novel relating the history of modern Israel through the eyes of Palestinian Arabs. This venture to Israel also resulted in a second husband-wife collaboration *Jerusalem: Song of Songs* (1981) which tells the story of Jerusalem from biblical to modern times. The Urises spent most of 1980 traveling through Central America, the Caribbean, and Israel, with another month-long visit to Ireland. Since the mid-1980s, he has limited his travels, preferring to spend more time researching and writing at home, first in Colorado and later in New York.

MAJOR MULTICULTURAL THEMES

Gideon Zadok in *Mitla Pass* clearly speaks for Uris when he says that writers should strive to "make people angry . . . to stir them up" (350). Throughout his career, Uris has stirred up millions of readers with novels focusing on cultures that are tragically at odds. Historical though his subjects typically are, his obvious partisanship has led some to label his books as propaganda novels. In several books, Uris works to enlist the reader's sympathy for the Jews: *Jerusalem: Song of Songs* relates the history of zealous anti-Semitism in Palestine from biblical times to the 1980s; *Mitla Pass* describes the horrors of Jewish life in the Russian pale; and *Exodus, Mila 18, Armageddon,* and *QB VII* all bring to life the atrocities perpetrated against the Jews in the Holocaust. Abraham Cady in *QB VII* also speaks for the author on the need to repeat the story of the Holocaust: "We must continue to protest our demise until we are allowed to live in peace" (281). The impact of Uris's Jewish novels throughout the world has been profound. In overturning stereotypes of Jews as passive and weak by depicting them as courageous warriors, Uris has become one of the world's most recognized ambassadors for the Jewish people.

While few have faulted Uris for his sympathetic portrayal of Jews facing European anti-Semitism, some consider his depiction of Arabs oversimplified and offensive. In *Exodus* and *The Haj*, he suggests that Arabs are a backward people whose lives would be greatly improved by acceptance of the Jews in their midst. Uris has Palestinian Arabs in *The Haj* deem themselves lazy, treacherous, cowardly, misogynistic, and driven by hatred. One character, Dr. Mudhil, declares that "We Arabs are the worst. We can't live with the world, and even more terrible, we can't live with each other. . . . We, who tried to humiliate the Jews, will find ourselves humiliated as the scum of the earth" (545–46). While Uris is generally pessimistic in seeing no end to the Arab-Israeli conflict, he celebrates Jerusalem in *Jerusalem: Song of Songs* as the world's most multicultural city: "an incredible mix of fact, fantasy, legend, superstition and conjecture from three religions and dozens of sects representing more dozens of cultures from every corner of the earth, all blended into one enormous euphoric cauldron" (139).

The imperialist British have also drawn Uris's frequent ire. He levels harsh criticism against the British in *Exodus* and *The Haj* for their self-interested administration of the Palestine Mandate and their failure to support Israel in its infancy. In his three Irish books, Uris condemns the British for demeaning and subjugating Irish Catholics. In *Ireland: A Terrible Beauty. The Story of Ireland Today* he describes the British presence in Ireland as four centuries of "tortured foreign occupation" (5). In Uris's version of Irish history, Ulster, now the nation of Northern Ireland, was established as a British "plantation, a fortress outpost of colonial exploitation" peopled with British-descended Ulstermen whose hatred of Irish Catholics "smells strangely of Aryan supremacy . . . of Nazi ideology" (100). This theme of British cultural bigotry is central in both *Trinity* and *Redemption*. In the latter, British prejudice extends outward to include the Australians and New Zealanders sacrificed in Turkey in the ill-considered 1915 invasion of Gallipoli.

Uris's guiding aim throughout his career has been to dramatize the injustice of cultural prejudice. As he writes in *A God in Ruins*, "The seeds of hatred are within us all. . . . [W]e must face the demand of a MORAL IMPERATIVE with the goal of eradicating racism. Racism from person to person, tribe to tribe, and nation to nation is the greatest blight on the people of this land, of this world" (480–81). This moral imperative of eradicating the bigotry that so often separates cultures lies at the heart of all of Leon Uris's work.

SURVEY OF CRITICISM

The one book-length study of Uris is Kathleen Shine Cain's *Leon Uris: A Critical Companion* (1998), a general survey of his novels through *Redemption*. While some little attention has been directed towards Uris's portrayal of the Irish in his fiction, most scholarly discussion centers on his depiction of the Arab-Israeli conflict. Jeremy Salt (1985) questions Uris's historical accuracy and condemns *The Haj* as a "a conscious attempt to show that the culture of an entire people is rotten to the core" (61–62). Elise Salem Manganaro (1988) also condemns Uris for the subversive technique of having multiple narrators appear to project a Bakhtinian mixture of dialogical voices, when all the narrative voices effectively coalesce into one monologic authorial voice that Manganaro considers "dangerous" given Uris's wide audience (3). Andrew Furman (1997) suggests that Uris stereotypes Arabs as "grotesque distortions" of Jews and portrays Israelis in positive ways satisfying "the pervasive American Jewish desire to forge a new, strong but sensitive Jewish identity in the wake of the Holocaust" (51). Bennett Lovett-Graff (1997) also considers Uris's impact in winning American support for the cause of Israel, partly through blending history and "religious drama" (442). Sharon D. Downey and Richard A. Kallan (1982) discover in Uris's fiction the rhetorical strategy of "semi-aesthetic detachment," a melding of fictional and actual worlds through a variety of techniques such that Uris "addresses an immediate, specific, external world concern" and encourages his readers to respond actively in seeking to right the wrongs he identifies in his novels (192–93).

SELECTED BIBLIOGRAPHY

Works by Uris

Battle Cry. New York: Putnam, 1953.
The Angry Hills. New York: Random House, 1955.
Exodus. Garden City, N.Y.: Doubleday, 1958.
Exodus Revisited. Garden City, N.Y.: Doubleday, 1960.
Mila 18. Garden City, N.Y.: Doubleday, 1961.
Topaz. New York: McGraw Hill, 1967.
QB VII. Garden City, N.Y.: Doubleday, 1970.
——— and Jill Uris. *Ireland: A Terrible Beauty. The Story of Ireland Today*. Garden City, N.Y.: Doubleday, 1975.
Trinity. Garden City, N.Y.: Doubleday, 1976.
Uris, Jill, and Leon Uris. *Jerusalem: Song of Songs*. Garden City, N.Y.: Doubleday, 1981.
The Haj. Garden City, N.Y.: Doubleday, 1984.
Mitla Pass. Garden City, N.Y.: Doubleday, 1988.
Redemption: A Novel. New York: HarperCollins Publishers, 1995.
A God in Ruins: A Novel. New York: HarperCollins Publishers, 1999.

Selected Studies of Uris

Cain, Kathleen Shine. *Leon Uris: A Critical Companion.* Westport, Conn.: Greenwood Press, 1998.

Downey, Sharon D. and Richard A. Kallan. "Semi-Aesthetic Detachment: The Fusing of Fictional and External Worlds in the Situational Literature of Leon Uris." *Communication Monographs* 49, no. 3 (1982): 192–204.

Furman, Andrew. "Embattled Uris." In Andrew Furman, *Israel through the Jewish-American Imagination: A Survey of Jewish-American Literature on Israel, 1928–1995,* 39–57. Albany: State University of New York Press, 1997.

Lovett-Graff, Bennett. "Leon Uris." *Contemporary Jewish-American Novelists: A Bio-Critical Sourcebook.* Ed. Joel Shatzky and Michael Taub, 439–47. Westport, Conn.: Greenwood Press, 1997.

Manganaro, Elise Salem. "Voicing the Arab: Multivocality and Ideology in Leon Uris' *The Haj.*" *MELUS* [*Multi-Ethnic Literature of the United States*] 15, no. 4 (1988): 3–13.

Salt, Jeremy. "Fact and Fiction in the Middle Eastern Novels of Leon Uris." *Journal of Palestine Studies* 14, no. 3 (1985): 54–63.

VLADIMIR NIKOLAEVICH VOINOVICH

(1932–)

D. Lynne Walker

BIOGRAPHY

Vladimir Nikolaevich Voinovich was born in Dushanbe (previously called Stalinabad), the capital city of Tajikistan. His mother—of Jewish heritage—was a schoolteacher. His father—of Serbian heritage—translated Serbian poetry and worked as a journalist; he was arrested in 1936 for a remark he had made during a private conversation about Stalin's ideas. Subsequent to the release of Voinovich's father in 1941, the family moved frequently to avoid further arrests. Voinovich entered trade school for carpentry in 1945. From 1952–1955, he served in the army (aviation mechanics) and started writing poetry. After graduating from evening school in 1956, he relocated to Moscow in 1958. There, he worked as a railway repairman and a carpenter and was admitted to the history department of the Krupskaia Pedagogical Institute. He was employed as an assistant editor in the Department of Satire and Humor of the All-Union Radio in Moscow (1960–61), began publishing prose ("My zdes' zhivem," 1961), and was accepted into the Writers' Union.

Liberalism in the arts ended in 1962; after the publication of "Khochu byt' chestnym" (1963), newspapers started to print negative comments about Voinovich. An early version of *Zhizn' i neobychainye prikliucheniia soldata Ivana Chonkina* was accepted by *Novyi mir* in 1964, but not published except in samizdat. In 1966, Voinovich signed two letters of protest. In one, he—along with 62 other writers—requested reconsideration of the harsh sentences imposed on Andrei Sinyavsky and Yuly Daniel. In the second—to the Supreme Soviet of the USSR—he requested reconsideration of two articles recently added to the Criminal

Code that defined deliberately false verbal criticism of the state as a criminal offense. By 1968, conditions worsened for Voinovich because of his active role in the human rights movement and his signing of more letters. He submitted *Zhizn' i neobychainye prikliucheniia soldata Ivana Chonkina* to the Writers' Union for publication in 1969. The manuscript was "lost," and subsequently—without Voinovich's authorization—published by an émigré press (Posev publishing house in West Germany). Voinovich was not expelled from the Writers' Union because he agreed to write a letter (published in *Literaturnaia gazeta*) protesting the unauthorized publication of *Chonkin* abroad. However, he adamantly refused to renounce his novel.

He was expelled from the Writers' Union in 1974 (and thus could no longer publish in the USSR) because of his publications in the West and, to a lesser extent, for his defense of the recently exiled Alexander Solzhenitsyn. However, the primary reason for his expulsion was his highly satirical letter to the newly created "Soviet Agency for the Protection of Authors' Rights." In 1975, he charged the KGB with attempting to poison him with a tainted cigarette (see "Proisshestvie v 'Metropole,'" 1975). The sequel to *Chonkin*, entitled *Pretendent na prestol: novye prikliucheniia soldata Ivana Chonkina*, was published in Paris in 1979 and excerpts were broadcast over Deutsche Welle. Consequently, Voinovich officially was asked to consider emigration.

In December 1980 an exit visa was granted, and he left the Soviet Union with his family, settling in Munich (Stockdorf) at the invitation of the Bavarian Academy of Arts. Voinovich was deprived of his Soviet citizenship in 1981 by Leonid Brezhnev for "activities undermining the prestige and reputation of the Soviet state" (David Treadwell, "Life's Absurdities 'Forced' Soviet to Become Satirist," E29). Voinovich published a response to Brezhnev in which he stated, "I could not possibly have undermined the prestige of the Soviet state. Thanks to the efforts of Soviet leaders, yourself included, the Soviet state has no prestige" (Treadwell, E29).

Voinovich was recognized as a candidate for the Neustadt International Prize for Literature in 1982. He visited Moscow in 1989, having been invited by Mosfilm to discuss a possible film version of *Chonkin*. The film subsequently opened in London on October 27, 1995. In 1990, Mikhail Gorbachev restored Voinovich's citizenship (as did he that of Solzhenitsyn and others). Voinovich was also granted a Moscow apartment and received an apology from the Writers' Union; he currently maintains the Moscow apartment and a home in Munich (his "dacha"). Sixty-one of the Soviet Union's leading writers (including Voinovich, Andrei Sinyavsky, Andrei Voznesensky, Ludmilla Petrushevskaya, and Andrei Bitov) formed a new Union of Independent Writers in 1991, signaling the collapse of the government-sanctioned Writers' Union. In 1994, Voinovich finished part I of his autobiography *Zamysel* (first published in the review *Znamia* in 1994) and also took up painting (his first exhibit was in Moscow in 1996). The latter activity has delayed the writing of part II of his autobiography. He received the Triumph Literary Award (1996) for a lifetime of achievement in Russian letters. He and Ludmilla Petrushevskaya were the major speakers at a 2001 Nottingham, England, conference: "Two Centuries of Russian Humor and Satire." A visiting writer, fellow, and scholar at a number of institutions in the United States and Europe, he received an honorary Ph.D. from Middlebury College in the United States in 2001. Currently he writes a column in the Russian newspaper *Izvestia* and maintains a highly informative Web site.

Voinovich's works (novels, short stories, plays, poems, essays, and feuilletons) have been translated into at least thirty languages.

MAJOR MULTICULTURAL THEMES

At the beginning of *Antisovetskii Sovetskii Soiuz* (1985), a collection of essays that describe Soviet society—both the *apparatchiki* (representative of the system) and the indomitable citizen trying to attain what he needs from that system—Voinovich notes that the Soviet people are like the beetles that live in the half-filled rain barrel outside his dacha. Their world is formed by that barrel; the most intelligent suspect that other worlds exist and the most freedom-loving try to escape by climbing up the sides of the barrel, only to fall back in. For the occasional beetle who does escape, there is a new world of boundless freedom—but a world in which one has to fight for survival. The natural response to this situation? "Quick, back in the barrel!" (*The Anti-Soviet Soviet Union*, trans. Richard Lourie, xvi–xvii). This metaphor serves to introduce what has consistently been Voinovich's thematic objective—to depict the Soviet/Russian world and the individual's negotiation of that world, and to interrogate man's responsibilities to himself and to others. As a young writer, Voinovich thought that Khrushchev's "freedom" was sufficient, and his first prose publication, "My zdes' zhivem," was a realistic reflection of worker dissatisfaction, not of socialist realist heroics. However, with Khrushchev's 1962 departure from his earlier policy of liberalism in the arts and the increasingly negative press occasioned by Voinovich's second work, "Khochu byt' chestnym" (in which a building supervisor refuses to submit an unfinished building to inspection), the author recognized that although "[he] wanted to be a normal realist, to depict life as it is . . . real life in the Soviet Union is so absurd, it forced [him] to become a satirist" (quoted in Treadwell, E1). Voinovich as satirist emerged with *Zhizn' i neobychainye prikliucheniia soldata Ivana Chonkina* and its sequel, *Pretendent na prestol: novye prikliucheniia soldata Ivana Chonkina*, in which he foregrounds the very absurdity of the Soviet system, of its 1941 policies during World War II, and of the individuals—including Stalin—who implemented those policies. Only a fool such as Ivan Chonkin could be the "hero" of such a novel. In addition, Voinovich's satirical voice surfaced in such nonfiction works as *Ivankiada, ili rasskaz o vselenii pisatelia Voinovicha v novuiu kvartiru* (1976), in which he recounts his difficulty obtaining a larger apartment. His most glaring satire, however—while he was still in the Soviet Union—took the form of "open" letters to various authorities (see "Putem vzaimoi perepiski," 1973).

Voinovich has continued to address the theme of emigration, remaining—in his own words—very much a Russian writer (*The Anti-Soviet Soviet Union*, ix). Nevertheless, his Russian perspective has expanded to become multicultural. Evidence of this appears in both his fiction, in which the narrator is often a well-traveled emigrant living in Munich, Germany, and also in his nonfiction. *Antisovetskii Sovetskii Soiuz* is geared toward a Western audience. Like his 1993 work, "Delo No. 348–40" (in which he details his accusation that the KGB attempted to poison him), and his 1997 collection of essays, *Zapakh shokolada: povesti i rasskazy* (in which the title essay—Proustian in nature—addresses memory and the value of one's personal history), *Antisovetskii Sovetskii Soiuz* questions humans' responsibility to themselves and others and foregrounds Voinovich's passionate belief in individual sovereignty. His bitingly satirical novel, *Moskva 2042* (1987), is an entertaining diatribe against totalitarian regimes—in whatever guise. This work, like his *Skazki dlia vzroslykh* (1996), illustrates Voinovich's ever-intensifying commitment to democratic government. In *Shapka* (1988), a novel about the Writers' Union, Voinovich returns to a satirical style more Horatian in nature (similar to that in *Ivankiada*). In his autobiographical *Zamysel* and in his novel *Monumentalnaia propaganda* (1995), Voinovich again addresses memory and history in both a personal context and a social one. The latter work surveys the Soviet era from Lenin to the present, questioning practices and policies from an "everyman" perspective.

SURVEY OF CRITICISM

Danile Rancour-Laferriere (1991), focusing on *Chonkin* as the introduction of Voinovich's satirical voice, discusses the way in which the author ridicules Stalin by portraying him as a castrated leader, as the individual who was responsible for the Soviet Union's initial inability to curb the Nazi invasion. He notes that this reading demands an "awareness of subtexts from Stalinist culture . . . and a rudimentary knowledge of certain unconscious fantasy material customarily dealt with by psychoanalysis" (36). Natalia Olshanskaya (2000) cites the Voinovich of *Moskva 2042* as a literary descendant of Evgeny Zamyatin and George Orwell, who plays with the generic conventions of anti-utopia (Bakhtin's "parodic stylisation" [428]) to take "the reader on a nightmarish journey into the future where the well-known absurdities of Soviet life are hyperbolized to create the most corrupt totalitarian world one can imagine" (426). In discussing *Moskva 2042*, Karen Ryan-Hayes (1994) outlines Voinovich's rejection of all tyranny and his conviction that it can never be justified. She then interrogates Voinovich's "scathing portrait of Solzhenitsyn through the character of Sim Simych Karnavalov" (453), concluding that "for Voinovich, . . . Solzhenitsyn's dismissal of Western democracy and championing of authoritarianism represent dangerous trends in the ongoing debate about Russia's future" (472). Edith W. Clowes's book (1993) examines what she terms "meta-utopian fiction," which interrogates "the question of social imagination: how alternative worlds are framed and what impact they have on our perception of social 'reality' and our behavior in society" (ix). She discusses Voinovich's concern about "the defixation of memory and imagination" (216) and "the resurgence of a simple, nostalgic, unreflected utopianism in various forms of neoconservatism" (218). Clowes notes that this concern belongs not only to Voinovich vis-à-vis Russia, but also to others vis-à-vis the West.

In his article (1996) on *Shapka*, Barry Lewis focuses on the Gogolian in Voinovich (an influence that the author acknowledges), in which a mediocre man does battle with authority and a piece of clothing is representative of position. Moreover, Voinovich is skillful in his depiction—and ridicule—of the hierarchical, the bizarre, and the comic in Soviet society, directing his most potent criticism at certain "intellectuals," the Soviet bureaucratic mind, and "materialistic Party careerists" (24). Throughout the text, Voinovich also ridicules the Soviet propensity for abbreviation by producing amusing—and often crude—acronyms and abbreviations of his own. Lewis also links the events portrayed in *Shapka* with Voinovich's own experiences with the Writers' Union.

SELECTED BIBLIOGRAPHY

Works by Voinovich

"My zdes' zhivem." *Novyi mir* 1 (Moscow) (January 1961): 21–71.

"Khochu byt' chestnym." *Novyi mir* 2 (Moscow) (February 1963): 150–86.

Zhizn' i neobychainye prikliucheniia soldata Ivana Chonkina. Part I. *Grani* 72 (Frankfurt-am-Main) (July 1969): 3–83. [*The Life and Extraordinary Adventures of Private Ivan Chonkin.* Trans. Richard Lourie. New York: Farrar, Straus and Giroux, 1977.]

"Putem vzaimoi perepiski." *Grani* 87–88 (Frankfurt-am-Main) (January–April 1973): 122–91. [*In Plain Russian.* New York: Farrar, Straus and Giroux, 1979.]

"Proisshestvie v 'Metropole.'" *Kontinent* 2–5 (West Berlin) (1975): 51–97.

Ivankiada, ili rasskaz o vselenii pisatelia Voinovicha v novuiu kvartiru. Ann Arbor: Ardis, 1976. [*The Ivankiad: or, The Tale of the Writer Voinovich's Installation in His New Apartment.* Trans. David Lapeza. New York: Farrar, Straus and Giroux, 1977.]

Pretendent na prestol: novye prikliucheniia soldata Ivana Chonkina. Paris: YMCA Press, 1979. [*Pretender to the Throne: The Further Adventures of Private Ivan Chonkin.* Trans. Richard Lourie. New York: Farrar, Straus and Giroux, 1981.]

"Fiktivnii brak." *Vremia i my* 72 (Moscow) (May–June 1983): 228–44.

Tribunal: Sudebnaia komediia v trekh deistviiakh. London: Overseas Publications Interchange, 1985.

Antisovetskii Sovetskii Soiuz. Ann Arbor: Ardis, 1985. [*The Anti-Soviet Soviet Union.* Trans. Richard Lourie. New York: Harcourt Brace Jovanovich, 1986.]

Moskva 2042. Ann Arbor: Ardis, 1987. [*Moscow 2042.* Trans. Richard Lourie. New York: Harcourt Brace Jovanovich, 1987.]

Shapka. London: Overseas Publications Interchange, 1988. [*The Fur Hat.* Trans. Susan Brownsberger. San Diego: Harcourt Brace Jovanovich, 1989.]

"Delo No. 348–40" (1993). *Delo No. 348–40: sovershenno nesekretno.* Moscow: Tekst, 1994.

Zamysel (1994). *Zamysel: Kniga.* Moscow: Vagrius, 1995, reprint 1999.

Monumentalnaia propaganda (1995). Moscow: Izd-vo "EKSMO-Press," 2000.

Maloe sobranie sochinenii: v 5 tomakh. 5 vols. Moscow: Fabula, 1995–96.

Skazki dlia vzroslykh. Moscow: Vagrius, 1996.

Zapakh shokolada: povesti i rasskazy. Moscow: Vagrius, 1997.

http://www.voinovich.ru

Selected Studies of Voinovich

Bek, Tat'iana. "Iz russkoi literatury ia ne uezzhal nikuda." *Druzhba narodov* (Russia) 12 (1991): 245–61.

Clowes, Edith W. *Russian Experimental Fiction: Resisting Ideology after Utopia.* Princeton, N.J.: Princeton University Press, 1993.

Fletcher, M. D. "Voinovich's 'Consumer' Satire in *2042.*" *International Fiction Review* (Canada) 16, no. 2 (Summer 1989): 106–108.

Lewis, Barry. "Homunculi Sovietici: The Soviet 'Writers' in Voinovich's *Shapka.*" *Australian Slavonic and East European Studies* 10, no. 1 (1996): 17–28.

Obukhov, Viktor. "Sovremennaia rossiiskaia antiutopiia." *Literaturnoe obozrenie* (Russia) 3, no. 269 (1998): 96–98.

Olshanskaya, Natalia. "Anti-Utopian Carnival: Vladimir Voinovich Rewriting George Orwell." *Forum for Modern Language Studies* (Scotland) 36, no. 4 (October 2000): 426–37.

Pearce, Carol Elizabeth. "The Prose Works of Vladimir Voinovich." Ph.D. diss., University of Washington, 1982.

Rancour-Laferriere, Daniel. "From Incompetence to Satire: Voinovich's Image of Stalin as Castrated Leader of the Soviet Union in 1941." *Slavic Review* 50:1 (Spring 1991): 36–47.

Rishina, Irina. "Ia vernulsia by . . . " *Literaturnaia gazeta* (Russia) 25, no. 5299 (June 20, 1997): 8.

———. "O tom o sem i okolo." *Literaturnaia gazeta* (Russia) 1–2, no. 5636 (January 15, 1990): 10.

Ryan-Hayes, Karen. "Voinovich's *Moskva 2042* As Literary Parody." *Russian, Croatian and Serbian, Czech and Slovak, Polish Literature* (Amsterdam) 35, no. 4 (November 15, 1994): 453–80.

Treadwell, David. "Life's Absurdities 'Forced' Soviet to Become Satirist." *Los Angeles Times* (December 10, 1989): E1, E28, E29.

DEREK WALCOTT
(1930–)

Jim Hannan

BIOGRAPHY

Even if Derek Walcott had never left his native Caribbean island of St. Lucia, he would qualify as a multicultural author. St. Lucia bears the cultural traces, found throughout the Caribbean, of indigenous Amerindians, colonizing Europeans, Africans brought as slaves, and the neighboring United States and Latin America. A British colony at the time of Walcott's birth, St. Lucia, like other Caribbean islands, frequently changed hands between European colonial powers. Walcott's English-speaking, Methodist family of modest means differed from the predominantly French-Creole-speaking, Catholic population of St. Lucia. Walcott's grandparents were Afro-Caribbean and white West Indian. His white paternal grandfather arrived in St. Lucia from Barbados, an island with strong English sensibilities. In Caribbean society and in Walcott's work, race and color continue to be important. His art forges a regional consciousness that profits from the influence in the Caribbean of the Americas, Africa, and Europe.

Walcott's father, Warwick, died one year after the birth of Derek and his twin brother. The twins and an older sister were raised by their mother Alix, a teacher and occasional principal of the Methodist primary school in St. Lucia's capital, Castries. Alix Walcott was part of Castries's Anglophone élite; thus Walcott received an excellent British colonial education and associated with important local cultural figures. As a youth, he studied as both poet and painter, and he continues to paint. Reflecting his background in painting, he regularly attends to landscape, color, light, and visual images in his poetry.

A published poet at eighteen, Walcott studied at the University College of the West Indies (UCWI), Mona, Jamaica, between 1950 and 1953. Bruce King reports that Walcott disliked the British pretensions of UCWI and the cultural and social differences between Jamaican students and those, like himself, from the southern West Indies (*Derek Walcott: A Caribbean Life*, 86–89). After a year in New York on a Rockefeller Fellowship (1958–59), Walcott settled in Port of Spain, Trinidad, where he founded and directed what would become the Trinidad Theatre Workshop. In addition to his work as a poet and dramatist, he wrote about culture for the *Trinidad Guardian* (1960–68). Unusual for most writers from the Caribbean, who often migrated to England, the United States, and Canada, Walcott lived in Trinidad throughout the 1960s and 1970s. During this time, his work as a poet and dramatist took him increasingly to the United States and places outside the Caribbean.

Since the 1980s, Walcott's career has taken on an extraordinarily international character. Seemingly always on the move, he appears at poetry and theater events throughout the United States, the Caribbean, Britain, and Europe. In 1981, he received a John D. and Catherine T. MacArthur Foundation Fellowship and began teaching at such institutions as Columbia, Harvard, and Boston Universities. He received the Queen's Gold Medal for Poetry (1988) and the Nobel Prize for Literature (1992). By the late 1990s, Walcott had divided his residence between St. Lucia and the United States. Never out of touch with the Caribbean, he has produced a body of work that speaks of local and global issues to an audience that knows no cultural or geographical boundaries.

MAJOR MULTICULTURAL THEMES

Walcott established himself among readers of West Indian poetry when, at the age of 18, he published *25 Poems* (1948). Praise from Frank Collymore, a leading literary figure in the Caribbean, helped build Walcott's reputation. A few poems from *25 Poems* appear in Walcott's first major collection, *In a Green Night: Poems 1948–1960* (1962). In such poems as "A Far Cry from Africa," "Ruins of a Great House," and "Bronze," as well as "Origins" (*Selected Poems*, 1964), Walcott addresses his and the Caribbean's racially mixed, culturally creolized heritage. As elsewhere in his poetry, he joins historical perspective with personal reflection, answers the violence of history with compassion, and celebrates the Caribbean for its beauty, creativity, and diversity. Walcott uses Creole dialect in "Parang" and "Tales of the Islands: Chapter VI," and in later poems he occasionally mixes local variants of English and French patois with standard English. No usage is natural or exotic; instead, this linguistic variability reflects the culturally complex Caribbean.

The Castaway, and Other Poems (1965) contains material previously published in *Selected Poems*, and includes the important new poems

"Laventille" and "Crusoe's Journal." In "Laventille," Walcott grimly connects the economic condition of a slum above Port of Spain to the Atlantic slave trade. Crusoe functions as a figure cut off from his past who makes something new in the world, emblematic of the Caribbean poet who must name the new world in which he lives. Some poems in *The Castaway* concern Walcott's early visits to the United States, and in *The Gulf, and Other Poems* (1969) he is critical of the political and racial climate of 1960s America. "Exile" imagines points of contact and displacement for an East Indian writer who has left the Caribbean for England. "Air" hauntingly inscribes the unrecoverable traces of the Carib and Arawak Indians in Caribbean history.

In *Another Life* (1973), Walcott's first long poem, he portrays his artistic development, his interest in painting and the visual arts, and his place as an artist in and of the Caribbean and the New World. He evokes Odysseus in the title poem in *Sea Grapes* (1976) as a figure who represents his own condition as a "sea-wanderer" navigating complex personal and public demands. "Party Night at the Hilton" and "Parades, Parades" express contempt for the unfulfilled promises of postindependence Caribbean politicians, while "Sainte Lucie" celebrates the people, landscape, sounds, spirituality, earthiness, and beauty of Walcott's native island. Though relatively short, *The Star-Apple Kingdom* (1979) contains some of Walcott's most powerful poetry. "The Schooner Flight" and the title poem ruminate on the history and current sociopolitical climate of the Caribbean and touch on the Middle Passage, racial and cultural difference in the region, and the quest for a freedom uncorrupted by power. Reflecting his increasingly international life, Walcott infuses *The Fortunate Traveller* (1981) and *Midsummer* (1984) with wide geographical and cultural references. "North and South" (in *The Fortunate Traveller*) shows Walcott as an exile at the end of colonialism in a period increasingly marked by displacement. Although Walcott divides *The Arkansas Testament* (1987) into sections entitled "Here" (the Caribbean) and "Elsewhere," his thoroughly international career challenges the significance of such distinctions. For example, "The Light of the World" finds the poet returning to his native St. Lucia only to stay in a hotel "full of transients like myself."

Omeros (1990), Walcott's longest poem, is his most acclaimed and critically studied work. Its expansive narrative addresses the way all people of the Caribbean, uprooted and transplanted, must make themselves at home in a region marked by the coexistence of cultural differences and unities. *The Bounty* (1997), which begins with an elegy for Walcott's mother and contains a brilliant elegy for Russian poet Joseph Brodsky, finds Walcott in France, Italy, Spain, and St. Lucia, preoccupied with mortality. He returns to his artistic development and his relationship to the Caribbean in his third long poem, *Tiepolo's Hound* (2000), as he reflects on the circumstances under which the painter Camille Pissarro, a

Jew of Portuguese descent born in St. Thomas, pursued his artistic vocation in France.

Walcott has devoted much of his career to writing and directing plays and to leading the Trinidad Theatre Workshop. Throughout his plays, he mixes French patois with standard and Creole English to indicate class, color, and community status. This varied use of language expresses his vision of a Caribbean united within cultural diversity. *Drums and Colours* (1961), commissioned for the 1958 opening of the First Federal Parliament of the West Indies, stages a historical pageant stretching from European conquest to the mid-nineteenth century and features historical figures, everyday characters, and music, song, and dance. *Dream on Monkey Mountain and Other Plays* (1970) addresses the insidious effects of the colonial obsession with race and the quest for origins. Rejecting white supremacy, the play shows Africa as a potent but illusory source of strength and hope for the descendents of slaves in the Caribbean. Both *Remembrance and Pantomime* (1980) and *The Last Carnival* (1986) refer to Trinidad's Black Power movement. *Remembrance and Pantomime* features a man whose humanist values earn him mockery as a "white nigger man" (8). *The Last Carnival* addresses the declining fortunes of a French Creole family in contemporary Trinidad. *The Odyssey: A Stage Version* (1993) is Walcott's condensed adaptation of the Homeric epic.

Three of Walcott's essays, collected in *What the Twilight Says* (1998), stand out for his penetrating comments about Caribbean culture, the artist in Caribbean society, and his position as a leading artist in the region. In the title essay, which originally prefaced *Dream on Monkey Mountain and Other Plays*, Walcott proclaims himself a "mongrel" (9) and states that "the forging of a language" (15) has delivered the West Indian writer from servitude; "The Muse of History" (1974) contains Walcott's pronouncement that "maturity is the assimilation of the features of every ancestor" (36); and "The Antilles: Fragments of Epic Memory" (1992) is his memorably eloquent Nobel lecture, in which he remarks that "Antillean art is [the] restoration of our shattered histories . . . our archipelago becoming a synonym for pieces broken off from the original continent" (69).

SURVEY OF CRITICISM

Robert D. Hamner (1993) brings his formidable knowledge of Walcott's work to bear in his compact, comprehensive, solid study of the poetry and plays. For Hamner, Walcott is a literary humanist who concentrates on the local, specific context of the Caribbean as a way to express universal values. Hamner (1997) contradicts Walcott's own description of *Omeros* and argues that the long poem constitutes a new epic form suitable to the experiences of Caribbean peoples. Bruce King's thorough biography (2000) offers valuable insights into the early British influences on Walcott's poetry, provides an astonishing amount of information about the writing and production of many of Walcott's plays, and situates Walcott in his Caribbean, North American, and European contexts. He plays down the political content of Walcott's work and emphasizes his place as a writer sharing a Commonwealth sensibility of literary universality. In her study of Walcott's ideology and art, Paula Burnett (2000) argues for a politically engaged writer who actively decenters European cultural and social hegemony. For criticism of Walcott's poetry, plays, and essays, see Stewart Brown (1991), who recognizes that Walcott's work belongs to an "International Hyperculture" (7), but directs attention to his Caribbean social and cultural context.

SELECTED BIBLIOGRAPHY

Works by Walcott

25 Poems. Port of Spain, Trinidad, privately printed, 1948; Bridgetown, Barbados: Advocate, 1949.

Drums and Colours. Caribbean Quarterly 7, no. 1–2 (1961): 1–104.

In a Green Night: Poems 1948–1960. London: Jonathan Cape, 1962.

Selected Poems. New York: Farrar, Straus, 1964.

The Castaway, and Other Poems. London: Jonathan Cape, 1965.

The Gulf, and Other Poems. London: Jonathan Cape, 1969.

Dream on Monkey Mountain and Other Plays. (Includes *The Sea at Dauphin; Ti-Jean and His Brothers; Malcochon, or the Six in the Rain; Dream on Monkey Mountain*). New York: Farrar, Straus and Giroux, 1970.

Another Life. New York: Farrar, Straus and Giroux, 1973.

Sea Grapes. London: Jonathan Cape; and New York: Farrar, Straus and Giroux, 1976.

The Star-Apple Kingdom. New York: Farrar, Straus and Giroux, 1979.

Remembrance. Remembrance and Pantomime: Two Plays. New York: Farrar, Straus and Giroux, 1980.

The Fortunate Traveller. New York: Farrar, Straus and Giroux, 1981.

Midsummer. New York: Farrar, Straus and Giroux, 1984.

Three Plays. (Includes *The Last Carnival; Beef, No Chicken; A Branch of the Blue Nile.*) New York: Farrar, Straus and Giroux, 1986.

The Arkansas Testament. New York: Farrar, Straus and Giroux, 1987.

Omeros. New York: Farrar, Straus and Giroux, 1990.

The Odyssey: A Stage Version. New York: Farrar, Straus and Giroux, 1993.

The Bounty. New York: Farrar, Straus and Giroux, 1997.

What the Twilight Says: Essays. New York: Farrar, Straus and Giroux, 1998.

Tiepolo's Hound. New York: Farrar, Straus and Giroux, 2000.

Selected Studies of Walcott

Baer, William, ed. *Conversations with Derek Walcott.* Jackson: University Press of Mississippi, 1996.

Breslin, Paul. *Nobody's Nation. Reading Derek Walcott.* Chicago: The University of Chicago Press, 2002.

Brown, Stewart, ed. *The Art of Derek Walcott.* Bridgend, Mid Glamorgan, Wales: Seren Books, 1991.

Burnett, Paula. *Derek Walcott: Politics and Poetics.* Gainesville: University Press of Florida, 2000.

Davis, Gregson, ed. *The Poetics of Derek Walcott: Intertextual Perspectives.* Special issue. *South Atlantic Quarterly* 96, no. 2 (1997): 227–380.

Hamner, Robert D. *Derek Walcott* (1981). Updated edition, New York: Twayne Publishers, 1993.

———. *Epic of the Dispossessed: Derek Walcott's "Omeros."* Columbia: University of Missouri Press, 1997.

King, Bruce. *Derek Walcott and West Indian Drama: "Not Only a Playwright but a Company," The Trinidad Theatre Workshop 1959–1993.* Oxford: Clarendon Press, 1995; New York: Oxford University Press, 1995.

———. *Derek Walcott: A Caribbean Life.* Oxford and New York: Oxford University Press, 2000.

WANG MENG
(1934–)

M. Cristina Pisciotta

BIOGRAPHY

Named minister of culture in 1986 (and dismissed in 1989 after the
Tiananmen events), Wang Meng has represented both the political-
administrative and the literary career modes at his country's highest level.
As a writer and the foremost representative of the so-called literature of
protest, he has personally paid the price of his courage in denouncing
what was failing to work in his society. Labeled "right-wing" in 1957 for
his blunt and direct criticism of the Communist bureaucracy (Q*ingnian
wansui*, 1953, in *Wang Meng chuanji* and *Zuzhibu xinlaide qingnianren*,
1956, in *Wang Meng xiaoshuo baogao wenxue xuan*), Wang Meng began
with stories in the dry style of reportage fiction, marked by brutal frank-
ness and caustic humor. In the 1960s, his style changed little by little,
taking on a softer and more comprehensive tone, but the critics still bela-
bored him, now branding him as an "esthete" because of the excessive
elegance of his strongly Westernized style. In contrast to the May 4th
Generation, so called from the profound cultural renovation identified
with the movement of May 4, 1919—which took form in Europe, America, and Japan and thus was strongly and directly influenced by Western
culture—the generation of Wang Meng, experiencing the tragic and
agonizing period of the Cultural Revolution, lacked the possibility of
studying or traveling abroad until the 1980s. Thus their knowledge of
Western literature is more indirect and, moreover, has been opposed by
the authorities who tend to give preference to national forms and to
reject foreign cultural elements. As a result of harsh criticisms, Wang
Meng in 1963 was exiled for years to the frontiers of Xinjiang, where, out

of interest in the local culture, he learned Uighur and, beginning in 1973, worked in Urumchi as a translator of Uighur literature. After having been a member of the Communist Party at the age of 14, he reentered it as a member of the Central Committee after his rehabilitation in 1978 and from there began his political and literary ascent.

Viscerally attached to the party despite the years of reeducation, Wang Meng insists on the one hand on freedom as the "condition and sister of literary creation" ("Guanyu yishiliu de tongxin," in *Wang Meng chuanji*, 124) and, on the other, on the responsibility that this freedom continues to impose on writers. Deeply versed in Anglo-American literature, he translates and disseminates in China the critics and writers who were occupied in the 1950s and 1960s with the stream of consciousness technique—the theories of Melvin Friedman, Robert Scholes, Seymour Chatman, Lawrence E. Bowling, Robert Humphrey, and Dorrit Cohn, and the works of Henry James, William Faulkner, James Joyce, and Virginia Woolf. All of the Chinese critics see in Wang Meng the exemplar and introducer of the "stream of consciousness narrative" (*yishiliu xiaoshuo*), which, without doubt, is one of the most innovative aspects of the new modernist literature (*xiandaipai wenxue*), born in China with the fall of the Gang of Four (1976). Wang was inspired by the American stream of consciousness literature not only in terms of theory and technique, but also in those of terminology. His linguistic experimentation, his new descriptive techniques, his creation of a different conception of literature are seen in China as fundamental to the overcoming of the old cultural stereotypes.

The greater part of Wang's writings date from the period 1978–84. The four volumes of *Selected Works of Wang Meng* (1989) include, in addition to the essays in literary criticism, a great number of stories (among the most significant, *The Bolshevik Salute—Buli, The Eyes of Night—Yede yan, The North Wind—Fengzheng piaodai, The Butterfly—Hudie, The Voice of Spring—Chen zhi sheng, The Dream of the Sea—Haide meng*); novels (for example, *Metamorphoses—Huodongbian renxing, Two Aspects Difficult to Reconcile—Xiang jian shi nan*), and condensed narratives, a traditional genre dear to the writers of the empire.

During the 1980s, Wang finally made a series of trips abroad, to Germany, America, Mexico, and the Soviet Union, which became ever more frequent in the 1990s. His works were published in translation all over the world, and he was awarded various literary prizes, for example the Mondello Prize in 1987. Vice president of the Association of Chinese Writers and editor in chief of the two most prestigious Chinese literary reviews (*Chinese Pen, Renmin wenxue*), Wang Meng is interested in analyzing the "complexity of life" (*Selected Works of Wang Meng* 1, 378), the contrast between Western and Oriental culture, and the transformation of the individual in modern China, a process rich in advantages but also in painful losses. Beyond his sarcastic humor, which often overflows into satire, his style is characterized by impeccable logic and precise metaphors; one is struck by the force of his reflection and the acuteness of his thought.

MAJOR MULTICULTURAL THEMES

The cultural liberalization of the post-Mao era involves not only the choice of themes but also, and more significantly, the stylistic and structural form. Through the new narrative techniques, the authors are actually trying to get away from the rigid perspective of the literature of the Cultural Revolution. They emphasize the complexity, the duality, and illogicality of human existence, which had hitherto been perceived in too simplistic and one-sided a manner. The description of society is no longer based on external observation but arises from within, from the subjective perceptions of its protagonists. In the new narrative structures, causal relationships, chronological, and spatial order are no longer respected; the point of view is constantly changing hand in hand with the sensations of the characters. Finally, the language, too, is profoundly changed in line with the transformation of the narrative structure, frequently becoming metaphoric, symbolic, and abstract. Technical experimentation is the dominant feature of Chinese modernism, which is expressed above all in the form of poetry, the theater, and the stream of consciousness narrative. In the creation of the modernist literature of the 1980s, the writers have very few Chinese models to refer to, and consequently look to the Western modernist works of the twentieth century, which use the stream of consciousness techniques—internal monologue, absence of plot and narrative progression, emphasis on individual psychology, and lack of any educational social message.

Wang Meng, as a profound connoisseur and translator of Anglo-American literature, is the undisputed protagonist of this stylistic renewal of Chinese fiction, based upon a deep-rooted synthesis of the two cultures. Translations of foreign modernist literature reached China beginning in 1979–80, but commenced to be really diffused between 1980 and 1983, primarily among young students and intellectuals, who appear completely captivated by this new literary experience. Thus, in the cultural ferment of those years, the publication of six stories by Wang Meng gave rise to a broad debate on the use of the stream of consciousness descriptive technique, and, in general, on the introduction of Western narrative techniques in Chinese literary experimentation of this new period. This very widespread debate was not only the subject of a whole series of articles appearing in the most broadly representative press, but also of many symposia. In the following years, from 1981 to 1988, the strong interest of the press was matched by an outburst of compilations of all of Wang Meng's narrative fiction, his critical articles and essays in literary theory, as well as his translations of Anglo-American literature.

To characterize his style, Wang Meng also borrows the Western terms and expressions utilized in this type of fiction. Illustrating the innovative elements with respect to both the preceding and the contemporary literary production, he speaks in fact of the employment of a free association of ideas (*ziyou lianxiang*), internal monologue (*neixing dubai*), psychological structure of the narrative (*xiuli jiegou*), and technique of symbolic metaphor (*xiangzheng yinyu*).

After 40 years of narrative in which the individual is always considered in his social role, Wang Meng transfers attention to his or her internal subjectivity. As in the current of the stream of consciousness of Anglo-American literature that he himself follows, it is psychological time that counts; one follows an extremely rapid narrative pace in which time and space are being continuously extended. It is, in the main, a liberation of the consciousness of the individual, the effort to describe his subjective sensations, his psychic activity, to reduce as much as possible the distance between the spiritual world of the personages and real life. The language, in this experimentation of Wang Meng, constitutes the direct realization of his artistic conception: the inversion of metaphors, the changes of subjects, the individualistic use of punctuation, and the absence of quotation marks in direct discourse. If it is true that the multicultural synthesis is represented in Wang Meng primarily in formal and structural experimentation, it is equally true that the themes of his works are also concentrated on the problem of the loss of identity of the individual in modern China, his or her slow transformation and continuing suspension between the two sharply contrasting cultures, the Western and the Oriental, provoking a progressive and inevitable alienation. As a most significant example, one could take the story of the romance *Xiang jian shi nan* (1982), in which a Chinese-American woman professor is torn between two civilizations, the antique charm of Beijing and the modern efficiency of the American metropolises, in an interior conflict which consumes her. Wang Meng concentrates upon her two separate identities that do not succeed in coexisting but provoke an ever-increasing alienation. The principal difficulty consists precisely in the encounter of the two personalities and in coming to know them in depth.

SURVEY OF CRITICISM

Fang Shunjing (1980) reviews the entire development of Wang Meng's narrative fiction, illustrating the use of the distinctive techniques of Western modernism and the American stream of consciousness narrative. He demonstrates with precise examples how Wang Meng has applied them not mechanically and blindly but in a critical manner.

Song Dan (1988) and Song Yaoliang (1986), by contrast, concentrate at length on the problem of the difference between the Anglo-American narrative of this type and the Chinese example of Wang Meng. The special distinction of the latter consists in the fact that there is no trace of decadence or nihilism in his stories; according to both Song Dan and Song Yaoliang, he pays particular attention to the inseparable links between subjectivity and objectivity, consciousness and existence, and to the figurative character of the consciousness of the characters. Deepening the contrast is the fact that Wang Meng purposefully controls the spontaneity, the autonomy, the disordered activity of his characters' consciousness, consistently favoring the content of the rational level over that of the emotional level. The fiction of Wang Meng is further distinguished by the perceptible presence of the author, who intervenes directly with his comments, in contrast to the normal procedure.

Edward Gunn (1991) studies the innovative role of Wang Meng in the new Chinese prose, his capacity for assimilating diverse stylistic techniques, and the characteristics of his strongly Westernizing language. D. E. Pollard (1985) and Tay William (1984) analyze the debates that accompanied the introduction of stream of consciousness in China. Finally, He Xilai (1982) closely examines the narrative structure of some of Wang Meng's works and the themes he treats.

SELECTED BIBLIOGRAPHY

Works by Wang

"Guanyu yishiliu de tongxin" (1980). In *Wang Meng chuanji*, 122–27. Guizhou: Renmin chubanshe, 1984.
Wang Meng xiaoshuo baogao wenxue xuan. Beijing: Beijing chubanshe, 1981.
Le papillon: Nouvelles. Beijing: Littérature chinoise, 1982.
Wang Meng chuanji. Guizhou: Renmin chubanshe, 1984.
Selected Works of Wang Meng. Trans. Denis C. Mair. Beijing: Foreign Languages Press, 1989.
Alienation. Trans. Nancy T. Lin and Tong Qi Lin. Hong Kong: Hong Kong Joint Publishing Co., 1993.

Selected Studies of Wang

Duke, Michael S. *Blooming and Contending: Chinese Literature in the Post-Mao Era.* Bloomington: Indiana University Press, 1985.
Fang Shunjing. "Chuangzao xinde yishu shijie—Shilun Wang Meng jinnianlaide yishu tansuo." *Wenyi pinglun* 8 (1980): 33–37.
Gunn, Edward. *Rewriting Chinese: Style and Innovation in Twentieth-Century Chinese Prose.* Stanford: Stanford University Press, 1991.
Hagenaar, Elly. *Stream of Consciousness and Free Indirect Discourse in Modern Chinese Literature.* Leiden: Centre of Non-Western Studies, Leiden University, 1992.
He Xilai. "Xinglingde bodong yu qingtu—Lun Wang Meng de chuangzuo." *Xin wenxue congshu* 2 (1982): 145–70.
Kinkley, Jeffrey C., ed. *After Mao: Chinese Literature and Society, 1978–81.* Cambridge, Mass.: Council on East Asian Studies, Harvard University, 1985.

Lan Tianyu, "Wang meng jinzuo yixie zhide zhuyide wenti." *Wenxue pinglun* 1 (1982): 74–81.

Pollard, D. E. "The Controversy over Modernism, 1979–1984." *China Quarterly* 104 (1985): 641–56.

Song Dan. "Lun xinshiqi xiandaipai xiaoshuode zhongguohua taishi." *Yishu Guangjiao* 1 (1988): 45–49.

Song Yaoliang. "Yishiliu wenxue dongfanghua guocheng." *Wenxue pinglun* 1 (1986): 33–40.

William, Tay. "Wang Meng, Stream of Consciousness, and the Controversy over Modernism." *Modern Chinese Literature* 1, no. 1 (1984): 7–24.

Yan Gang. "Xiaoshuo chuxian xin shoufa—Du Wang Meng jinzuo." *Beijing shiyuan xuebao* 4 (1980): 189–99.

Zhang Zhong. "Wang Mengde xin tansuo—Tan *Hudie,* deng liu pan xiaoshuo biaoxian shoufade tedian." *Guangmin ribao* (September 28, 1980): 4.

ELIE WIESEL
(1928–)

Michèle Ratsaby

BIOGRAPHY

The only son among the four children of a close-knit Jewish Hassidic family, Elie Wiesel was born in Sighet, then part of Hungary and now belonging to Romania. He studied the Torah and the Talmud, and was eager to learn the mysteries of Kabbalah. Both his father, a leader in the Jewish community of Sighet, and his mother, daughter of a renowned rabbi, encouraged him to spend more time on secular studies and learning Hungarian and modern Hebrew.

In 1944 the town's Jews were moved to the concentration camps in Poland. His mother and younger sister were killed in Auschwitz. Wiesel, then 15, and his father, were sent to Buchenwald, where the father died of exhaustion. He himself survived, was liberated, and was sent to France in April 1945, where an agency placed him in an orphanage for Jewish children. His two older sisters also survived and found him in Paris.

Having learned French, the multilingual Wiesel began to study literature, philosophy, and psychology at the Sorbonne in 1948. He soon became involved in journalism, writing in French for the French Jewish newspaper *L'Arche* and in Hebrew for the Israeli newspaper *Yedioth Ahronoth*. His journalistic work now became his main occupation. As *Yedioth Ahronoth*'s correspondent in Paris, he traveled to Israel, the Far East and, in 1956, New York.

At first, Wiesel was unwilling and unable to speak or write about the concentration camp horrors, but while writing for *L'Arche* he met the French writer and Nobel laureate François Mauriac who persuaded him to change his mind. This resulted in his first book, *La nuit* (1958). The original manuscript of this work, written in Yiddish (*Un di Velt hot geshvign*, 1956), was 864 pages long; two years later it appeared in the 127-page French version, a terrifying biographical account of a Nazi death camp by a young Jewish boy who witnessed the death of his family, as well as the loss of both his innocence and his faith. *La nuit* has been translated into 25 languages.

Since then, Wiesel has assumed the role of a witness of the Holocaust and, as a survivor, a relentless messenger and teacher of this worst of all evils : "The fear of forgetting. . . . Gather the names, the faces, the tears. If, by a miracle, you come out of it alive, try to reveal everything, omitting nothing. Such was the oath we had all taken" (Elie Wiesel, quoted in Rosenfeld and Greenberg, ed. *Confronting the Holocaust. The Impact of Elie Wiesel*, 201). In his fictional works, in his memoirs and essays, he sees it as his duty to address everyone's conscience, using his terrible experiences to fight "man's inhumanity toward man" (Elie Wiesel, "Words from a Witness," 42), for "to remain silent and indifferent is the greatest sin of all" (Elie Wiesel, *Souls on Fire. Portraits and Legends of Hasidic Masters*, 97).

Assigned to New York in 1956 to cover the activities of the United Nations, Wiesel suffered an automobile accident that confined him to a wheelchair for a year. He decided to make his home in the United States, and has since been living in New York with his wife Marion, also a survivor of the concentration camps, who collaborates with him by translating his work into English. In 1976 he became Andrew Mellon Professor of Humanities at Boston University. For his literary and human rights activities, he has received numerous awards, including the Presidential Medal of Freedom, the United States' Congressional Gold Medal, and the Medal of Liberty. He was awarded the Nobel Prize for Peace in 1986 for his efforts to fight indifference to human suffering all over the world. Shortly afterwards, he established the Elie Wiesel Foundation for Humanity, whose mission, based on the memory of the Holocaust, is to advance the cause of human rights.

MAJOR MULTICULTURAL THEMES

Whenever he is asked what it means to be a writer, Elie Wiesel responds that it means to become a universal messenger, creating hope and fighting against injustice and suffering. The art of the witness is to testify by telling stories. In true Hassidic fashion, most of his novels take place before or after the events of the Holocaust and deal with various aspects of his experiences. They evolve from bitter despair to religious belief and hope, *in spite* of what humans are able to do to humans. *L'aube* (1960) is the tale of a Holocaust survivor who plans to kill the enemies of the new state of Israel. In *La ville de la chance* (1962), Wiesel deals with the silence of the non-Jewish population in the face of the Holocaust, and with returning to his hometown after the war. *Le mendiant de*

Jérusalem, récit (1968) is about the six-day Arab-Israeli war. *Le serment de Kolvillag* (1973) tells about an accusation of ritual murder in a small Carpathian town, while *Le cinquième fils: Roman* (1983) analyses the forces of good and evil in humans. *Le crépuscule, au loin: Roman* (1987) questions the sanity of the Nazis, who could combine European culture with horrible crimes against humanity.

Since the 1960s, Wiesel has written on behalf of oppressed people in the Soviet Union, Africa, Vietnam, Biafra, and Bangladesh. He has also defended the Nicaraguan Miskito Indians, Argentina's *desaparecidos*, Cambodian refugees, the Kurds, victims of famine in Africa, and victims of apartheid in South Africa. After learning about the persecution of Soviet Jews in the USSR, Wiesel became politically involved, traveled to the Soviet Union in 1965, and later published his study, *Les Juifs du silence* (1966). In 1992 he was invited by the presidents of Bosnia and Serbia to visit the war-stricken zones of former Yugoslavia.

In the declaration of the aims of the Elie Wiesel Foundation for Humanity, the author writes: "When human lives are endangered, when human dignity is in jeopardy, national borders and sensivities become irrelevant. Whenever men or women are persecuted because of their race, religion or political views, that place must become the center of the Universe" (Elie Wiesel Foundation for Humanity, available at eliewieselfoundation.org/, home page).

SURVEY OF CRITICISM

Vincent Engel (1989) analyzes the evolution of Wiesel's deep religious faith in view of the supreme evil encountered in the concentration camps. Art and writing are for him the best means of fighting against "a meaningless world and the silence of God" (51). For Engel, Wiesel's writings are one long and painful trial of God, who is accused of letting his people be slaughtered without reason. Therefore madness—God's and humans' madness—is an essential element of Wiesel's writings. Fifty years after the Holocaust, in a conversation with Wiesel, Jorge Semprun (1995) notes the complex feelings encountered by the survivors of deportation. They were the living, embarrassing proof of what humanity is capable of (14) and were seldom encouraged to tell their stories. In reality, the 1945 victory over the fascist regimes never was complete and it did not stop evil, racial hatred, and fanaticism in the world (25). Alan Rosen (1998) points out that Wiesel, having survived and turned his survival into a mission of peace, is one of the most important people of the twentieth century (10). Rosen stresses the almost biblical nature of Wiesel's memoirs, where "without forgiving the unforgivable, excusing the unexcusable, he searches for peace" (54).

In a parallel with Sophocles's *Oedipus*, John Silber (1998) develops the element of fate in Wiesel's work and his wonder at the complexity and mystery of human existence. He notes that, contemplating Auschwitz, Wiesel writes : "It forces us to question everything, the very foundations of culture, of faith, of science. Educated men and women, gifted, refined lovers of literature, music and art were able to commit those most hideous crimes. How can we explain such an abdication of culture and morality?. . . . For me the mystery of Auschwitz remains intact" (quoted in Silber, 200). Like Sophocles, Wiesel affirms the complexity of humanity both in its grandeur and in its depravity.

SELECTED BIBLIOGRAPHY

Works by Wiesel

La nuit (1958). [*Night*. Trans. Stella Rodway. New York: Hill and Wang, 1960.]

L'aube (1960). [*Dawn*. Trans. Frances Frenaye. New York: Hill and Wang, 1961.]

La ville de la chance (1962). [*The Town Beyond the Wall*. Trans. Stephen Becker. New York: Avon, 1964.]

Les Juifs du silence (1966). [*The Jews of Silence: A Personal Report on Soviet Jewry*. Trans. and afterword Neal Kozodoy. New York: Holt, Rinehart and Winston, 1966.]

"Words from a Witness." *Conservative Judaism* 21 (Spring 1967): 40–53.

Le Mendiant de Jérusalem, récit (1968). [*A Beggar in Jerusalem: A Novel*. Trans. Lily Edelman and Elie Wiesel. New York: Random House, 1970.]

"To remain Human in face of Inhumanity." *The Jewish Digest* 17 (September 1972): 37–42.

Souls on Fire. Portraits and Legends of Hasidic Masters. Trans. from the French Marion Wiesel. New York: Random House, 1972.

Le serment de Kolvillag (1973). [*The Oath*. Trans. Marion Wiesel. New York: Random House, 1973.]

Le cinquième fils: Roman (1983). [*The Fifth Son: A Novel*. Trans. Marion Wiesel. New York: Summit Books, 1985.]

Le crépuscule, au loin: Roman (1987). [*Twilight*. Trans. Marion Wiesel. New York: Summit Books, 1988.]

From the Kingdom of Memory: Reminiscences. New York: Summit, 1990.

Silences et mémoire d'hommes: Essais, histoires, dialogues. (1989). [*Sages and Dreamers: Biblical, Talmudic, and Hasidic Portraits and Legends*. New York: Summit, 1991.]

Tous les fleuves vont à la mer (1994). [*All Rivers Run to the Sea. Memoirs*. New York: Knopf, 1995.]

Et la mer n'est pas remplie (1999). [*And the Sea is Never Full: Memoirs, 1969-*. Trans. Marion Wiesel. New York: Knopf, 1999.]

Selected Studies of Wiesel

Cohen, Brigitte-Fanny. *Elie Wiesel*. Lyons: La Manufacture, 1987.

Engel, Vincent. *Fou de Dieu ou Dieu des Fous: l'oeuvre tragique d'Elie Wiesel*. Brussels: De Boeck, 1989.

Patterson, David. *In Dialogue and Dilemma with Elie Wiesel.* Wakefield, N.H.: Longwood Academic, 1991.

Rosen, Alan, ed. *Celebrating Elie Wiesel: Stories, Essays, Reflections.* Notre Dame, Ind.: University of Notre Dame Press, 1998.

Rosenfeld, Alvin H., and Irving Greenberg, ed. *Confronting the Holocaust. The Impact of Elie Wiesel.* Bloomington: Indiana University Press, 1978.

Semprun, Jorge. *Se taire est impossible.* Paris: Arte, 1995.

Sibelman, Simon P. *Silence in the Novels of Elie Wiesel.* New York: St. Martin's Press, 1995.

Silber, John. "From Thebes to Auschwitz: Moral Responsibility in Sophocles and Wiesel." In *Celebrating Elie Wiesel: Stories, Essays, Reflections.* Ed. Alan Rosen, 173–202. Notre Dame, Ind.: University of Notre Dame Press, 1998.

YI MUNYŎL
(1948–)

Maurizio Riotto

BIOGRAPHY

Yi Munyŏl, the well-known contemporary Korean novelist, is believed to have been born in the village of Yŏngyang in the North Kyŏngsang province of South Korea, although other sources state that he was born in Seoul. At the age of three, in the middle of the Korean War, he lost his father, who fled to communist North Korea and thus permanently divided his family. Yi Munyŏl consequently grew up not only as practically an orphan, but also under strict surveillance by the South Korean anticommunist police. Habitually enveloped in a cloak of suspicion, he was compelled as a youth to move frequently and prevented from following a regular course of study, so that his intellectual formation necessarily became that of an autodidact. It was undoubtedly his difficult youth that forged Yi Munyŏl's characteristics as a man and writer, leading him to the unique style and pessimistic view of reality that distinguish him among contemporary Korean fiction writers.

After a rather modest debut at the end of the 1970s, the novelist's embarkation in the following decade on an irresistible ascent was marked by prestigious literary prizes—such as the Yi Sang Prize, awarded him in 1987 for the novel *Uridŭr-ŭi ilgŭrŏjin yŏngung*, which contributed to making him the country's most-read author. As one of the writers most translated abroad, he continued to hold first place on the South Korean best-seller lists despite the opposition of some critics and of the student movement which at times burst into open and clamorous objection to him and his works.

Admittedly a "troublesome" writer, known for a most accurate and erudite vocabulary but also for an extremely disenchanted view of the world, Yi Munyŏl has made the plots of his novels into real, tragic human destinies that are repellent to many more rightly thinking readers. Among his most significant novels, in addition to *Uridŭr-ŭi ilgŭrŏjin yŏngung*, mention may be made of *Saram-ŭi adŭl* (1979), *Kŭde tasi-nŭn kohyang-e kaji mothari* (1980), *Chŏlmŭn nar-ŭi ch'osang* (1981), *Kŭmsijo* (1982), *Hwang je-rŭl wihayŏ* (1982), *Yŏngung sidae* (1984), and *Siin* (1991).

MAJOR MULTICULTURAL THEMES

The qualities that most strike the admirer of Yi Munyŏl are his nihilism and constructive pessimism, often misrepresented by his detractors as "whatever-ism" and defeatism. In reality, the writer's entire body of work is marked by a quest for freedom in the most absolute sense, a value which, to his mind, cannot and must not be limited either by any spatial or temporal bounds or by any ideological, political, or religious obstacles. From this context emerges one of the most controversial points in the work of Yi Munyŏl, his total distrust of human institutions, which to him are seen, from an absolutely apolitical standpoint, not as a civic instrument for the advancement of humanity but as an inexorable and pitiless machine against which humanity needs to defend itself. In *Uridŭr-ŭi ilgŭrŏjin yŏngung*, the analysis of the relationship between the masses and the holders of power leads to the bitter conclusion that the people, subordinating everything else to the supreme objective of survival, always end by taking the stronger side and thus obstructing the rare individual who has the will, though not the authority, to change the course of events.

The novel that best reflects the author's critical vision in regard to constituted authority is certainly *Siin*. Taking its departure from the life of the nineteenth-century poet Kim Sakkat—a real person, who, though possessing exceptional ability and an illustrious lineage, is sidelined and rejected by society for a crime committed by his grandfather—the writer examines the corrupt instruments by which the state oppresses and even suppresses its own citizens. As might be expected, Yi Munyŏl's own personal story is merged with that of the protagonist; the fatherless childhood and the systematic persecution for an uncommitted offense are recollections too painful to be ignored. Self-realization, for Yi Munyŏl, is possible only at an intimate and personal level, without the help of third parties and, above all, without the help of society. Power, he holds, corrupts the human being just as the human being corrupts the structures of power, irrespective of what orientation, faith, or doctrine inspires him or her. Within the framework of this extremely pessimistic view of life, Yi Munyŏl stigmatizes even the aggregative nature of the human being as an Aristotelian "political animal" (*zòon politikòn*). For him, the "plague" that for other writers like Thucydides, Giovanni Boccaccio, Daniel Defoe, and Albert Camus is symbolically bound up with particular historical circumstances (e.g., for Thucydides, with Athenian imperialism; for Camus, with Nazism), is part and parcel of history itself, and thus of human society.

It is understandable that such a view of reality, perhaps acceptable to experienced Western readers accustomed to confronting the defects even of democracies, should by contrast arouse a part of the Korean public to indignation and attacks against what they saw as vulgar "whatever-ism." Koreans were for a long time deprived of their fundamental rights by dictatorial regimes, and the conduct of politics in a democratic society came to be looked upon as a sort of panacea capable of rescuing the entire community. Now that democracy has been laboriously achieved, the distrust of institutions as a matter of principle is understandably viewed by a section of the Korean public as extremely negative and censurable.

Considering the tributes paid him by Western critics, it is natural that Yi Munyŏl should be considered a multicultural writer even if his sources of inspiration are somewhat problematical. Through his own efforts he acquired a vast erudition that has embraced different camps and has developed in very heterogeneous directions. In this respect, Yi Munyŏl has much in common with existentialism and with Sartre. The typical existentialist concept of human freedom linked to one's choices (understood in the sense that any choice irremediably conditions human liberty) is well adapted to the idea of liberty that emerges from Yi Munyŏl's pages. In *Siin*, this idea is exploited to the maximum, with the assertion that the essence of poetry resides not so much in a "creation" (thus an act of will and a definite choice), as simply in rediscovering what is already there but has been obscured by obstacles and conditions generated by society and culture, placed before the eyes of humans, and causing them to see not the reality but only its image. Hence the necessity of freeing oneself from the rules in order to achieve self-realization. When every link with the structured world of humans shall have been broken, Yi Munyŏl implies, the individual will be able to return to his or her primordial essence, that very "liberty" that will make him or her at one with the world and with nature.

SELECTED BIBLIOGRAPHY

Works by Yi

Saram-ŭi adŭl. Seoul: Minŭmsa, 1979.

Kŭdae tasi-nŭn kohyang-e kaji mothari. Seoul: Minŭmsa, 1980.

Chŏlmun nar-ŭi ch'osang. Seoul: Minŭmsa, 1981.

Hwangje-rŭl wihayŏ. Seoul: Tonggwang, 1982. [*Hail to the Emperor!* Trans. Sol Sun-bong. Seoul: Si-sa-yong-o-sa and Arch Cape, Oregon: Pace International Research, 1986.]

Kŭmsijo. Seoul: Tongsŏ munhwasa, 1982. [*The Golden Phoenix*. Trans. Suh Ji-moon (with the editorial assistance of Daisy Lee Yang). In *The Golden*

Phoenix: Seven Contemporary Korean Short Stories. Ed. Suh Ji-moon, 11–45. London: Lynne Rienner, 1998.]

Yŏngung sidae (first published serially in the review *Segye-ŭi munhak* beginning summer 1983). Seoul: Minŭmsa, 1984.

Uridŭr-ŭi ilgŭrŏjin yŏngung (first published in summer 1987 issue of the review *Segye-ŭi munhak*). Seoul: Munhaksasang ch'ulp'ansa, 1987. [*Our Twisted Hero.* Trans. Kevin O'Rourke. New York: Hyperion East, 2001.]

Siin. Seoul: Mirae munhak, 1991. [*The Poet.* Trans. Chung Chong-wha and Brother Anthony of Taizé. London: The Harvill Press, 1995.]

Selected Studies of Yi

Cherchi, Grazia. "Il dittatore e i camaleonti." Book supplement to *L'Unità* (April 6, 1992): 1.

Crown, Bonnie R. "Yi Munyŏl. *Our Twisted Hero.*" *World Literature Today* 76, no. 1 (Winter 2002): 138.

Kim, Subok, and Yang Ŭnch'ang, eds. "Yi Munyŏl." In *Han'guk hyŏndae sosŏl.* Ed. Subok Kim and Unch'ang Yang, 601–5. Seoul: Hallim ch'ulp'ansa, 1990.

Kwŏn, Yŏngmin. *Han'guk hyŏndae munhaksa.* Seoul: Minŭmsa, 1993.

Noiret, Gérard. "La dissidence intime." *L'Humanité* (November 3, 1992).

Velter, André. "Le poète qui se cachait du ciel." *Le Monde* (October 2, 1992).

"Yi Munyŏl." In *Who's Who in Korean Literature.* Ed. Korean Culture and Arts Foundation, 505–8. Elizabeth, N.J., and Seoul: Hollym, 1996.

"Yi Munyŏl." In *Han'guk hyŏndae munhak chagŭn sajŏn.* Various editors, 421–23. Seoul: Karam Kihoek, 2000.

MARGUERITE YOURCENAR
(1903–1987)

Marlène Barsoum

BIOGRAPHY

The prolific writer Marguerite Yourcenar is celebrated for her literary creations that gained her entry into the Académie française on March 6, 1980, making her the first woman to be elected to that august institution. Although she lived for 48 years in the United States, she remained profoundly rooted in French culture and the French language.

Yourcenar was born Marguerite de Crayencour on June 8, 1903 in Brussels to Michel de Crayencour, a French diplomat native to the region of Béthune in northern France, and a Belgian (Walloon) mother, Fernande de Cartier de Marchienne, who died at childbirth. About her heritage, Marguerite Yourcenar has expressed the following sentiments: "I am as much French as I am Flemish. . . . What is more important and more objective than these criteria of blood and language is that I am French by culture. . . . I have several cultures, just as I have several homelands. I belong to all" (*With Open Eyes: Conversations with Matthieu Galey*, trans. Arthur Goldhammer, 214). In a gesture to affirm her independence, she chose the pen name "Yourcenar," an anagram of her family name, in order to put some distance between herself and the family tradition and to set herself free from possible family fetters (*With Open Eyes*, 35).

When she was six weeks old, she and her father moved to Mont-Noir, in northern France. She was educated by teachers at home, which was not unusual at the time. She was versed in Latin, which she began to learn at the age of 10, and Greek, reading at the age of 15 Homer, Plato, and Virgil. Her knowledge of languages, including English, enabled her later to translate the poems of Constantin Cavafy in collaboration with

Constantin Dimaras, as well as Virginia Woolf's *The Waves*. But it was her father, "a man of letters of the old school, who read because he loved books" who proved to be her greatest influence (*With Open Eyes*, 9). Besides initiating her to the world of literature, her father, whom she described as *cet homme aux semelles de vent* (the man with soles of wind), who felt at home everywhere and nowhere, also introduced her to the thrill of travel (Josyane Savigneau, *Marguerite Yourcenar: l'invention d'une vie*, 400).

Nomadic and cosmopolitan, she traveled quite extensively—to France, England, Switzerland, Austria, Portugal, and especially to her symbolic land, Greece—before settling in the United States in 1939. She explained that she ended up in the United States by pure chance. She had gone for a few months to attend conferences, by the end of which France had fallen into enemy hands. She therefore decided to remain in the United States, making her residence on Mount Desert Island, off the coast of Maine, with Grace Frick, her companion and translator.

From 1949 until her death, she lived there in a house called Petite Plaisance that she considered to be her *cella del conoscimento di sé* (a cell for self-knowledge), an expression she borrowed from Saint Catherine of Siena. It was in this idyllic nineteenth-century cottage that she wrought her heroes Hadrian and Zeno. She found on that island retreat the solitude she regarded as indispensable to the practice of her art. She also started taking a greater interest in the environment. Throughout her life, she maintained an interest in ecological problems and was involved in activities that would "lay the groundwork for a cleaner, purer world to come" (*With Open Eyes*, 247).

Except for a 12-year teaching stint (1941–53) at American colleges—Hartford Junior College, Connecticut College, and Sarah Lawrence—Yourcenar was free from the worry of earning a living. This privileged situation allowed her to devote her time to writing and to seeing the world. Between the two world wars, she traveled widely in the Mediterranean countries that served as a setting for many of her works. Her wanderlust did not abate with age. After Grace Frick's death in 1979, she continued traveling with her young companion, Jerry Wilson, going as far as India, Japan, Thailand, Egypt, and Kenya. Yourcenar subscribed to the words of Zeno, the protagonist of *L'oeuvre au noir* (1968): "Who would be so besotted as to die without having made at least the round of this, his prison?" (*With Open Eyes*, 63). Marguerite Yourcenar died on December 17, 1987. Her ashes were placed in an Indian basket swathed in the white silk shawl she wore at her induction to the Académie française.

MAJOR MULTICULTURAL THEMES

In spite of the many years Yourcenar spent in the United States, her writing was untouched by American culture, with the exception of *Fleuve profond, sombre rivière* (1964, a translation of what she refers to as Negro Spirituals, accompanied by a lengthy preface outlining the history and condition of African-Americans in the United States), an essay on the American poet Hortense Flexner, and a study of the city of Hartford, Connecticut, where she lived briefly in the 1940s.

While she insulated herself from the culture of her adopted land as well as from its language, which she feared might invade her writing that was always done in French, she was open to distant cultures as borne out by her lifelong fascination with the Far East. In 1921, at the age of 18, she sent a book of her poems to Rabindranath Tagore. He replied immediately, inviting her to India. She was unable to take the trip but always wondered how her life and thinking might have changed had she done so (Savigneau, 71). The culture of Japan also gripped her imagination. When asked which woman writer she admired most, she promptly named Lady Murasaki Shikibu, author of *The Tale of Genji*. Her interest in Japan spurred her to study Japanese, which culminated in a published translation of five Nō plays in 1984. She also wrote a biographical study of Mishima Yukio entitled *Mishima, ou, La vision du vide* (1980). Her passion for Japanese as well as Chinese literature can also be attested by two short stories, "Le dernier amour du prince Genghi" and "Comment Wang-cho fut sauvé," which can be found in *Nouvelles orientales* (1938). This collection also includes a Hindu tale, "Kali décapité," as well as stories set in Greece and the Balkans.

Her study of Eastern religion (she had an affinity for Buddhism in particular) and philosophy made available to her contemplative methods which she used to create. "The writer must soak up the subject completely as a plant soaks up water, until the ideas are ready to sprout" suggested Yourcenar (*With Open Eyes*, 114). To do so, she used to strive to achieve what the Hindu sages described as a state of "attentiveness" (*With Open Eyes*, 119). This involved subduing her personality and effacing herself in order to receive her creations. These techniques made it better to hear, better to give herself over to the characters she was trying to comprehend. She envisioned the writer as a medium: "I feel like an instrument through which currents, vibrations have passed" (*With Open Eyes*, 259). It is by such a technique that Hadrian was created.

Mémoires d'Hadrien (1951) and *L'oeuvre au noir* are considered her masterpieces. By the age of 20, she had already sketched Hadrian and Zeno, the heroes of these two novels. But it was not until she settled in the calm of Petite Plaisance that she fleshed out the emperor and the physician, making them into full-fledged characters.

A visit to the Villa Adriana in Tivoli when she was 20 sparked the idea of bringing the Roman emperor back to life (*With Open Eyes*, 117). *Mémoires d'Hadrien* is the depiction of the slow ascent to power and self-mastery of "an exceptional man at a unique moment in history" (*With Open Eyes*, 73, xiv). Hadrian was both a man of letters and a man of action; he was an artist, patron of the arts, lover, and statesman. The *Mémoires d'Hadrien* exacted that Yourcenar immerse herself in the period (the second century) and learn about the Roman world.

In *L'oeuvre au noir*, she resurrects the political turmoil of Flanders during the Renaissance. She first conceived the idea of writing this work because of her interest in the histories of the families and towns in the area where she grew up. An anonymous work, *Mémoire anonymes sur les troubles des Pays-Bas*, became the basis of *L'oeuvre au noir*, just as Dio Cassius served as the foundation of the *Mémoires d'Hadrien*. She also consulted genealogical documents (*With Open Eyes*, 131). Tommaso Campanella, Giordano Bruno, and Erasmus inspired the creation of the Zeno character.

To breathe life into Zeno, she studied Renaissance medicine, magic, theology, and philosophy. *L'oeuvre au noir* is anti-institutional; this man of the cloth who also practiced medicine was against everything: the universities, the family, the monastery, the authorities, and so forth (*With Open Eyes*, 134). Here again, we have a protagonist who is both a man of action and a meditative man. Zeno chooses to make tabula rasa of all the ideas and prejudices of his century in order to see where his own thinking would lead him (Savigneau, 295).

The plots of *Denier du rêve* (1934), *Feux* (1935), and *Le coup de grâce* (1938) have diverse settings. Yourcenar wrote *Denier du rêve* when she was living in Italy. The action takes place at the time of or shortly after the assassination of the Italian Socialist leader Giacomo Matteotti. Several of the novel's characters, some of whom were based on people she knew, belonged to antifascist groups. Through them she "shared in the excitement and emotion of the moment" (*With Open Eyes*, 59). In *Feux*, she depicts characters inspired by the Bible and Greek history. While writing this story she was traveling in the Near East, which provided the backdrop for the stories (*With Open Eyes*, 70). *Le coup de grâce* is based on a true story. It evokes the Baltic Wars of 1919–21 and relates "[t]he human drama of three isolated young people set against the larger drama of war, poverty and conflicting ideologies" (*With Open Eyes*, 88).

Mon choix de vie n'est pas celui de l'Amérique contre la France. Il traduit un goût du monde dépouillé de toutes frontières (My choice of life is not that of America as opposed to France. It conveys rather a penchant for a world shorn of all frontiers), Yourcenar explained in a 1976 interview (quoted in Savigneau, 210). She lived in exile in both space and time (Savigneau, 368). This situation allowed her to develop an individualistic philosophy of life and gave her writing a timeless quality. Her wish to remain indelibly in touch with the universal led her tirelessly to try to fathom how each word and act fit into the larger scheme, into a vaster conception of the world. Her writings bear the mark of an effort to delve beneath the surface in order to grasp the truth about the human condition.

SURVEY OF CRITICISM

A wealth of studies have been written on Marguerite Yourcenar. This survey will be limited to her published conversations with Matthieu Galey (1984) and Josyane Savigneau's 1990 biography. Galey, a journalist from *L'Express*, interviewed Yourcenar in Petite Plaisance. The outcome was a book, over 250 pages in length, in which Yourcenar speaks about her childhood, her education, the craft of writing, love, her philosophy of life, her relationship to the United States, solitude, and her opinion of writers she admired.

Savigneau's magisterial biography brings Yourcenar back to life. This dense, thoroughly researched work traces the author's life through letters, interviews, critical articles, entries in agendas and diaries, and conversations with people who knew her. Savigneau succeeds not only in relating all the important events of Yourcenar's life, providing precise dates, but also conveys the larger-than-life spirit of the heroine of her book.

SELECTED BIBLIOGRAPHY

Works by Yourcenar

Denier du rêve. Paris: Bernard Grasset, 1934; revised edition, Paris: Plon, 1959.

Feux. Paris: Bernard Grasset, 1935.

Les vagues (Translation of Virginia Woolf's *The Waves*). Paris: Stock, 1937; rpt. 1974.

Nouvelles orientales. Paris: Gallimard, 1938; revised edition, 1963.

Le coup de grâce. Paris: Gallimard, 1939.

Mémoires d'Hadrien. Paris: Plon, 1951.

Fleuve profond, sombre rivière; Les "Negro Spirituals," commentaires et traductions. Paris: Gallimard, 1964.

L'oeuvre au noir. Paris: Gallimard, 1968.

Présentation critique d'Hortense Flexner, suivie d'un choix de poèmes. Trans. Marguerite Yourcenar. Paris: Gallimard, 1969.

Mishima, ou, La vision du vide. Paris: Gallimard, 1980.

Les yeux ouverts: Entretien avec Matthieu Galey. Paris: Le Centurion, 1980. [*With Open Eyes: Conversations with Matthieu Galey*. Trans. Arthur Goldhammer. Boston: Beacon Press, 1984.]

Selected Studies of Yourcenar

Savigneau, Josyane. *Marguerite Yourcenar: L'invention d'une vie*. Paris: Gallimard, 1990. [*Marguerite Yourcenar: Inventing a Life*. Trans. Joan E. Howard. Chicago: University of Chicago Press, 1993.]

Servan-Schreiber, Claude. "Marguerite Yourcenar s'explique." *Lire* (July 1976). In Josyane Savigneau, *Marguerite Yourcenar: l'invention d'une vie*, 210. Paris: Gallimard, 1990.

ALEXANDER ZINOVIEV
(1922–)

Christopher W. Lemelin

BIOGRAPHY

Alexander Alexandrovich Zinoviev was born in Pakhtino, a village in the Kostroma region of Russia, 375 miles northeast of Moscow. He received his secondary education in Moscow and entered the department of philosophy at Moscow State University in 1939. Here he voiced his anti-Stalinist opinions openly, and this lack of discretion cost him his place at the university and led to his arrest. He managed to escape the NKVD agents and spent a couple of years on the run from the authorities.

During World War II, the efforts of the secret police turned elsewhere; Zinoviev managed to volunteer for the army and was decorated several times. After the war, he was allowed to return to Moscow and his education. He graduated in 1951 and entered graduate study at Moscow State in the department of logic. His dissertation was published in 1954, and by 1972 he had published several studies in logic. But his work leaned increasingly toward sociological analysis, and his critical stance toward Soviet society again riled the authorities, causing him to lose his teaching position in 1974. At this point Zinoviev turned to fiction, and in 1976 his first literary work, *Ziiaiushchie vysoty*, appeared in the West. This satire of the USSR led to the end of Zinoviev's career as an academic. Two years later, the Soviet authorities granted him permission to leave Russia under the pretext of his employment at the University of Munich. That same year his second work of fiction, *Svetloe budushchee*, appeared in the West and won the 1978 Prix Médicis. Zinoviev continued to write longer fictional works, but he also produced short essayistic pieces in which he could present more overt social commentary. He became known as an expert on Soviet society and lectured frequently throughout Europe. Yet his opinions often clashed with those of the émigré community and Western Sovietologists. In the twelve years after his emigration, he produced about a dozen works of fiction and published numerous essays, articles, interviews, and lectures in smaller collections.

After the collapse of the Soviet Union, there was a hiatus in Zinoviev's writing, which prompted Michael Kirkwood (1998) to note that Zinoviev was born the year the Soviet Union was officially recognized and fell silent at its dissolution (923). But beginning in 1995, Zinoviev again began producing a steady stream of work, both fictional and essayistic; clearly, his career has outlived the government he so frequently brought to task.

MAJOR MULTICULTURAL THEMES

Zinoviev's writing covers a wide range of genres and styles, from his early treatises on logic to his later work in fiction. These later works are difficult to classify because they are dense and complex, and Zinoviev himself admits that he writes books that are not easy to understand. His fiction is always satirical, with each book forming a stylistic collage comprised of brief chapters, some as short as a few lines, each with a title. His works become a patchwork of shifting styles, genres, points of view, and opinions—a style originally used, perhaps, to make it easier to smuggle Zinoviev's work to the West. Yet he has continued to use this style in his later works as well (Kirkwood, 1993, 30). Such kaleidoscopic presentation demands particular attention and skill from the reader to perceive the work as a whole.

Zinoviev's multiculturalism is the offspring of Russia's eternal identity crisis: is Russia part of the West or part of the East? Zinoviev's exposure to the West has deepened and complicated his stance on this issue. His concern is not simply to compare East and West, but to expose and examine the misunderstandings, incongruities, and individual flaws of the two cultures. This theme is constantly recast in his work, often framed as a conflict between "civilization" and "communism." His position is unique because he refuses to align himself completely with either side of the debate. He is critical of Soviet culture and the Soviet man, but the West offers no panaceas. Yet this ambivalent position is not merely hedging—for Zinoviev, *both* systems must exist in order for human society to continue to move forward.

The theme of East versus West appears in Zinoviev's early works, but a new perspective appears in *Zheltyi dom: romanticheskaia povest', s predosterezheniem i nazidaniem* (1980), which was begun in Russia and finished in Germany. His experience in the West caused a shift in his views. Direct experience with Western society has shown Zinoviev that "some features which he had believed were specific to Soviet society are to be found also in Western societies" (Tait, 26), and that "the West is equally in the grip of its own ideology" (Kirkwood, 1988, 55). While his early essays gained him fame as a Sovietologist, his exposure to Western culture actually moved him away from standard Western views on Soviet society because he refused to reject Sovietism and embrace Western ideals completely.

One novel of note here is *Gomo sovetikus* (1982). The introduction to this fictional work gives a clear and straightforward description of Zinoviev's position: "This book is about Soviet Man. He is a new type of man, Homo Sovieticus. . . . I have a dual relationship with this new being: I love him and at the same time I hate him; I respect him and I despise him. . . . I myself am [Homo Sovieticus]. Therefore I am merciless and cruel when I describe him" (*Homo Sovieticus*, trans. Charles Janson, 5). As in most of Zinoviev's works, it is difficult to find a plot in *Gomo sovetikus*. The main character is a Russian émigré living in the West. The narrator satirizes both the Western society he lives in and his fellow émigrés. He tries to be hired as a spy, and his interviews with Western officials show them to be logical to the point of ridiculousness and, consequently, illogical. Yet the Russian émigrés are emotional and irrational. Neither culture can understand the other and neither offers true solutions. One of Zinoviev's more recent works, *Russkii eksperiment* (1995), moves the theme of *Gomo sovetikus* in the other direction. The hero, Writer, returns to Russia after a long time abroad. His most significant companion is Philosopher, a retired academic who has spent his whole life in Soviet and post-Soviet Russia. The perspectives of these two characters, coming from different cultural norms, provide the strong multiculturalism in this work.

Zinoviev's numerous essays on Russian culture, its transformations, and its interaction with the West are also significant works of multiculturalism. In his essays Zinoviev's stance is more clearly stated, though no less complex. *My i Zapad: stat'i, interviu, vystupleniia 1979–1980 gg.* (1981) opens with a very sympathetic portrait of the Stalin years, but one should not conclude that Zinoviev is a Stalin supporter. He supports the general idea of Sovietism, but he does not idolize the Great October Revolution. Neither does he like the Romanov tsars, particularly those after Peter the Great. Zinoviev searches for something uniquely Russian and finds that both the tsars and the Communists were too beholden to the West. In the long essay *Ni svobody, ni ravenstva, ni bratstva: Stat'i, publichnye vystupleniia i otryvki iz vystuplenii v 1980–1981 gg.* (1983), Zinoviev states that both the West and the Soviets are "destroying the bulwarks of civilization built up over centuries which were designed to . . . constrain the spontaneous forces of people's social environment" (Kirkwood, 1988, 56).

SURVEY OF CRITICISM

There are not many critical works on Zinoviev, for several reasons. Foremost is the difficulty of the writer's style and language, especially for a non-native speaker (translations, of course, are insufficient to convey the depth of Zinoviev's perception). In addition, satire—a method of expression perhaps more common in Russia—is not an easily accessible form of literature. The stance of Zinoviev the writer is no less difficult to discern than his texts themselves, which poses problems for the critic. Finally, critical assessment of Zinoviev's importance varies: some feel his writing is overrated, others feel that "anyone who wants to understand the [former] Soviet Union . . . must take Zinoviev into account" (Hanson and Kirkwood, 11).

One of the foremost specialists on Zinoviev is Michael Kirkwood, who has translated several of the works, written a full-length analysis of Zinoviev's oeuvre (1993), and edited, with Philip Hanson, a collection of essays on the writer (1988). Much of Kirkwood's focus is on Zinoviev's style and ideological stance, but the latter cannot be fully separated from the writer's multiculturalism. In Kirkwood's analysis, multicultural experience did not alter Zinoviev's view on Soviet society as much as it shifted his views on the West. Yet Kirkwood also seems to classify Zinoviev more as a Westernizer than as a Slavophile. Arch Tait (1988) offers the slightly different opinion that Zinoviev's changing view of the West did cause him to reassess his earlier opinions on Soviet life.

SELECTED BIBLIOGRAPHY

Works by Zinoviev

Ziiaiushchie vysoty. Lausanne: L'Âge d'Homme, 1976. [*The Yawning Heights.* Trans. Gordon Clough. New York: Random House, 1979.]

Svetloe budushchee. Lausanne: L'Âge d'Homme, 1978. [*The Radiant Future.* Trans. Gordon Clough. New York: Random House, 1980.]

Zheltyi dom: romanticheskaia povest', s predosterezheniem i nazidaniem. Lausanne: L'Âge d'Homme, 1980. [*The Madhouse.* Trans. Michael Kirkwood. London: Gollancz, 1986.]

Kommunizm kak real'nost'. Lausanne: L'Âge d'Homme, 1981. [*The Reality of Communism.* Trans. Charles Janson. New York: Schocken Books, 1984.]

My i Zapad: stat'i, interviu vystupleniia 1979–1980 gg. Lausanne: L'Âge d'Homme, 1981.

Gomo sovetikus. Lausanne: L'Âge d'Homme, 1982. [*Homo Sovieticus.* Trans. Charles Janson. London: Gollancz, 1985.]

Moi dom—moia chuzhbina. Lausanne: L'Âge d'Homme, 1982.

Ni svobody, ni ravenstva, ni bratstva: Stat'i, publichnye vystupleniia i otryvki iz vystuplenii v 1980–1981 gg. Lausanne: L'Âge d'Homme, 1983.

Russkii eksperiment. Moscow: Nash Dom; and Lausanne: L'Âge d'Homme, 1995.

Post-kommunisticheskaia Rossiia: Publitsistika 1991–1995 gg. Moscow: Respublika, 1996.

Global'nyi cheloveinik. Moscow: Tsentrpoligraf; and Lausanne: L'Âge d'Homme, 1997.

O Rossii, o Zapade, o zagranitse, i o sebe. Moscow: ISPI RAN, 1998.

Russkaia sud'ba: Ispoved' otshchepentsa. Moscow: Tsentrpoligraf, 1999.
Zapad. Moscow: Tsentrpoligraf, 2000.

Selected Studies of Zinoviev

Fassio, Fabrice. *La nature du communisme selon Alexandre Zinoviev.* Lion-sur-Mer, France: Editions Arcane-Beauniex, 1991.

Hanson, Philip and Michael Kirkwood, eds. *Alexander Zinoviev as Writer and Thinker: An Assessment.* New York: St. Martin's Press; and Basingstoke: Macmillan, 1988.

Kirkwood, Michael. "Ideology in the Works of Alexander Zinoviev." In *Alexander Zinoviev as Writer and Thinker: An Assessment.* Ed. Philip Hanson and Michael Kirkwood, 44–60. New York: St. Martin's Press; and Basingstoke: Macmillan, 1988.

_____. *Alexander Zinoviev: An Introduction to his Work.* London: Macmillan Press, 1993.

_____. "Aleksandr Aleksandrovich Zinov'ev." In *A Reference Guide to Russian Literature*, 923. Ed. Neil Cornwell. London: Fitzroy Dearborn, 1998.

Tait, Arch. "Alexander Zinoviev on the Role of Literature in Society." In *Alexander Zinoviev as Writer and Thinker: An Assessment.* Ed. Philip Hanson and Michael Kirkwood, 26–43. New York: St. Martin's Press; and Basingstoke: Macmillan, 1988.

Tolstykh, Valentin. "Vy chto, boites' Zinovieva?" *Nezavisimaia gazeta* (September 29, 1992): 8.

SELECTED BIBLIOGRAPHY

Achebe, Chinua. *Things Fall Apart*. London: Heinemann, 1958. [In Swahili: *Shujaa okonkwo*. Nairobi: East African Publishing House, 1973.]

———. "The African Writer and the English Language." In *Morning Yet on Creation Day*, 55–62. London: Heinemann Educational, 1975.

———. *Home and Exile*. Oxford and New York: Oxford University Press, 2000.

Aciman, André. "Shadow Cities." *New York Review of Books* (December 18, 1997): 35–37.

Afrika, Jan [Breyten Breytenbach]. *Papierblom: 72 gedigte uit 'n swerfjoernaal*. Cape Town: Human and Rousseau, 1998.

Agamben, Giorgio. *Quel che resta di Auschwitz: L'archivio e il testimone*. Turin: Bollati Boringhieri, 1998. [*Remnants of Auschwitz: The Witness and the Archive*. Trans. Daniel Heller-Roazen. New York: Zone Books, 2000.]

Akas, Munir, and Khaled Mattawa, eds. *Post-Gibran: Anthology of New Arab American Writing*. West Bethesda, Md.: Kitab, 1999.

Aldrich, Robert. "From *Francité* to *Créolité:* French West Indian Literature Comes Home." In *Writing Across Worlds. Literature and Migration*, ed. Russell King, John Connell, and Paul White, 101–24. London and New York: Routledge, 1995.

Ali, Tariq. *Fear of Mirrors*. London: Arcadia, 1998.

———. "Mullahs and Heretics." *London Review of Books* (February 7, 2002): 7–14.

Allen, Roger. "Literary History and the Arabic Novel." *World Literature Today* 75, no. 2 (Spring 2001): 205–13.

Anagnost, Ann. *National Past-Times: Narrative, Representation, and Power in Modern China*. Durham, N.C.: Duke University Press, 1998.

Annan, Gabriele. "Ghosts." *New York Review of Books* (September 25, 1997): 29–30.

———. "Nesting Dolls." *New York Review of Books* (July 16, 1998): 35–36.

Antelme, Robert. *L'espèce humaine* (1947). Paris: Gallimard, 1978. [*The Human Race*. Trans. Jeffrey Haight and Annie Mahler. Marlboro, Vt.: Marlboro Press, 1992.]

Appel, Allan. *High Holiday Sutra: A Novel*. Minneapolis, Minn.: Coffee House Press, 1997.

Appelfeld, Aharon. *Kol Asher Ahavti*. Jerusalem: Keter, 1999.

———. *Kutonet Veha-passim* (1983). [*Tzili: The Story of a Life*. Trans. Dalya Bilu. New York: E. P. Dutton, 1983.]

———. *Mesilat barzel* (1991). [*The Iron Tracks*. Trans. Jeffrey M. Green. New York: Schocken, 1998.]

———. *Mikreh Ha-Kerah*. Jerusalem: Keter, 1997.

———. *Tor ha-pelaʾot* (1978). [*The Age of Wonders*. Trans. Dalya Bilu. Boston: D. R. Godine, 1981.]

Appiah, K. Anthony. "The Multiculturalist Misunderstanding." *New York Review of Books* (October 9, 1997): 30–36.

Appiah, Kwame Anthony, and Henry Louis Gates Jr., eds. *The Dictionary of Global Culture*. New York: Knopf, 1997.

Axford, Barrie, Daniela Berghahn, and Nick Hewlett, eds. *Unity and Diversity in the New Europe*. New York: Peter Lang, 2000.

Aziz, Nurjehan, ed. *Her Mother's Ashes and Other Stories by South Asian Women in Canada and the United States*. Toronto: Tsar, 1994.

———. *Her Mother's Ashes 2: More Stories by South Asian Women in Canada and the United States*. Toronto: Tsar, 1998.

Bach, Bernard. *Entre peur et révolte: La littérature d'expression allemande en Alsace (1945–1980)*. New York: Peter Lang, 1995.

Baker, Colin. *Key Issues in Bilingualism and Bilingual Education*. Clevedon, Avon: Multilingual Matters, 1988.

Banville, John. "The Dawn of the Gods." *New York Review of Books* (January 14,1999): 16–18.

———. "A Life Elsewhere." *New York Review of Books* (November 20, 1997): 24–26.

Barkan, Elazar, and Marie-Denise Shelton, eds. *Borders, Exiles, Diasporas*. Stanford, Calif.: Stanford University Press, 1998.

Bayley, John. "Too Polish for the Poles." *New York Review of Books* (October 6, 1994): 13–15.

———."Under the Overcoat." *New York Review of Books* (June 25, 1998): 42–44.

Beardsmore, Hugo Baetens. *Bilingualism: Basic Principles*. Clevedon, Avon: Multilingual Matters, 1986.

Bernabé, Jean, Patrick Chamoiseau, and Raphaël Confiant. *Eloge de la créolité*. Paris: Presses Universitaires Créoles, 1989.

Bernstein, Jeremy. "The Road to Lhasa." *New York Review of Books* (June 12, 1997): 45–49.

The Best of Granta Travel. London: Granta, 1991.

Bhatt, Sujata. *Point No Point: Selected Poems*. Manchester, England: Carcanet Press, 1997.

Blanton, Casey. *Travel Writing: The Self and the World*. New York: Twayne, 1997.

Bolger, Dermot, ed. *Ireland in Exile: Irish Writers Abroad*. Dublin: New Island, 1993.

Booker, M. Keith. *The African Novel in English: An Introduction*. Oxford: James Currey, 1998.

Borges, Jorge Luis. *Borges A/Z: La Biblioteca de Babel.* Ed. Antonio Fernández Ferrer. Madrid: Siruela, 1988.

Borland, Isabel Alvarez. *Cuban-American Literature of Exile.* Charlottesville: University Press of Virginia, 1998.

Brandys, Kazimierz. *Miesiace, 1982–1984.* Paris: Institut Littéraire, SARL, 1984. [*Paris, New York: 1982–1984.* Trans. Barbara Krzywicki-Herburt. New York: Random House, 1988.]

Breckenridge, Carol A., Sheldon Pollock, Homi K. Bhabha, and Dipesh Chakrabarty, eds. *Cosmopolitanism.* Durham, N.C.: Duke University Press, 2002.

Brennan, Timothy. *At Home in the World: Cosmopolitanism Now.* Cambridge, Mass.: Harvard University Press, 1997.

Breytenbach, Breyten. *The True Confessions of an Albino Terrorist* (1982). London and Boston: Faber and Faber, 1984.

Britton, Celia. *Édouard Glissant and Postcolonial Theory: Strategies of Language and Resistance.* Charlottesville: University Press of Virginia, 1999.

Bull, Malcolm. "Hate Is the New Love." *London Review of Books* (January 25, 2001): 23–24.

Buruma, Ian. "Down and Out in East Tokyo." *New York Review of Books* (June 25, 1998): 9–12.

Butler, Judith, Ernesto Laclau, and Slavoj Zizek. *Contingency, Hegemony, Universality: Contemporary Dialogues on the Left.* New York: Verso, 2000.

Caminero-Santangelo, Marta. "Contesting the Boundaries of Exile Latino/a Literature." *World Literature Today* 74, no. 3 (Summer 2000): 507–17.

Campomanes, Oscar V. "Filipinos in the United States and Their Literature of Exile." In *Reading the Literatures of Asian America*, ed. Shirley Geok-lim and Amy Ling, 49–78. Philadelphia: Temple University Press, 1992.

Canetti, Elias. *Die gerettete Zunge: Geschichte einer Jugend.* Munich: C. Hanser, 1977.

Carpenter, Bogdana. "The Gift Returned." *World Literature Today* 73, no. 4 (Autumn 1999): 631–36.

Certeau, Michel de. *Culture in the Plural.* Trans. Tom Conley. Minneapolis: University of Minnesota Press, 1998.

Césaire, Aimé. *Cahier d'un retour au pays natal* (1939). Paris: Présence Africaine, 1956. [*Notebook of a Return to My Native Land.* Trans. Mireille Rosello with Annie Pritchard. Newcastle upon Tyne, England: Bloodaxe, 1995.]

———. *Discours sur le colonialisme.* Paris: Présence Africaine, 1955. [*Discourse on Colonialism.* Trans. Joan Pinkham. New York: Monthly Review Press, 1972.]

Chamoiseau, Patrick. *Solibo Magnifique.* Paris: Gallimard, 1988. [*Solibo Magnificent.* Trans. Rose-Myriam Réjouis and Val Vinokurov. New York: Pantheon, 1998.]

Chamoiseau, Patrick, and Raphaël Confiant. *Lettres Créoles: Tracées Antillaises et Continentales de la littérature.* Paris: Karthala, 1992.

Chatwin, Bruce. *In Patagonia.* London: Cape, 1977.

———. *On the Black Hill.* London: Cape, 1982.

———. *The Songlines.* London: Cape, 1987.

———. *The Viceroy of Ouidah.* New York: Summit, 1980.

Cheng, Ch'ing-wen. *Three-Legged Horse.* Ed. Pamg-yuan Chi. New York: Columbia University Press, 1999.

Cheung, Dominic (Chang Ts'o). *Drifting.* Copenhagen and Los Angeles: Green Integer, 2000.

Chevrel, Yves. *Comparative Literature Today: Methods and Perspectives.* Trans. Farida Elizabeth Dahab. Kirksville, Mo.: Thomas Jefferson University Press, 1994.

Clarke, George Elliott. *Odysseys Home: Mapping African-Canadian Literature.* Toronto: University of Toronto Press, 2002.

Clifford, James. *The Predicament of Culture: Twentieth-Century Ethnography, Literature, and Art.* Cambridge, Mass.: Harvard University Press, 1988.

———. *Routes: Travel and Translation in the Late Twentieth Century.* Cambridge, Mass.: Harvard University Press, 1997.

Coetzee, J. M. "Against the South African Grain." *New York Review of Books* (September 23, 1999): 51–53.

———. "Blowing Hot and Cold." *New York Review of Books* (July 17, 1997): 50–53.

Confiant, Raphaël. *Commandeur du sucre: Récit.* Paris: Ecriture, 1994.

———. *Régisseur du rhum.* Paris: Ecriture, 1999.

Dabydeen, David. *A Harlot's Progress.* London: Cape, 1999.

Dai Sijie. *Balzac and the Little Chinese Seamstress.* Trans. Ina Rilke. London: Chatto, 2001.

Davis, Robert Murray. "Out of the Shadows: Slovene Writing after Independence." *World Literature Today* 75, no. 1 (Winter 2001): 59–65.

———. "Slovak Writers after 1993." *World Literature Today* 73, no. 1 (Winter 1999): 93–96.

Desai, Anita. *Baumgartner's Bombay.* Boston: Houghton Mifflin, 2000.

———. *In Custody.* New York: Harper and Row, 1984.

Didier, Béatrice. *Dictionnaire universel des littératures.* 3 vols. Paris: Presses Universitaires de France, 1994.

Divakaruni, Chitra Banerjee. *The Mistress of Spices.* London: Transworld, 1997.

———. *Sister of My Heart.* New York and London: Doubleday, 1999.

Djebar, Assia. *Vaste est la prison.* Paris: Albin Michel, 1995.

———. *Ces voix qui m'assiègent . . . en marge de ma francophonie.* Paris: Albin Michel, 1999.

Dodd, Philip, ed. *The Art of Travel: Essays on Travel Writing.* London: Cass, 1992.

Duffy, Patrick. "Literary Reflections on Irish Migration in the Nineteenth and Twentieth Centuries." In *Writing Across Worlds: Literature and Migration,* ed. Russell King, John Connell, and Paul White, 20–38. London and New York: Routledge, 1995.

Durrell, Lawrence. *Justine.* In *The Alexandria Quartet,* 13–203. London: Faber and Faber, 1968.

Eco, Umberto. *Serendipities: Language and Lunacy.* Italian Academy Lectures. Trans. William Weaver. New York: Columbia University Press, 1998.

Edwards, John. *Multilingualism.* London and New York: Routledge, 1994.

Fanon, Frantz. *Les damnés de la terre.* Preface by Jean-Paul Sartre. Paris: Maspéro, 1961.

———. *Peau noire, masques blancs.* Paris: Seuil, 1952. [*Black Skin, White Masks.* Trans. Charles Lam Markmannn. New York: Grove Press, 1967, 1982; London: Pluto, 1986.]

Farah, Nuruddin. "A Country in Exile." *World Literature Today* 72, no. 4 (Autumn 1998): 712–15.

———. *Yesterday, Tomorrow: Voices from the Somali Diaspora.* London and New York: Cassell, 2000.

Flores, Lauro, ed. *The Floating Borderlands: Twenty-five Years of U.S. Hispanic Literature.* Seattle: University of Washington Press, 1998.

Frank, Edwin. "Passage to Brooklyn." *New York Review of Books* (December 4, 1997): 53–54.

Fredrickson, George M. "America's Caste System: Will It Change?" *New York Review of Books* (October 23, 1997): 68–75.

Gao, Xingjian. "The Case for Literature: The 2001 Nobel Lecture." Trans. Mabel Lee. *World Literature Today* 75, no. 1 (Winter 2001): 4–11.

Gelfant, Blanche H. *Cross-Cultural Reckonings.* New York: Cambridge University Press, 1995.

Ghosh, Amitav. *The Circle of Reason.* London: H. Hamilton, 1986.

———. *In an Antique Land.* New Delhi: Ravi Dayal, 1992.

Ginzburg, Carlo. *Occhiacci di legno: Nove riflessioni sulla distanza.* Milan: Feltrinelli, 1998.

Glad, John. *Russia Abroad: Writers, History, Politics.* Tenafly, N.J.: Hermitage; Washington, D.C.: Birchbark, 1999.

Glazer, Nathan. *We Are All Multiculturals Now.* Cambridge, Mass.: Harvard University Press, 1997.

Glissant, Edouard. *Le discours Antillais.* Paris: Seuil, 1981.

———. *Malemort.* Paris: Seuil, 1975.

———. *Tout-monde.* Paris: Gallimard, 1993.

Gnisci, Armando, ed. *La letteratura nel mondo.* Rome: Sovera Multimedia, 1993.

———. *Noialtri Europei: Saggi di letteratura comparata su identità e luoghi d'Europa.* Rome: Bulzoni, 1994.

Gnisci, Armando, and Franca Sinopoli, eds. *Letteratura comparata: Storia e testi.* Rome: Sovera Multimedia, 1995.

Goldman, Francisco. *The Long Night of White Chickens.* New York: Atlantic Monthly Press, 1992.

———. *The Ordinary Seaman.* New York: Atlantic Monthly Press, 1997.

Goonetilleke, D. C. R. A., ed. *Perspectives on Postcolonial Literature.* London: Skoob, 2001.

Gordimer, Nadine. *The Pickup.* London: Bloomsbury, 2001.

Gracq, Julien. *Autour des sept collines.* Paris: J. Corti, 1988.

———. *Le rivage des Syrtes.* Paris: J. Corti, 1951.

Granta 57: India! The Golden Jubilee. Issue to commemorate India's fiftieth year of independence. London: Granta, 1997.

Grosjean, François. *Life with Two Languages.* Cambridge, Mass.: Harvard University Press, 1982.

Grossman, David. ʿAyen ʿerekh—ahavah (1986). [*See Under—Love.* Trans. Betsy Rosenberg. New York: Farrar, Straus and Giroux, 1989.]

Ha Jin. *In the Pond.* Cambridge, Mass.: Zoland, 1998.

———. *Ocean of Words: Army Stories.* Cambridge, Mass.: Zoland, 1996.

———. *Waiting.* New York: Pantheon, 1999; London: Heinemann, 2000.

al-Hakim, Tawfiq. *Usfur min al-Sharq* (1938). [*Bird of the East.* Trans. R. Bayly Winder. Beirut: Khayats, 1966.]

Hakuta, Kenji. *Mirror of Language.* New York: Basic, 1986.

Hamers, Josiane, and M. Blanc. *Bilingualité et bilinguisme.* Brussels: Pierre Mardaga, 1983.

Hammoud, Hani. *L'occidentaliste.* Beirut: Éditions Dar An-Nahar, 1997.

Hanania, Tony. *Unreal City.* London: Bloomsbury, 1999.

Handke, Peter. *Noch einmal für Thukydides* (1990). [*Once Again for Thucydides.* Trans. Tess Lewis. New York: New Directions, 1998.]

Harnisch, Antje, Anne-Marie Stokes, and Friedemann Weidauer, eds. and trans. *Fringe Voices: An Anthology of Minority Writing in the Federal Republic of Germany.* Oxford and New York: Berg, 1999.

Head, Bessie. *Serowe: Village of the Rain Wind.* London: Heinemann, 1981.

Heighton, Steven. *Flight Paths of the Emperor* (1992). London: Granta, 1997.

Heller, Peter. *In Transit.* New York: Peter Lang, 1996.

Hill, Justin. *A Bend in the Yellow River.* London: Phoenix House, 1997.

———. *The Drink and Dream Teahouse.* London: Weidenfeld, 2001.

Hitchens, Christopher. "Goodbye to All That." *New York Review of Books* (July 17, 1997): 20–23.

Hofmann, Michael. *Corona, Corona.* London: Faber and Faber, 1993.

Hout, Syrine C. "Of Fathers and the Fatherland in the Post-1995 Lebanese Exilic Novel." *World Literature Today* 75, no. 2 (Spring 2001): 285–93.

Huntington, Samuel P. *The Clash of Civilizations and the Remaking of World Order.* New York: Simon and Schuster, 1997.

Hutcheon, Linda, and Marion Richmond, eds. *Other Solitudes: Canadian Multicultural Fictions.* Toronto: Oxford University Press, 1990.

Huot, Claire. *China's New Cultural Scene: A Handbook of Changes.* Durham, N.C.: Duke University Press, 1999.

Ibnifassi, Laila, and Nicki Hitchcott, eds. *African Francophone Writing: A Critical Introduction.* Herndon, Va.: Berg, 1996.

Ignatieff, Michael. *Asya.* London: Chatto and Windus, 1991.

———. "In the Center of the Earthquake." *New York Review of Books* (June 12, 1997): 31–33.

———. *The Russian Album.* London: Chatto and Windus, 1987.

Iriye, Akira. *Cultural Internationalism and World Order.* Baltimore: Johns Hopkins University Press, 1997.

Issawi, Charles. *Cross-Cultural Encounters and Conflicts.* New York: Oxford University Press, 1998.

Jack, Ian, ed. *The Granta Book of Travel.* London: Granta, 1998.

Jameson, Fredric, and Masao Miyoshi, eds. *The Cultures of Globalization.* Durham, N.C.: Duke University Press, 1998.

Jhabvala, Ruth Prawer. *East into Upper East: Plain Tales from New York and New Delhi.* Washington, D.C.: Counterpoint, 1998.

Jones, Rosemarie. "*Pied-noir* Literature: The Writing of a Migratory Elite." In *Writing Across Worlds: Literature and Migration,* ed. Russell King, John Connell, and Paul White, 125–40. London and New York: Routledge, 1995.

Kadare, Ismail. *Nëntori i një kryeqyteti* (1975). [*Novembre d'une capitale.* Trans. Jusuf Vrioni. Paris: Fayard, 1998.]

———. *Nepunesi i pallatit te ëndrrave* (1981). [*The Palace of Dreams.* Trans. Barbara Bray, from the French translation of Jusuf Vrioni. London: Harvill, 1993.]

———. *Pluhuri mbreteror* (1995). [*The Pyramid.* Trans. David Bellos, from the French translation of Jusuf Vrioni. London: Harvill, 1996.]

Kamenetz, Rodger. *The Jew in the Lotus: A Poet's Rediscovery of Jewish Identity in Buddhist India.* San Francisco: HarperSanFrancisco, 1994.

Kapur, Geeta. "Globalization and Culture: Navigating the Void." In *The Cultures of Globalization*, ed. Fredric Jameson and Masao Miyoshi, 191–217. Durham, N.C.: Duke University Press, 1998.

Kapuściński, Ryszard. *Heban* (1998). [*The Shadow of the Sun.* Trans. Klara Glowczewska. New York: Alfred A. Knopf, 2001.]

———. *Imperator.* Moscow: Nauka, 1992. [*Imperium.* Warsaw: Czytelnik, 1993. *Imperium.* Trans. Klara Glowczewska. New York: A. A. Knopf, 1994.]

———. *Wojna futbolowa* (1990). [*The Soccer War.* Trans. William Brand. New York: A. A. Knopf, 1991.]

Khair, Tabish. *Babu Fictions: Alienation in Contemporary Indian English Novels.* New Delhi, New York: Oxford University Press, 2001.

Khalfa, Jean, with Jérôme Game. "Pustules, Spirals, Volcanoes. Images and Moods in Césaire's *Cahiers d'un retour au pays natal.*" *Wasafiri* 31 (Spring 2000): 43–51.

Killam, Douglas, and Ruth Rowe, eds. *The Companion to African Literatures.* Oxford: James Currey, 2000.

Kim, Elaine H., and Eui-Young Yu. *East to America: Korean American Life Stories.* New York: New Press, 1996.

King, Desmond. *Making Americans: Immigration, Race, and the Origins of the Diverse Democracy.* Cambridge, Mass.: Harvard University Press, 2000.

King, Russell, John Connell, and Paul White, eds. *Writing Across Worlds: Literature and Migration.* London and New York: Routledge, 1995.

Klíma, Ivan. *Between Security and Insecurity.* Trans. Gerry Turner. New York: Thames and Hudson, 1999.

———. *Moje zlata remesla* (1990). [*My Golden Trades.* Trans. Paul Wilson. London: Granta, in association with Penguin, 1992.]

———. *Poslední stupeň důvěrnosti* (1996). [*The Ultimate Intimacy.* Trans. A. G. Brain. London: Granta, 1997.]

———. *The Spirit of Prague: And Other Essays.* Trans. Paul Wilson. New York: Granta, 1994.

Kobal, Ivan. *Men Who Built the Snowy.* Rydalmere, New South Wales: I. Kobal, 1984.

Kokis, Sergio. *Le pavillon des miroirs.* La Tour d'Aigues, France: L'Aube, 1999.

Kongoli, Fatos. *Dragoi i fildishtë.* Tiranë, Albania: Çabej, 1999. [*Le dragon d'ivoire.* Trans. Edmond Tupja. Paris: Rivages, 2000.]

Kristeva, Julia. *Étrangers à nous-mêmes.* Paris: Librairie Fayard, 1988.

Kundera, Milan. "You're Not in Your Own House Here, My Dear Fellow." *New York Review of Books* (September 21, 1995): 21–24.

Kushner, Eva, and Milan V. Dimič, eds. *Acculturation: Proceedings of the XIth Congress of the International Comparative Literature Association.* New York: Peter Lang, 1994.

Kushner, Eva, and Haga Toru, eds. *Dialogues of Cultures. Dialogues des cultures.* New York: Peter Lang, 2000.

Kymlicka, Will. *Multicultural Citizenship: A Liberal Theory of Minority Rights.* Oxford: Clarendon Press; New York: Oxford University Press, 1995.

Lamming, George. *The Emigrants.* London: Michael Joseph, 1954.

———. *In the Castle of My Skin.* London: Michael Joseph, 1953.

———. *The Pleasures of Exile.* London: Michael Joseph, 1960.

———. *Water with Berries.* London: Michael Joseph, 1971.

Lawrie, Steven W. *Erich Fried: A Writer without a Country.* New York: Peter Lang, 1996.

Lê, Linda. *Fuir: Roman.* Paris: La Table Ronde, 1988.

Leonardo, Micaela di. *Exotics at Home: Anthropologies, Others, American Modernity.* Chicago: University of Chicago Press, 1998.

Lessing, Doris. *The Grass Is Singing.* New York: Crowell, 1950.

———. *Mara and Dann.* New York: HarperFlamingo, 1999.

Leys, Simon. "The Archaeological Me." *New York Review of Books* (March 26, 1998): 34–39.

Li, David Leiwei. *Imagining the Nation: Asian American Literature and Cultural Consent.* Stanford, Calif.: Stanford University Press, 1998.

Li-Chun Lin, Sylvia. "Between the Individual and the Collective: Gao Xingjian's Fiction." *World Literature Today* 75, no. 1 (Winter 2001): 12–18.

Lidman, Sara. *Samtal i Hanoi.* Stockholm: Bonnier, 1966.

Lien Chao. *Beyond Silence: Chinese Canadian Literature in English.* Toronto: Tsar, 1997.

Lindqvist, Sven. *Utrota varenda javel* (1992). [*Exterminate All the Brutes.* Trans. Joan Tate. London: Granta, 1997.]

Lipman, Jonathan N. *Familiar Strangers: A History of Muslims in Northwest China.* Seattle: University of Washington Press, 1998.

Liu, Lydia H. *Tokens of Exchange: The Problems of Translation in Global Circulations.* Durham, N.C.: Duke University Press, 1999.

Loomba, Ania. *Colonialism/Postcolonialism.* New York and London: Routledge, 1998.

Loughman, Celeste. "The Seamless Universe of Ōe Kenzaburō." *World Literature Today* 73, no. 3 (Summer 1999): 417–22.

Luis, William. *Dance between Two Cultures: Latino Caribbean Literature Written in the United States.* Nashville, Tenn.: Vanderbilt University Press, 1998.

Maalouf, Amin. *Les identités meurtrières.* Paris: Grasset, 1998.

Magill, Frank N., ed. *Great Women Writers.* New York: Henry Holt, 1994.

Mahjoub, Jamal. "An Interview with Mehdi Charef." *Wasafiri* 31 (Spring 2000): 37–40.

Malcolm, Noel. "In the Palace of Nightmares." *New York Review of Books* (November 6, 1997): 21–24.

Malouf, David. *An Imaginary Life.* London: Chatto and Windus, 1978.

Mankekar, Purnima. *Screening Culture, Viewing Politics: An Ethnography of Television, Womanhood, and Nation in Postcolonial India.* Durham, N.C.: Duke University Press, 1999.

Maurer, Doris, and Arnold E. Maurer. *Guida letteraria dell'Italia.* Parma: Guanda, 1993.

McCourt, Frank. *Angela's Ashes: A Memoir.* New York: Scribner, 1996.

———. *'Tis: A Memoir.* New York: Scribner, 1999.

Melzer, Arthur M., Jerry Weinberger, and M. Richard Zinman, eds. *Multiculturalism and American Democracy.* Lawrence: University Press of Kansas, 1998.

Mezzadra, Sandro. "La cucina etnica dell'identità'." *Il Manifesto* (September 18, 1999): 21–22.

Miller, Christopher L. *Nationalists and Nomads: Essays on Francophone African Literature and Culture.* Chicago: University of Chicago Press, 1999.

Miller, John J. *The Unmaking of Americans: How Multiculturalism Has Undermined America's Assimilation Ethic.* New York: Free Press, 1998.

Miner, Earl R. "Gli studi comparati interculturali." In *Letteratura comparata: Storia e testi,* ed. Armando Gnisci and Franca Sinopoli, 179–204. Rome: Sovera Multimedia, 1995.

———. *The Japanese Tradition in British and American Literature.* Princeton, N.J.: Princeton University Press, 1958.

Minta, Stephen. *Aguirre: The Re-creation of a Sixteenth-Century Journey across South America.* New York: Henry Holt, 1994.

Mishra, Pankaj. "The Last of His Kind." *New York Review of Books* (September 23, 1999): 12–13.

———. "A Spirit of Their Own." *New York Review of Books* (May 20, 1999): 47–53.

Mlakar, Frank. *He, the Father.* New York: Harper, 1950.

Modiano, Patrick. *Voyage de noces* (1990). [*Honeymoon.* Trans. Barbara Wright. London: Harvill, 1992.]

Mohanram, Radhika, and Gita Rajan, eds. *English Postcoloniality: Literatures from around the World.* Westport, Conn.: Greenwood, 1996.

Mokeddem, Malika. *L'interdite.* Paris: Grasset, 1993. [*The Forbidden Woman.* Trans. K. Melissa Marcus. Lincoln: University of Nebraska Press, 1998.]

Mondesir, Simone. "Far from the Madding Crowd." *High Life* (August 1998): 52–55.

Moser, Gerald M. "Neglected or Forgotten Authors of Lusophone Africa." *World Literature Today* 73, no. 1 (Winter 1999): 19–22.

Moving Worlds: A Journal of Transcultural Writings (biannual). Ed. Shirley Chew. Leeds: School of English, University of Leeds.

Mudimbe, Valentin Y. *The Idea of Africa.* Bloomington: Indiana University Press, 1994.

———, ed. *Nations, Identities, Cultures.* Durham, N.C.: Duke University Press, 1997.

Mukherjee, Bharati. *Darkness.* New York: Penguin, 1985.

———. *The Middleman and Other Stories.* New York: Grove Press, 1988.

———. *Jasmine.* New York: Grove Weidenfeld, 1989.

"Multilingualism in Europe." *International Herald Tribune,* January 26, 1998, 15.

Myrdal, Jan. *Rapport från kinesisk by* (1963). [*Report from a Chinese Village.* Trans. Maurice Michael. New York: Pantheon, 1965.]

———. *Samtida bekännelser av an Europeisk intellektuell.* Stockholm: Norstedt, 1964. [*Confessions of a Disloyal European.* New York: Pantheon, 1968.]

Naikan Tao. "Building a White Tower at Night: Zhai Yongming's Poetry." *World Literature Today* 73, no. 3 (Summer 1999): 409–16.

Naipaul, V. S. *Among the Believers: An Islamic Journey.* London: A. Deutsch, 1981.

————. *Beyond Belief: Islamic Excursions among the Converted Peoples.* New York: Random House, 1998.

————. *Half a Life.* London: Picador, 2001.

————. *India: A Million Mutinies Now.* London: Heinemann, 1990.

Nettle, Daniel, and Suzanne Romaine. *Vanishing Voices: The Extinction of the World's Languages.* New York: Oxford University Press, 2000.

Nguyên, Văn Sâm. *Khói sóng trên sông.* San José, Calif.: Văn, 2000.

Nkosi, Lewis. *Home and Exile, and Other Selections.* London and New York: Longman, 1983.

Nooteboom, Cees. *Omweg naar Santiago.* Amsterdam: Atlas, 1992. [*Roads to Santiago: Detours and Riddles in the Lands and History of Spain.* Trans. Ina Rilke. London: Harvill, 1997.]

————. *De Zucht naar het Westen.* Amsterdam: Arbeiderspers, 1985.

O'Hearn, Claudine Chiawei, ed. *Half and Half: Writers on Growing Up Biracial and Bicultural.* New York: Pantheon, 1998.

Oliveira, Claire de. *La poésie allemande de Roumanie: Entre hétéronomie et dissidence (1944–1990).* New York: Peter Lang, 1995.

Ollier, Claude. *Le jeu d'enfant.* Paris: Flammarion, 1958–75.

————. *Marrakch medine.* Paris: Flammarion, 1979.

————. *Mon double à Malacca.* Paris: Flammarion, 1982.

————. *La vie sur Epsilon.* Paris: Gallimard, 1972.

Ousmane, Sembene. *O pays, mon beau peuple!* Paris: Amiot-Dumont, 1957.

Paik Nak-chung. "Nations and Literatures in the Age of Globalization." In *The Cultures of Globalization,* ed. Fredric Jameson and Masao Myoshi, 218–29. Durham, N.C.: Duke University Press, 1998.

Panikkar, Kavalam Madhava. *The Afro-Asian States and Their Problems.* London: Allen and Unwin, 1959.

————. *Asia and Western Dominance: A Survey of the Vasco da Gama Epoch of Asian History, 1498–1945.* London: Allen and Unwin, 1953.

————. *In Two Chinas, Memoirs of a Diplomat.* London: Allen and Unwin, 1955.

Pantoja Hidalgo, Cristina. "The Philippine Novel in English into the Twenty-first Century." *World Literature Today* 74, no. 2 (Spring 2000): 333–36.

Pasolini, Pier Paolo. "Alì dagli occhi azzurri." In *Poesia in forma di rosa,* 93–99. Milan: Garzanti, 1964.

Pattanayak, Debi Prasanna, ed. *Multilingualism in India.* Philadelphia: Multilingual Matters, 1990.

p'Bitek, Okot. *Song of Lawino: A Lament.* Nairobi: East African Publishing House, 1966.

————. *Song of Ocol.* Nairobi: East African Publishing House, 1966.

Pelevin, Victor. *Chapaev i Pustota* (1996). [*Buddha's Little Finger.* Trans. Andrew Bromfield. New York: Viking, 2000.]

Pellegrini, Carlo, ed. *Venezia nelle letterature moderne.* Venice: Fondazione Giorgio Cini, 1961.

Pérez Firmat, Gustavo. *Cincuenta lecciones de exilio y desexilio.* Miami: Universal, 2000.

Phillips, Caryl. *The Atlantic Sound.* London: Faber, 2000.

————. *The Nature of Blood.* New York: Knopf; London: Faber, 1997.

————, ed. *Extravagant Strangers: A Literature of Belonging*. New York: Vintage, 1999.

Pichová, Hana. *The Art of Memory in Exile: Vladimir Nabokov and Milan Kundera*. Carbondale: Southern Illinois University Press, 2001.

Pierce, David, ed. *Irish Writing in the Twentieth Century: A Reader*. Cork, Ireland: Cork University Press, 2001.

Pineau, Gisèle. *L'exil selon Julia*. Paris: Stock, 1996.

Pullinger, Kate, ed. *Border Lines: Stories of Exile and Home*. London: Serpent's Tail, 1993.

Queneau, Raymond. *Histoire des littératures*. (Encyclopédie de la Pléiade). 3 vols. Paris: Gallimard, 1958.

Ramras-Rauch, Gila. "Aharon Appelfeld: A Hundred Years of Jewish Solitude." *World Literature Today* 72, no. 3 (Summer 1998): 493–500.

Riggan, William. "Hebrew Literature in the 1990s: Introduction." *World Literature Today* 72, no. 3 (Summer 1998): 477–78.

————. "Nuruddin Farah's Indelible Country of the Imagination: The 1998 Neustadt International Prize for Literature." *World Literature Today* 72, no. 4 (Autumn 1998): 701–2.

————. "Of Obstacles, Survival, and Identity: On Contemporary Canadian Literature(s)." *World Literature Today* 73, no. 2 (Spring 1999): 229–30.

Ritchie, J. M. *German Exiles: British Perspectives*. New York: Peter Lang, 1997.

Rodgers, Lawrence R. *Canaan Bound: The African-American Great Migration Novel*. Chicago: University of Illinois Press, 1997.

Rudman, Mark. "To Live Like a Bird." *London Review of Books* (June 1, 2000): 38.

Rushdie, Salman, and Elizabeth West, eds. *Mirrorwork: 50 Years of Indian Writing 1947–1997*. New York: Henry Holt, 1997.

Ryle, John. "Nomad." *New York Review of Books* (December 4, 1997): 6–7.

Said, Edward W. "In Memory of Ibrahim Abu-Lughod." *London Review of Books* (December 13, 2001): 19–20.

————. *Orientalism*. New York: Pantheon, 1978.

————. "*Orientalism*, an Afterword." *Raritan: A Quarterly Review* 14, no. 3 (1995): 32–59.

————. "Orientalism Reconsidered." *Cultural Critique* 1 (1985): 89–107.

————. *Out of Place: A Memoir*. New York: Knopf, 1999.

————. *Reflections on Exile and Other Essays*. Cambridge, Mass.: Harvard University Press, 2000.

Salih, al-Tayyib. *Mawsim al-Hijrah ilaɔ al-Shamal*. Cairo: Dar al-Hilal, 1966. [*Season of Migration to the North*. Trans. Denys Johnson-Davis. London: Heinemann Educational, 1969.]

Sarachchandra, Ediriwira R. *Foam upon the Stream: A Japanese Elegy*. Trans. from the Sinhalese by the author. Singapore: Heinemann Asia, 1987.

————. *With the Begging Bowl*. Delhi: B. R., 1986.

Saracino, Maria Antonietta. "In Africa: Scrittura e Censura." In *Le lettere rubate: Forme, funzioni e ragioni della censura*, ed. Annalisa Goldoni and Carlo Martinez, 1–20. Naples: Liguori, 2001.

————, ed. *Altri lati del mondo*. Rome: Sensibili alle foglie, 1994.

Scammell, Michael. "Loyal Toward Reality." *New York Review of Books* (September 24, 1998): 36–40.

Schulze, Ingo. *Augenblicke des Glücks* (1995). [*33 Moments of Happiness: St. Petersburg Stories*. Trans. John E. Woods. New York: A. A. Knopf, 1998.]

———. *Simple Storys: Ein Roman aus der ostdeutschen Provinz*. Berlin: Berlin, Verlag, 1998.

Selvon, Samuel. *The Lonely Londoners*. London: A. Wingate, 1956.

———. *Moses Ascending*. London: Davis-Poynter, 1975.

———. *Moses Migrating*. Harlow, Essex: Longman, 1983.

Senghor, Léopold Sedar, ed. *Anthologie de la nouvelle poésie nègre et malgache de langue française. Précédée de "Orphée noir" par Jean-Paul Sartre*. Paris: Presses Universitaires de France, 1948.

Sernet, Milton C. *Bound for the Promised Land: African American Religion and the Great Migration*. Durham, N.C.: Duke University Press, 1997.

Seth, Vikram. *The Golden Gate: A Novel in Verse*. New York: Random House, 1986.

Shallcross, Bozena. *Through the Poet's Eye: The Travels of Zagajewski, Herbert, and Brodsky*. Evanston, Ill.: Northwestern University Press, 2001.

Sidhwa, Bapsi. *An American Brat*. Minneapolis, Minn.: Milkweed, 1993.

Škvorecký, Josef. *Headed for the Blues: A Memoir*. Trans. Káca Poláčková Henley. Hopewell, N.J.: Ecco Press, 1996. Trans. Peter Kussi, Káca Poláčková Henley, and Caleb Crain. London: Faber and Faber, 1997.

Smith, Carolyn D., ed. *Strangers at Home: Essays on the Effects of Living Overseas and Coming "Home" to a Strange Land*. New York: Aletheia, 1996.

Smith, Paul. "Refuge for the Aristocracy." *London Review of Books* (June 21, 2001): 30–31.

Soar, Daniel. "Willesden Fast-Forward." *London Review of Books* (September 21, 2000): 30–31.

Soyinka, Wole. *The Burden of Memory, the Muse of Forgiveness*. New York: Oxford University Press, 1999.

Spence, Jonathan D. *The Chan's Great Continent: China in Western Minds*. New York: W. W. Norton, 1998.

Stam, Robert. *Tropical Multiculturalism: A Comparative History of Race in Brazilian Cinema and Culture*. Durham, N.C.: Duke University Press, 1998.

Stavans, Ilan, ed. *Mutual Impressions: Writers from the Americas Reading One Another*. Durham, N.C.: Duke University Press, 1999.

Steiner, George. *After Babel*. London: Oxford University Press, 1975.

Sturrock, John, ed. *The Oxford Guide to Contemporary Writing*. Oxford: Oxford University Press, 1996.

Suarez, Lucia M. "Gisèle Pineau: Writing the Dimensions of Migration." *World Literature Today* 75, no. 3–4 (Summer/Autumn 2001): 9–21.

Tamai Kobayashi. *Exile and the Heart*. Toronto: Women's Press, 1998.

Tanner, Tony. *Venice Desired*. Oxford: Blackwell, 1992.

Taylor, Charles. *Multiculturalism and "The Politics of Recognition": An Essay*. Princeton, N.J.: Princeton University Press, 1992.

Todorov, Tzvetan. *Vie commune* (1939). [*Life in Common: An Essay in General Anthropology*. Trans. Katherine Golsan and Lucy Golsan. Lincoln: University of Nebraska Press, 2001.]

Tolstaya, Tatyana. "The Way They Live Now." *New York Review of Books* (April 24, 1997): 13–15.

Venclova, Tomas. *Forms of Hope: Essays.* Riverdale-on-Hudson, N.Y.: Sheep Meadow, 1999.

———. *Winter Dialogue.* Foreword by Joseph Brodsky. Dialogue between Czesław Miłosz and Tomas Venclova. Trans. Diana Senechal. Evanston, Ill.: Hydra, 1997.

Verma, Nirmal. *India and Europe: Selected Essays.* Ed. Alok Bhalla. Shimla, India: Indian Institute of Advanced Study, 2000.

Veteto-Conrad, Marilya. *Finding a Voice: Identity and the Works of German-Language Turkish Writers in the Federal Republic of Germany to 1990.* New York: Peter Lang, 1996.

Waas, Margit. *Language Attrition Downunder: German Speakers in Australia.* New York: Peter Lang, 1996.

Walcott, Derek. "A Letter to Chamoiseau." *New York Review of Books* (August 14, 1997): 45–48.

———. *What the Twilight Says.* New York: Farrar, Straus and Giroux, 1998.

Walzer, Michael. *On Toleration.* New Haven, Conn.: Yale University Press, 1997.

Wasafiri 31 (Spring 2000). [Special issue on migrant writing in Europe.]

Wendt, Albert, ed. *Nuanua: Pacific Writing in English since 1980.* Honolulu: University of Hawaii Press, 1995.

Weschler, Lawrence. *Calamities of Exile: Three Nonfiction Novellas.* Chicago: University of Chicago Press, 1998.

Williams, Robert C. *Russia Imagined: Art, Culture, and National Identity, 1840–1995.* New York: Peter Lang, 1997.

Wilpert, Gero von. *Lexikon der Weltliteratur.* 3 vols. Stuttgart: Alfred Kröner, 1968, 1975, 1993.

Wilson, Rita, and Carlotta von Maltzan, eds. *Spaces and Crossings: Essays on Literature and Culture in Africa and Beyond.* New York: Peter Lang, 2001.

Wittgenstein, Ludwig. *Tractatus logico-philosophicus* (1921). London: Routledge and Kegan Paul, 1974.

Wu, Fatima. "Gao Xingjian: *Soul Mountain.*" *World Literature Today* 75, no. 1 (Winter 2001): 101.

Wylie, Hal, and Bernth Lindfors, eds. *Multiculturalism and Hybridity in African Literatures.* Trenton, N.J.: Africa World Press, 2000.

Yehoshua, A. B. *Kohah ha-nora shel ashmah ketanah: Ha-heksher ha-musari shel ha-tekst ha-sifruti.* Tel Aviv: Yedi'ot aharonot: Sifre hemed, 1998. [*The Terrible Power of a Minor Guilt: Literary Essays.* Trans. Ora Cummings. Syracuse, N.Y.: Syracuse University Press, 2000.]

———. *Masaʾ el Tom ha-elef: Roman bi-sheloshah halakim.* Tel Aviv: Ha-Kibuts ha-meʾuhad, 1997. [*Voyage to the End of the Millennium.* Tel Aviv: Ha-Kibuts ha-meʾuhad, 1997.]

———. *Mul ha-yeʾarot; sipurîm* (1968). [*Facing the Forests.* Trans. Miriam Arad. Tel Aviv: Institute for the Translation of Hebrew Literature, 1997.]

Yi-fu Tuan. *Cosmos and Hearth: A Cosmopolite's Viewpoint.* Minneapolis: University of Minnesota Press, 1996.

Zizek, Slavoj. *The Zizek Reader.* Ed. Elizabeth Wright and Edmond Wright. Oxford: Blackwell, 1999.

INDEX

Page locators in **boldface** indicate main entries.

ABOUT THE EDITORS
AND CONTRIBUTORS

ALBA AMOIA is Associate Professor Emerita, Department of Romance Languages, Hunter College of the City University of New York. She has published several literary biographies (Edmond Rostand, Jean Anouilh, Albert Camus, Feodor Dostoevsky), as well as studies of the Italian literary and theatrical scenes (*Women on the Italian Literary Scene*, 1992, *20th-Century Italian Women Writers*, 1996). *No Mothers We!* (2000) analyzes the revolt of Italian women writers against maternity. Her coedited volume (with Bettina L. Knapp), *Multicultural Writers from Antiquity to 1945*, appeared in 2002.

BETTINA L. KNAPP is Thomas Hunter Professor of French and Comparative Literature (Emerita) at Hunter College and the Graduate Center of the City University of New York. The author of over 50 books, the most recent of these are *Gambling, Game, and Psyche* (2000); *Voltaire Revisited* (2000); and *French Fairy Tales: A Jungian Approach* (2003). Editor of the annual review *Antemnae*, she is also a Knight in the Order of Arts and Letters.

ROSA AMATULLI, a doctoral candidate at the City University of New York, teaches Italian language and literature at Hunter College and Queens College. She has written about medieval and Renaissance Italian authors (Dante, Ariosto), as well as twentieth-century Italian writers (Anna Banti, Edith Bruck).

GIORGIO AMITRANO is Professor of Japanese at the Oriental Institute of the University of Naples, Italy. He has translated into Italian works by Nakajima Atsushi, Miyazawa Kenji, Kawabata Yasunari, Yoshimoto Banana, and Murakami Haruki. He is the author of *The New Japanese Novel: Popular Culture and Literary Tradition in the Work of Murakami*

Haruki and Yoshimoto Banana (1996). The Italian edition of Kawabata Yasunari's collected works appeared in 2003.

PAUL J. ARCHAMBAULT is Professor of French at Syracuse University, New York, where he directs the French program. He has written many books and articles dealing with autobiography, the most recent book being *A Monk's Confession: The Memoirs of Guibert de Nogent* (1996). He delivered four lectures at the Collège de France in 1998 on the relation between autobiographical discourse and historical narrative. Currently he is working on a comparative study of Jean-Jacques Rousseau's *Confessions* and Giambattista Vico's *Autobiography*.

SONIA ASSA is Associate Professor of French and Spanish in the Department of Humanities and Languages at the State University of New York, College at Old Westbury. Her two most recently published articles, on Assia Djebar, are "De l'auteure en lectrice: Fonction de l'Histoire du captif dans *Vaste est la prison*" (*Le Maghreb littéraire* IV.8, December 2000: 31–49) and "Pour étaler la pièce principale ou rien: Démontages de la fiction dans la trilogie maghrébine d'Assia Djebar" (in *Collectif Assia Djebar*, Toronto: Éditions La Source, 2002).

ABDELLATIF ATTAFI, originally from Tangier, Morocco, completed his doctorate in Lille, France. He is currently Associate Professor of French at the University of Charleston in South Carolina. His research interests include the brain drain phenomenon of North African students in France, and North African literature, specifically that of Tahar Ben Jelloun.

LEE BAGINSKI teaches in the English Department at Trident Technical College in Charleston, South Carolina. In addition to two ethnographic studies (1993 and 1998), she has written "'Upon the Hearth the Fire is Red': The Search for Home in J.R.R. Tolkien's *The Lord of the Rings*" (1984).

THOMAS BAGINSKI is Associate Professor of German at the University of Charleston, South Carolina. He is the author of *Psychologie und Zeitkritik in Oskar Loerkes Traumgedichten* (1990) and *Gesichtspunkte* (1994) and a contributor to the *Encyclopedia of German Literature* (2000). His articles "Traumerfahrung als Erkenntnisweg: Oskar Loerkes Gedicht 'Die Hand'" (in *Monatshefte* 93.2) and "Von Mullahs und Deutschen: Annäherung an das Werk des iranischen Exillyrikers Said" (in *German Quarterly* 74.1) were published in 2001.

MARLÈNE BARSOUM is Assistant Professor of French at Hunter College of the City University of New York. She is the author of *Théophile Gautier's "Mademoiselle de Maupin": Toward a Definition of the 'Androgynous Discourse'* (2001), articles on Andrée Chedid, and two articles on the traveler Ibn Battuta.

INGEBORG BAUMGARTNER is Professor of German and Russian language and literature at Albion College, Michigan. Her research and publications are on nineteenth- and twentieth-century literature, particularly the novella and Thomas Mann. Recent publications include "Czechoslovakia's 'Beautiful Gesture': Thomas Mann as Citizen of Czechoslovakia 1936–1944" (in *Michigan Academician* 30, no. 2 [March 1998]: 123–30) and "Johann Gottfried Herder and German Romanticism" (in *From Kant to Weber: Freedom and Culture in Classical German Social Theory*, 19–36, ed. Thomas M. Powers and Paul Kamolnick. Malabar, Fla.: Krieger Publishing Company, 1999).

LUCILLE FRACKMAN BECKER is Professor Emerita of French at Drew University in Madison, New Jersey. She has lectured on modern French literature at universities throughout the world. The author of numerous articles and reviews, she has published seven books, the most recent of which is *Georges Simenon Revisited* (1999).

BETTY BEDNARSKI is Professor of French and the Coordinator of Canadian Studies at Dalhousie University, Halifax, Nova Scotia, Canada. A literary translator well known for her English translations of Quebec writer Jacques Ferron, she is also the author of numerous studies on Quebec literature and an award-winning essay on the act of translation, *Autour de Ferron: littérature, traduction, altérité* (1989).

JANE BENARDETE, Professor Emerita of English at Hunter College of the City University of New York, is an Americanist who specializes in the literature of the nineteenth and early twentieth centuries. She is the editor of Hamlin Garland's *Crumbling Idols* (1962), author of *American Realism: A Shape for Fiction* (1972), and coeditor of *Companions of Our Youth* (1980), an edition of tales for children by well-known American women writers of the nineteenth century. She has also written numerous essays and reviews.

CRISTINA BOIDARD BOISSON is Titular Professor in the Department of French Philology at the University of Cádiz, Spain. Her doctoral dissertation (1991) was on Georges Henein and Surrealism, and she has published several articles on Henein and other contemporary Francophone writers of Egypt and the Mahgreb. Her latest published articles are "La didactique de la matière de Civilisation à la croisée de l'An 2000" (2000) and "Réflexion sur le recueil de nouvelles *Femmes d'Alger dans leur appartement* d'Assia Djebar dans une perspective féministe" (forthcoming).

ARTA LUCESCU BOUTCHER was born in Sibiu, Romania. After emigrating to Paris (1970), then to the United States (1971), she earned the Ph.D. in French literature at the Graduate Center of the City University of New York. The publication of her study of Benjamin Fondane, a Jewish-Romanian poet and a victim of the Holocaust, is forthcoming. She is Professor of French at the College of Saint Elizabeth in Morristown, New Jersey. She is also a member of the Ceres Art Gallery in Greenwich Village, New York City, where she regularly exhibits her oil paintings.

SUSAN BRANTLY is Professor of Scandinavian Studies at the University of Wisconsin, Madison. A specialist in Scandinavian literature, she has published articles on August Strindberg, Pär Lagerkvist, Tove Ditleven, E. T. A. Hoffmann, and other topics. Author of *Understanding Isak Dinesen*, she has also written a biography of Laura Marholm, a turn-of-the-century woman writer and translator of Scandinavian literature into German.

ROBERT E. CLARK holds a Ph.D. from Columbia University. He is an editor and writer living in New York City.

JUDY COCHRAN is Professor of French at Denison University in Granville, Ohio, where she teaches literature and writing. She has published articles on intertextuality and myth in Andrée Chedid's works. Her book *Selected Poems of Andrée Chedid* (1995) is the first French-English anthology of the poet's work. A second book of Chedid's verse, *Territories of Breath/Territoires du souffle: A Bilingual Anthology*, is forthcoming.

SUSAN D. COHEN is an independent scholar. She served as guest editor for the special issue on Marguerite Duras of *L'Esprit Créateur* (1990); published *Women and Discourse in the Fiction of Marguerite Duras: Love, Legends, Language* (1993); and recently contributed "La Scène, le jeu et l'enjeu" to the volume *Lire Duras* (2000).

ANNE D. CRAVER received her doctorate in comparative literature (French/Persian/Arabic) from Washington University, Saint Louis, Missouri, in 2000. Her dissertation was entitled: "The Persistence of Vision in Andrée Chedid's Poetry." She was made Chevalier dans l'Ordre des Palmes Académiques by the French government in 2001.

JOHN DOLIS is Associate Professor of English at Penn State University, Scranton, Pennsylvania. His publications include articles in literary, philosophical, and psychoanalytic journals; two volumes of poetry, *Bl( )nk Space* and *Time Flies: Butterflies;* and a book on Hawthorne, *The Style of Hawthorne's Gaze: Regarding Subjectivity*. His most recent publications include "Thoreau's Nature: Tending to Matter, Minding ItSelf" (2000) and "Domesticating Hawthorne: Home is for the Birds" (2001). At present he is completing a book on Thoreau, *Tracking Thoreau: Double-Crossing Nature and Technology*.

NADINE DORMOY is the Director of *Europe Plurilingue* (*Plurilingual Europe*) and is on the faculty at the Université de Paris VIII-Saint-Denis, France. She formerly was Associate Professor of French at Herbert H. Lehman College of the City University of New York. Her most recent publication, *L'écriture ou la vie* (1999), is a translation of Isabelle Hoog Naginski's *George Sand: Writing for Her Life*.

ELENA DÚZS is Professor in the Russian Department of Dickinson College, Carlisle, Pennsylvania.

GISÈLE FÉAL is Professor Emerita of French, State University of New York, College at Buffalo. She has published three books and numerous articles, mainly on twentieth-century French theater. Her latest published work is *Ionesco. Un théâtre onirique* (2001).

BRUNO FERRARO is Associate Professor of Italian in the School of European Languages and Literatures of the University of Auckland, New Zealand. Among his recent publications are "Antonio Tabucchi e il fascino della pittura" (in *I Segni incrociati. Letteratura italiana del '900 e Arte Figurativa*, 829–48, ed. Marcello Ciccuto and Alexandra Zingone. Viareggio and Lucca: Mauro Baroni editore, 1998) and "Antonio Tabucchi's 'returned gaze': art, fiction and reality" (in *Una bella Menzogna: Zur italienischen Erzählliteratur der Gegenwart*, 31–41, ed. H. Felten and D. Nelting. Frankfurt: Peter Lang, 2000).

ANTÓNIO FOURNIER specializes in medieval and modern Portuguese literature. He has taught at the University of Madeira, Portugal, and is presently a lecturer at the Camões Institute of the University of Pisa, Italy. His three most recently published contributions (2001) to colloquia at Portuguese universities are "Natália Correia e a tradução da lírica trovadoresca galego-portuguesa in *Sobre o Tempo*," "Bamba: a construção de uma exemplaridade—a propósito da figura do refundidor da 'Crónica Geral de Espanha de 1344' in *Figura*," and "'Quando traduzes/o amor, tu sabes/que é já outro o seu nome'—Albano Martins e tradução poética in *Uma flauto de areia*."

GIUSEPPE GARGIULO, a specialist in the philosophy of language, teaches methodology of textual analysis and the history of ideas in modern and contemporary Italy at the Université de Paris X-Nanterre. He is particularly interested in relationships between visual and spoken language, literary and electronic hypertexts, multimedial literature, and automatic narrative sequences applied to Giovanni Giacomo Casanova's *Mémoires* and to eighteenth-century erotic literature "sous le manteau" between Italy and France (cf. "Un masque de saisie électronique pour démasquer le récit érotique de Casanova" in *Récit et Informatique*, 1993). He has directed video clips on linguistic communication and on the theatrical works of Torquato Tasso and Casanova.

KAIAMA L. GLOVER is Assistant Professor of Francophone literature at Barnard College, Columbia University. After receiving the B.A. in French history and literature and Afro-American studies from Harvard University, she spent a year in Paris as a Fulbright scholar, then entered the Columbia University doctoral program, where she specialized in the literature of the French-speaking Caribbean. Her Ph.D. dissertation was a comparative analysis of the works of Haitian "Spiralists" Frankétienne, Jean-Claude Fignolé, and René Philoctète and those of Martinican writer-theorist Édouard Glissant.

JIM HANNAN is completing a dissertation at the University of Chicago in the Department of English Languages and Literatures on modernity, globalism, and locality in Anglophone Caribbean fiction.

ANNE MULLEN HOHL has taught at the University of Cincinnati as a Taft Postdoctoral Fellow and at Seton Hall University in South Orange, New Jersey, where she is currently Assistant Professor of French and Director of the French Program of Study Abroad (Paris). She specializes in nineteenth- and twentieth-century French literature, in particular the works of Gustave Flaubert and Maryse Condé. Her publications include *Exoticism in* Salammbô: *The Languages of Myth, Religion, and War* (1995), 12 entries in *A Gustave Flaubert Encyclopedia* (ed. Laurence M. Porter, Greenwood Press, 2001), and articles on Gustave Flaubert, Maryse Condé, and Sony Labou Tansi.

STUART KNEE is Professor of History at the University of Charleston in South Carolina. He is the author of *The Concept of Zionist Dissent in the American Mind 1917–1941* (1979), *Hervey Allen (1889–1950): A Literary Historian in America* (1988), and *Christian Science in the Age of Mary Baker Eddy* (1994).

JERZY R. KRZYŻANOWSKI is Professor Emeritus of Slavic Languages and Literatures at Ohio State University. He specializes in the history and criticism of contemporary Polish literature. The author of a number of studies in English and Polish, he has also published several novels in Polish, the latest of which is *Myślę, że wrócę kiedyś* (London, 2001).

CHRISTOPHER W. LEMELIN is an instructor in Russian at Dickinson College in Carlisle, Pennsylvania. He is completing his Ph.D. at Yale University, writing on the influence of Prague on Marina Tsvetaeva's lyric poetry. Among his other research interests are Romanticism, film and performing arts, and Slavic linguistics.

B. AMARILIS LUGO DE FABRITZ is Mellon Postdoctoral Fellow in the Department of Russian and East Asian Languages and Cultures at Emory University in Atlanta, Georgia. She specializes in Soviet culture and cinema.

MARINA MACKAY is a tutor in English literature at the University of East Anglia, Norwich, England, where she was awarded the Ph.D. in 1999. Her dissertation was on the novels of Angus Wilson, and she has published essays on Wilson in *Pretext* and the *Journal of Modern Literature*.

ROGER MCKNIGHT is Professor of Scandinavian Studies at Gustavus Adolphus College in Saint Peter, Minnesota. Author of articles and a book on Vilhelm Moberg, his latest publication is "Father-Son Saga: Leif Ericsson and the Christianization of Medieval Greenland" in *Christian History* 18 (1999).

ARIANNA MAIORANI holds the *laurea* from the University of Rome, and a Research Doctorate in Sciences of Culture from the Scuola Internazionale di Alti Studi della Fondazione San Carlo of Modena. Her dissertation, "L'esotico ricreato: forme letterarie dell'altrove orientale tra

Ottocento e Novecento," was published in shortened form in 2001. She teaches English and French language and literature in Modena at the *liceo* level and English linguistics at the University of Bologna. She has translated several books for Italian publishers, and her essays and articles have appeared in various specialized Italian and foreign reviews. She also teaches classical and contemporary dance, and has published a children's book on the subject of dance.

CLÉMENT MBOM is Professor of French at Brooklyn College of the City University of New York. The most significant of his 14 books are *Le théâtre d'Aimé Césaire* (1979), *Réflexions de Léopold Sédar Senghor sur les Antécédents et la genèse de la Négritude senghorienne de Martin Stein* (1999), *La femme et l'enfant camerounais, symboles de l'intégration en Afrique* (1999). He has published more than sixty articles and presented papers at more than one hundred conferences the world over.

BRUCE MERRY held the chair of Italian at the University of the Witwatersrand, Johannesburg (1980–1987) and is now Associate Professor in the Department of English Literature at Kuwait University. He has written books on Eugenio Montale (1977), G. G. Belli (1978), Beppe Fenoglio (1978), and Dacia Maraini (1997), as well as *Anatomy of the Spy Thriller* (1977) and *Women in Modern Italian Literature* (1990). He recently published *The Basil Plant: An Analysis of Eros in the Modern Novel* (2001). He whiles away the cooler seasons in Kuwait working on a bibliography of modern Greek literature.

ALESSANDRO MONTI is Professor of English Language and Postcolonial Literatures and Languages at the University of Torino, where he holds the Chair of Shakespearean Studies. He is author of studies on Indian literature in English and Associate Editor of the *Atlantic Literary Review* (Delhi). He has published, among other works, *Durga Marga* (1994) and *The Time after Cowdust* (2000), and edited *Hindu Masculinities Across the Ages: Updating the Past* (2002).

MAI MOUNIAMA is Associate Professor of French Language and Literature at the University of L'Aquila, Italy. She is a member of the International Society for Eighteenth-Century Studies and the Centre de Recherche sur la Littérature des Voyages of the Université de Paris (IV). Her published articles include "Un naturalista in Senegal" (1997), "Un récit de voyage minimaliste: *Le palais des saveurs accumulées* de P. Boman" (1998), and "L'ansia della perfezione" (1999).

JOSEPH NNADI is Professor in the Department of French Studies and German Studies at the University of Winnipeg, Canada. A specialist in nineteenth-century French literature, he is the author of *Visions de l'Afrique dans l'oeuvre de Baudelaire* (1980) and *Les Négresses de Baudelaire* (1994) as well as numerous articles on French and Francophone literatures.

MAX. E. NOORDHOORN is Professor of German Literature at Albion College, Michigan. His main areas of interest are lyric poetry from the seventeenth century to the present and popular culture, ranging from Wilhelm Busch to the Wiener Volkstheater.

BENEDETTA ORIGO, the eldest daughter of Iris Origo, has worked for many years as publisher of Edizioni dell'Elefante in Rome. She is co-author (with John Dixon Hunt, Morna Livingston, and Laurie Olin) of *La Foce, a Garden and Landscape in Tuscany* (Philadelphia: Pennsylvania University Press, 2001). She directs the La Foce estate in Val d'Orcia, organizing cultural events such as the chamber music festival "Incontri in Terra di Siena."

MARIA GRAZIA ORSI is Researcher at the University of Pisa and is specializing in Lusitanian studies at the University of Bari, Italy, where the subject of her postdoctoral dissertation is the work of the Angolan writer José Luandino Vieira. Her research project at the Fundação Calouste Gulbenkian in Lisbon was entitled *Da História à história através dos mitos e tradições orais em Agustina Bessa Luís e Ungulani Ba Ka Khosa* (1999–2000).

MARIA TERESA ORSI is Professor of Japanese Language and Literature at the University of Rome, Italy. She has published many articles on Japanese literature and has edited and translated into Italian numerous classical and modern Japanese texts. Her prize-winning translation of Sakaguchi Ango's work, *Sotto la foresta di ciliegi in fiore* (1993), was followed by her edition and translation of Ishikawa Jun's *I demoni guerrieri (Shura)* (1997) and *Fiabe giapponesi* (1998). Her latest publication is "La standardizzazione del linguaggio: il caso giapponese" (2001) in *Il romanzo* (edited by Franco Moretti).

JAMES O. PELLICER is Professor in the Department of Romance Languages at Hunter College of the City University of New York. His most recent publication is *El "Facundo," significante y significado*. In preparation are two textbooks, *Structures of Modern Spanish* and *Advanced Spanish Writing*. His field of interest is the history of ideas in Spanish America, mainly in the nineteenth century.

ROLANDO PEREZ is a librarian and the philosophy- and Romance Languages-bibliographer at Hunter College of the City University of New York. He publishes widely in fields ranging from philosophy and literary criticism to poetry and fiction. Some of his works include *Severo Sarduy and* the *Religion of the Text* (1988), *The Odyssey* (1990), *On An(archy) and Schizoanalysis* (1990, on the work of French philosophers Gilles Deleuze and Felix Guattari), *The Divine Duty of Servants: A Book of Worship* (1999, based on the artwork of Bruno Schulz), *The Electric Comedy* (2000; a modern version of *La Divina Commedia)*, and *The Lining of Our Souls* (1995–2001, poetic excursions into selected paintings of Edward Hopper).

PATRICIA PERKINS writes about the secret that Paul Bowles understood about long-term traveling: that the Self we take out there is never the Self we bring back. She has been writing full time for nine years. Her award-winning literary travel essays and articles have appeared in national magazines. This is her third essay about Paul Bowles.

DEBORAH PHELPS is Associate Professor of English, specializing in Victorian literature and women's studies, at Sam Houston State University, Texas. Her presentation at the Modern Language Association convention (2000) was entitled "'My Mind Saw Double': Margaret Atwood and Canadian Nationalism." She has published numerous scholarly essays and a chapbook of poetry entitled *Deep East* (2001).

M. CRISTINA PISCIOTTA is Professor of Chinese Language and Literature at the Oriental Institute of the University of Naples, Italy. She has earned degrees in modern Chinese language and literature at the University of Rome, the École des Hautes Études Chinoises of the Sorbonne, and the Language Institute and the University of Beijing, and has taught at the University of Venice and the University of Rome. Her recent publications include the translation and edition of Lu Wenfu, *Vita e passione di un gastronomo cinese* (1991) and "Nuove tendenze del teatro di prosa contemporaneo in Cina" (*Atti del Convegno sulla letteratura cinese contemporanea*, 2000).

JEANINE PARISIER PLOTTEL is Professor Emerita at Hunter College and the Graduate Center of the City University of New York. A scholar of nineteenth- and twentieth-century French literature, her recent publications deal with Victor Hugo and Rodin, and morality and literature in France during the World War II German occupation.

ELIZABETH POWERS, besides her publications in the field of German literature, also writes on literary and cultural matters for U.S. national newspapers and magazines. She is currently completing a memoir of religion and reading in late-twentieth-century America.

MICHÈLE RATSABY, Associate Professor at Saint John's University in New York, has taught French literature at Tel Aviv University in Israel. Her latest publication is "Une femme sous la révolution: Olympe de Gouges (1748–1793). Auteur dramatique et pamphlétaire révolutionnaire" (in *Antemnae* 2 [2000]: 60–78.)

MAURIZIO RIOTTO is Associate Professor of Korean Language and Literature at the Oriental Institute of the University of Naples, Italy. His titles include Research Fellow at Seoul National University, Visiting Scholar at Kyoto's Doshisha University, and Visiting Scholar at Seoul's Hanyang University. The author of numerous books, articles, and translations in the field of Korean language and literature, his most recent publication, *Il sogno delle nove nuvole* (2001), is his Italian translation and annotated edition of the classical Korean novel by Kim Manjung.

A. L. ROGERS II is Visiting Instructor in English at the College of Charleston, South Carolina. He received the B.A. from Duke University (1985), the M.A. from the University of North Carolina in Charlotte

(1992), and the Ph.D. in English literature from the University of Tennessee in Knoxville (2002). He contributed chapters on Charles Dickens and Percy Bysshe Shelley to *Multicultural Writers from Antiquity to 1945* (2002).

MARTHA L. RUBÍ is Adjunct Professor of Spanish at Hunter College of the City University of New York, and sometime Director of the Hunter College Study Abroad program in Madrid, Spain. Her published article on María Luisa Bombal appeared in 2001; works in progress are *Twentieth-Century Themes in the Poetry of Hispanic American Women: A Selected Anthology* and *Spanish American Feminist Literary Theory: An Approach Through the Concept of Willing and Willingness.*

DIEGO SAGLIA is Lecturer in English Literature at the University of Parma, Italy. He has published widely on topics of the Romantic period, with essays appearing in *Studies in Romanticism, ELH, Studies in the Novel, Textus, Women's Writing, Nineteenth-Century Literature*, and *Comparative Literature*. He is the author of two books: *Byron and Spain: Itinerary in the Writing of Place* (1996) and *Poetic Castles in Spain: British Romanticism and Figurations of Iberia* (2000). He is currently working on a book about Orientalism as an intersection of texts and objects in the Romantic period.

MARIA ANTONIETTA SARACINO is Researcher and Lecturer in Postcolonial Literature in English in the Department of English of the University of Rome, Italy. She has written extensively on themes and authors in contemporary African, Caribbean, and Indian literature in English. Her two most recent publications (2000) are *Africa bambina* and *Il calypso e la Regina*. She is the recipient of the international literary Mondello Prize (2003) for the best work of translation *(Il giorno della libertà*, translation of Ralph Ellison's *Juneteenth).*

ROSS SHIDELER is Professor in the Department of Comparative Literature and Scandinavian at the University of California in Los Angeles, and has served as Vice-President and President of the Society for the Advancement of Scandinavian Study (1997–2001). In addition to a wide range of articles, he has published books on Gunnar Ekelöf and Per Olov Enquist. His most recent book is *Questioning the Father: From Darwin to Zola, Ibsen, Strindberg, and Hardy* (1999).

GIOVANNA SILVANI is Professor of English Literature at the University of Parma, Italy. She has published widely in the field of nineteenth-century literature (Oscar Wilde, Dante Gabriel Rossetti, Algernon Charles Swinburne, Mary Shelley), on early modern women's writing (Margaret Cavendish, Lady Mary W. Montagu), on William Shakespeare and Christopher Marlowe, and on literary utopias and the Gothic tradition (Joseph Sheridan Le Fanu). Her most recent publications are the monograph *Il cerchio di narciso: Figure e simboli dell'immaginario wildiano* (1998) and the coedited volume *Shakespeare e Verdi* (2000).

RICHARD SUSSMAN has taught physics in New York City high schools for over 35 years. He is currently writing a study of the concept of nature in the work of the English philosopher R. G. Collingwood (1889–1943).

SANDRA TERONI is Professor of French Language and Literature at the University of Cagliari, Italy. She has published books and essays on nineteenth- and twentieth-century French authors (Stendhal, Baudelaire, Maupassant, Mallarmé, Jabès, Céline, Malraux, Benda, Sartre), as well as on the genre of travel literature. A frequent contributor to literary reviews, newspapers, and book-information periodicals, she collaborated in the Bibliothèque de la Pléiade edition of Jean-Paul Sartre's theatrical works (2001).

HENRY URBANSKI is Distinguished Service Professor of Foreign Languages at the State University of New York at New Paltz, where he teaches Russian language, culture, and literature, and where he founded and now directs the Language Immersion Institute.

LUISA VALMARIN is Professor of Romanian language and literature at the University of Rome. Founder and director of the review *Romània Orientale*, in which her work on philological and linguistic problems has appeared (1997–1998 and 1999), she is also President of the Italian Association of Southeastern European Studies and Vice President of the Italian Association for Romanian Studies. She has also written on Romanian classical and contemporary literature. Her most recent publication is *Percorsi rumeni, fra storia e letteratura* (1999).

MARIA GIOIA VIENNA is Lecturer in Modern and Contemporary Japanese Literature at the University of Rome and also teaches Japanese language and literature at the Università per Stranieri in Siena. Her doctoral dissertation was on the Japanese writer Ôba Minako (b. 1929), and she obtained the "Dottorato di Ricerca" in Oriental Studies from the University of Naples in 1999 with a monograph on adolescent characters in the modern and contemporary Japanese novel. Among her publications are the translation into Italian (1993) of the short story *Watashiwa tamago* by Uchida Shungiku (b. 1959), and a translation and critical edition in Italian (2003) of the same author's autobiographical novel *Father Fucker*.

D. LYNNE WALKER teaches in the Department of Slavic Languages and Literatures at the University of Washington, Seattle, where she is a Ph.D. candidate in Russian literature and critical theory. Her doctoral dissertation is about Vladimir Nabokov's madmen and misfits.

KRISTEN WELSH is Faculty Fellow in Russian at Colby College, Waterville, Maine. She is working on a book on Vladimir Nabokov, Vladislav Khodasevich, and the literary polemics in the Russian émigré community between the two world wars. She has participated in seminars and symposia at the V. V. Nabokov Museum in St. Petersburg, and has presented her work at numerous professional meetings. Her other research interests include the reception of Augustinian thought in pre-revolutionary Russia and the role of the visual in early twentieth-century literature.

BILL WOLF holds a master's degree in British literature from Montclair State University. He is currently a teacher of English at The Livingston Alternative High School, Livingston, New Jersey. His chapter on Henry Miller appeared in *Multicultural Writers from Antiquity to 1945: A Bio-Bibliographical Sourcebook* (2002). He is a Sunday painter, a published poet, and a contributor to the American journal *The Flying Lady*.

LORENA ZACCAGNINO holds the *laurea* in French literature from the University of Bari with a thesis entitled "La dialettica della presenza in Yves Bonnefoy." Presently she is preparing a doctorate in French studies at the University of Bari, concentrating on Edmund Husserl's influence on Bonnefoy. Her article on Bonnefoy, "Un poeta fenomenologo," was published in the on-line philosophy review *Dialegesthai* (November 21, 2000).